"Corky Lee put in the center of his frame working-class women, children, and men who have been erased from the annals, capturing their struggle and solidarity with grit, dedication, and beauty. *Corky Lee's Asian America* is an enduring and important book about Asian American resistance that will help change the way we look at American history."

—**CATHY PARK HONG**, author of *Minor Feelings*

"Corky Lee's remarkable images demonstrate how crucial it is to make sure that Asian Americans are seen, first and foremost, as themselves. His oeuvre is a valuable and moving record of Asian American existence, culture, and activism. Not least, his work is a critical testimony to the Asian American movement of which he was a part, and which he helped to preserve through his photographs."

—**VIET THANH NGUYEN**, author of *A Man of Two Faces*

"These stunning photographs by Corky Lee and the stirring essays by those who knew him will take your breath away. For fifty years Corky was the fly on the wall of Asian American–Pacific Islander life. Every image he produced was that of an artist with deep knowledge and commitment to his subject, not that of some outsider searching for easy stereotypes."

—**JUAN GONZÁLEZ**, cohost of *Democracy Now!*

"What a fantastic celebration of both the documented and the documenter! To see Asian American history as it was made, and to feel the power of witness—this is the tribute to Corky Lee that he amply deserves, and a gift of incalculable value to American history."

—**GISH JEN**, author of *Thank You, Mr. Nixon*

"Corky Lee and his photographs not only documented the most significant transformations in Asian America, they also inspire us to work toward justice. *Corky Lee's Asian America* is the book that we have been waiting for. It will become an instant classic that inspires the next generation of artists and activists to continue the work that Corky began."

—**ERIKA LEE**, professor of history, Harvard University

"*Corky Lee's Asian America* makes visible the unseen contours of a vibrant, dynamic, and diverse Asian American community. This selection will no doubt become an invaluable resource and inspiration for all who want to 'think and know more' about the individuals who became artists, protestors, educators, and activists fostering a sense of Asian American community, together."

—**STEPHANIE H. TUNG**, Byrne Family Curator of Photography, Peabody Essex Museum

CORKY LEE'S ASIAN AMERICA

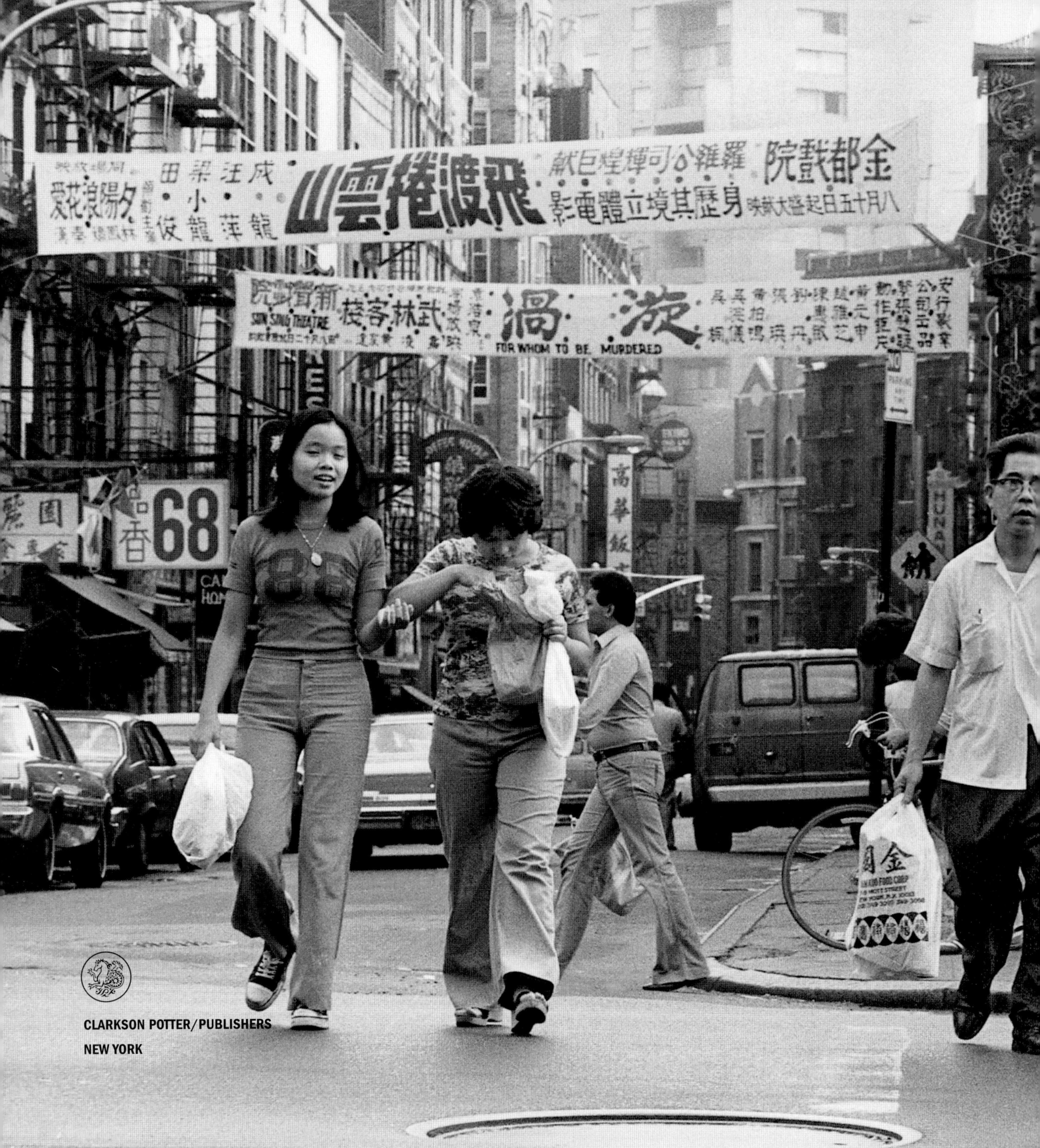

CLARKSON POTTER/PUBLISHERS
NEW YORK

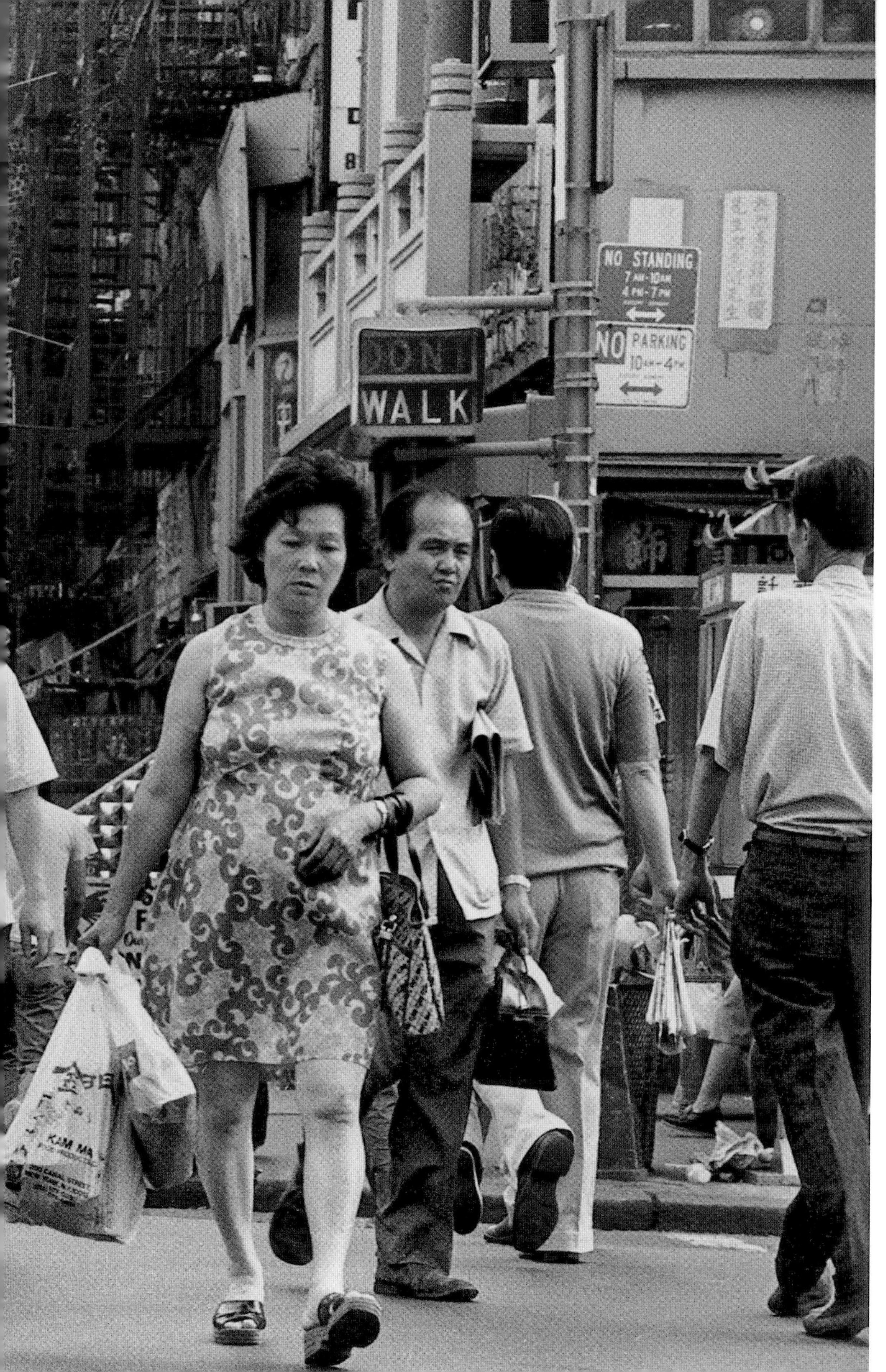

CORKY LEE'S ASIAN AMERICA

FIFTY YEARS OF PHOTOGRAPHIC JUSTICE

PHOTOGRAPHS BY
CORKY LEE

EDITED BY
CHEE WANG NG
& MAE NGAI

To the Asian American–Pacific Islander communities in the United States who strive for recognition, respect, and equality and who inspired these photographs

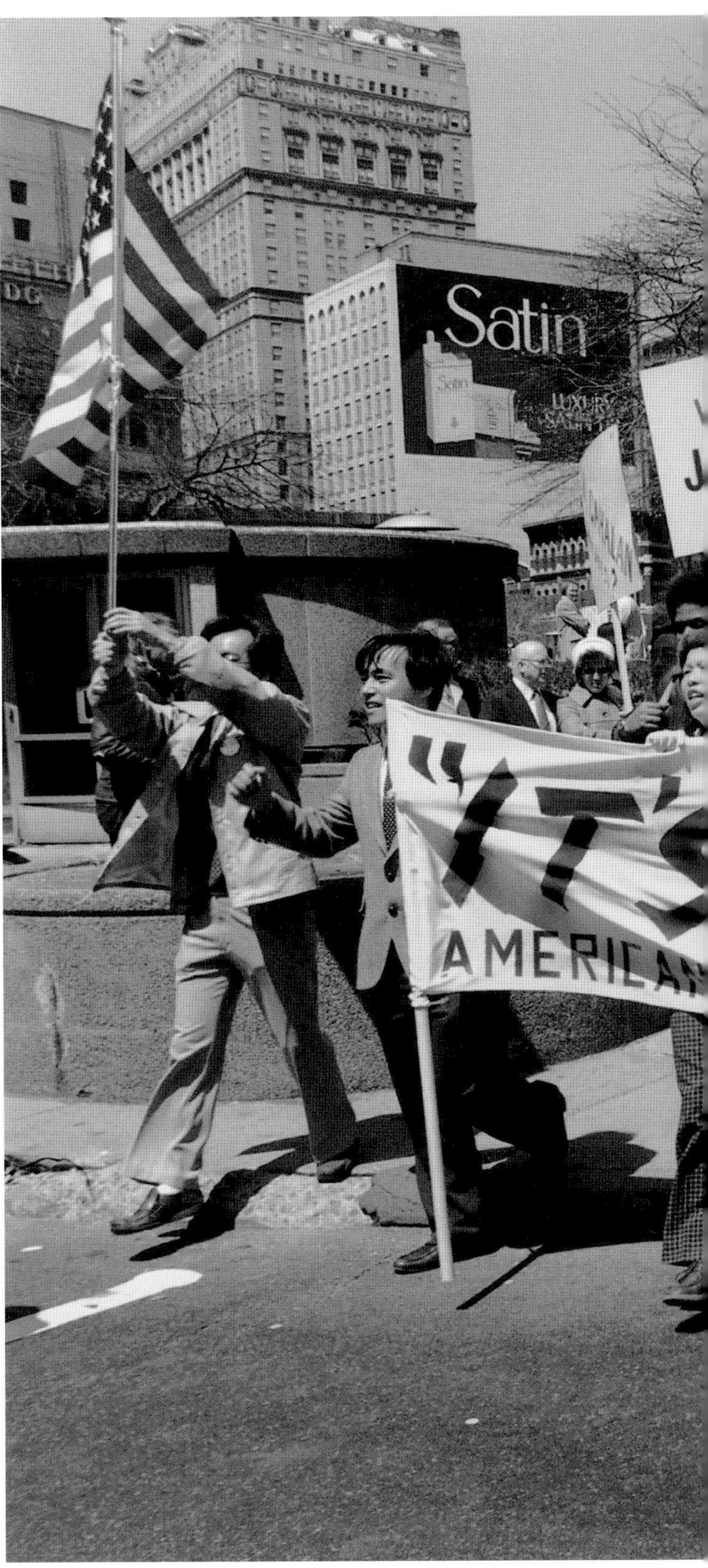

Protesting the killing of Vincent Chin.
Detroit, 1983.

Previous pages: Crossing Canal Street.
Chinatown, New York, early 1970s.

Overleaf: The Day of Remembrance.
New York, 1989.

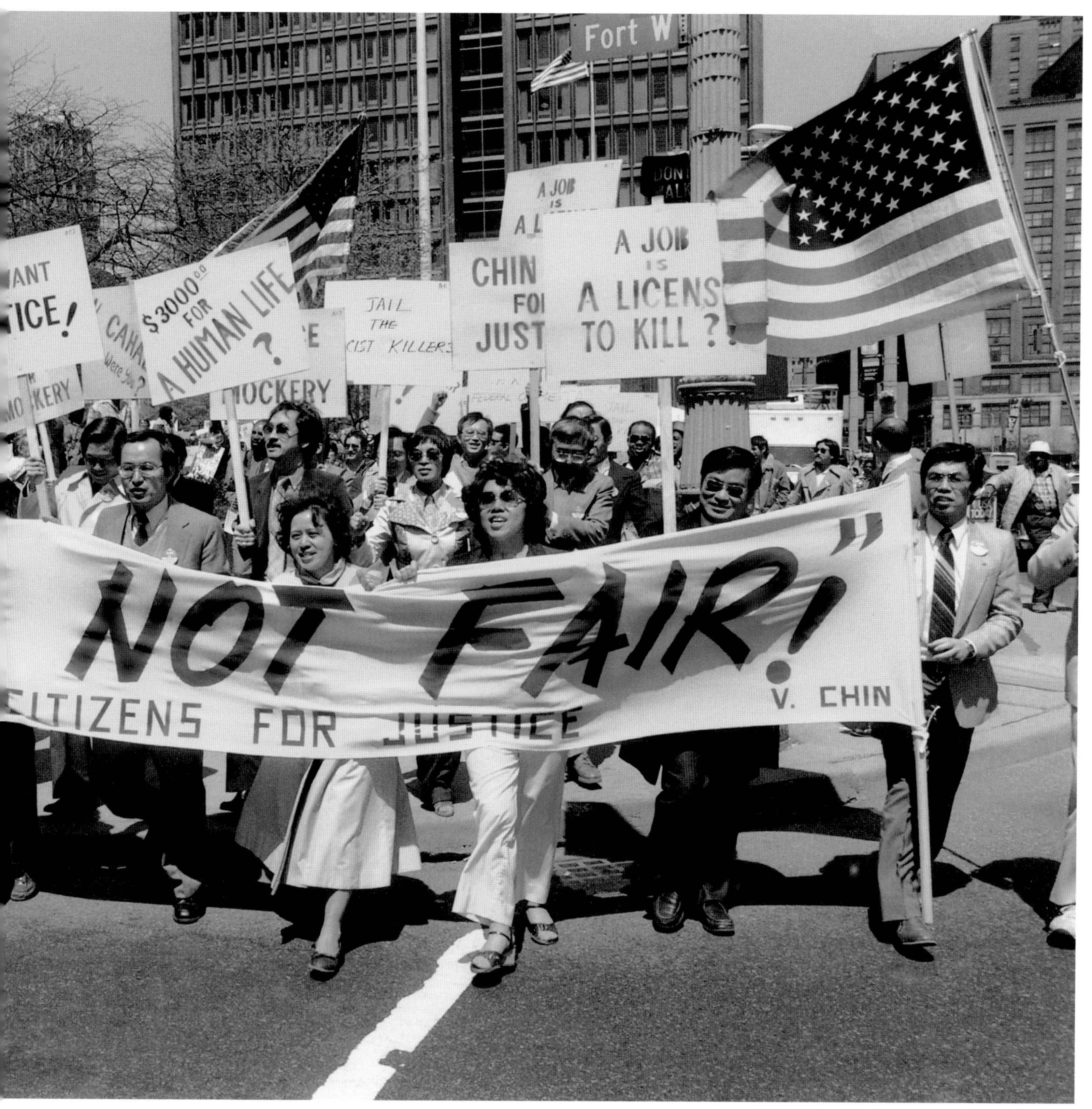
Fort W
A JOB IS A LICENS TO KILL ?
$3000.00 FOR A HUMAN LIFE ?
JAIL THE
MOCKERY
"NOT FAIR!"
V. CHIN
CITIZENS FOR JUSTICE

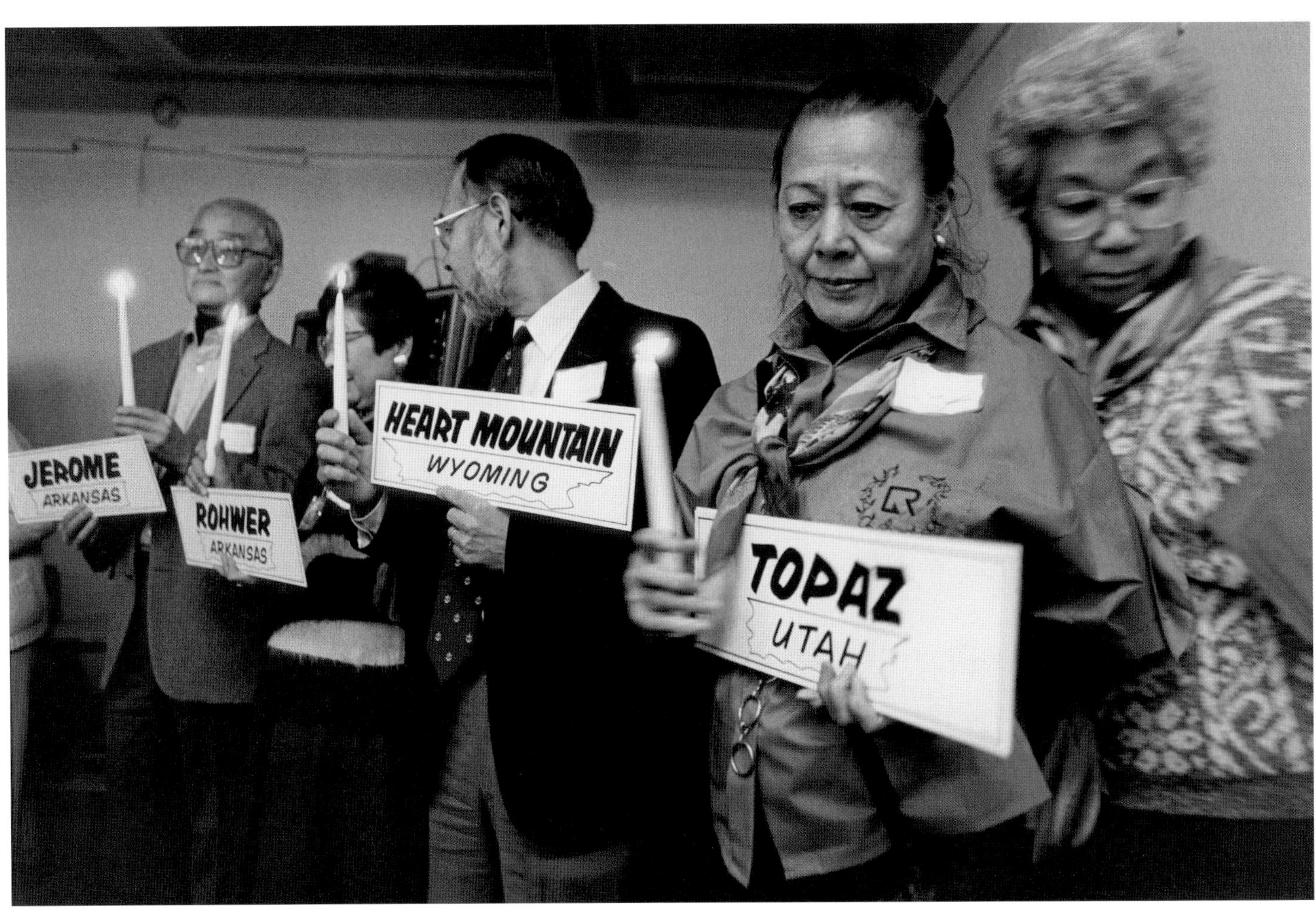
JEROME
ARKANSAS
ROHWER
ARKANSAS
HEART MOUNTAIN
WYOMING
TOPAZ
UTAH

Contents

Chapter introductions
by Mae Ngai

Foreword

HUA HSU

Staff writer for *The New Yorker,* author of the Pulitzer Prize–winning *Stay True*, and professor at Bard College

It's probably one of the most useless conversations I can have with a young person: *the way things used to be.* You can't imagine the effort it once took to take a simple picture. It required not just possession of an actual camera but also the foresight to carry it around with you, not to mention lighting, manual focus, the cost of film. Nowadays I take more pictures on an average day than I did in entire years in the eighties or nineties, of things I would have never thought to chronicle back then: plates of food, funny street signs, chance encounters with friends. We are awash in images. They feel inevitable.

I'd tell this imaginary young person that we were once so starved for pictures of the world that we would study the ones we had over and over. We would horde and exchange them; entire movements grew out of photographs that captured humanity at its very worst. I would want to explain to this person that we are so lucky that Corky Lee never wavered, never seemed to feel tired or jaded. For fifty years he devoted himself to chronicling the Asian American community—a tricky proposition given the diverse complexities of the category, but he never ran from the complications of this assignment. For Corky, photography was more than the daily registration of our whereabouts. Photography was a way of seeing. And, for generations, Corky taught us how to see ourselves—as individuals and as a community.

Corky was everywhere. The protests and concerts, rallies and opening-night premieres, demonstrations and parties, as well as the rehearsals and planning sessions that preceded them. He took some of the only photos that survive of Chinatown in the seventies, back when it was a nexus of activism: protests against the Vietnam War or police brutality or cruel bosses or miserly landlords. "Every time I take my camera out of my bag," he once said, "it is like drawing a sword to combat indifference, injustice, and discrimination and trying to get rid of stereotypes." But he was still just a photographer; he had to show up and wait for the right moment.

Some don't expect to be noticed at all; they've been conditioned to see themselves outside of American history, even when they are central to it. These were the people of Corky's community, the spirit that runs through his portraits of forgotten merchants, old couples showing off their cramped apartments, kids dancing and playing in the street. Pictures of restaurants, factories, cabs, newsstands, and laundries, full of people who didn't comprehend why he was bothering to take pictures of them. Chinatown rock gigs and beauty pageants, teenagers hanging out on the corner trying to look as cool as possible for the man with the camera. Sparsely attended readings or community meetings that suddenly seemed important since Corky had shown up to document them. Perhaps they were doing something important after all. For Corky, the commitment to community required constant renewal and reaffirmation. Each new organization or collective could be the one that changed the world.

It's humbling to survey the range and breadth of Corky's five decades of work, as the tight focus on Manhattan's Chinatown widens to consider neighborhoods, experiences, and ethnicities throughout the nation. There are factions and disagreements, moments when stress is applied to any sense of common purpose. The Asian American community remains an unfinished project. But for Corky, the work that remained was a reason for hope, not despair.

My imaginary young friend, by now weary from my lecture, gives a perfunctory nod. We no longer feel invisible, the way Corky once did, even if we sometimes still feel unseen. And this young person, fed up with playing the part of a stereotype, finally scoffs. These pictures aren't meant to anchor us to the past; they are meant as gifts for the future, too. My young friend would recognize that Corky's gifts were his patience and curiosity. The point of Corky's work, they would continue, was never to dictate a single way forward. His pictures are as much about honoring overlooked visionaries and leaders as they are attempts to valorize the masses, the possibility of change that draws strangers together, across neighborhoods and generations. And this young person would leave me behind and go into the world in search of their own interpretation of community.

Back then was the same as now, it's just the cameras that have changed. We await our moment, in pursuit of the picture that Corky envisaged, a portrait of a community that is too large and too brilliant, it can only come into focus in these beautiful, fleeting fragments.

Introduction

JOHN J. LEE,
CHEE WANG NG
& MAE NGAI

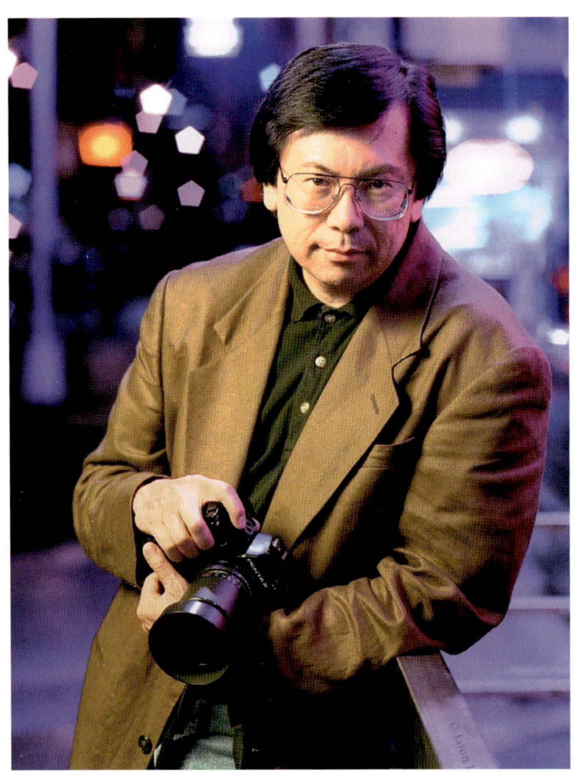

"The Undisputed, Unofficial, Asian American Photographer Laureate," 1997. *Jason Jem*

This is the story of a man who endeavored to change the world, one photograph at a time. Who dared to create a record of an upheaval—of thoughts and beliefs that held a people down, of an ignorant nation that prevented the growth of ideas new and better. The truth and a bit of justice. This is the story of our brother and friend, whom the world came to know as Corky Lee.

With each photograph he took, Corky aimed to break the stereotype of Asian Americans as docile, passive, and above all, foreign to the United States. He insisted that Asian Americans are Americans, that they were, and are, part of this country, of its history and the ongoing project of its making. As he wrote after 9/11, "Do not let anyone tell you to go back to the country of your ancestors. You belong here. Immigrants built America. It was created for you and me."

Corky Lee documented Asian American–Pacific Islander communities for fifty continuous years, from 1970 to 2020, until we lost him to Covid-19 in January 2021, at the age of seventy-three. This book is a retrospective of his life's work, a selection of the best photographs from his vast collection, starting in New York's Chinatown and extending to diverse Asian American communities across the country.

If Corky aimed to break stereotypes one photograph at a time, his photographs, taken together, show the amazing growth and diversity of Asian peoples in America in the late twentieth and early twenty-first centuries. They offer a view—a long view—of the rise and development of the Asian American movement for civil rights and social justice.

Corky Lee was a social photographer—he had little interest in haute art or commercial photography. He sometimes described himself, and was described by others, as a photojournalist. But he was always aware of the limits on photojournalism imposed by editorial gatekeepers and remained true to his first calling as a documentarian of the Asian American community and movement. His intention was to use photography to educate and organize. He avidly photographed protest demonstrations and cultural celebrations as well as children at play, families in their homes, and people at work, be they restaurant kitchen workers or, more atypically, cops and firefighters, pizza and bagel makers, and women taxi drivers, boxers, and pool sharks.

Following trends in politics and culture, Corky used the pan-ethnic identifier "Asian American–Pacific Islander" (AAPI) to refer to his subject matter. His photographs track the growth of the AAPI movement for equality and social justice, spanning a range of issues, from demonstrations against police and racist violence to protests against racial stereotyping in film and theater productions. In the early 1990s, when tension developed between Korean grocers and their Black customers in Brooklyn, Corky documented it. When racism erupted against Sikh Americans in the aftermath of 9/11, Corky was there with his camera. He photographed the rise of the Basement Workshop, a collective of Asian American artists and activists, in the 1970s, and the National Queer Asian Pacific Islander Alliance in the 2000s. He recorded solidarity between Asian Americans and other communities of color, like the Black Lives Matter movement. As cultural heritage events proliferated in number and diversity, reflecting the new Asian immigrations in the 1980s and 1990s—parades for India Day, Sikh Day, Korea Day, and the like—Corky was there to show us what they looked like.

While Corky photographed diverse AAPI cultures, New York City's Chinatown remained at the center of his social and photographic world. His long association with this community generated a high level of photographic achievement.

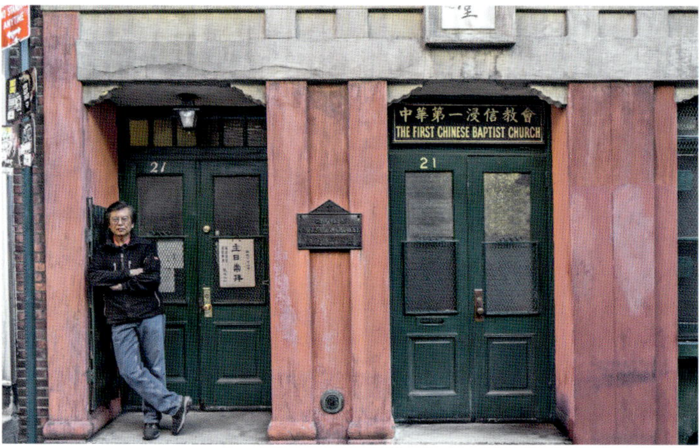

Corky Lee in front of 21 Pell Street, the First Chinese Baptist Church, where he organized arts and media programming for the community. Chinatown, New York, 2015.
Jook Leung

Corky knew and loved Chinatown deeply, calling it "a part of my soul." His portrayal of Chinatown life was at once social and personal, documentary and artistic. He captured ordinary people in their social environment and objects in still-life compositions, like a tenement fire escape. Some of his photographs of community events, like dragon boat races, express joyous energy, but others are intimate, like an opera singer sitting on a park bench, adjusting her hairpiece. Some show provocative juxtapositions, like American Legion members and beauty pageant contestants lined up for the Chinatown Fourth of July parade. His late photos, taken of a lonely and shuttered Chinatown in 2020 during the first year of the coronavirus pandemic, reveal that over decades of experience in the community, he had honed a very special kind of eye.

Corky considered his greatest triumph to be a 2014 photograph in which 250 Asian Americans, including direct descendants of Chinese railroad workers, reenact the completion of the transcontinental railroad. He had long sought to correct the famous photograph taken of the railroad's completion in 1869, which had no Chinese in it, even though upward of twenty thousand Chinese workers had built the western part of the line, including the arduous tunneling of the Sierra Nevada. Corky called his reenactment a work of "photographic justice."

This book is the result of a collaboration between John J. Lee, Corky Lee's sole surviving brother and executor of his estate; Mae Ngai, a professor of history and Asian American studies at Columbia University; and Chee Wang Ng, an artist-photographer and Corky's longtime colleague.

Mae first met Corky in the early 1970s, when she—like scores of other young people—moved to New York's Chinatown to join the emerging Asian American movement. She joined the radical group I Wor Kuen, then got a job as a nurse's aide at Gouverneur Hospital, where she became active in the labor movement. She later moved away from Chinatown and eventually became a professor, specializing in immigration and Asian American history. Her last contact with Corky was in the late fall of 2019, when she invited him to mount a photo exhibition at the ethnic studies center at Columbia University. Corky took measurements at the gallery and mused about a potential theme. A few months later, though, the pandemic shut everything down, and the exhibition never materialized.

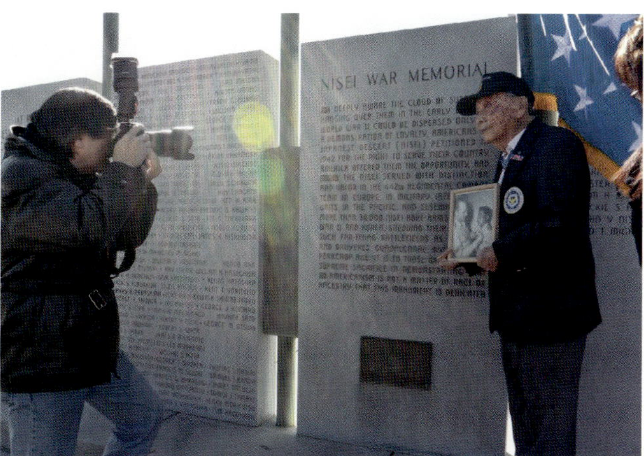

Corky Lee photographs George "Joe" Sakato, a veteran of the all-Nisei 442nd Regimental Combat Team in World War II and a Medal of Honor recipient, at the Nisei Veterans Memorial. Fairmount Cemetery, Denver, 2014. *Gil Asakawa*

Chee Wang Ng's personal and professional friendship with Corky was thirty years long. Born in Kuala Lumpur, Malaysia, he came to the United States in the 1980s and earned a bachelor of fine arts in architecture at the Rhode Island School of Design. An artist-photographer, he has been active in the Chinatown–Asian American art and photography scene since the 1990s. In 2002, when Corky was invited to do a solo show at the Asian American Arts Centre in Chinatown, he instead chose to exhibit the work of eight other Asian American photographers, knowing they had limited opportunities in New York at the time, and Chee Wang was one of them. Over the years, Chee Wang worked with Corky as a graphic designer, participated in group shows with him, and helped him curate and prepare for many of his exhibitions.

In the fall of 2021, John reached out to Mae and Chee Wang to help him fulfill his late brother's dream of publishing a book of his photographs. Our job as co-editors, as we saw it, was to select the best of Corky's work and to present it in a historical and social context. Still, it was a daunting challenge. Corky once estimated that he took an average of two hundred photographs a week. Over the course of his fifty-year career, that adds up to a half-million images. How would we select the photographs for the book?

We started with the photographs that Corky himself had selected in 2011 for a book that he intended to self-publish. He chose one hundred photos, gave the book a title, *Not on the Menu*, and created a mock-up with Chee Wang. A friend donated the funds for the purchase of paper for the publication. But as with many things in life, the book was put aside in the everyday crush of work and other matters.

To that selection, we added photographs that Corky took in the last decade of his life. We considered the most important to be those that he chose for exhibitions or loaned out for films and other creative projects. Taken together, they represent the ones Corky himself considered to be his best work.

Finally, we have added some never-before-seen gems from Corky's archive. We found some of them in old metal boxes of slides and on newer digital storage disks. Others were sent to us by Corky's friends and acquaintances from their personal collections.

Corky Lee's fifty-year quest for "photographic justice" unfolds in these pages. The initial essay by Mae Ngai, "An ABC from NYC," situates his life and career in the context of American history and the history of photography. Then the book presents Corky Lee's photographs, organized in three chronological chapters. The sequence tracks AAPI social movements' struggle for recognition and rights and simultaneously Corky's artistic development as a social photographer and activist. Each chapter begins with an introduction that situates the time and place of the photographs within it. Essays by Asian American writers, artists, activists, and friends of Corky's—including filmmaker Renee Tajima-Peña, writer Helen Zia, historians Gordon Chang and Vivek Bald, playwright David Henry Hwang, and photographer Alan Chin—give greater context to each chapter's major themes and reflect on their relationship to Corky.

"The Birth of the Movement" focuses on the 1970s and the beginnings of both Corky Lee's photographic career and New York's Asian American movement. New York's Chinatown was the center of the Asian American civil rights struggle on the East Coast; Corky was both a participant and a chronicler of that energetic scene. He also created portraits of ordinary people and streetscapes. He captured the 1970s as a moment of historical transition, not only in Chinatown's community politics and activism but also in everyday life, as longtime residents and new immigrant families shared parks, streets, and shops.

"Empowerment" covers the explosive growth of AAPI communities in the 1980s and 1990s and the widening range of struggles for social justice. As the Asian American population grew, communities became more organized and more insistent in claiming equal rights and representation for themselves. But their increased visibility also provoked opposition from mainstream institutions, whether the government, the criminal justice system, or the arts and media establishment. Demographic change is not destiny, yet it creates new conditions for what is possible.

"Resilience" tracks the Asian American experience in the first two decades of the new millennium. While immigrant and working-class communities continued to face longstanding

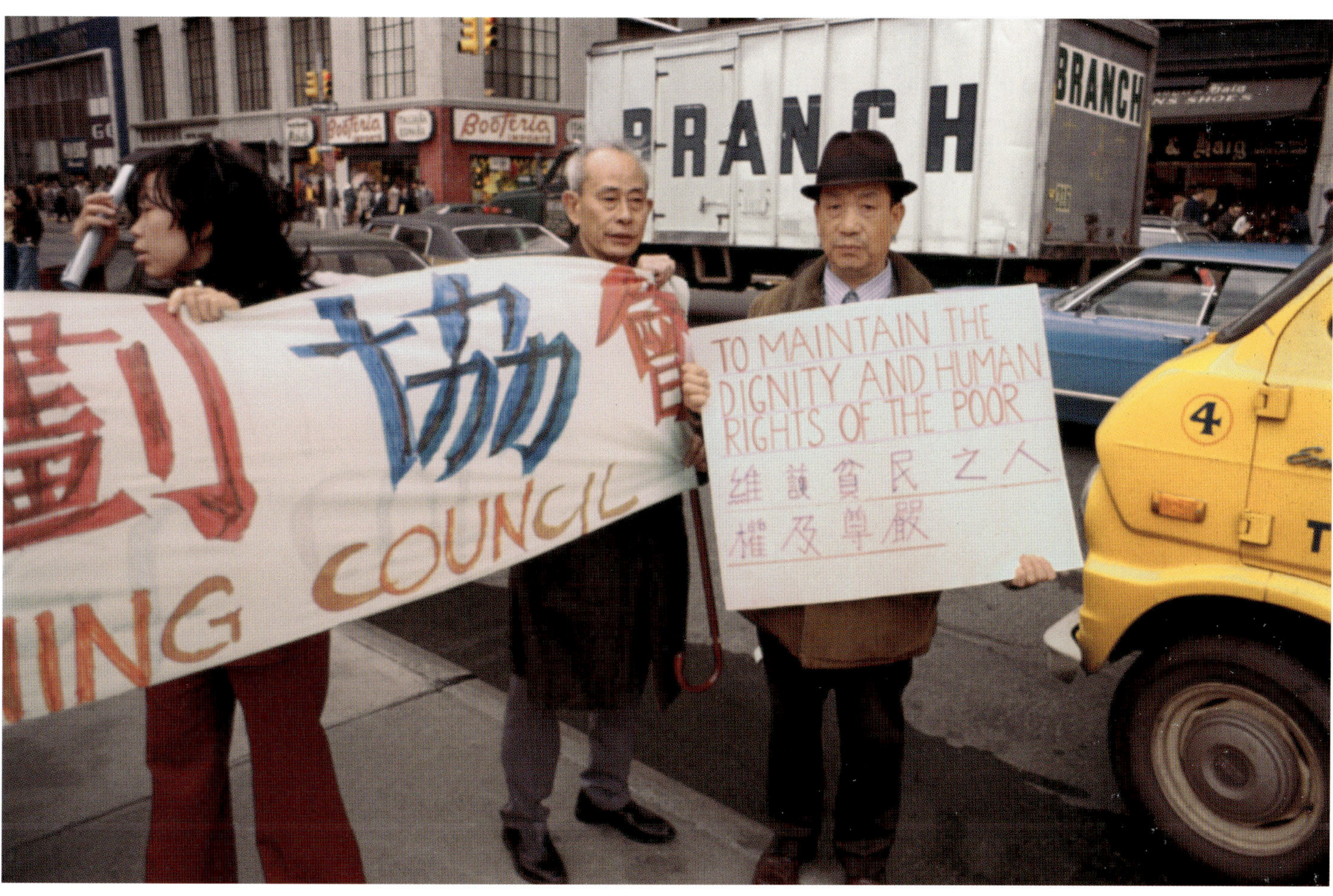

The Office of Economic Opportunity, created in 1964, administered most of the Johnson administration's War on Poverty programs. It funneled $21 million a year to New York City for Head Start, job training, senior centers, and more. When its termination was threatened, the Chinatown Planning Council took part in a protest with five thousand people at city hall. New York, April 1974.

In 1996 students at Columbia University demanded the creation of an ethnic studies program, including Asian American and Latino studies. Some students went on a hunger strike and occupied a building. The campaign led to the formation in 1998 of the Center for the Study of Ethnicity and Race. New York, 1996.

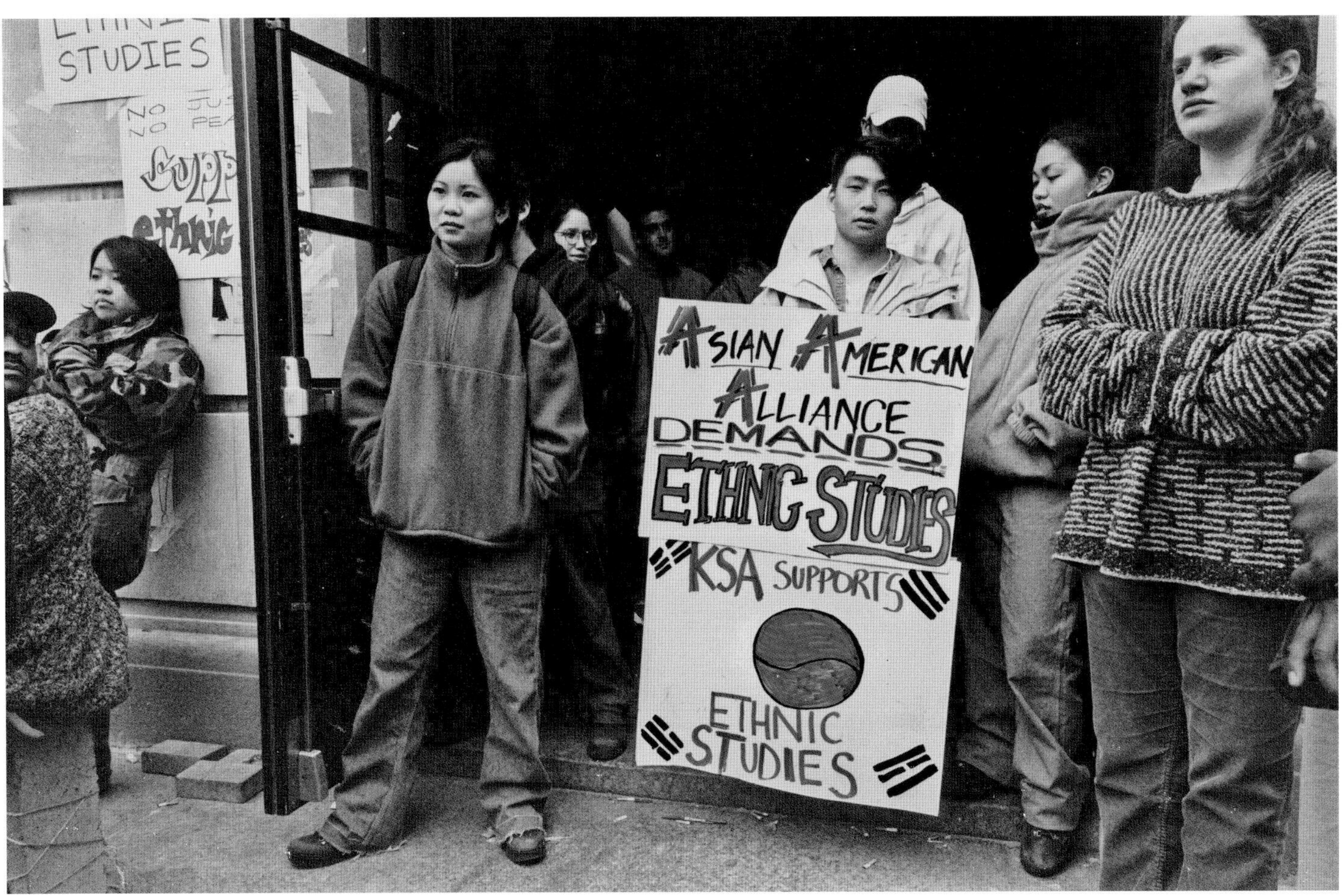

problems in housing and jobs, middle- and upper-middle-class Asian Americans made inroads in business, the professions, and electoral politics. But these two decades also saw the backlash against South Asians (perceived as Muslims) after September 11, 2001, and the outpouring of anti-Asian racism during the coronavirus pandemic of 2020. Corky's photographs can be understood as a study of resilience and hope in the face of ongoing challenges. They can also be read as a story whose conclusion remains to be written.

History is not a simple chronology of facts and events. It is a narrative, written usually by history's winners. In his junior high school history classes, young Corky Lee wondered why Asian Americans were invisible in the mainstream story of who built America and who was an American. And so he set about producing a different narrative, using his camera as his pen and his sword, to write a history of inclusion, resistance, ethnic pride, and patriotism. His photographs comprise a remarkable documentation of history in the making, a history that Asian Americans continue to make. We have tried to capture that story, imbued with Corky Lee's own intentions and values, and we hope Corky is pleased with this book, *his* book.

An ABC from NYC

The Life and Times of Corky Lee (1947–2021)

MAE NGAI

Corky Lee often introduced himself as an "ABC from NYC"—an American-born Chinese from New York City.

In this way he conveyed a story about himself. Corky was a legendary storyteller. He loved to regale others with the story behind every photograph he took, whether they were classes of students, journalists, or visitors at exhibitions. Every photograph contained a mini-lesson in Asian American history and community life that he was eager to share. He had an easy manner that connected to people; he was never didactic. He told you not only the story in the photo but also the backstory of how he came to take it.

He often pointed out things that the casual viewer did not notice but that to him held important meaning. In a 1975 photograph of New York Chinatown youths leading a demonstration against police brutality, for example, he liked to point out a young Black man in the crowd. The man was smiling, Corky surmised, because Chinese Americans were protesting police violence, something that Black people had been doing for years. In this small story, Corky conveyed that the Black freedom struggle paved the way for and inspired Asian Americans and other communities of color to make their claims for equal rights. At the same time, he highlighted the potential for interracial solidarity.

Compared to Corky's storytelling, his description of himself as an "ABC from NYC" was uncharacteristically pithy. Yet it sets the framework for this book, which intertwines the story of his life and career with that of the Asian American movement for civil rights and social justice. These two stories meet in the photographs that Corky Lee took from 1970 to 2020.

Corky's self-description as an ABC from NYC refers to a specific generation of Asian Americans: those who were born in the United States to Chinese immigrants in the two decades following World War II. His life and photographic career bear the marks of this distinctive hinge of history, between the Chinese exclusion era (1875–1943) and the immigration reforms of the 1960s.

The Chinatown that Corky photographed was one where the new immigrants did not displace the older community so much as layer and mix with it. At the same time, he documented the remaking of Asian America as a whole, as Koreans, South Asians, Vietnamese, and other Asian ethnic groups arrived in the United States. He experienced those changes directly, as a contemporary, but also as someone who had lived during the preceding era. That gave him a unique perspective, one that was at once historical and anticipatory.

Members of the ABC-NYC generation grew up in the 1950s and 1960s in the prototypical Chinese immigrant family of the hand laundry, the sewing factory, the restaurant. During that time, an estimated one-quarter of Chinese in America were so-called paper sons, those who had entered the United States with fake documents bearing the names of Chinese Americans who had claims to U.S. citizenship. Paper sons like Corky's father were the latest in a long chain of unauthorized migration dating back to the late nineteenth century. By claiming to be U.S. citizens, they circumvented the exclusion laws, which barred all Chinese laborers from immigrating to the United States and denied all Chinese naturalized citizenship.

The exclusion laws were deeply racist: their logic was that Chinese were innately incapable of assimilation and therefore a threat to American society and to national security. The paper sons and daughters were not proud that they broke the law, but it was the only way they could join their families in America. To their minds, exclusion was unjust, even if it was legal.

The Chinese are the only ethnic or racial group that the U.S. government ever singled out for exclusion by name. During the exclusion era, Chinese who were living in the country—citizens, legal immigrants such as merchants, and paper sons—encountered extreme discrimination in the labor market and marginalization in social and political life. State laws, especially in the West, forbade Chinese to marry whites, to testify against whites in court, to buy homes in white neighborhoods, or to hold professional and commercial licenses. And since they were denied citizenship, they could not vote. By the 1920s, the Chinese exclusion laws extended to all Asians (save for Filipinos, who were colonial subjects of the United States).

During World War II, when China was an American war ally, Congress repealed the Chinese exclusion law in an attempt to counter Japan's claim that the United States was a racist country. But even after the repeal, Congress set an extremely low quota for Chinese immigration—105 a year for all persons in the world with half-Chinese ancestry—reflecting ongoing racism and suspicion. After the Chinese

Wedding photograph of Jung Ping Hung and Lee Yin Chuck, Corky Lee's parents. Hong Kong, 1934. *Courtesy of John J. Lee*

After their wedding celebration, Corky carries his bride, Margaret Dea, up the stairs to their home. Jamaica, Queens, New York, October 1974. *Courtesy of John J. Lee*

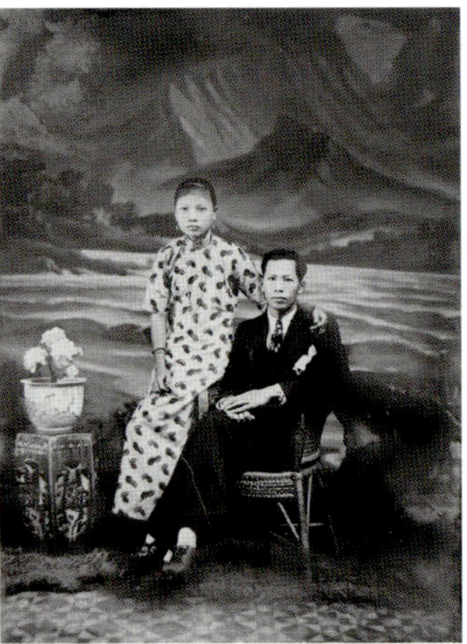

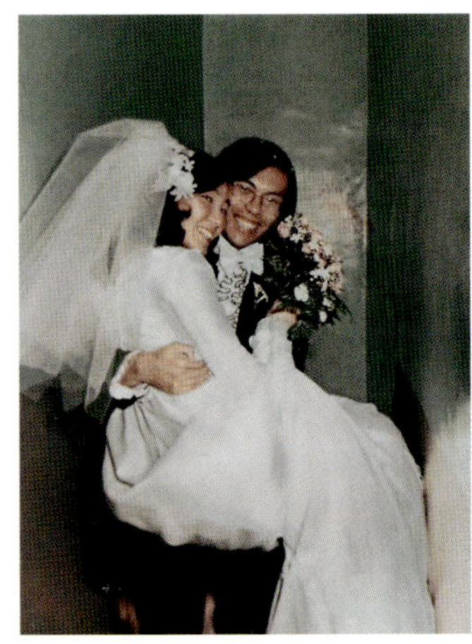

revolution of 1949 and during the Korean War and the Cold War, American mainstream opinion associated Chinese Americans with Communist China, a double threat that was both racial and ideological.

Throughout the Cold War, New York Chinatown's social life was dominated by the Chinese Consolidated Benevolent Association, an umbrella group composed of traditional associations organized according to clan and region. Its leaders were staunchly conservative and anti-Communist. So-called tongs ran gambling houses and extorted local businesses for "protection," using youth gangs to do their bidding. Violence between gangs and by police was endemic. To avoid detection and controversy, everyday people kept their heads down. Stay quiet. A raised nail invites the hammer.

Such was the milieu of Corky's childhood. He was born in 1947, at the tail end of the exclusion era and at the onset of the Cold War. Three generations of the Lee family—parents, five kids, and a grandmother—lived above their hand laundry business in Jamaica, Queens. At the time there were few other Chinese in the area. The family's paper name was Quoork (Guo) and when a white kid in the neighborhood began calling the boy "Corky," it stuck. Corky and his brothers worked in the laundry after school and during the summer. By the time he was in junior high school, he knew how to run the laundry.

But that life—the life of his father and that of several generations of Chinese laborers before him—was not to be the fate of the ABC generation.

During the 1960s, when Corky Lee was coming of age, Asian Americans were beginning to emerge from the shadows cast by the exclusion era. American-born Chinese were going to college and obtaining semiprofessional or professional jobs in engineering and health care, teaching, and social services. These opportunities resulted from the expanding domestic economy and from the shift in racial policies led by the African American civil rights movement. As that movement defied Jim Crow segregation in the South, the Supreme Court struck down segregation in schools and prohibitions on interracial marriage. In 1964–65, Congress passed the Civil Rights Act and the Voting Rights Act, as well as the Immigration and Nationality Act. Corky's father, unlike his more conservative peers, was sympathetic to the civil

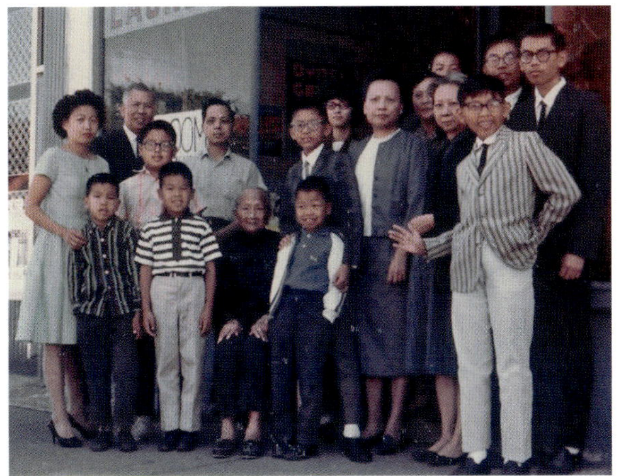

The extended family in front of Lee Laundry in Queens: Corky Lee's father, Lee Yin Chuck *(second from left)*; his paternal grandmother (*seated*); his mother, Jung Ping Hung *(in blue jacket),* flanked by her sons John *(to her right)*, Richie *(waving)*, Corky (*back row, far right*), and Jimmy (*to his right*). The others are the families of Louie Lee, his father's nephew, and Poy Lore, a childhood friend of his mother. All the adults in the photo ran laundries. Jamaica, Queens, New York, circa 1962. *Courtesy of John J. Lee*

rights movement. He understood that the Rev. Martin Luther King, Jr., and the movement's tireless work would have reverberations far beyond the Black community, that Chinese Americans would benefit from its effects. Though he was an immigrant hand laundry man, Corky's father had educated himself, he had lived in Jim Crow Baltimore, and he had served in the army during the war, which gave him a broad worldview.

Corky attended Queens College of the City University of New York, which then had few Asian students. He put himself through school by working at part-time jobs—a Chinese takeout joint in Queens, a florist's stand in a subway station. He majored in American history and served as president of the Chinese Student Association. He admired the revolutionaries of the Black Panthers and the Puerto Rican group the Young Lords, because they were militant and because they served the people with free breakfast programs and medical clinics. Like many of his generation, he opposed the war in Vietnam as imperialist and racist.

Upon his graduation in 1969, Corky's draft status was reclassified as 1-A (available for military service). He declared himself a conscientious objector and received a draft exemption, with alternative service with Vista, the forerunner to AmeriCorps. He was assigned to work at Two Bridges Neighborhood Council, in an area just east of Chinatown where Chinese, Black, and Puerto Rican residents lived in dilapidated tenements. Corky visited them and organized rent strikes, putting the tenants' rent money into escrow accounts until the landlords made repairs. To document tenants' needs, he took photographs of their living conditions.

In the 1960s and early 1970s, government antipoverty funds trickled into the Lower East Side and Chinatown. In addition to Two Bridges, several other social service agencies sprang up: the Chinatown Planning Council, Mobilization for Youth, and Project Reach. Government funding also gave renewed energy to the nearby older settlement houses, like Henry Street and Hamilton-Madison. All these organizations provided badly needed social services; tackled problems such as substandard housing and gang violence; and established an infrastructure that educated and mobilized residents to stand up for their rights. Some set up storefront organizations that espoused more radical politics and offered alternative services such as acupuncture clinics and food co-ops.

Corky Lee at the Women's March against Donald Trump. Midtown Manhattan, January 2017. *David "Dee" Delgado*

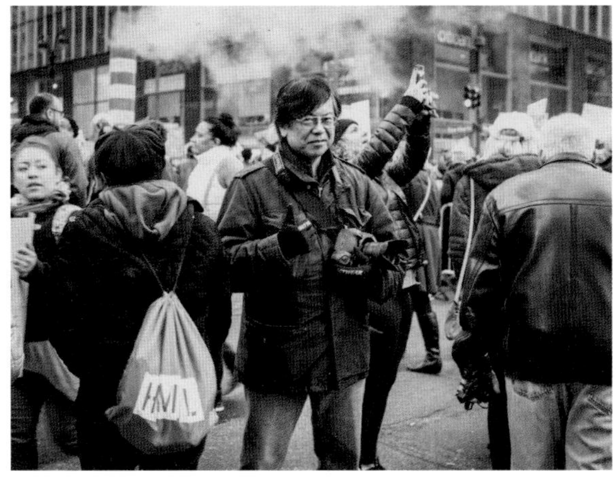

These social service organizations hired young college graduates as social workers, youth counselors, housing advocates, and community organizers. The young activists hailed from both working-class and middle-class backgrounds; some, like Corky, had attended New York's public universities while others came through Columbia, Yale, and Princeton.

Chinatown was opening up. Change was in the air. Immersed in Chinatown's street life, Corky became interested in photographing the community. His interest would later reach beyond Chinatown to diverse Asian American communities in the New York City metropolitan area and beyond. But in the early 1970s, he mainly took slides and composed slideshows for presentations to students and community groups. In 1974 and 1975 he sold photographs to the *New York Post*, adding photojournalism to his repertoire. Soon he sold photos to *The New York Times*, the New York *Daily News*, *Time*, and other periodicals.

Corky Lee's portrayals of Chinatown and Asian Americans amounted to nothing less than a radical break in the history of American photography. In the late nineteenth and early twentieth century, some white American photographers had pursued a fascination with Chinatown, especially in San Francisco. Isaiah Taber, Arnold Genthe, Charles Weidner, and others developed different styles as they moved from portraiture to aesthetic photography, yet they all represented Chinatown and its people as foreign to and separate from America and Americans. They perceived Chinatown through a lens that combined desire and difference, as art historian Anthony Lee has analyzed. Their gaze was Orientalist, casting the Chinese "other" as an object against which Euro-Americans composed themselves as civilized, rational, and modern. Well into the twentieth century, photography books, tourist guidebooks, and journalistic accounts continued to portray Chinatown as alien and exotic, a closed society.

Only a handful of Chinese American photographers captured Chinatown from the inside. During World War II and the postwar years, James Wong Howe and Kem Lee showed a different aspect of San Francisco. Corky Lee was the first to photograph New York's Chinatown from within. "I see a different part of Chinatown that the general public does not see," he would say. "It's not a drive-by tourist destination but a living community." His gaze was that of the son, the

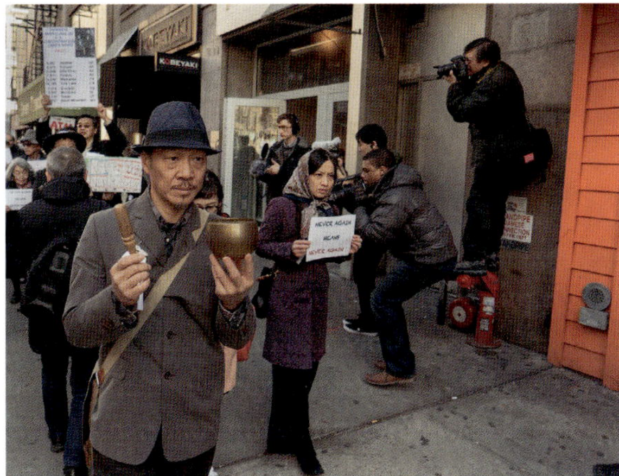

Corky Lee photographs the Silent March commemorating the Japanese American internment, with actor Perry Yung in the lead. Midtown Manhattan, 2017. *Stan Honda*

older brother, the comrade, and he wanted Asian Americans to see themselves as he saw himself and as he saw them. In this way, he differed from other social photographers like Lewis Hine and Dorothea Lange, who famously portrayed child laborers and migrant farmworkers as abject subjects in order to elicit sympathy from elites.

Corky, a self-taught photographer, was often said to be streetwise. That was partly true, but he also worked deliberately at honing his craft and advancing his career. When the San Francisco photographer Barry Chin came to New York on assignment for the Associated Press in the 1970s, Corky shadowed him for several weeks. Corky studied the work of photojournalists and urban street photographers like Weegee, the mid-twentieth-century crime-scene sensationalist, and *The New York Times*'s fashion photographer, Bill Cunningham, who rode a bicycle around town to snap photos of New Yorkers dressed in the latest styles. Corky learned from rejections how to better select photos to pitch to editors.

At a 1975 protest against police brutality, Corky darted around a line of press photographers "like a wide receiver" and grabbed a quick shot of police dragging away a bloodied Chinese American man (see page 86). Then he sprinted over to the *New York Post*'s building on South Street in time for the newspaper's afternoon edition. The photo made the front page. It was a great shot, but it was also a lucky one, he knew.

In the late 1970s Corky moved from the Pentax screw-mount to the bayonet lens. (He would switch to a Nikon digital in the late 1990s.) He held three artist-in-residencies, at the Asian Pacific American Studies Institute at New York University, the Asian American Studies Center at UCLA, and the Lightbox at Syracuse University, where he worked on darkroom technique.

Many people have remarked that Corky seemed to be "everywhere," at every AAPI event. He was, indeed, always on the move. In addition to his freelance work and paid gigs (gala events and weddings), he held a day job as account executive at Expedi from 1983 to 2011. Expedi was a progressive minority-owned print shop where left-wing and ethnic community groups printed their weeklies, bulletins, and posters. The owner, Sam Chen, hired many Chinese international students and striving artists (including a young Ai Weiwei in the 1980s) as production workers. (For the protest against the 1989 Tiananmen massacre, the artists made a giant papier-mâché replica of China's Goddess of Liberty in Expedi's loft.) Corky befriended the diverse Asian American and other minority groups who brought their business to Expedi, and by having advance knowledge of their events—this was before email and social media—he was able to be on the scene to photograph them.

In 1979 Corky took a photograph of elderly Chinatown women protesting Yves Saint Laurent's Opium perfume (see page 39) and brought it to the *New York Post*'s news editor, who turned it down. Corky later went to the night editor, who accepted it. The sly move infuriated the news editor, who told Corky the *Post* would not run any more of his photographs. To Corky, the incident exemplified the mainstream media's disregard for AAPI issues. He often lamented that he did not receive the respect and recognition that he deserved. But he remained undeterred in his mission to break stereotypes. His choice was both political and aesthetic.

His first business card for "Corky Lee, Photographer" gave Expedi's address and the quip, "Ordinary skills, Extraordinary will. Someone hip but not a lot of lip. If that's the plan, I'm the man." He later modified it to express his politics: "Ordinary skills, extraordinary will—to practice photographic justice to right the wrongs," and tagged himself, "*b*. New York City, activist photographer." In the 1990s, when his reputation was well established, he printed a card with his adopted moniker, "Undisputed, Unofficial Asian American Photographer Laureate."

Corky's wry business cards hint at the evolution of his persona from hipster to activist to photographer laureate. And over time, he honed his thinking in another way. He continued to submit freelance work to outlets with AAPI audiences, such as *Downtown Express*, which covered Lower Manhattan, and *Asian American News*, with its national readership. But he came to feel that the word *photojournalism* diminished the scope of his ambition. It was no longer enough for him merely to capture the action of a moment, to "get the shot," so to speak. Instead he gained a more purposeful, conceptual, and artistic focus, creating intentional compositions that made a statement: the grieving mother of Vincent Chin, a Sikh man draped in an American flag, and portraits of everyday people and everyday life. He liked to compose photos that showed both the "Asian" and the "American"—Asians in ethnic dress waving American flags, Muslim schoolgirls in front of McDonald's golden arches, Filipinos riding Harleys—the ease with which Asian Americans adopted American cultural symbols. He created visual narratives that are by turns serious, joyous, political, quirky; always conscious of the zeitgeist that was Asian America.

The photographs in this book speak to Corky Lee's evolution as an activist-photographer. His genius was to capture in his compositions something of the personality of his subjects, each one distinctive and each with their own story, each bearing their own sense of personal dignity. He presents them as individual human beings and historical actors, not as clichéd agit-prop. That is what makes his photos of Asian Americans, separately and in aggregate, so powerful.

At the United Nations, Filipino Americans and their supporters protest the U.S.-backed dictatorship of Ferdinand Marcos in the Philippines. New York, 1979.

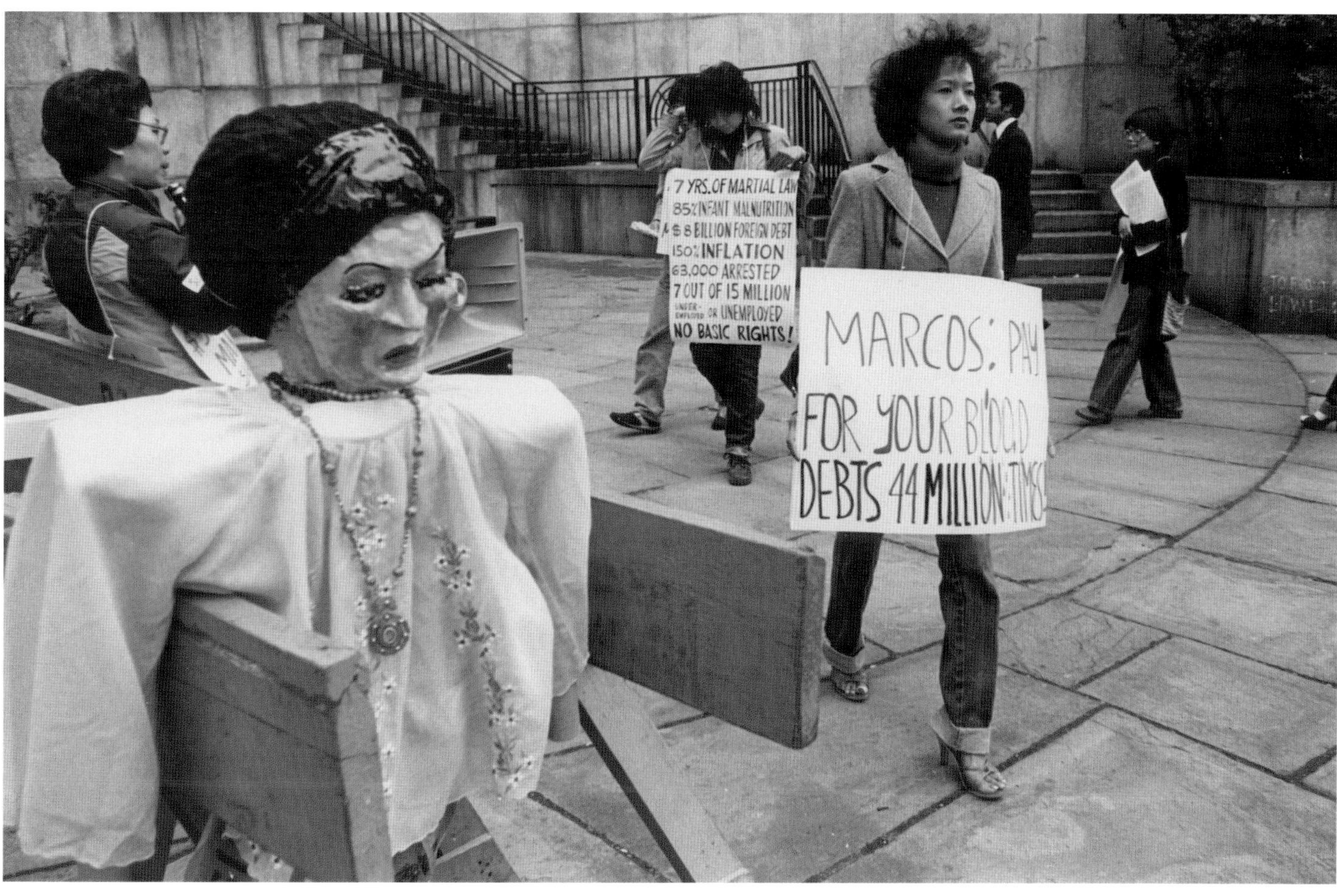

On Composition

CORKY LEE

Corky Lee was interviewed in 2011 by the late Peter Kwong, a professor of Asian American Studies at Hunter College of the City University of New York. Kwong was preparing to write an introduction for a book that Corky intended to self-publish but did not complete. In this excerpt Corky discusses his craft.

To me, composition of a picture is the most important thing. You want to be able to give the right lighting, the right angle with a clear story to tell. And it should inspire people to think and want to know more. . . . It took lots of experience to put all that together. For instance, I saw a number of sewing machines on the sidewalk in front of a factory recently. To most people it was nothing significant. But knowing Chinatown, I realized that the machines were being moved out because the factory was closing. . . . The backstory of these eight sewing machines lying out there is the decline of Chinatown's manufacturing industry and the end of an era. This is the kind of story I like to tell.

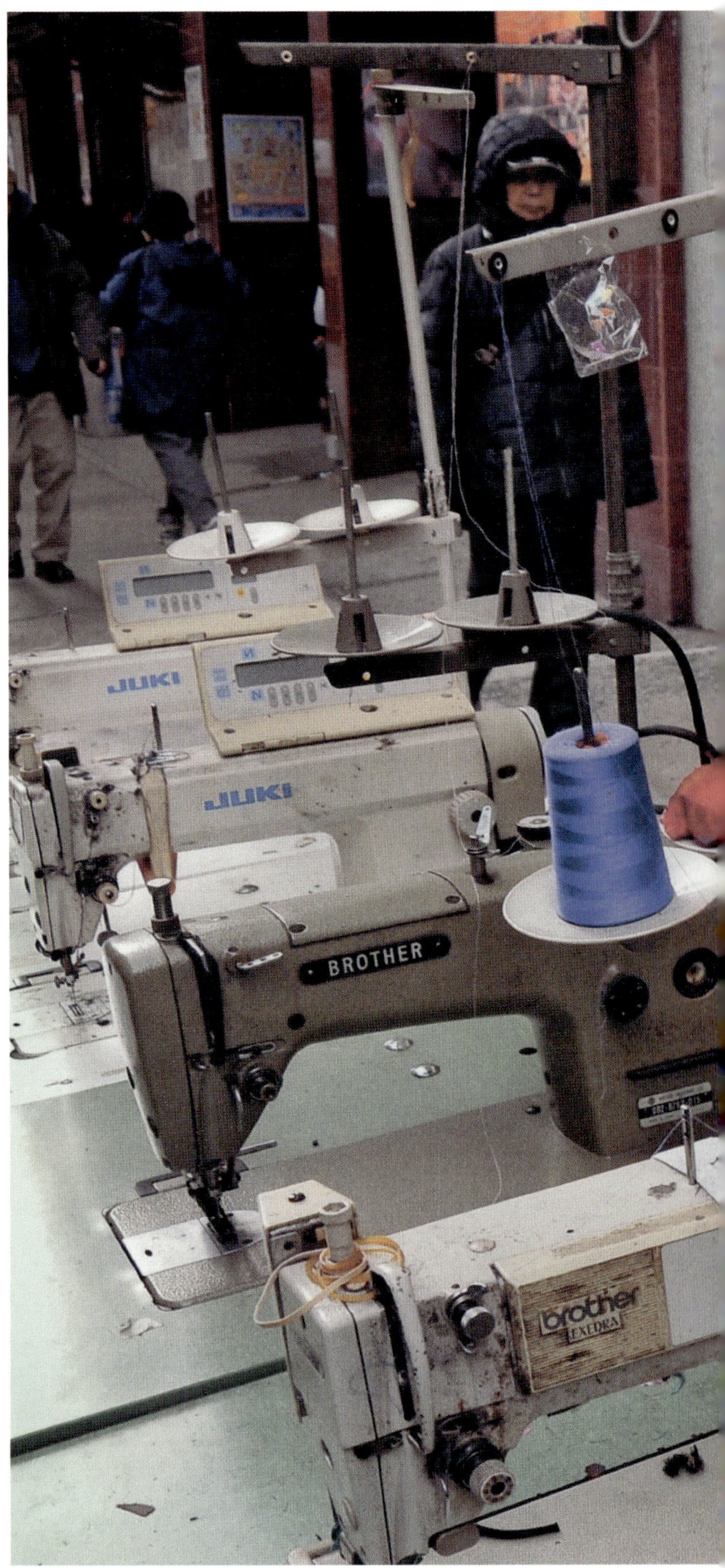

Discarded sewing machines on a Chinatown sidewalk after a garment shop closing. New York, 2011.

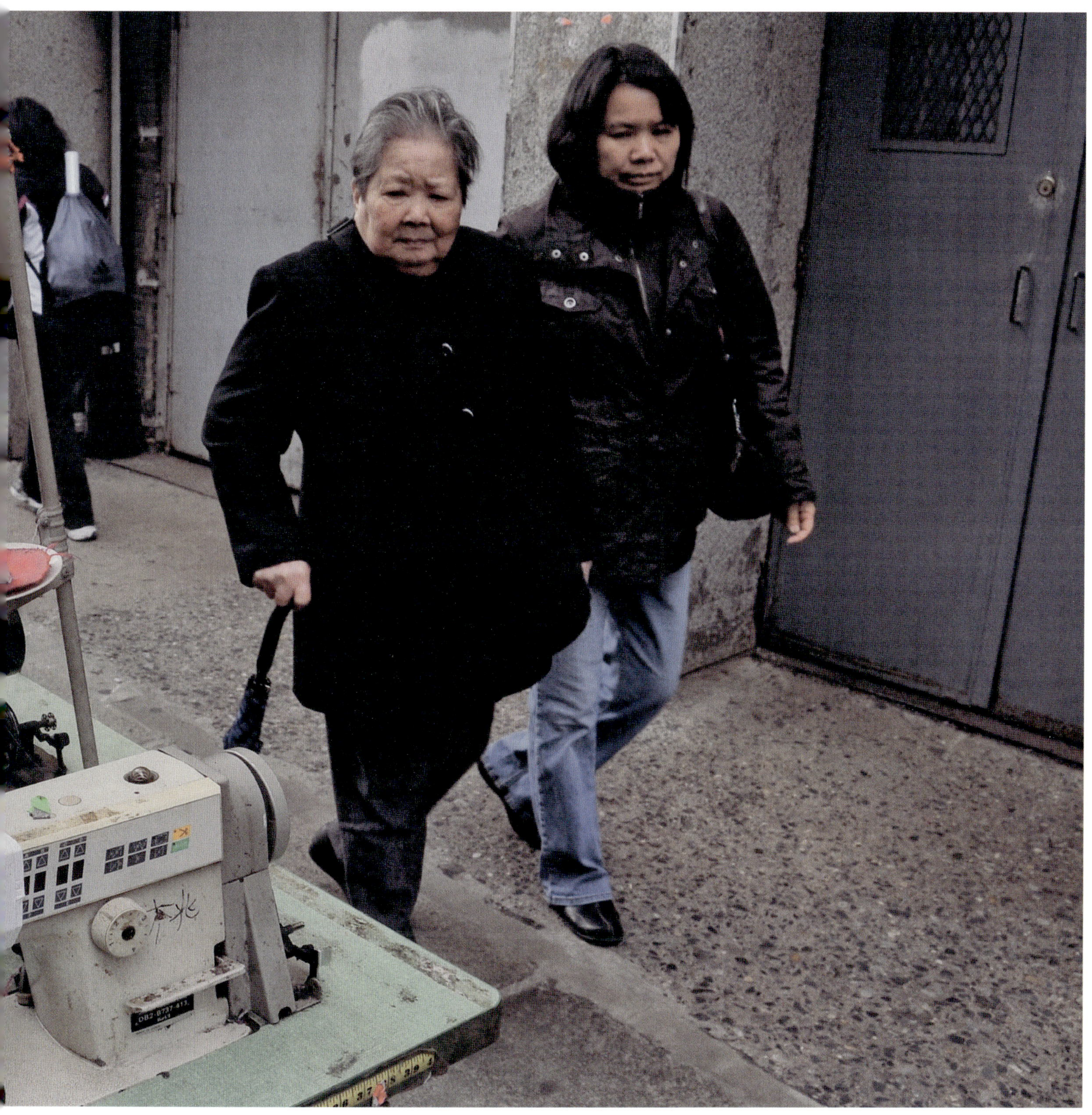

THE BIRTH OF THE MOVEMENT

1970s

Corky Lee. 1973.
Bob Hsiang

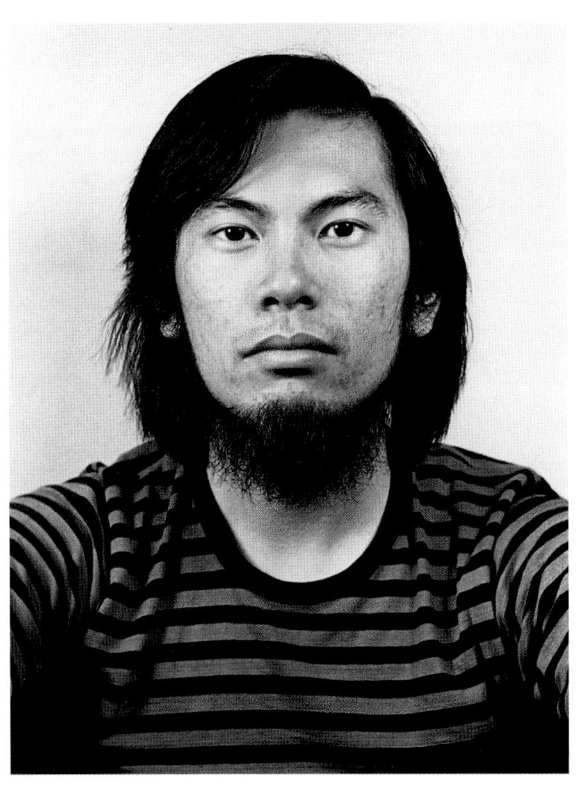

In 1969, when Corky Lee began working at Chinatown's Two Bridges Neighborhood Council, the Black freedom movement was in full swing and so was the federal government's War on Poverty. These two trends were complementary, but they also generated tension. The civil rights movement had led the government to concede massive funding for services and improvements in poor and minority communities, but the reforms often fell short of substantive structural change. The Great Society programs of the Lyndon Johnson administration promoted "equal opportunity" in employment but not actual job creation. New housing developments would take years to break ground as politicians and experts conducted lengthy studies. A door to equal rights and social justice had opened, but only partially. Hope mingled with frustration.

The door was also always in danger of being slammed shut. The bloody assassinations of the Rev. Martin Luther King, Jr., Malcolm X, and Black Panther leader Fred Hampton were but the most extreme instances of the violent repression of the Black freedom struggle. Across the left, civil rights, student, and antiwar activists faced government surveillance, police violence, and political persecutions. The war against the Vietnamese people's right to self-determination raged on and, among other things, fed the stereotype that Asian Americans were not Americans. Indeed, Asian Americans and Pacific Islanders were not listed in the Economic Opportunity Act of 1964 and were not even officially recognized by the federal government as a "minority" group until 1977. Although studies in the 1960s and 1970s showed that crushing poverty prevailed in Chinese immigrant communities (upward of 70 percent in New York), the city agencies that were charged with distributing federal War on Poverty funds virtually ignored Chinatown until the late 1970s.

Nevertheless, some federal funds did trickle into Chinatown and support new agencies, like the Chinatown Planning Council; or they were made available through agencies in the multiethnic Lower East Side, like Two Bridges. Corky was one of scores of young Asian Americans who were being hired by these agencies or who were starting their own radical storefront organizations like I Wor Kuen (*yihequan*), named after the anti-imperialist Boxer Rebellion of the late Qing dynasty. A door that opens, even a little, allows for a glimpse of another horizon.

Through his work at Two Bridges and its parent agency, Hamilton-Madison House, Corky worked with other activists. In 1969, as a community youth activity, they organized a pushcart derby down Mott Street, through the center of Chinatown. Engineering students designed the pushcarts, neighborhood kids steered them, and jocks pushed them. It was not only fun but brought together people from diverse backgrounds.

One of the biggest problems facing the Chinese community was the lack of access to medical services, even as many immigrants suffered from diabetes, hypertension, and tuberculosis. In the summer of 1971, a broad community coalition organized a ten-day health fair on Mott Street. Corky was one of the leaders, and his resourcefulness was already apparent: he knew how to get Mott Street closed to traffic, and he directed the young people in building the booths. At the fair, volunteers staffed educational tables and administered free blood pressure tests to more than two thousand residents. The Chinatown Health Fair, and grassroots organizing led by the late community health advocate Thomas Tam, resulted in the formation of the Chinatown Health Clinic later that year. In 1972 a new city hospital, Gouverneur,

Corky Lee directs a pushcart derby in Chinatown, with his fiancée, Margaret Dea (*right*). New York, 1969. *Courtesy of John J. Lee*

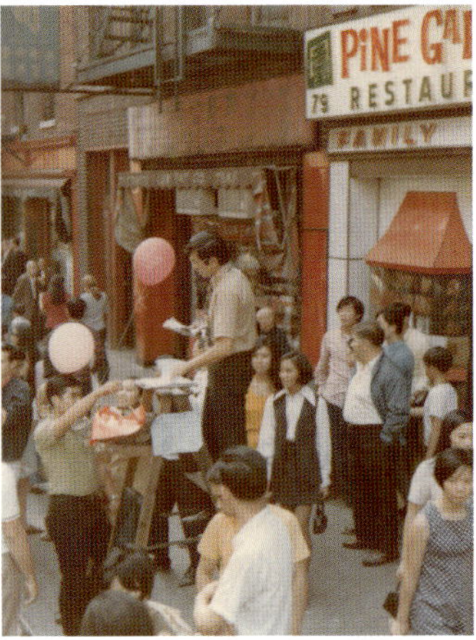

opened near Chinatown, with full services and a Chinese-speaking staff.

Corky's interest in photography began while he was working at Two Bridges, where he used a camera borrowed from an acquaintance. Bob Hsiang was an artist and a photographer who had recently graduated from college. Now living in Chinatown, Bob founded the Asian Media Collective. As Corky moved from photographing tenements to Chinatown scenes, Bob brought him into the collective. The group became part of the Basement Workshop, a vibrant arts center that was founded in 1970 by Asian American poets, writers, visual artists, dancers, actors, and musicians. The Basement's creative energies and radical expressions of identity epitomized the new Asian American movement.

Corky channeled his activist spirit into photography, documenting street fairs, protest demonstrations, and student conferences as well as everyday community life. He photographed a visit by members of the Black Panther Party to the Chinatown storefront of I Wor Kuen (IWK) and the Asian American contingents in anti–Vietnam War protests in New York and Washington, D.C.

In 1971 the United Nations voted to restore China's seat on the Security Council to the People's Republic of China. The following year President Richard Nixon visited China and shook hands with Chairman Mao Zedong and Premier Zhou Enlai. The United States would not formally recognize the People's Republic until 1978, but the era of "ping-pong diplomacy" that Nixon opened overseas transformed Chinatown in New York. The Fujian Association flew the five-star flag of the People's Republic on East Broadway. Young people and old-timers alike packed the IWK storefront to watch revolutionary films from the PRC.

Around this time Mr. and Mrs. Ching Yeh Chen, young graduate students from Taiwan and political activists, opened a small retail store at 22 Catherine Street that would become known as the Pearl River Mart. It sold goods from mainland China—cotton kung fu slippers, sandalwood soap, Mao jackets—as a means of building "friendship," a kind of people-to-people diplomacy. Corky bought the iconic canvas schoolbag emblazoned with "serve the people" in Mao's calligraphy at the shop and used it as his first camera bag.

In 1972 Corky participated in an Asian American youth delegation to China, one of the first groups invited by the PRC after Nixon's visit. His

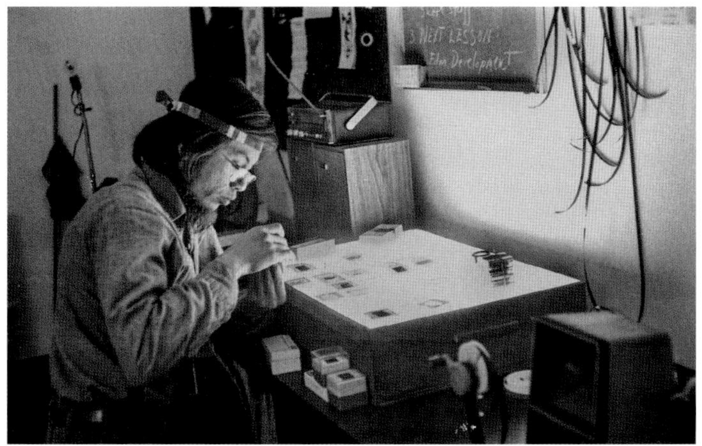

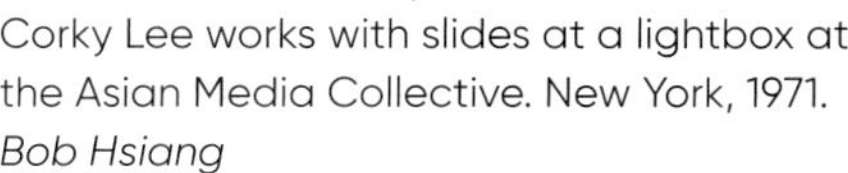

Corky Lee works with slides at a lightbox at the Asian Media Collective. New York, 1971. *Bob Hsiang*

father was ecstatic and urged him to visit the family's ancestral village and to tell the people back home that the folks in America were all right. On his way to China, in Hong Kong, Corky bought his first camera, a 35mm single-lens reflex Pentax Spotmatic with a screw-mount lens, and shot twenty-four rolls of film on the trip.

Also during the 1970s, Corky worked as a television reporter for Chinese Cable TV (CCTV), the forerunner of Asian CineVision. But most enduringly he documented the explosive growth of Asian American activism in Chinatown: protests that criticized tour bus companies for steering business to restaurants that were on the take; protests by tenants against their tenement landlords; protests demanding the hiring of Asian American workers for the construction of the Confucius Plaza housing complex; protests calling for bilingual education at the local junior high school and for Asian American studies at City College; and the near-constant demonstrations against the war in Vietnam.

Corky's protest photographs are often intergenerational portraits of senior citizens, workers, and young people marching together. They are evidence of the new infrastructure of social services and new interactions between students and workers and seniors, immigrants and ABCs. Their activism transformed Chinatown's political landscape. No longer did the Chinese Consolidated Benevolent Association (CCBA), the tongs, and the gangs hold the community in thrall. A new political spectrum emerged that extended from liberal civil-rights reformism to revolutionary activism. Liberals led social service agencies like the Chinatown Planning Council and the local Democratic Party Club, accruing mainstream political and social capital. Meanwhile the more radical Basement Workshop, I Wor Kuen, and Asian Americans for Equal Employment (AAFEE) valorized and mobilized people at the grass roots. Their phrases "serve the people," "power to the people," and "oppressed peoples of the world unite" captured the era's radical ethos.

Moderates, liberals, and radicals worked together or opposed one another, depending on the issue. Everyone supported the historic 1971 Chinatown Health Fair, and even the CCBA's conservativism moderated under the leadership of Man Bun Lee, who welcomed the African American boxing hero and anti–Vietnam War activist Muhammad Ali to Chinatown. But at times activists also opposed the CCBA and the liberals. In 1972–73 IWK organized tenants

Corky Lee interviews New York mayor Ed Koch for Chinese Cable TV. New York, late 1970s. *Courtesy of CCTV, © 1980 Asian CineVision*

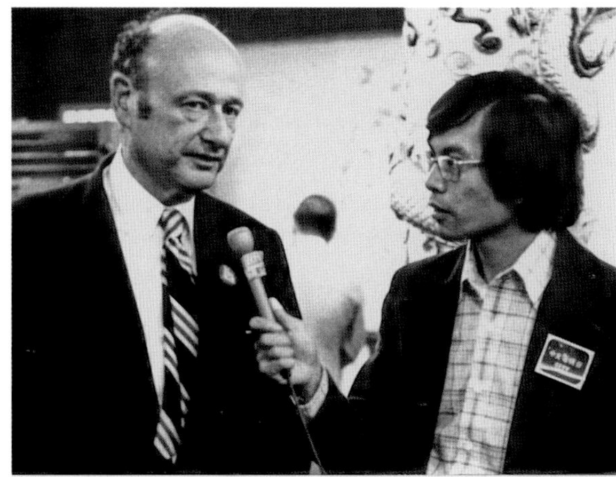

against their slumlord, a prominent immigration lawyer whose family were Democratic Party leaders. In 1975 the AAFEE pushed the CCBA to openly oppose police brutality. While community politics were heterodox, the organizing energies of the left suffused the emerging Asian American movement. Calls for empowerment and solidarity challenged the power structure of slumlords, police, and local and national politicians; of racism, capitalism, and imperialism.

The Asian American movement was ethnically diverse from its beginnings. Japanese Americans and Filipino Americans worked in Chinatown community organizations. The Basement Workshop and the anti–Vietnam War movement were pan-Asian affairs. The annual Days of Remembrance, commemorating the internment of Japanese Americans during World War II, and protests against the Marcos dictatorship in the Philippines drew participants from diverse Asian ethnic groups.

In their struggles for access to health care, housing rights, and jobs, the activists were often remarkably successful, and some efforts had a long-lasting impact. The Chinatown Health Clinic evolved to become one of the community's most enduring institutions: the Charles B. Wang Community Health Center is today the major health care provider in the Manhattan and Flushing Chinatowns. When the New York Telephone Company planned to demolish tenements, tenant organizing by Two Bridges and I Wor

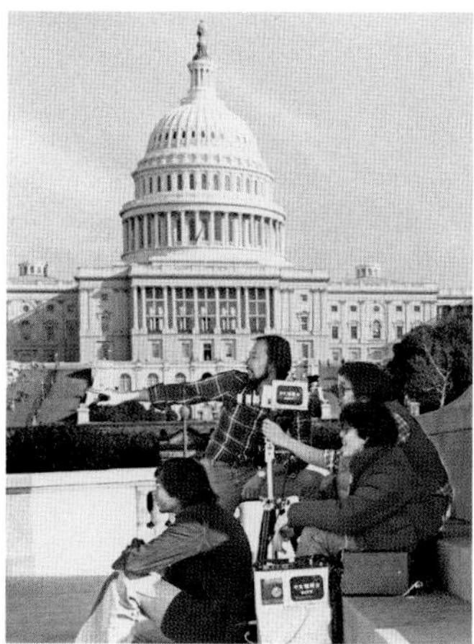

Corky Lee (*front, left*), on assignment with a CCTV crew, covers demonstrations supporting affirmative action, during the Supreme Court's hearings in *Regents of the University of California v. Bakke*. Washington, D.C., 1977. *Thomas Chin*

Kuen defeated it in a "We Won't Move" campaign. Asian Americans for Equal Employment succeeded in getting jobs for Chinese construction workers at Confucius Plaza. A community-wide uprising against police brutality resulted in the removal of the police officers who had beaten Peter Yew (see page 88) and in reforms in the department. The door opened a bit wider.

Corky was both a participant in the emerging movement and, with his camera, an observer. Though garrulous, he was actually a very private person. Being behind the camera may have been more comfortable for him, but for whatever reason, it became his persona. He was ecumenical and took photographs of activities regardless of the organizers' political persuasion. He eschewed formal membership in any organization, which enabled him to stay above the political fray.

Corky's interest in documenting the daily lives of ordinary people also dates to these early years. To his mind, struggling against racism included combating stereotypes of Chinatown and Chinese people. To that end, during the 1970s he took hundreds of photographs of people at work, seniors in their homes and in the park, and children playing. He photographed Chinatown street scenes. He was getting his feet wet, experimenting with composition and light. His portraits are iconic representations of Chinatown life at the moment of transition from the exclusion era to the new immigration.

Young Kok: "To Be Praiseworthy of the Nation"

JOHN J. LEE

Corky Lee's younger brother, a retired public defender in Southern California

Corky was a product of his times, but he was also, more directly, a product of his family. We grew up in the 1950s and 1960s in an apartment in Jamaica, Queens, above our parents' Chinese hand laundry. On occasion our mom, Jung Ping Hung (Zhong Pinghong), worked in a garment factory in Manhattan's Chinatown, an hour away by subway. Like many garment workers, she often brought work home, to sew at an industrial Singer machine in our grandmother's bedroom. Our sister's wedding picture hung on the wall above.

Our father, Lee Yin Chuck (Li Renzhuo), came to the United States in 1925, at the age of seventeen. Dad hailed from Taishan, Guangdong province, the home county of most Chinese immigrants before 1965. He evaded the racist Chinese exclusion laws by immigrating as a paper son, using fake papers with the surname Quoork (Guo) that claimed he had been born in China to a Chinese person who had American citizenship.

Most Chinese immigrant men believed they would eventually return to their home villages, even if they remained in America for decades and were relegated to "feminine" jobs, like cooking and washing clothes, where they did not compete with white male workers. But our father had a different sort of grit. Although he had only three years of formal education, he availed himself of every opportunity, shadowing Chinese university students on weekends and seeking training and employment beyond the insular Chinese community. He eventually became an industrial welder at the naval shipyards in Camden, New Jersey, and was drafted into military service in 1943. He served in China in aircraft maintenance for the Fourteenth Air Division, the famous Flying Tigers.

In the last year of World War II, Dad longed to return to his homeland, but the Chinese civil war was raging, he was getting no younger, and he wanted sons of his own to carry on his name. He relinquished his sojourner status and resolved to raise his children as Americans. In 1946 he brought our mother (whom he had married on a visit home in 1934), our sister, Fee, and our adopted brother, Bing, to join him in New York. On September 5, 1947, Lee Young Quoork (Li Yangguo), destined to be nicknamed Corky, was born. By January 1952, three more boys had joined the family.

Although Dad's own ambitions had been constrained, he took pains to ensure that his kids would not have that problem. An astute and thoughtful observer of his adopted country, he made use of the modest educational resources

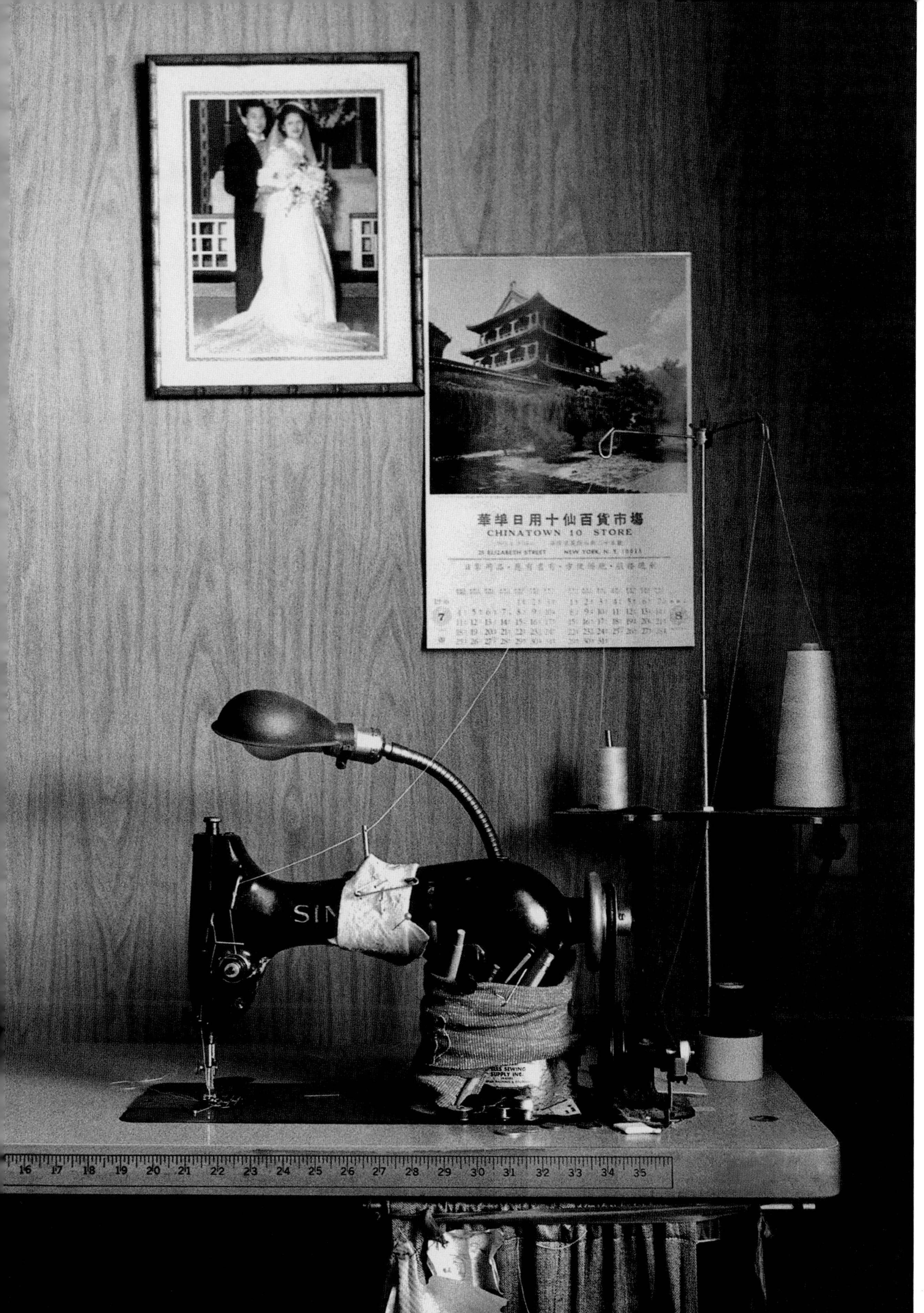

Corky Lee's mother, Jung Ping Hung, used this industrial sewing machine in the Lee family apartment. Jamaica, Queens, New York, 1976.

that were available, both for himself and for his offspring. He procured for us a set of the *Encyclopaedia Britannica* and took us on frequent visits to the public library. He tuned the radio to the morning news before school, discussed current events with us over the dinner table, and shared the evening TV news with us. He posed Socratic queries and conversed with us about the civil rights movement. We imbibed our parents' lessons of perseverance and took pride both in our Chinese heritage and in American democracy and patriotism.

Corky and I shared a bedroom as kids and later, when he went to college, an apartment. I took to shadowing him to the public library and then to meetings and other events in the emerging Asian American movement. We both chafed at the "model minority" stereotype.

In the 1970s, Asian American activism, for all its righteousness and later successes, was not a popular endeavor. Our parents, knowing all about the internment of Japanese Americans during World War II and the Chinese red scares during the Korean War, feared for their two sons. Corky's college sweetheart, Margaret Dea, also worried about the potential negative consequences of Corky's activism. But Marge came to understand the depth of Corky's commitment to his mission, and they married in 1974. She remained his devoted wife for twenty-six years and supported him in her tender, loving, and modest manner before she passed away from cancer in 2001. Their love affair was as intense and pure as it was private.

In the mid-1970s, the pace and scope of Asian American activism continued to grow. We brothers took different routes toward our shared goal of social justice. I decided to become an attorney because I thought the movement should have its own lawyers. I left New York in 1975 for the West Coast, where I attended law school and had a legal career serving indigent clients. Corky settled into his vocation of photojournalism. He soldiered ahead, camera in hand, living up to the name our father had given him, Young Kok, "to be praiseworthy of the nation." By recording the stories and the achievements of the forgotten, he told the story of a hitherto invisible piece of the American social and historical fabric, casting sparks with each click of his shutter.

Chinatown residents protest Yves Saint Laurent's Opium perfume as offensive to Chinese people. New York, 1979.

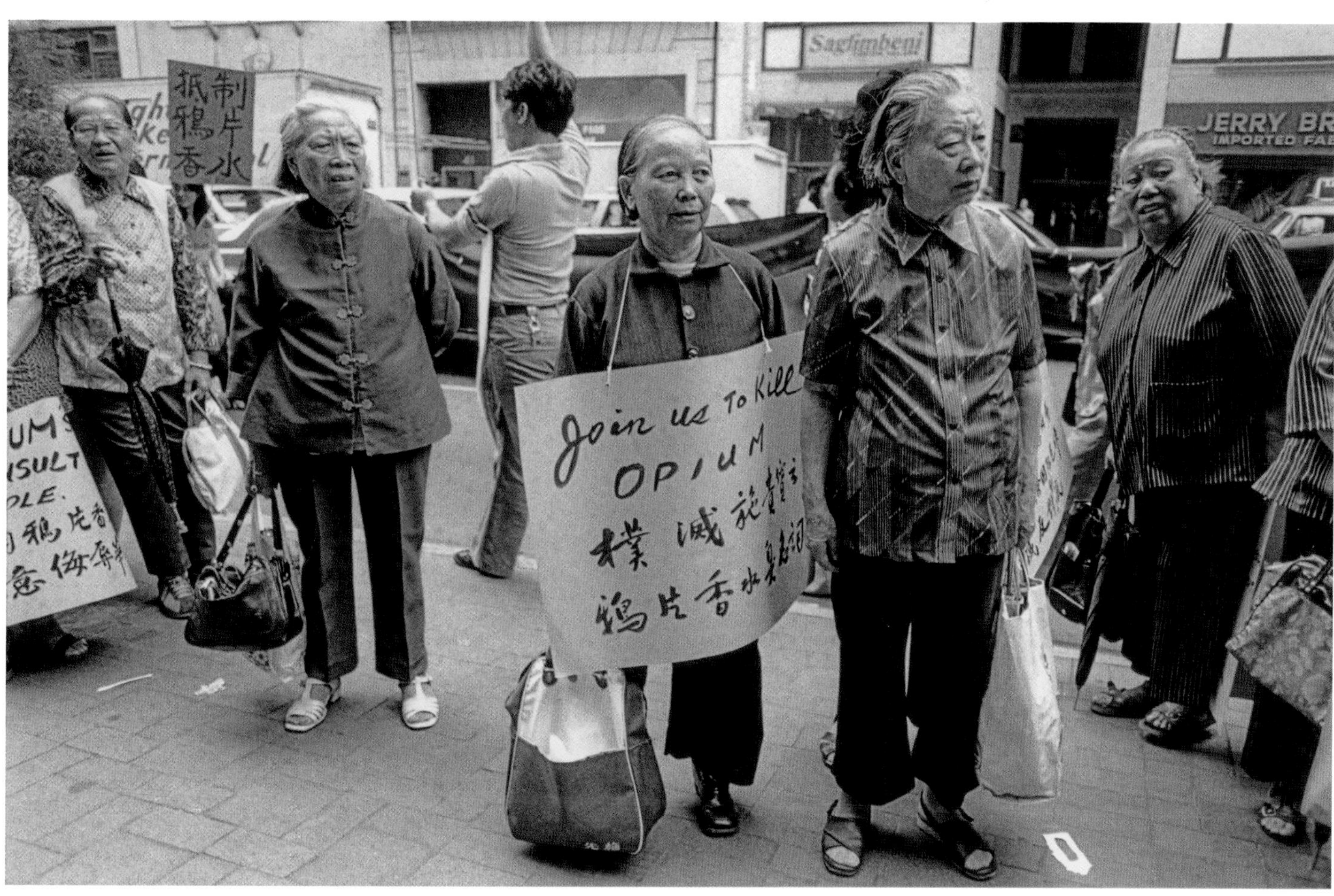

Chinese American families came into Chinatown on the weekends for a meal, some shopping, Chinese-language school for the children, and perhaps to attend church services. New York, early 1970s.

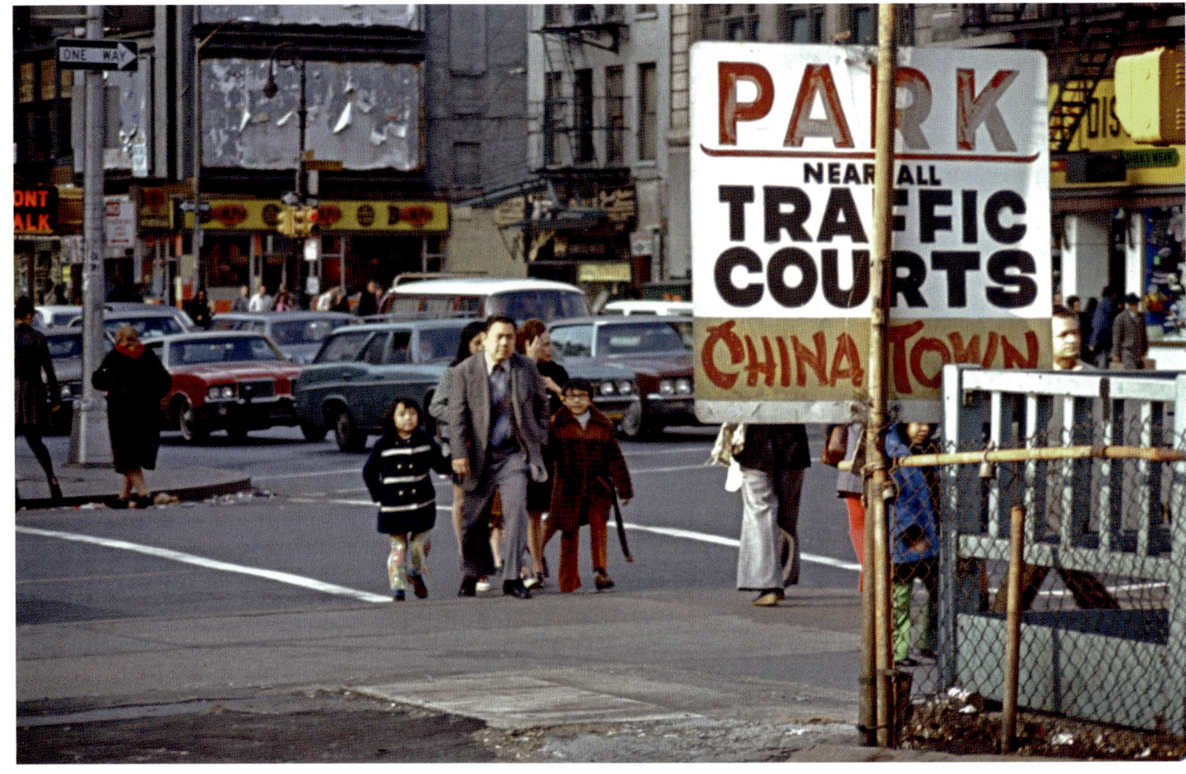

A tour bus at the corner of Bowery and Bayard. New York, early 1970s.

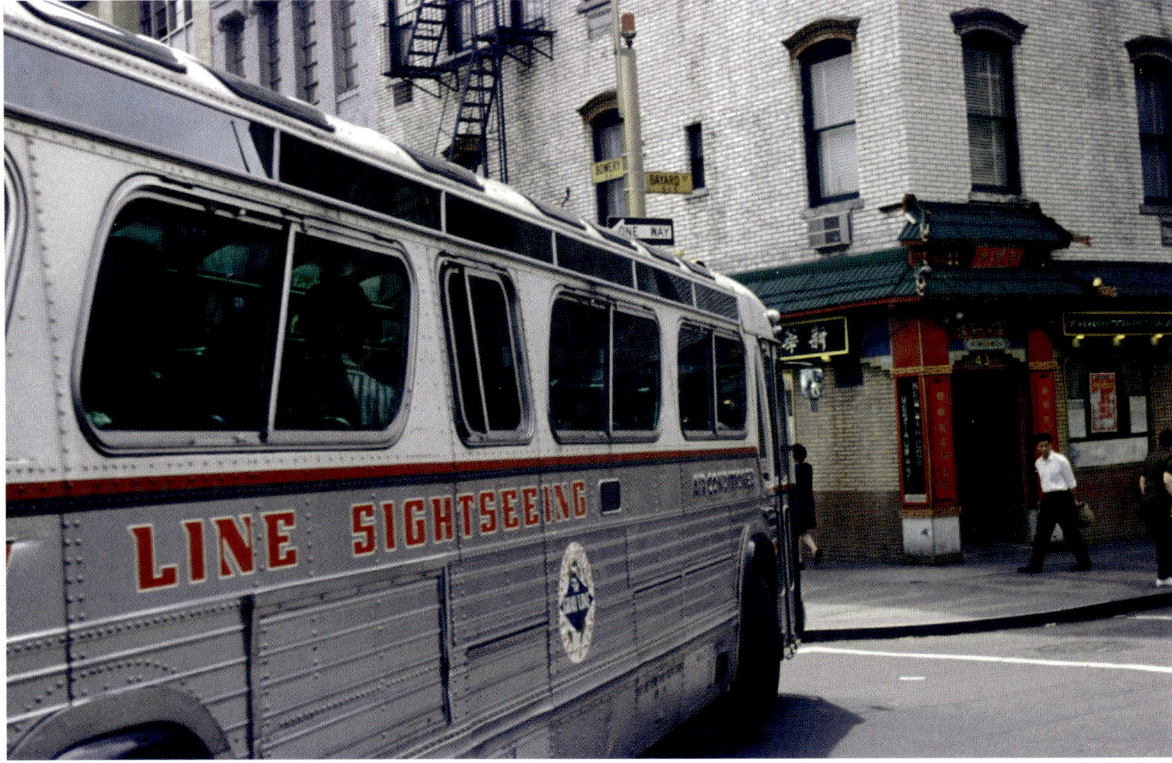

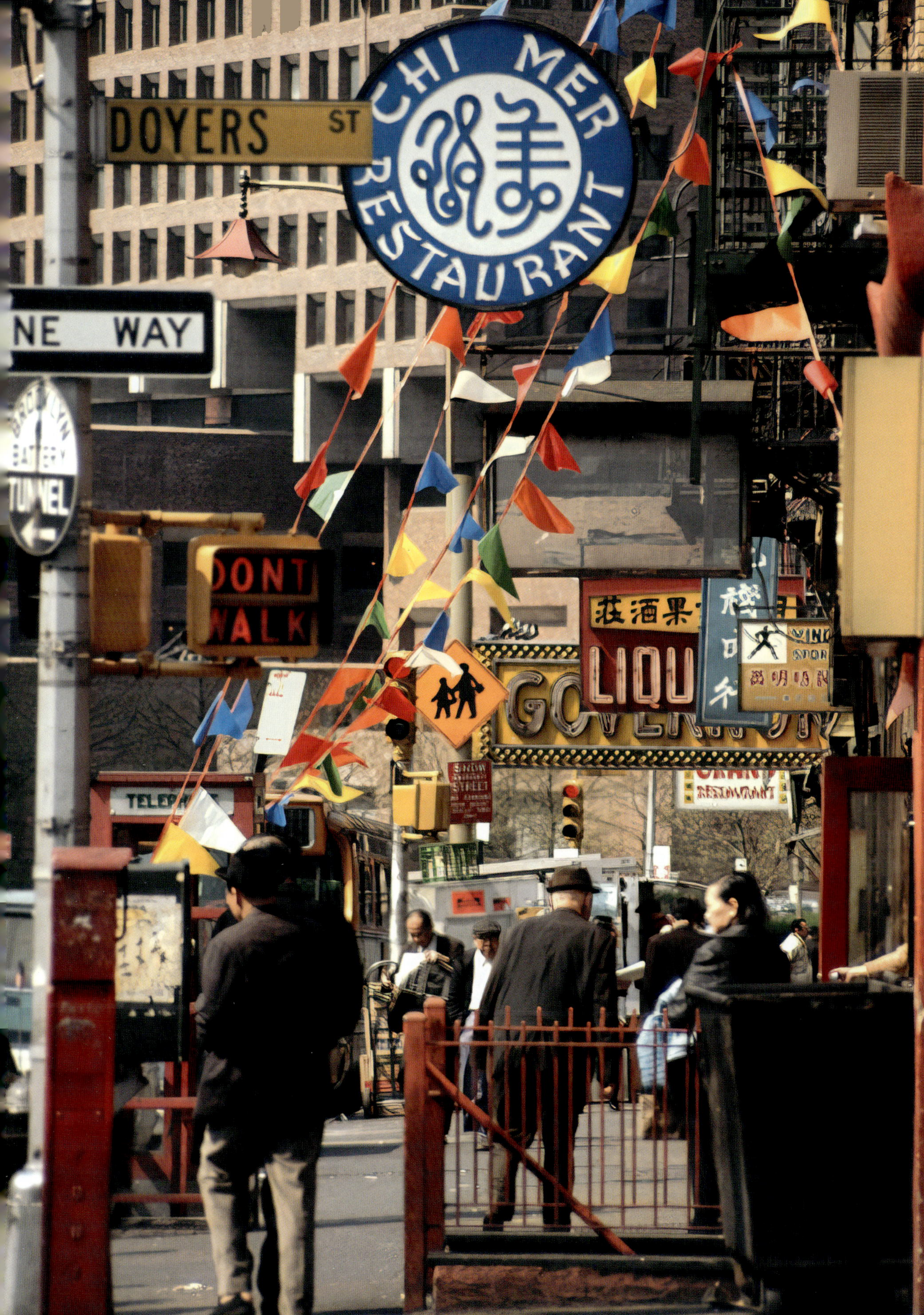

Doyers Street. New York, early 1970s.

The 1971 health fair on Mott Street included Ping-Pong at twenty-five cents a game to raise money for the fair. New York, 1971.

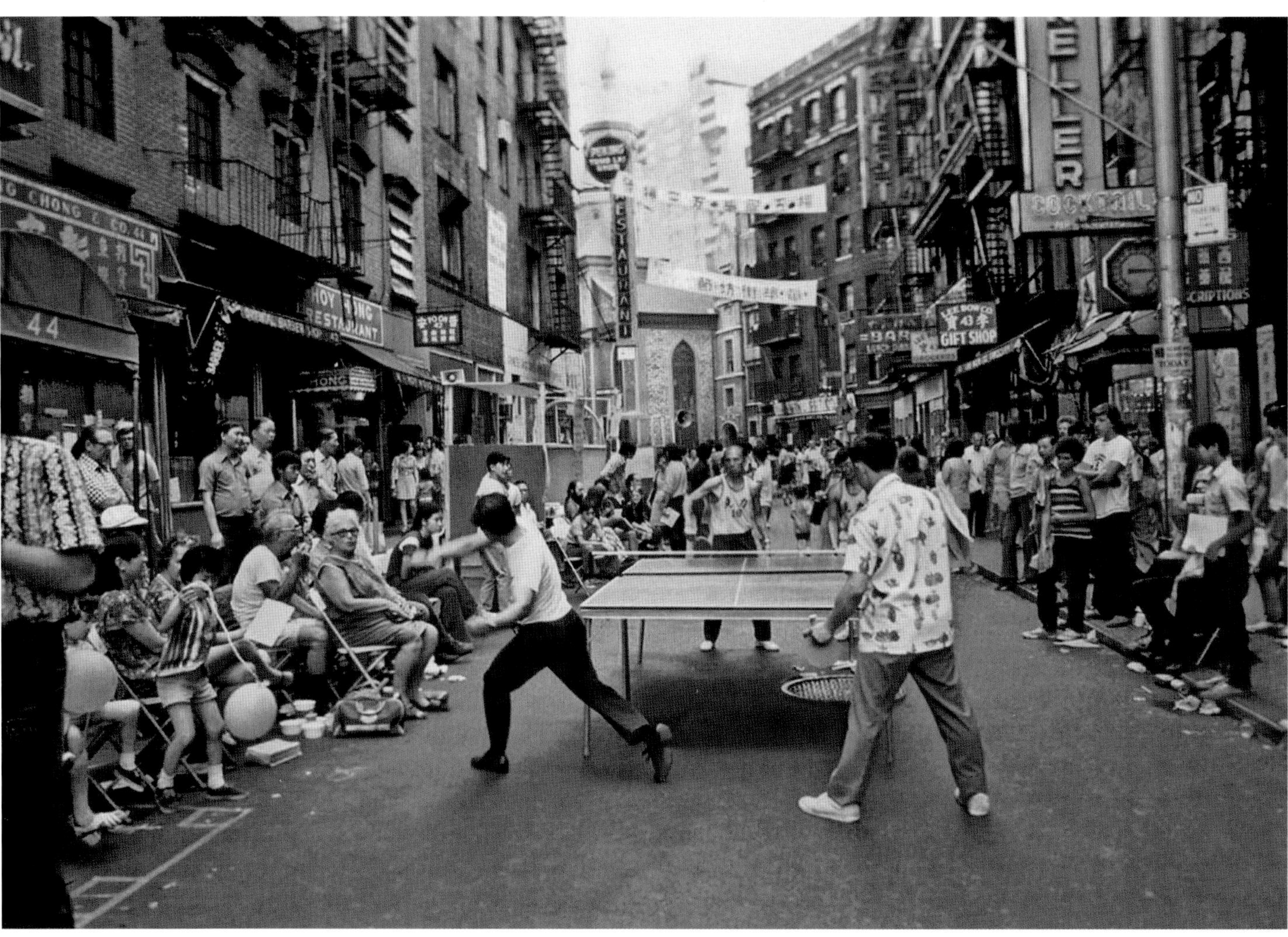

Old-time sojourners, *lo wah que* (*lao huaqiao*), in Chinatown. New York, early 1970s.

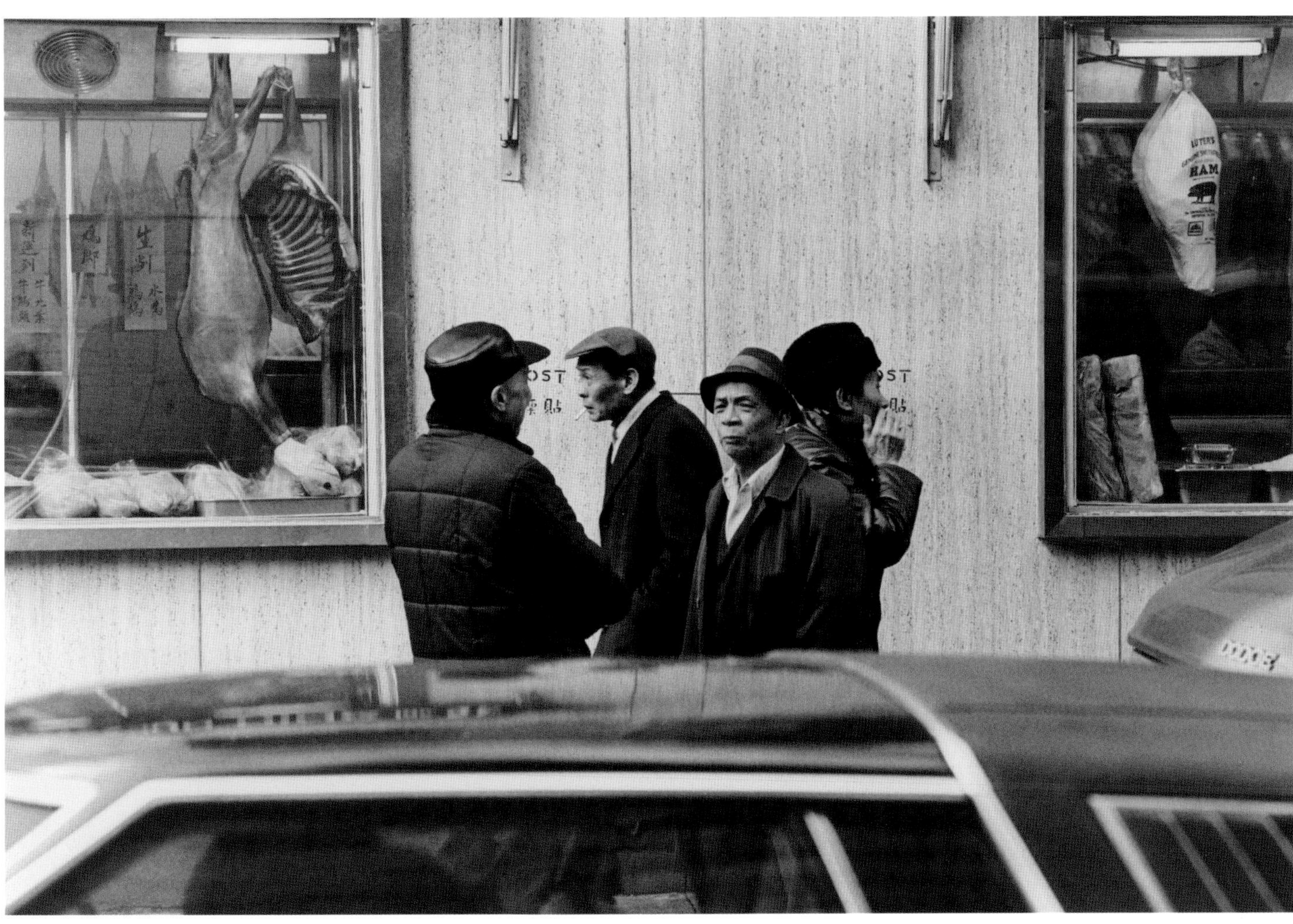

Chinatown in the 1970s

ALAN CHIN

Contributing photographer and writer to *Business Insider*; adjunct professor of photojournalism at Columbia University and the New School

In the 1970s, New York's Chinatown underwent explosive growth and cultural evolution. The Taishanese variant of Cantonese that had always been spoken there was replaced by the standard Cantonese that many immigrants had learned in Hong Kong. Many of the new immigrants came from Taiwan and other parts of China as well. Some formed an urban working class that toiled in sweatshop garment factories, while others created small businesses in manufacturing, in farming, and in marketing products to Asian Americans. Enough of them graduated from college that for the first time they could assert their parallel priorities of assimilation and identity simultaneously.

Corky Lee's images of the era became iconic. He was the first photographer from within Chinatown to document Chinese Americans' lives and experiences with the intentionality of an activist asserting their legitimacy and uniqueness. Fifty years later his photographs constitute a nostalgic record of a vanished world.

Since their community was still small and sometimes insular, most Chinese Americans in New York lived and worked in and around Chinatown. Up to a dozen Chinese-language newspapers were published daily, representing divergent pro-KMT (Guomindang) and pro-Communist perspectives as well as regional differences. Movie theaters screened the latest films from Hong Kong and Taiwan, usually in double bills pairing a period or martial arts film with a contemporary comedy or drama. Traditional clan and chamber of commerce associations thrived, in a few cases incubating youth gangs infamous for committing acts of sensational violence. In Columbus Park and other public spaces, men and women remained largely socially segregated. The society was still reeling from the Chinese Exclusion Act and other racist laws that for eighty years had forbidden almost any ethnic Chinese to set foot on American soil.

But China was a Second World War ally, and the work of the Flying Tigers did much to ameliorate racial attitudes. So did the American-educated first lady of China, Soong Mei-ling (Madame Chiang Kai-shek). As a result, the Chinese Exclusion Act was finally repealed in 1943. Chinese Americans participated in the wartime military as a larger percentage of the population than any other minority group. Some who served in Asia returned with Chinese "war brides" who were now permitted to enter the country. That was how Corky's father, a veteran, brought his wife over from Taishan after the war. But national quotas and other restrictive laws remained, and the Chinese Communist Revolution of 1949 nded U.S.-Chinese diplomatic relations for more han twenty years.

In 1965 came the sea change: President Lyn- lon B. Johnson signed into law the Immigration and Nationality Act. The signing ceremony took place on Ellis Island, where the president was surrounded by high government officials. The only nonwhite people in the crowd were two Japa- nese Americans, Senator Daniel Inouye of Hawaii and the official White House photographer, Yoi- chi Okamoto. The Immigration and Nationality Act is often forgotten as a part of the Great Soci- ety, but it was as instrumental as the Voting, Civil Rights, and Fair Housing acts in defining con- temporary American life. All of a sudden, long- separated families could reunite. Every ten years after that, just about, the Chinese American pop- ulation would double and double again.

With increased immigration, young immi- grants and American-born Chinese challenged what they perceived as their elders' passive sub- mission in the face of discrimination. Nonprofit social services provided health care, English classes, childcare, and job training. Dance troupes, music ensembles, and arts initiatives formed. Chi- nese American activists, inspired by the anti- Vietnam War and civil rights movements, took to the streets to protest inadequate housing, poor working conditions, and police brutality. The dif- ferent generations, the diverse regional and lan- guage groupings, and the various social classes struggled to code-switch not just with mainstream white Americans but with one another, as well.

My own father, like Corky's, was a paper son. His uncle Sing Chin (Chen Dongcheng) left Tai- shan in 1927 and lived for seven years in Cuba, then traveled to the United States on a harrowing voyage hidden in the coal hold of a steamer. Like many Chinese immigrants of his generation, my great-uncle claimed that they were born in California but their documents had been destroyed in the 1906 San Francisco earthquake and fire.

Sing then arranged for my father to become a paper son. My dad arrived in 1951, taking the name Doo Gawn Chin (Chen Ziguan) instead of his real one, Fow Sang Chin (Chen Fusheng). That was the name he used to sign documents and label photographs with. Even during my childhood in the 1970s, his old friends would still call him that. But his paper identity was that of a single man, whereas in fact he had a wife and two children back in Taishan and then Hong Kong.

Finally my father took advantage of the U.S. government's Chinese Confession Program (1956–65)—which offered legalization of one's status in exchange for "confessing" to using a fake name—to regain his true identity. For him—as for many—confession was the necessary first step to reuniting his family, and he was able to truthfully answer the question "Are you now or have you ever been a member of the Communist Party?" with the necessary no.

When Nixon's and Kissinger's visits to China and their ping-pong diplomacy resulted in official recognition of the People's Republic in 1979, Chi- nese American groups debated and contested the international politics. Corky's photographs captured how these tensions played out in Chinatown.

Meanwhile, in the 1970s New York City lost almost a million people to white flight, even as the Chinese American community was growing. Chi- nese Americans had to navigate a cultural revolu- tion in American life, finding their way through racial conflict, street crime, and changing genera- tional expectations, often encapsulated in indi- vidual family narratives. The "model minority" stereotype became fixed both inside and outside the community, even as Chinese Americans especially the elderly, continued to be the poorest of all the demographic groups in New York.

Looking back at Corky's photographs from the 1970s, I marvel at the store signs that once advertised businesses, now long gone; the Orientalist pagoda adornments on buildings; the chop suey lettering fonts intended to lure tourists; the mailboxes of involuntary bachelors—today all these remind us of a time that was more overtly racist but was also more suffused with the youthful activist energy of assertion and discovery. The elderly men and women whom Corky photographed have passed on, some of them born in the twilight of the Qing Dynasty, when China was an empire. Others, both outsiders and Chinese Americans, had photographed the community before. But perhaps no one had done so with an eye toward establishing both a distinct Chinese American identity and history.

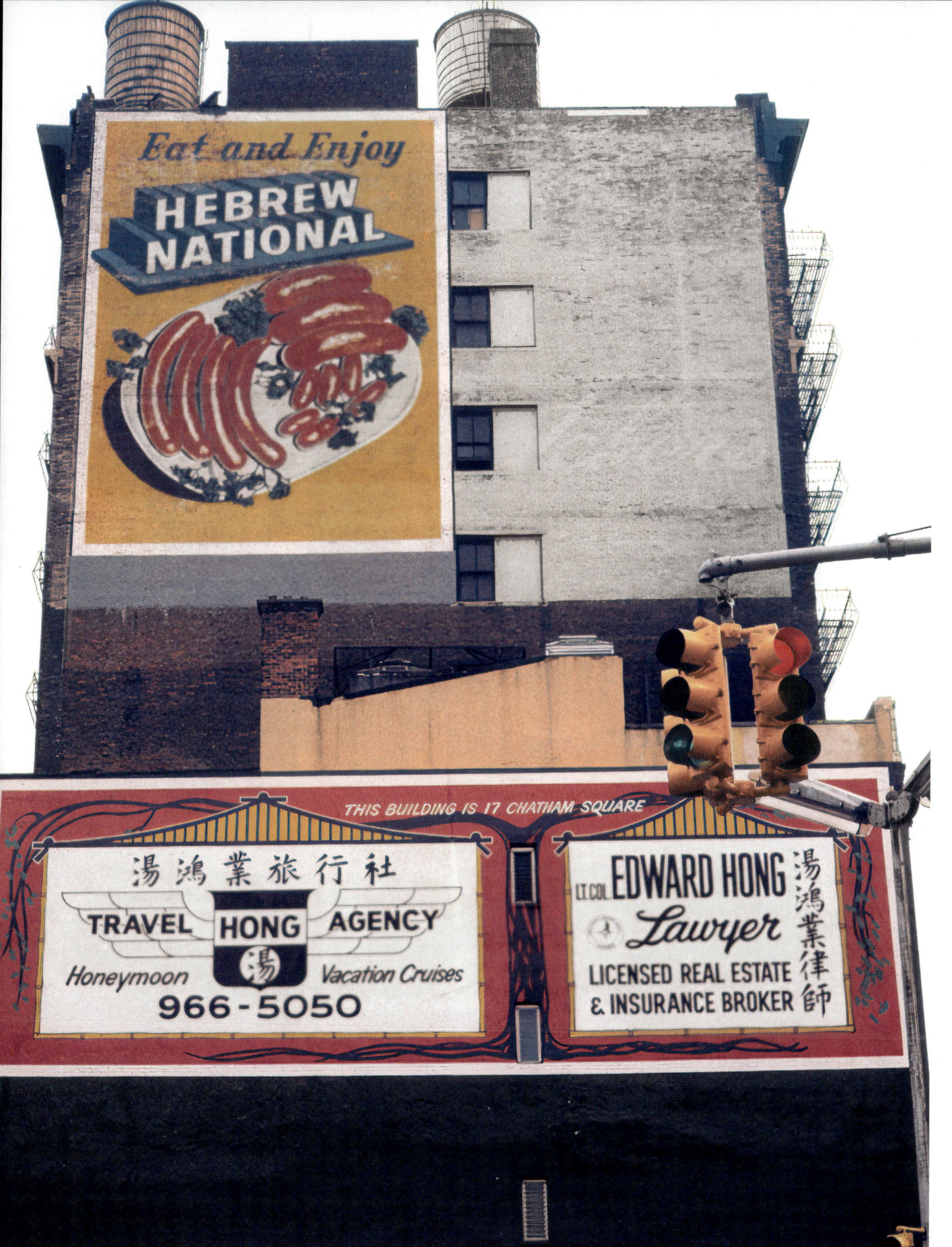

New and old signage at Chatham Square. New York, early 1970s.

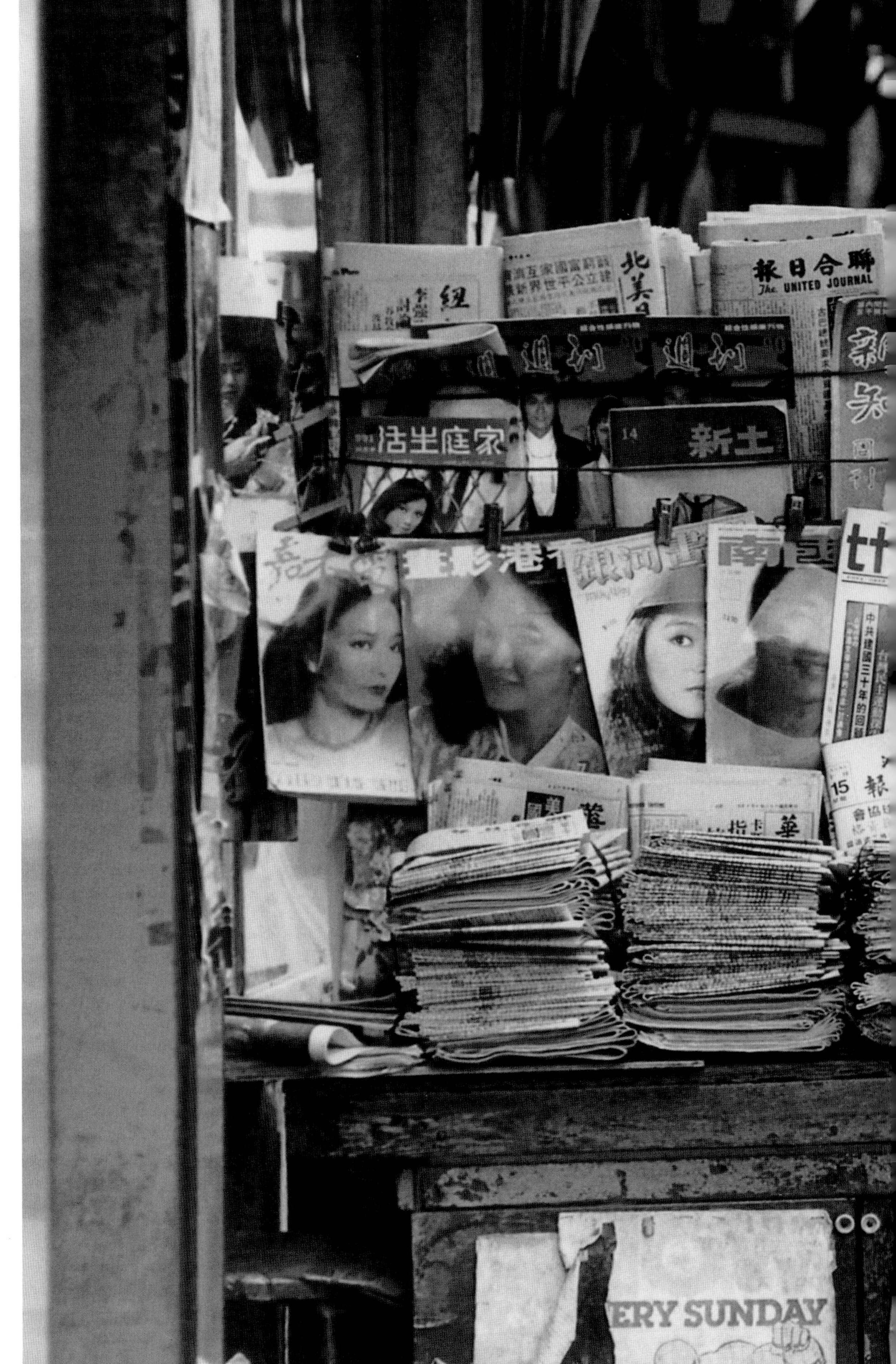

Newsstand at the corner of Mott and Canal in Chinatown. New York, 1979.

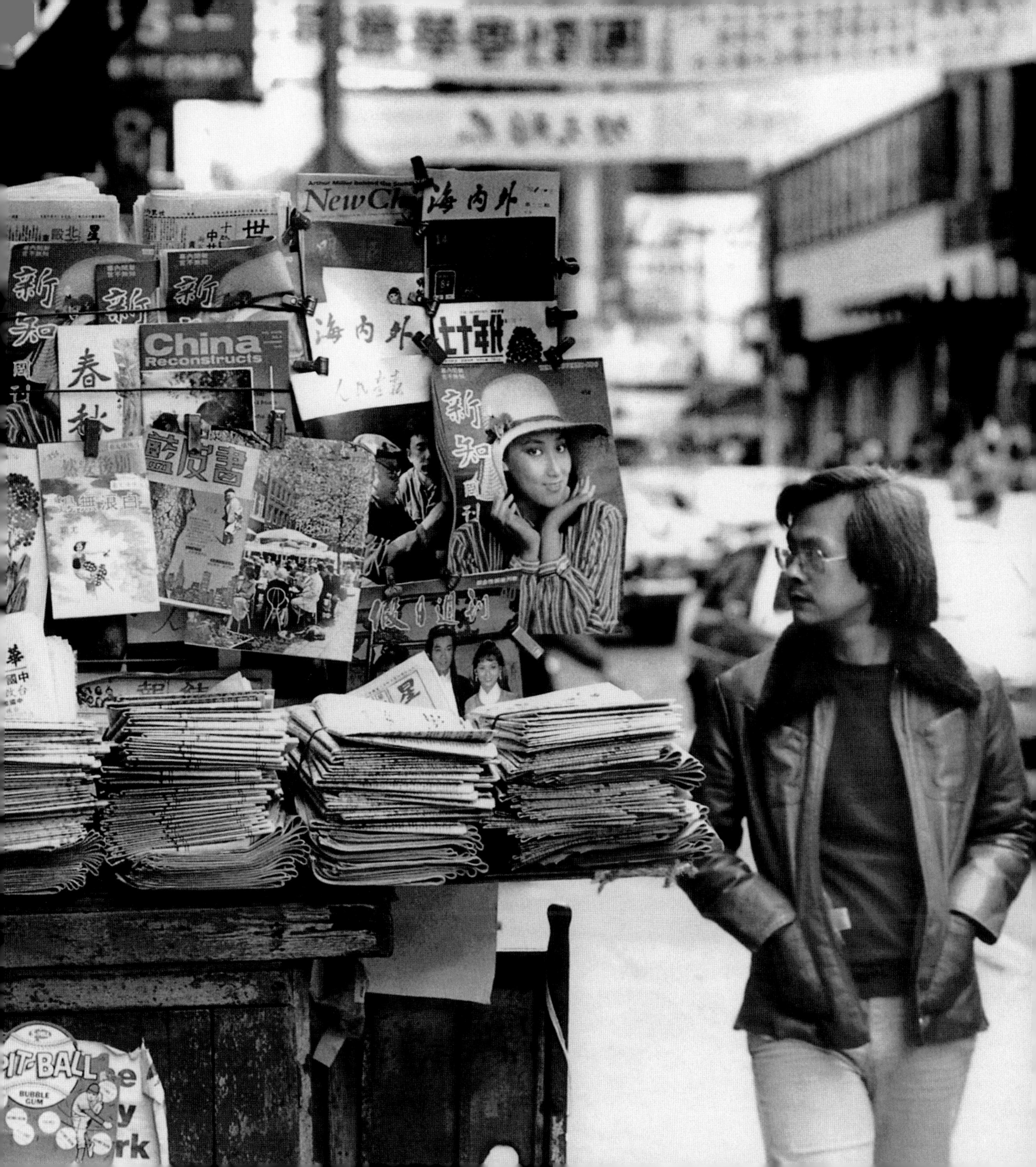
NewCh
海內外
China
Reconstructs
海內外
春秋
藍皮書
BUBBLE
GUM

Sojourners' mailboxes at 51 Bayard Street.
New York, 1976.

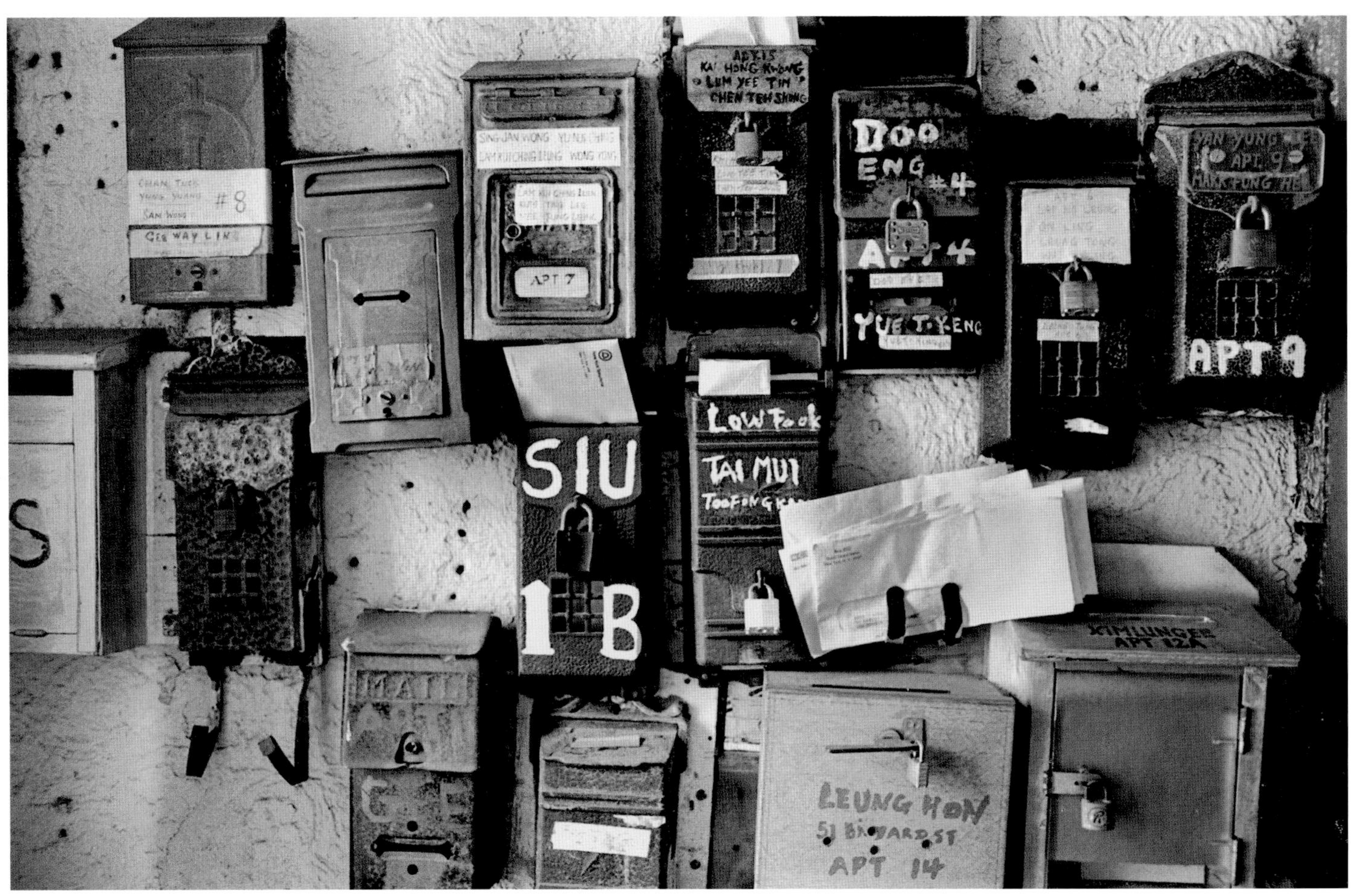

The Chinese American Food Market in Chinatown. New York, early 1970s.

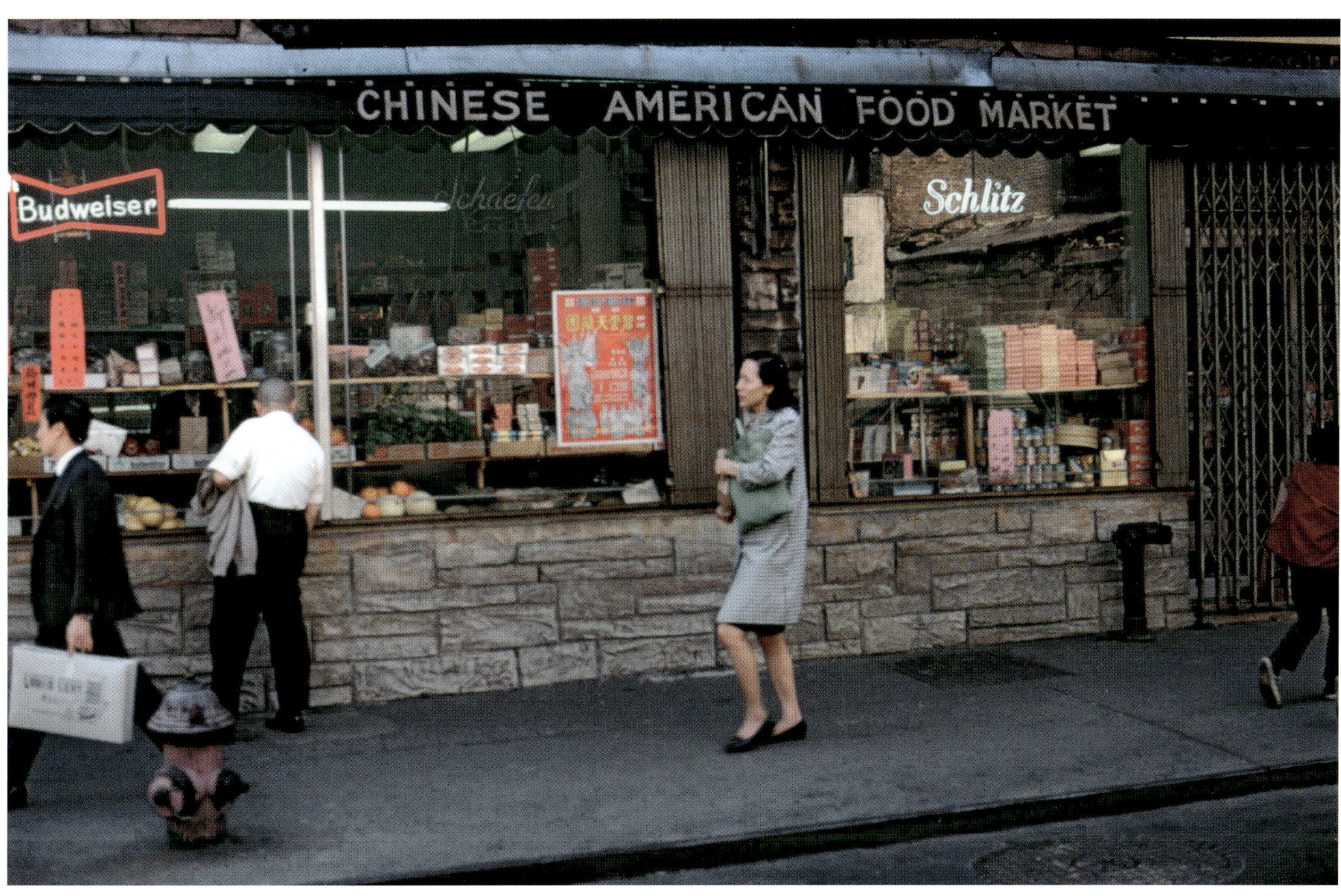

Brothers, 56 Mulberry Street. New York, 1977.

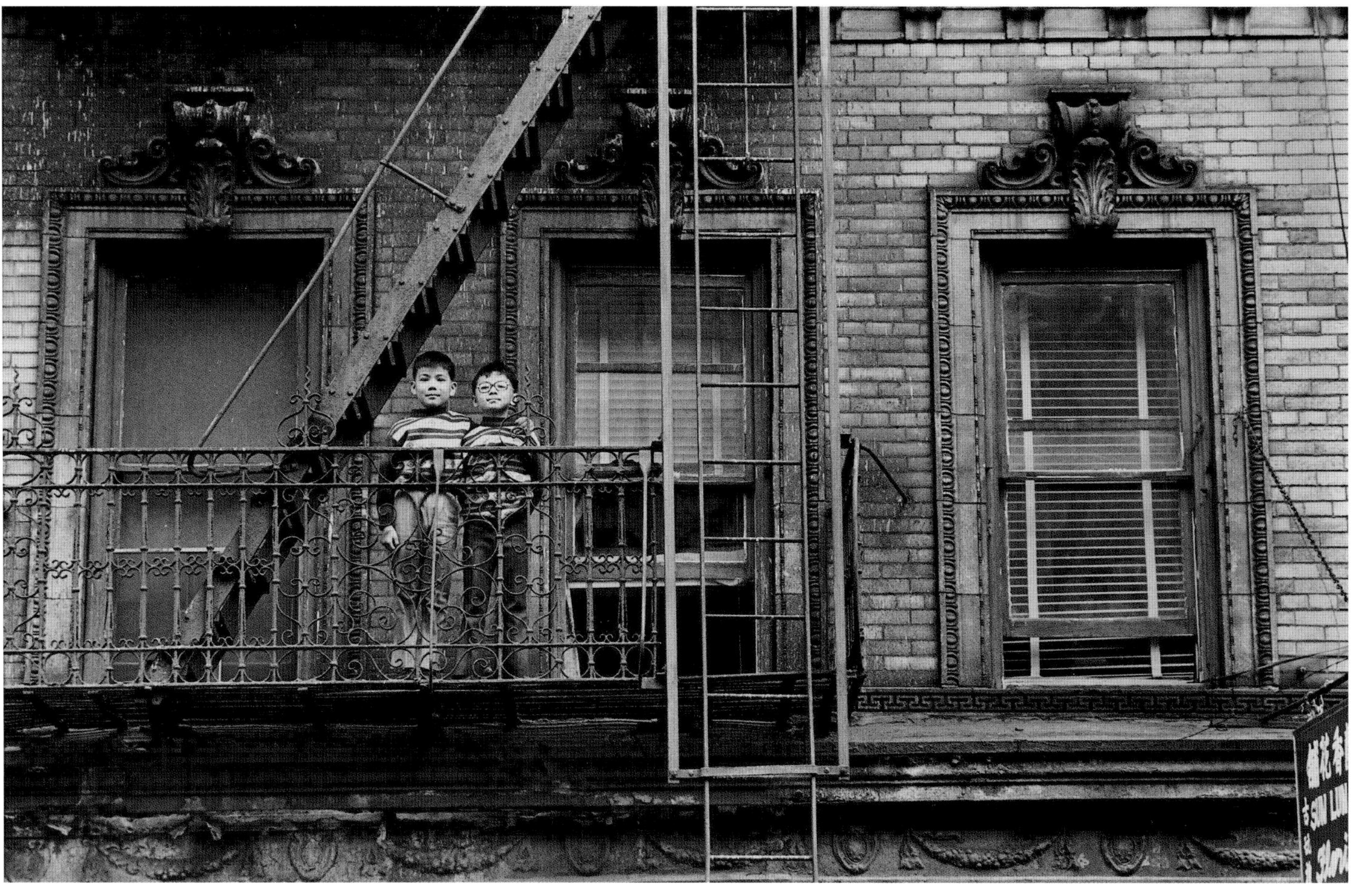

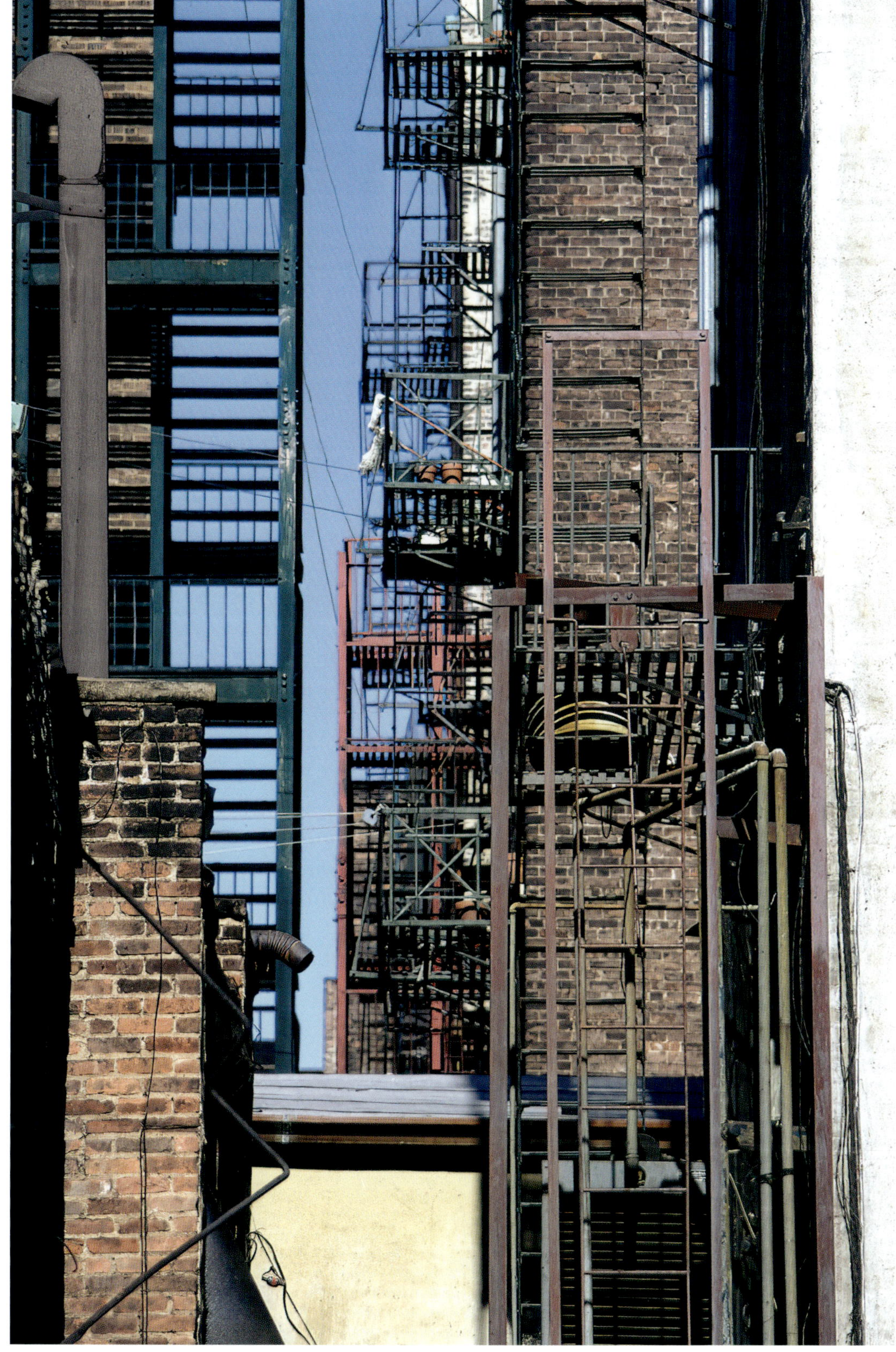

As Corky Lee documented people, conditions, and issues in Chinatown, he also experimented with abstract compositions. New York, early 1970s.

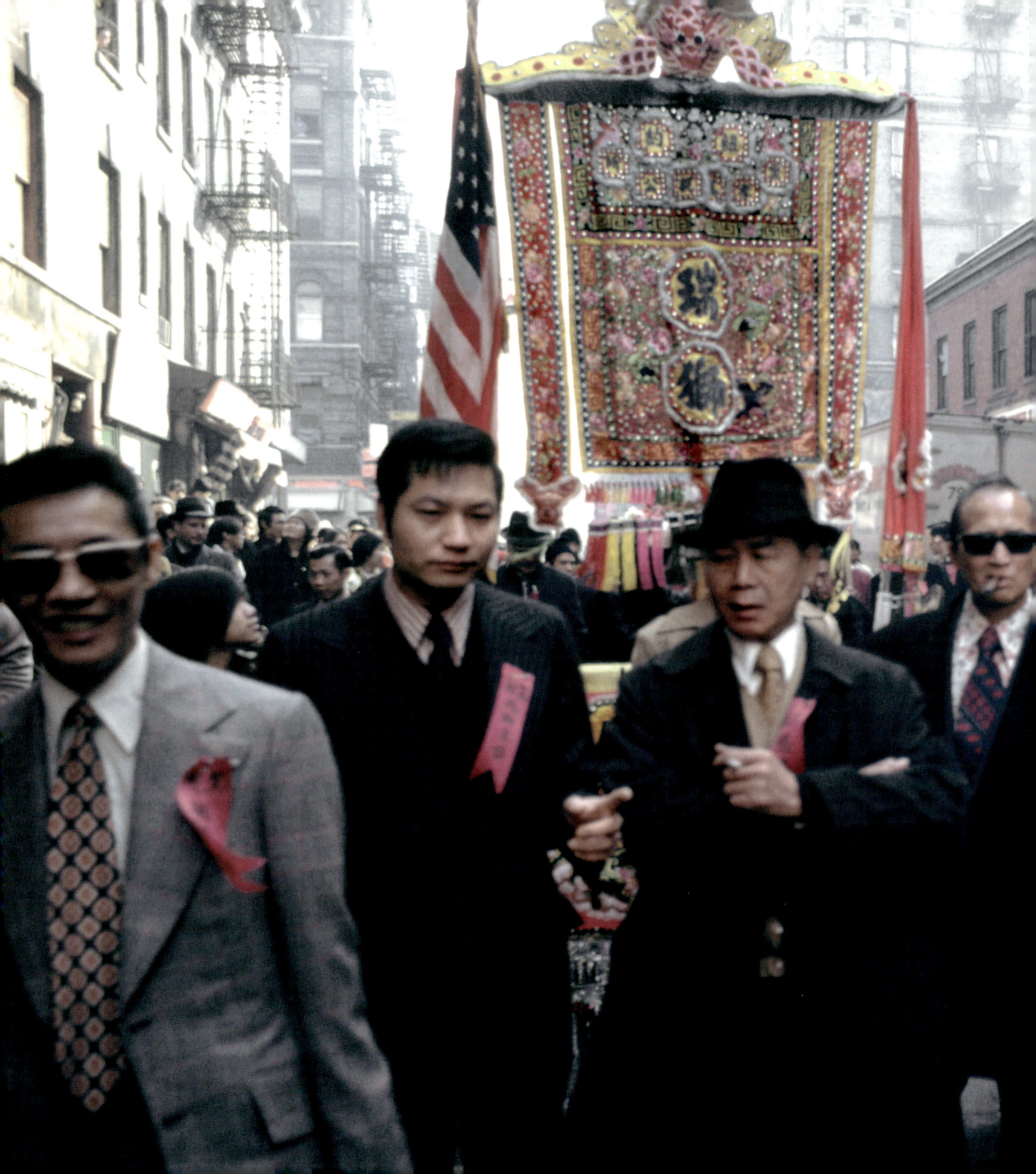

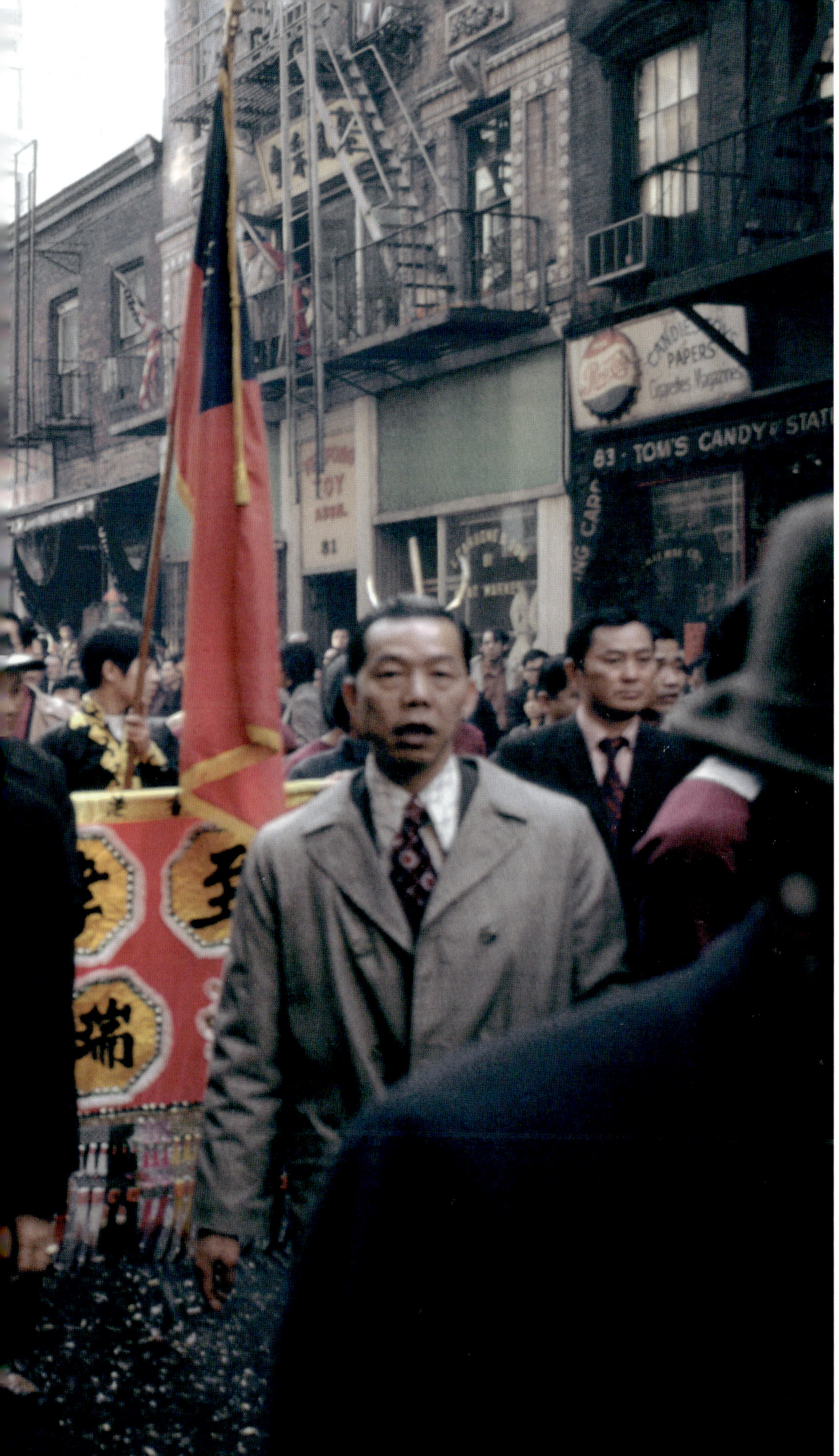

Leaders of the Chinese Consolidated Benevolent Association at the Chinatown Lunar New Year parade, with the flag of the Republic of China and the KMT (Guomindang). New York, early 1970s.

The new immigration brought demands that New York City address the needs of Chinese schoolchildren. At a rally in Chinatown's Chatham Square, students and teachers from Junior High School 65 (now Middle School 131) called for bilingual education. New York, 1971.

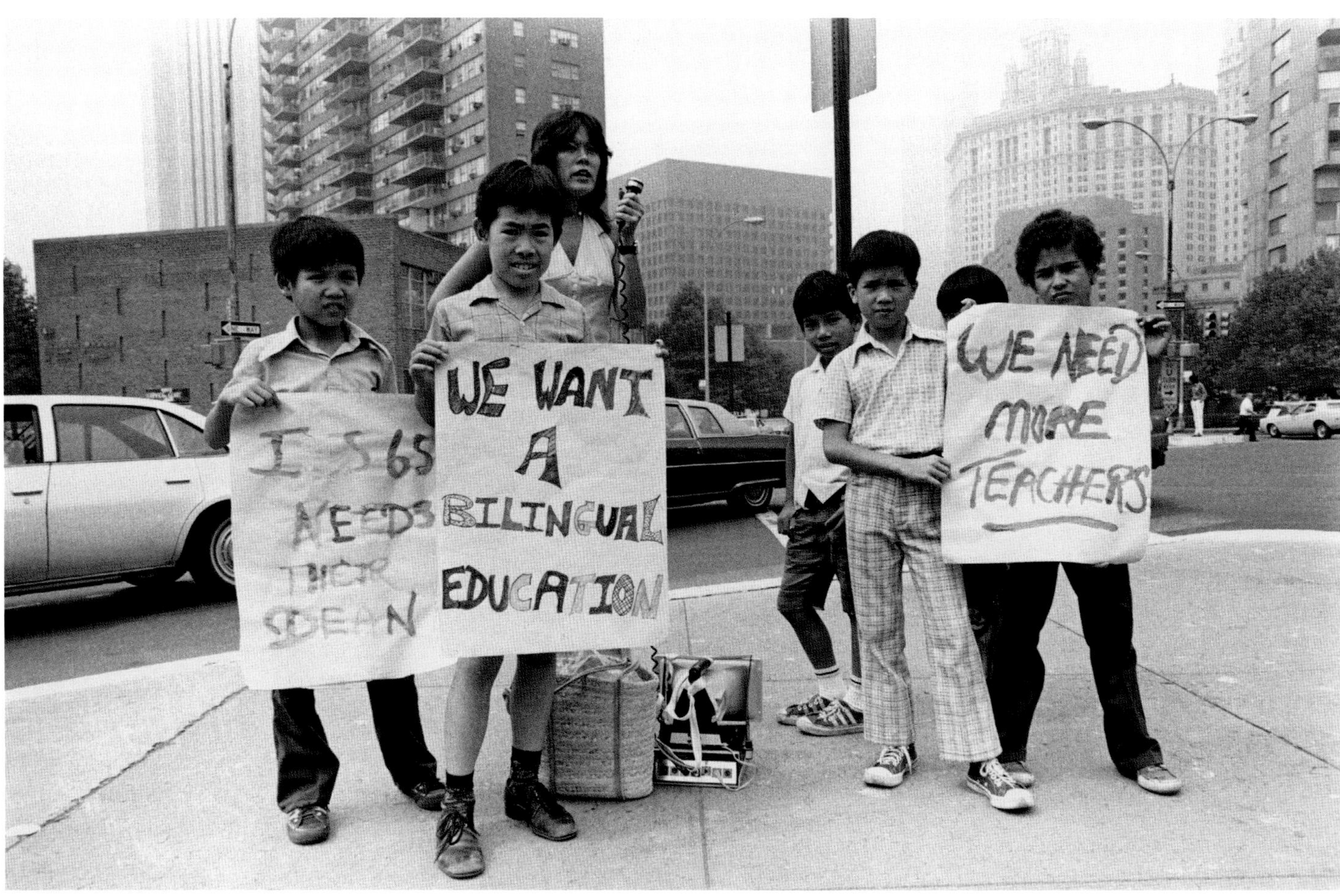

A Mongolian dance performance at the annual summer festival of the New York Chinese Cultural Center in Chinatown's Columbus Park. New York, 1978.

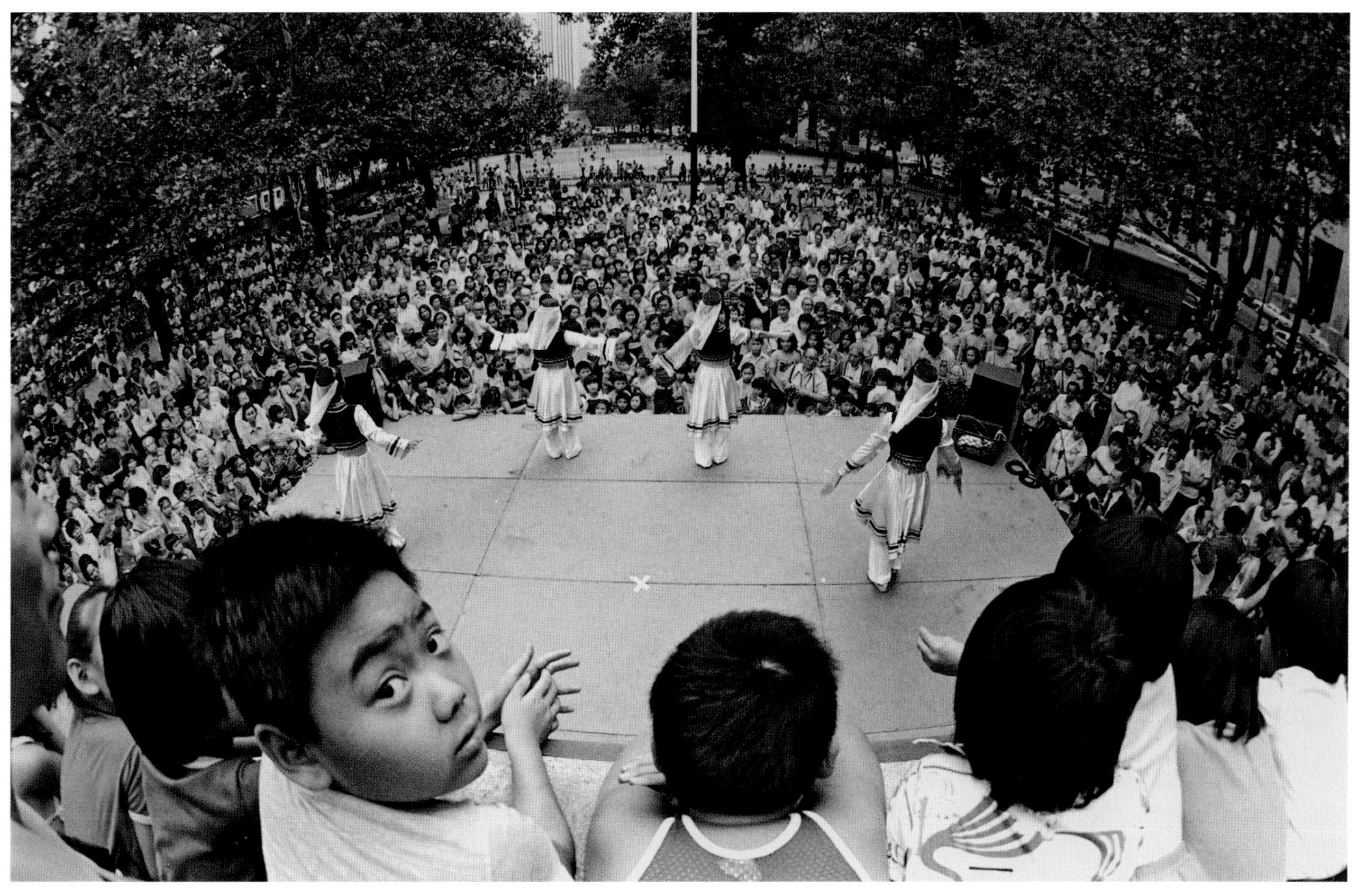

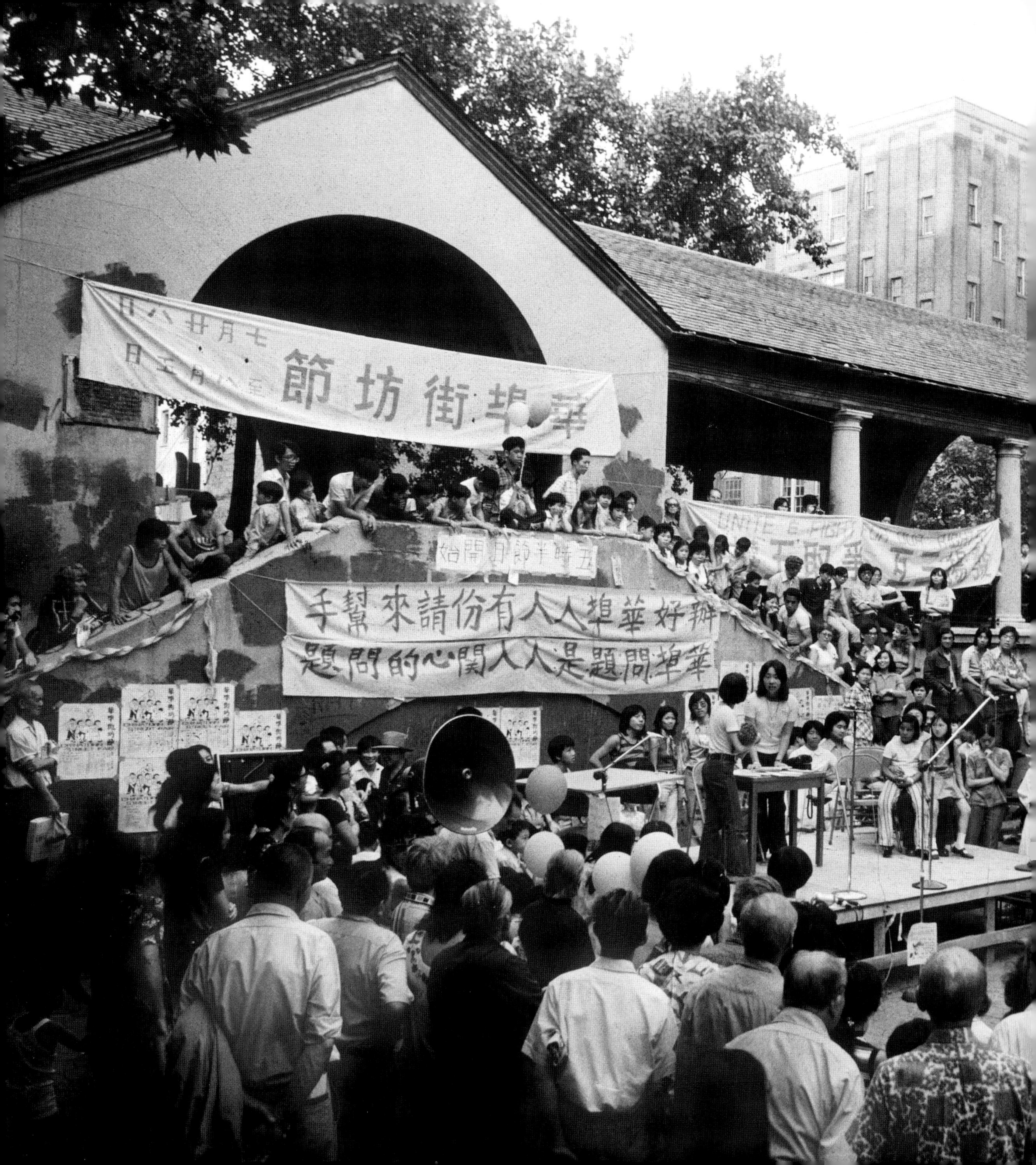

七月廿八日
至八月三日
華埠街坊節
辦好華埠人人有份請來幫手
華埠問題是人人關心的問題

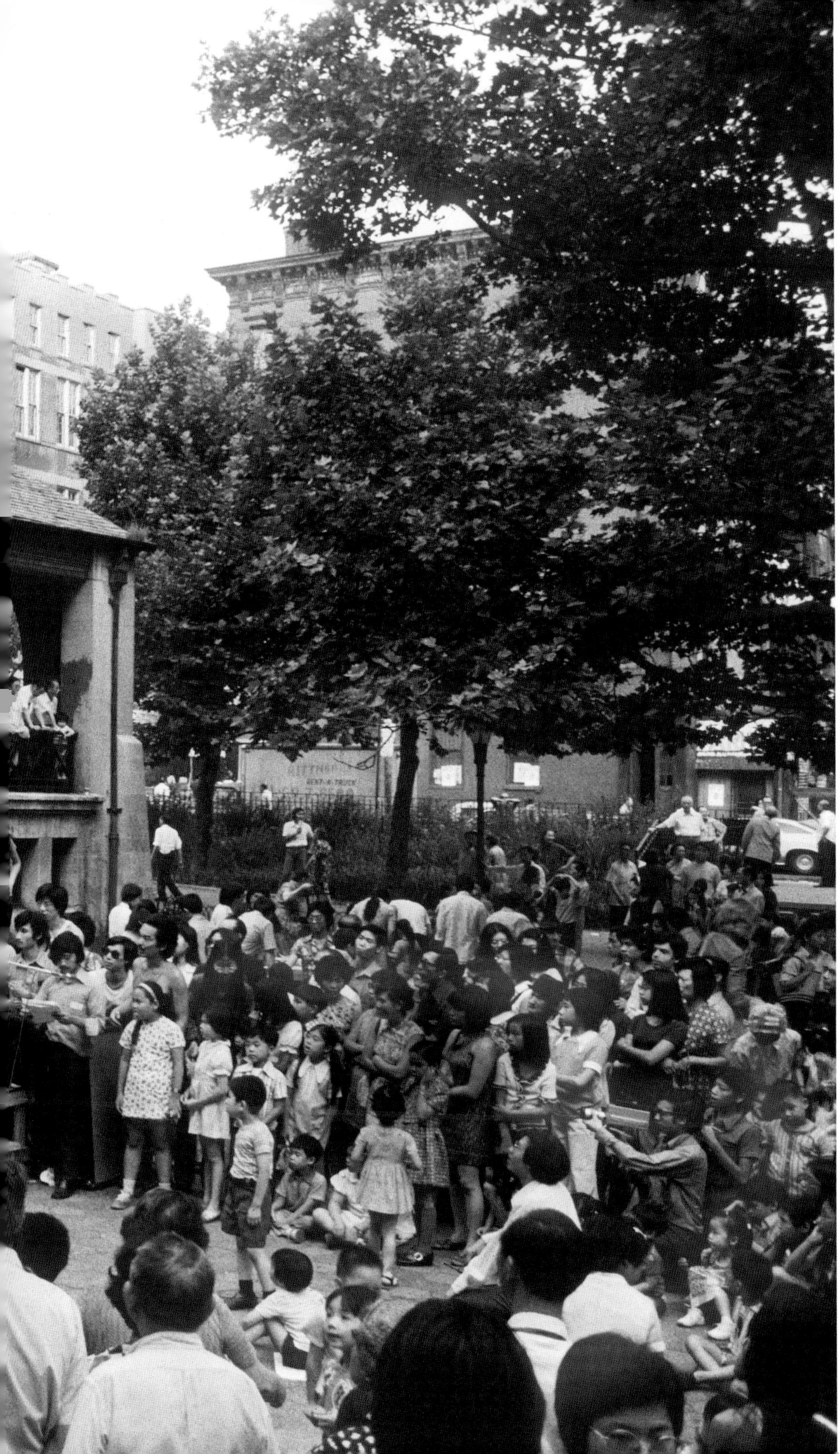

The first Chinatown Health Fair, held over the course of a week in the summer of 1971, brought the examining room into the community. Volunteer doctors and nurses screened more than 2,500 residents for hypertension, tuberculosis, diabetes, and other chronic illnesses. Young volunteers from Two Bridges, I Wor Kuen, and the Catholic and Baptist churches built and staffed the booths. The fair also featured games of Ping-Pong (twenty-five cents a game, to raise funds for the fair) and cultural programs. The health fair led to the opening of the Chinatown Health Clinic later that year. In 1999 it became the Charles B. Wang Community Health Center and now serves the most Asian Americans in New York.

The health fair included a cultural performance in Columbus Park. The top banner in Chinese reads, "Chinatown neighborhood festival." New York, 1971.

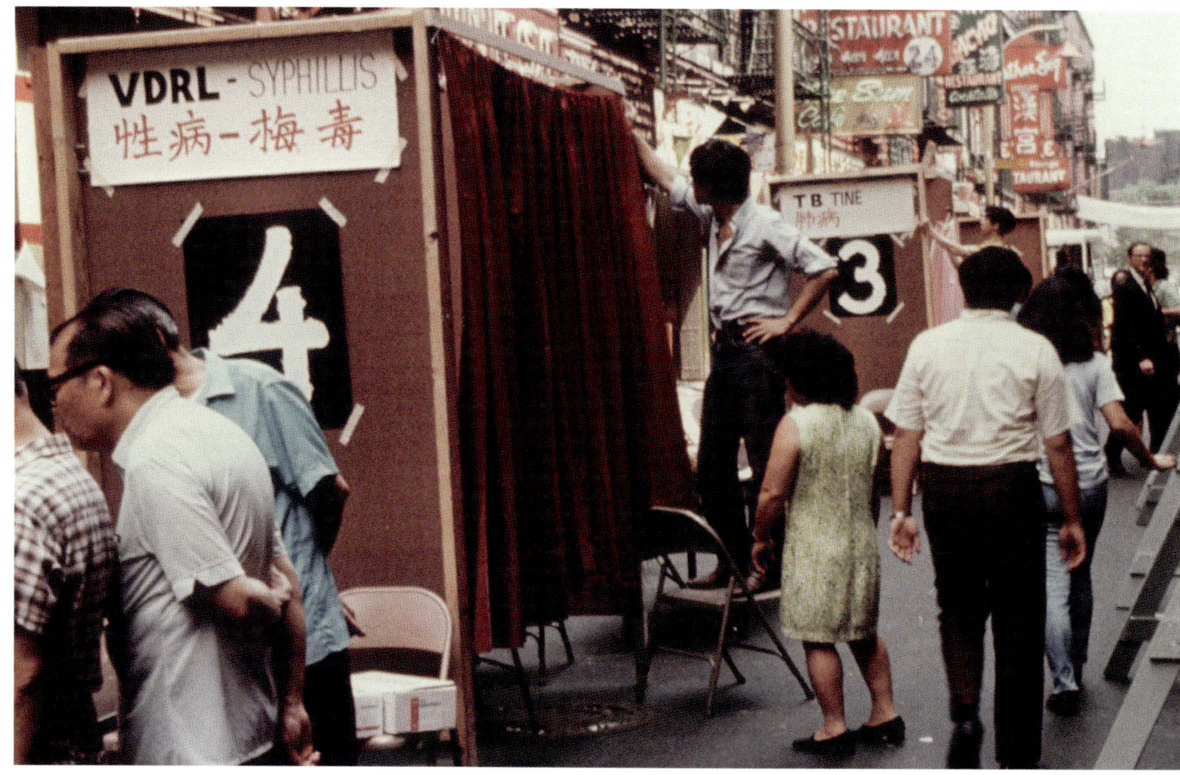

Testing for sexually transmitted diseases. New York, 1971.

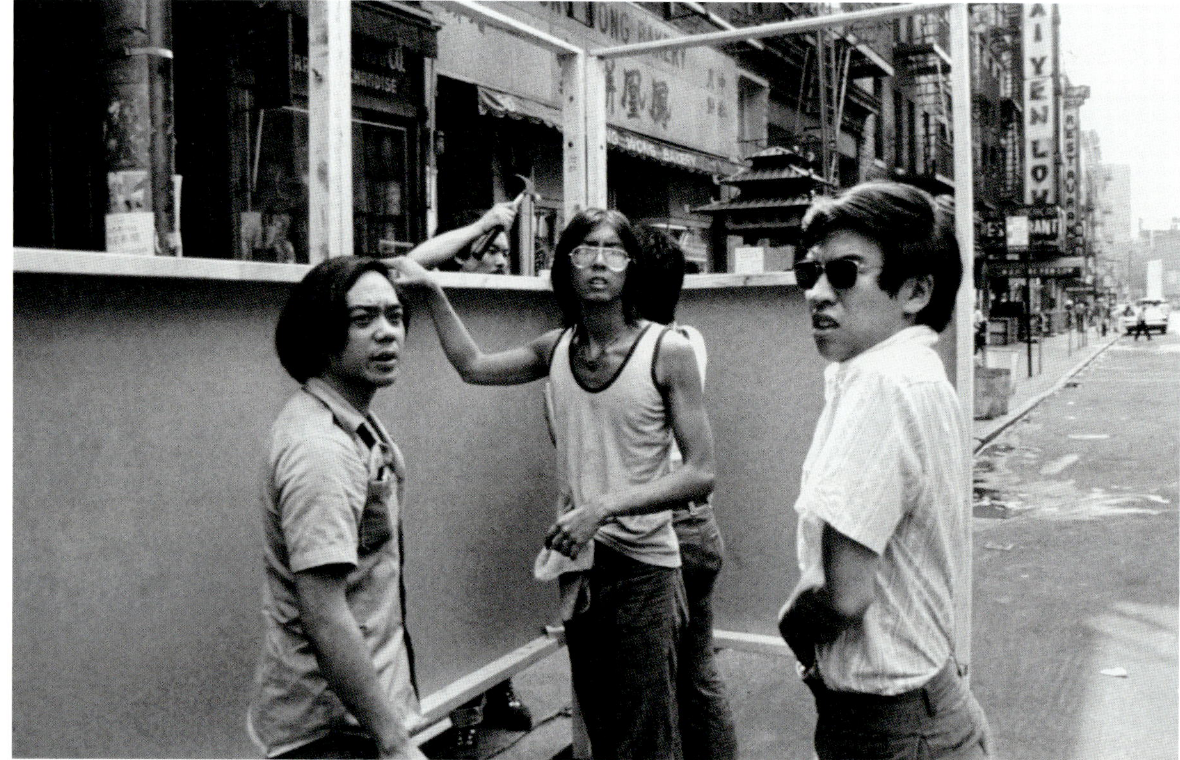

Richie Lee (*center*), Corky's youngest brother, and Hugh Mo (*right*), a student activist and future deputy commissioner of the New York Police Department, with an unnamed companion, building booths for the health fair. New York, 1971.

Taking blood pressure at the health fair.
New York, 1971.

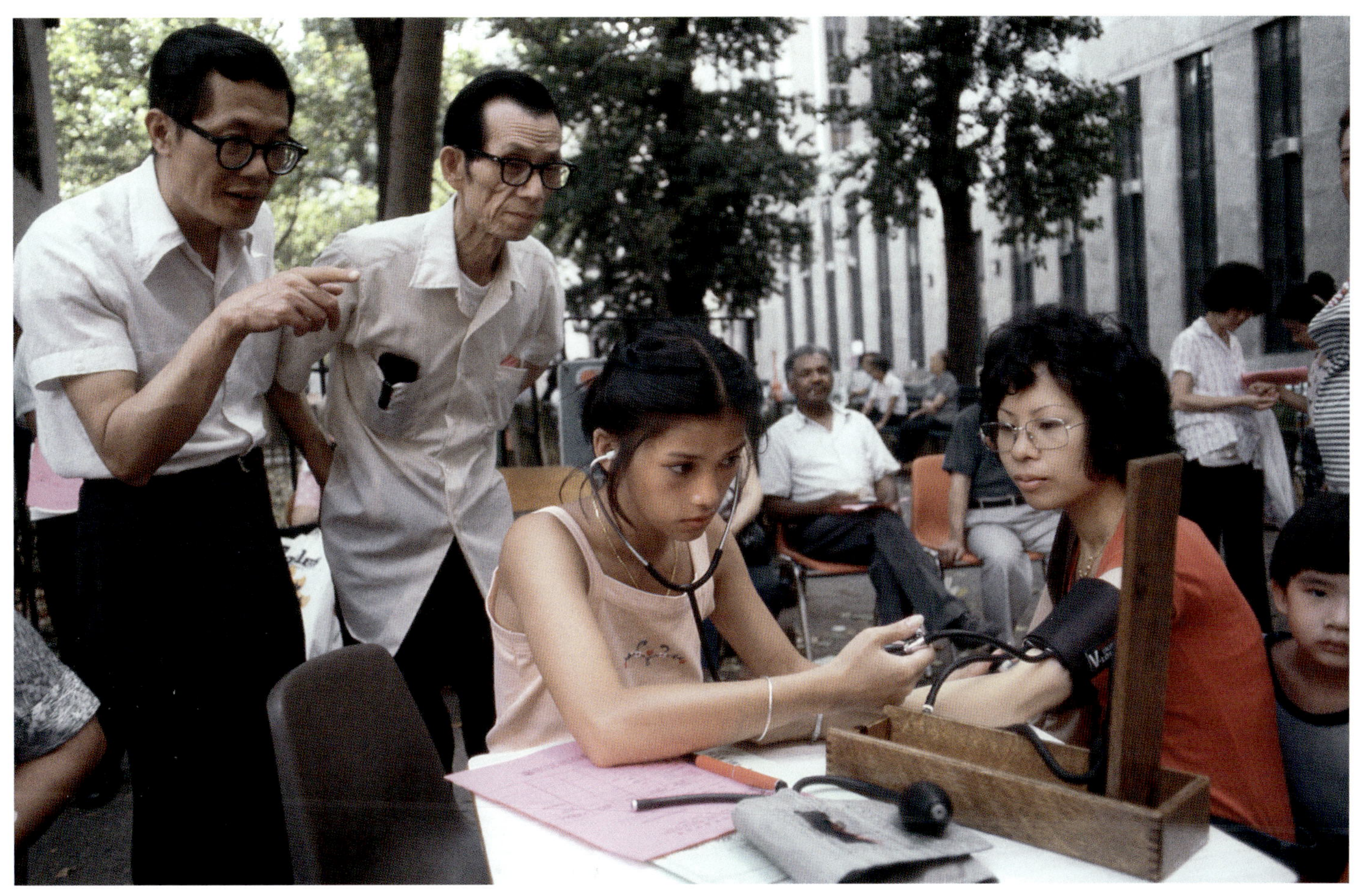

The fair provided information about housing, including how to navigate landlords' demands for "key money," in addition to health issues. New York, 1971.

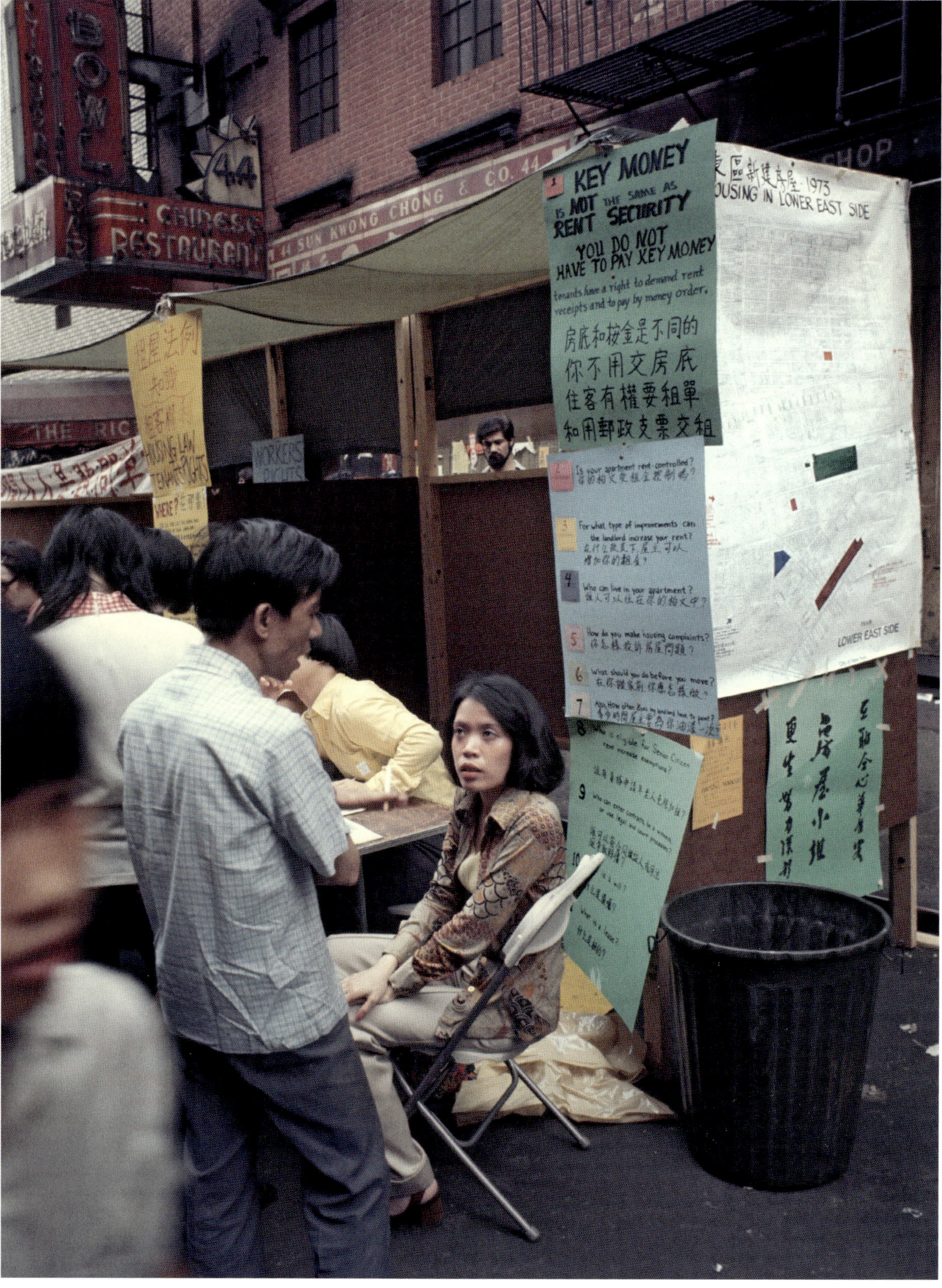

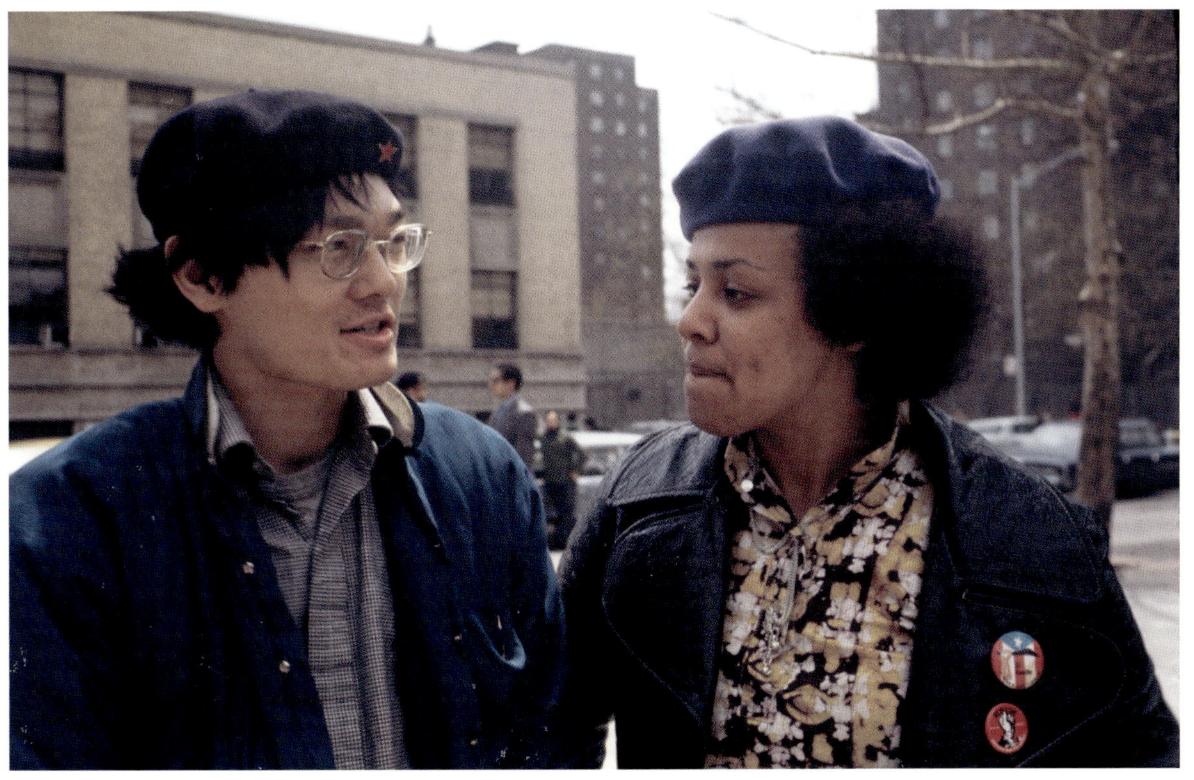

Virgo Lee of I Wor Kuen with Aida Causcut, minister of health of the Young Lords Party, at a rally at the site of the proposed new Gouverneur Hospital. New York, circa 1971.

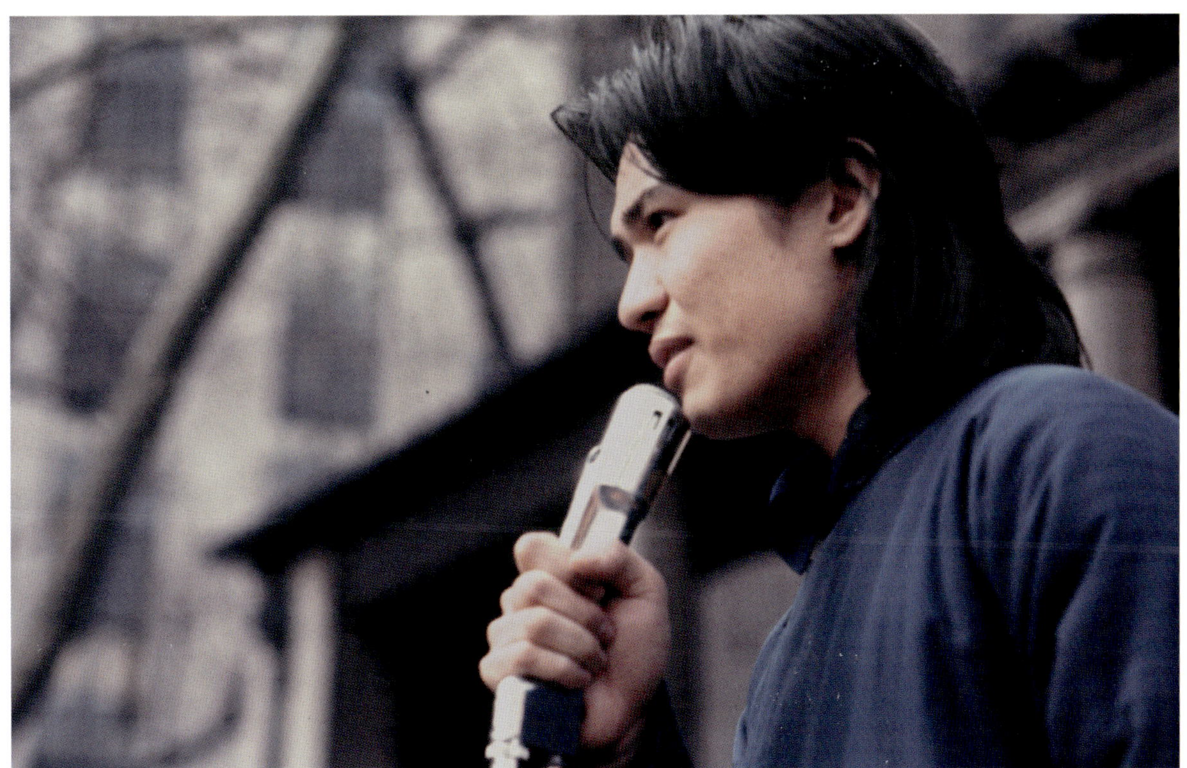

The Chinatown Health Fair was initiated by health care activist Thomas Tam (1946–2008), who also led the effort to form the Chinatown Health Clinic. Tam later became the founding director of the Asian American/Asian Research Institute at the City University of New York and the first Asian American trustee of CUNY. New York, 1971.

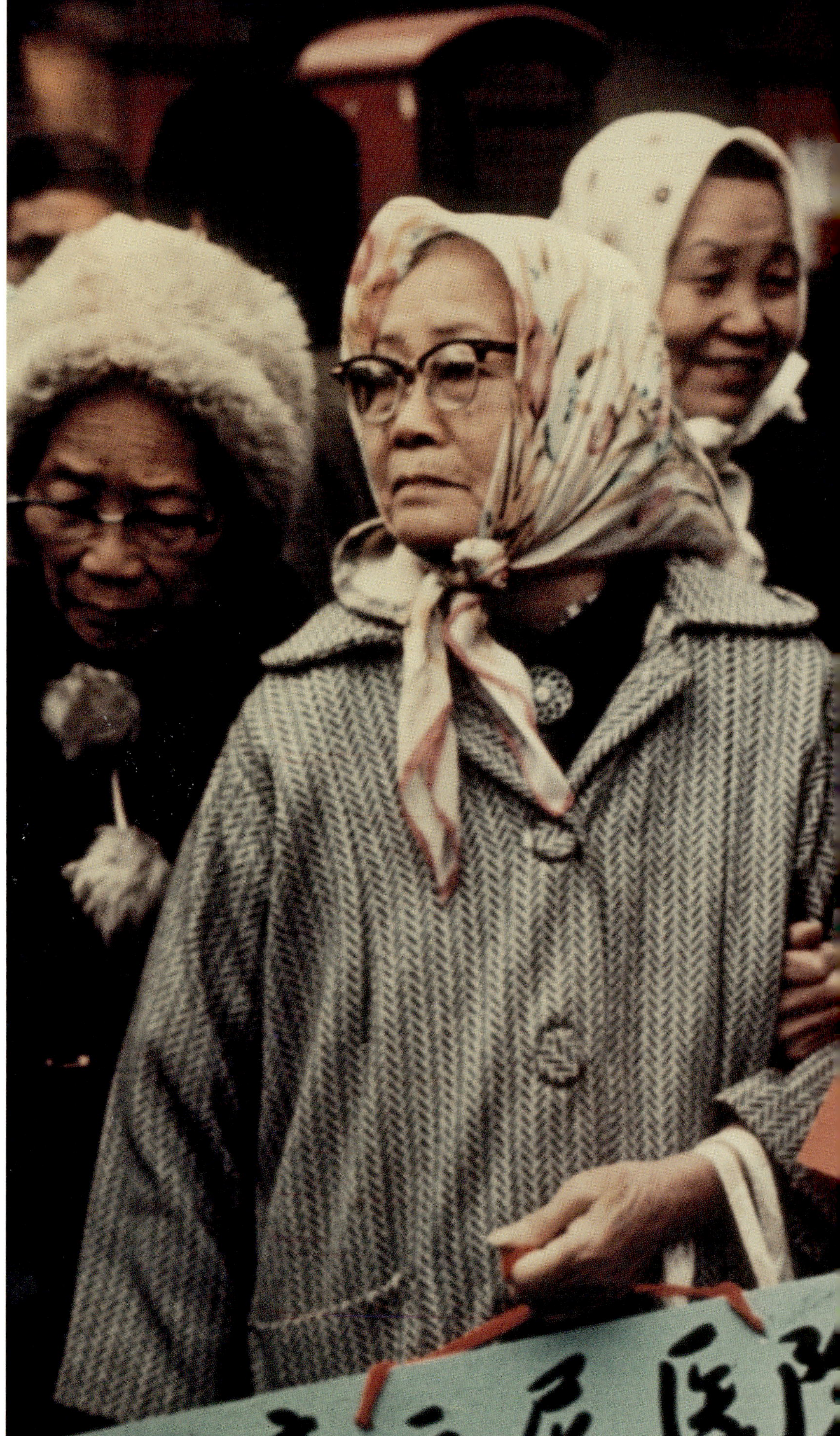

Community residents demanded that Gouverneur, the new city hospital built east of Chinatown, provide bilingual Chinese staff and other culturally sensitive services. This protest took place in front of the Health and Hospitals Corporation. New York, 1972.

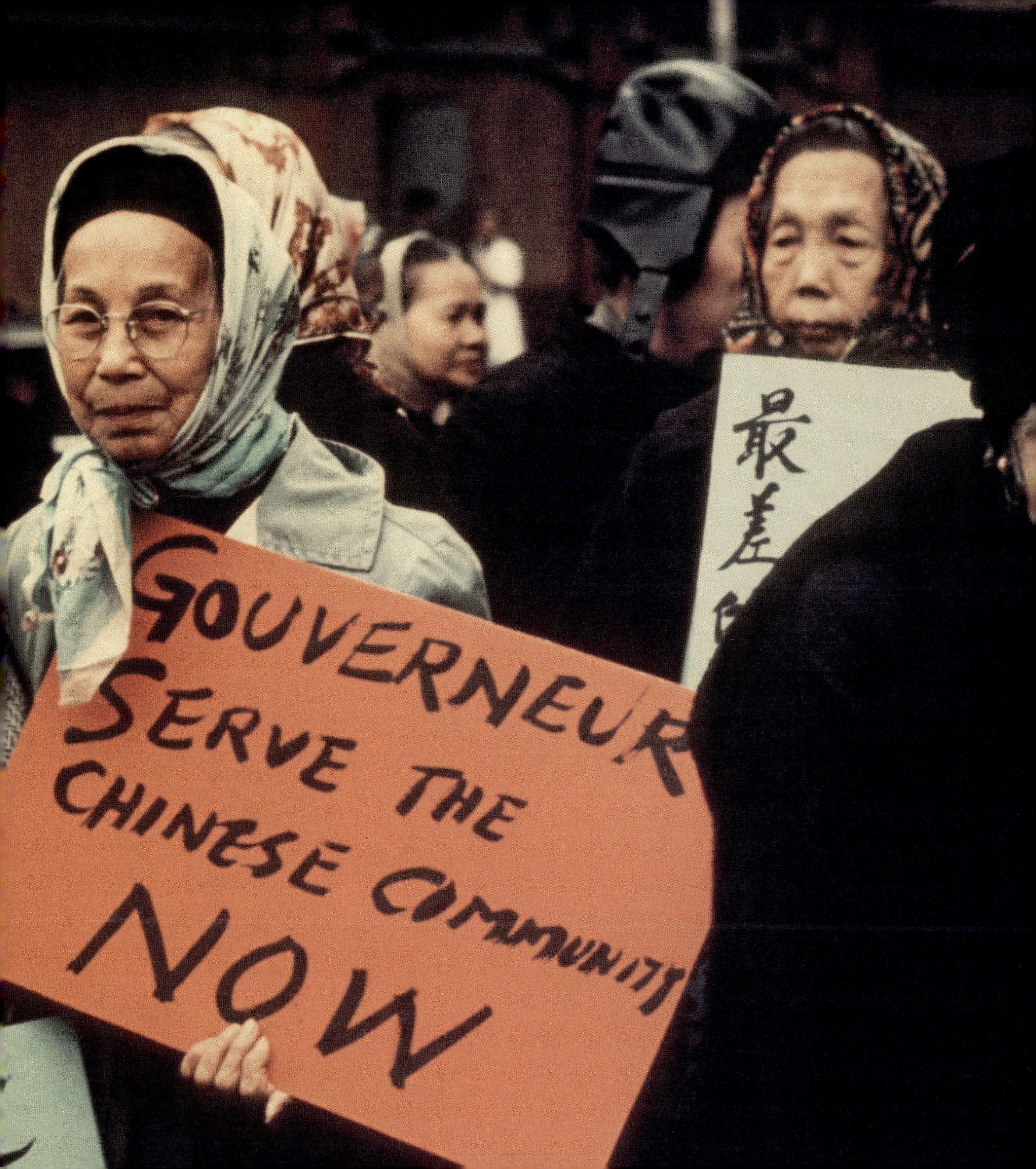
GOUVERNEUR
SERVE THE
CHINESE COMMUNITY
NOW
最差

When the International Ladies Garment Workers Union ran a publicity campaign that blamed Japan for the loss of U.S. garment workers' jobs, a multiethnic crowd protested in front of the union's headquarters in the garment district in Midtown Manhattan. The demonstration was organized by Asian Americans for Action, whose leaders included Japanese Americans who had been interned during World War II. New York, 1972.

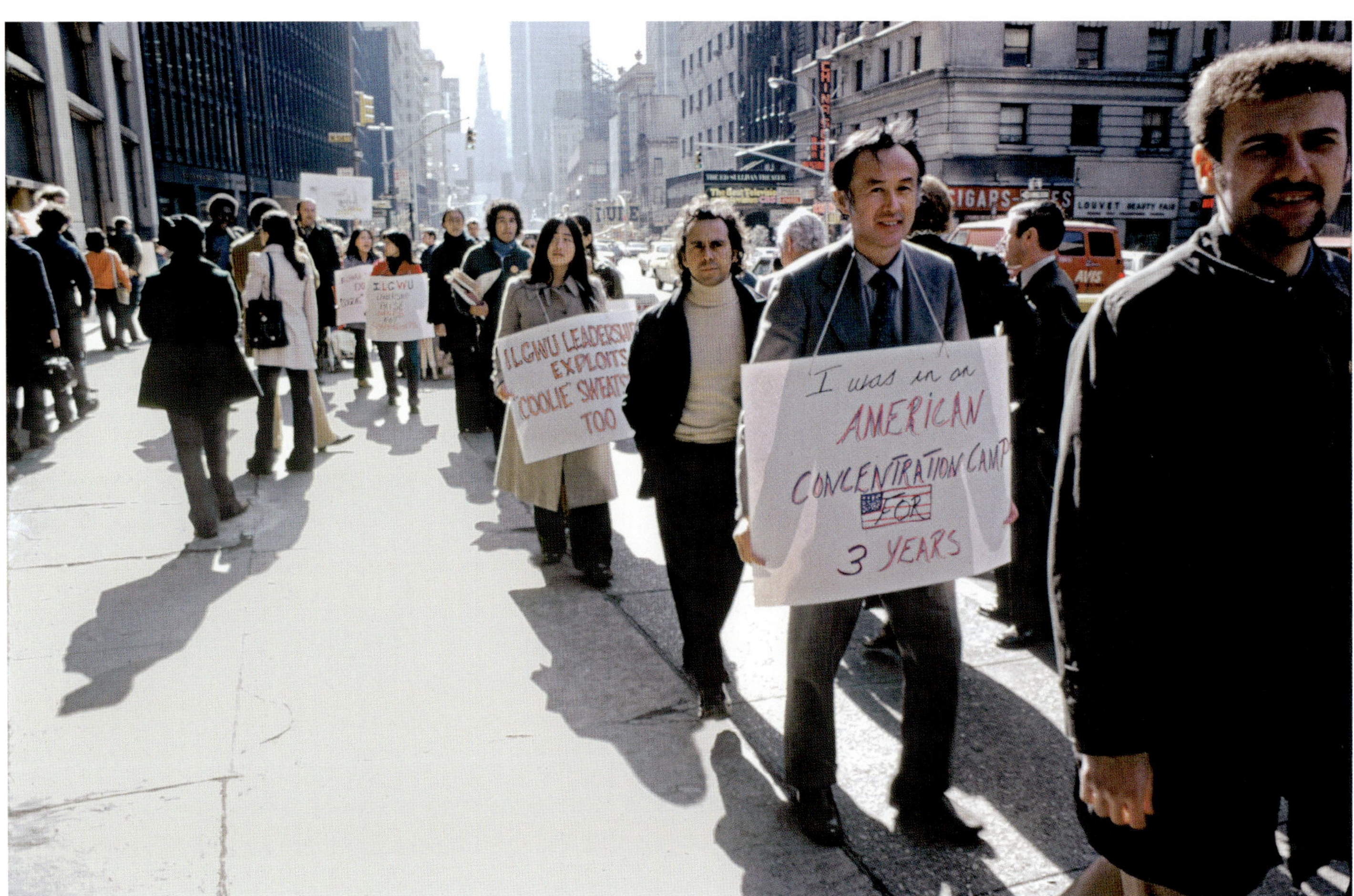

Kazu Iijima (1918–2007), *left,* and Minn Matsuda (1911–2003) were mothers in their fifties in 1969 when they formed Asian Americans for Action, the first pan-Asian political organization on the East Coast. Here these two longtime activists and friends celebrate the fifth anniversary of "Triple A." New York, 1974.

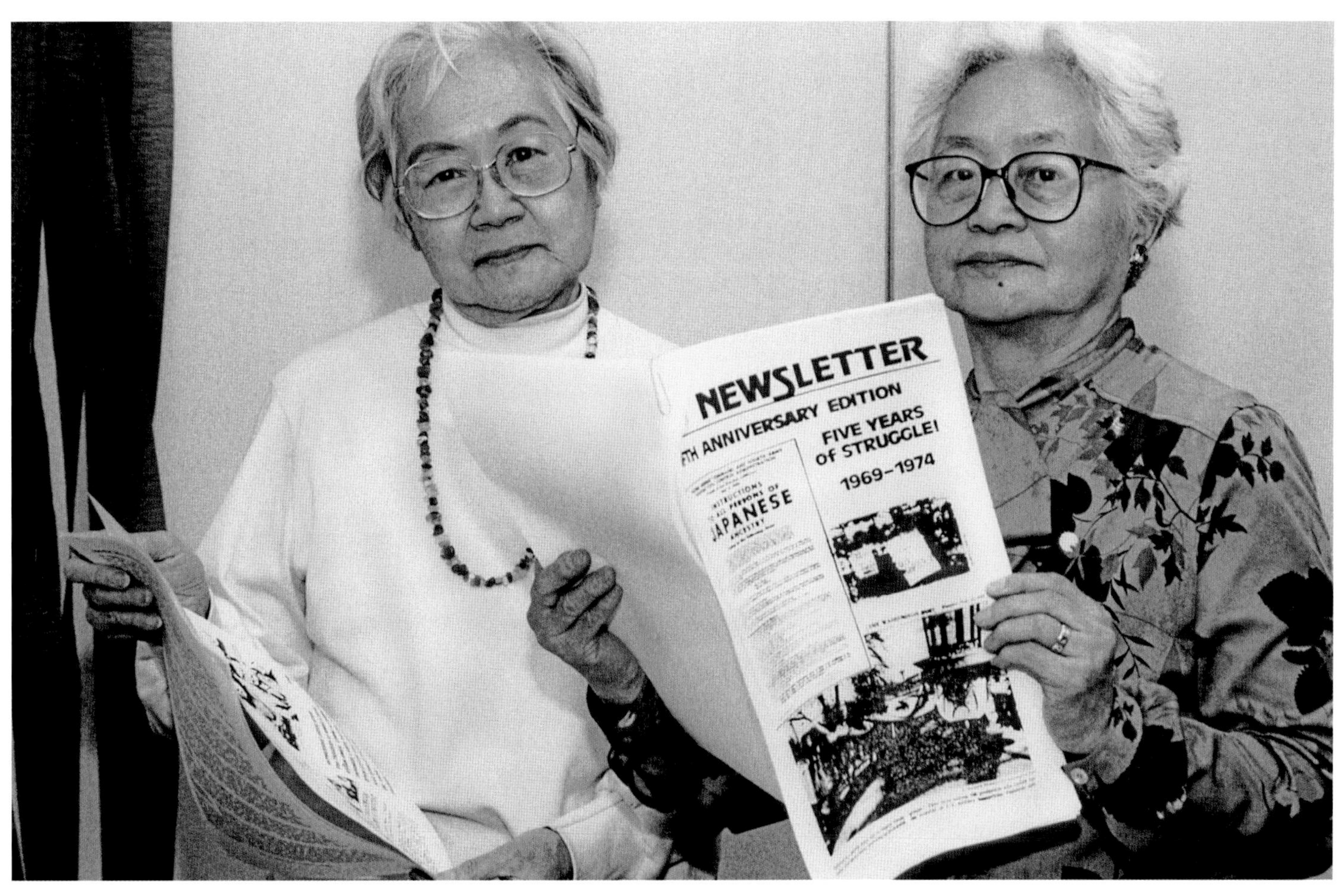

The Early Days of the Asian American Movement

ROCKY CHIN

Activist and attorney; member of the New York City Commission on Human Rights

Corky Lee and I were born two months apart in the Year of the Pig. We both graduated from high school in 1965, the year racially restrictive immigration laws were eliminated. And as our college graduations in 1969 approached, we both found ways to avoid getting drafted to fight in the war in Vietnam. Corky declared himself to be a conscientious objector and asked his draft board to assign him to community service as an alternative to combat duty. I began a two-year graduate program in city planning and continued to receive a student deferment.

My program required me to identify a community where I could focus on its history, explore its challenges, and envision its future. I chose New York's Chinatown. There, in the fall of 1969, I met Corky, who was then a tenant organizer at the Two Bridges Neighborhood Council.

"We're taking on Ma Bell!" he boasted to me that day. He impressed me as a bit cocky although clearly passionate about community organizing. He had stature and confidence, and I could see that he envisioned himself as a modern-day David confronting New York Telephone (later AT&T)'s Goliath. The phone company had planned to erect a thirty-two-story switching station in Manhattan's Lower East Side, a neighborhood along the East River where Black, Puerto Rican, Italian, Jewish, and Chinese families lived side by side in walk-up tenements and public housing. The station would have displaced hundreds of families. Corky was exuberant when he told me several months later that the phone company had given up. It was a hard-fought victory for the "We Won't Move" coalition.

My studies also put me in touch with Danny N. T. Yung, a Hong Kong–born architect–urban planner engaged in graduate studies at Columbia University's Center for Urban Research and Policy. At the time, Corky was working closely with Danny and his team of community-oriented professionals on a survey of Chinatown. They recruited bilingual residents and activists to participate. The resulting Chinatown Study Report, which came out in 1970, was groundbreaking because it based its important findings on critical empirical data, touching on housing conditions, demography, employment, occupations, educational attainment, and immigration.

The burgeoning Asian American student movement, initially galvanized by opposition to the Vietnam War, wanted to learn about conditions in Chinatown. In the spring of 1970, I invited Corky and Danny to lead a workshop called "Chinatown and Its Problems" at the "Asians in America" conference at Yale University

That conference brought together three hundred Asian American students and young people, the first activist gathering on the East Coast in the early 1970s. A summer and fall of marches, rallies, and meetings—and discussions of national and global current events, like the Black freedom struggle and the war in Vietnam—fueled the growth of the Asian American movement. In the winter of 1970, twice as many people attended a second gathering, the "Asian American Reality" conference at Pace University in Lower Manhattan, a stone's throw from Chinatown. The veteran revolutionary activist Grace Lee Boggs gave a rousing keynote. The Asian American movement was fired up!

Meanwhile, Danny had been searching for a home for the documents and data that had been collected for the Chinatown Study Report. A basement space at 54 Elizabeth Street, just north of Canal, became the Basement Workshop. It moved twice to ever larger spaces and for some fifteen years would remain New York's largest and most beloved Asian American community art and cultural center.

The Basement Workshop produced several projects that are iconic emblems of the early Asian American movement. In the summer of 1971, it launched *Bridge Magazine.* Headed up by *New York Times* journalist Frank Ching, *Bridge* would publish news analyses, essays, criticism, and poetry until 1986. The Basement also launched the Asian American Resource Center, where I took charge. Corky eagerly assumed an unofficial role as a Basement promoter. More and more new projects started. The Basement's success in those early years stemmed from its being an open forum for many voices, diverse views, and joyous creativity.

During these years folk singers Joanne Nobuko Miyamoto, Chris Kando Iijima, and "Charlie" Chin came together to form the group Yellow Pearl. They performed in the folk-music style of vocals and acoustic guitar, with the occasional accompaniment by bongo drums, bass, and *dizi,* a Chinese flute. At a time when the most famous folk singers (like Pete Seeger and Peter, Paul, and Mary) were white, Yellow Pearl created the sound of the new Asian American movement. Their songs captured the spirit of the new Asian American identity and expressed solidarity with Black, Latinx, and Third World liberation movements. In 1972 the Basement published the first collection of Asian American graphic art, poetry, and music and lyrics, in an art book also called *Yellow Pearl.*

In the liner notes for their album *A Grain of Sand: Music for the Struggle by Asians in America* (1973), the musicians wrote:

You are the music
You are the song
You are the ones
To whom the future belongs

Corky Lee captured and embodied that spirit.

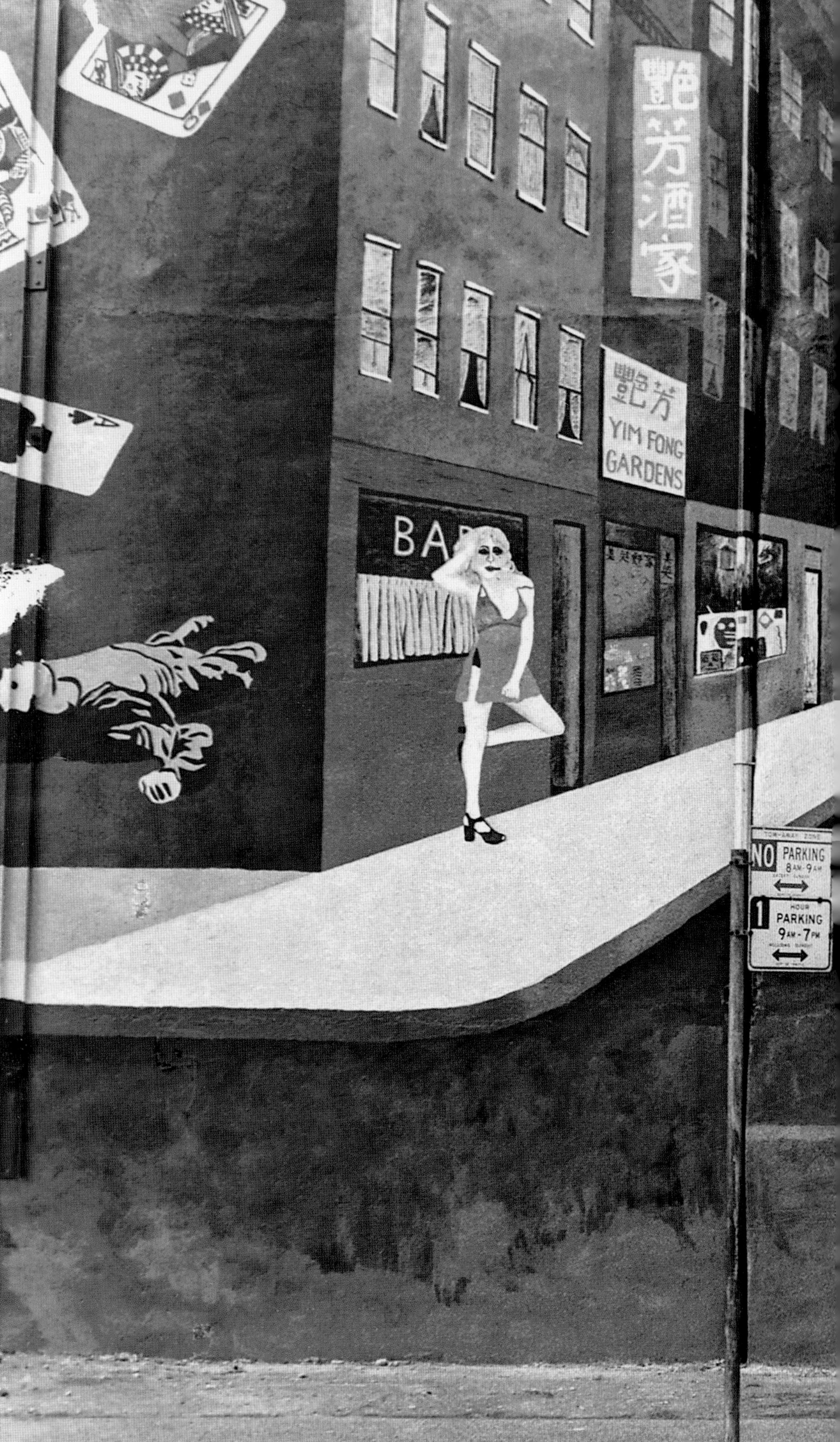

Chinatown Today was a mural painted on Pike Street in 1973 by Alan Okada, with Fay Chu, Mimi Eng, Nancy Lee, Valerie Velazquez, Sheila Washington, and Grace Yung. It showed young people amid tourists, a sex worker, gamblers, and drug dealers, along with Grandpa's, a bar on East Broadway whose proprietor let kids do their homework in the back of the bar after school, to keep them off the streets. It was one of several murals painted in Chinatown between 1972 and 1978, in summer-long projects of artists (many of them from the Basement Workshop) and youth sponsored by CityArts Workshop and Project Reach. By the 1990s, the murals had been painted over or their buildings torn down. New York, 1976.

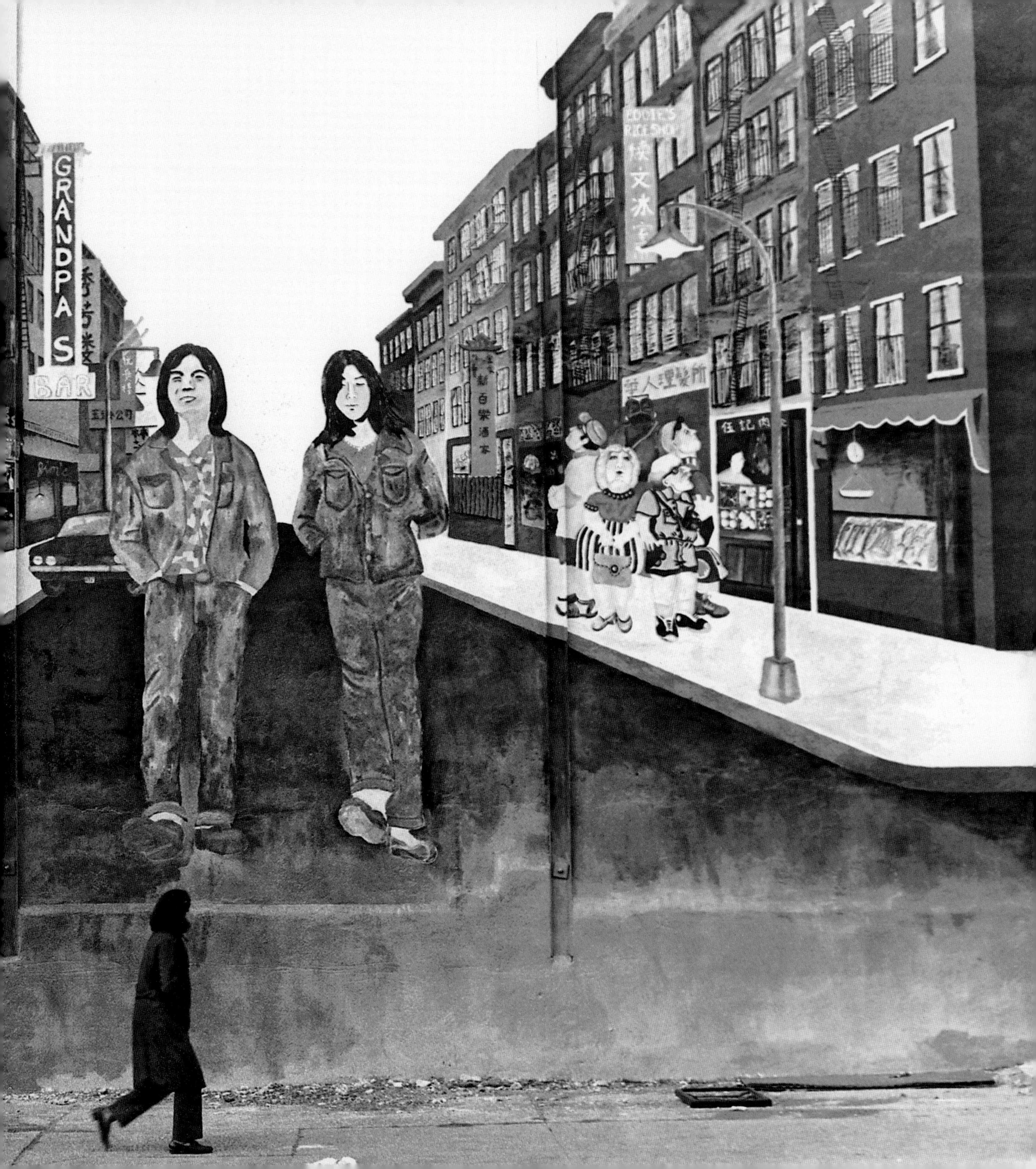
GRANDPAS
BAR

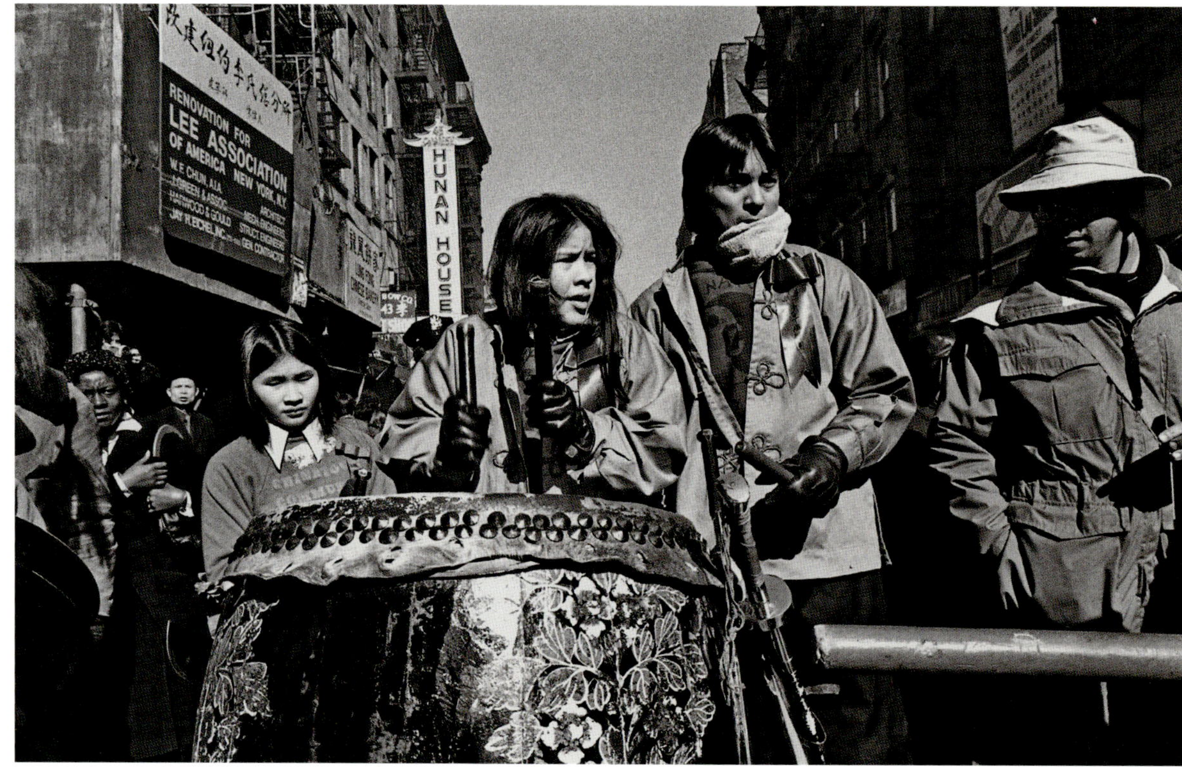

A young woman beats the drum—traditionally a male role—during a lion dance performance at the Chinatown Lunar New Year parade. New York, 1977.

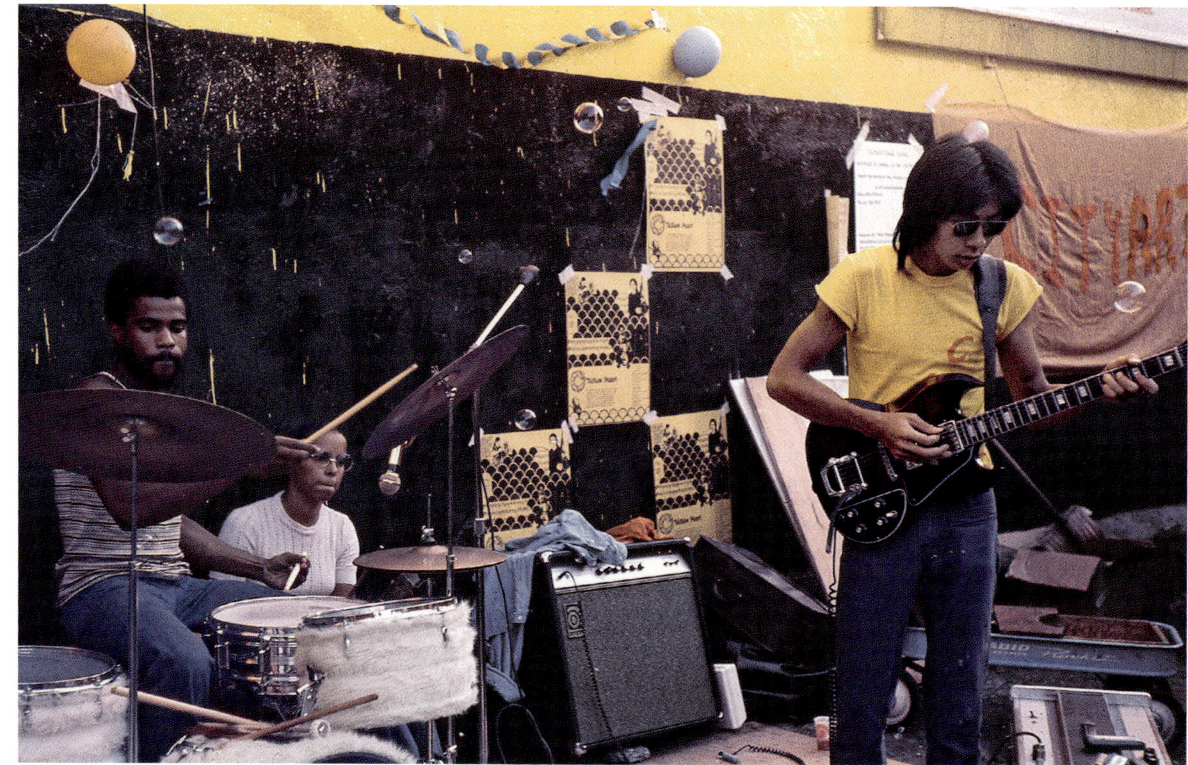

Partygoers celebrate the completion of the CityArts mural on the history of Chinese immigration to the United States, led by Alan Okada and painted at Chatham Square. The rock musician, actor, and activist Geoff Lee (1952–2022), a member of the Basement Workshop, and two colleagues performed at the party. New York, 1972.

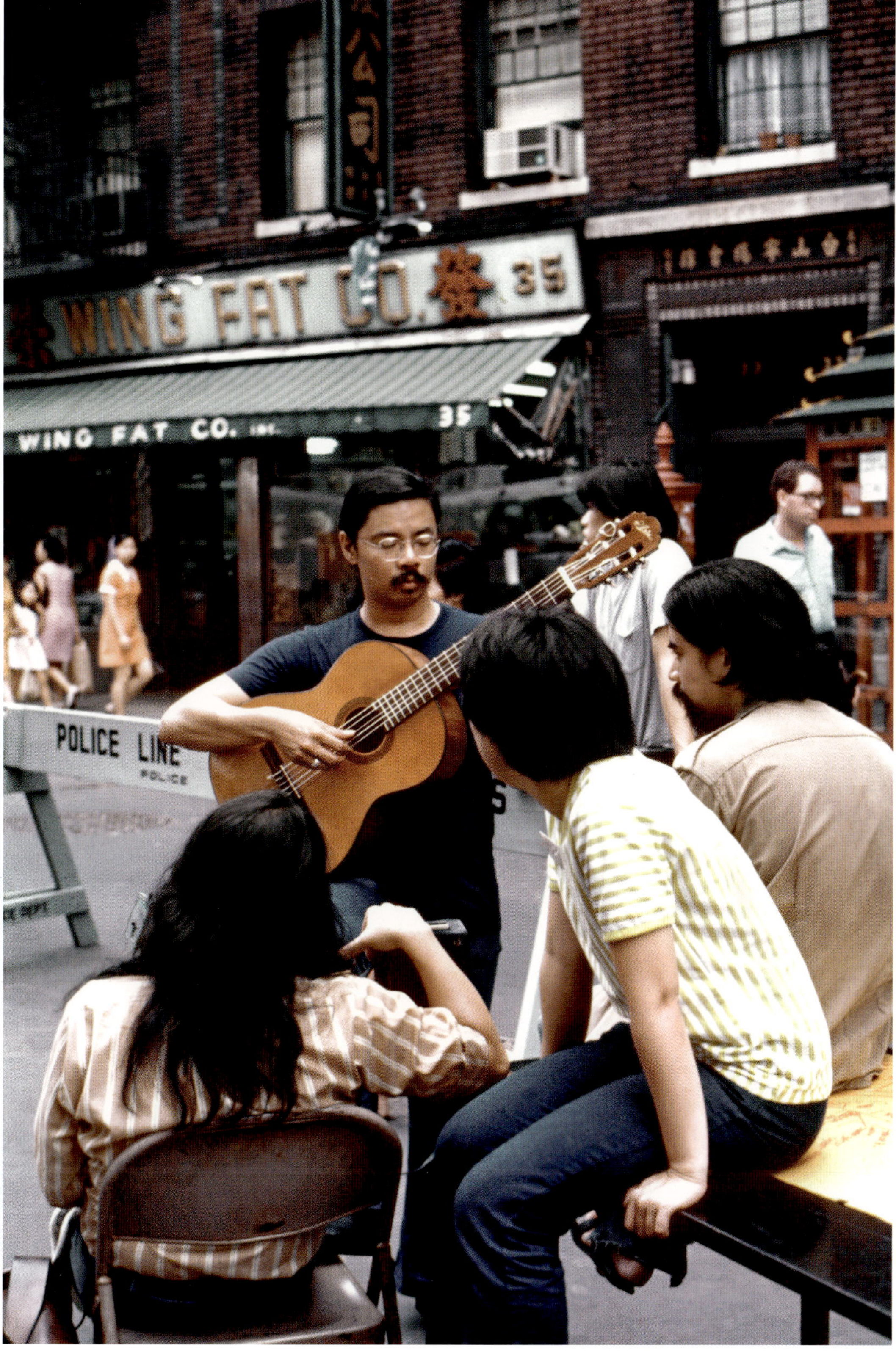

Folk singer "Charlie" Chin performs at the Chinatown Health Fair. New York, 1971.

The early issues of *Bridge Magazine* were edited by journalist Frank Ching and published by the Basement Workshop. New York, 1974.

Opposite: During the summer of 1975, actor Tzi Ma was cast in his first leading role, in a production of *Monkey King in the Yellow Stone Dream* (adapted from the classic Chinese fable *Journey to the West*). The show was to open at the La MaMa Experimental Theatre Club. In preparation for the role, on the rooftop of 22 Catherine Street in Chinatown, Ma was practicing kung fu, and Corky took photos to help him with his form. Tzi Ma would go on to have a long career in theater, television, and film, performing in David Henry Hwang's *The Dance and the Railroad* (1981), *Rush Hour* (1998), *24* (2005–7), *The Man in the High Castle* (2016), *Mulan* (2020), and *Kung Fu* (2021–present). New York, 1975.

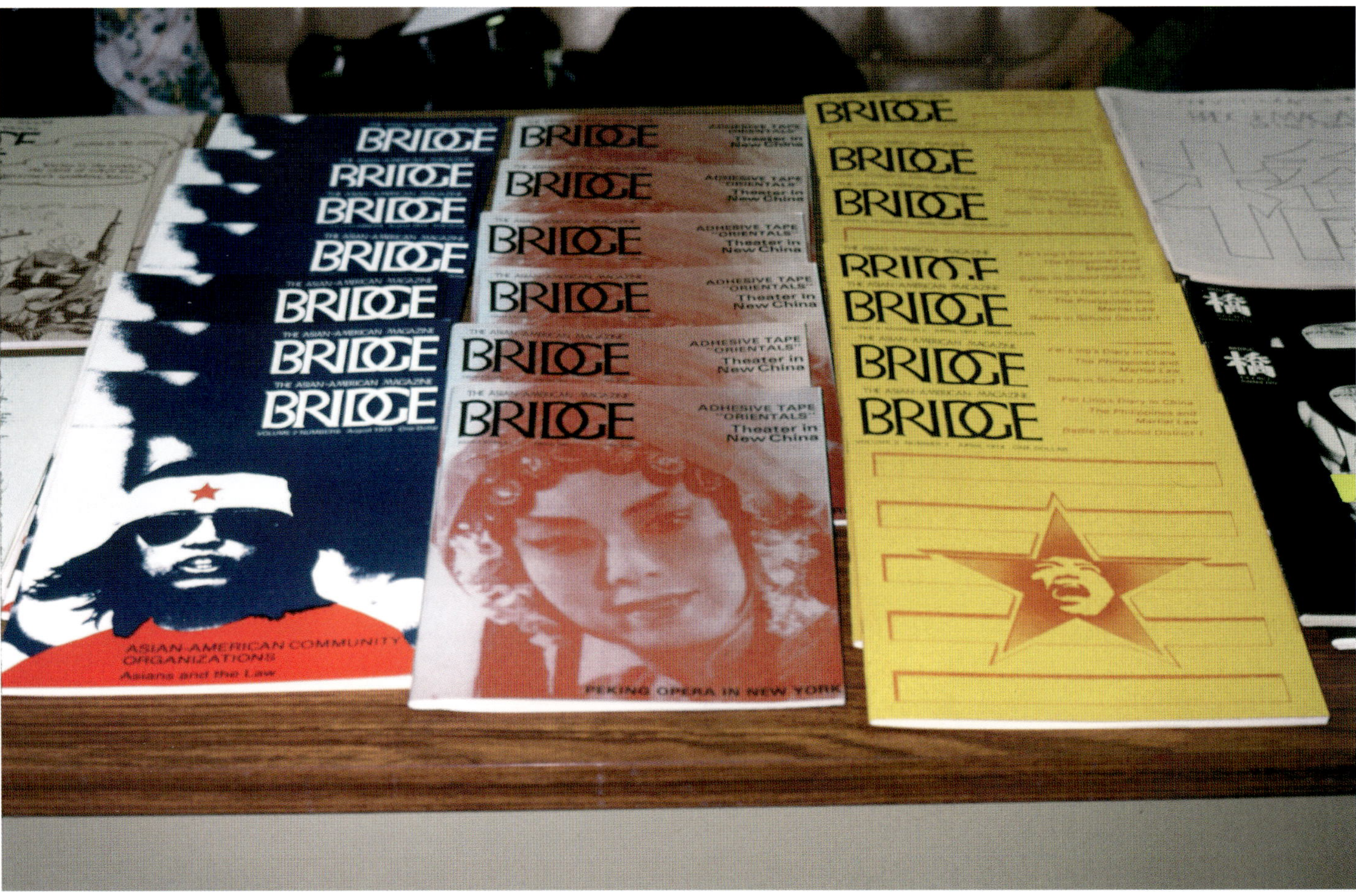

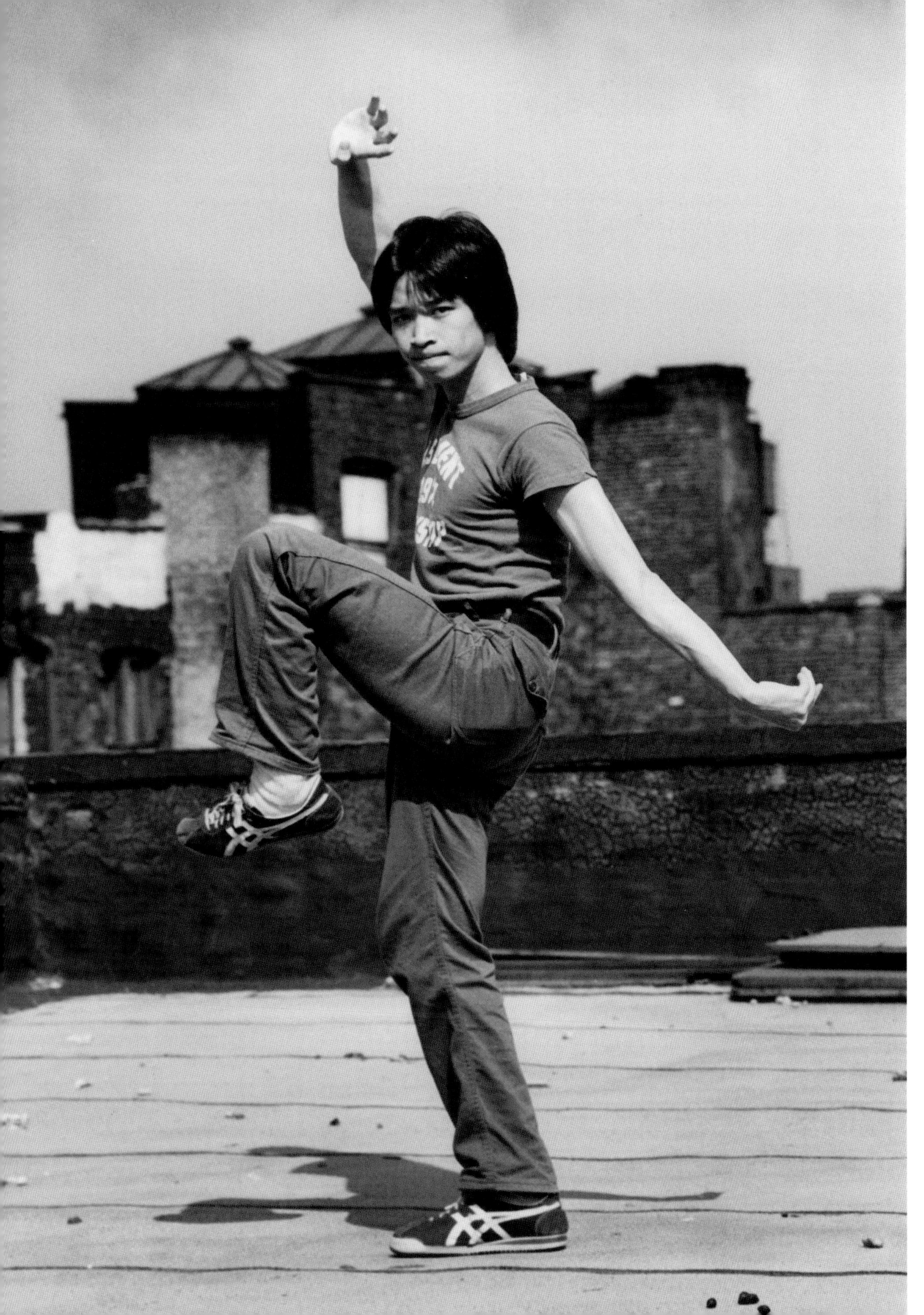

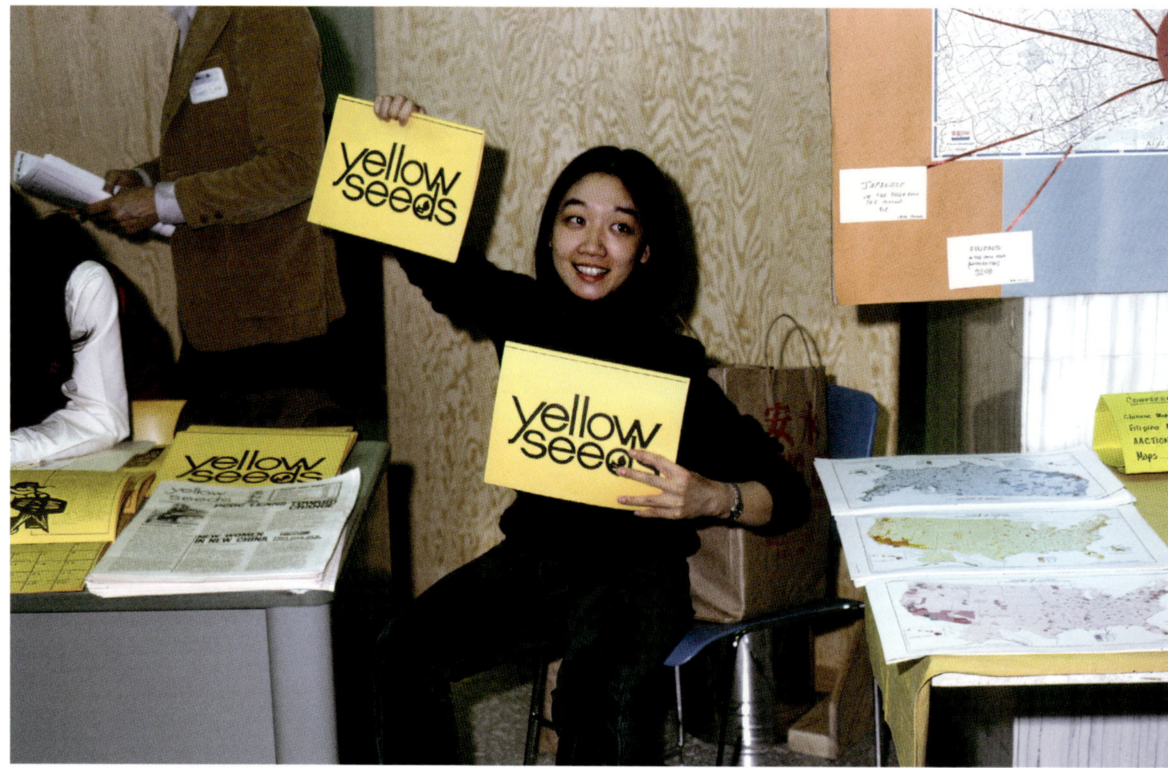

In Philadelphia in the 1970s, Miao Shao Gee of the Asian American youth organization Yellow Seeds published a Chinese-English newspaper by the same name and fought the building of an expressway that threatened to destroy the local Chinatown. Here she attends an Asian American conference. New York, 1974.

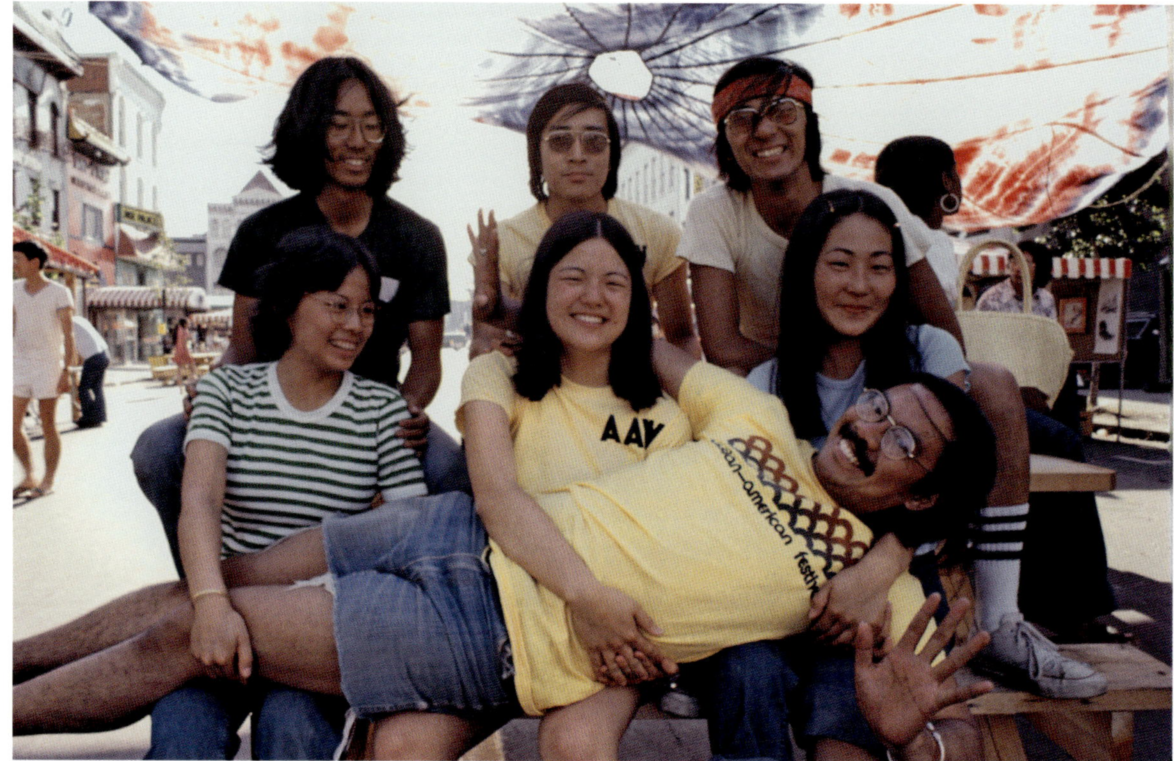

In Washington, D.C., at the Asian American summer festival sponsored by the local group Eastern Wind, folk singer "Charlie" Chin (*horizontal*) poses with Corky's brother John Lee (*back row, right*), then an instructor at Oberlin College, and Oberlin students who had worked on their senior projects with Corky earlier that year. Washington, D.C., 1974.

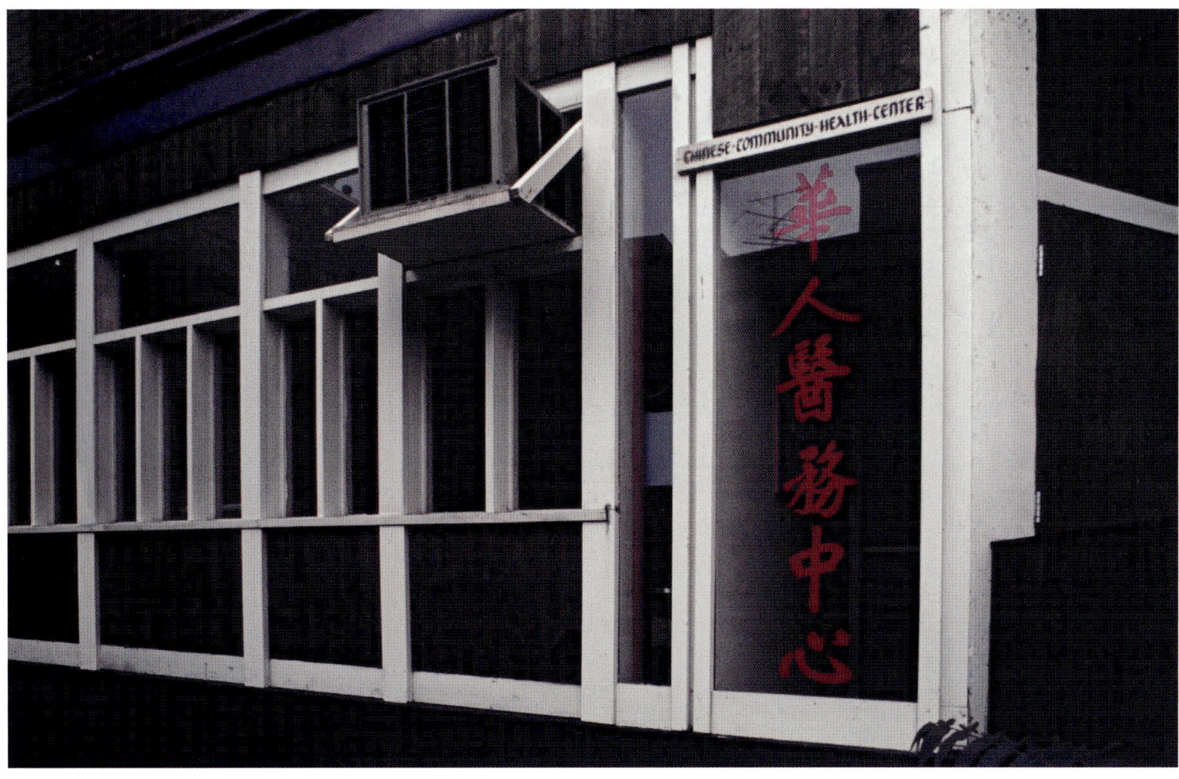

Chinatown's health center. Boston, 1972.

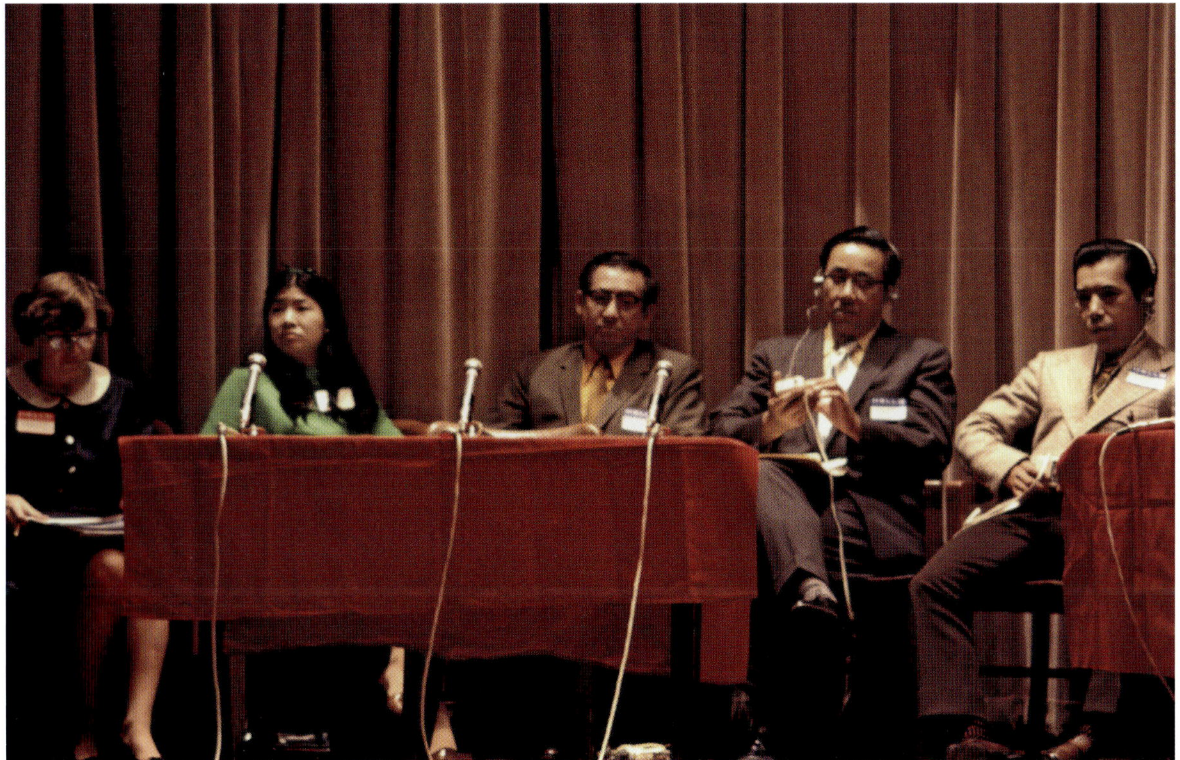

Community activists in Boston's Chinatown addressed similar issues of housing and health care. A Future of Chinatown conference, called by the Chinese American Civic Association, was held at the headquarters of the On Leong Association, where participants discussed the threat to the community posed by the expansion of Tufts–New England Medical Center. Boston, 1972.

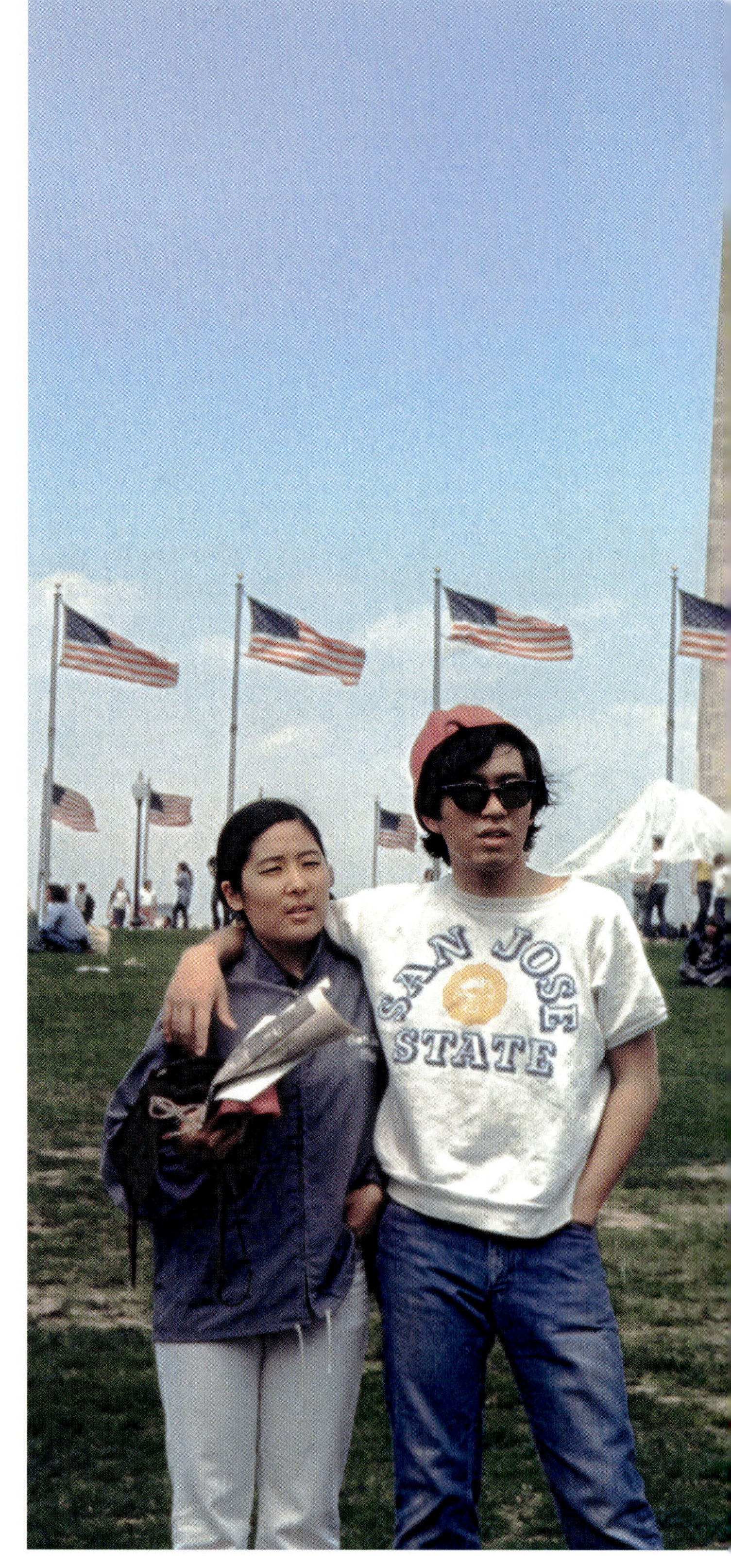

During a demonstration of one million Americans against the Vietnam War, the revolutionary activist Grace Lee Boggs (1915–2015) spoke to the Asian American contingent at the Washington Monument. Washington, D.C., 1971.

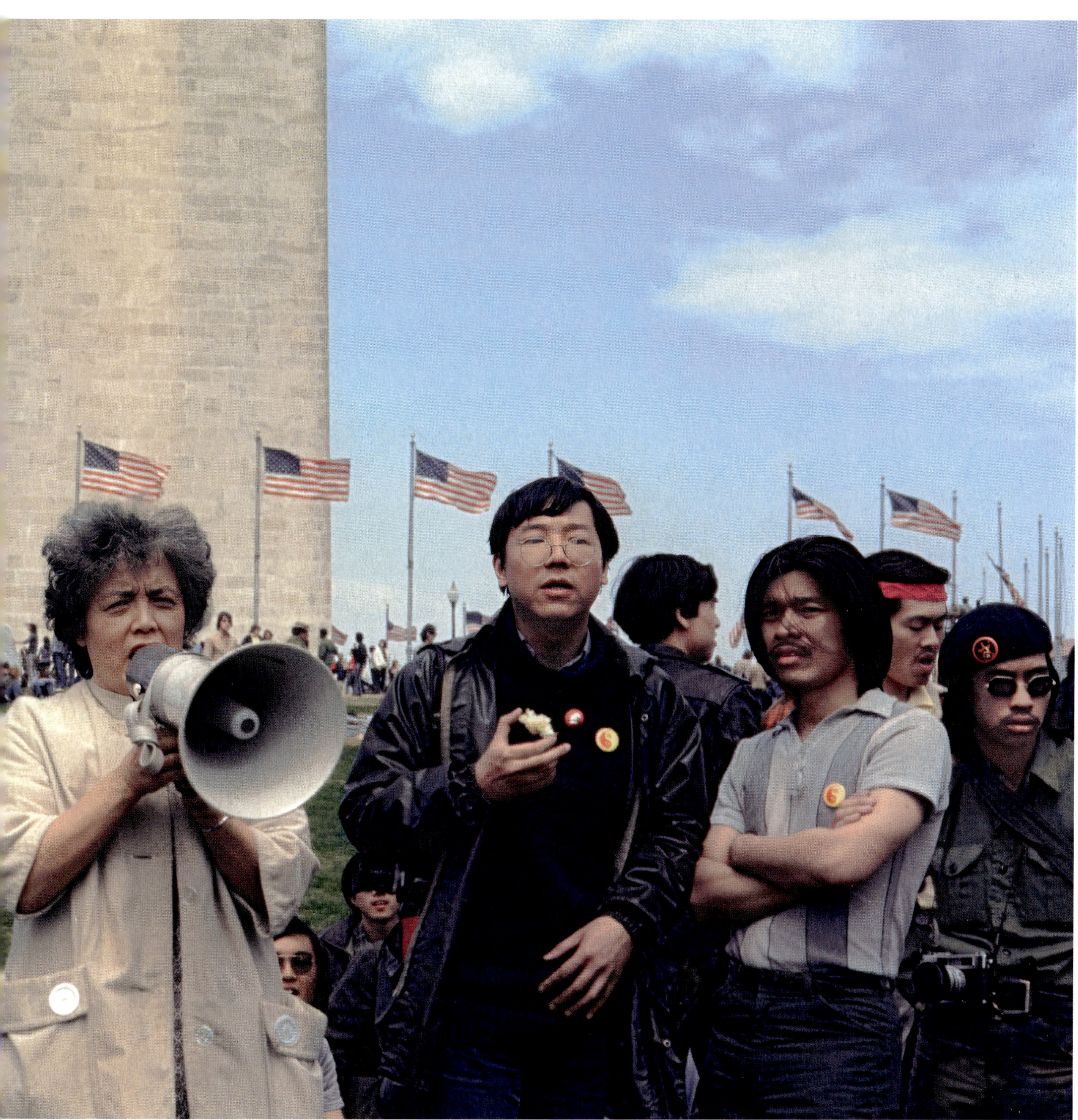

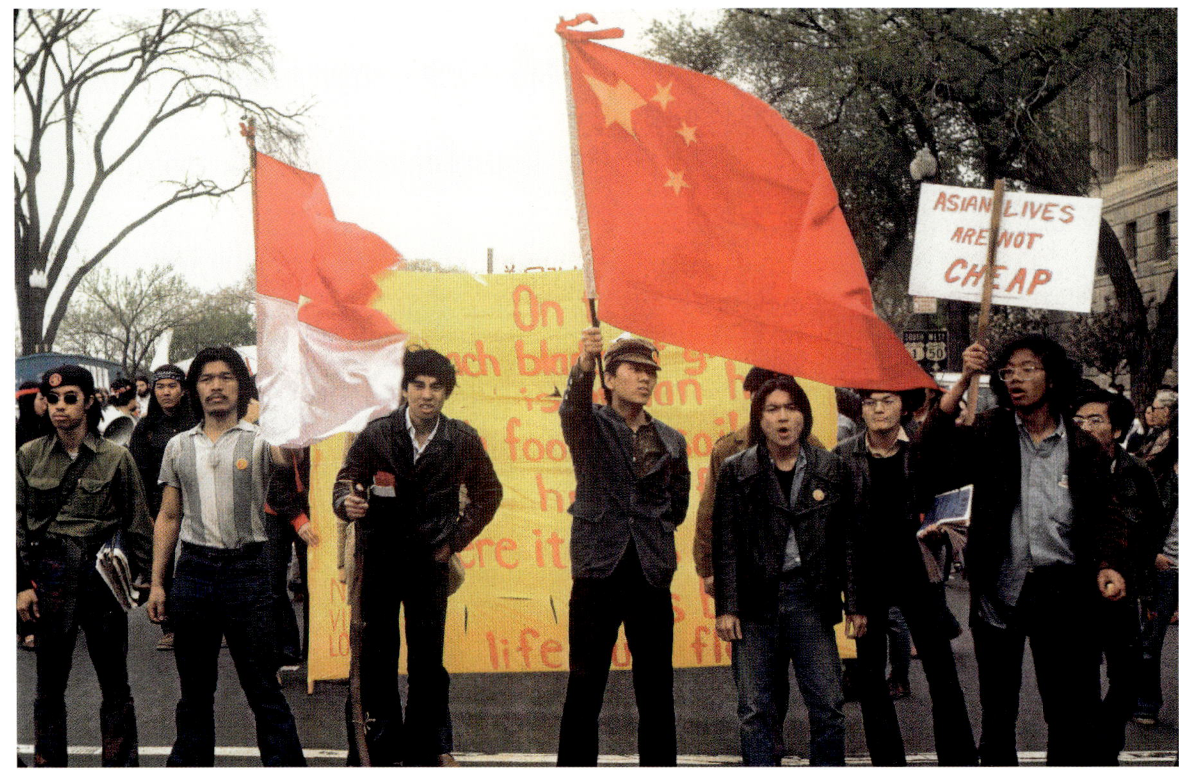

At the demonstration, the Asian American contingent marched against the war with the flags of the People's Republic of China (*center*) and the North Vietnamese Army (*left*). Washington, D.C., 1971.

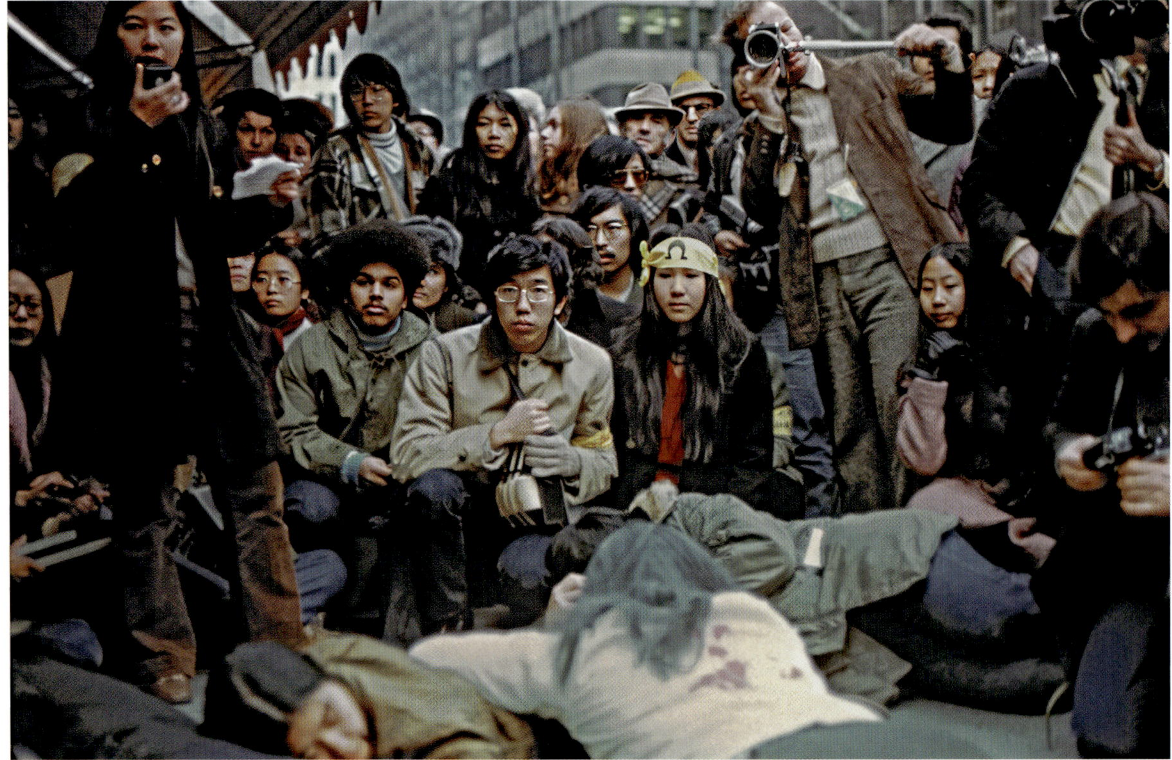

Rocky Chin (*center*) and Asian American students participated in an anti–Vietnam War march and "die-in" in Midtown Manhattan. New York, circa 1971.

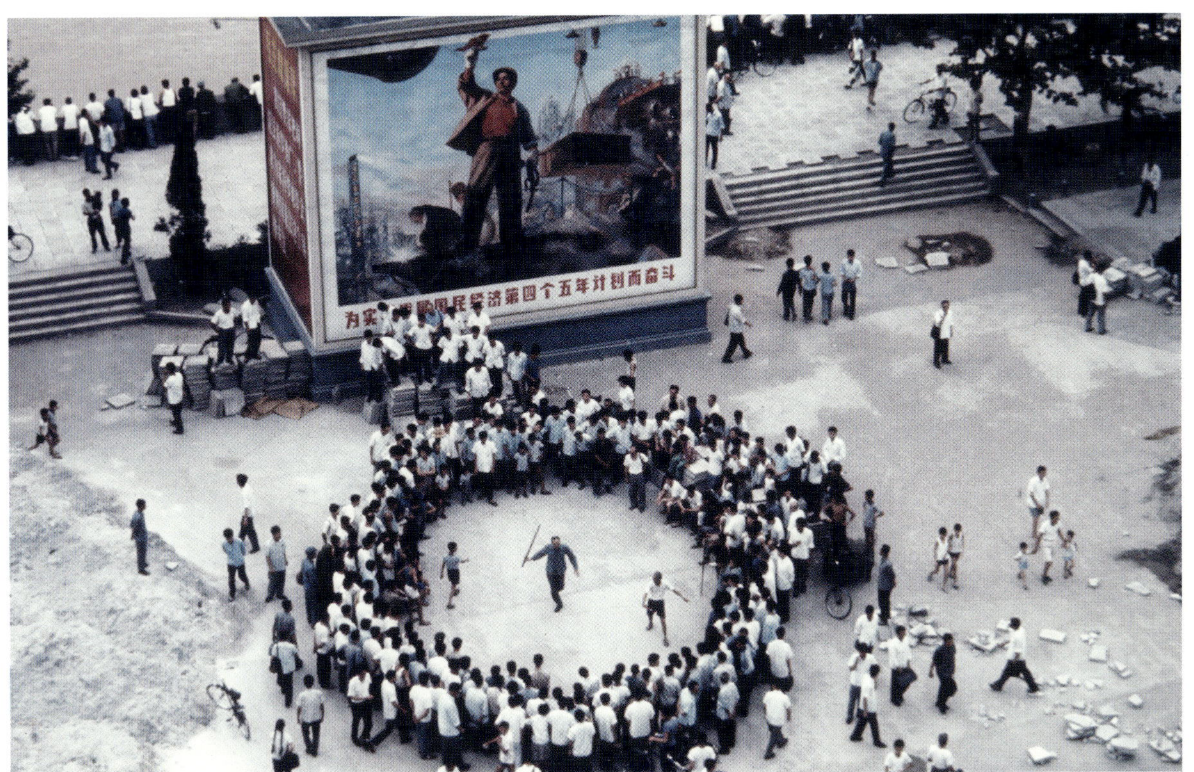

In 1972, Corky Lee went to the People's Republic of China as part of an Asian American youth delegation, one of the first groups to go to China after Nixon's visit. The group visited rural communes, schools, factories, and community centers.

Morning tai-chi exercise outside the Peace Hotel on the Bund. Shanghai, 1972.

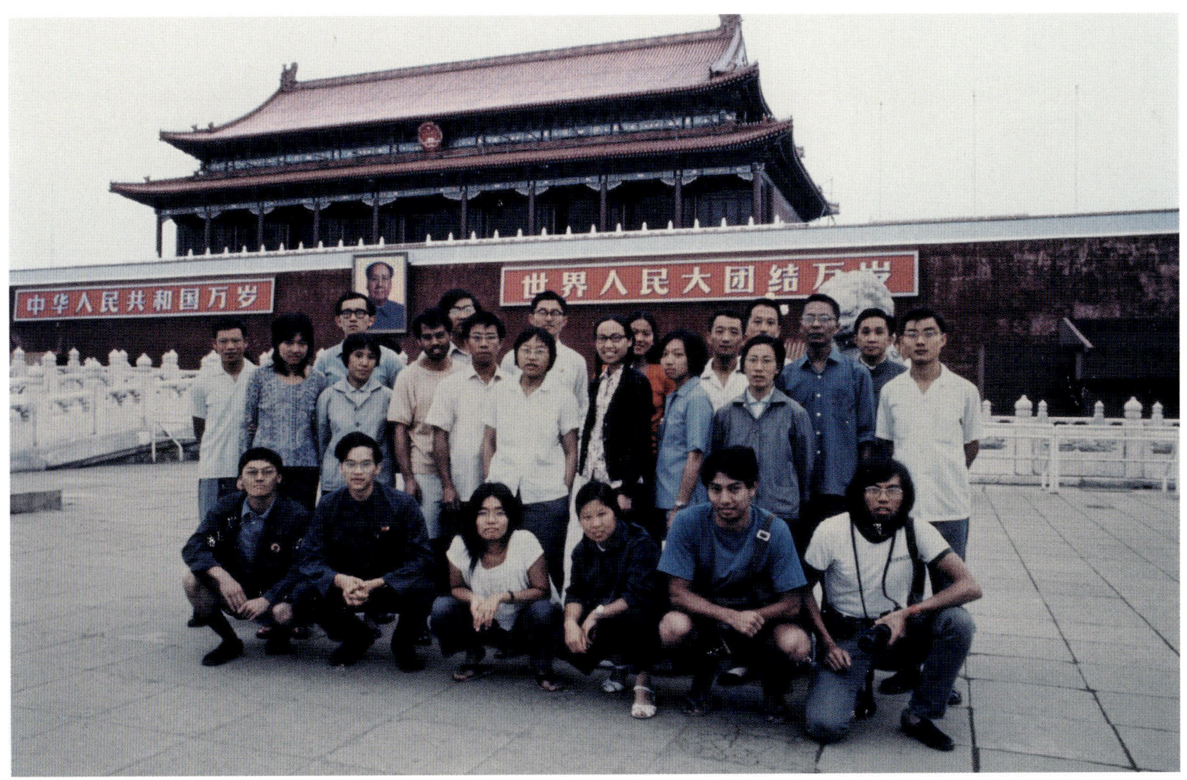

Corky took group photos with a tripod and timer. The delegation included young activists and future leaders Evelyn Yoshimura, founder of the Little Tokyo Service Center in Los Angeles; Leonard Hoshijo (1951–2021), who became an officer of the longshoremen's union in Hawaii; and Helen Lo, who heads the handbag company Lo and Sons. Tiananmen Square, Beijing, 1972.

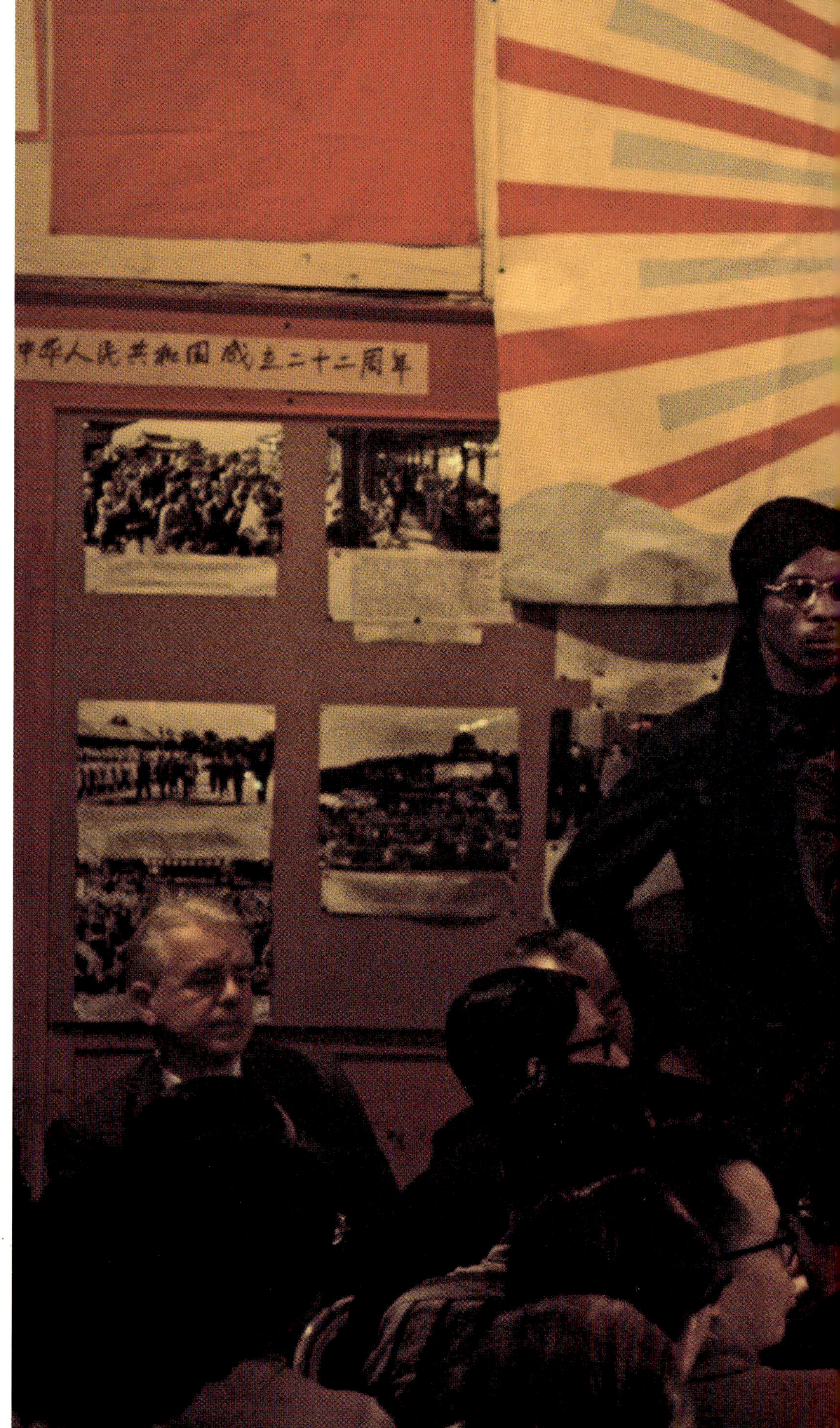

At the celebration of the twenty-second anniversary of the founding of the People's Republic of China, members of the Black Panther Party spoke at the I Wor Kuen storefront. The program, before a packed audience, also featured a screening of the classic *East Is Red* film in 16mm. New York, October 1971.

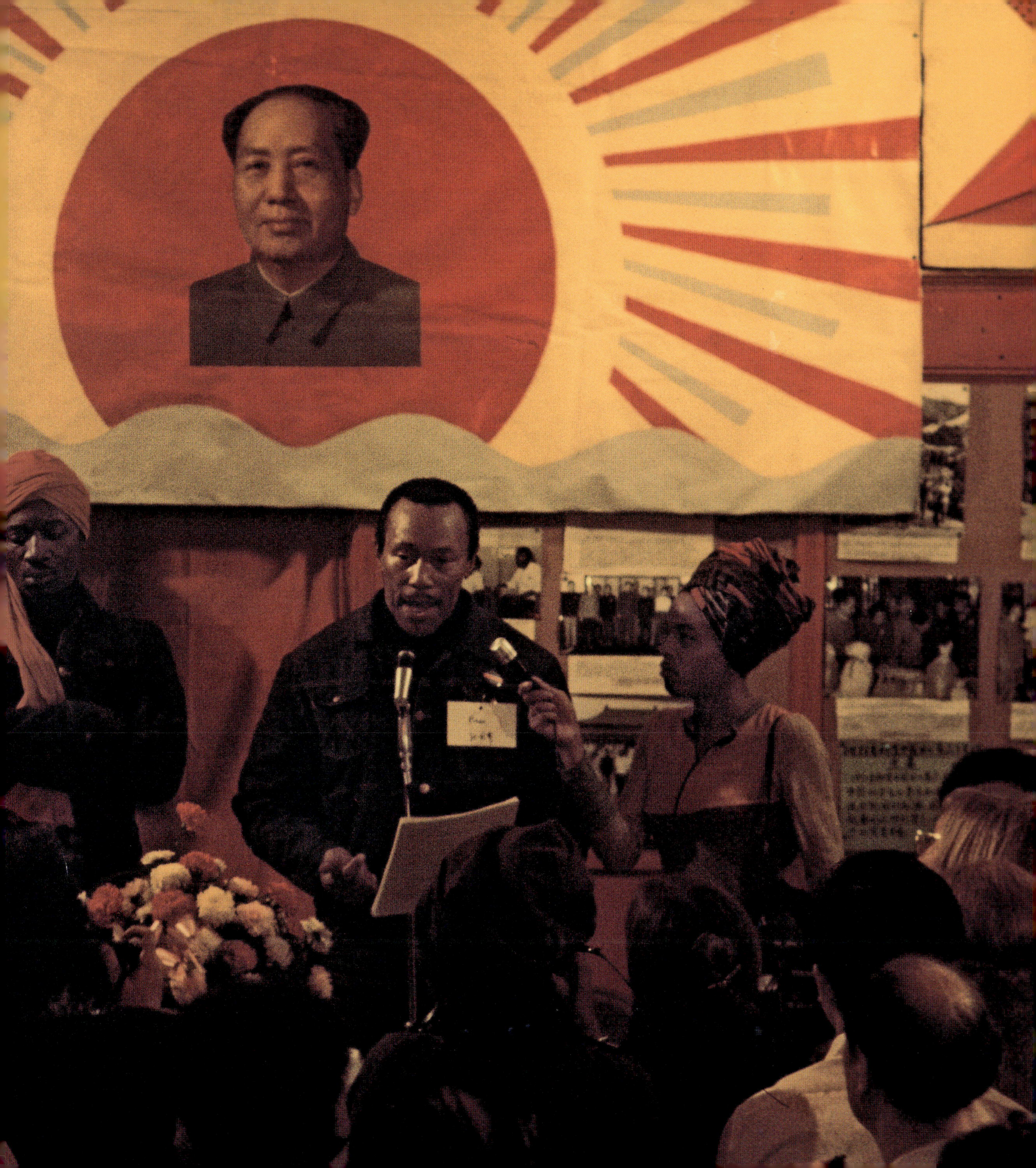

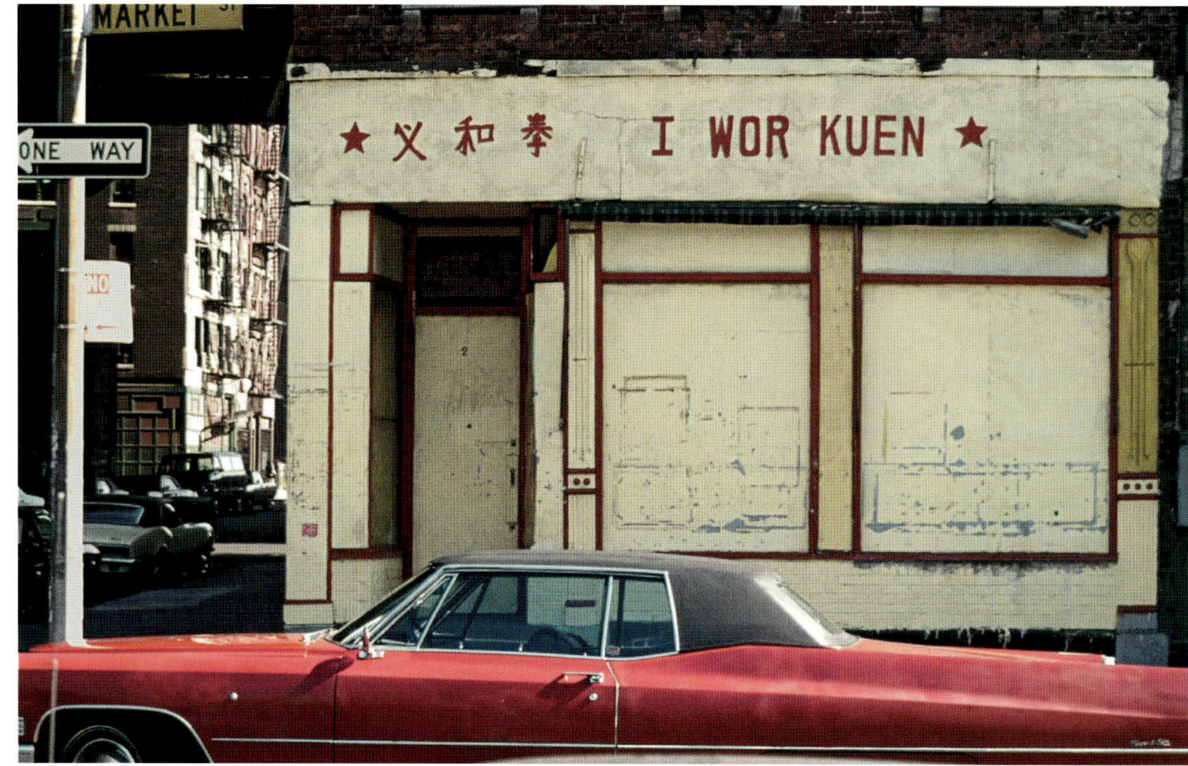

The storefront of I Wor Kuen at 24 Market Street in Chinatown. IWK published an English-Chinese newspaper, *Getting Together,* and espoused a revolutionary ideology in solidarity with all those fighting racism and imperialism. It screened films from the People's Republic of China, hosted free health and acupuncture clinics, and organized tenants and young people. New York, 1973.

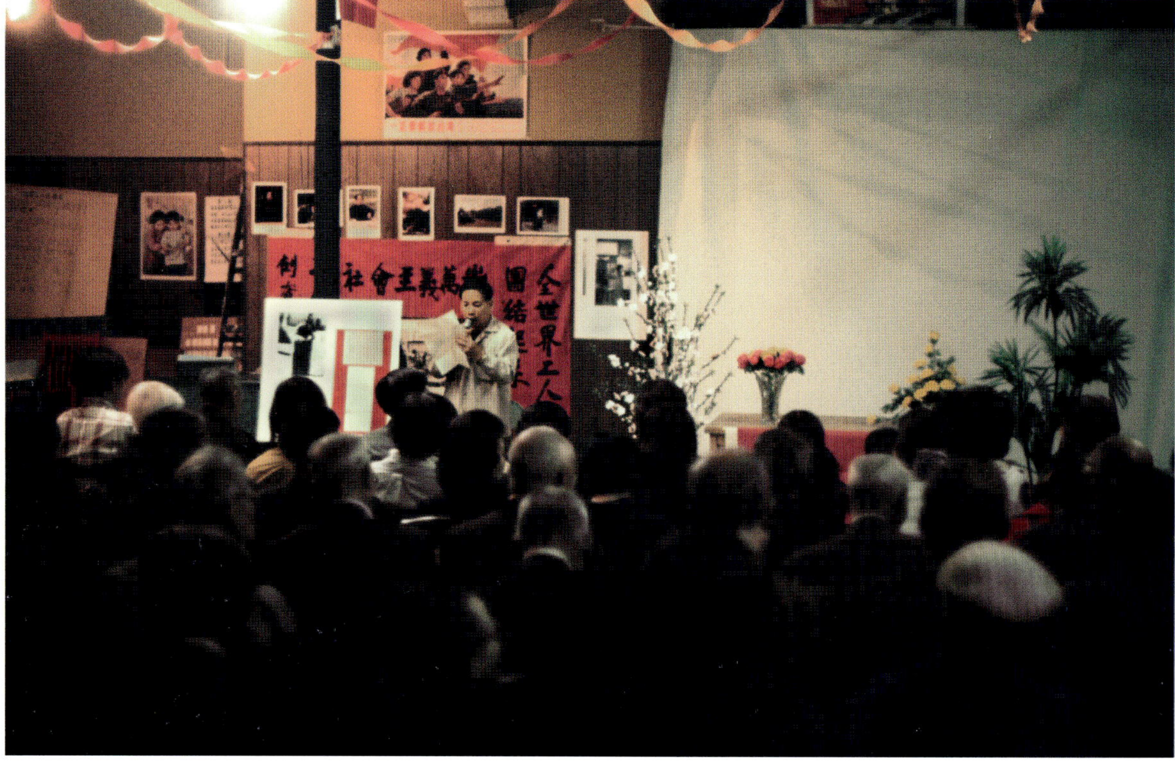

A celebration of International Workers Day, hosted by IWK at a community center in the International Hotel in Chinatown/Manilatown. San Francisco, 1972.

In this building at 22 Catherine Street in Chinatown, Pearl River Mart was founded in 1971. Its original Chinese name Sixin Shangdian (Four News Shop) was a nod to a Chinese revolutionary slogan promoting new customs, new culture, new habits, and new ideas. That same year, on the second floor, the Chinatown Health Clinic opened; the Basement Workshop on the third floor would arrive in 1972. When the store moved in 1978, it was rebranded as Pearl River, referring to the Cantonese origins of the Chinatown community. Lunar New Year, New York, 1974.

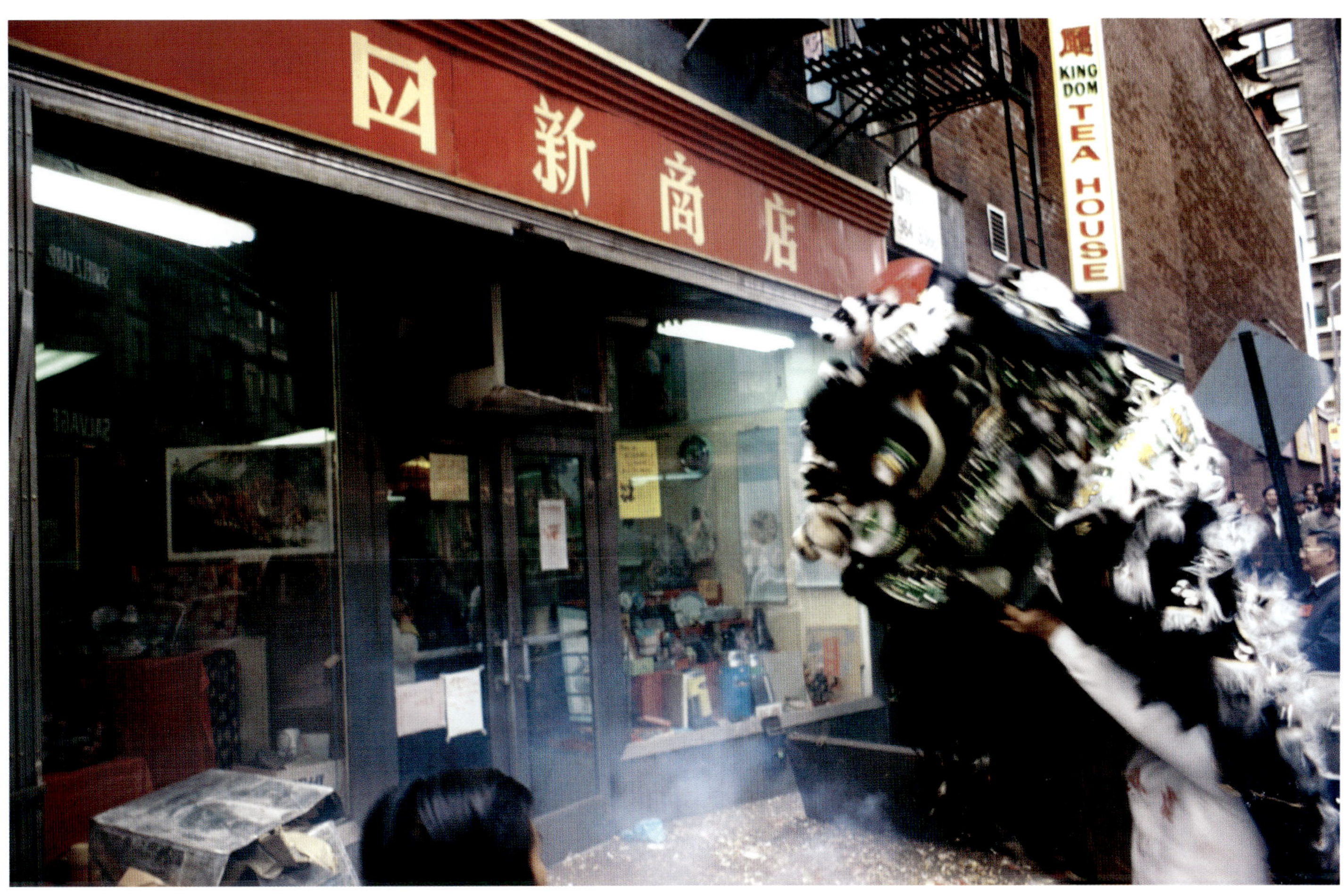

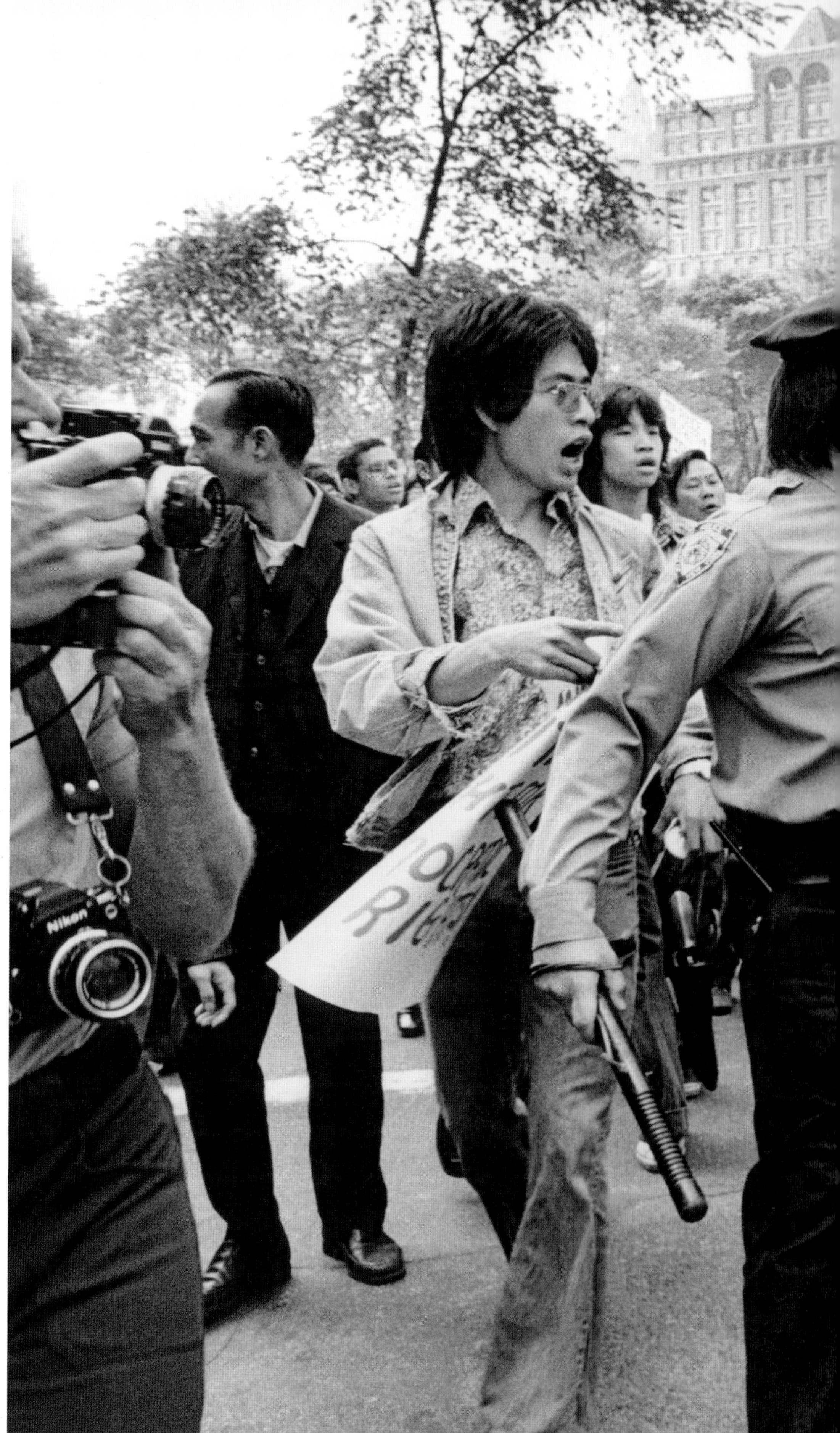

In April 1975 Peter Yew was arrested and beaten by police at the Fifth Precinct in Chinatown after he protested police treatment of a bystander in a traffic dispute. On May 12, several thousands marched to demand justice for Peter Yew, in a protest called by Asian Americans for Equal Employment, and a week later, on May 17, more than twenty thousand marched again, when the Chinese Consolidated Benevolent Association called for a community-wide protest that shut down shops and workplaces. Corky Lee captured a melee with police at city hall, which resulted in beatings and arrests. A protester pictured here was among those beaten. The photograph was published on the front page of the *New York Post* that day. New York, 1975.

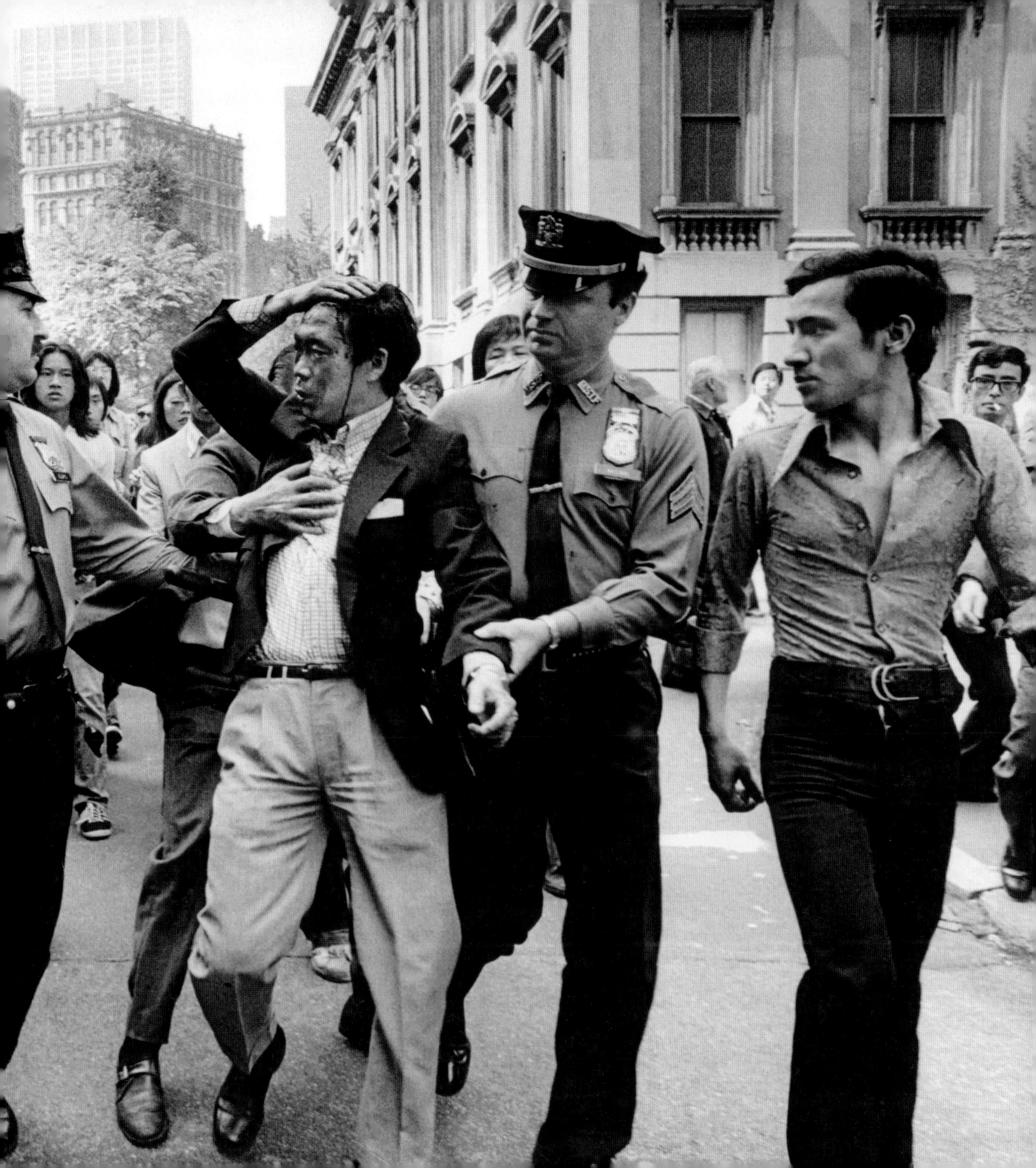

Corky Lee's Police Brutality Photographs

KEN CHEN

Poet and writer; assistant professor and associate director of creative writing at Barnard College

On December 3, 1974, two cops stalked some Chinatown youths into the Jade Chalet bar on Worth Street, on the edge of Chinatown. One of them fired his weapon. The bullet struck Tsu Yi Wu, a bystander, who died simply from being there. The officer faced no consequences.

A few months later, on April 26, 1975, a Saturday afternoon, an argument broke out over a traffic incident. Then an angry crowd of Chinatown residents gathered on Elizabeth Street in front of the Fifth Precinct police station. Policemen stepped out, forced the crowd back, and knocked down a teenager.

"Don't push like that," someone in the crowd reportedly yelled. His name was Peter Yew, a twenty-seven-year-old mechanical engineering student. The police attacked him, too, then dragged him inside, where they stripped him and beat him, wounding his forehead and spraining his wrist.

Afterward none of the officers who assaulted Yew were held accountable for their actions. On the contrary, Yew found himself charged with felonious assault. From the point of view of the police, Chinatown had too many roaming Chinese men, whom they interpreted as criminals. Yew wasn't a criminal or a recalcitrant teenager. His beating suggested to the community that police violence was indiscriminate, that it could reach even the educated middle class.

On the day before Yew's hearing, May 12, five thousand people turned out for a protest organized by Asian Americans for Equal Employment, which connected police brutality to the simultaneous cuts in social services and discrimination against Asians who were looking for city jobs. Some protesters threw eggs at the building of the Chinese Consolidated Benevolent Association (CCBA), home of the community's conservative leadership, which hadn't supported the march.

Under community pressure, the CCBA called for a protest march a week later on May 17. An unlikely coalition between merchants and militants brought out an astonishing twenty thousand marchers, but also hid underlying fissures. Shopkeepers shut their doors. Gambling parlors closed for the day. Women garment workers joined in, carrying placards identifying their shops, showing the breadth of support from that industry. Other marchers carried signs that said "End All Oppression" and "Jobs for All—Not Welfare." Corky Lee photographed the march as a river of wide lapels and floral shirts, denim jackets and Asian perms. In another famous photograph, he captured a line of young Asians—students from Brooklyn Technical High School who had skipped school for the day—proudly linking arms.

The march proceeded to city hall, where the deputy mayor and the police commissioner met with the CCBA, the Chinese Chamber of Commerce, and other Chinatown business leaders. The meeting excluded the radical youth, who split away from their elders and blocked traffic on Broadway. That was when the police rolled out.

The NYPD had called for reinforcements, and at least another four hundred officers showed up and clashed with the protesters. By the end of the day, four protesters would land at Beekman Downtown Hospital, but so would eleven policemen. Lee took a photograph of one such confrontation, a man who had just been struck by a cop. The photo reads like a baroque frieze of gestures, bustling with horizontal action. The background looks dodged, history in the process of being forgotten. The sight lines of the protesters and the police all track toward the wounded activist. He is the one being restrained, not the officer carrying a club. Two cops flank him, bracketed by a surly white man and an agitated Asian protester who literally holds a sign protesting police brutality, a pairing that seems to express the historical transition of the Asian American from third-world radical to NYPD booster. The center of attention, the protester, looks as if he has one too many hands. Someone else's grip presses against his heart. He clutches his wound. He pushes his head down, as if to keep his crown from ejecting from pure rage. Staring furiously, wounded like a martyr in a Caravaggio painting, he looks unwilling to be a victim.

By capturing the assault, Lee did more than represent movement politics—he catalyzed it. The photograph would become one of the most circulated images of Asian American radicalism up to that time, providing a picture of the police's rough abandon. It became an entry point into conversations about the NYPD's role as an occupying force in Chinatown. Within a week after the second protest, the head of the Fifth Precinct was removed. In July, charges against Yew were dropped, and a grand jury indicted the two officers who assaulted him.

What I love about the photograph of the wounded protester is how confusing it is to look at now. In our time, the foremost Asian American politician, Andrew Yang, campaigned for greater police protection. We imagine Asian seniors as perfect victims and conservatives as needing to be educated out of anti-Blackness by their sophisticated liberal children. Such assumptions evaporate when we glance at another Corky Lee photograph (see page 91).

In this photograph, two women emanate a sense of their own strength and individuality. The elderly woman, stout-faced, powerful, surveys the scene, her hands clasped around a placard that says, in Chinese, "Down with racist oppression / Justice for Peter Yew now / Unite and fight to victory." Her younger companion stands with lapels wide, her glance slanted, and her leg cocked out, a posture I associate for some reason with the 1970s. Her sign says in English, "Minorities Unite! Fight for Democratic Rights!" Something unique about these protests was their unity across race and class.

The cross-class solidarity would not last. In 1995 the NYPD killed sixteen-year-old Yong Xin Huang by shoving the boy face-first into a glass pane and shooting him in the back of the head. The grand jury failed to indict the officer. This time, in contrast to the Peter Yew protests, only forty people came to the courthouse vigil, which Lee photographed (see page 140). Unlike Lee's usual depictions of packed crowds, this one strikes you with its emptiness. Instead of masses of people, you see a cardboard shrine, some sidewalk detritus, and a cop staring you in the eye. Where did all that power go? The worker community had fractured, split between documented and undocumented, Taishanese and other Chinese, Manhattan and Brooklyn, where Yong Xin Huang lived.

This arc is only one way of representing the decline of Asian American politics. For many children of post-1965 immigrants, every photograph in Lee's visual archive vibrates with radical potential. There is something moving about the sheer number of people Corky Lee decided were worth remembering. Looking at his photos, I thought about the tremendous courage it would take to proffer yourself to a country that considers you its terrorist. What bravery it requires to rebut a cop or your boss, or to transplant yourself from your home into some dismal American sweatshop. Unlike identifying with someone just like yourself, solidarity suggests that "you" constitutes something suppler than the cell of yourself.

Lee's prints emanate a heterogeneous light. They are a magic mirror that reflects a person different from their onlooker.

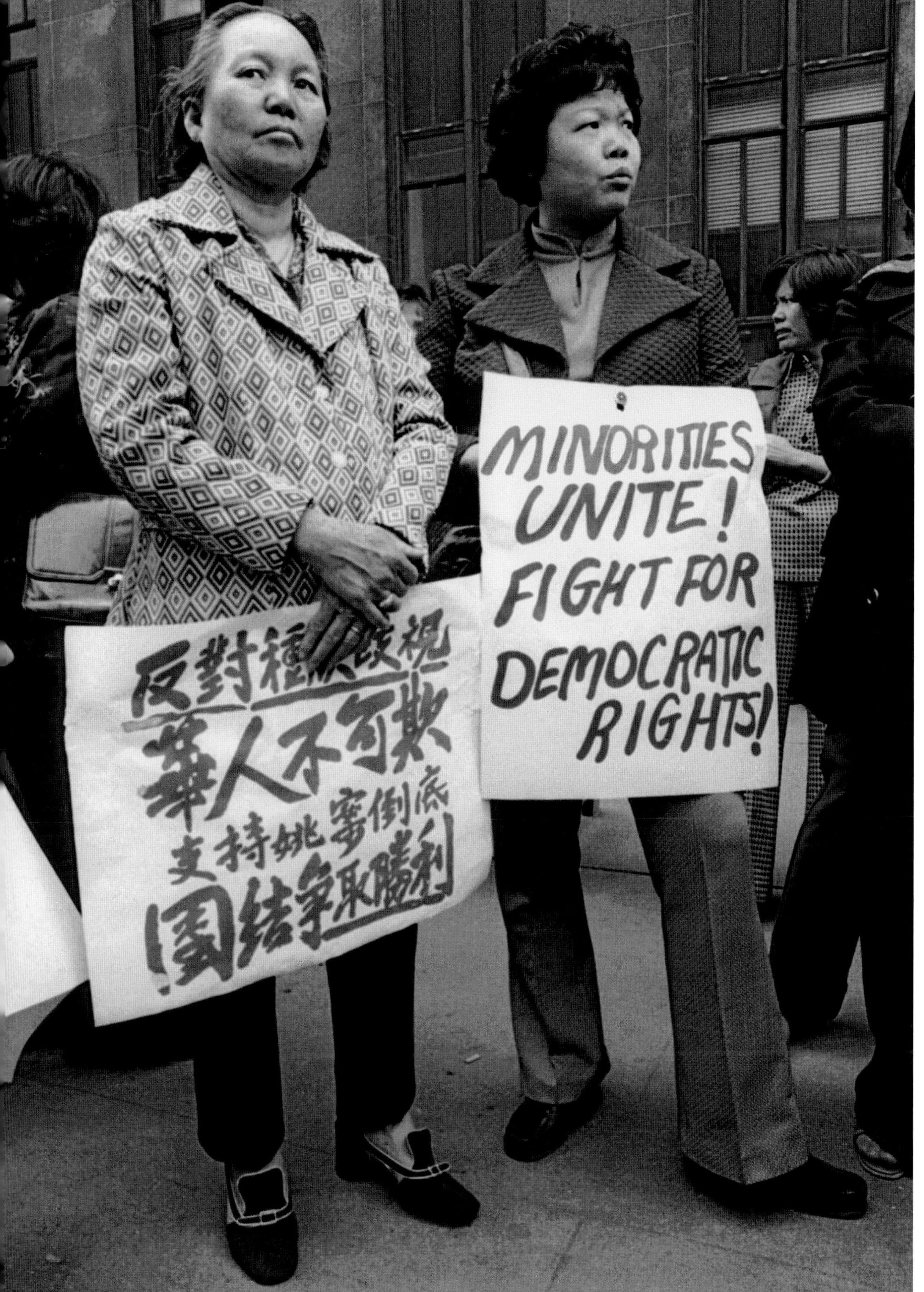

The sign in Chinese reads: "Down with racist oppression/ Justice for Peter Yew now/Unite and fight to victory." New York, 1975.

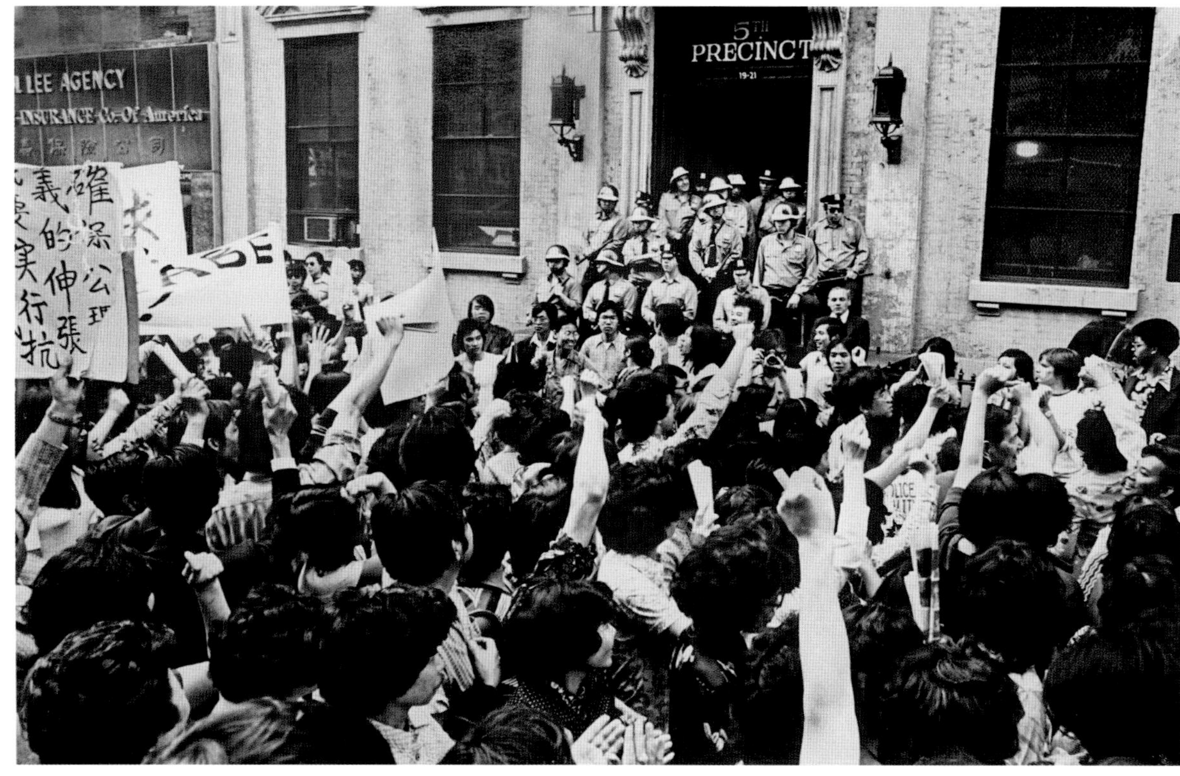

Protesters gathered in front of the Fifth Precinct in Chinatown, where Peter Yew was arrested and beaten by police. New York, 1975.

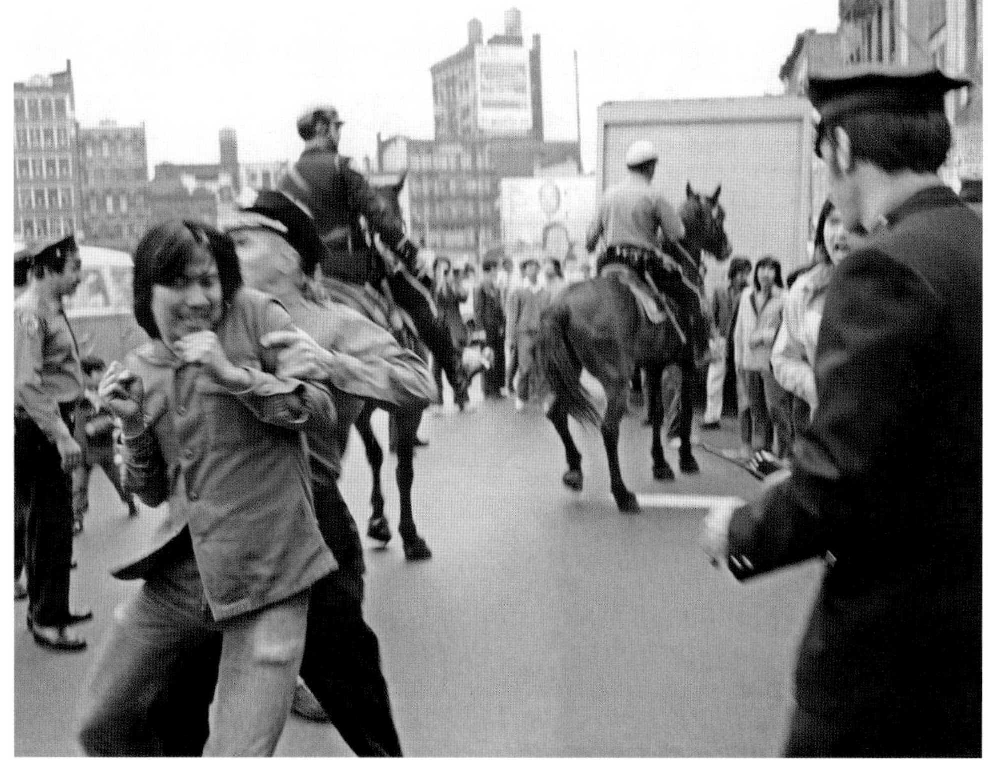

Police, some mounted on horseback, disperse activists demanding justice for Peter Yew. New York, 1975.

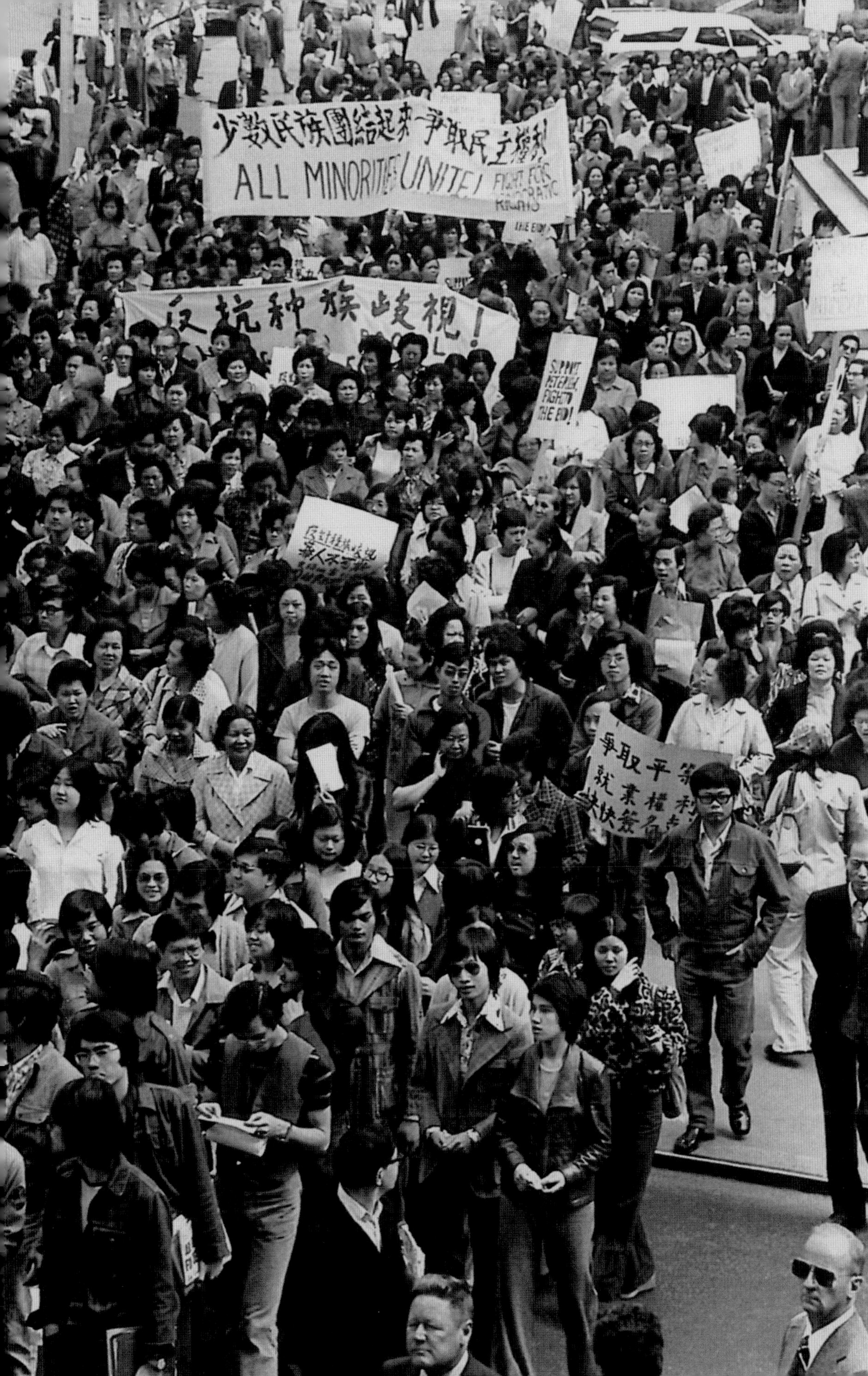

Thousands marched from Chinatown to city hall to protest police brutality. New York, 1975.

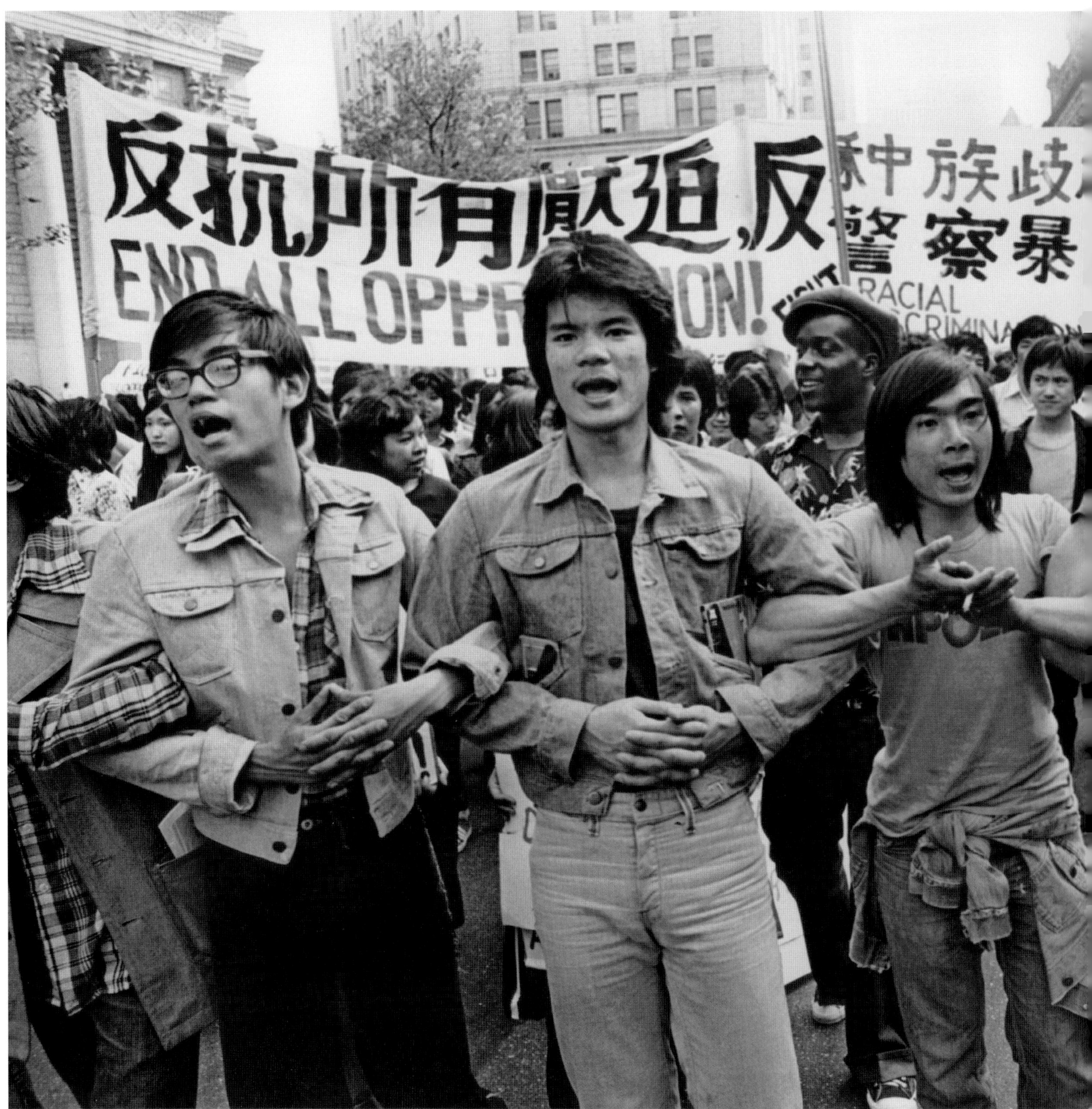

反抗所有壓迫,反
END ALL OPPR
ION!
族歧
警察暴
RACIAL

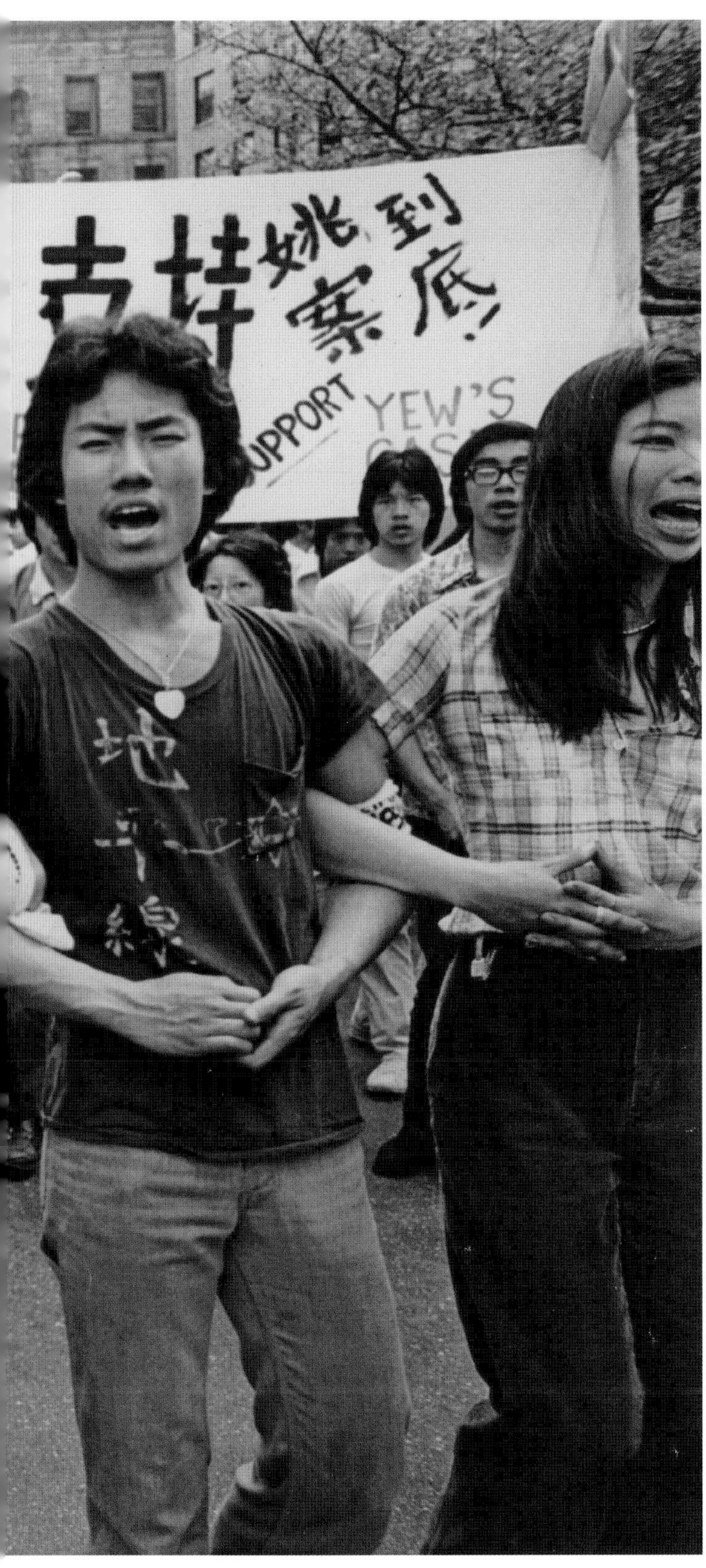

Students from Brooklyn Technical High School skipped school and marched with arms locked to demand justice for Peter Yew. *From left:* Warren Chin, Kam Wong, Michael Chan, Charles Wong, and Susan Yung. New York, 1975.

The Two Bridges Neighborhood Council campaigned against New York Telephone's plan to raze blocks of housing. In its storefront window, the poster "Public Enemy No. 1" featured the phone company's logo. New York, 1971.

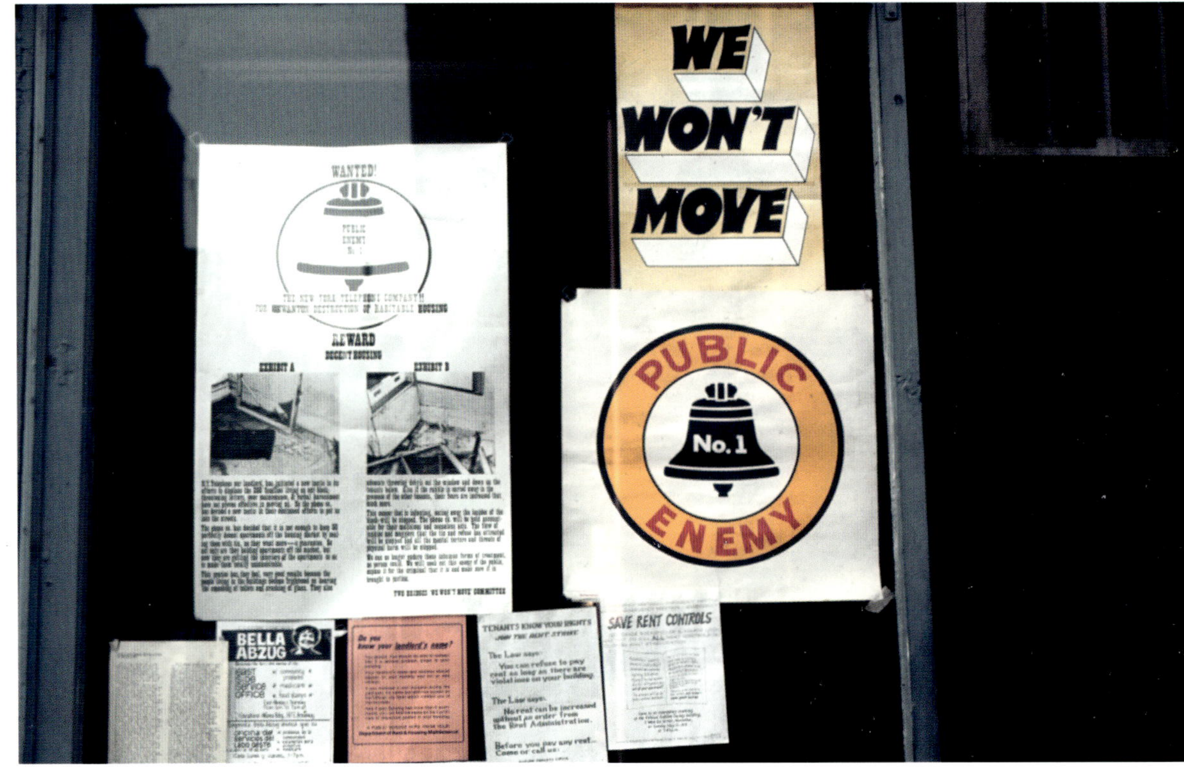

Representative Bella Abzug, whose district included Lower Manhattan, supported the campaign against New York Telephone in 1970 and contributed funds to the 1971 Chinatown Health Fair. Here she speaks at a community meeting in Chinatown. New York, 1971.

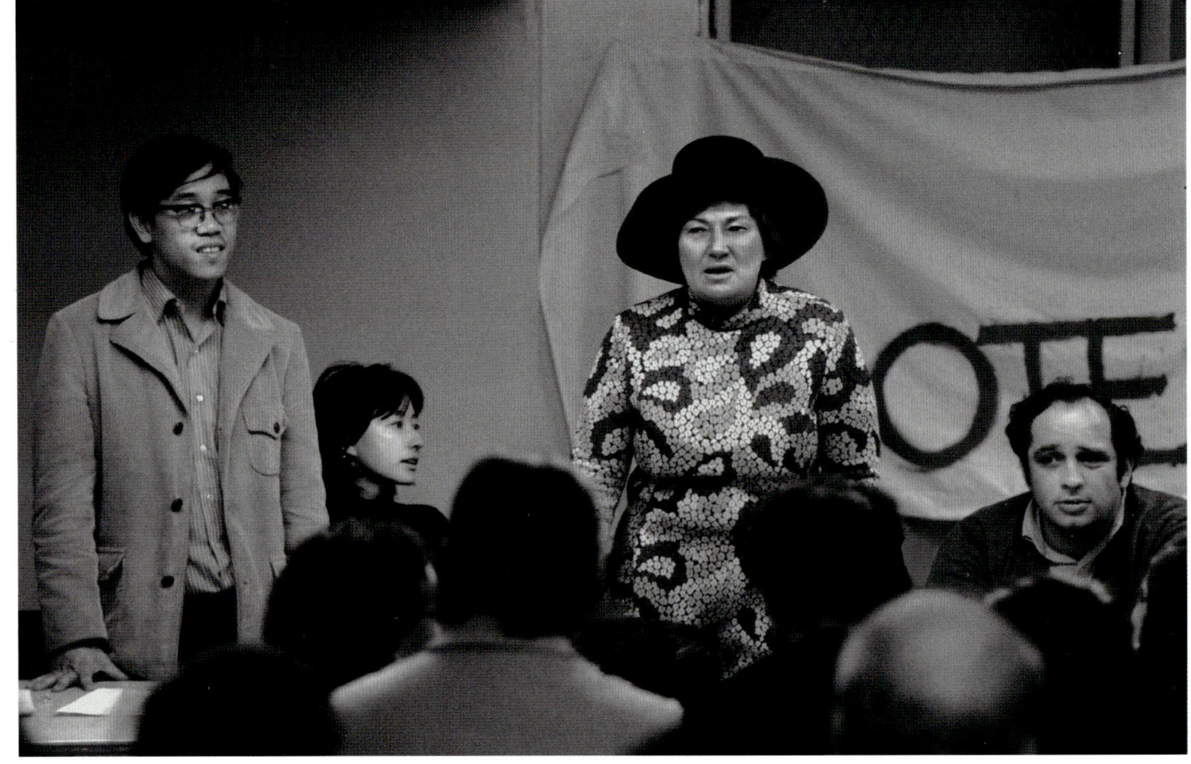

Chinatown and Lower East Side residents demonstrate against the Department of Housing and Urban Development's urban renewal plan. Activist Thomas Tam holds a sign that reads, "Housing for the Poor Now." New York, 1974.

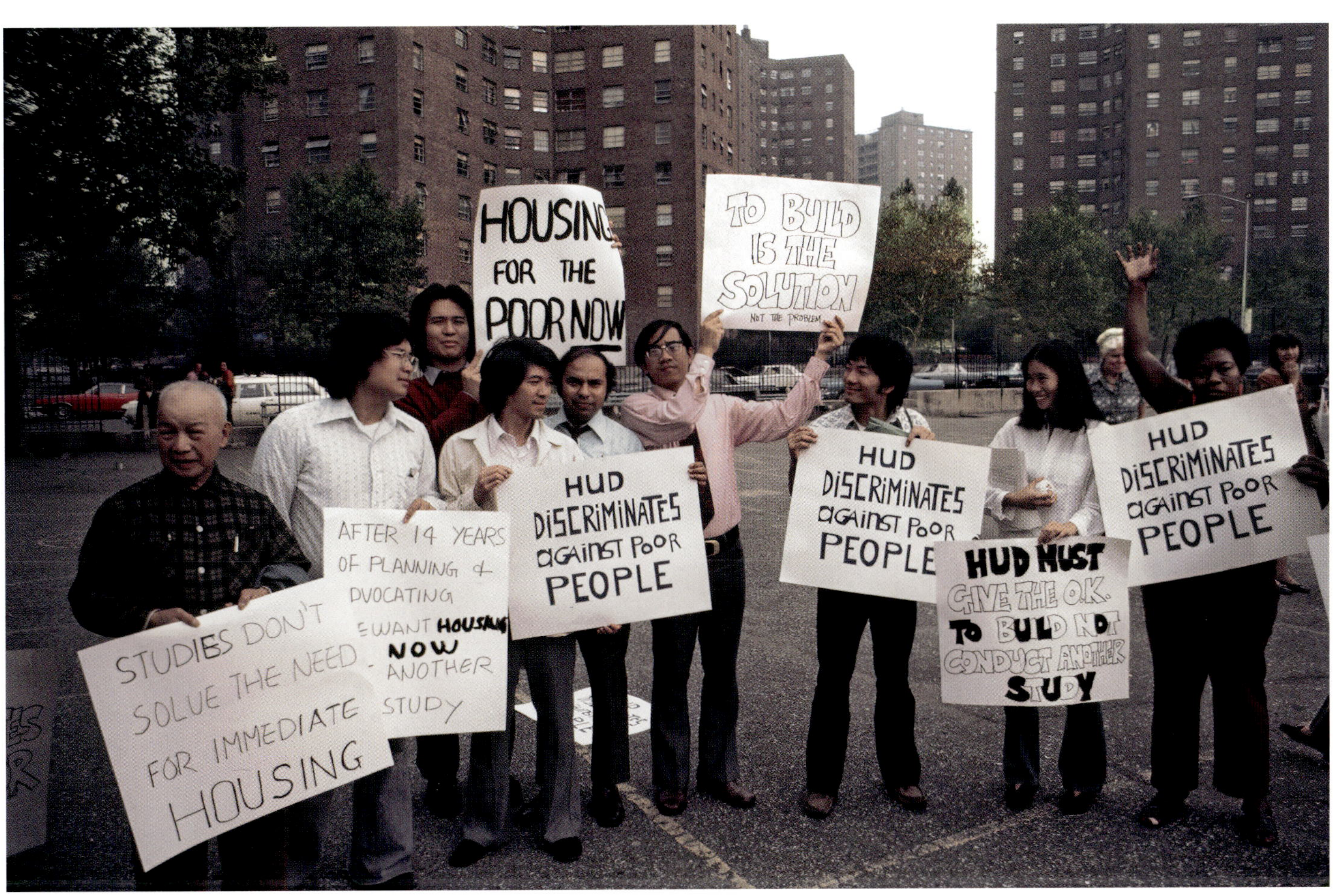

Even after three fires in the building at 28 Market Street, the owner, one of Chinatown's largest landlords, refused to make repairs. Tenants met with IWK organizer Lorraine Leong *(in the foreground)*. New York, 1972.

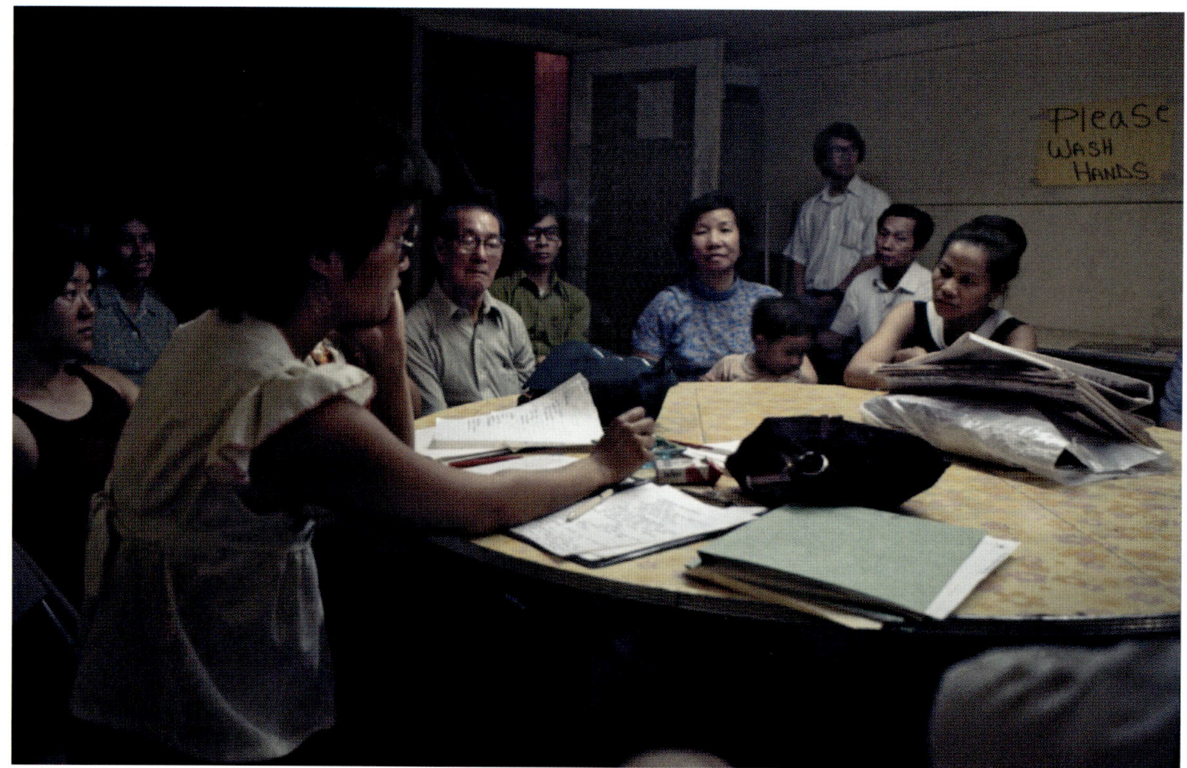

Tenants and supporters protested in front of the landlord's Chinatown office. Among the protesters was Tsui Hark *(facing the camera with raised fist)*, the future Hong Kong film director. New York, 1972.

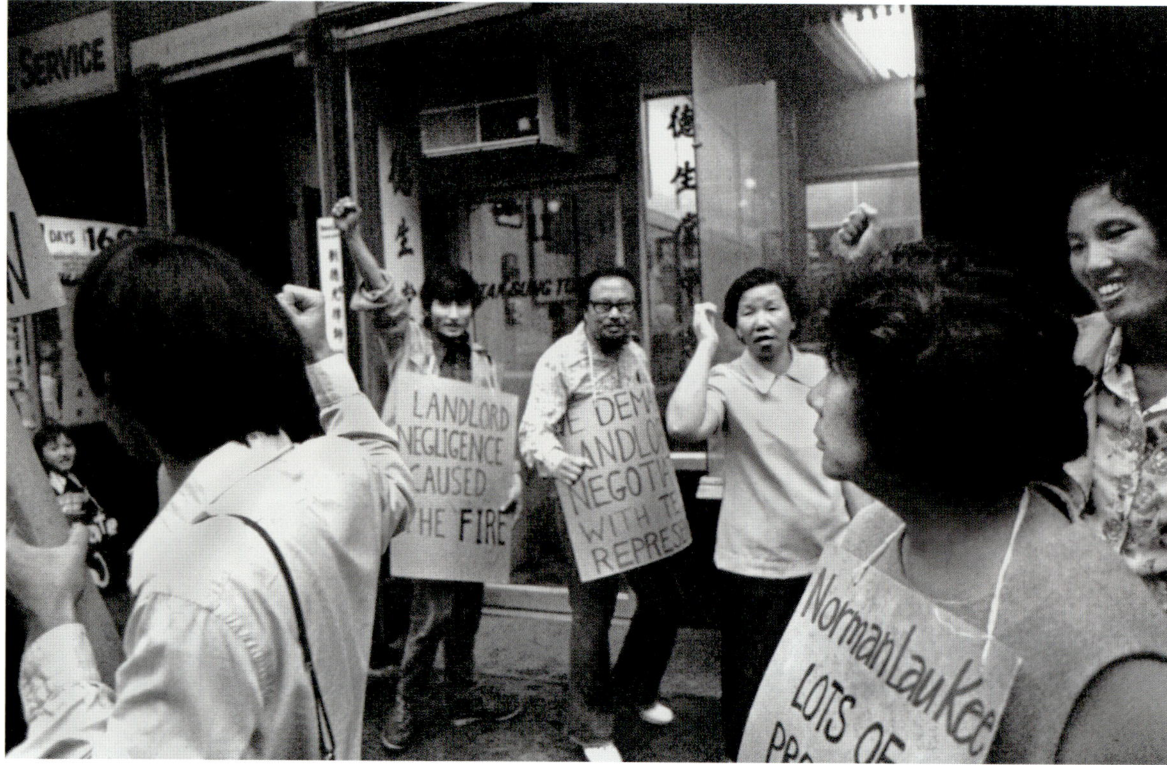

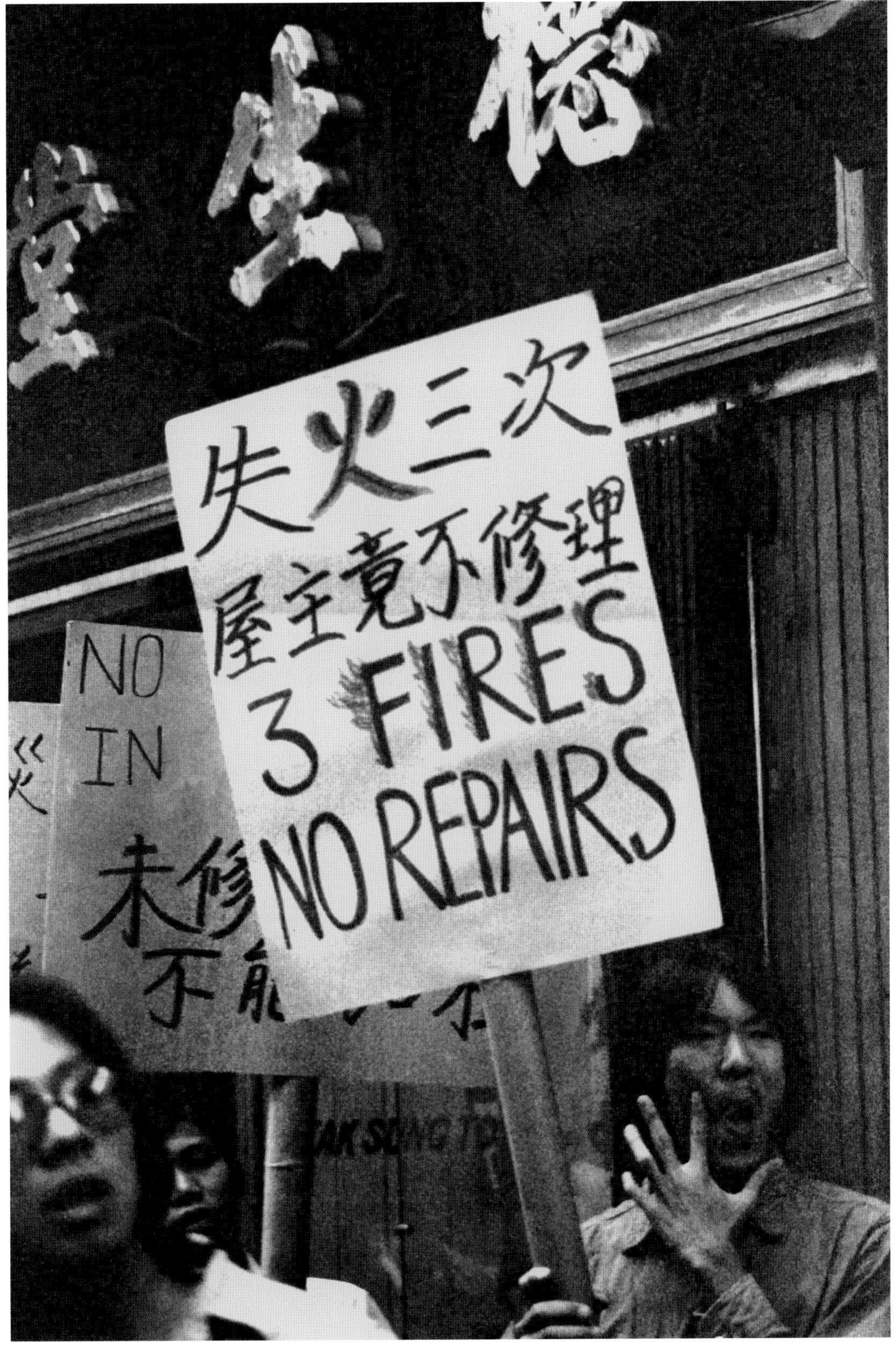

Protesting the Chinatown landlord who refused to make repairs. New York, 1972.

In 1974, developers planned to build Confucius Plaza, a $40 million housing development for middle-income families, in the middle of Chinatown. Asian Americans for Equal Employment led a campaign to demand jobs for Chinese workers on the project. At the construction site, AAFEE picketed and staged mass demonstrations and sit-ins. It succeeded in winning twelve positions for Asian American journeymen and twenty-seven trainees. Rebranded as Asian Americans for Equality, AAFE would go on to organize further for jobs and low-income housing and also become a housing developer itself.

Below: The construction site at Bowery looking south from Doyers Street. New York, 1974.

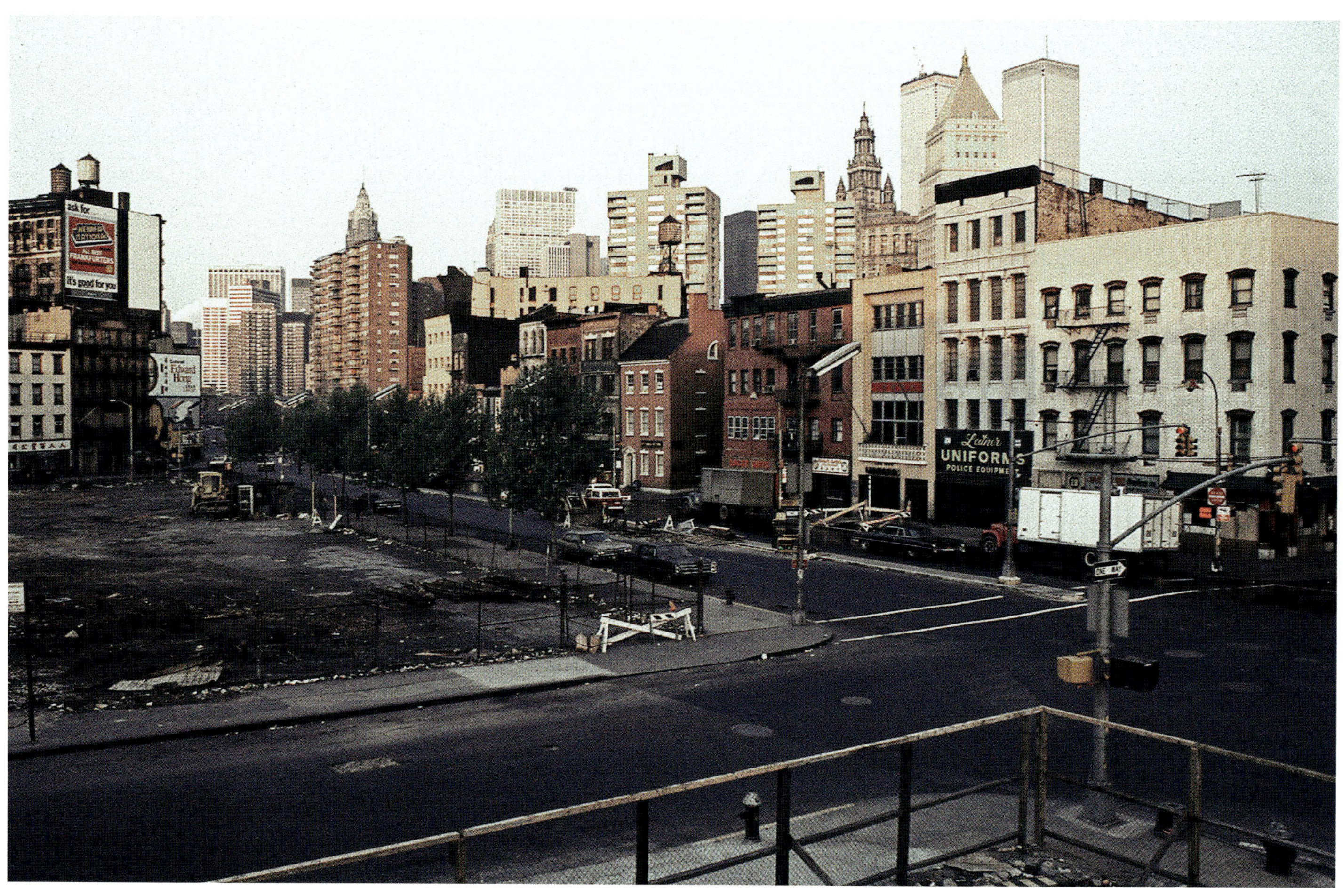

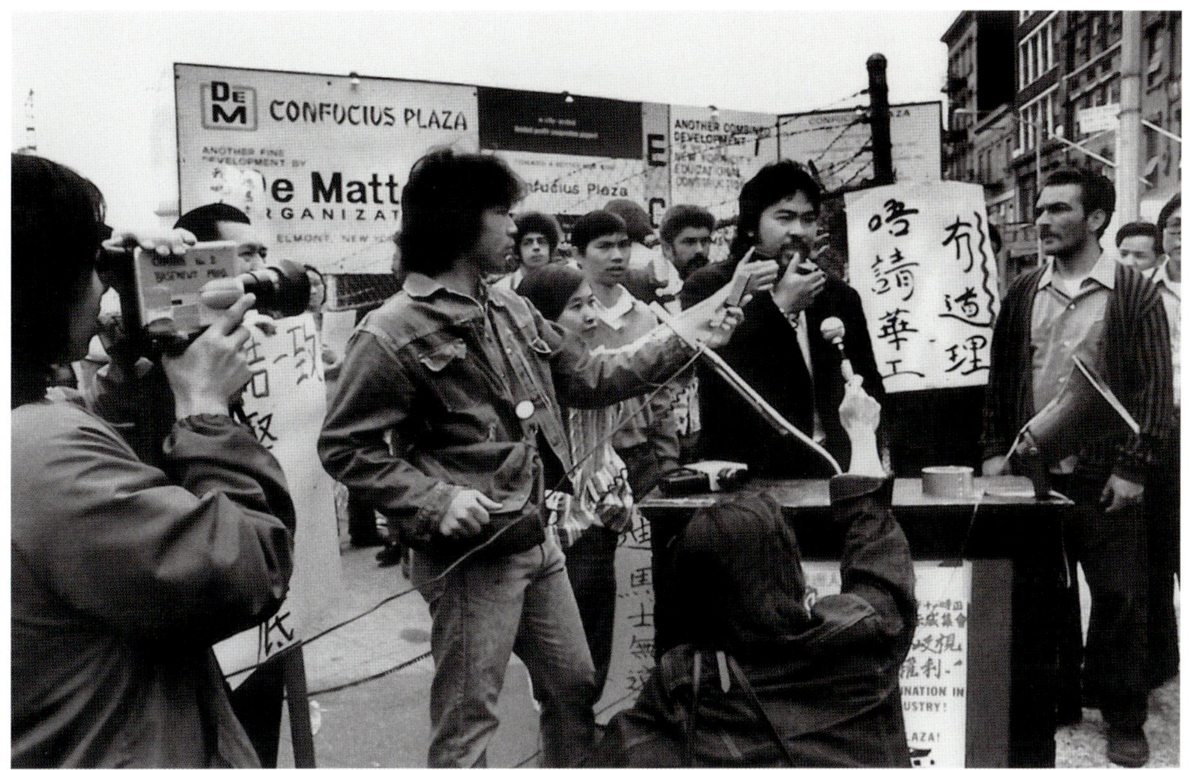

AAFEE leader Takashi Yanagida (1948–2021) addresses a protest rally at the construction site. The sign in Chinese reads, “No logical reason to not hire Chinese workers.” The rally was documented in Super 8mm film by a cameraman from the Basement Workshop. New York, 1974.

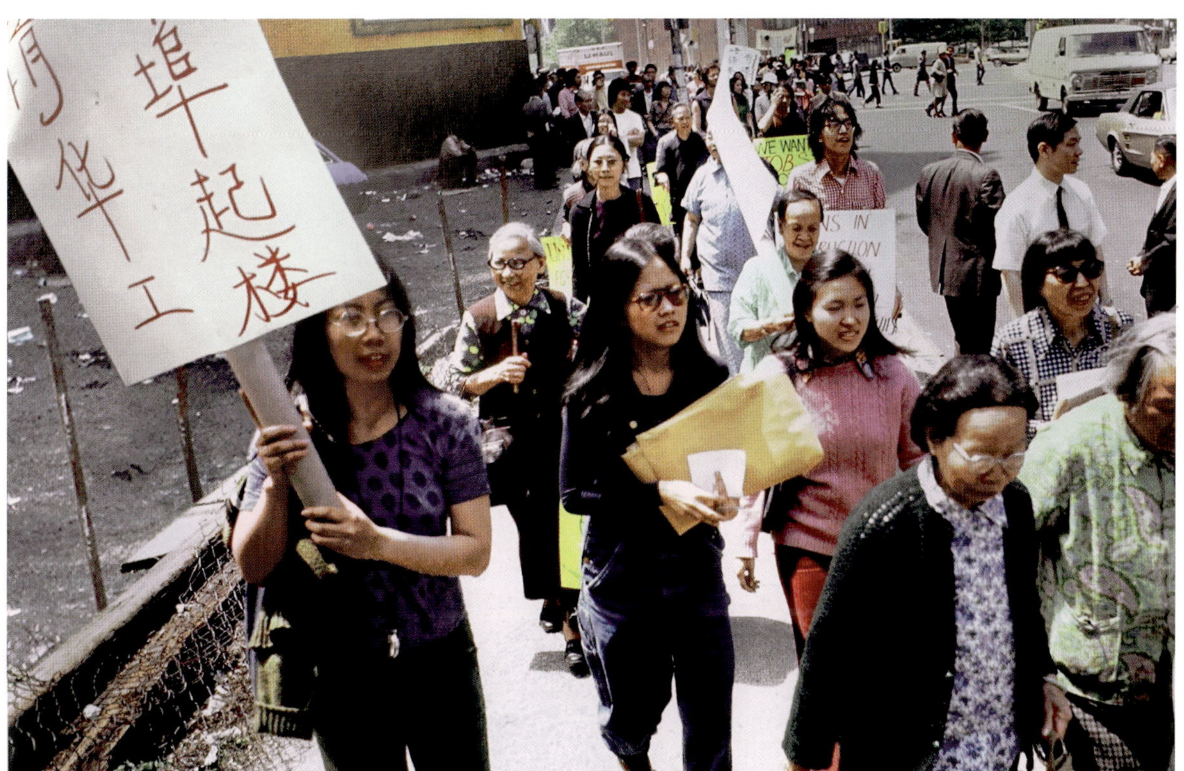

Fay Chiang (1952–2017), director of the Basement Workshop (*far left*), at a demonstration at Confucius Plaza. Her sign in Chinese translates as “Chinatown construct the building, hire Chinese workers.” New York, 1974.

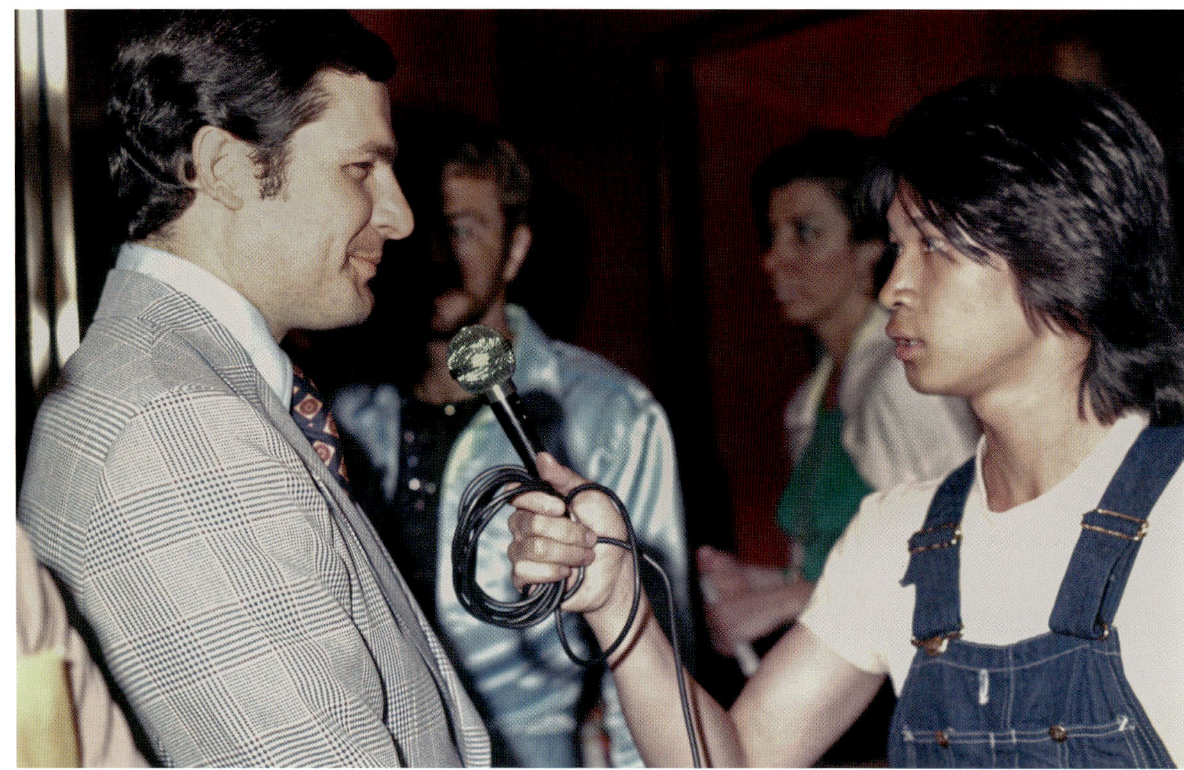

Ride the Winds, an ersatz samurai tale written and directed by John Driver, was produced on Broadway. On opening night, actor Tzi Ma interviewed Driver outside the theater. The production was panned by both critics and the Oriental Actors Association and closed after only three performances. New York, 1974.

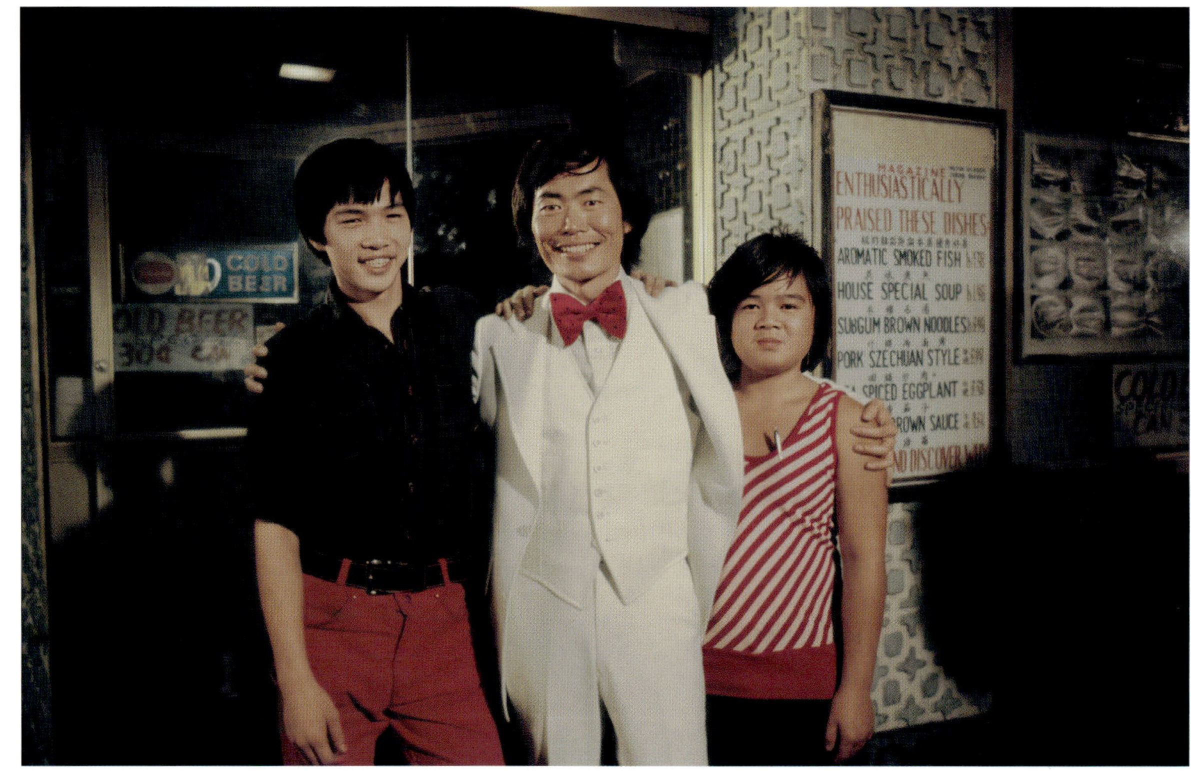

In 1975 actor George Takei starred in *Year of the Dragon*, a PBS television adaptation of Frank Chin's play about intergenerational conflicts and the meaning of identity. Takei played a Chinese American restaurant owner and family patriarch, shown here on set with the actors portraying his children. Takei considered the role to be the "most satisfying and fulfilling" he had had as an actor. New York, 1975.

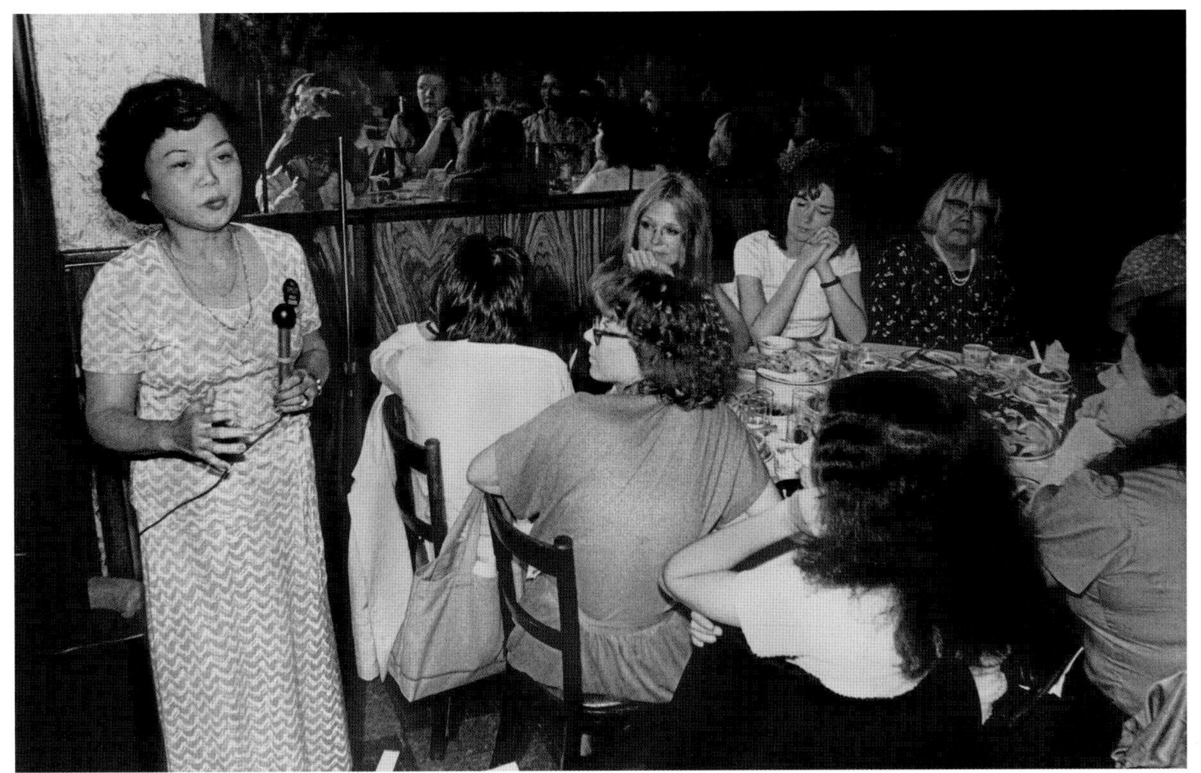

Representative Patsy Mink of Hawaii was the first woman of color in Congress and coauthor of Title IX, the 1972 law that prohibits sex discrimination in schools receiving federal assistance. Here she speaks to a group of feminists, including *Ms.* magazine publisher Gloria Steinem. New York, late 1970s.

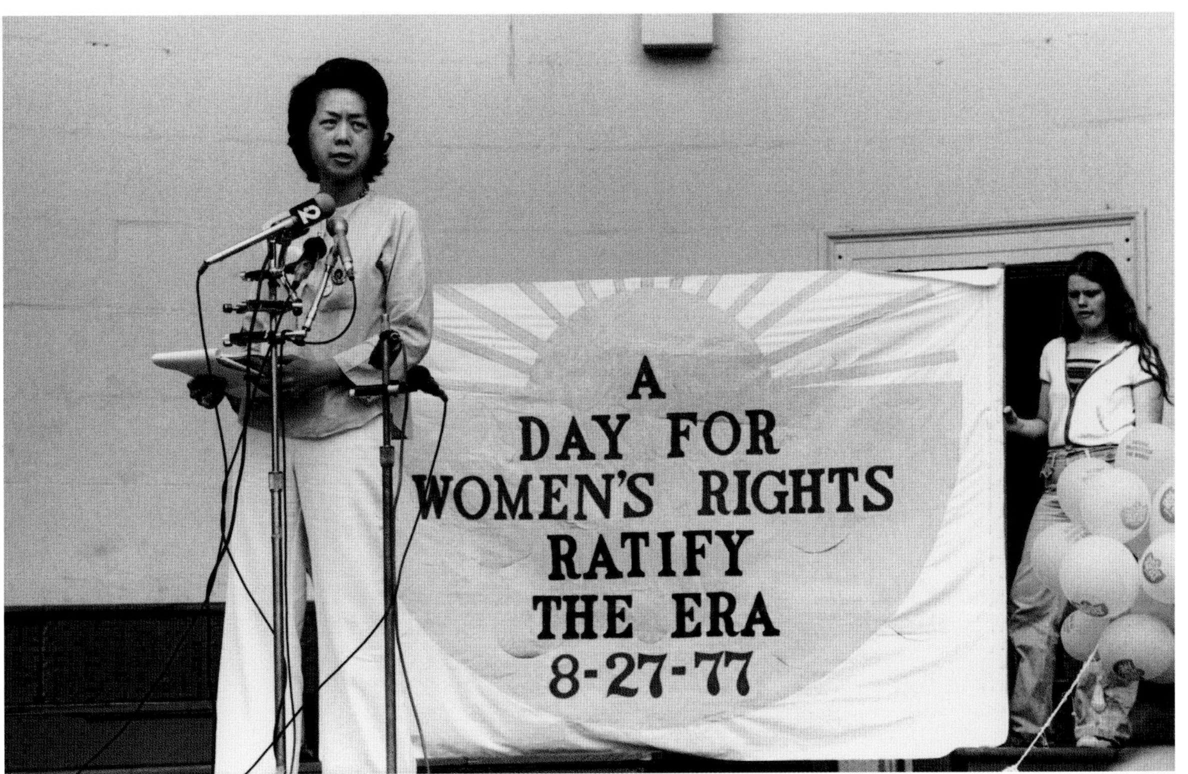

Goldie Chu, director of the Two Bridges Neighborhood Council, was an avowed feminist. Here she speaks at a rally supporting the Equal Rights Amendment. New York, 1977.

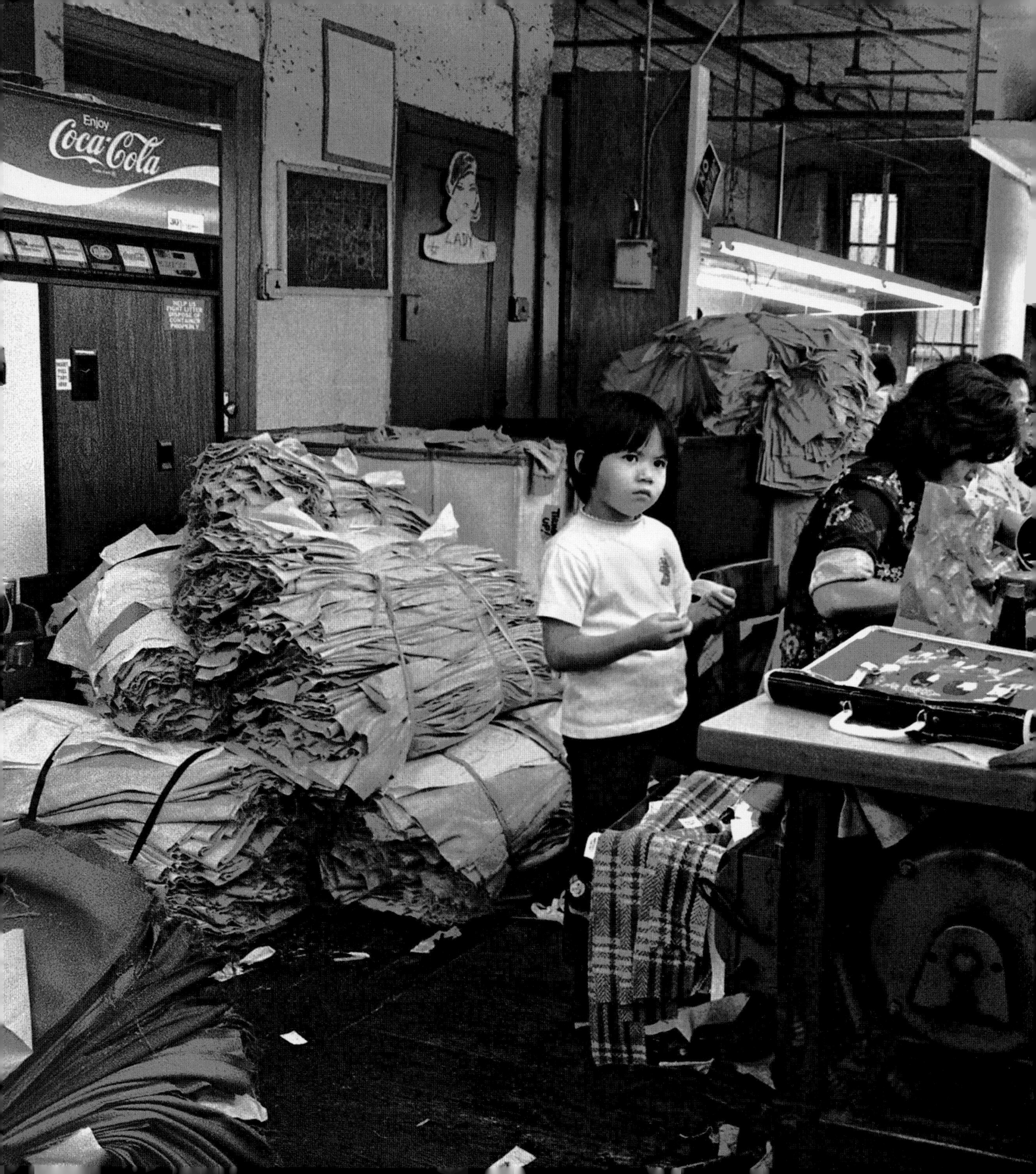
Enjoy
Coca-Cola
LADY

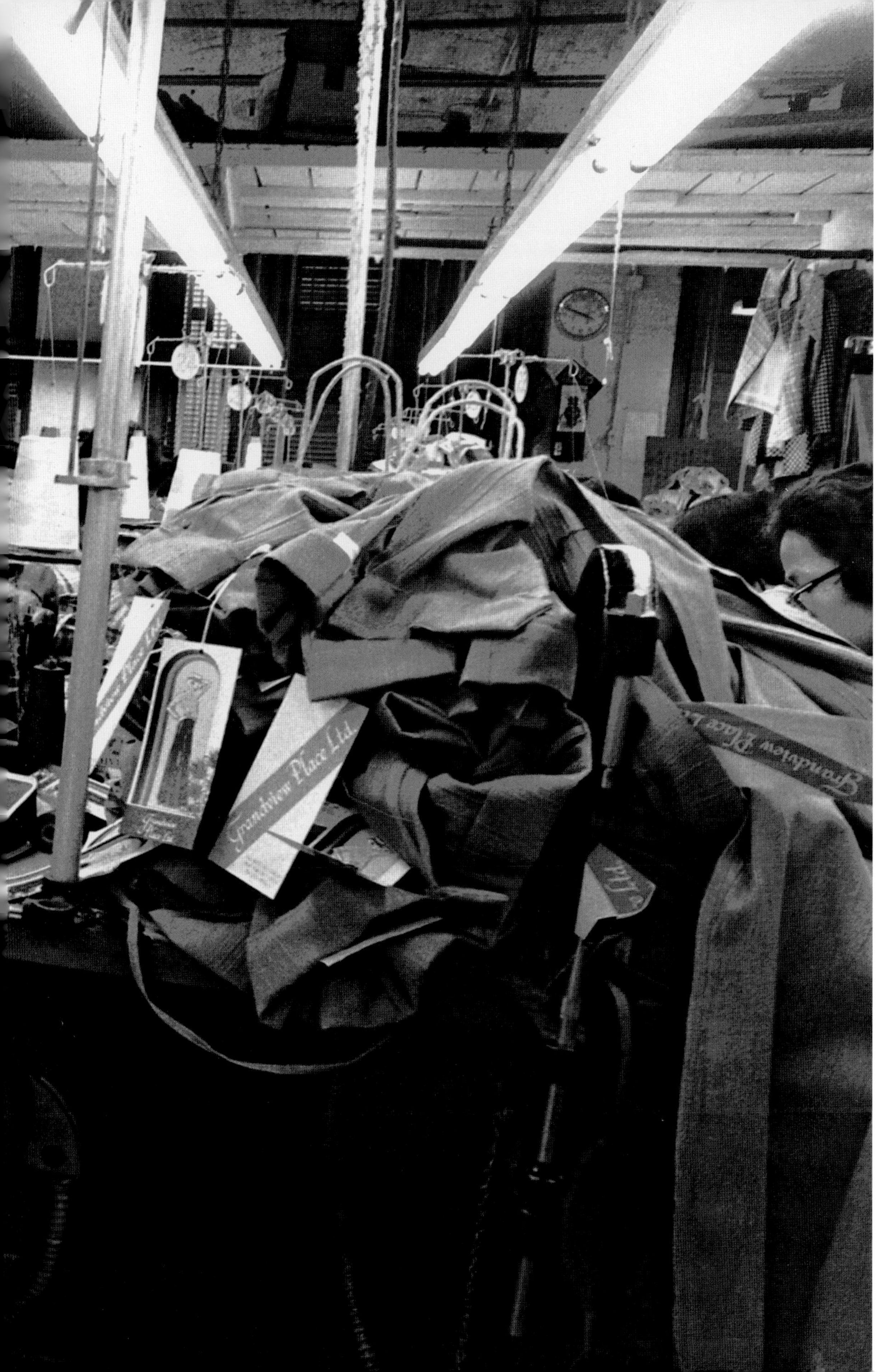

Many women brought their children with them to work in the factories until 1983, when the International Ladies Garment Workers Union opened a childcare center in Chinatown. New York, 1976.

In the 1970s, Chinatown became the new center of New York's garment industry, employing thousands of Chinese immigrant women, some in large factories run by whites and others in smaller shops run by Chinese subcontractors. New York, early 1970s.

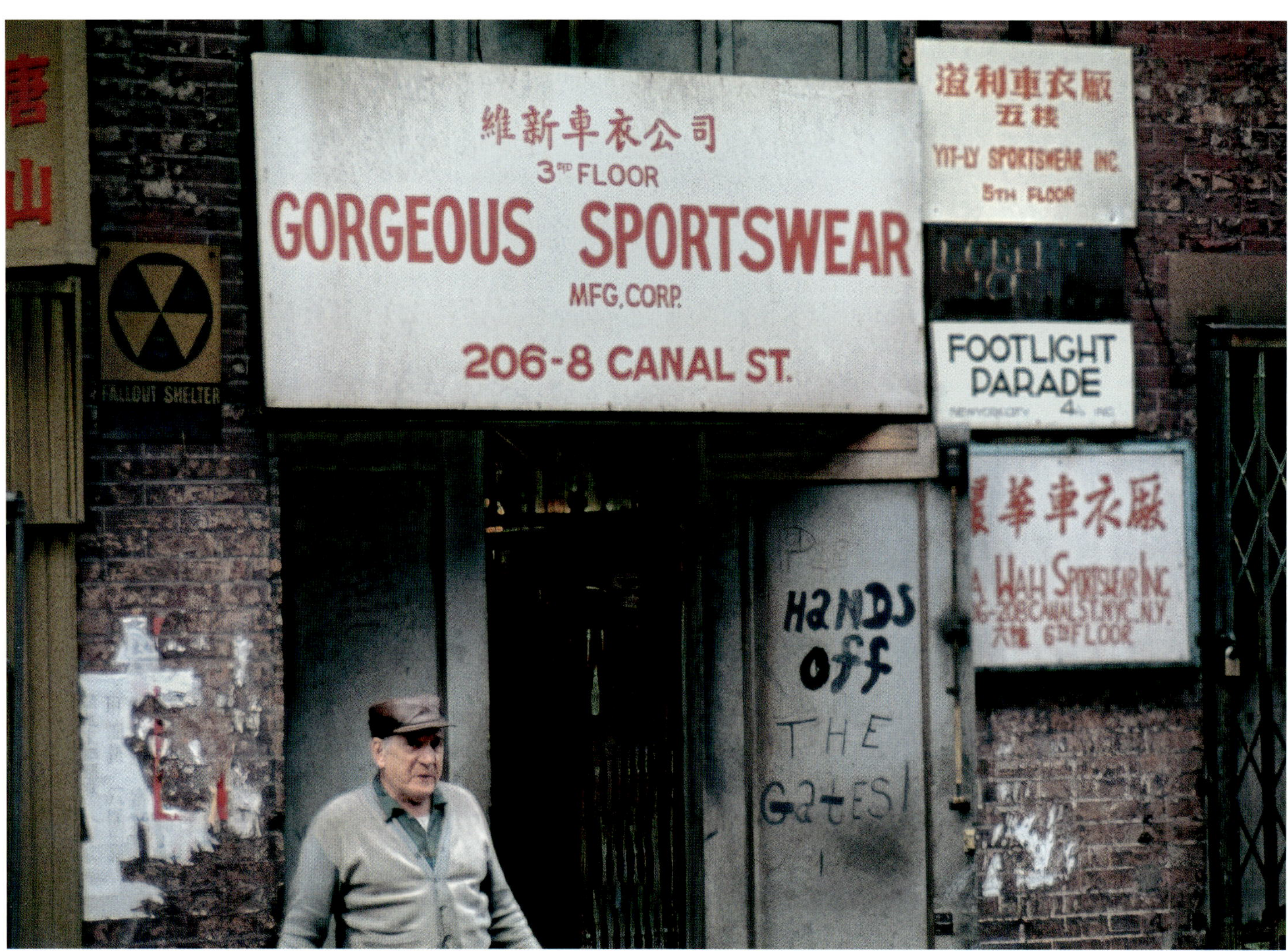

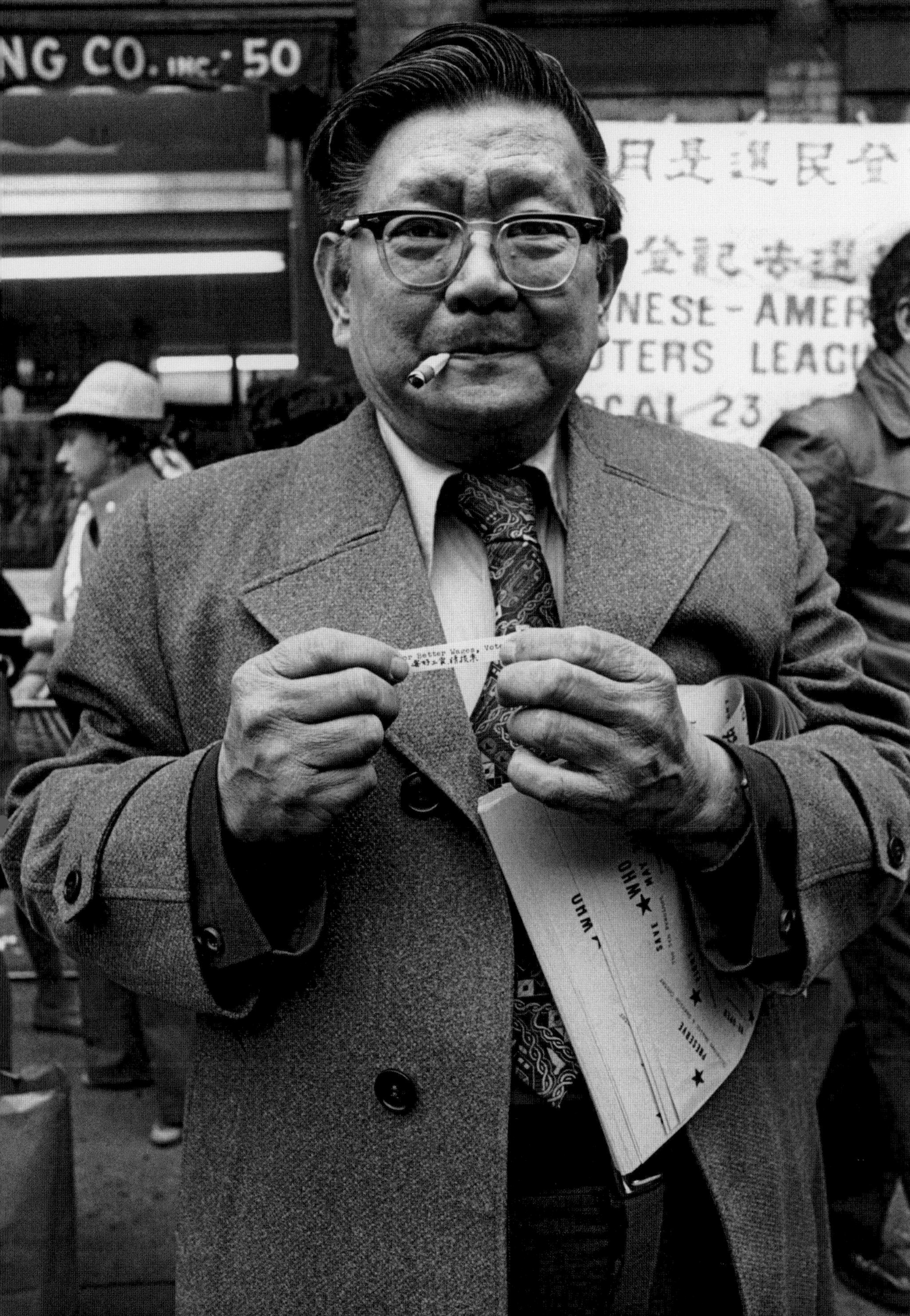

Ben Fee, veteran organizer of the ILGWU's Local 23-25, promotes voter registration in Chinatown with a bilingual fortune cookie slogan: "For better wages, vote." New York, 1976.

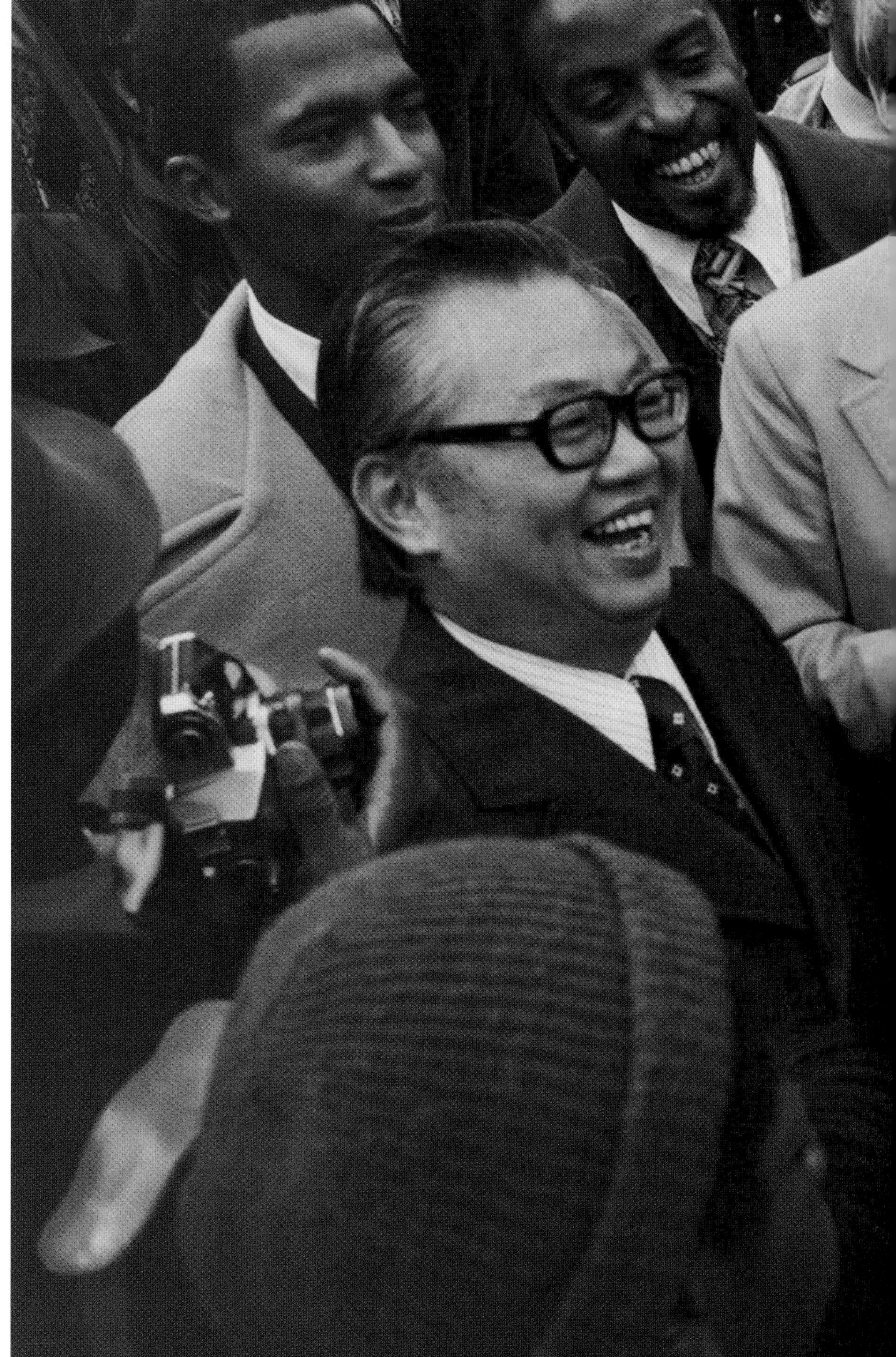

Muhammad Ali, the world champion boxer who refused to fight in Vietnam, stands with Man Bun Lee, president of the Chinese Consolidated Benevolent Association, during a visit to Chinatown. New York, December 1974.

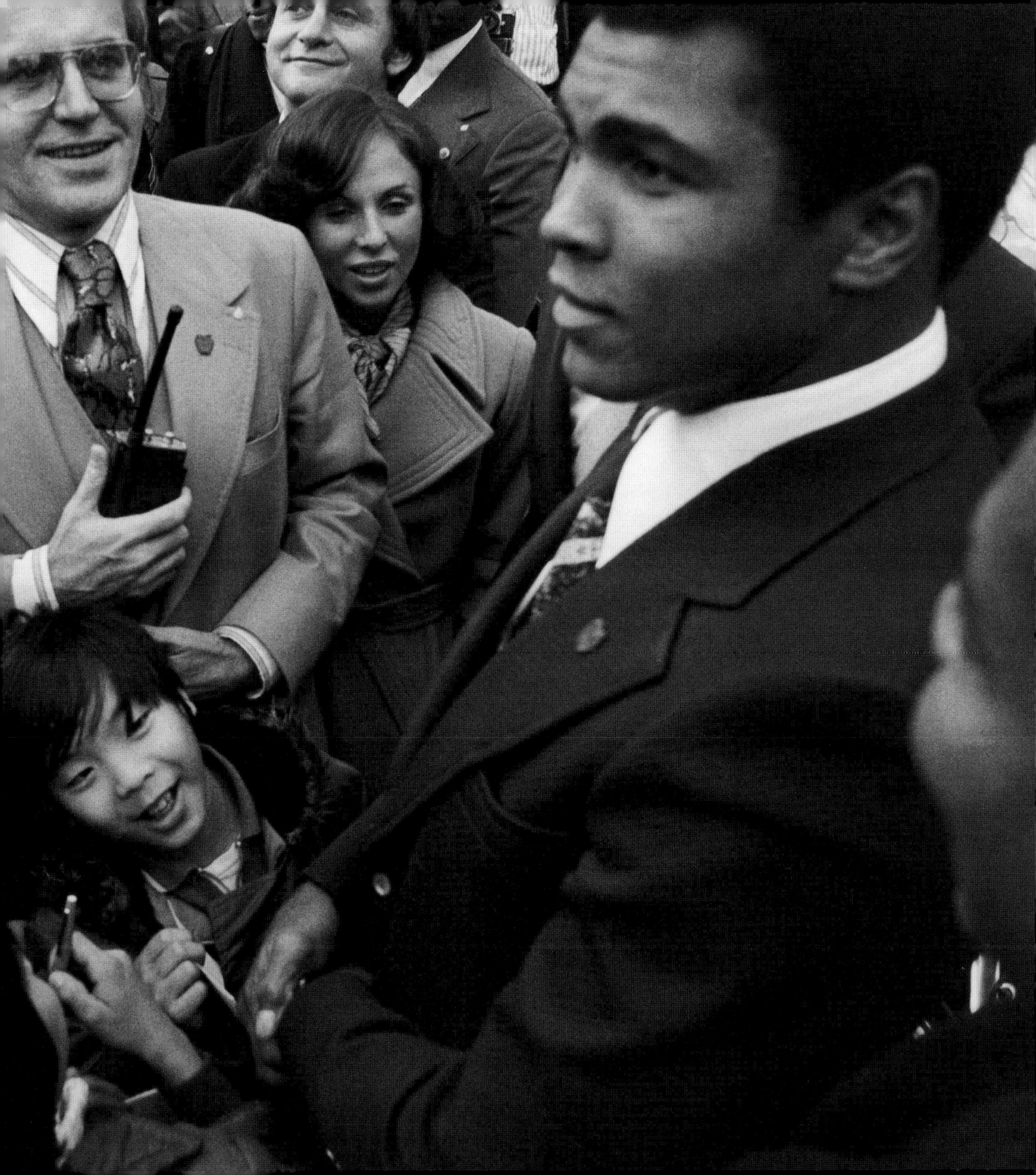

EMPOWERMENT

1980s—

—1990s

Corky Lee, self-portrait. New York, 1990s.

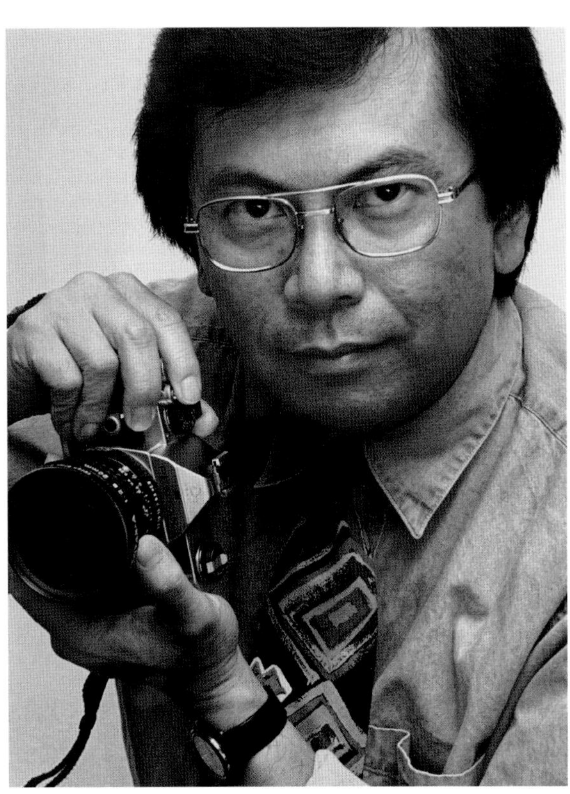

By the 1980s and 1990s, Corky Lee was covering Asian American events and issues that were more ethnically diverse and more geographically distant from Chinatown. The makeup of the Asian American–Pacific Islander population underwent a sea change. The Immigration and Nationality Act of 1965 opened the way for immigrants from South Korea, India, Hong Kong, and other parts of Asia. After the Vietnam War, the United States admitted refugees from Vietnam, Cambodia, and Laos. In a veritable demographic explosion, the number of Asian Americans and Pacific Islanders grew from 1.5 million in 1970 to nearly 12 million in 2020. New communities established, with new entrées into the labor market, new businesses, and new art.

Asian Americans became more visible in U.S. society, which brought both recognition and resentment from mainstream white America. Corky captured the trend toward empowerment in photographs of college students demanding ethnic studies, voter registration campaigns, protests against racist violence, and garment and restaurant workers standing up for their rights.

His photos also show the vibrancy of ethnic cultures on display during these years—buchaechum (Korean fan dance), taiko (Japanese drumming), bhangra (Punjabi harvest dance), pananadem (Meranao, southern Philippines, remembrance dance). These performances took place at parades and festivals, usually in May, which Congress declared in 1992 to be "Asian/Pacific American Heritage Month" (an upgrade from its "week" in 1979), meant for commemoration, reflection, and education. In 1979 Corky was one of the organizers of the first Asian American Heritage Festival in New York City, and he faithfully continued to document these cultural events over the years and decades, respecting them as moments of self-expression and recognition that AAPI communities were part of the mosaic of American culture.

Asian American and Pacific Islander, a term first officially used in the U.S. Census in 1980 (and modified to Asian American and Native Hawaiian/Pacific Islander in 2021), organizes various ethnic and nationality groups into a single category. It is the successor to Asian American, which student activists coined in the 1960s as a replacement for Oriental, much as how African American and Latino/a also became preferred terms during the era of civil rights and self-determination. Initially, Asian American referred to those of East Asian descent, but with new immigrations after 1970 it grew to include Southeast Asians and South Asians.

Asian American and AAPI do not eliminate ethnic or nationality distinctions or specific concerns. They are terms of art or, more precisely, of politics, that express solidarity and seek visibility and influence by coalition building and increasing numbers. The U.S. Census now identifies twenty-seven subgroups of Asian Americans and Pacific Islanders: Chinese, Korean, Bangladeshi, Thai, Cambodian, Samoan, Indonesian, Fijian, and others.

The proliferation of categories resulted from demands by Asian Americans and Pacific Islanders themselves to be included in the census. AAPI activists did not want to be counted just for its own sake; they understood that recognition is necessary in order to justify and enact antiracist policies. In this respect, Corky's photographs, showing real-life people and conditions, were a form of historical evidence that rebuked government neglect of AAPI communities.

As the Asian American population grew both in numbers and in visibility, Asian Americans participated in more political activity. They registered to vote and became sought-after constituencies for political-office seekers. Noting that Chinese Americans during the exclusion era had been "reluctant to exercise their democratic rights," Corky believed the turn to voting was one of the most "profound changes" of the post-1965 years. As early as the mid-1970s, New York Chinatown activists engaged in voter registration drives by distributing fortune cookies with a bilingual message: "For better wages, vote." During the 1980s, activists formed Asian Americans for Jesse Jackson and Asian Americans for David Dinkins (the first Black mayor of New York), signaling their identification with these candidates' invocations of the "Rainbow Coalition" and the "gorgeous mosaic" that was multiracial America. By the 1990s, all candidates running for local or national office, regardless of party affiliation, made a stop in Chinatown. And Asian Americans themselves began running for office—Gary Locke in Washington State, Judy Chu in Los Angeles, Margaret Chin in New York, and others.

Corky came out from behind the camera to advocate for voting rights. For years Asian Americans had asked New York City's board of elections to print bilingual English-Chinese ballots, but the board had rebuffed them on grounds that there was no room on the ballot. In the early 1990s the Asian American Legal Defense Fund sued the board, and Corky worked with them to show that it could be done: at Expedi he produced a sample bilingual ballot, meeting the board's requirement for a die-cut space with a little square where the lever would mark the voter's selection. By the 2000s, voter turnout in districts where Asian American candidates were winning election to local office was about 50 percent higher than the city's average.

The resurgence of 1970s activist energy was also evident in Chinese immigrants' labor struggles. Low wages and substandard conditions were long-standing issues, but now activists went into the factories and the unions to organize. In 1982, when the Chinatown sewing factory owners refused to sign a renewal of their union contract, some twenty thousand workers, members of Local 23-25 of the ILGWU, went on strike and won. In other battles, the Chinese Staff and Workers Association picketed and sued two of Chinatown's biggest dim sum restaurants and banquet halls—Silver Palace in 1980 and Jing Fong in 1995—for stealing workers' tips.

Similarly, third-generation Japanese Americans—college students in the 1960s and

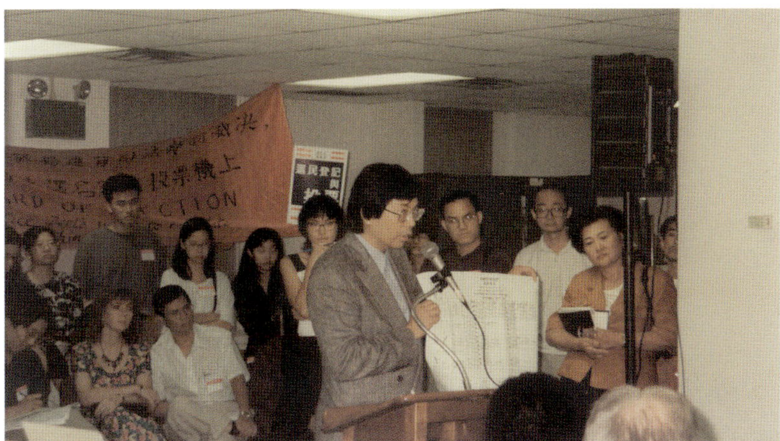

Corky Lee testifies at the New York City Board of Elections, showing a prototype of a bilingual ballot. New York, 1994. *Margaret Fung/AALDEF*

1970s—brought the issue of the government's internment of Japanese Americans during World War II out of the shadows of silence and shame. They began to make pilgrimages to the former campsites in 1969, and during the 1970s they made growing calls for redress. These efforts culminated in the 1980s with a nationwide campaign that rallied the community, young and old, to demand redress and reparations. The U.S. Congress passed the Civil Liberties Act of 1988, issuing a national apology and providing individual reparations of $20,000 to surviving detainees.

As an artist-photographer, Corky Lee was a founding member of the Asian American Arts Alliance (A4) and an advocate for photojournalists to join the Asian American Journalists Association. He photographed the rise of Asian American theatrical performers and productions, as well as protests against obstacles to inclusion. *The New York Times* printed Corky's photographs of protests against the Broadway musical *Miss Saigon*, which perpetuated racist stereotypes in its storyline and in casting a white actor in yellow face.

But even as Asian Americans increased their visibility and participation in politics and culture, they also experienced a rise in racial discrimination. The pharmaceutical, telecommunications, and health care industries hired large numbers of immigrants with professional and technical training from Taiwan, Hong Kong, the Philippines, and South Korea, but those workers faced discrimination in promotions, hitting the "bamboo ceiling."

After it was revealed that a few Chinese Americans in New York had improperly bundled campaign contributions to Bill Clinton's presidential campaign, the Democratic Party removed all donors with Chinese surnames from its lists and stopped seeking contributions from them, as if to blame all Chinese for the transgressions of a handful of people. Being of Chinese ethnicity could also bring scrutiny and persecution on grounds of national security. In 1999 Wen-ho Lee, a physicist at Los Alamos National Laboratory and a naturalized citizen, was falsely accused of passing secrets to China. He spent 278 days in solitary confinement without the possibility of bail before the government's case crumbled and he was freed.

Moreover, as their communities spread into new areas, Asian Americans increasingly became targets of racist violence. As early as 1975, on the streets of Jersey City, New Jersey, white supremacist youth gangs calling themselves "Dotbusters" assaulted immigrants from India, a menace that continued through the early 1990s. In 1982, during a trade war against imported Japanese products, two unemployed white autoworkers in Detroit beat a young Chinese American, Vincent Chin, to death, blaming him for "taking" their jobs. The perpetrators, arrested for second-degree murder, admitted to manslaughter in a plea bargain; the judge sentenced them to three years of probation (no jail time) and a fine of $3,000. A federal appeals court later overturned their conviction for violating Chin's civil rights. So much of what was wrong with that case was emblematic of Asian Americans' racial predicaments: the mistaking of a Chinese American for a Japanese person; the judge's obvious racial bias; the blaming of Japan for American auto companies' failure to meet consumer demand for high-gas-mileage cars; and the near impossibility of achieving justice through the courts. Corky understood the gravity of the Vincent Chin case and traveled to Detroit to document the grief and anger of Chin's family and the community.

Vincent Chin's killing catalyzed Asian American awareness and activism across the country. The 1987 film *Who Killed Vincent Chin?* by Renee Tajima-Peña and Christine Choy answered the question by illuminating the long history of racism and violence perpetrated against Asian Americans. The film became an instant classic—it has been taught in Asian American studies classes and shown to community audiences for thirty-five years and counting.

Corky Lee's photographs from the 1980s and 1990s document the ways in which Asian Americans pushed forward their efforts for equal rights and social justice—and pushed back against those who resisted. They teach us that while demography changes the conditions of what's possible, it is not destiny. Rather, it is a call to action.

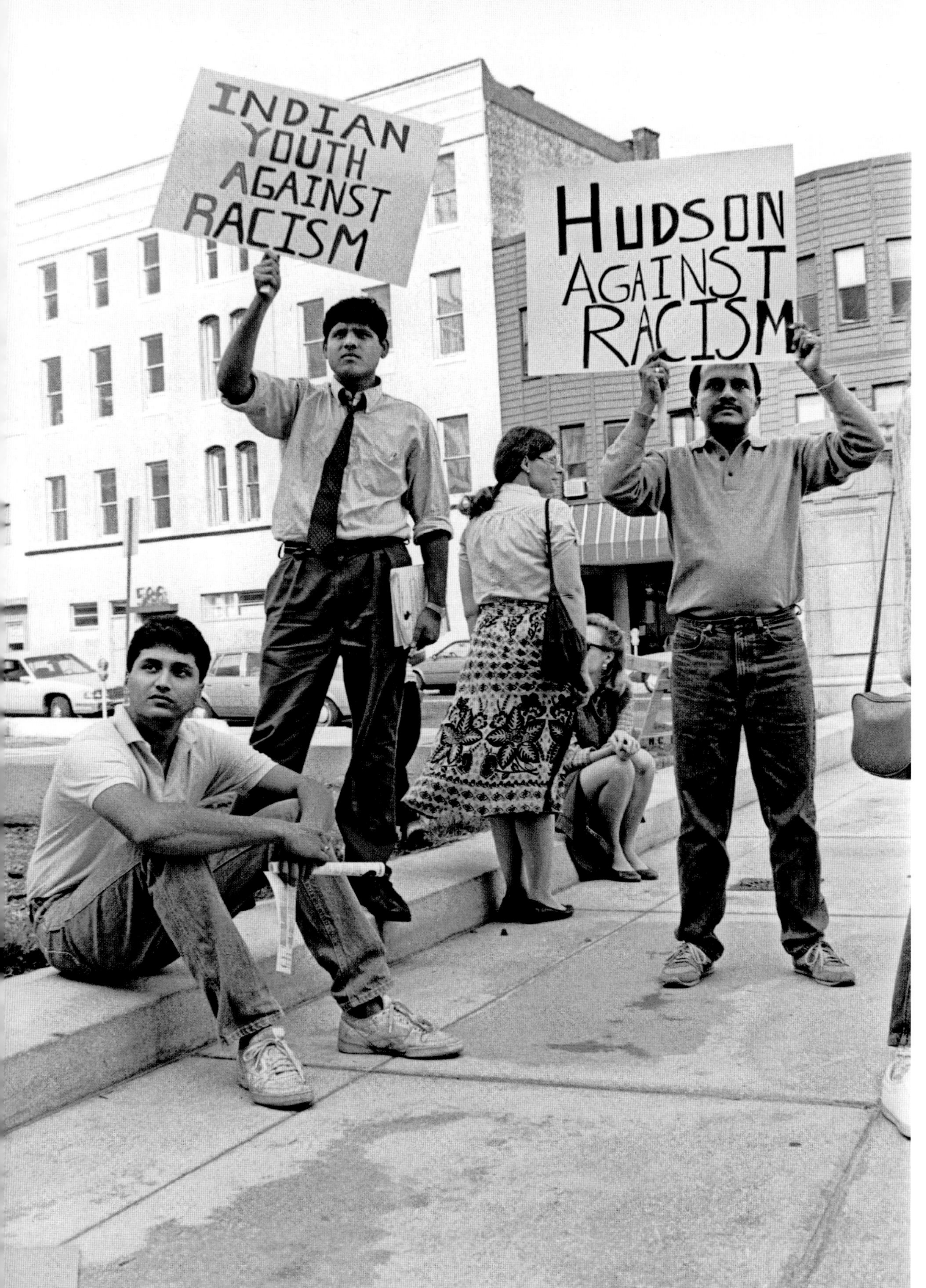

South Asians in New Jersey protest racial violence and killings by "Dotbusters." In September 1987, Navroze Mody, age thirty, died after members of the anti-Indian hate group beat him into a coma. He was one of several Indians attacked in Jersey City and Hoboken in the late 1980s and early 1990s. Jersey City, New Jersey, 1988.

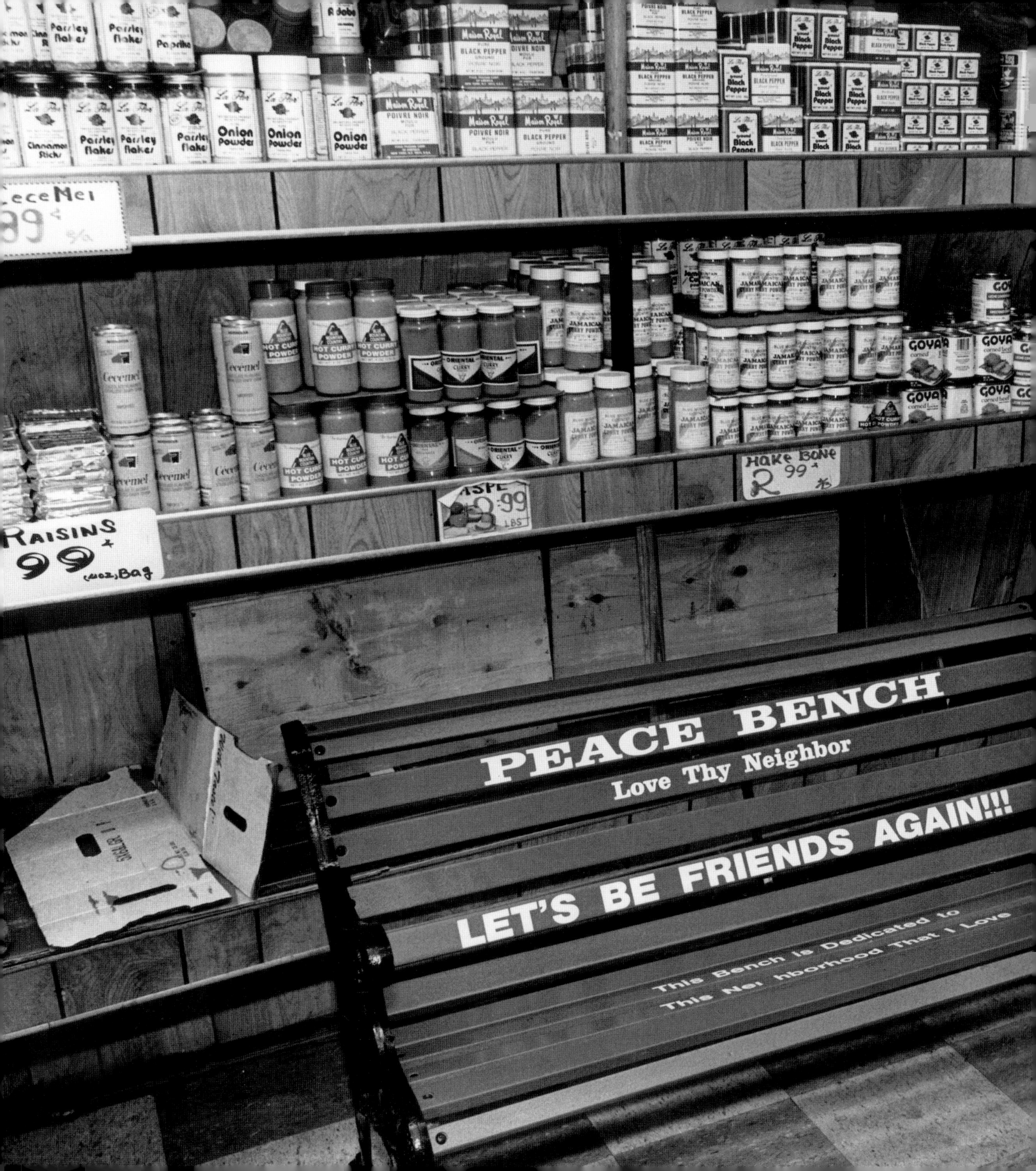

PEACE BENCH
Love Thy Neighbor
LET'S BE FRIENDS AGAIN!!!
This Bench is Dedicated to
RAISINS
99¢
Bag
Hake Bone
2.99
Parsley flakes
Paprika
Onion Powder
Maison Royal
BLACK PEPPER
POIVRE NOIR
HOT CURRY POWDER
ORIENTAL CURRY
JAMAICAN CURRY POWDER
GOYA

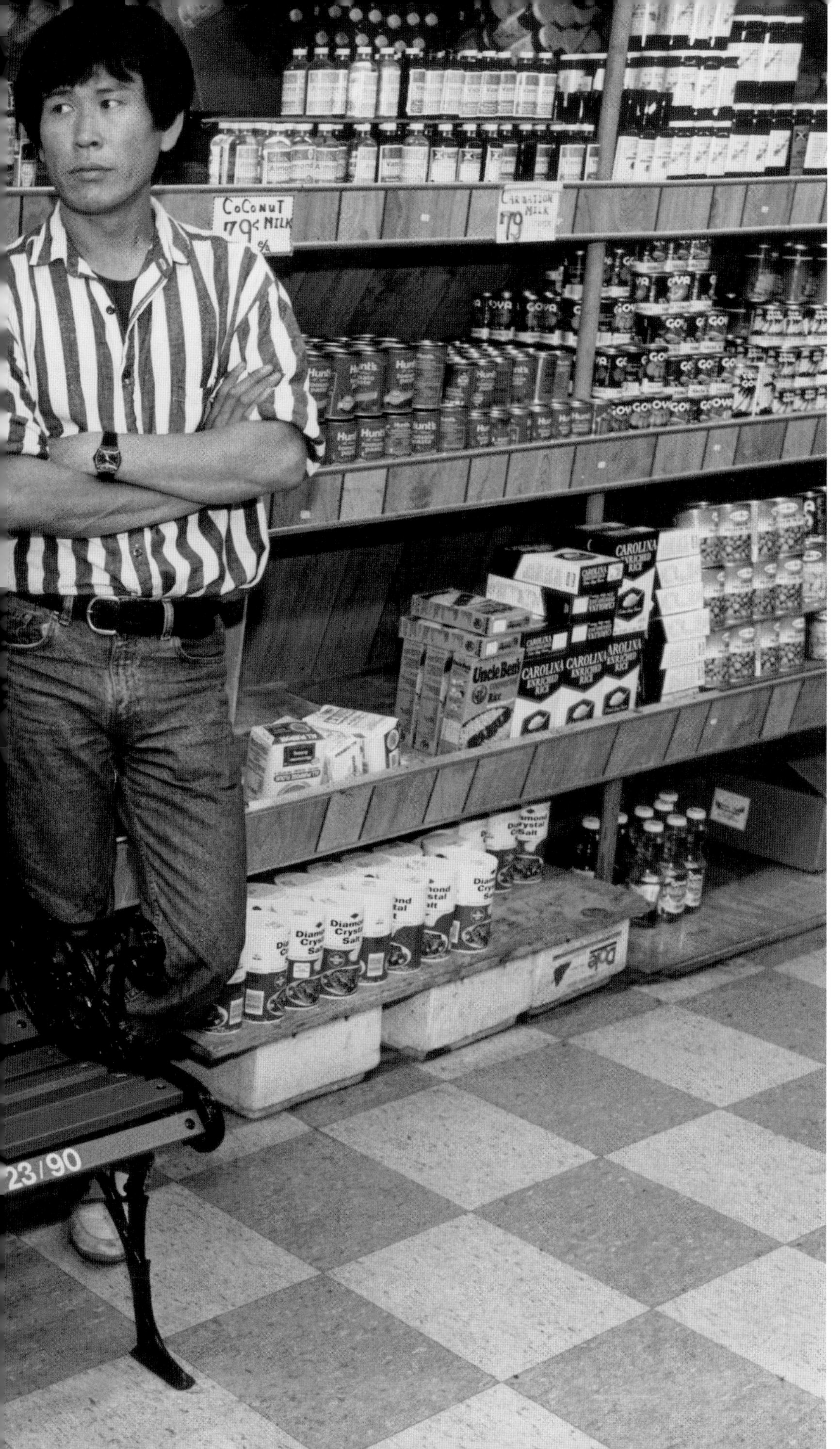

In the 1980s and 1990s racial tensions developed between the African American and Korean American communities on both the East and West coasts. Cultural differences, language barriers, and general economic inequality fueled misunderstanding, resentment, and occasional violence between Korean store owners and Black customers. In 1990, after an altercation between a Haitian woman and the Korean cashier at the Family Red Apple in Flatbush, local merchants presented owner Bong Jae Jang with a peace bench and urged an end to the Black community's boycott of the store. Brooklyn, New York, 1990.

Internment: "Never Again Means Now"

AKEMI KOCHIYAMA

Activist, writer, and co-director of the Yuri Kochiyama Archives Project

On November 23, 1981, Corky Lee photographed my grandfather, Bill Kochiyama, a native New Yorker and proud veteran of the all–Japanese American 442nd combat unit of the U.S. Army, testifying before the Commission on Wartime Relocation and Internment of Civilians.

Over the years, this photograph has become a symbol of the resilience and courage of the Japanese American community in the fight for redress and reparations and against the discrimination, racism, and disenfranchisement they faced during World War II. In February 1942, under President Franklin D. Roosevelt's Executive Order 9066, the U.S. government forcibly removed 120,000 people of Japanese descent— most of them natural-born U.S. citizens, like my grandparents—from their homes, farms, and businesses along the Pacific coast and incarcerated them in nine "relocation" camps across the western United States. These concentration camps were located in remote areas in deserts and mountains, sometimes adjacent to Native American reservations.

There was no due process. While the government rationalized the internment as a precautionary act to ensure the safety of American citizens, it was in fact driven by a long history of racism, anti-Asian propaganda, and white property interests in Japanese-owned farmland and businesses that predated World War II. The bombing of Pearl Harbor on December 7, 1941, provided an opportunity for those interests to use war hysteria and fear to fuel anti-Japanese sentiment and to seize Japanese American property. In his report on the Japanese evacuation from the West Coast, Lt. Gen. John DeWitt wrote, "The Japanese race is an enemy race."

Shortly after the signing of Executive Order 9066, the Japanese American Citizens League (JACL) persuaded the federal government to allow for the creation of an all-Japanese (segregated) volunteer combat unit in order to prove their loyalty. My grandpa Bill enthusiastically signed up. Eager to prove his loyalty to the country in which he was born and to escape Topaz, Utah, where he had been interned, Bill joined the 442nd. He was sent to Hattiesburg, Mississippi, to train at Camp Shelby, a segregated boot camp for Black and Japanese American soldiers about to ship out to the front lines of Europe. During his training in Hattiesburg, Bill met his future wife, my grandma Yuri, at an all-Japanese USO where she was working as a volunteer. Bill and his peers fought honorably and bravely; in the end, the 442nd was the most highly decorated unit in the entire U.S. Army during World War II.

But the JACL's insistence on acquiescence and compliance cast a layer of shame over the experience of internment. That feeling remained unarticulated by most Japanese Americans, and it lasted long after the war was over. Growing up, my grandparents always knew they had been a "minority" group that experienced discrimination. Their wartime experiences of forced relocation and incarceration informed a deep sense of themselves as people of color living under a racist government. Their understanding of the internment and of American racism strengthened in the postwar years as they built a family and community in Harlem, New York City.

In the 1960s and 1970s, a new generation began to demand an accounting of the internment. A nationwide campaign for redress and reparations brought together the entire Japanese American community, young and old, former internees, their descendants, and their allies from BIPOC communities. The campaign itself was empowering and created an opportunity for *yonsei* (fourth-generation Japanese Americans) like me and my cousin Zulu, who were kids at that time, to learn about internment and to watch our grandparents be part of a successful national movement for reparations.

The photograph of my grandfather is inspiring and important to me personally for so many reasons. It is frequently used in schools to teach about internment and reparations and in mobilizations of the Japanese American community to advocate on behalf of immigrants facing discrimination. When racists attacked Muslims and South Asians after 9/11, Japanese Americans responded in solidarity. When Trump separated migrant families and detained them in cages, Japanese Americans protested, "Never again means now." Today we are mobilizing support for H.R. 40 and reparations for Black people.

American history textbooks and institutions don't contain a lot of information about or images of Asian Americans. In fact, one of the few images of an Asian American in the Smithsonian's National Portrait Gallery is a photo of my grandmother, Yuri Kochiyama, marching with striking restaurant workers in New York City's Chinatown in 1980. The photo was taken by Corky Lee.

From cultural events to marches, Corky documented the critical moments of the Asian American movement for civil rights. The poignant images in his photographic archive of this movement provide powerful evidence of the struggles and resilience of Asian Americans that is important for the next generation of educators, organizers, activists, artists, and archivists. As Corky put it, he was "rectifying American history one photograph at a time."

Over the course of more than two decades of organizing my grandmother's archive, I've developed an understanding of her work not just as an activist and organizer but also as a disciplined and thoughtful archivist. Throughout her fifty years of community building and political organizing in many movements, she meticulously collected all the flyers, posters, books, invitations, and correspondence she received, and she documented every person she met, phone call she received, and meeting or event she attended. With each record, she was building an activist archive, one for social justice and BIPOC solidarity.

By taking hundreds of thousands of photographs and documenting every notable Asian American event and person in the second half of the twentieth century, Corky Lee single-handedly created a photographic archive for social justice and for the history of Asian American activism and civic engagement. By telling its own story, it reflects Corky's conviction that "We do matter."

The Day of Remembrance, an annual event in Japanese American communities, marks President Franklin D. Roosevelt's Executive Order 9066. Issued on February 19, 1942, it authorized the removal of Japanese Americans living on the Pacific coast. On the 1989 Day of Remembrance, community residents held a candlelight vigil and carried signs indicating the camp where they had been interned. Artist Miné Okubo (1912–2001) is second from the right. New York, 1989.

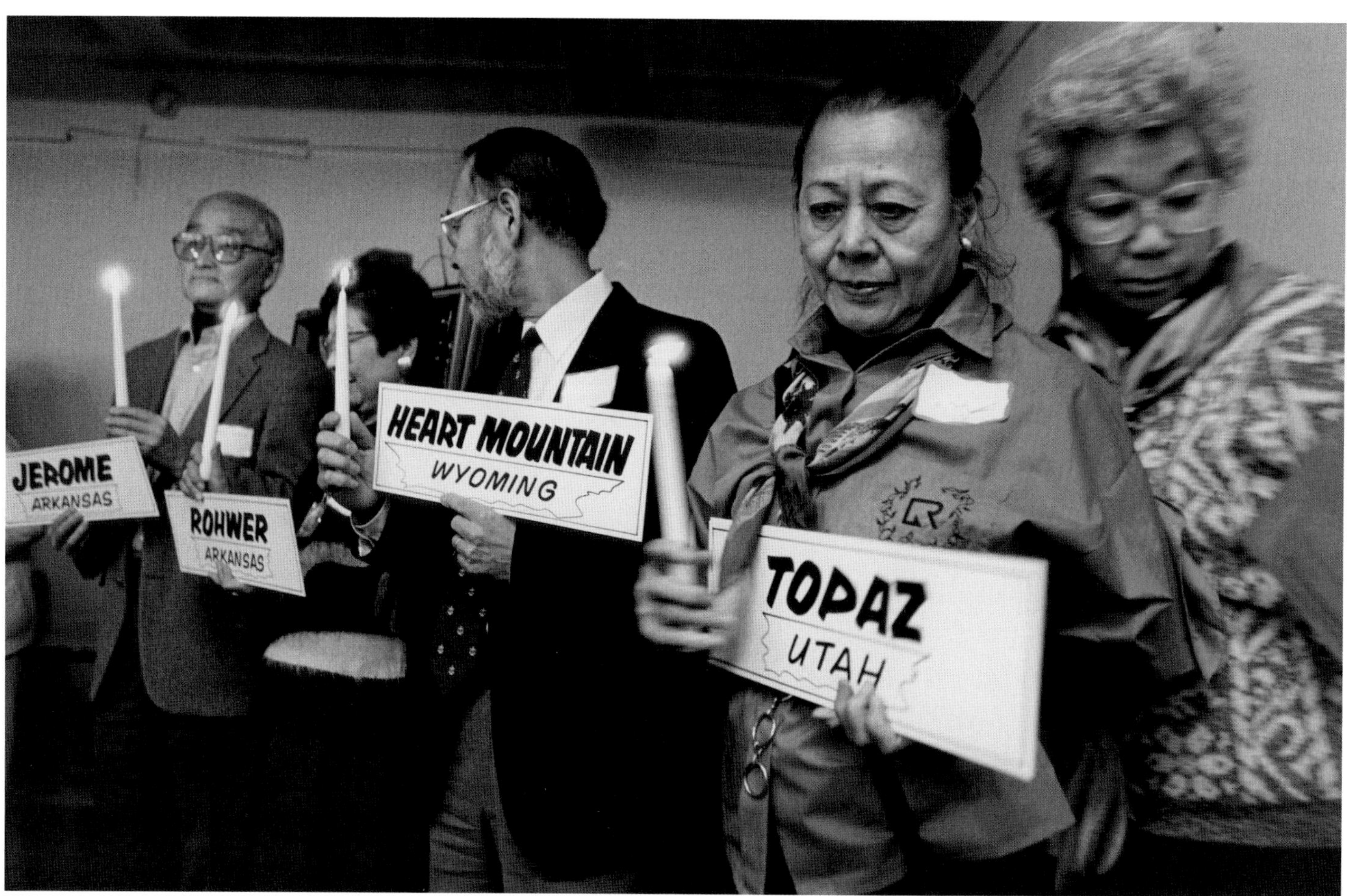

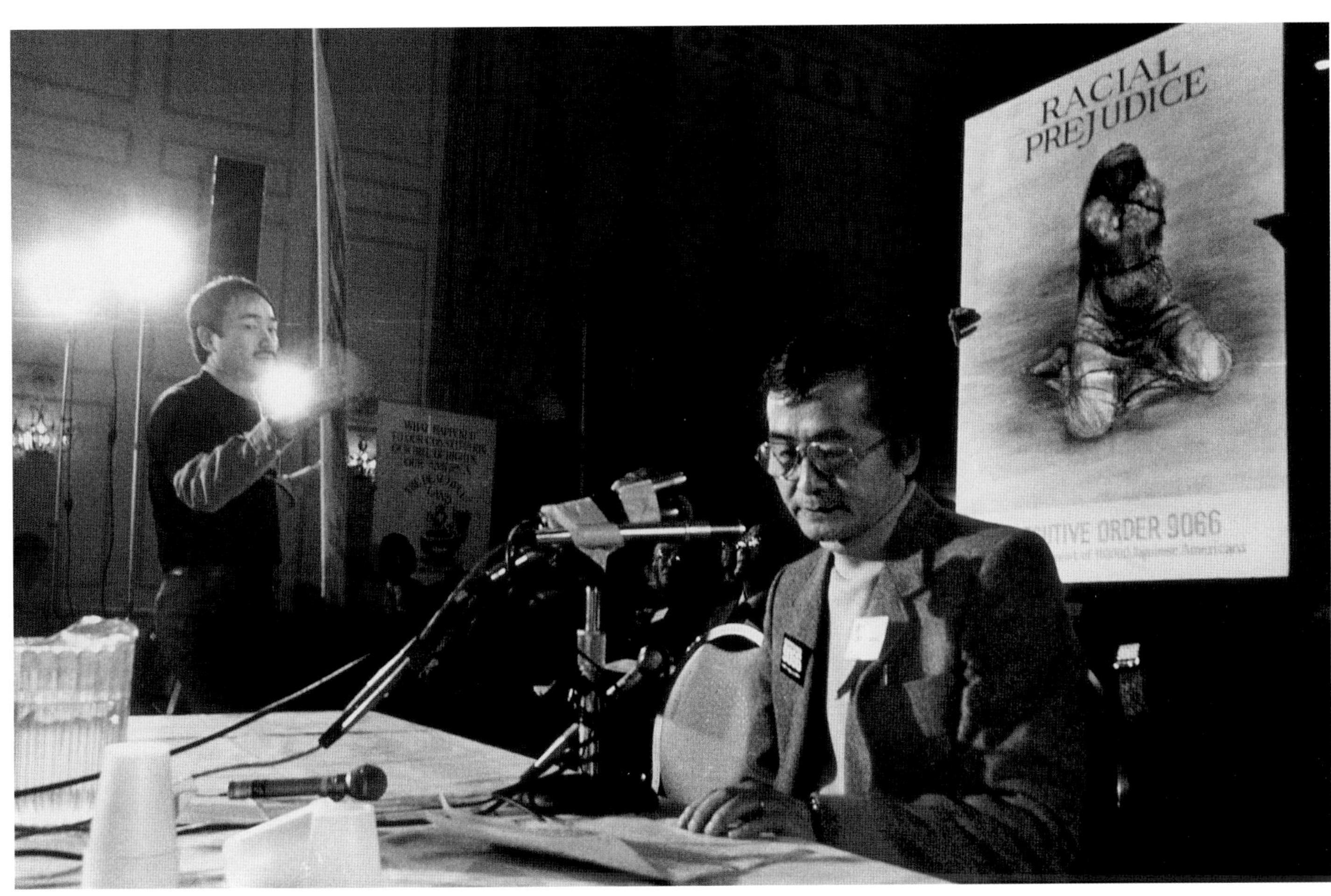

Bill Kochiyama (1921–1993) testifies at a congressional hearing on the Japanese American internment during World War II. New York, 1982.

Gordon Hirabayashi (1918–2012) (*left*) and Fred Korematsu (1919-2005) brought the landmark cases that challenged the government's violation of their civil liberties on account of their race. The Supreme Court's rulings in 1943 and 1944 upheld the military's right to detain civilians without having to show evidence of military necessity. Later, Japanese American activists discovered documents showing that the government had deliberately withheld from the court reports by the FBI and the Office of Naval Intelligence that concluded that Japanese Americans posed no threat to national security. In 1983 the court vacated Korematsu's original conviction but did not repudiate the ruling itself until 2018. Place unknown, late 1980s.

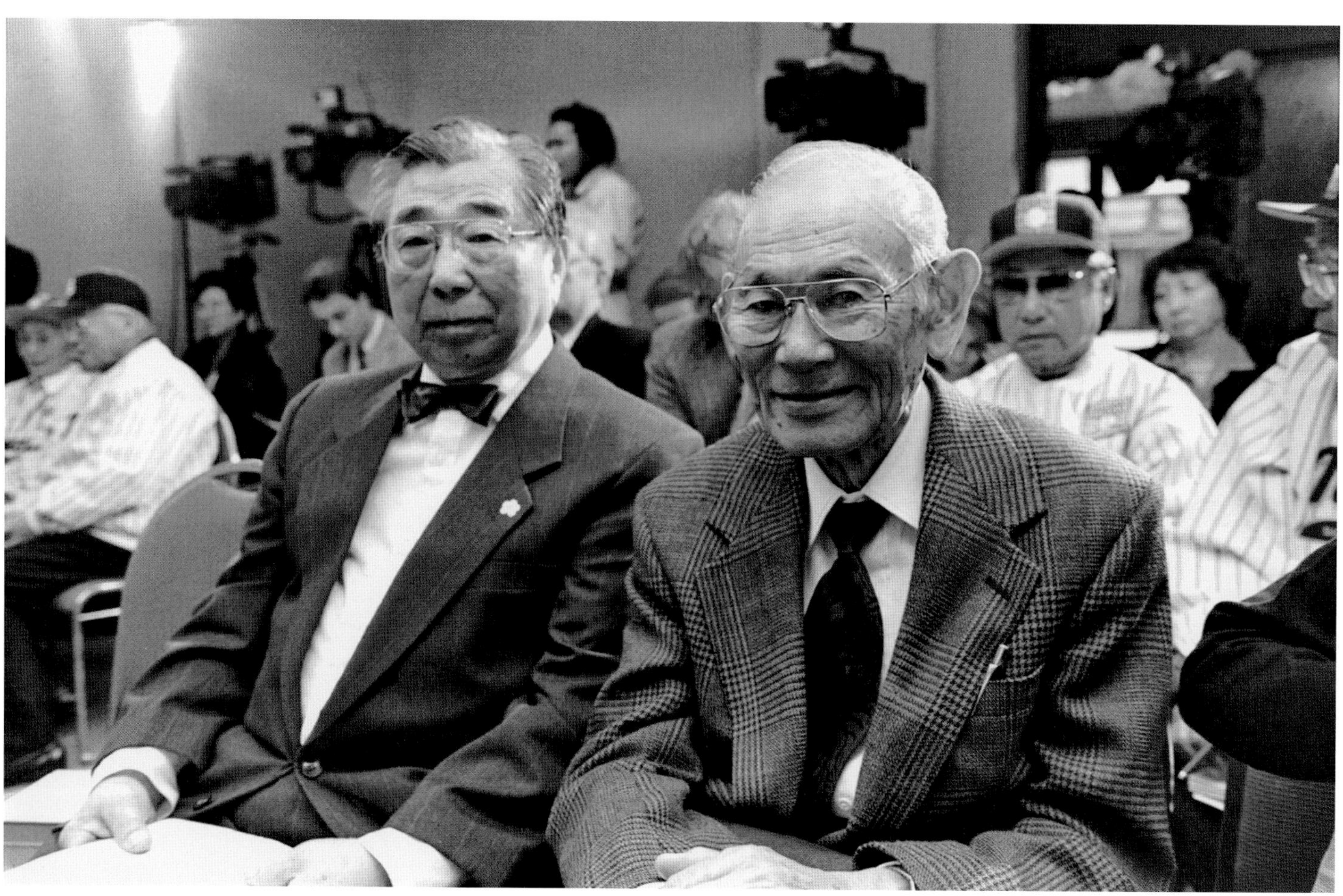

Artist Byron Goto (1919–2014) with antiwar posters that he and other artists created for congressional hearings on the internment. Congress refused to allow them to be shown in Washington, but they were displayed in other cities. One of Goto's posters appeared behind Bill Kochiyama as he testified. Place unknown, circa 1982.

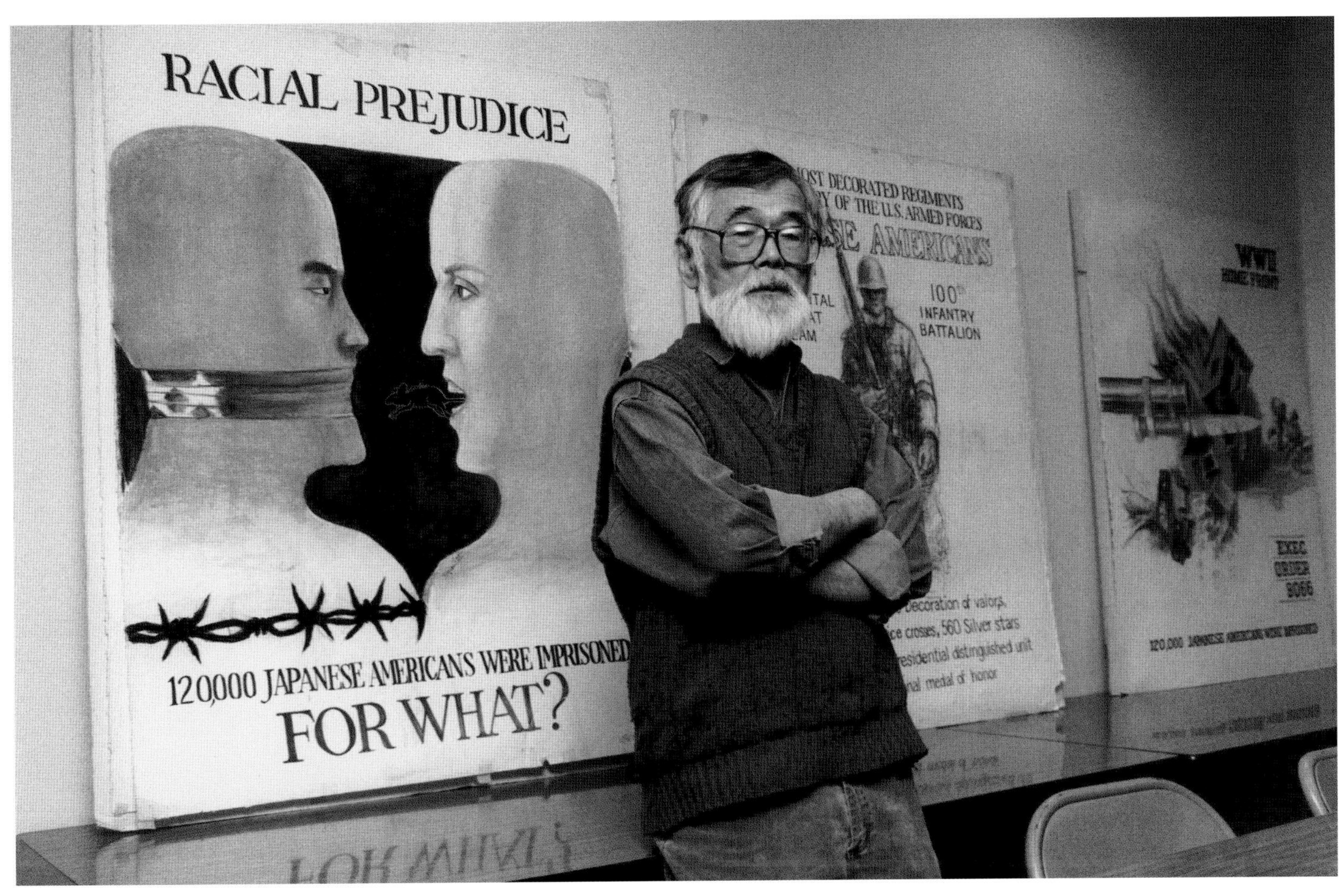

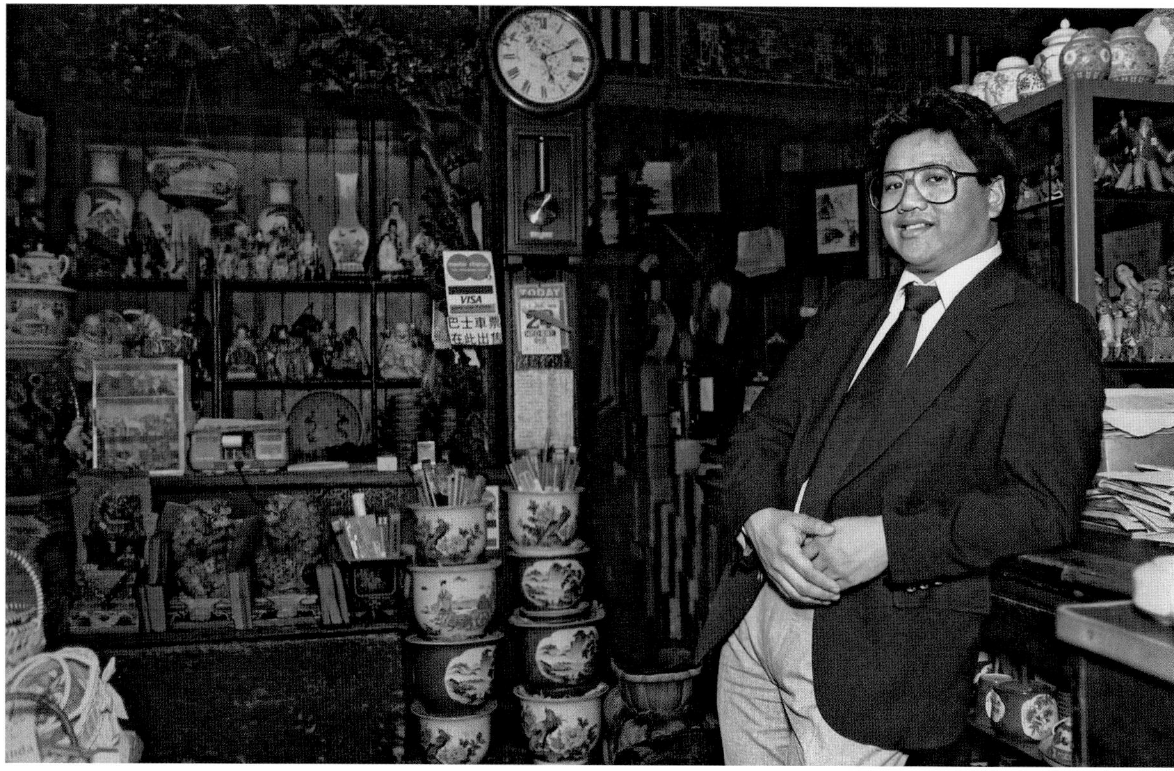

Paul J. Q. Lee (1950–2014) was the proprietor of Quong Yuen Shing (Mott Street General Store), the oldest shop in Chinatown. His grandfather opened the shop at 32 Mott in 1891. Lee was a civic leader, actor, and community raconteur, whom Corky Lee described as the "Al Sharpton of Chinatown." The shop closed in 2003. New York, 1988.

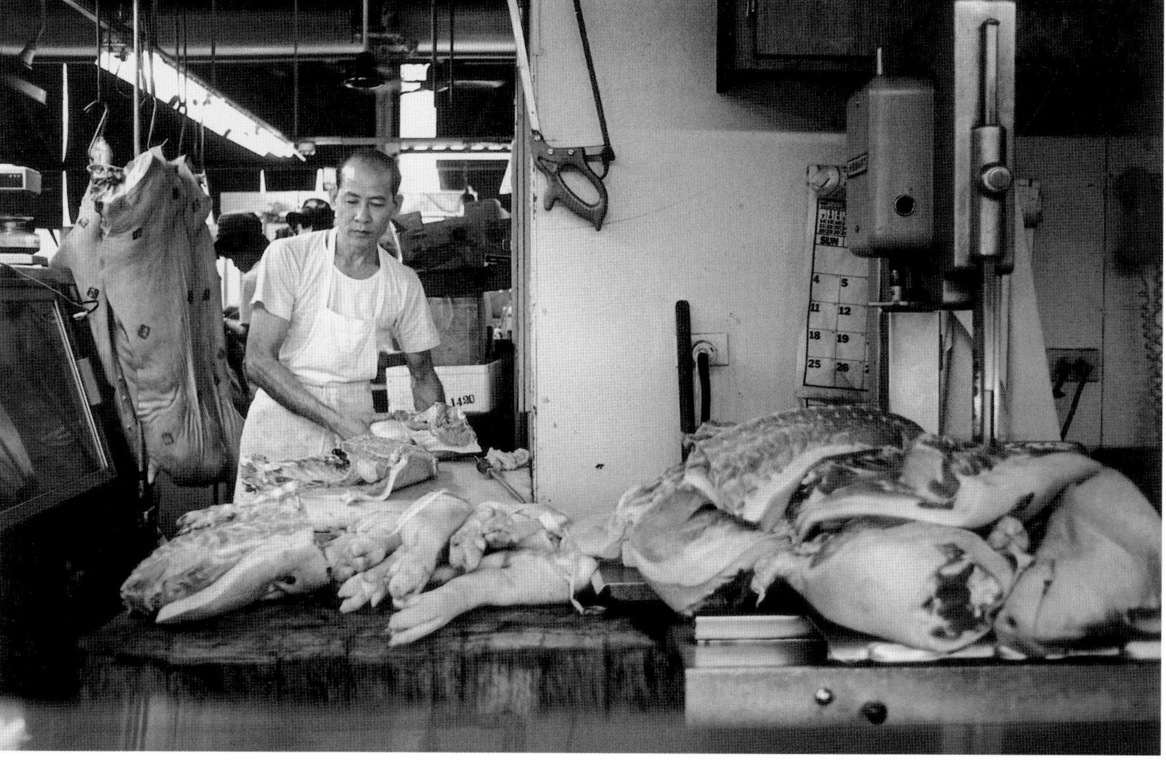

Chinatown butcher shop. New York, 1985.

"Greetings from Chinatown New York"
old postcard and contemporary scene.
New York, 1989.

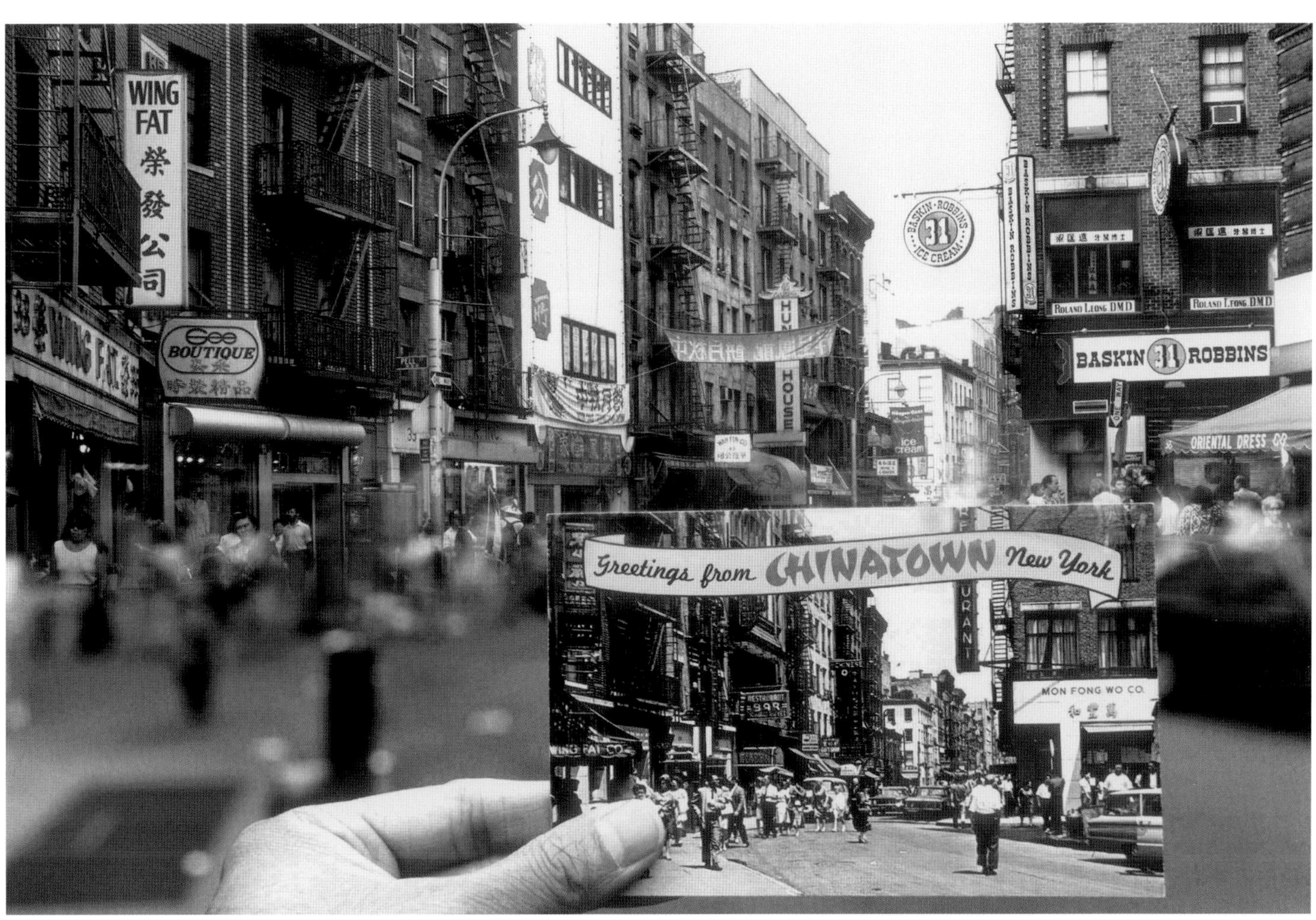

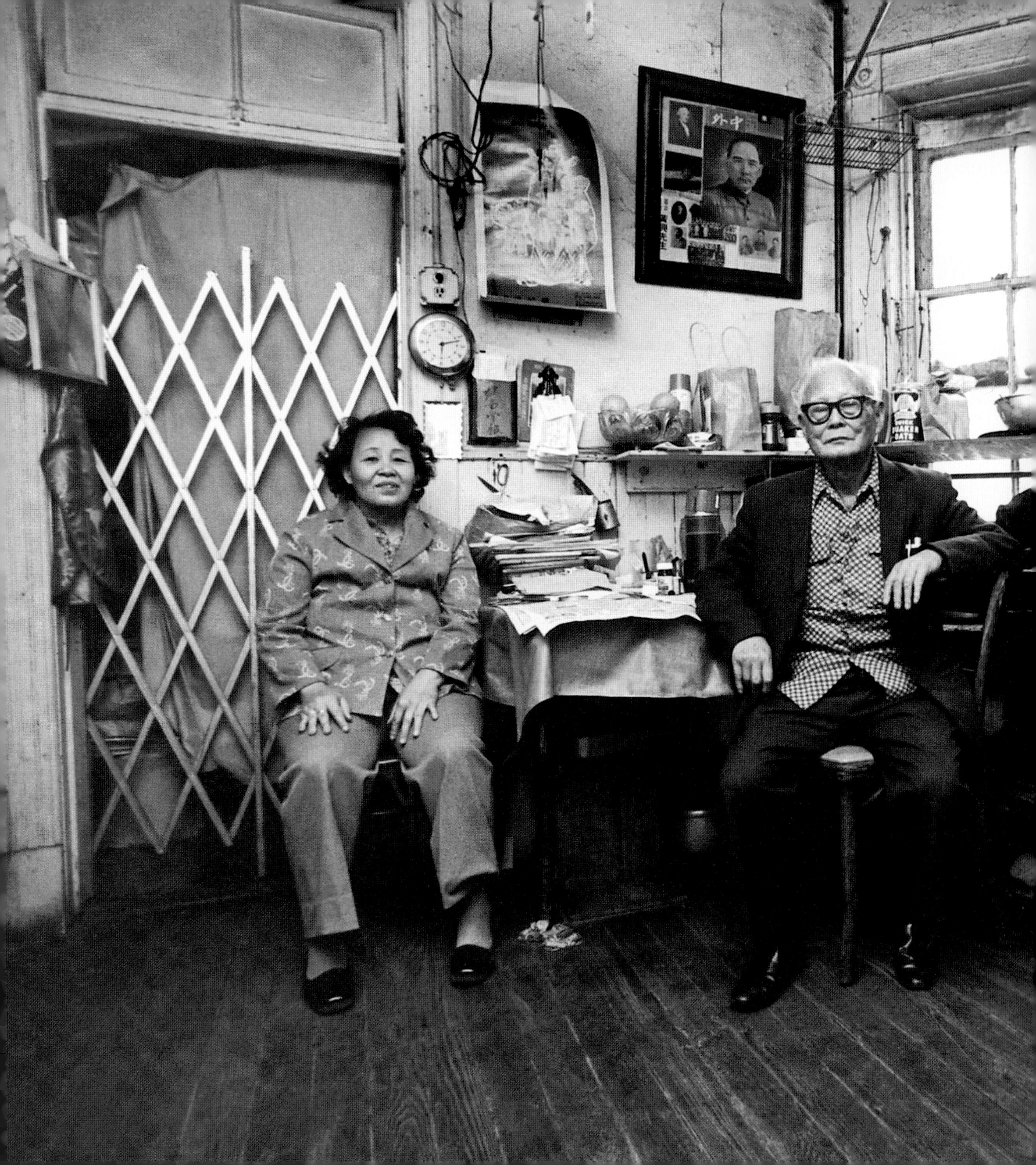
中外
QUAKER OATS

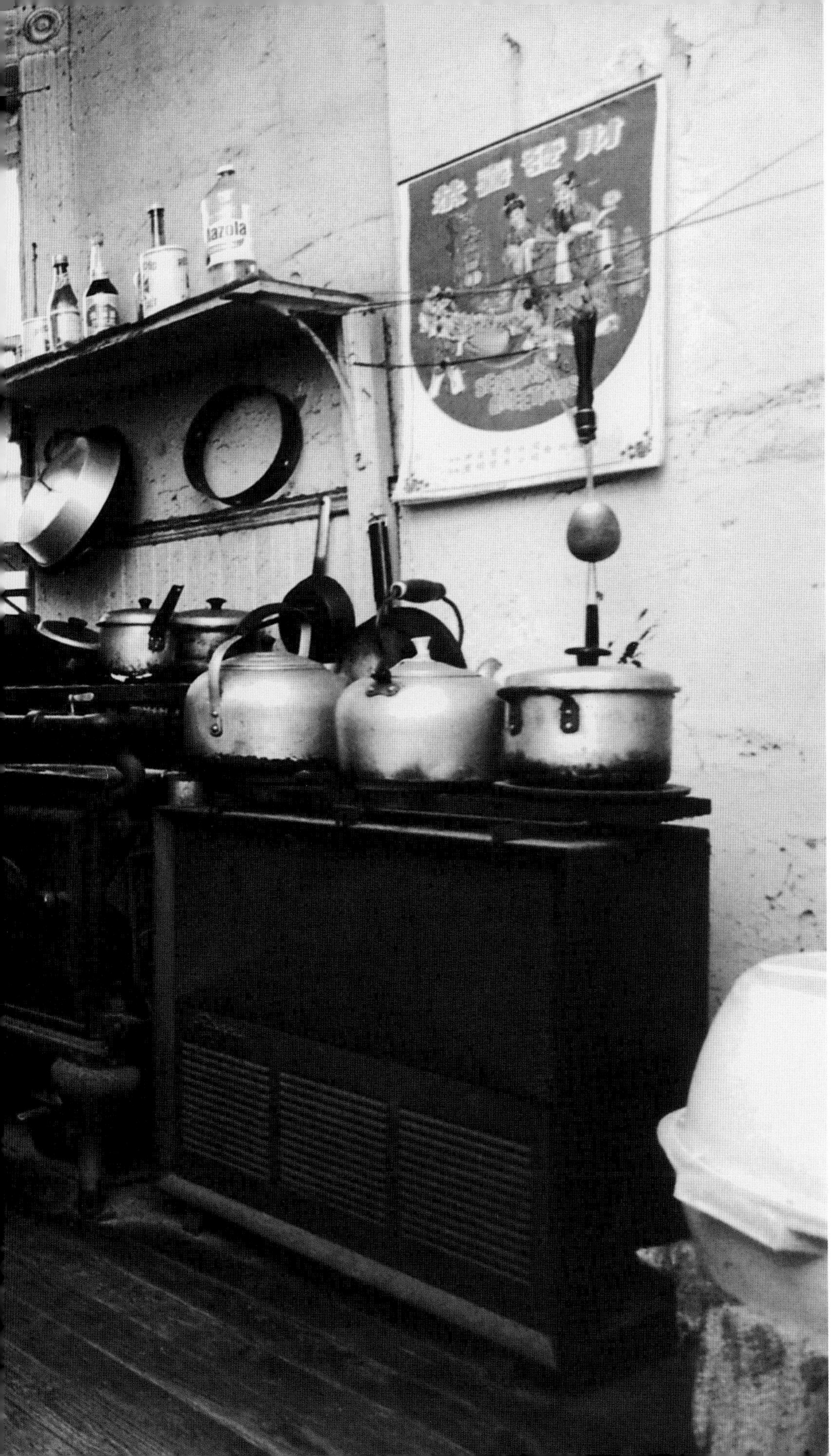

An elderly couple in their Mott Street apartment in Chinatown. The man, a cousin of Corky's mother, was barred from the United States by the Exclusion Act, so immigrated as a young man to Cuba. In the late 1970s he immigrated to the United States and brought his wife from Hong Kong. New York, 1981.

Tea Bac Nguon Chor (aka Ti Bac Nguon Chho), formerly a senator in Cambodia and an elder in the Cambodian refugee community, with the Buddhist shrine in his home in public housing. Jacksonville, Florida, 1988.

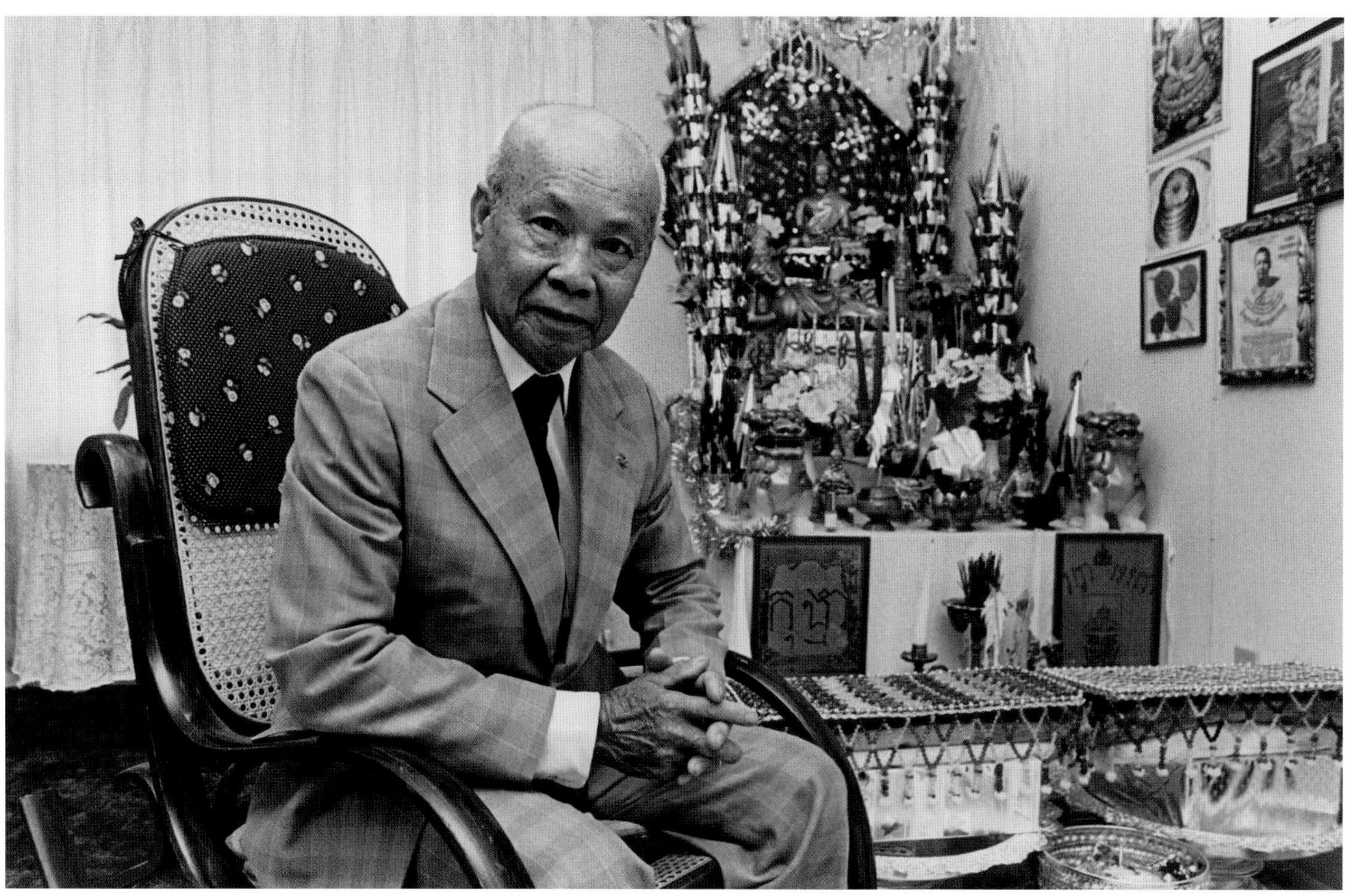

Ho Yung restaurant in Washington, D.C. Corky Lee noted the restaurant's use of the chop suey font, which had gone out of fashion in New York. Most of D.C.'s Chinatown would be destroyed in the 1990s by the construction of luxury housing and the Capitol One Arena. Washington, D.C., 1981.

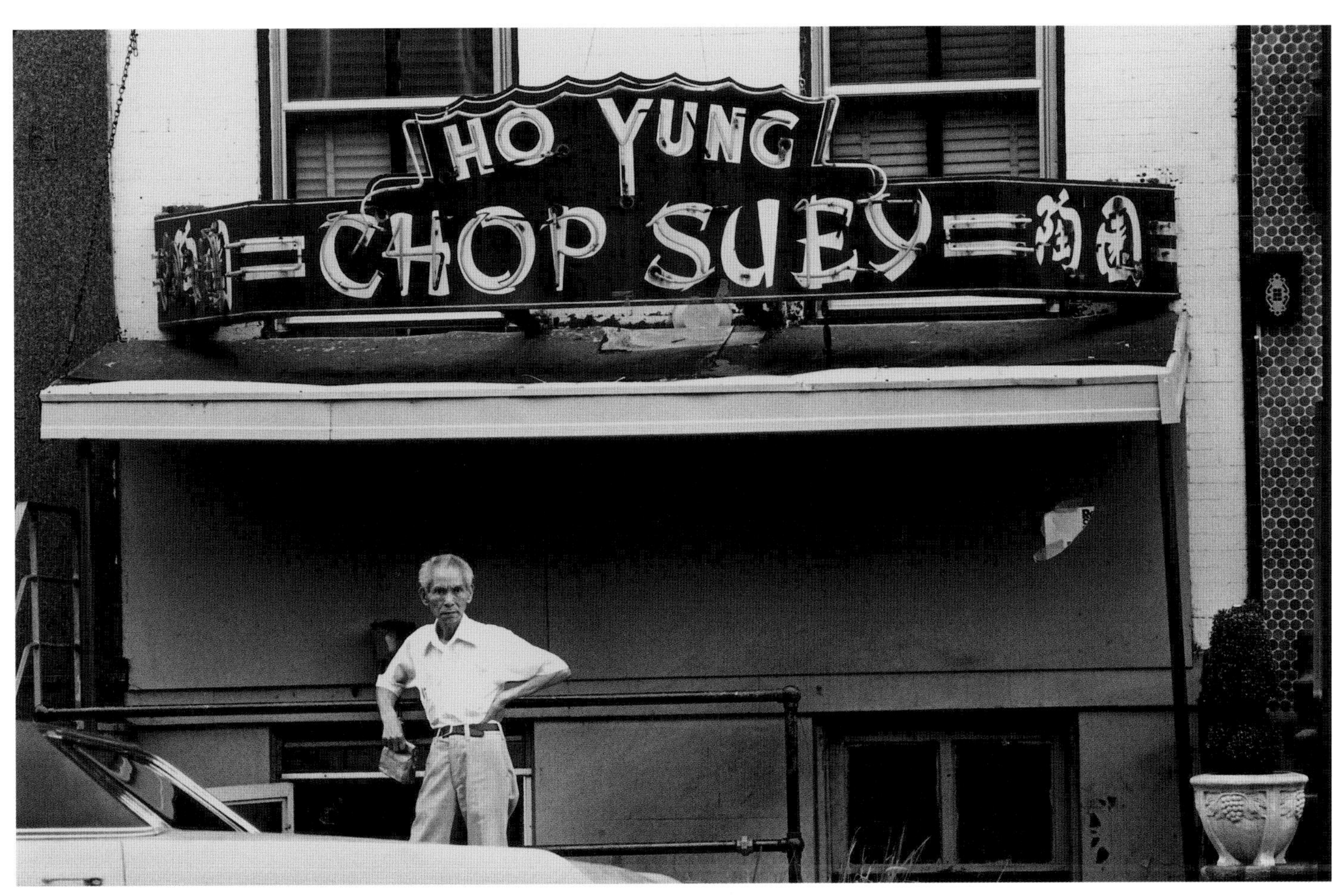

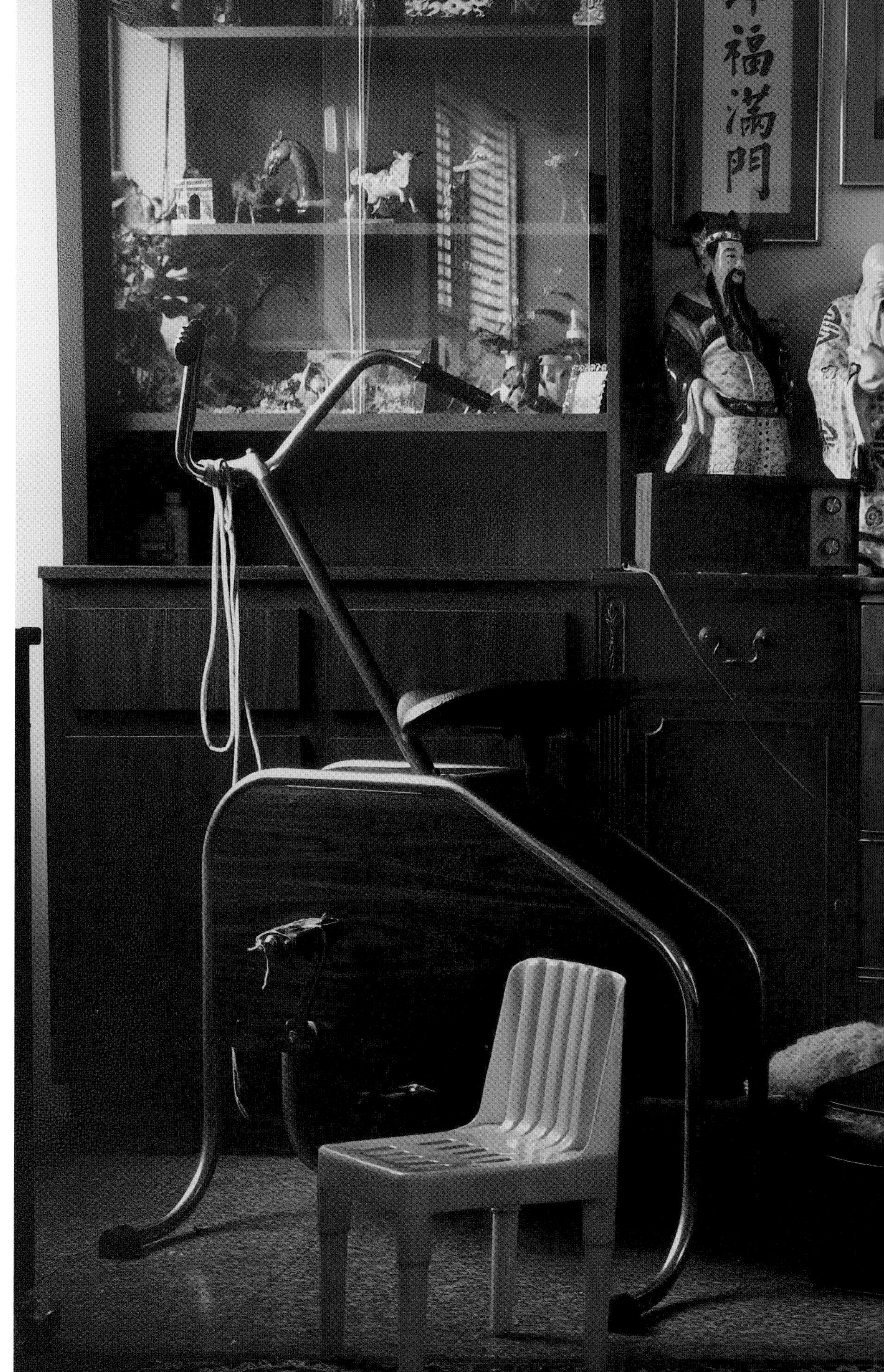

Jung Ping Hung,
Corky Lee's mother,
in her apartment in
Confucius Plaza
in Chinatown.
New York, 1980s.

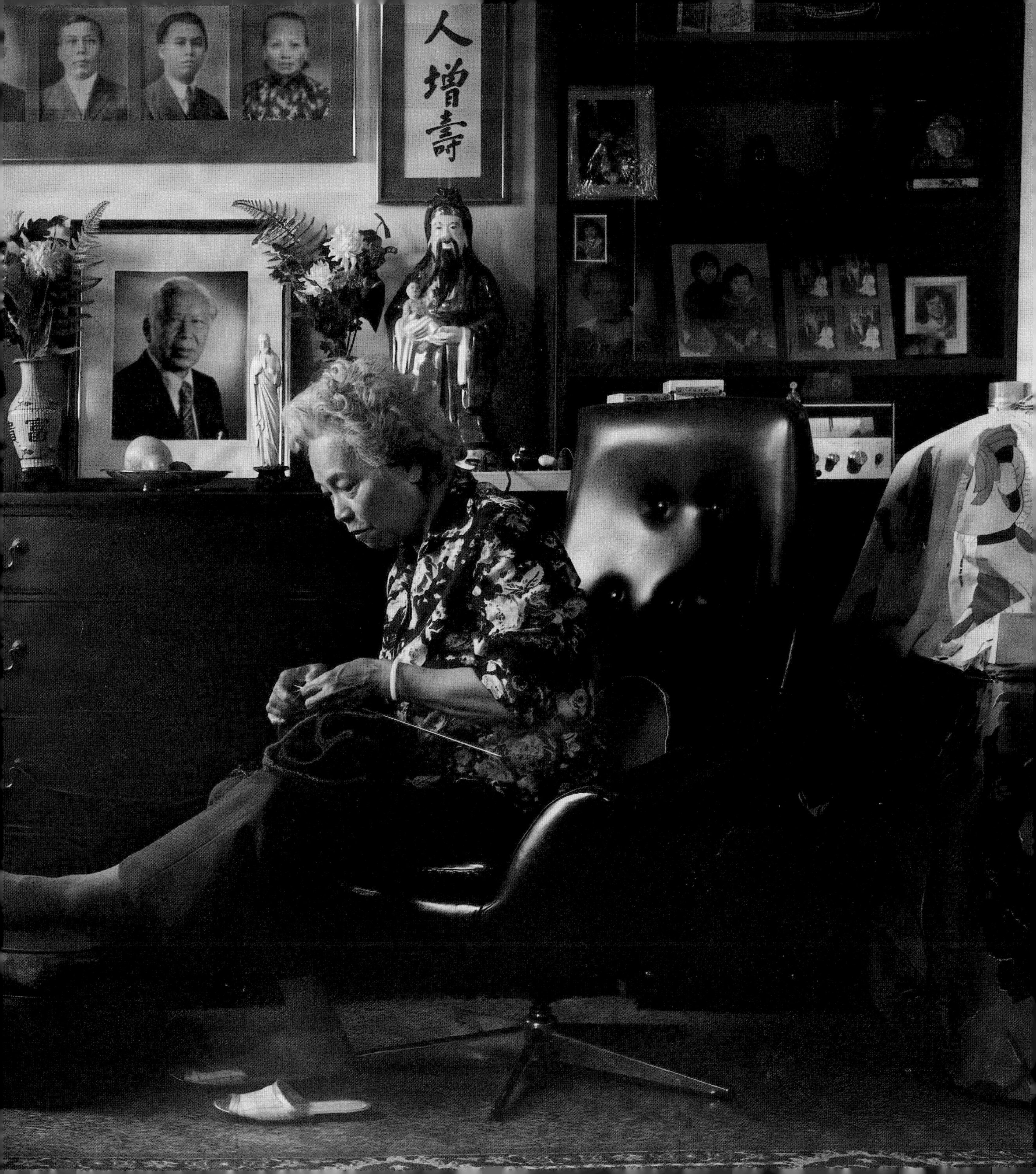
人增壽

Vincent Chin and the Long Struggle Against Anti-Asian Violence

HELEN ZIA

Activist and writer, author of *Last Boat Out of Shanghai*

My first encounter with Corky Lee took place in the early 1970s, when I was a college activist and he was evolving into the "photographer laureate" of the Asian American community. I had long forgotten about that chance crossing, but I know it took place, because decades later Corky gave me photographic proof. Somehow he had recognized a much younger, long-haired me at an antiwar rally in New York City.

In the years that followed, Corky focused his unwavering lens on the heart of our communities. So it wasn't entirely surprising to see him in Detroit on May 9, 1983, with his camera. That was the day the brand-new pan–Asian American group that we named American Citizens for Justice (ACJ) planned to hold a big protest over the injustices in the brutal killing of Vincent Chin and its aftermath. This young Chinese American had been beaten to death by two white unemployed autoworkers, who each received a sentence of no more than probation.

At that time, having been laid off as a worker at a Big Three auto factory, I was a journalist. I had become ACJ's press secretary. Vincent Chin's courageous mother, Lily, bravely stood before reporters and many other strangers and spoke about the racist attack on her son. She explained why Asian Americans were standing together for equal treatment under the law. Our news releases connected the economic recession and the anti-Asian hate of 1982 to earlier times when economic stress had led to bigotry: one hundred years earlier, the Chinese Exclusion Act of 1882 became the federal embodiment of "frontier justice" when white mobs, blaming Chinese workers for America's labor woes, destroyed Chinatowns and murdered and lynched Chinese with impunity.

For more than a century preceding Vincent Chin's murder, America's master narrative of white supremacy had labeled and positioned Chinese and other Asians in the United States as foreign invaders, as subhuman "Asiatic hordes" of disease-ridden vermin, intent on stealing jobs from "real" Americans by working harder for less pay and other evils. At different times, various Asian American ethnicities had tried to dissociate themselves from this dehumanizing stereotype, by trying to prove that they could be more acceptable and more compliant than the Asian immigrants who preceded them. But the 1907 expulsion of Sikhs from Bellingham, Washington, the anti-Filipino riots in Washington State in 1927 and in California in 1930, and the incarceration of all ethnic Japanese from the West Coast during World War II made clear that Asians from anywhere, whether yellow or brown, could become targets of American bigotry and hate. The proverbial "Chinaman's chance" meant that Asians had no way to escape the anti-Asian racism that was baked into America's infrastructure.

In the 1970s and early 1980s, America was facing another cycle of economic distress. Global oil crises led to nationwide gas shortages and increases in prices at the pump by a multiple of ten; inflation approached 20 percent; and the entire American manufacturing sector fell into a deep slump as the auto industry collapsed. At the same time, the Reagan administration sought to slash wages and the social safety net of government assistance. As the economic turmoil and misery deepened, demagogues blamed Japan, but not Germany, for making fuel-efficient cars that buyers preferred over Detroit's gas-guzzling dinosaurs. Once again anti-Asian racism and scapegoating emerged, tragically setting the stage for the brutal murder of Vincent Chin, whose white killers went unpunished.

But this time Asian Americans began to organize, despite ethnic, linguistic, cultural, generational, and class differences. Restaurant and laundry workers joined auto engineers and researchers in protest. In those pre-internet days, outreach required face-to-face meetings and long-distance phone calls, mailed appeals with information packets, and even telegrams. Activists cranked out press releases on typewriters and hand-delivered them. Asian American communities from New York, Chicago, and Toronto to San Francisco and Los Angeles mobilized support for the campaign for justice in Detroit. On April 18, 1983, *The New York Times* reported on our efforts.

Corky Lee learned of our plans and made his way to Detroit. At the May 9 pan-Asian protest, he photographed the multiracial, multiethnic crowd, with its many community, civil rights, and interfaith leaders. He captured the intense grief and strength of Lily Chin. Many of his pictures became iconic as his photojournalism bore witness to Asian American resistance to injustice and inequity.

Though Vincent Chin's name is known because of writers, filmmakers, and photographers like Corky, many others suffered from the anti-Asian hate that was unleashed by that economic downturn. Amid the many racially charged situations, avowed white nationalist groups like the White Student Union, Master Race, and Dotbusters committed racist attacks. In 1989 a mass shooter with white supremacist connections fired an AK-47 into a Stockton, California, elementary school where 80 percent of the students were Southeast Asian Americans, killing five eight-year-olds. Yet in this and many other instances law enforcement, public officials, and the media instantly and automatically responded by declaring that racism had played no part in the attacks, continually rendering Asian-ness invisible.

In this millennium, South Asian Americans as well as East and Southeast Asian Americans have been targeted, while Chinese (lumped together with other East Asians) are being blamed for Covid-19. Meanwhile, attacks driven by Islamophobic hate and the anti-Muslim policies that followed 9/11 have not subsided. In 2012, a white supremacist shot up a Sikh temple in Oak Creek, Wisconsin, while people were praying, killing six. Similarly, in April 2021, a mass shooter targeted a FedEx facility in Indianapolis where the majority of workers were Sikh, killing eight people, including four Sikh Americans. In March 2021 in Atlanta, a gunman who hunted for Asian-owned spas shot six East Asian women and two bystanders. Once again officials in both Indianapolis and Atlanta immediately dismissed the possibility of a racial motivation.

Such denials of racism underscore another vexing issue. The entrenched racist stereotype of Asian Americans as the model minority, as passive, complaisant, and uncomplaining, carries the implication that Asian Americans don't experience racism. It has set the bar higher for "proving" anti-Asian racism to gatekeepers in the government and the media. Back in the 1980s, witnesses heard Vincent Chin's killers say, "It's because of you mother—s that we're out of work" and "Let's get the Chinese," clearly targeting Chin and his Chinese friend. Yet in the absence of commonly accepted racial slurs or proof of the killers' KKK membership, those words weren't enough for a Cincinnati jury to see a racial motivation. Even two years after the Covid hate began and StopAAPIHate.org reported more than eleven thousand hate incidents, a 2022 survey by the Center for the Study of Hate and Extremism found that one-third of Americans are unaware that attacks against Asian Americans are increasing.

Corky Lee's work disrupts such systemic invisibility by showing AAPI community resistance to inequities and injustice. His photos offer instructive and powerful counternarratives, depicting Asian Americans of all ages and walks of life speaking out and standing up against violence and hate. Corky's lens reveals Asian Americans in their full personhood, empowered to fight back.

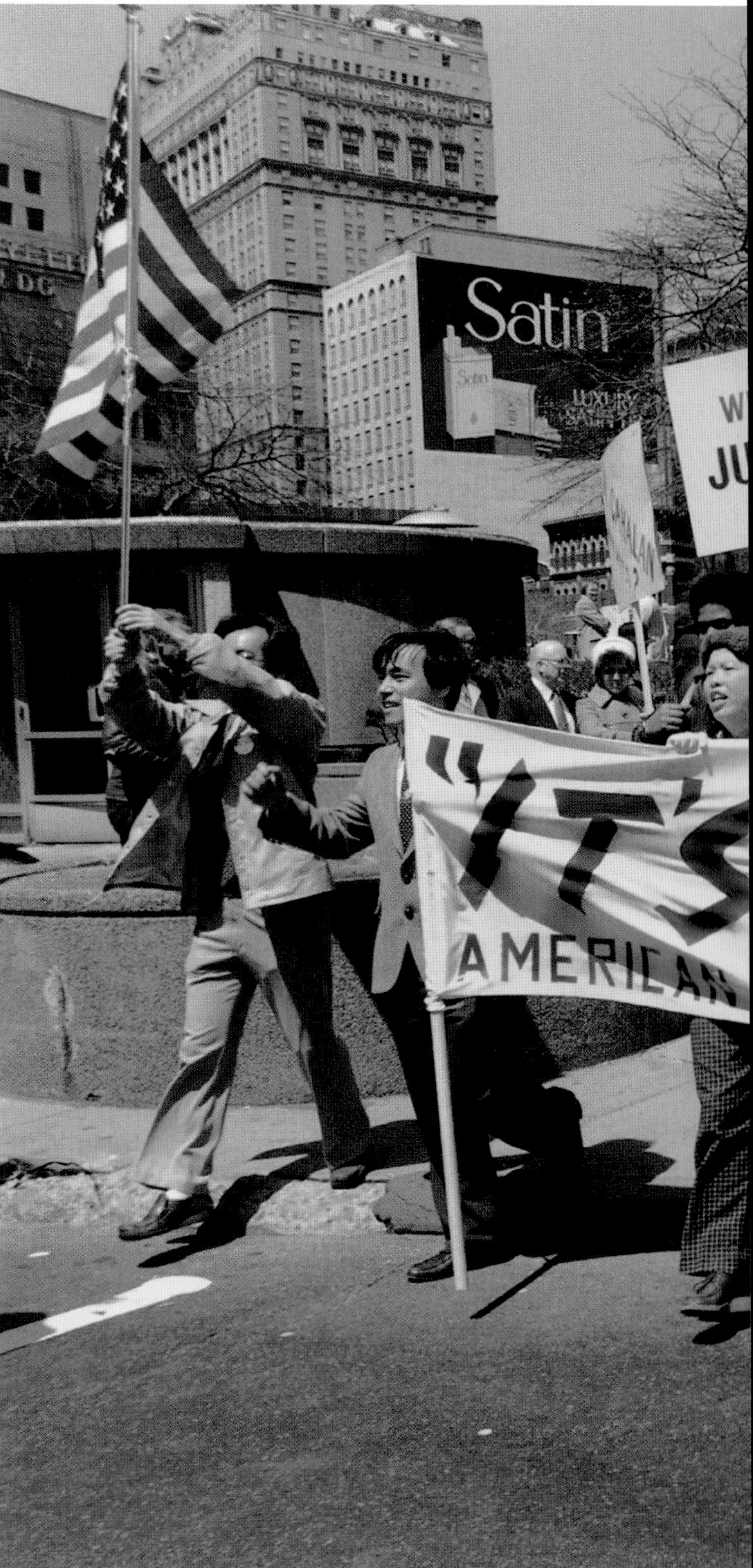

American Citizens for Justice led a mass protest when the court sentenced Vincent Chin's killers, who pleaded guilty to manslaughter, to probation and a fine. Detroit, 1983.

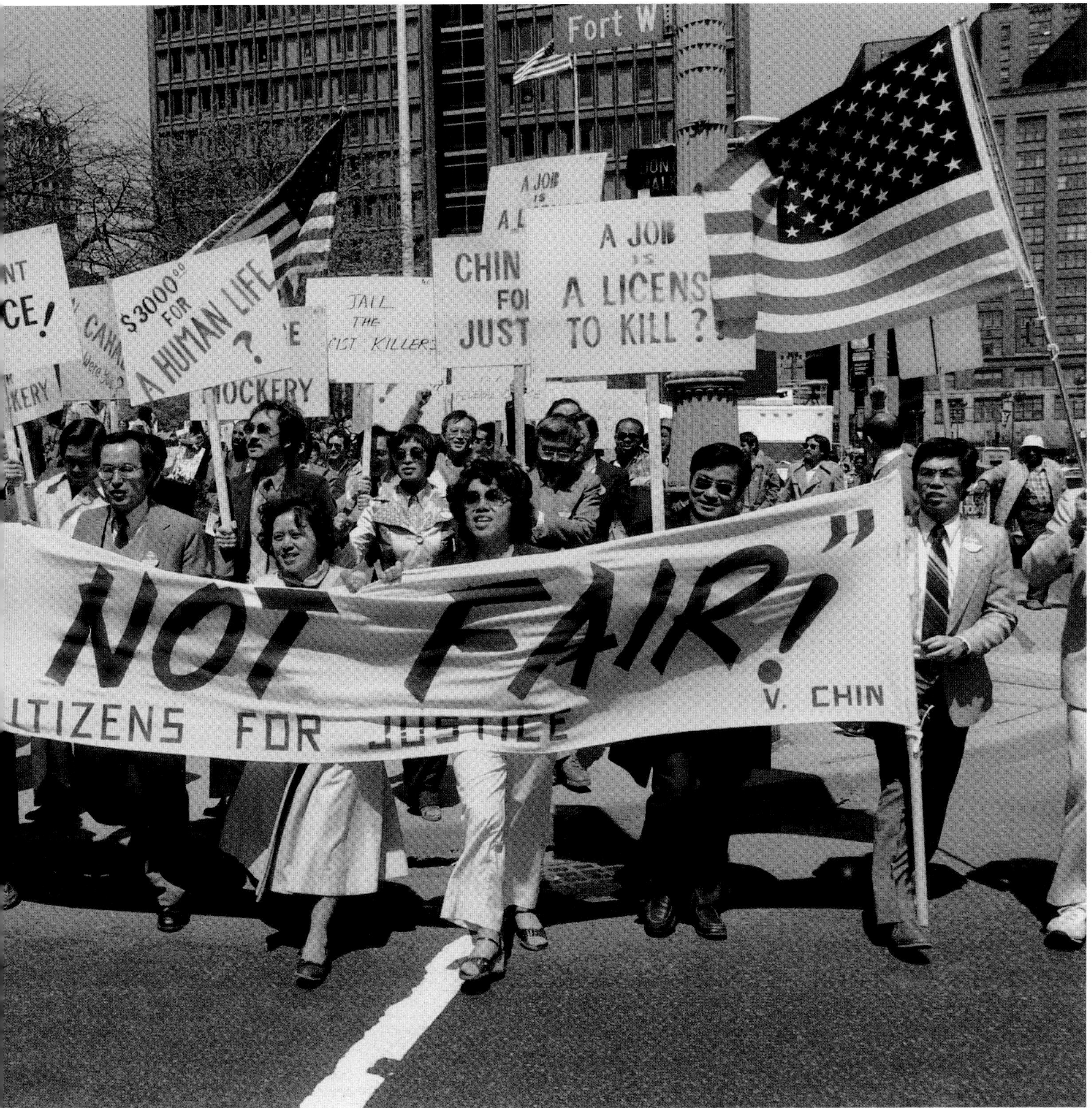

Fort W
A JOB IS A LICENS TO KILL ?
$3000.00 FOR A HUMAN LIFE ?
JAIL THE CIST KILLERS
CHIN FO JUST
MOCKERY
"NOT FAIR!"
V. CHIN
ITIZENS FOR JUSTICE

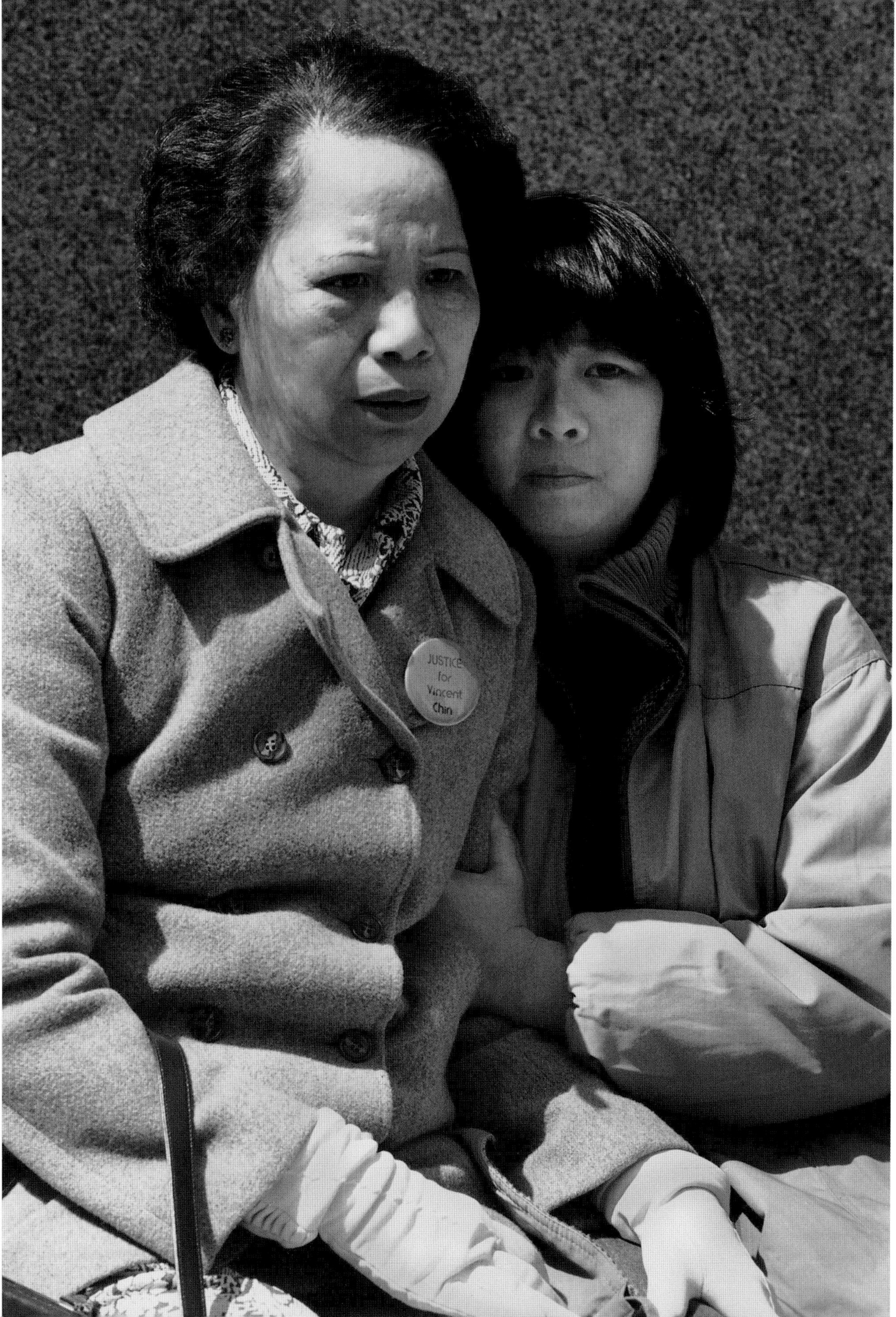
JUSTICE
for
Vincent
Chin

Below left: Organizer Helen Zia. Detroit, 1983.

Below right: Helen Zia (*center*) with filmmakers Christine Choy (*left*) and Renee Tajima-Peña, at the premiere of *Who Killed Vincent Chin?* The film was nominated for an Academy Award. New York, 1987.

Opposite: Vincent Chin's mother, Lily Chin, with her niece, Betty Li. Detroit, 1983.

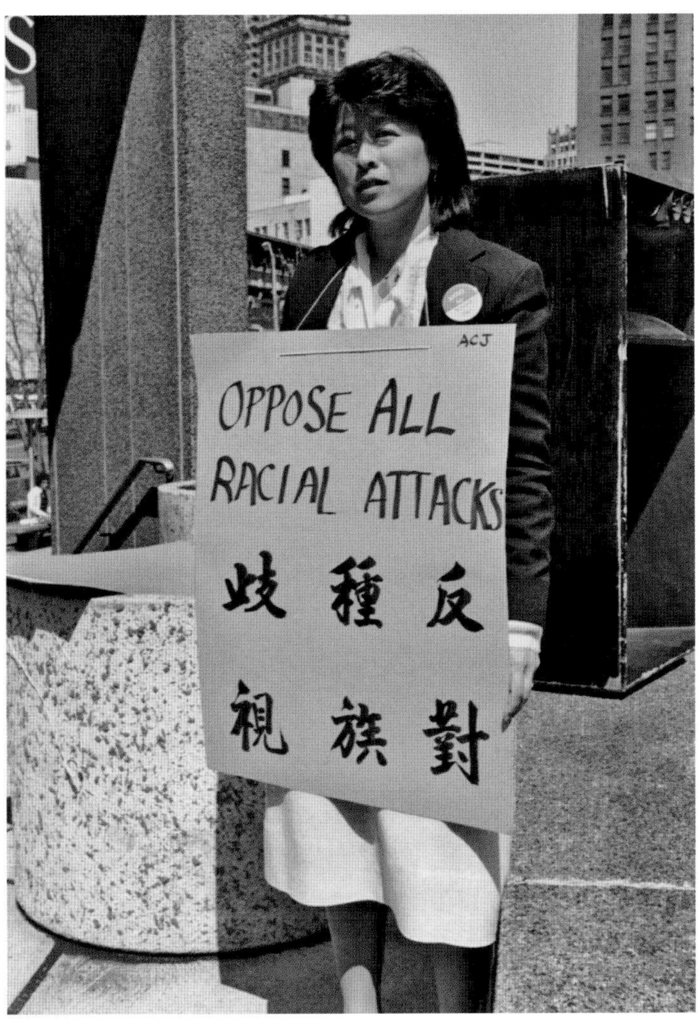

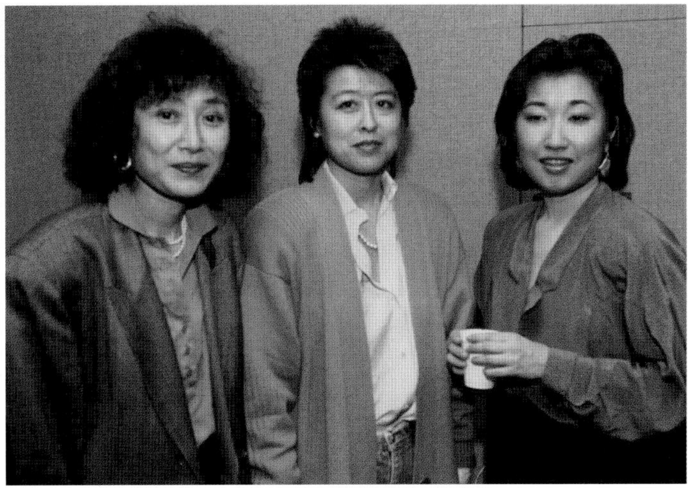

In 1995, in Brooklyn, New York, police officers killed Yong Xin Huang, a sixteen-year-old. Huang and his friends had been playing with a toy gun. Police shot Huang in the back of the head at point-blank range. The Asian American Legal Defense and Education Fund brought a federal civil rights lawsuit on behalf of the family, which the city settled for $400,000. Brooklyn, New York, 1995.

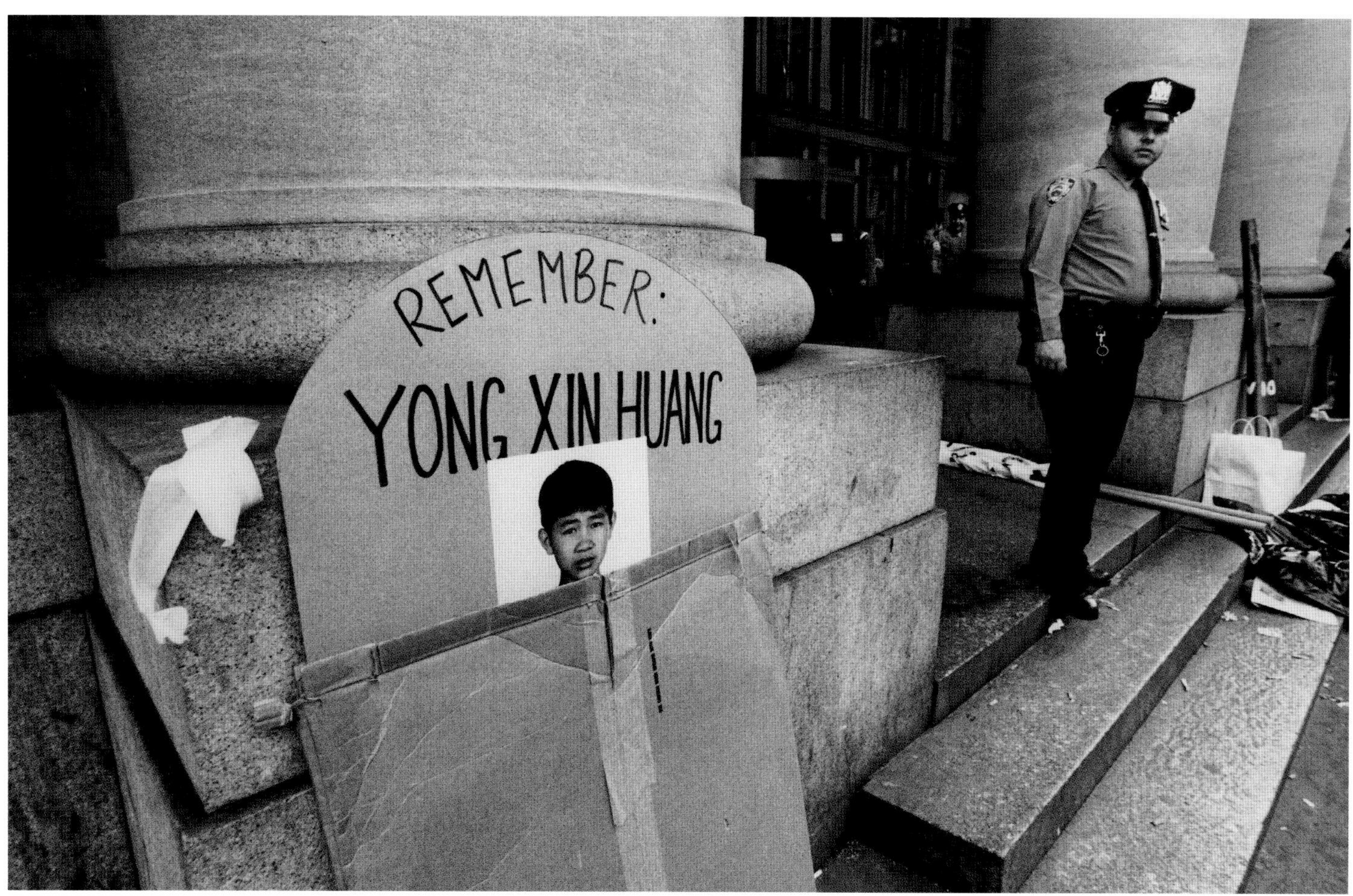

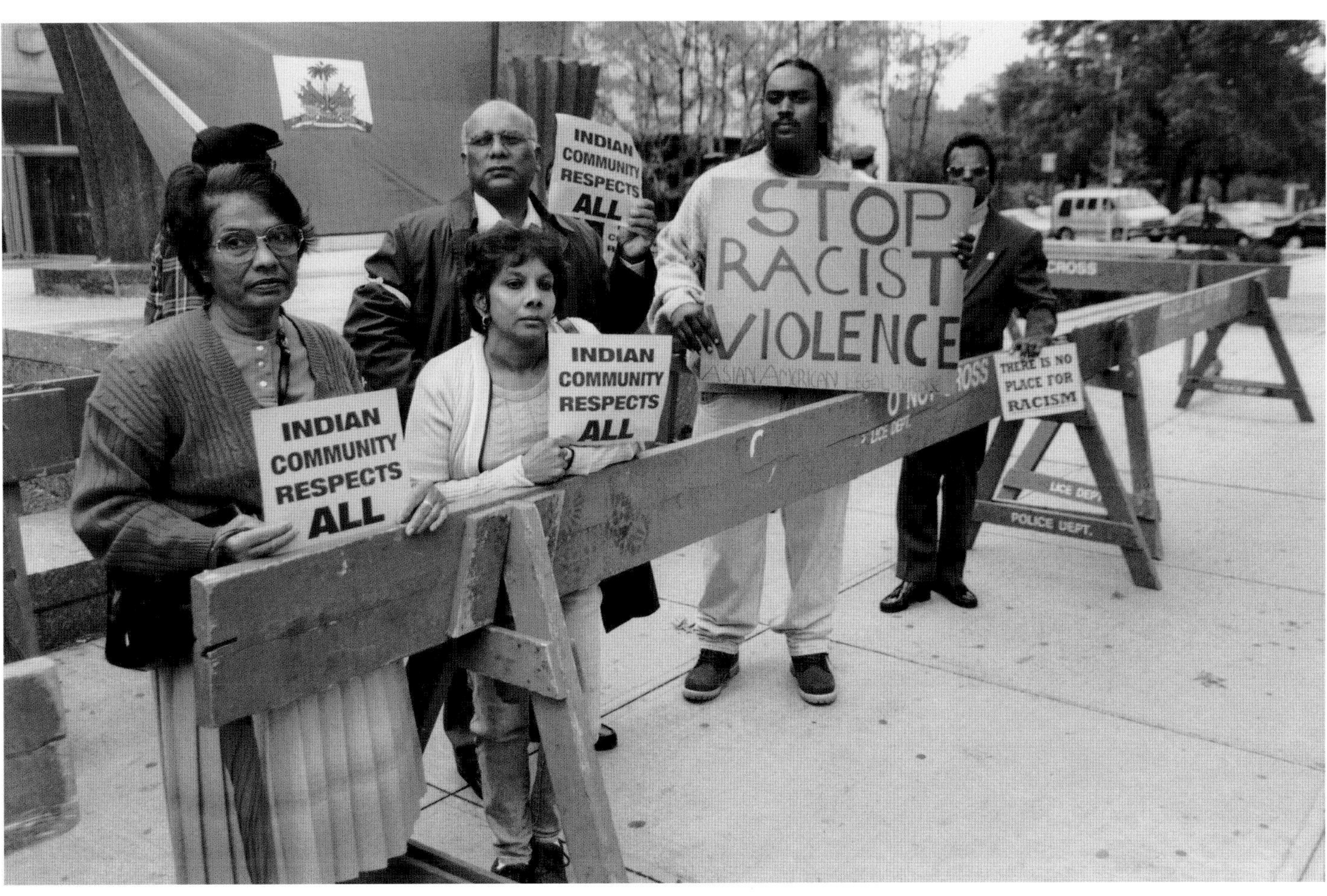

South Asian Americans joined in solidarity with the Black community to protest the police torture of Abner Louima, a Haitian immigrant. Brooklyn, New York, 1997.

“I work very hard and love to be independent”

LILY CHOW

Cabdriver and mother

In 1983, Asian Women United, an organization in Oakland, California, was compiling a book, With Silk Wings: Asian Women at Work. *The book's editors solicited profiles from Asian women around the country. Corky Lee took the photographs that accompanied the interviews with women in New York. His photograph of Lily Chow, a cabdriver, became iconic, but few know how she described her work in her own words.*

Some people think it's awful for a Chinese lady to drive a cab. They think ladies should stay home and take care of the kids. But I think it's great that I am a woman and can do the same work as a man.

I can be a cabdriver and also help at the family restaurant. During the slow periods, I pick up groceries for the restaurant. After I return the taxi to the company, I go to the restaurant, put on my apron, and work until eleven at night. My husband and kids can't understand why I'm so busy all the time. But I can't just sit around watching TV. I think Chinese women are very strong and smart and can do anything. I work very hard and love to be independent.

Do cabdrivers make a lot of money? Yes and no. You have to be at the right place at the right time. If you take someone to the airport and pick up a passenger coming back to Manhattan, when traffic isn't congested, you can make forty dollars an hour. But another hour you might make five or seven dollars. I keep 49 percent of the fares, and the boss gets the rest.

I've been driving a cab for seven years now. Most drivers won't drive at night, but I do. It can be dangerous. Sometimes passengers won't pay. Once I chased a passenger into his apartment building after he jumped out of my cab. I told him, “I don't need a knife. I don't need a gun. I know kung fu, so don't let me see you again!”

I'm never really scared, but I am careful. I'm already ready to face the situation.

Mrs. Lily Chow, mother of eight children and the first Chinese woman to drive a taxi in New York. New York, 1982.

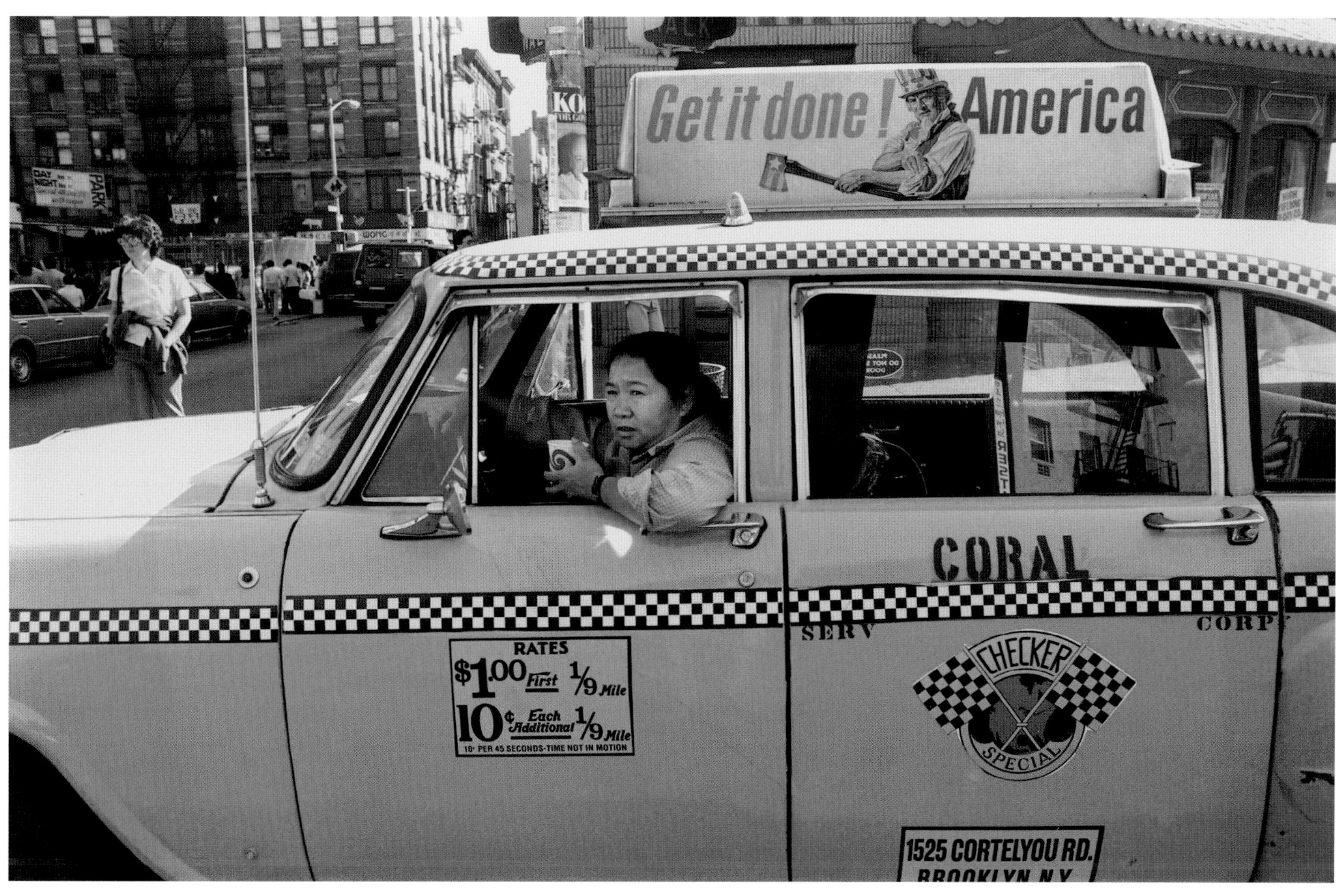

Workers picketing Silver Palace, one of Chinatown's largest banquet halls, in a protest organized by the Chinese Staff and Workers Association to oppose substandard wages and the theft of their tips by the employer. New York, 1980.

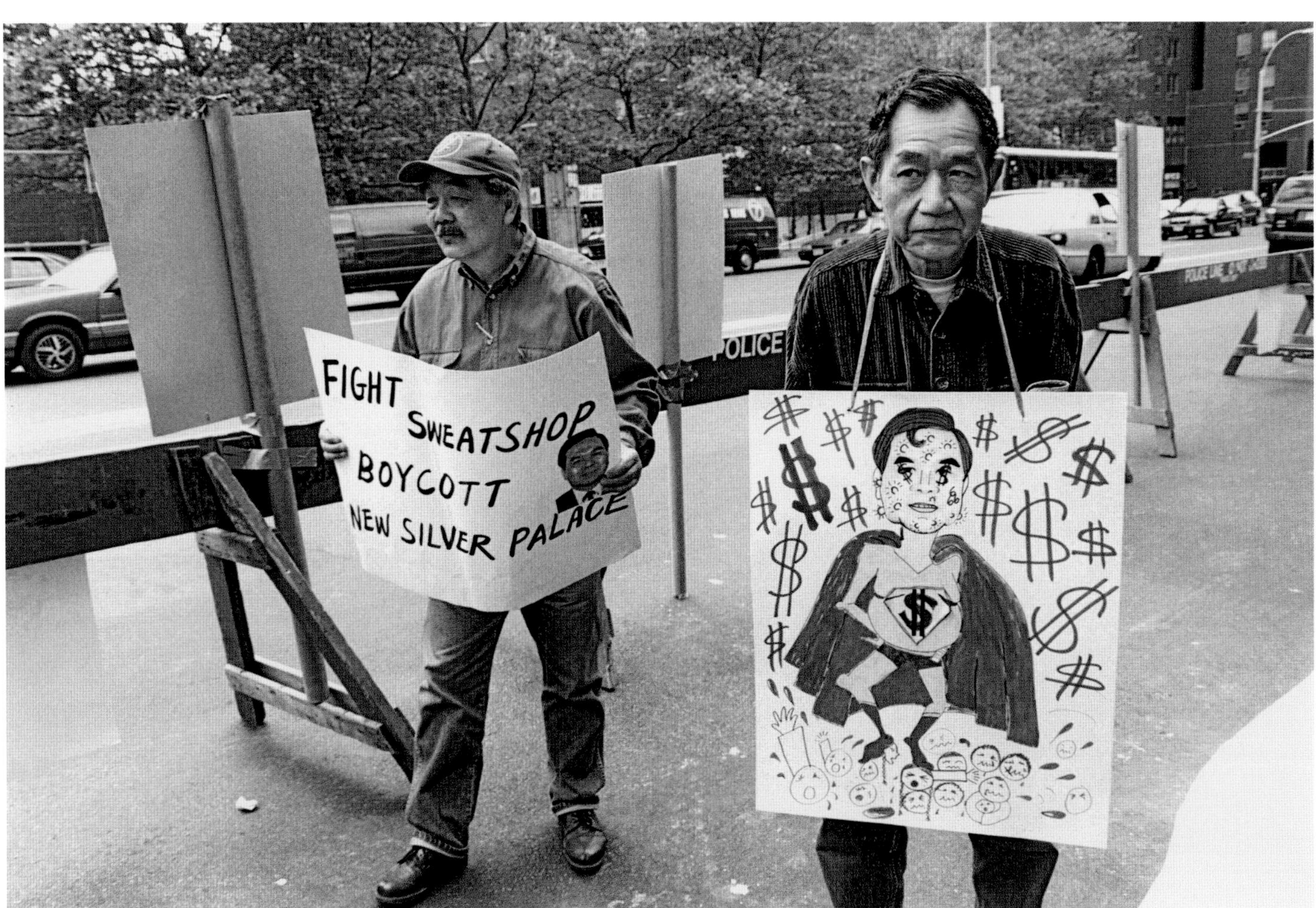

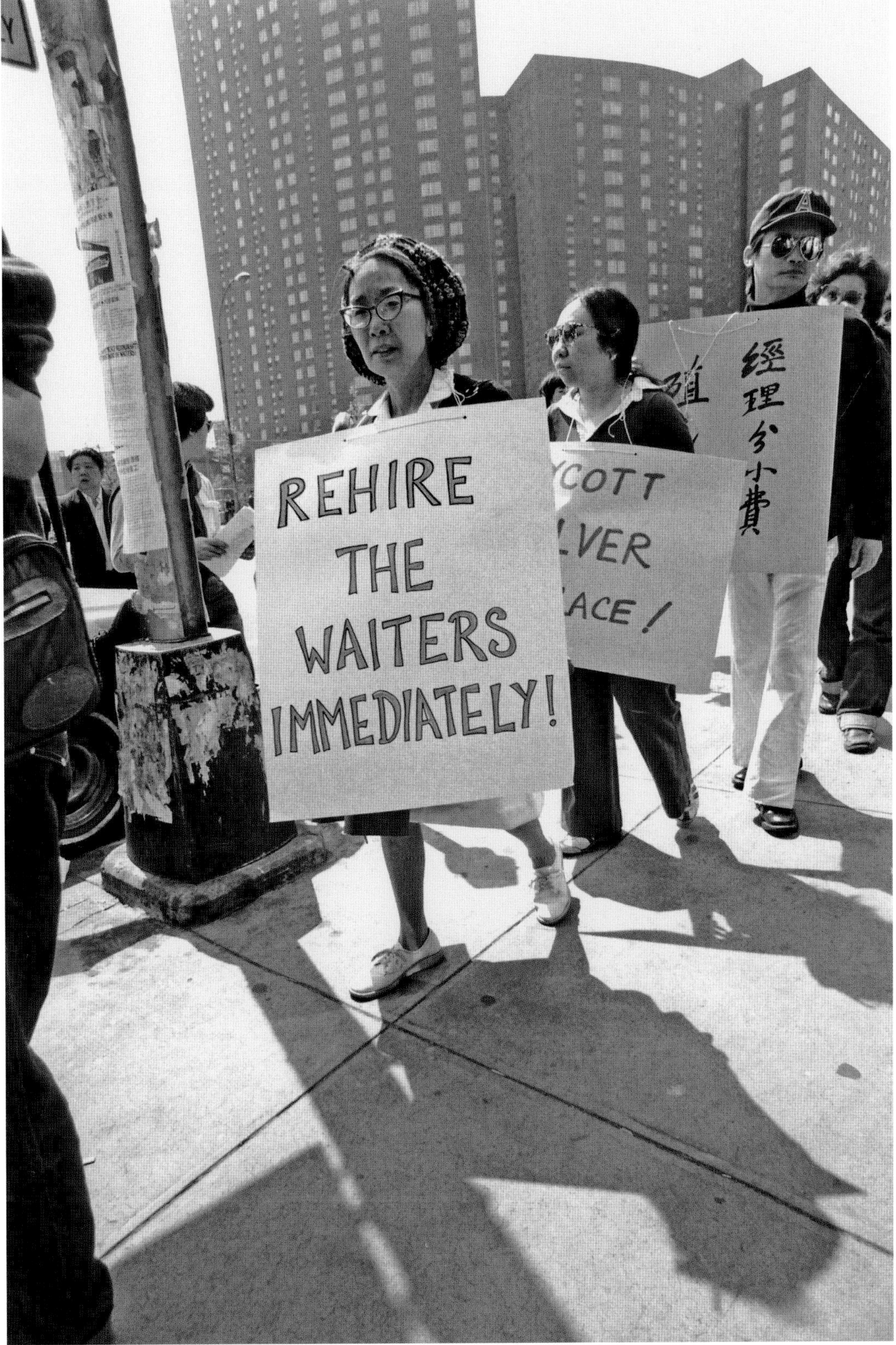

The Japanese American civil rights leader Yuri Kochiyama (1921–2014), along with activists Leslee Inaba Wong and GT Wong, marched with Silver Palace workers. The sign in Chinese reads, "Silver Palace steals tips." This photograph was acquired by the National Portrait Gallery of the Smithsonian Institution. New York, 1980.

In the summer of 1982, Chinatown's garment workers went on strike after their employers refused to sign their contract with the International Ladies Garment Workers Union. Chinatown shop owners assumed that the workers, Chinese immigrant women, would accept an inferior contract. But years of organizing had built a culture of union solidarity, in which shop workers were elected to union leadership positions and the union organized English and citizenship classes and a variety of social and cultural events. When Local 23-25 of the ILGWU called a strike on June 24, nearly 20,000 workers walked out of the factories and into the streets and held a rally in Columbus Park (*right*), the largest in the history of the union and in Chinatown. Their rallying cry was "We are One!" Almost immediately some of the employers agreed to sign the contract, and within a few weeks, the others fell into line. New York, 1982.

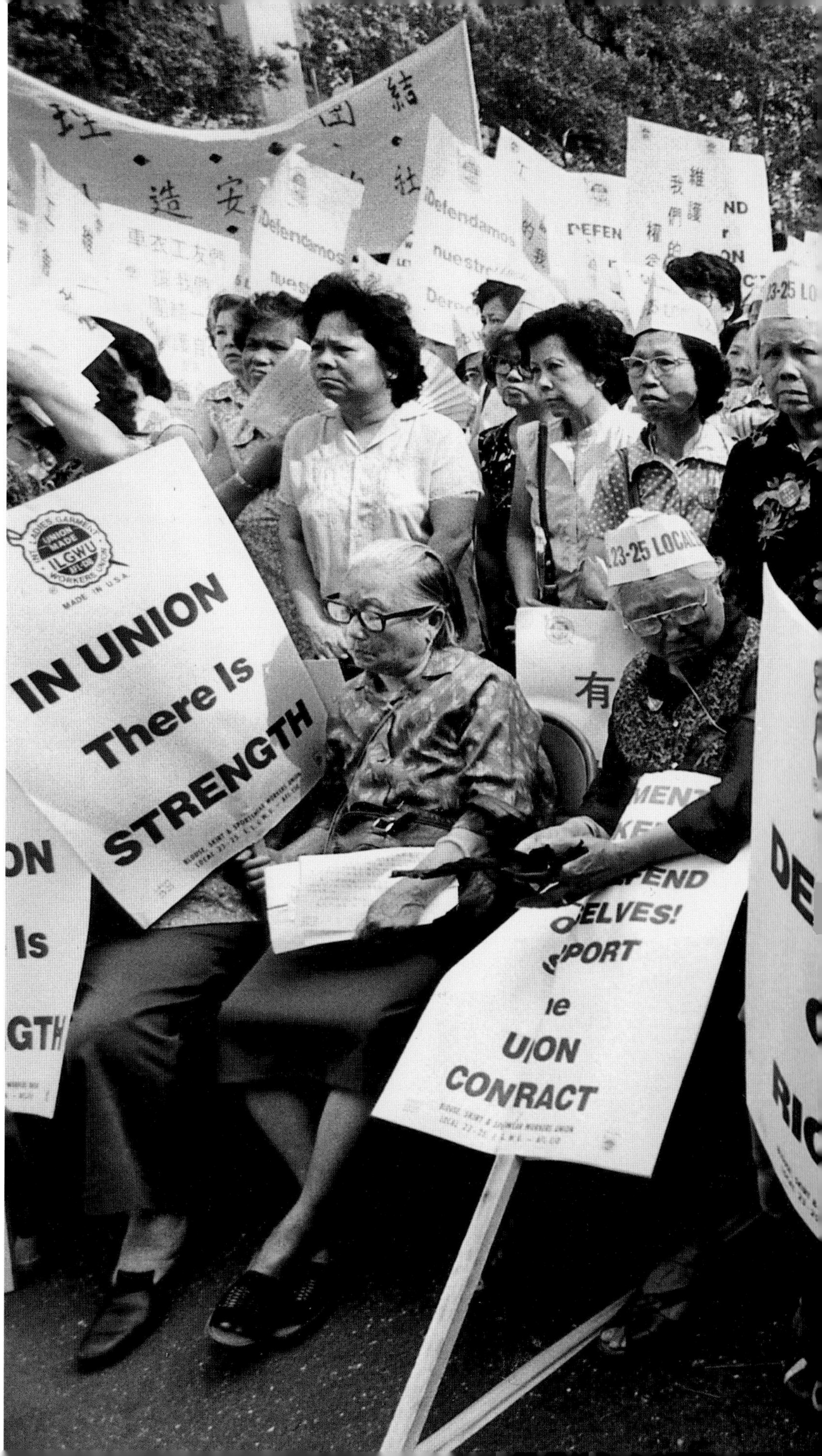

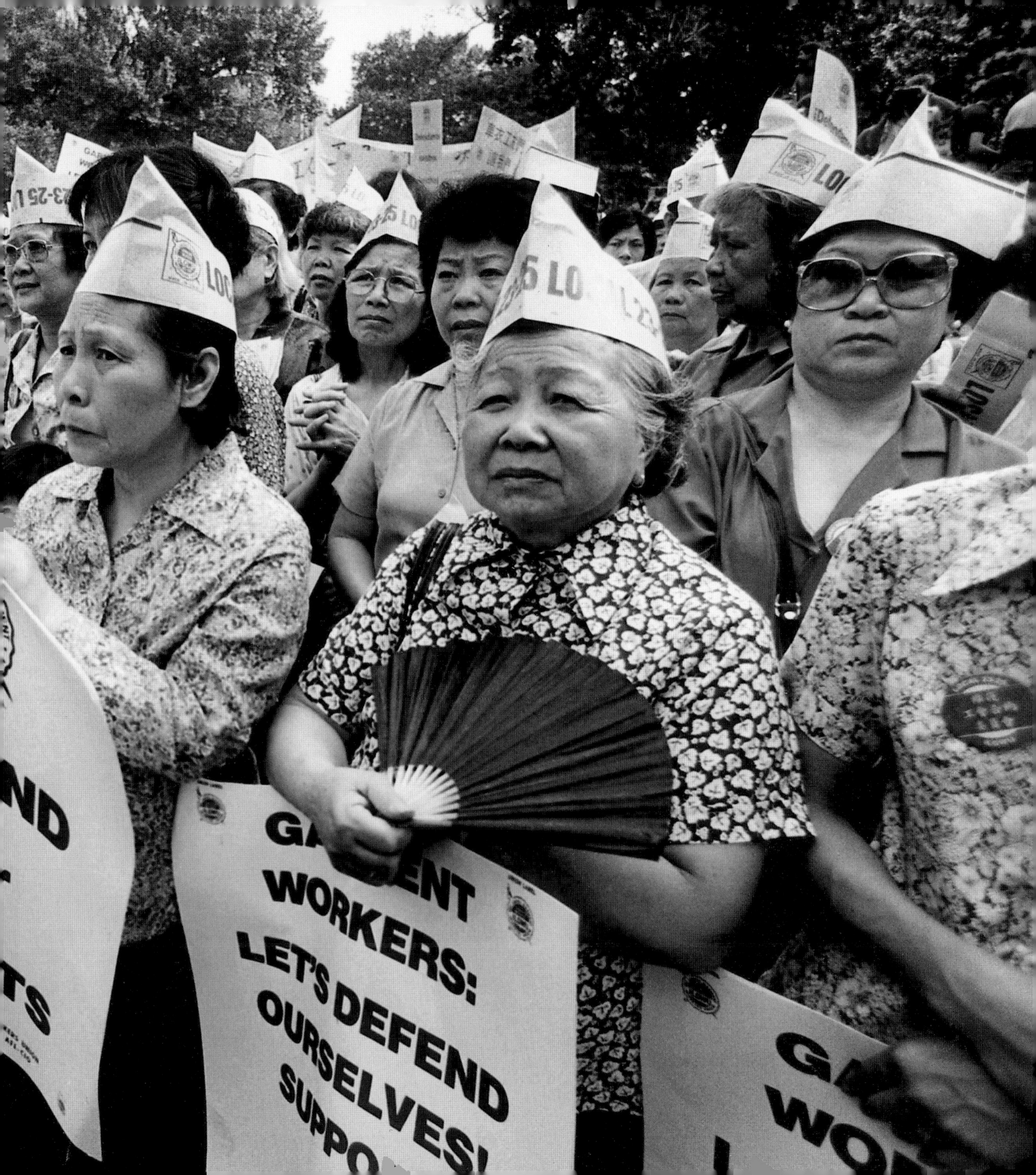
WORKERS:
LET'S DEFEND
OURSELVES!

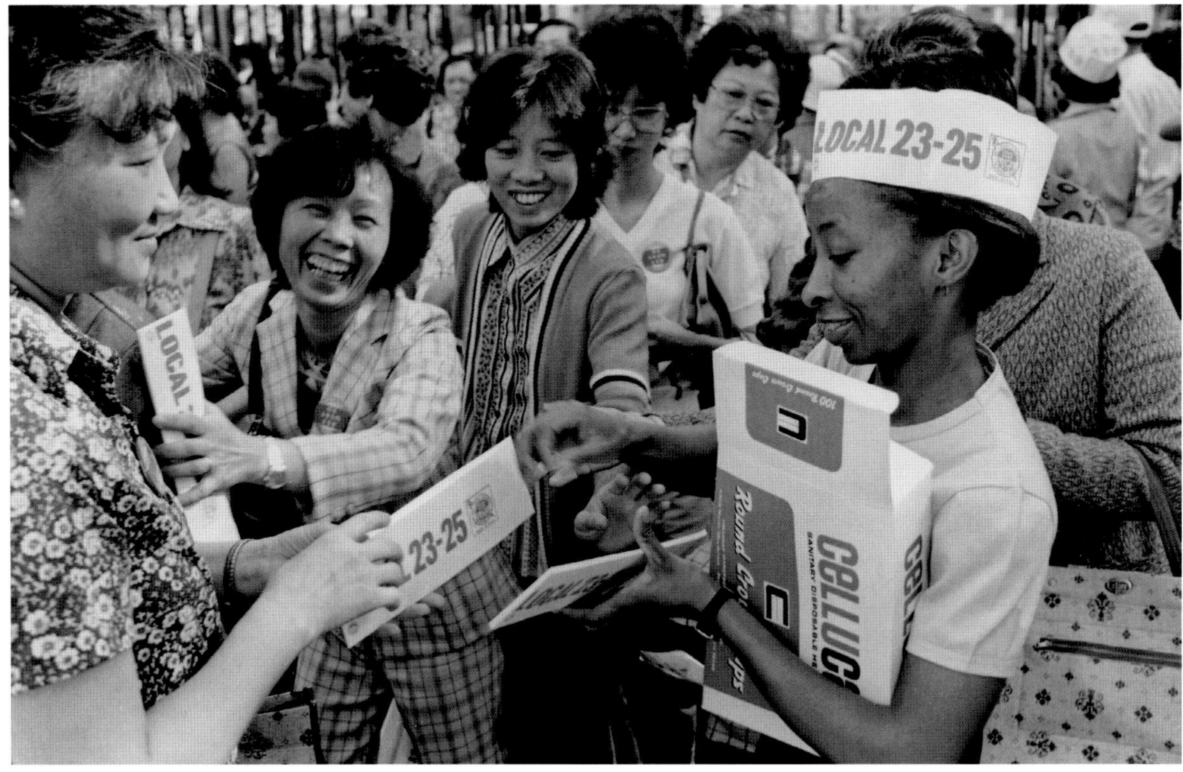

Workers gather at Columbus Park for a union rally. New York, 1982.

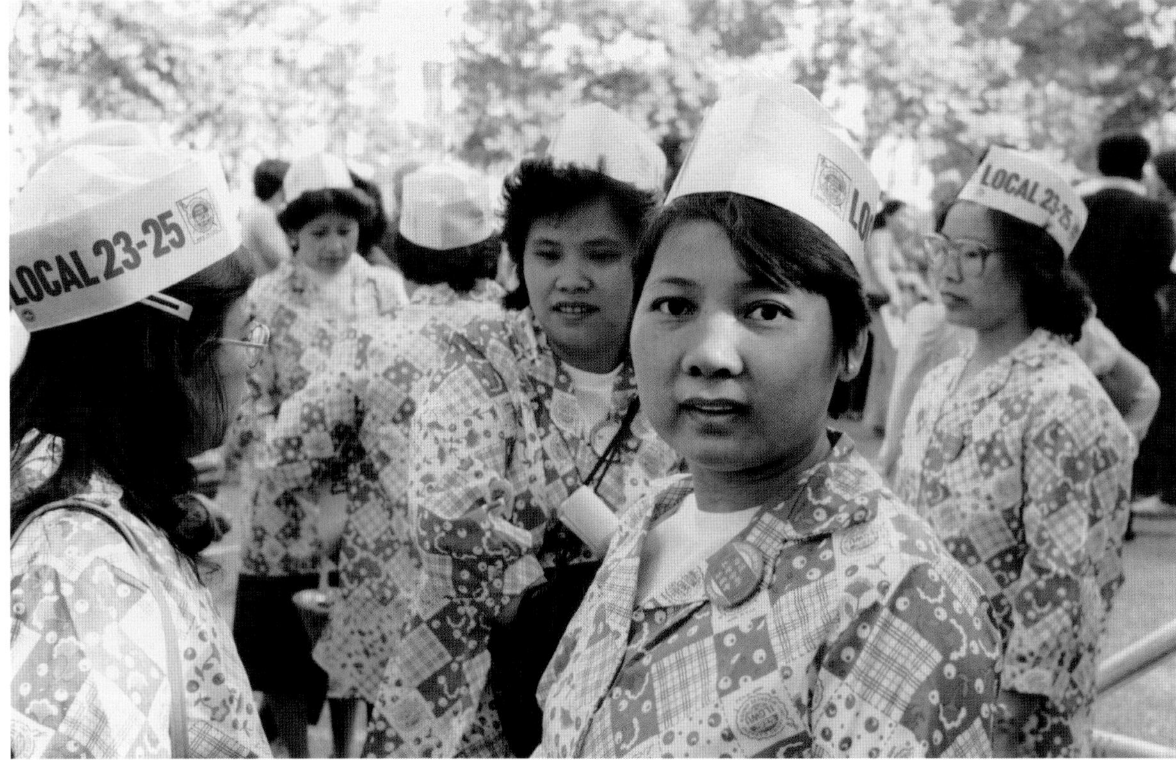

Striking workers wear hats and blouses with the union's name and logo. New York, 1982.

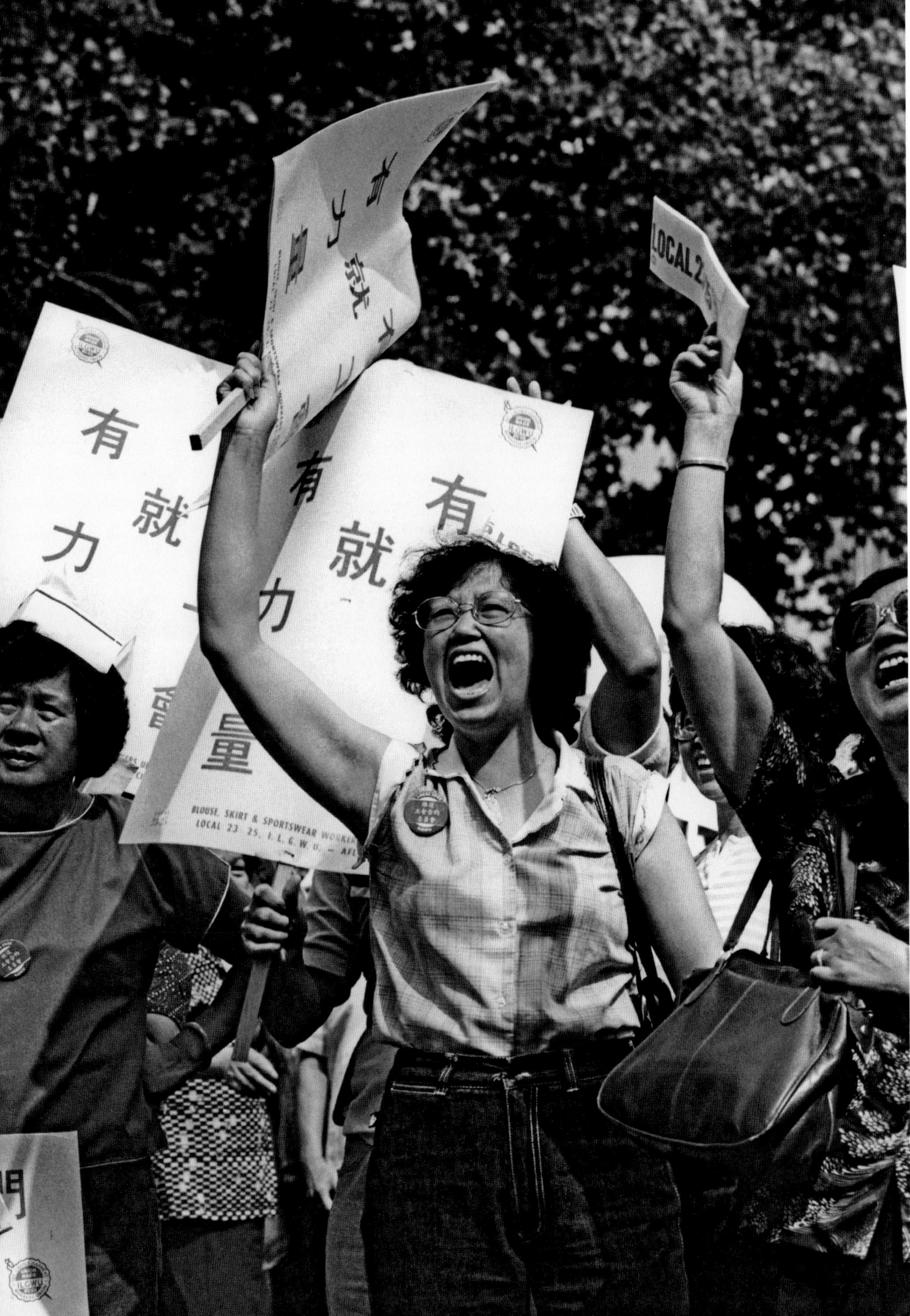

Signs in Chinese read, "In unity there is strength." New York, 1982.

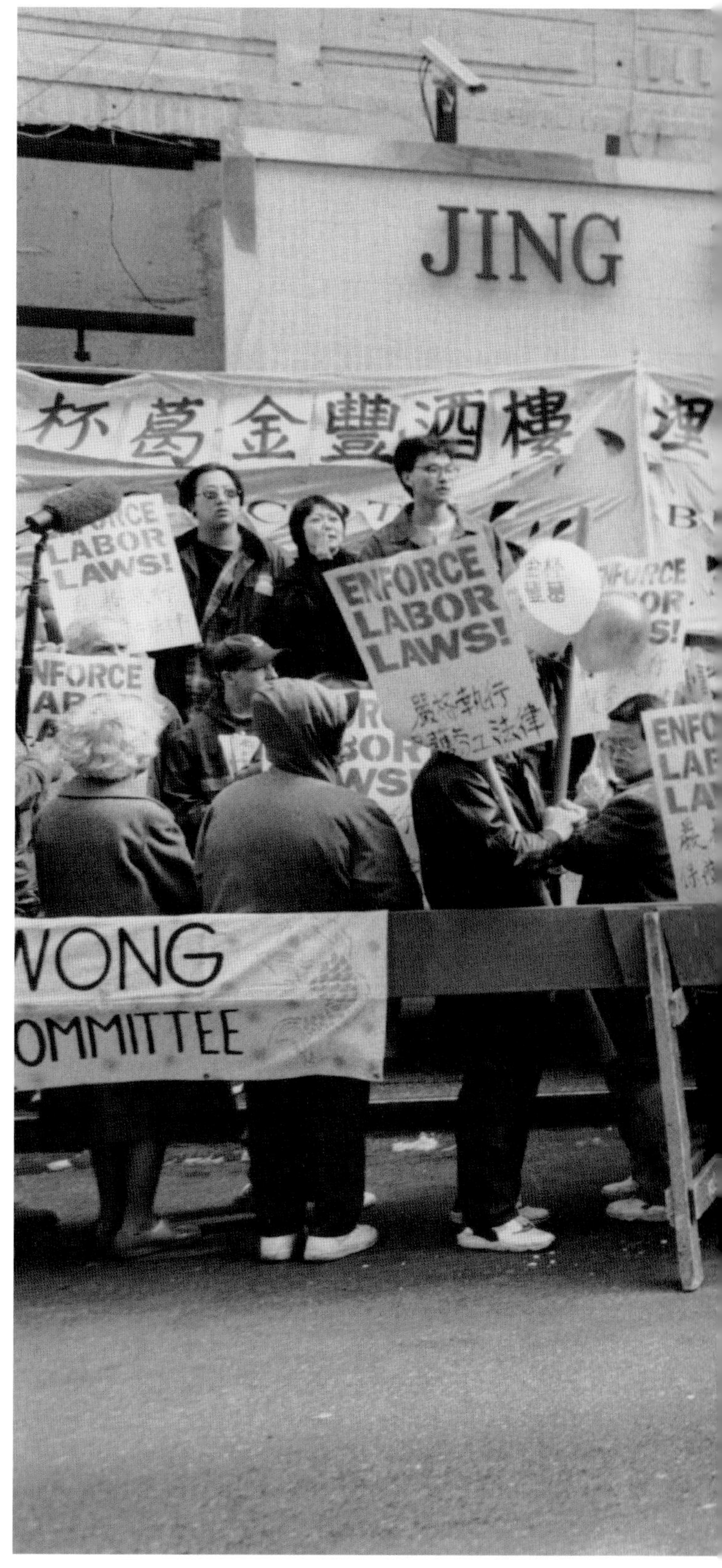

In 1995 restaurant workers and their supporters waged a campaign against Jing Fong restaurant for paying its workers a subminimum wage and keeping their tips. The Chinese Staff and Workers Association organized the protest, which included a petition of five thousand signatures that urged the city government to enforce labor laws in Chinatown. In 1997 the workers won a $1.1 million settlement for back wages and tips, in two suits brought by the Asian American Legal Defense and Education Fund and the New York State attorney general. New York, 1995.

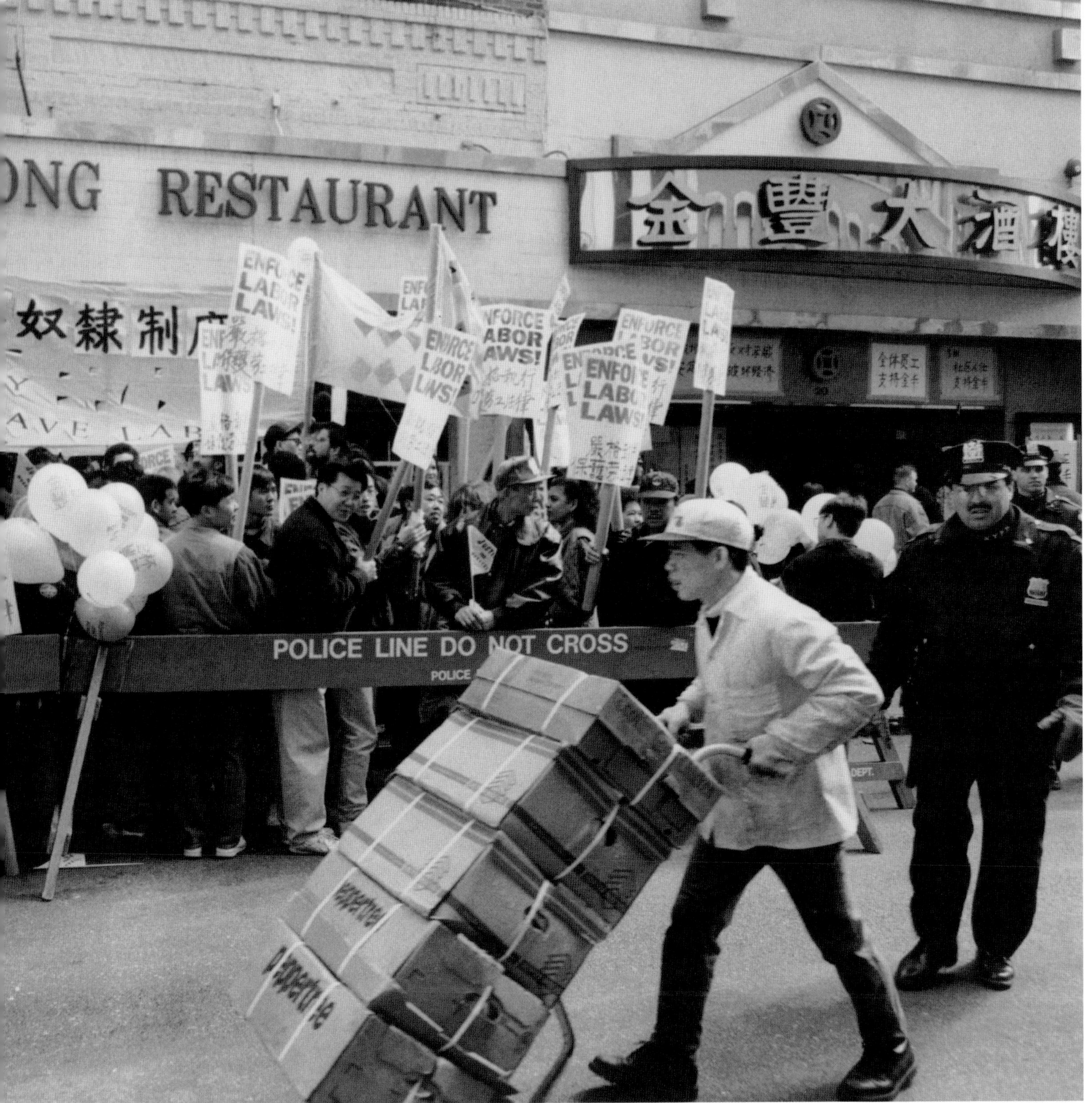
ONG RESTAURANT
金豐大酒樓
奴隸制
ENFORCE LABOR LAWS!
ENFORCE LABOR LAWS!
ENFORCE LABOR LAWS!
POLICE LINE DO NOT CROSS

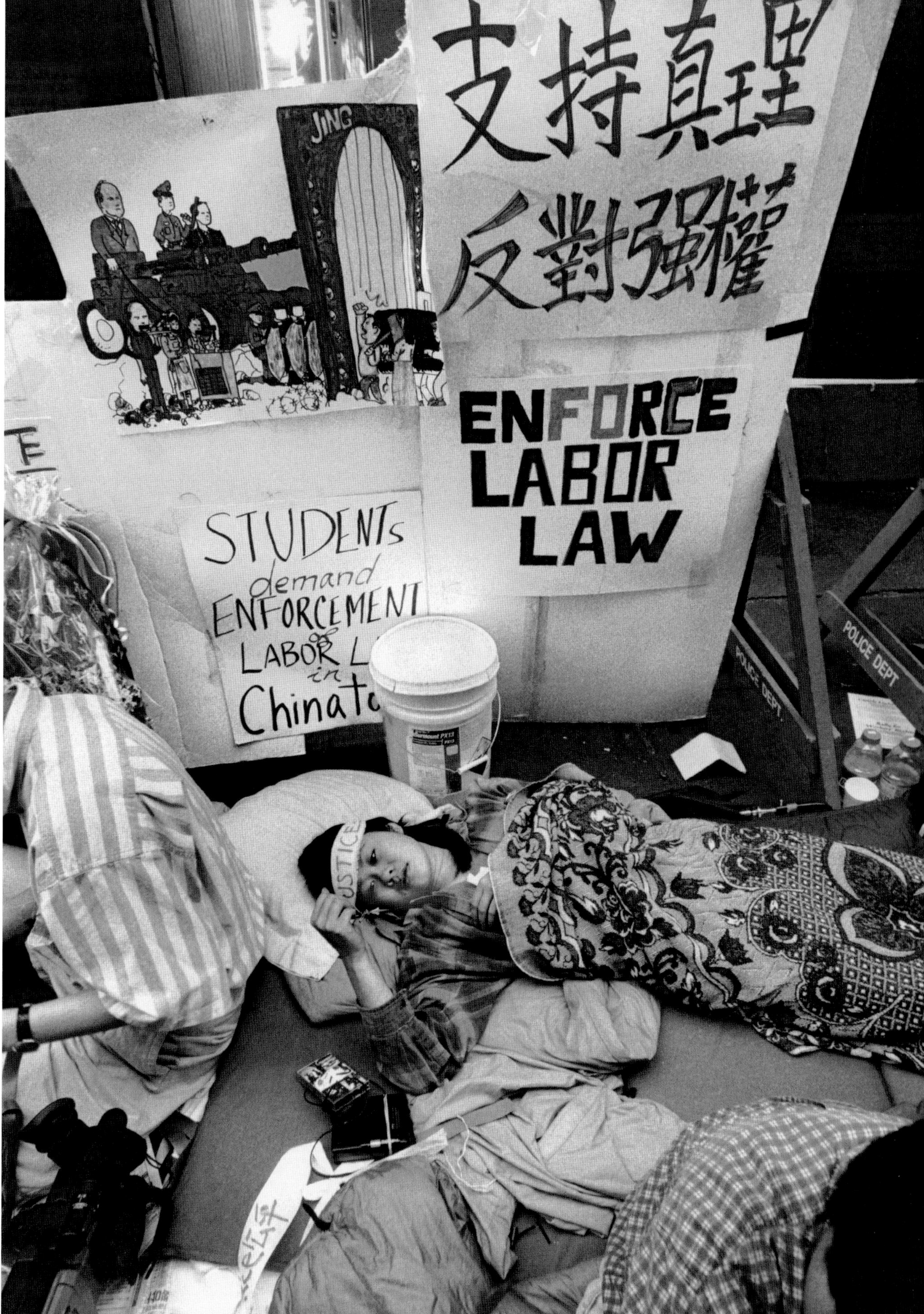

Students staged a weeklong hunger strike to bring attention to Jing Fong's theft of workers' wages and tips. New York, 1995.

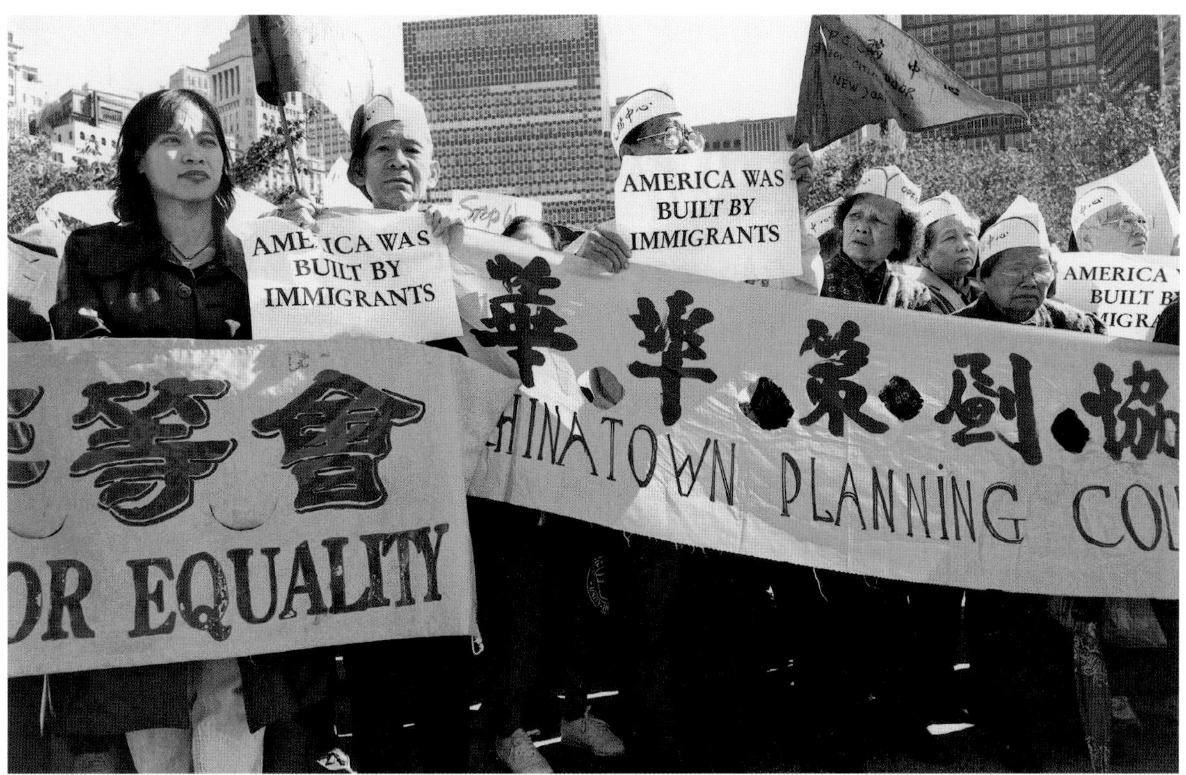

Asian Americans for Equality and the Chinatown Planning Council were among the Chinatown community organizations calling for immigration rights at Castle Clinton, in Lower Manhattan, across from the Statue of Liberty. New York, 1996.

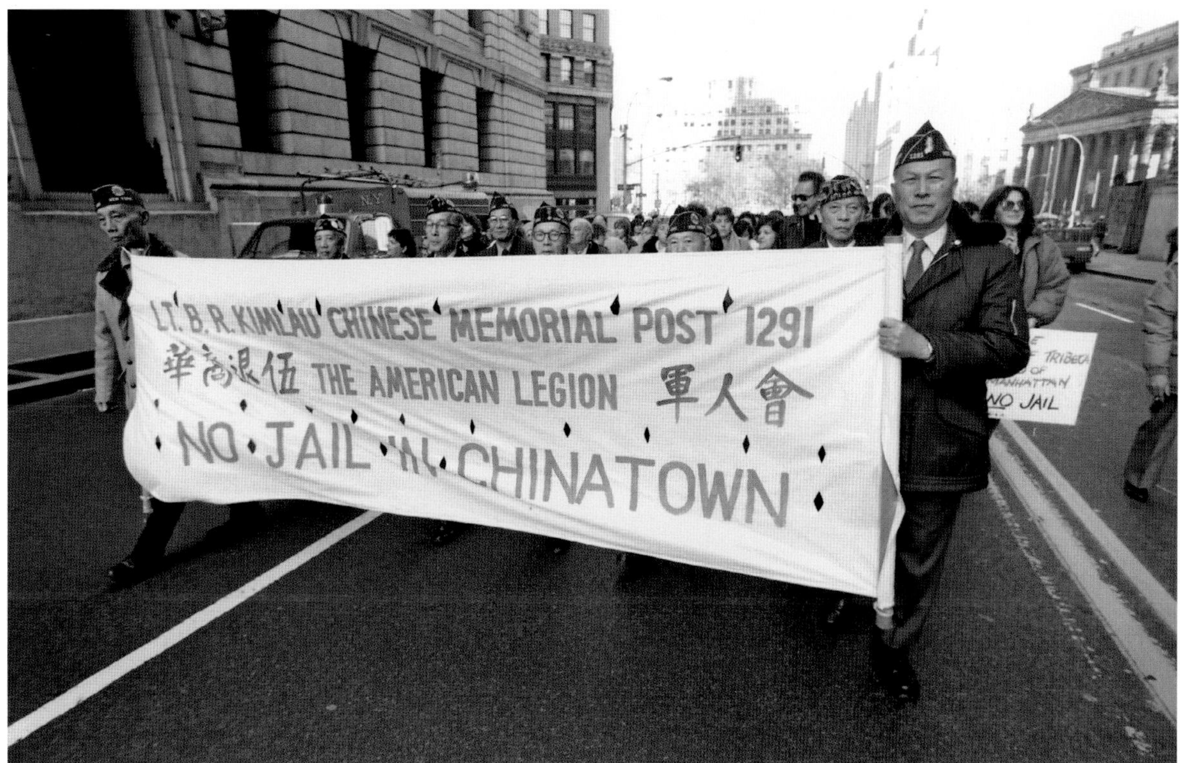

In 1982, when New York City proposed building a jail on the northern border of Chinatown, twelve thousand people marched from Chinatown to city hall in protest. Chinese American veterans, members of the American Legion's Lt. B. R. Kimlau Chinese Memorial Post 1291, took part. Mass opposition led the city to suspend the plan, but the controversial proposal reappeared in 2019. New York, November 1982.

When the U.S. government decided to build a new federal building at Foley Square in Lower Manhattan, the Chinese Staff and Workers Association demanded jobs for Chinese construction workers. As a result of the campaign, thirteen Chinese were hired for the site. New York, 1992.

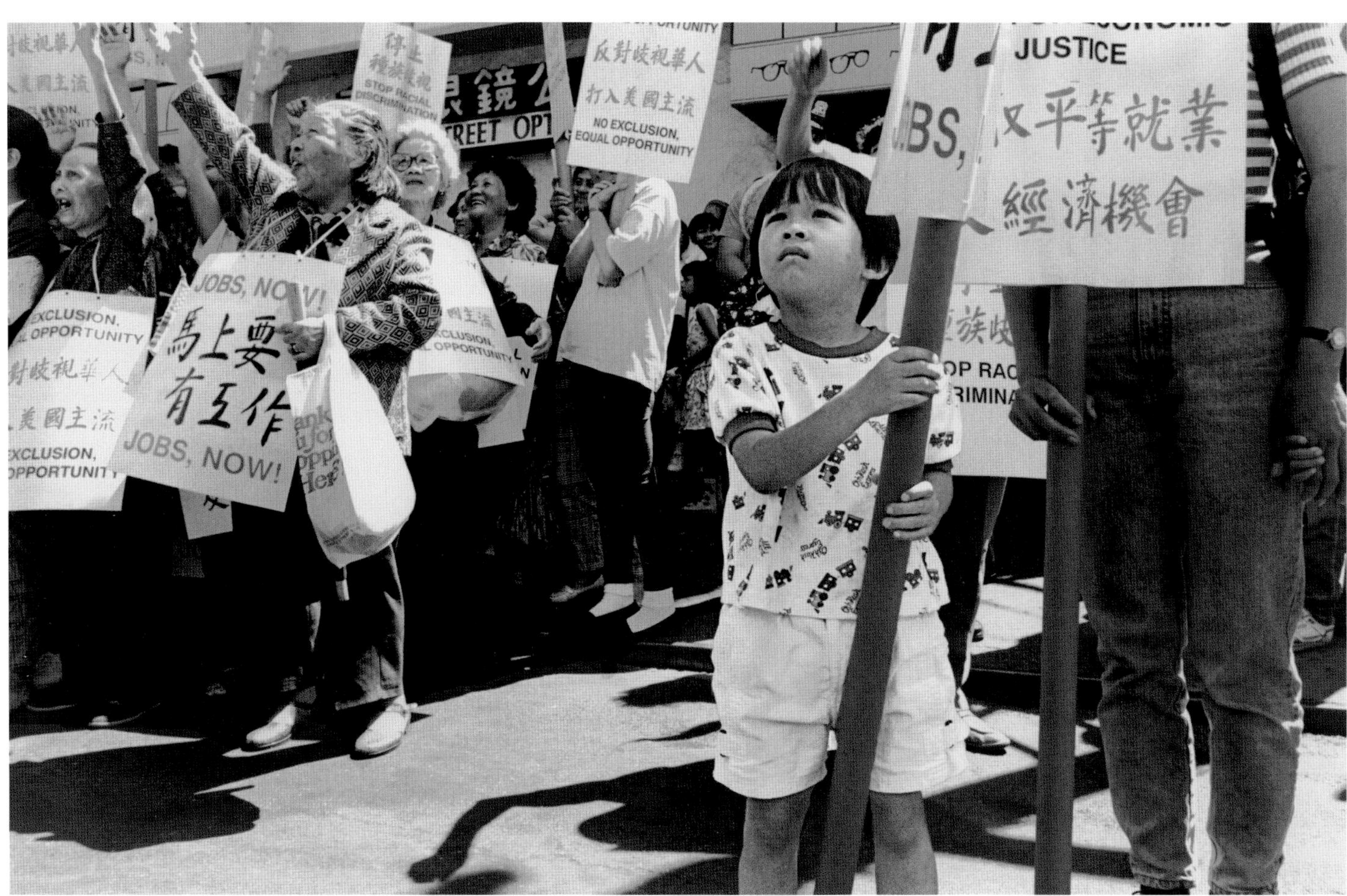

In 1997 community demonstrators called for one floor of the old police building on Centre Street, near Chinatown, to be used for a new senior citizens' center. Despite the dire need and support from Chinatown organizations, the city's Department for the Aging, and local elected officials, the landmark building remained reserved for luxury apartments. New York, 1997.

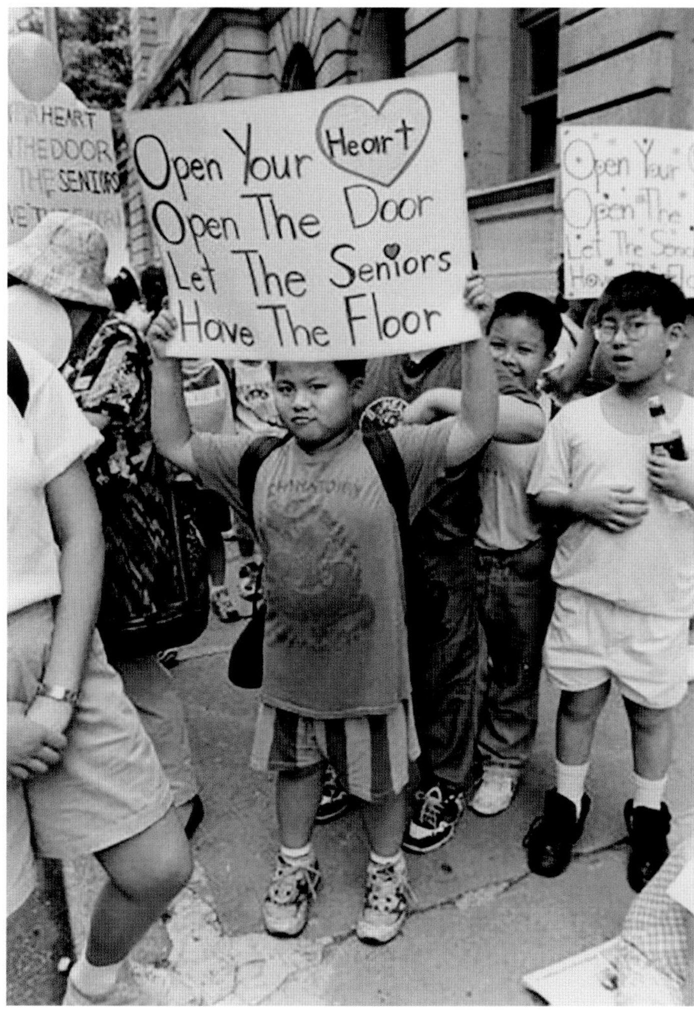

At the Chinatown Health Clinic. New York, circa 1984.

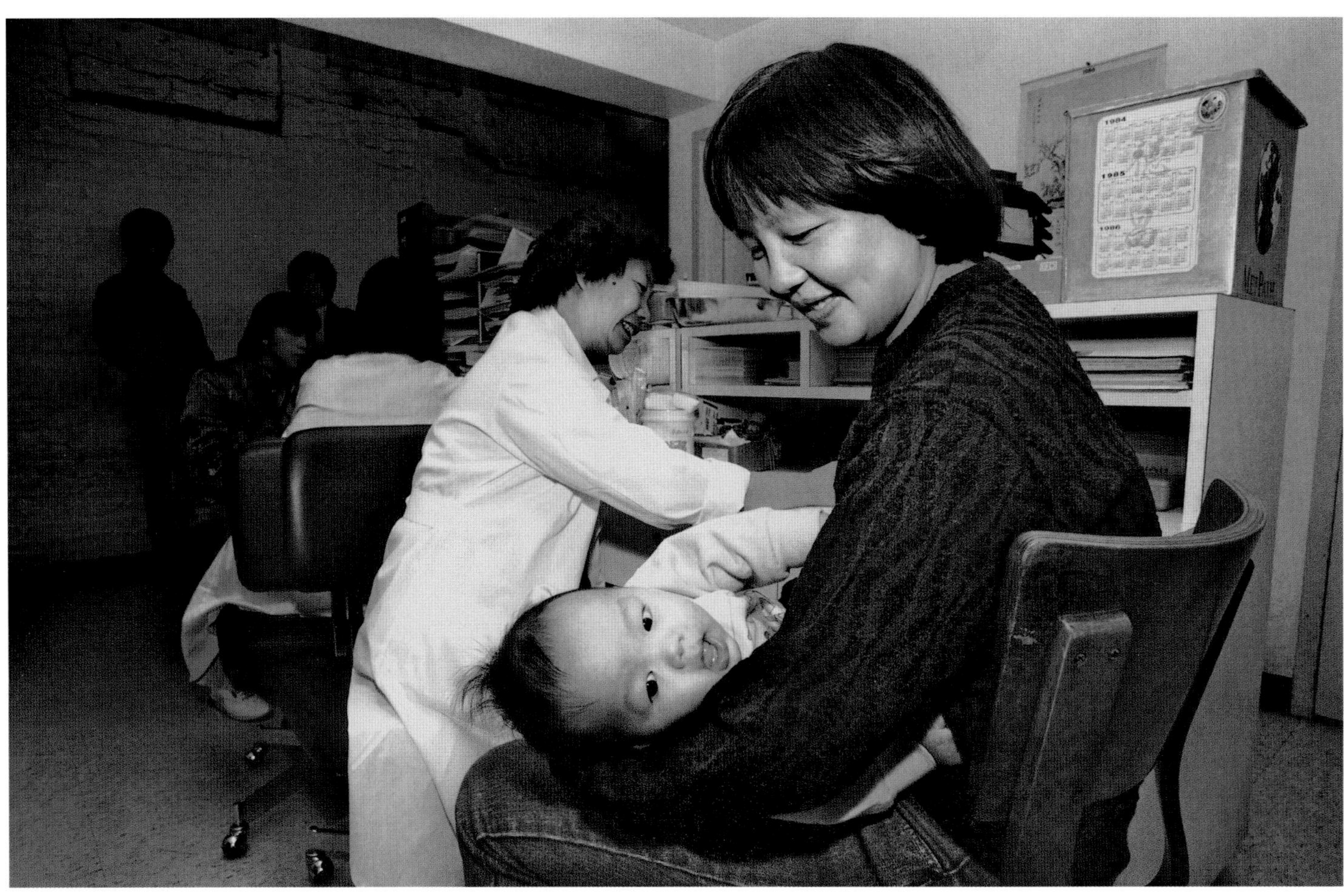

Backstage at the China Pavilion, Queens Festival. Flushing Meadows, Queens, New York, 1988.

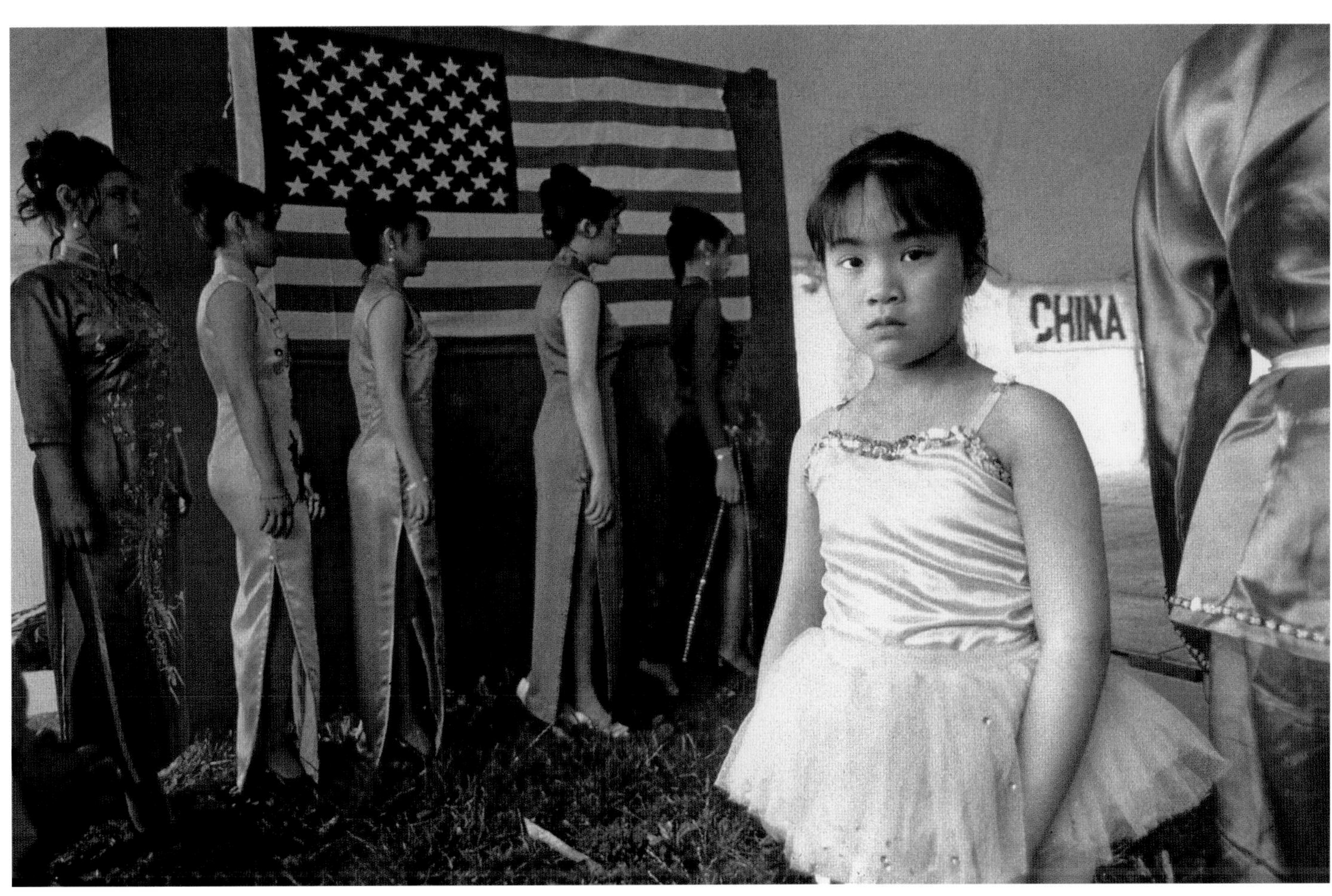

Dee Hamaguchi, a 105-pound boxer, forced the New York Golden Gloves to admit women competitors. New York, 1995.

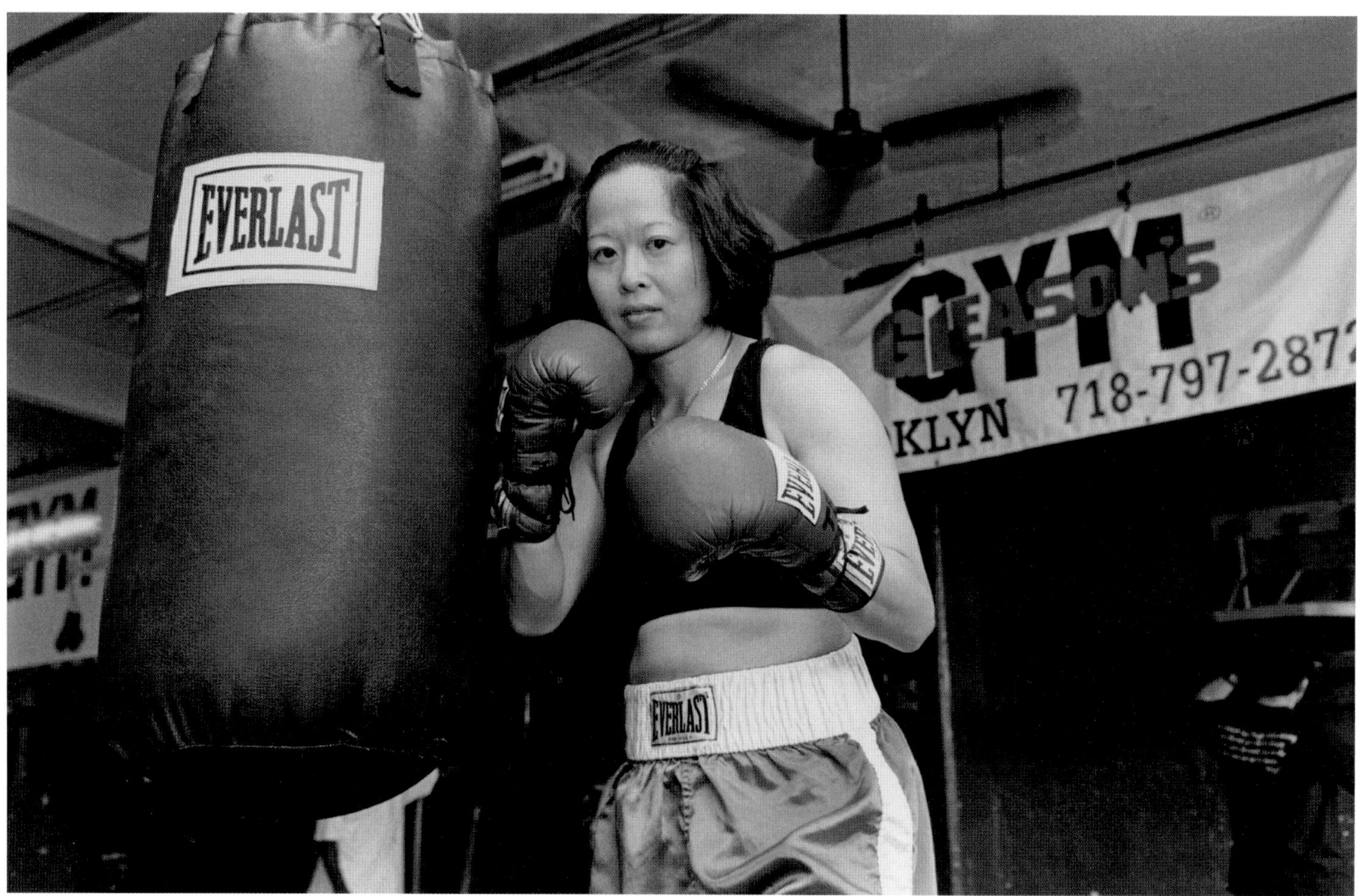

In the 1990s, Jeannette Lee, a Korean American pool shark known as the Black Widow, was ranked the world's number one female billiards player. New York, 1990s.

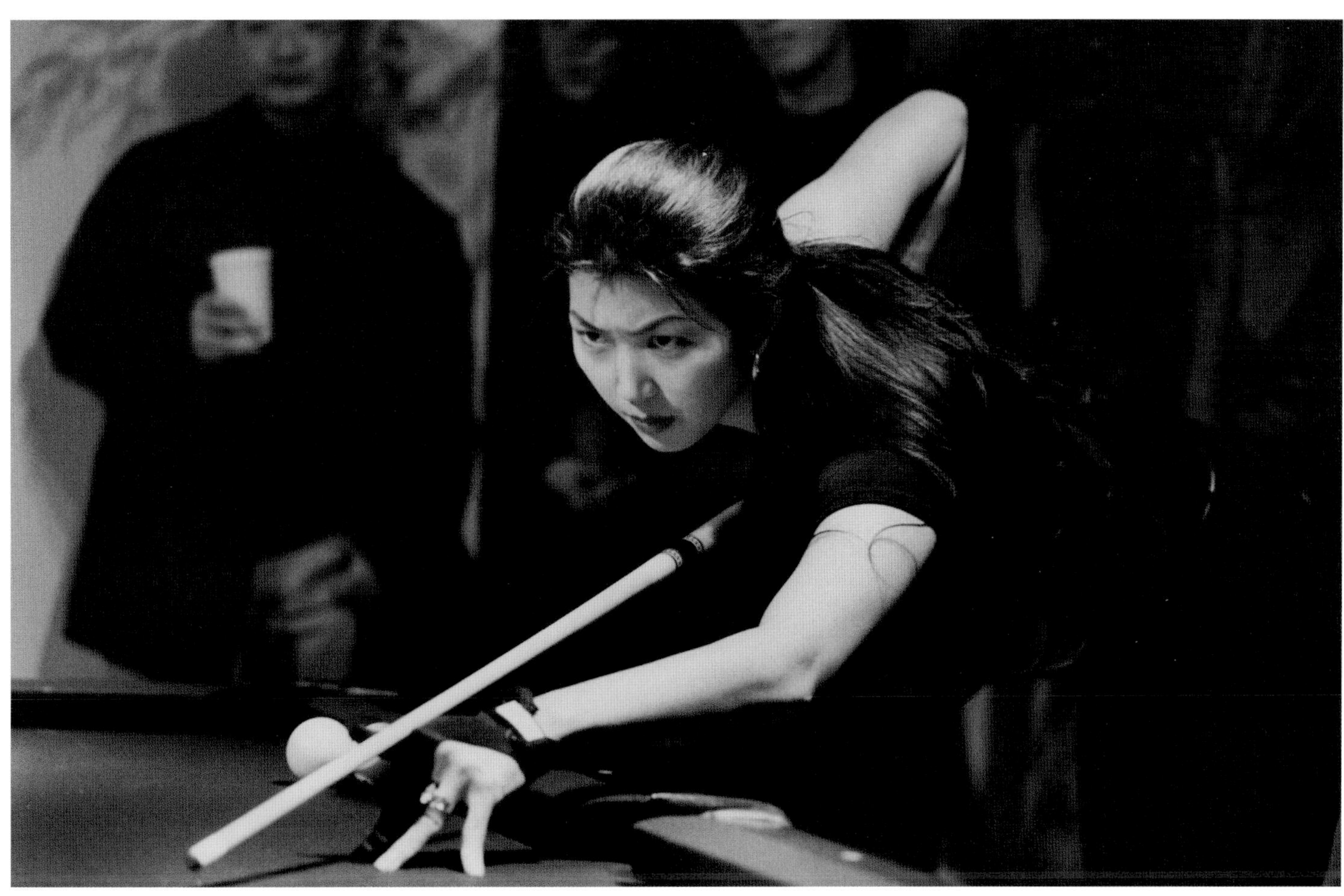

Margaret Dea Lee (Corky's wife) and her mother, Yun Yee Dea, in the Dea family's laundry in the Chelsea neighborhood of Manhattan. New York, 1999.

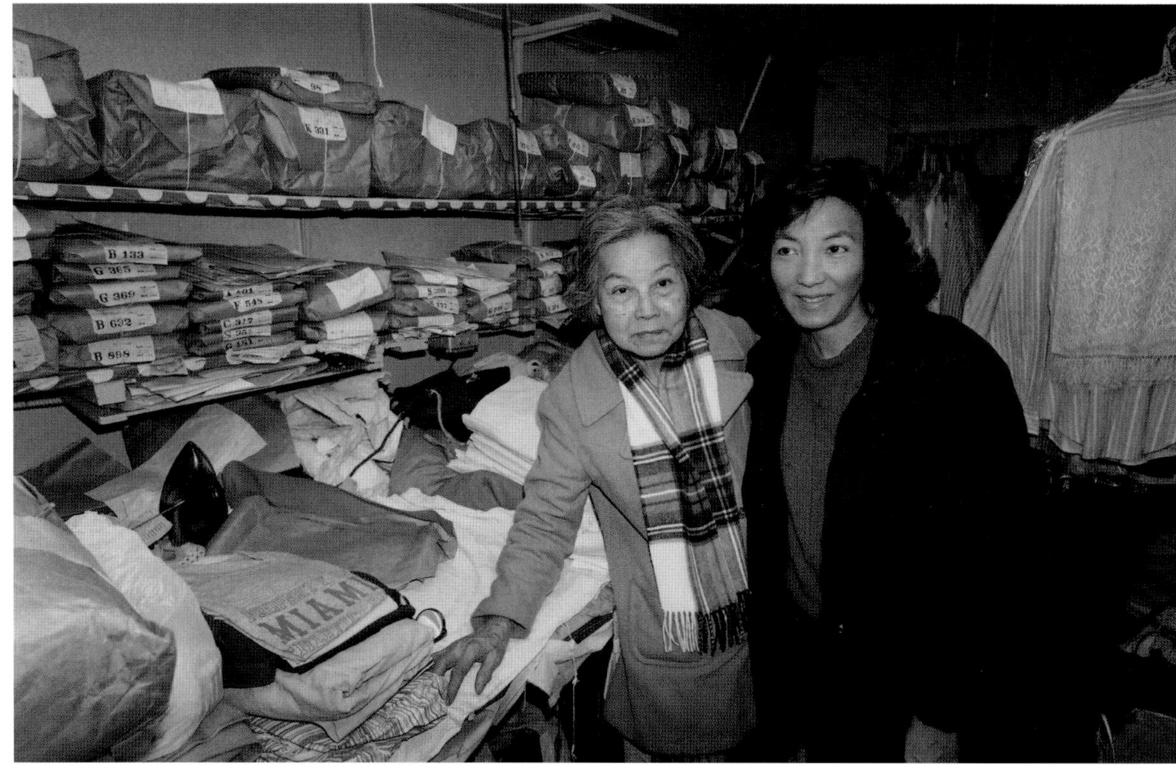

Laundry ready for pick up at the Dea's laundry. New York, 1999.

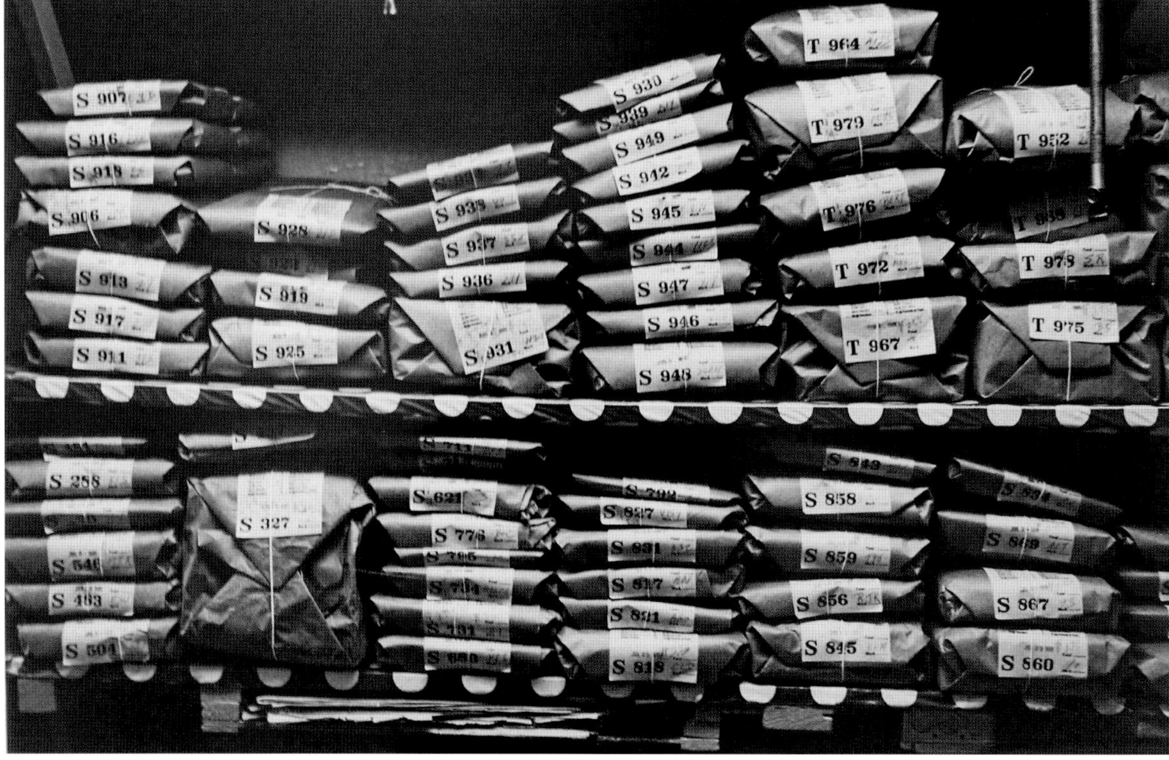

Young women taking a break in the girls room during a high school dance at the Chinese Methodist Church in Chinatown. Although none were smokers, Corky asked them to pose with a cigarette. From left: Jean Hom-Weng, Helen Lo-Lee, and Christine Chan-Yip. New York, 1987.

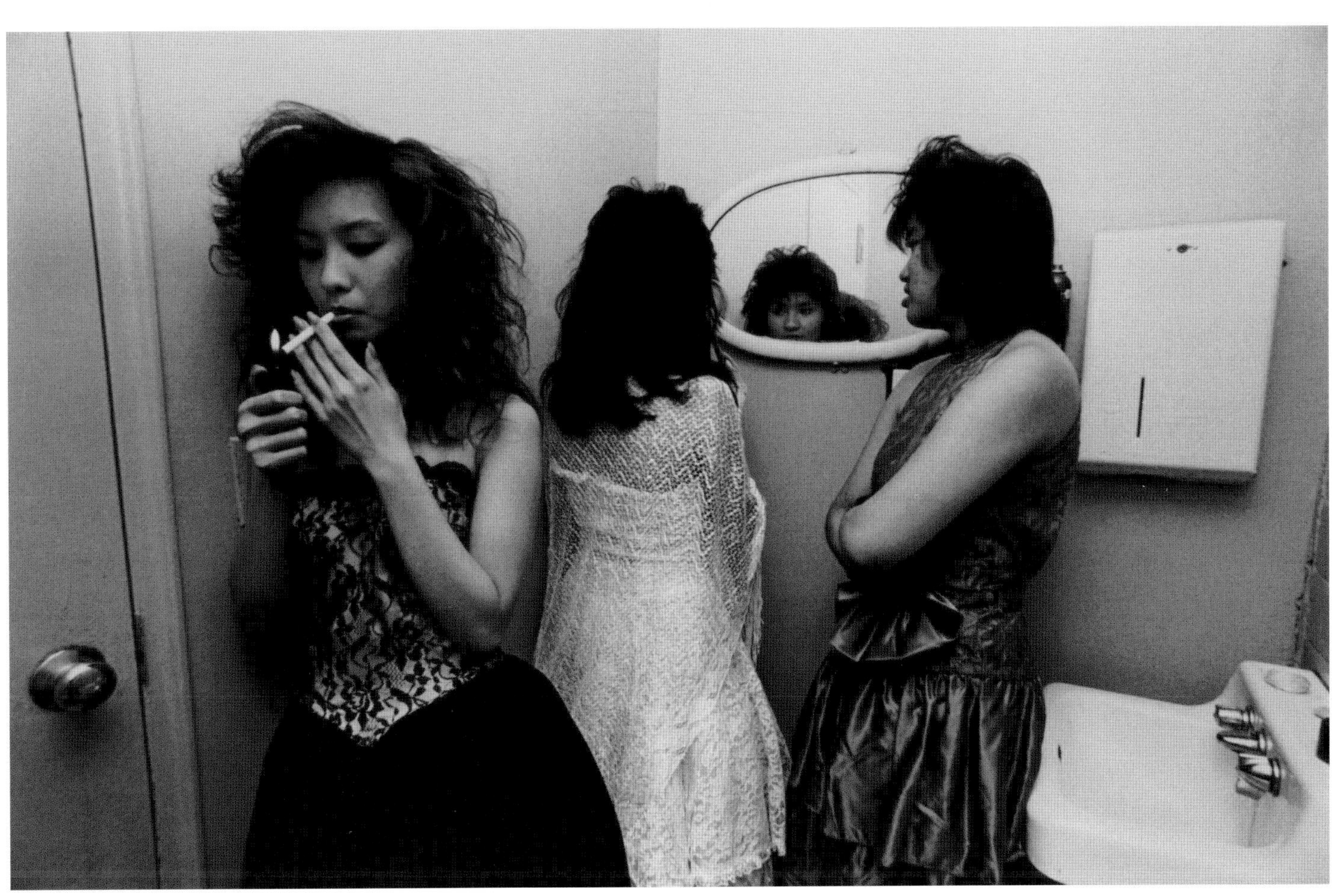

Filipina fashion designer Josie Natori.
New York, 1990s.

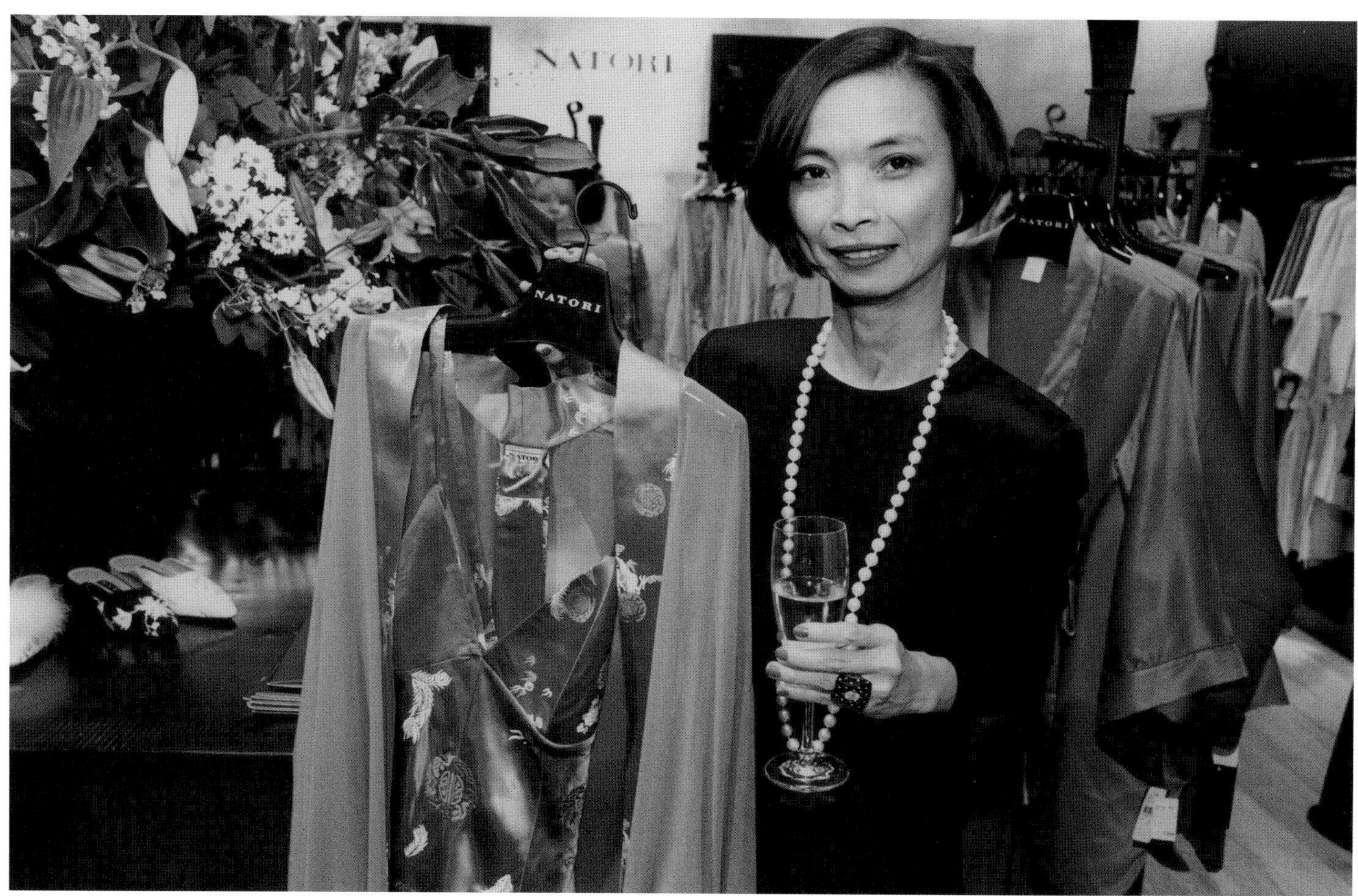

A parade celebrates Great Britain's return of Hong Kong to China. New York, 1997.

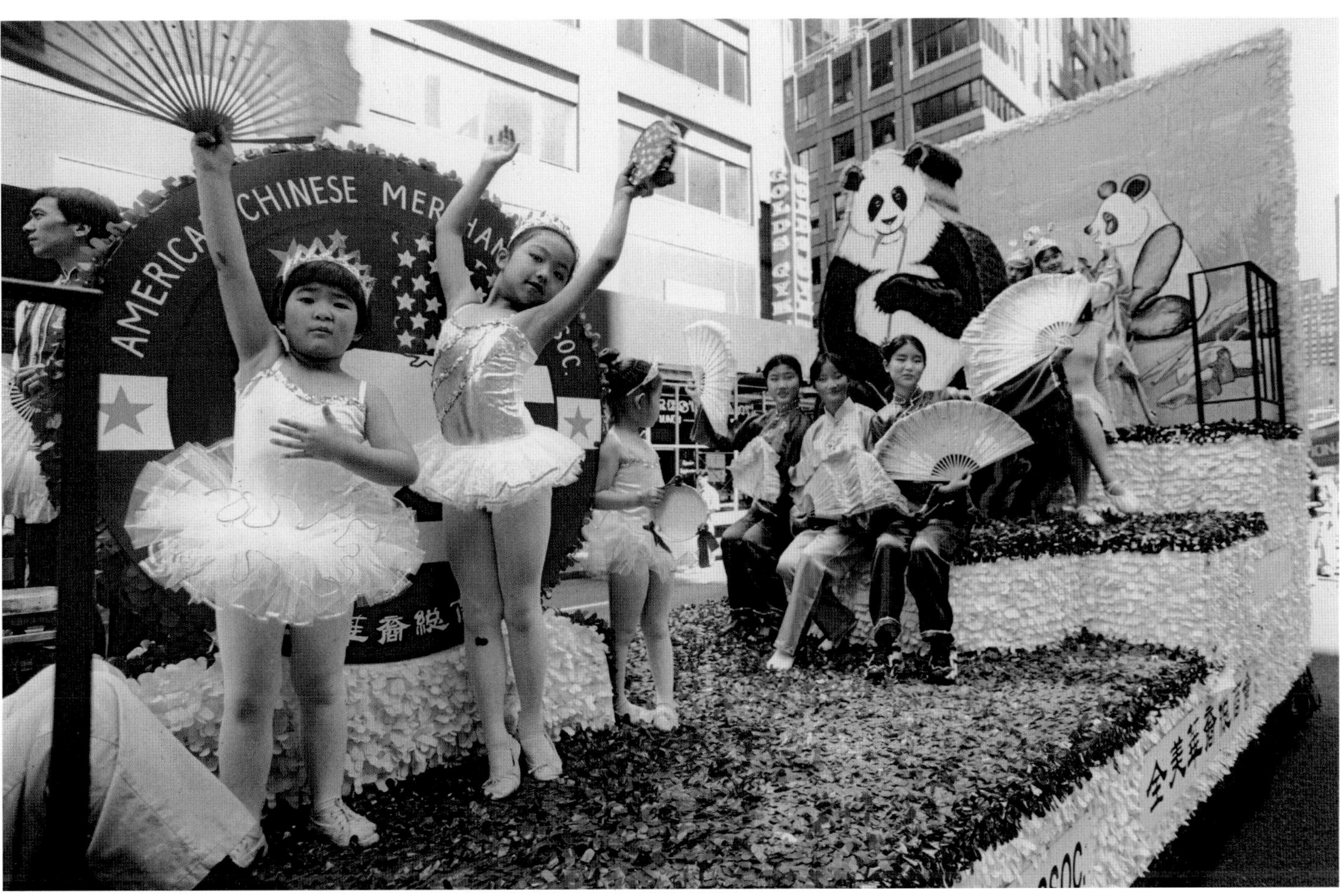

A bagel maker, name unknown. New York, 1993.

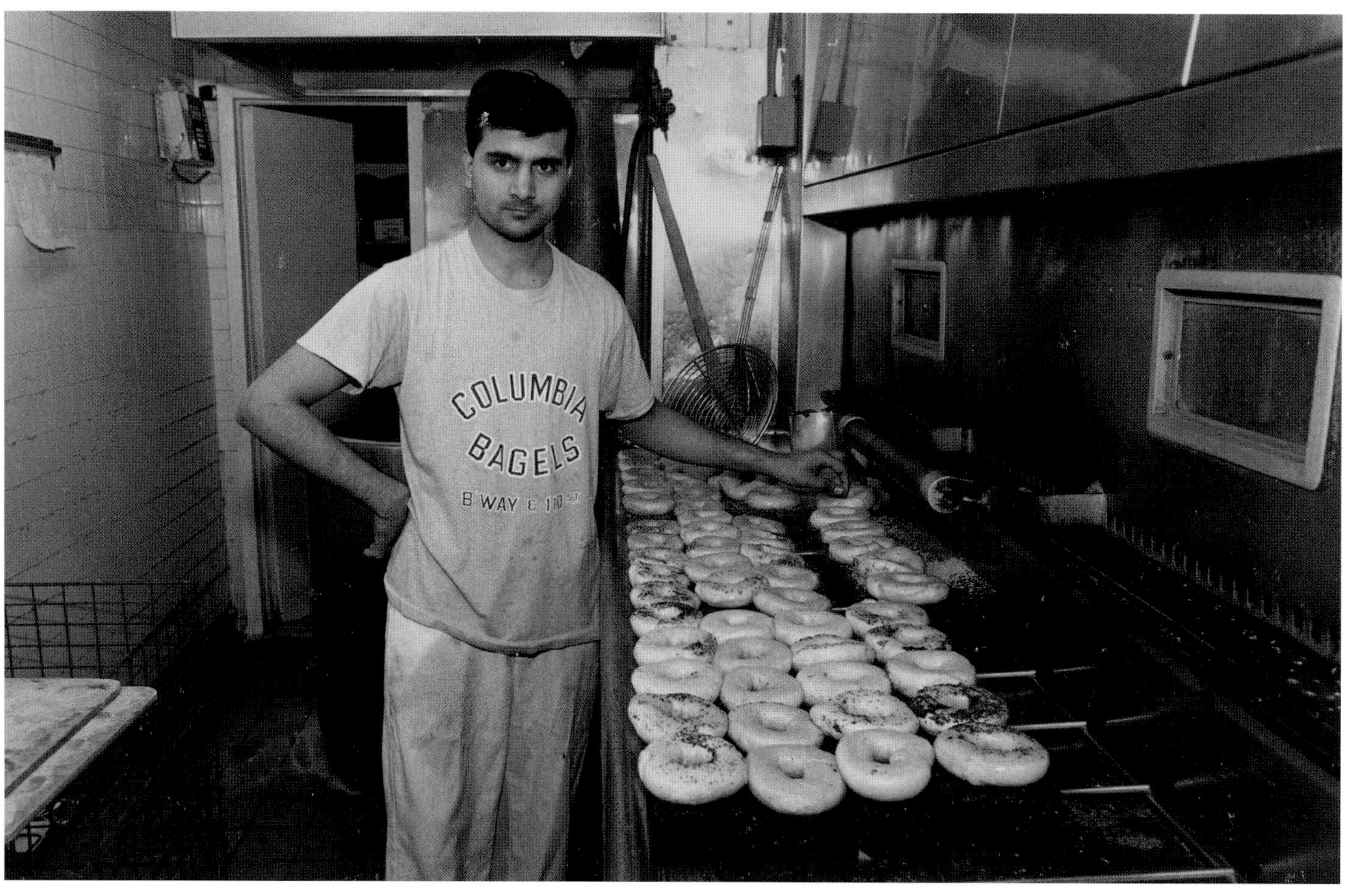

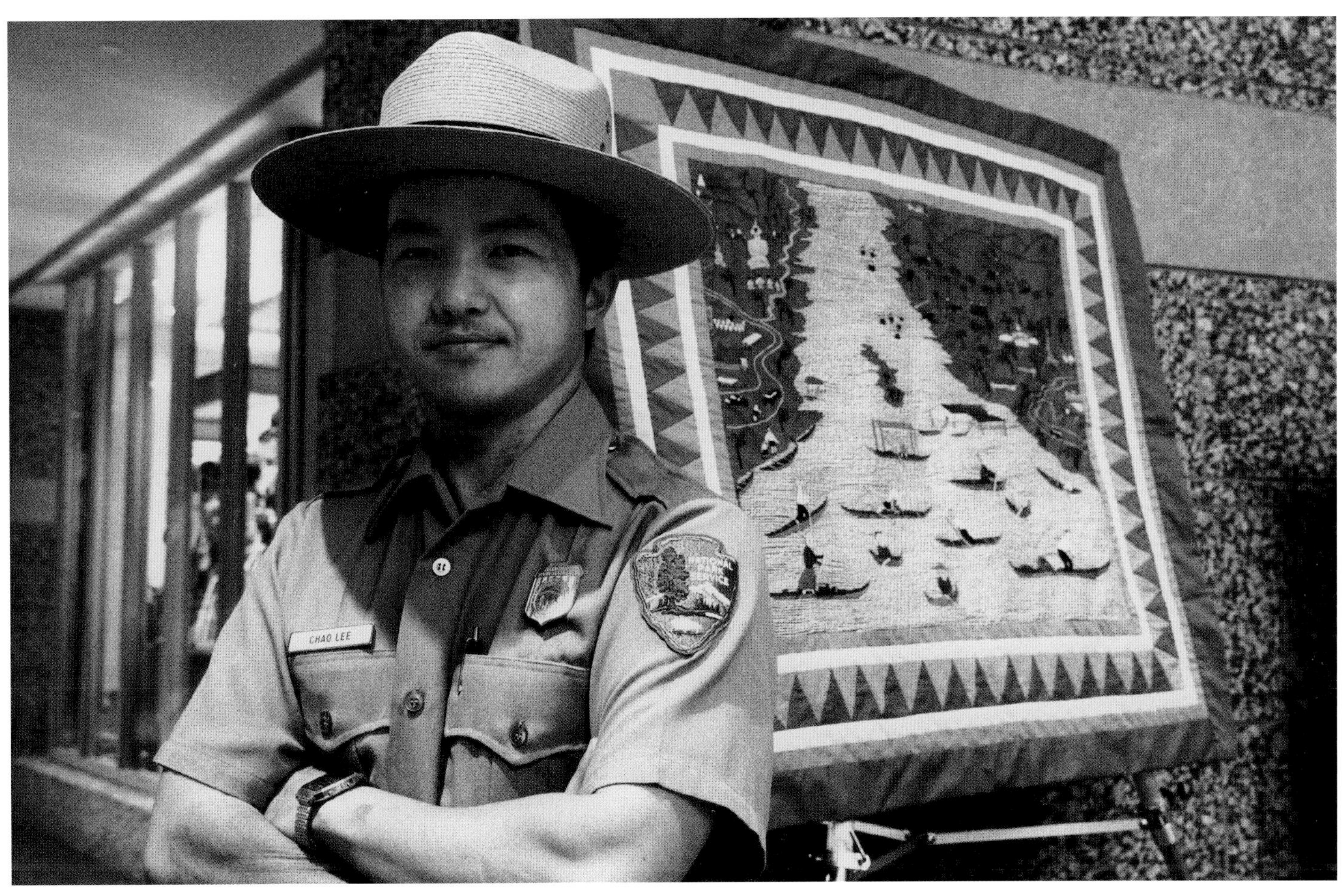

Chao Lee, a Chinese Hmong park ranger, with an embroidered "story cloth" showing Hmong refugees' journey from farming villages to refugee camps. Minneapolis, 1996.

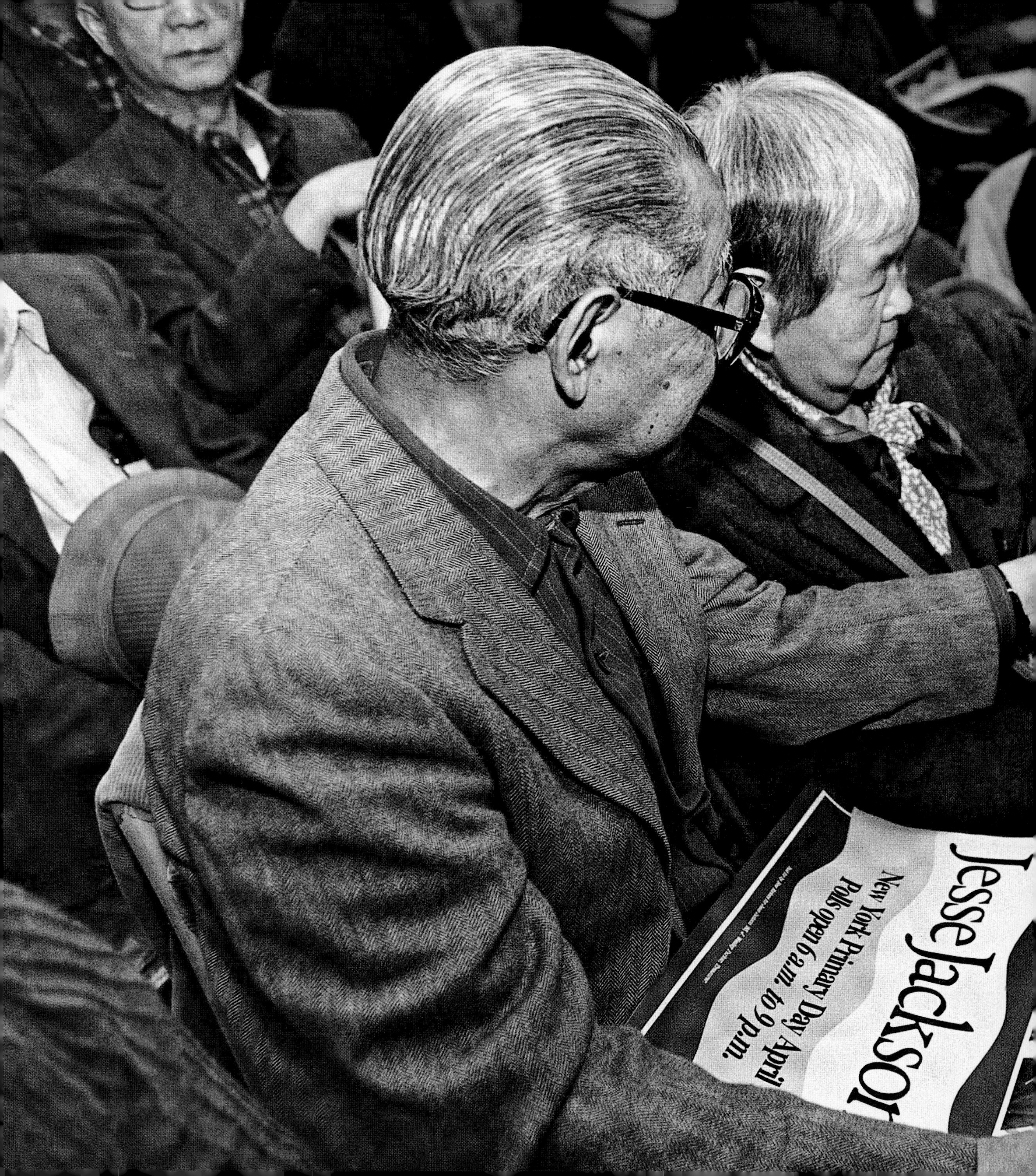
Jesse
New York Primary Day April
Polls open 6 a.m. to 9 p.m.

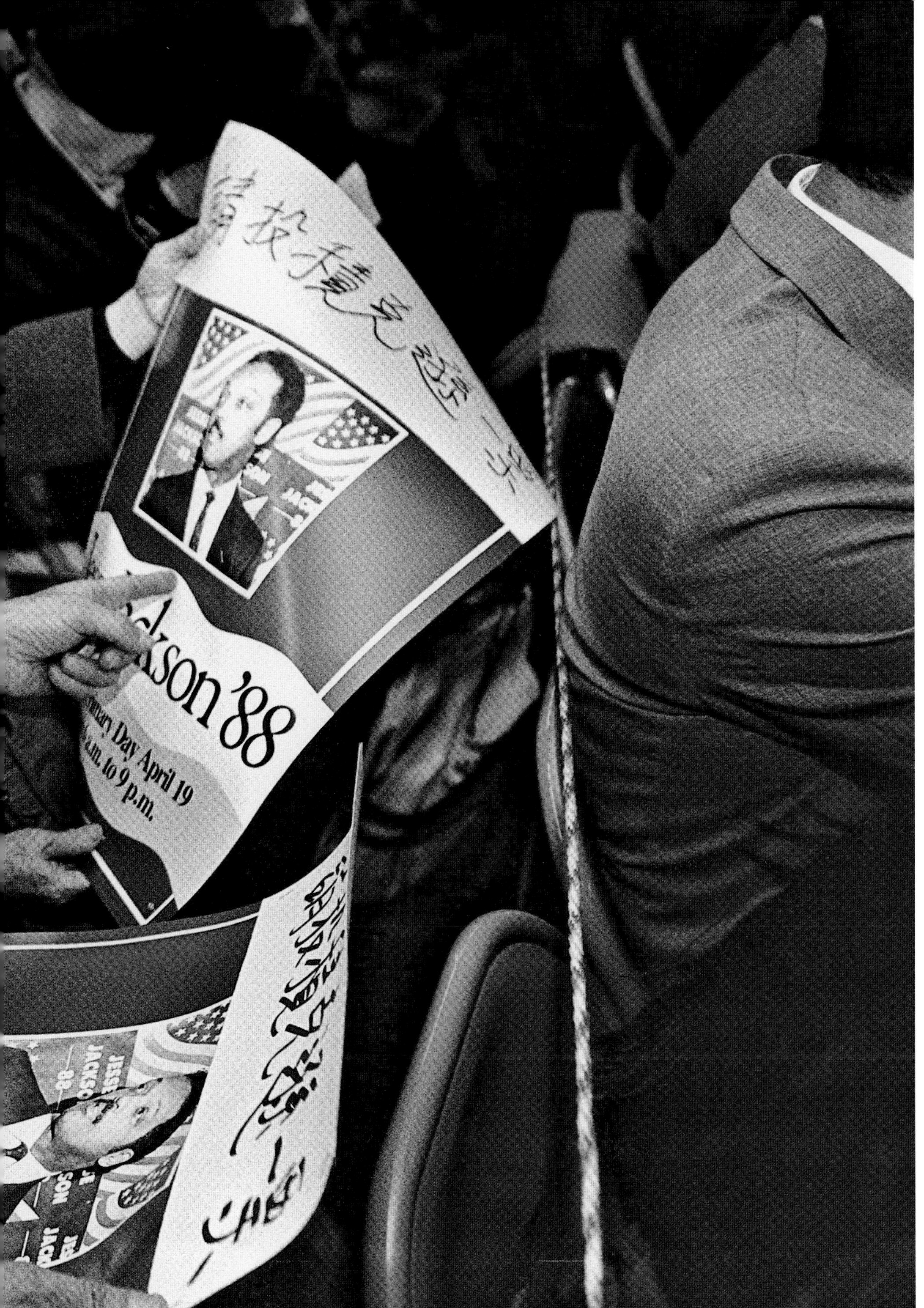

Asian Americans for Jesse Jackson sponsor a campaign rally at the Chinatown senior center. New York, 1988.

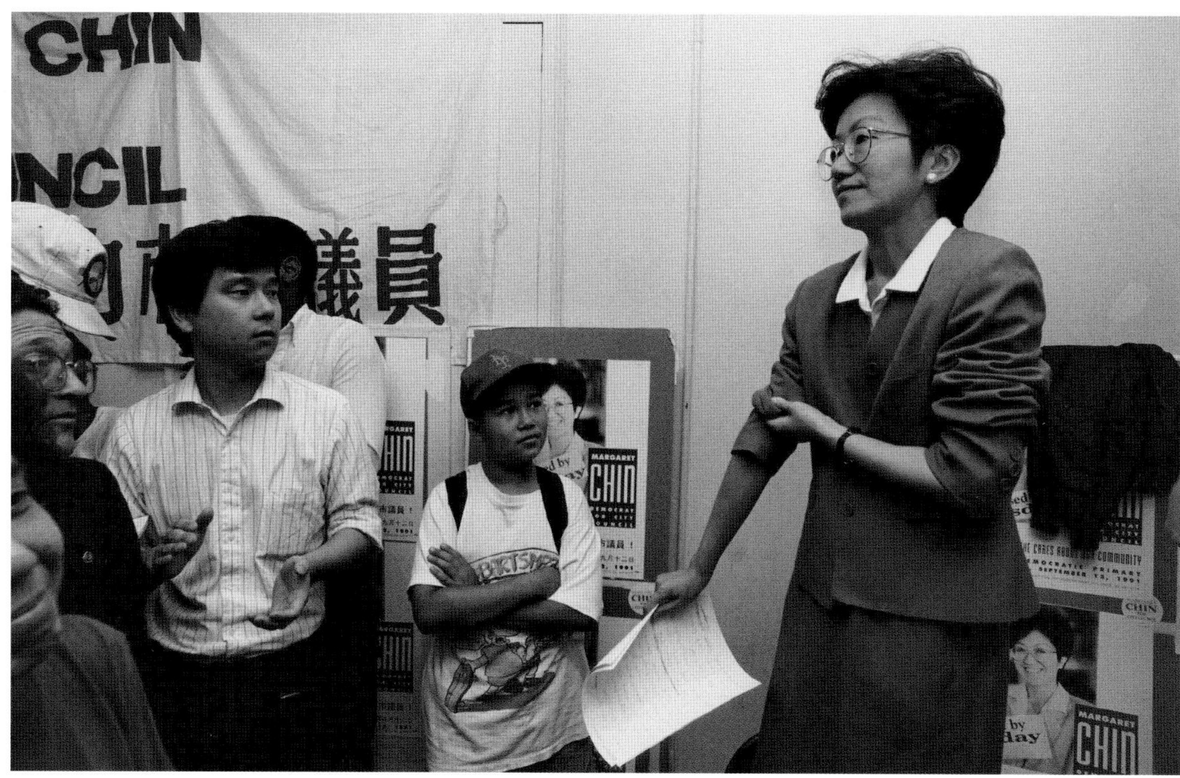

In 1991 two Asian Americans ran for the New York City Council in a newly drawn district in Lower Manhattan that included Chinatown: Margaret Chin, an activist with Asian Americans for Equality, and Fred Teng (*below*), a media executive. Neither won that year but Chin was elected in 2009 and served until 2020. New York, 1991.

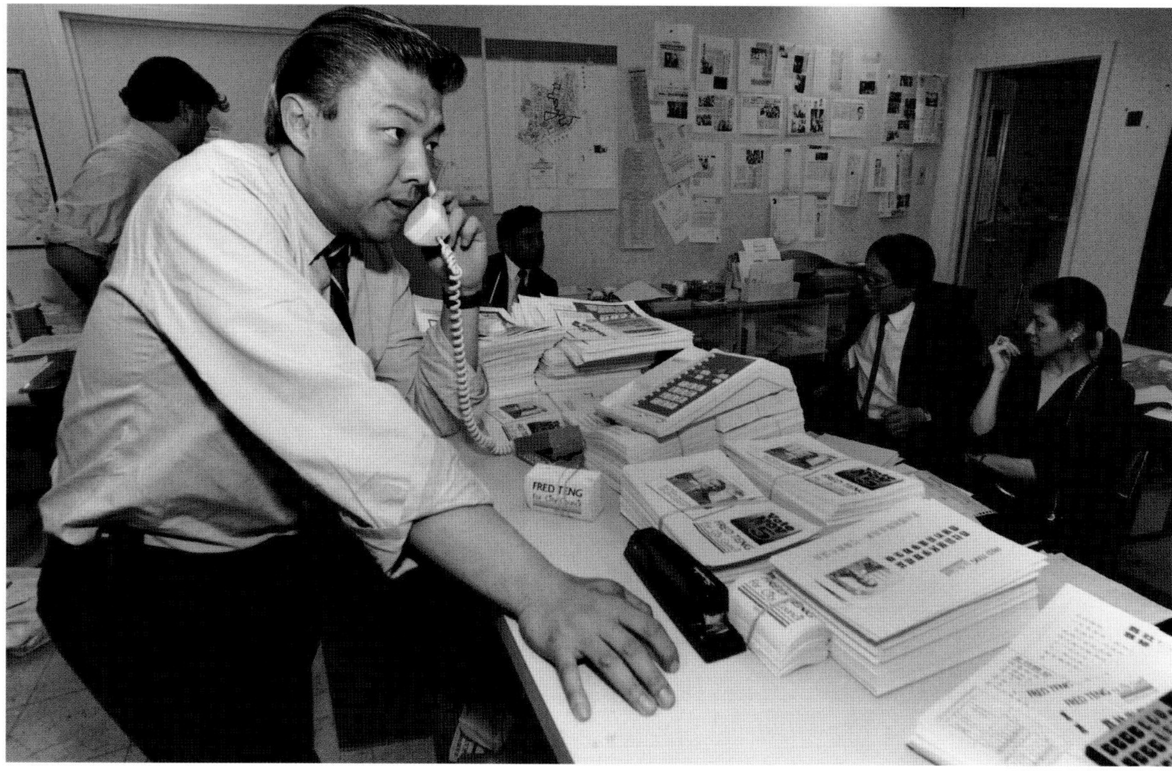

Members of the International Ladies Garment Workers Union register voters at the corner of Mott and Canal in Chinatown. New York, late 1980s.

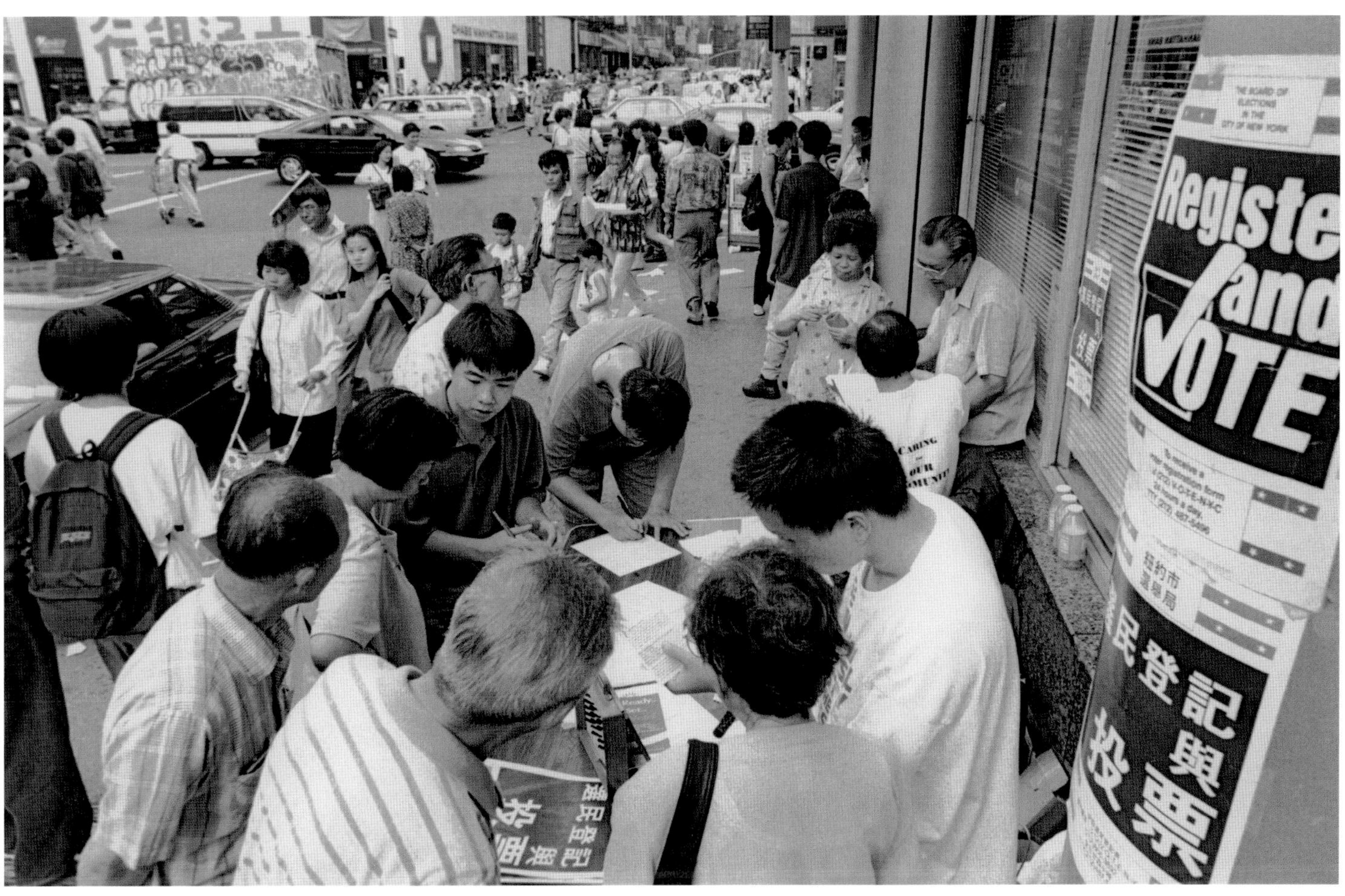

President Bill Clinton and actor Tamlyn Tomita, during Clinton's reelection campaign. New York, 1996.

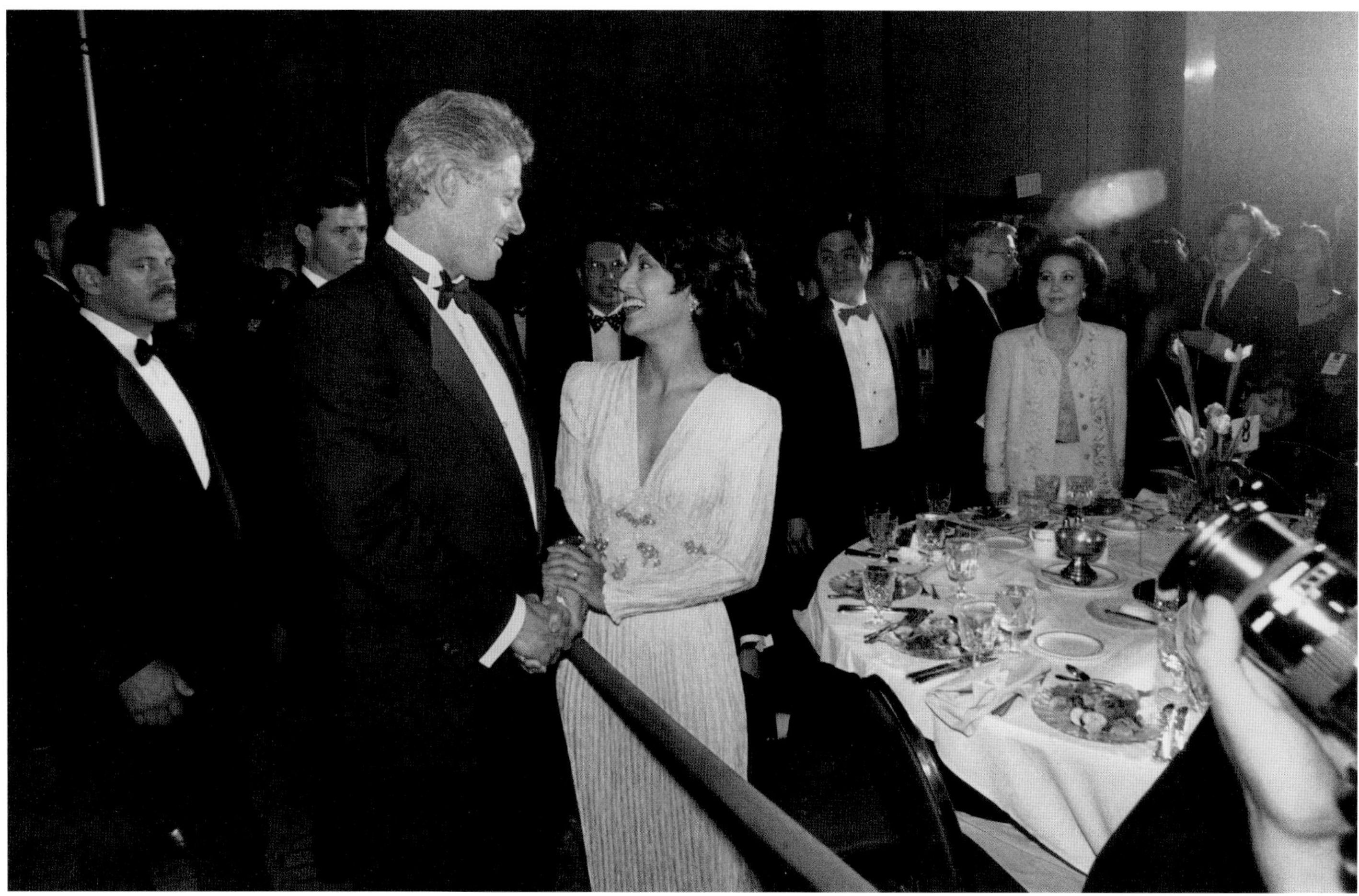

Washington's Gary Locke was the first Asian American to be elected governor in the continental U.S. He served two terms (1997–2005) and later served as U.S. secretary of commerce (2009–2011) and U.S. ambassador to China (2011–2014). Here Locke and his wife, Mona Lee, make a campaign visit. New York, 1996.

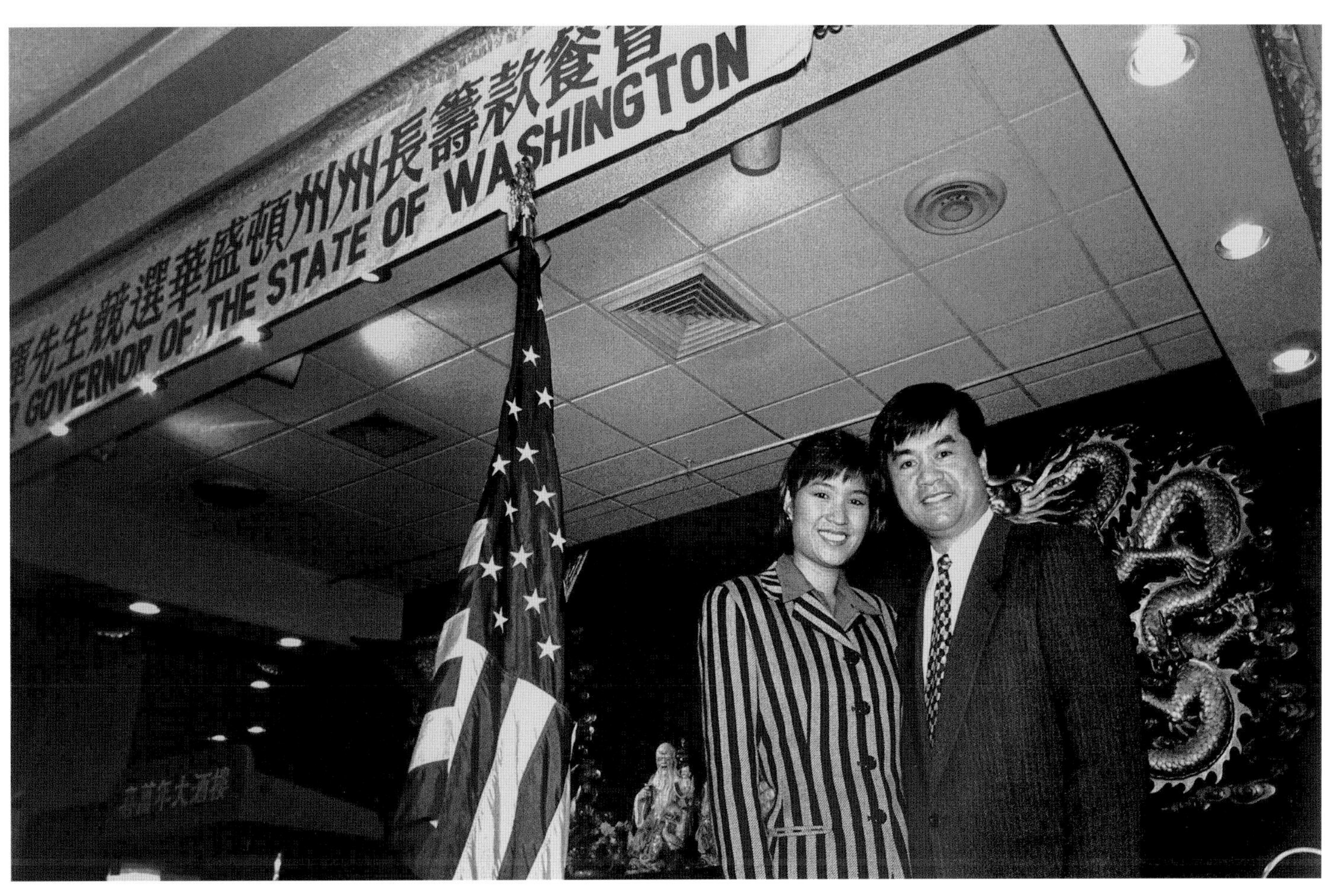

Tiananmen

AI WEIWEI
Artist

Corky Lee and I met in New York in the 1980s. I know that he was faithful to his photography and to the people he photographed. He was a brilliant photographer and comprehensively documented the life of the Chinese community.

This photo was taken by Corky during our protests in New York after the 1989 Tiananmen Square massacre. Without his photo, I would have only a very faint memory of that protest. Photography can never replace reality, but it is a reinforced version of reality. It solidifies our memories and enables us to search further and to rediscover. I would like to thank Corky Lee for his effort in building a very important foundation for our understanding of reality and history.

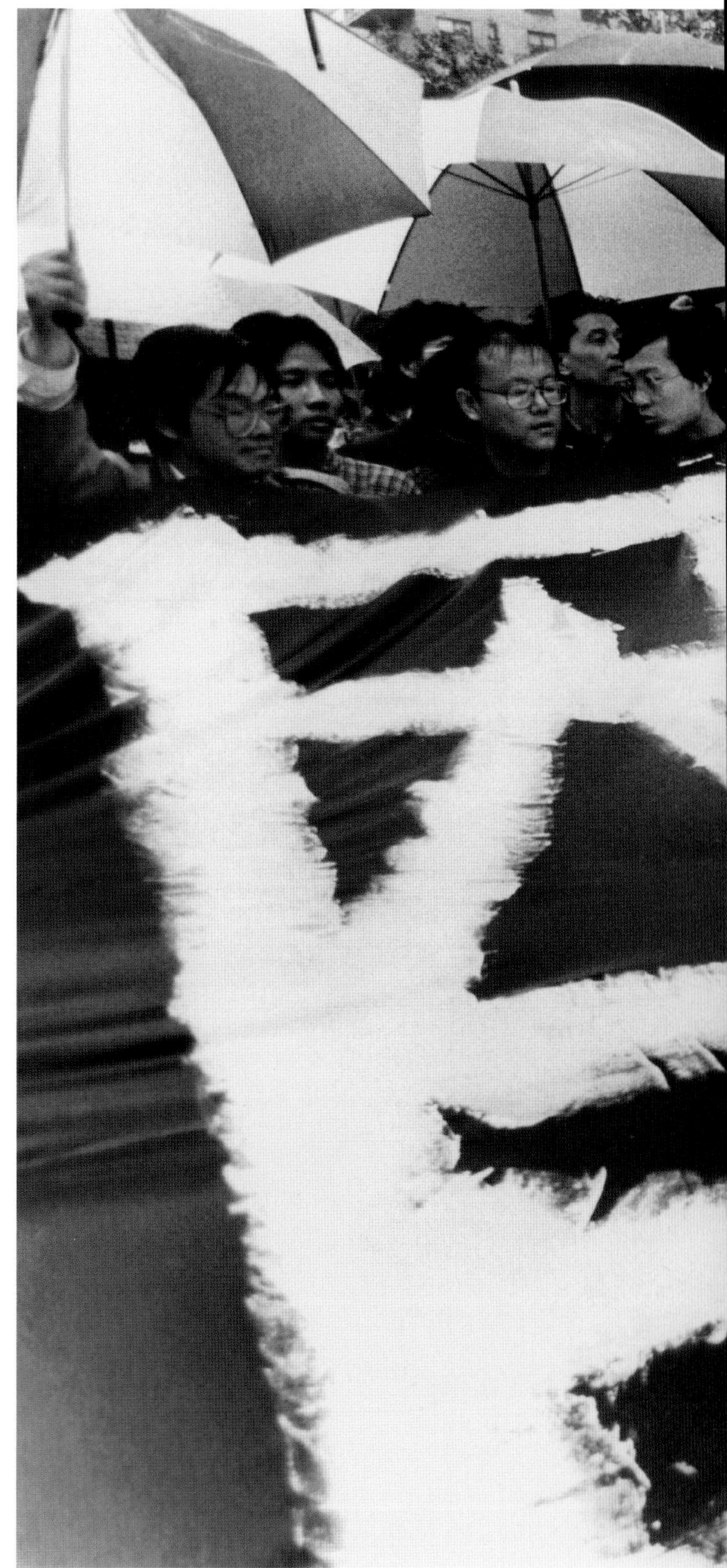

In 1989, more than six thousand Chinese international students and others gathered at the United Nations to protest the massacre of students demonstrating for democracy at Tiananmen Square in Beijing. The banner reads *guo shang*, or "national mourning." Artist Ai Weiwei is at the center with a white headband, traditionally worn at Chinese funerals. New York, June 5, 1989.

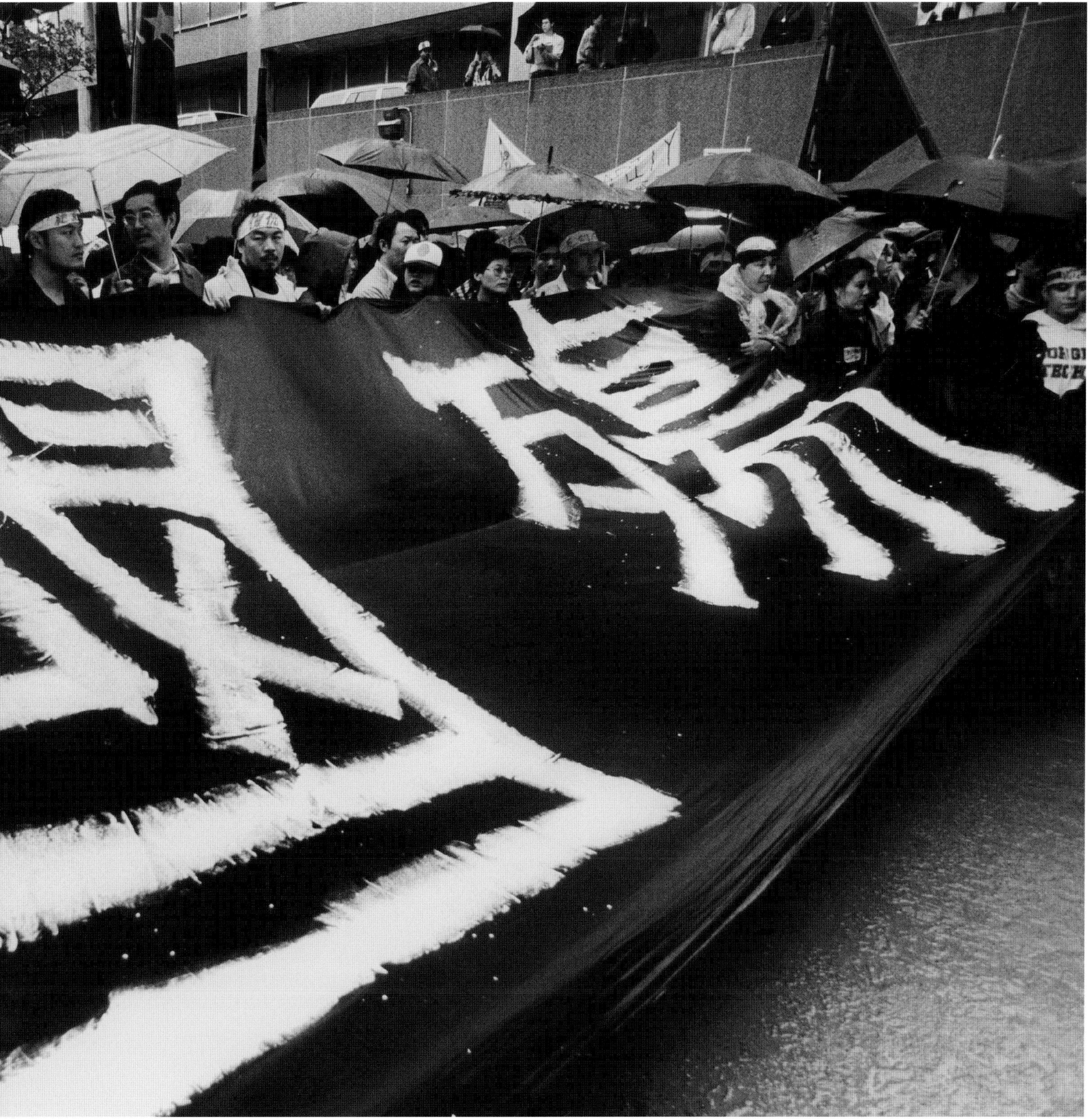

Below left: Chinatown residents protested the Tiananmen Square massacre with a march down Mott Street, holding copies of the local Chinese-language newspaper *United Journal* (*lianhe ribao*) (now defunct). New York, June 1989.

Below right: Five thousand Filipino Americans greet President Cory Aquino of the Philippines as she visits Fordham University to receive an honorary law degree. Aquino was elected in February 1986 after a peaceful democratic revolution toppled the twenty-one-year U.S.-backed dictatorship of Ferdinand Marcos. Her late husband, the opposition leader Benigno Aquino, Jr., had been assassinated by Marcos in 1983. On her visit, Aquino received other awards and spoke at the United Nations. New York, September 1986.

Bottom: Protesters march across 42nd Street from the Chinese consulate to the United Nations, opposing the Hong Kong government's decision to forcibly repatriate refugees ("boat people") from Vietnam. New York, 1989.

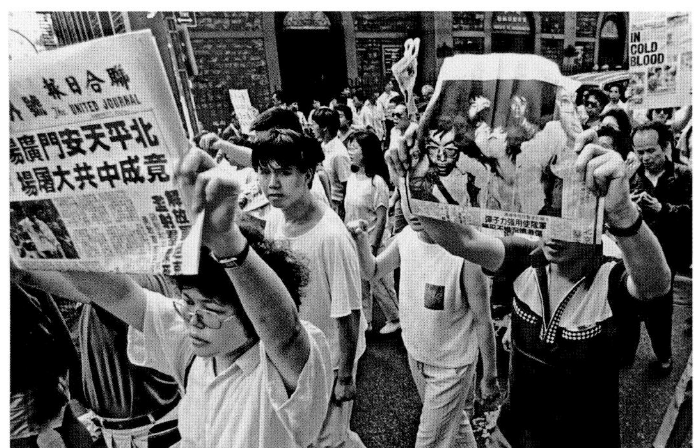

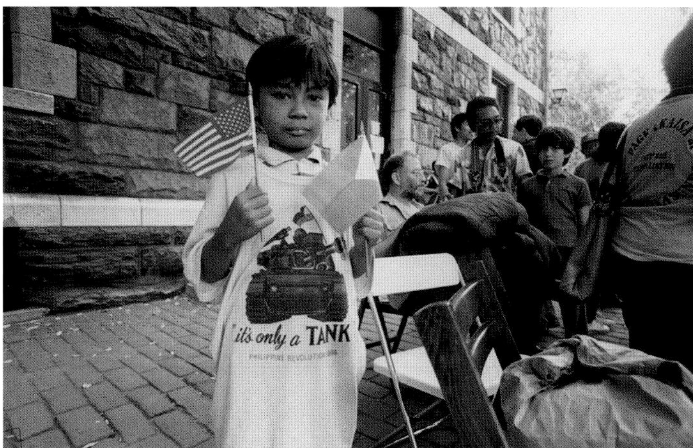

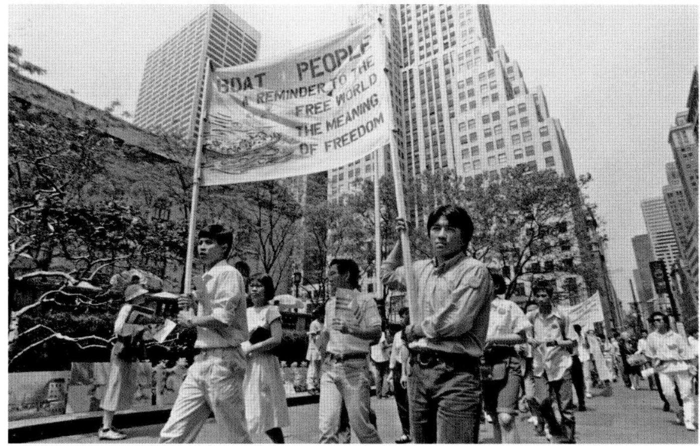

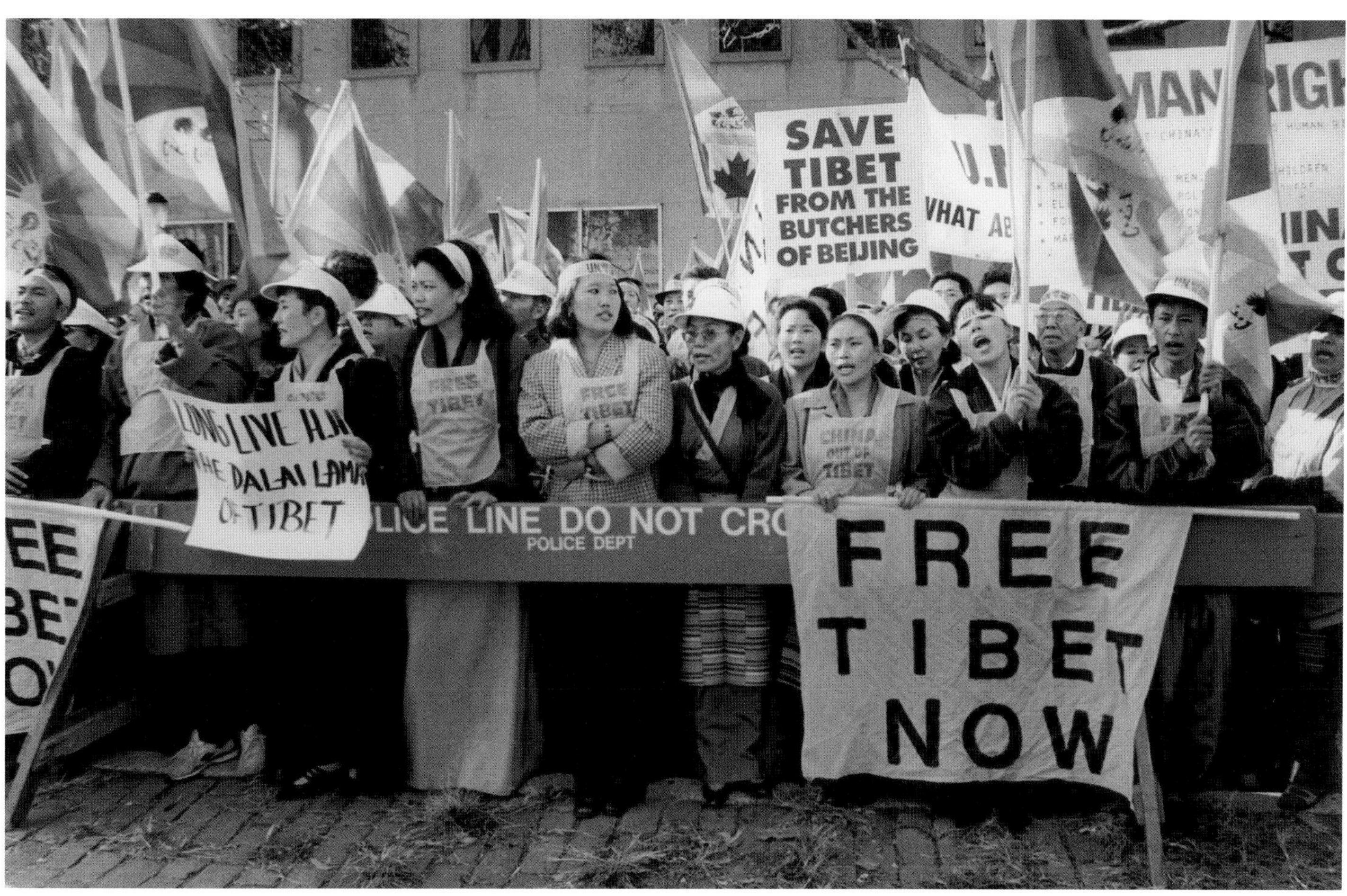

A "Free Tibet" demonstration at the United Nations. New York, circa 1996.

Asian American Arts in the 1990s

RENEE TAJIMA-PEÑA

Documentary filmmaker, producer of the PBS series *Asian Americans*, and professor of Asian American studies at UCLA

In 1991 the Whitney Museum of American Art Biennial served up 101 "it" artists of the day, as anointed by the influential curators who defined what was next in visual culture. Out of that number, there were as many artists named Kelly as there were Asian Americans. Three, to be exact.

This despite the fact that Asian migration was 150 years old by that time. And the previous year's 1990 U.S. census had elevated Asian Americans as the nation's fastest-growing population group. We were on the cusp of a future that was unforeseeable to the cultural gatekeepers but that Asian American artists on the margins were already imagining into an inevitable force.

Also in 1990 a group of New York artists formed the Godzilla Asian American Artists Network. As irreverent and oppositional as its name suggests, Godzilla was the ideological spawn of the seminal art and politics space Basement Workshop, which had been one of Corky's organizational homes back in the early 1970s. In response to the 1991 Whitney Biennial, the Godzilla collective launched its debut volley against art world homogeneity in the form of an open letter to the museum's director, David Ross, calling out the "conspicuous absence of Asian American visual artists" at the exhibition.

By that time, we were already deep into the 1980s and 1990s culture wars triggered by white replacement anxiety at the prospect of a majority "minority" nation. It recalled an earlier period of demographic change and division, the late 1800s and early 1900s, when new nonwhite populations were entering the American body politic: formerly enslaved Blacks; colonized populations from the continent's tribal lands and Mexico and territories in the Atlantic and the Pacific; and Asian immigrants from China, Japan, Korea, India, and the Philippines.

White Americans asked, *Are these people like us? Will they belong?* Their answer to their own questions was evident in the systemic racism that also evolved during this time. The ecosystem was made up not only of laws, such as Jim Crow and exclusionary immigration measures, but also of cultural representations of race and racial hierarchy. Gross distortions of dehumanized differences reinforced the idea that Asians would always be the perpetual foreigners. Or that they would be invisible.

The late-twentieth-century conflict over multiculturalism was one battle in this protracted war against the inevitable colorization of the United States. Defenders of the Western canon like Harold Bloom attacked creatives of color for upholding identity politics and for producing work of supposedly inferior quality. The same argument was made in every arena, from college admissions to Hollywood casting calls, that opening doors to people of color meant capitulation to mediocrity. But the cultural warriors on the right failed to notice, or to accept, that history was marching on with or without them.

Throughout the 1990s, Asian American artists continued to mobilize and create. Their communities flourished, and immigrants never stopped coming. This is the world that Corky captured in endless frames of film. They show Asian Americans' anger, joy, and pageantry, the stuff of everyday life, and history in the making. With his commitment to "photographic justice," Corky always reminded me of a camera-toting Tom Joad out of a Chinatown *Grapes of Wrath*: "Wherever they's a fight so hungry people can eat, I'll be there. Wherever they's a cop beatin' up a guy, I'll be there." Corky was always there.

He gave us the gift of our collective memory. Thanks to him, we can still see New York's Chinatown before the worst ravages of gentrification, and the burgeoning Little India in Jackson Heights, Queens. The Korean *ajummas*, the World War II veterans in full regalia, and the *obon* dancers at a summertime *matsuri* festival. We can see the indigenous Filipino dance theater company Kinding Sindaw when it first performed in 1992, because Corky was there to photograph it.

His photographs from the 1990s show an Asian America that was at the tipping point of the new millennium that would bring *Crazy Rich Asians*, the BTS ARMY, and Kamala Harris in the West Wing. The roots of the Asian American cultural explosion that we are experiencing now were in place, born out of the activism of the 1960s and 1970s and pollinated by demographic and social change.

By the 1990s, Asian American artists, writers, and filmmakers were slowly crossing over into the mainstream and gaining recognition: Ang Lee, Mira Nair, and Wayne Wang in film; David Henry Hwang in theater; Jhumpa Lahiri and Chang-rae Lee in literature; and performers as different as apl.de.ap, Mike Shinoda, and Yo-Yo Ma in music.

Sometimes breaking the glass ceiling required a brittle reach. In 1994 Margaret Cho's *All-American Girl* was the first Asian American network sitcom since *Mr. T and Tina* some twenty years before. But the mostly white writers' room squandered Cho's exceptional talent with caricature, ensuring that it would be another twenty years before *Fresh Off the Boat* appeared as a hit show. On Broadway, the eighteen-year-old Lea Salonga may have been a revelation as Kim in the 1989 London production of *Miss Saigon,* a musical based on Puccini's *Madama Butterfly*, set in Vietnam. But the show rehashed the old story of the tragic, hypersexualized Asian femme—with a yellow-faced Jonathan Pryce to boot.

Meanwhile, outside of Hollywood and away from Broadway, at community festivals and parades and screenings and student culture nights and underground clubs, Asian Americans were creating something new, the Western canon and the gatekeepers be damned. The 1990s were the time of B-boys, DJ Rekha spinning Basement Bhangra, and Beau Sia slamming verse at the Nuyorican Poets Café.

These culture makers were giving life to the novelist Viet Thanh Nguyen's counsel to emerging artists, to write like they're the majority, not a minority. "When I say write like a majority," he says, "I don't mean like a white person. I mean write as if we ourselves are speaking to ourselves, and let everyone else catch up. That's where you get interesting art, and even hopefully, great art, to come from." Asian Americans may have been culturally marginalized, but the ecosystem of white supremacy has always coexisted with an ecosystem of resistance. Creativity is resistance.

Established white-led institutions were beginning to take note, sometimes under duress, because people of color were lobbying for inclusion. Sometimes, too, funding became available for "multicultural" initiatives, although dollars for diversity were dispersed only in token amounts to the organizations of color that had been doing the work for years. Otherwise, cultural power and resources remained within white institutions, even as the reckoning over systemic racism roiled the art world.

Still, the Whitney Biennial of 1993 was a startling change in its intentional diversity of the artists on exhibition; it was co-curated by Thelma Golden, the museum's first Black curator. The show became known—mostly disparagingly—as the identity politics biennial, and major white critics like Robert Hughes and Hilton Kramer lined up for the kill.

I was a part of that show. The filmmaker-artist Shu Lea Cheang had convened a group of women of color artists to create *Those Fluttering Objects of Desire,* an installation of "tales of postcolonial interracial desire through reconstructed red phones, appropriating the 900-phonesex and 25-cent-per-peep pornography apparatus."

Basically, we produced phone sex tapes, art world critics be damned. My contribution was an audio remix of James Brown to quotations from Mao Zedong's Little Red Book as performed by the *Dogeaters* playwright Jessica Hagedorn and the writer-performance artist Robbie McCauley. Our main concern was that co-curator John Handhardt wouldn't let us charge museumgoers a quarter for each phone sex playback.

During the 1990s, Asian American culture was in flux. The 1965 immigration reforms and the diaspora from the war in Southeast Asia had remade America, writ large. Now the children of those immigrants were coming of age and staking out their place in the culture. Viet Thanh Nguyen was a part of that generation, schooled in college by the 1970s ethnic studies warriors-turned-professors. The future acting and writing team of Randall Park and Ali Wong were performing at UCLA in the first Asian American student theater company. At the UCLA Film School, Justin Lin and Quentin Lee were among the class of '97's Asian American feature filmmakers. These creatives would become central figures in the cultural transformations of the twenty-first century. Their works, ranging from Nguyen's 2015 novel *The Sympathizer* to Wong's 2016 comedy special *Baby Cobra* to Lin's 2002 crime feature *Better Luck Tomorrow,* are refreshingly short on respectability politics and long on irreverence and the confidence of speaking from the majority.

Corky Lee's genius was to capture what was possible and what would come next, often before anyone else noticed or cared. Whenever he showed up at a community event, large or small—and he always showed up—he photographed a collective act of creation. He immortalized Asian America as it was in the process of becoming.

At the Asian American Comedy Show. That night, Margaret Cho received the news that her show *All-American Girl* was picked up by ABC. *Left to right:* Christine Yang, Bob Kubota, Betty Wong, BD Wong, Margaret Cho, Jeff Yang, Maria Ho. New York, May 1994.

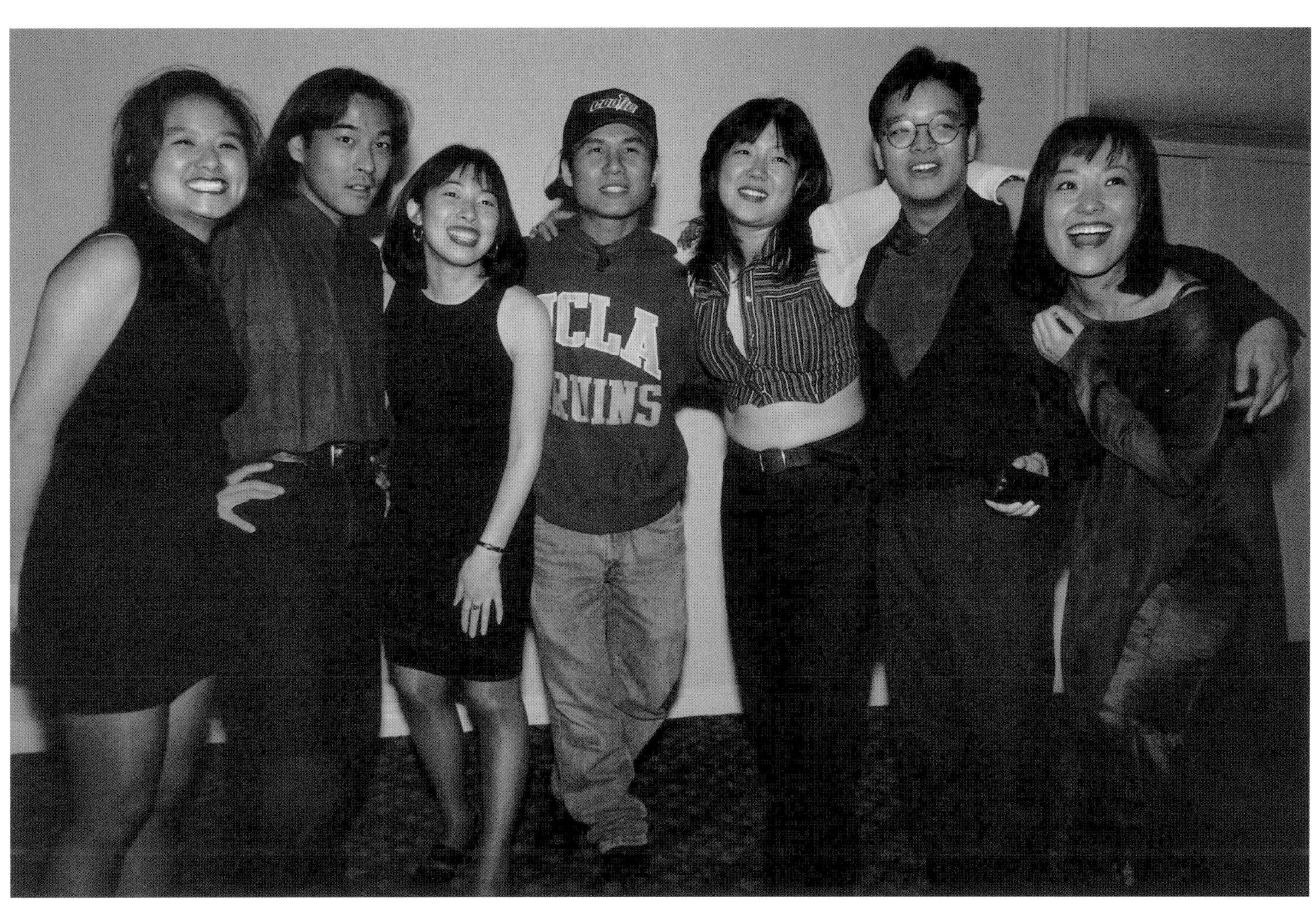

Asian Americans protested the 1991 Broadway production of the musical *Miss Saigon* in which the British actor Jonathan Pryce performed an Asian character in yellow face and with an eye prosthesis. The actors' union, Actors Equity, took the unusual step of refusing Pryce permission to perform in New York but reversed its position when the producer, Cameron Mackintosh, threatened to cancel the show. Critics condemned both *Miss Saigon*'s casting and its recycling of stereotypes portraying Asian women as prostitutes and helpless victims, long prominent in mainstream productions.

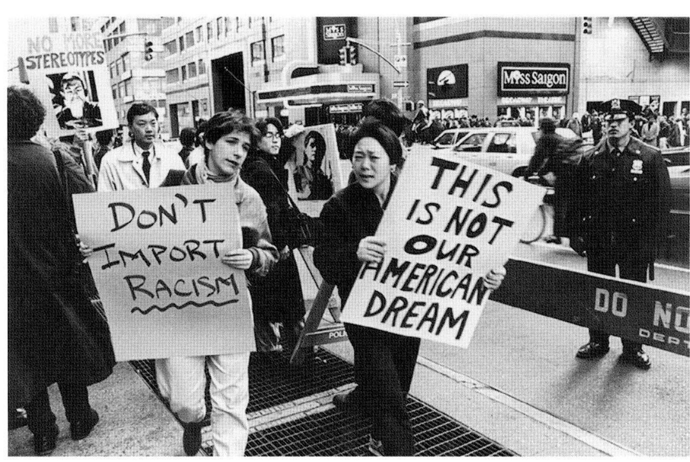

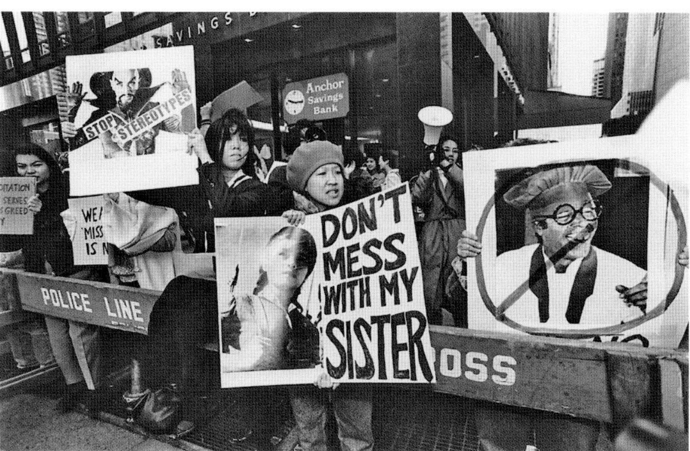

Demonstrators protest stereotypes in *Miss Saigon* on opening night. New York, 1991.

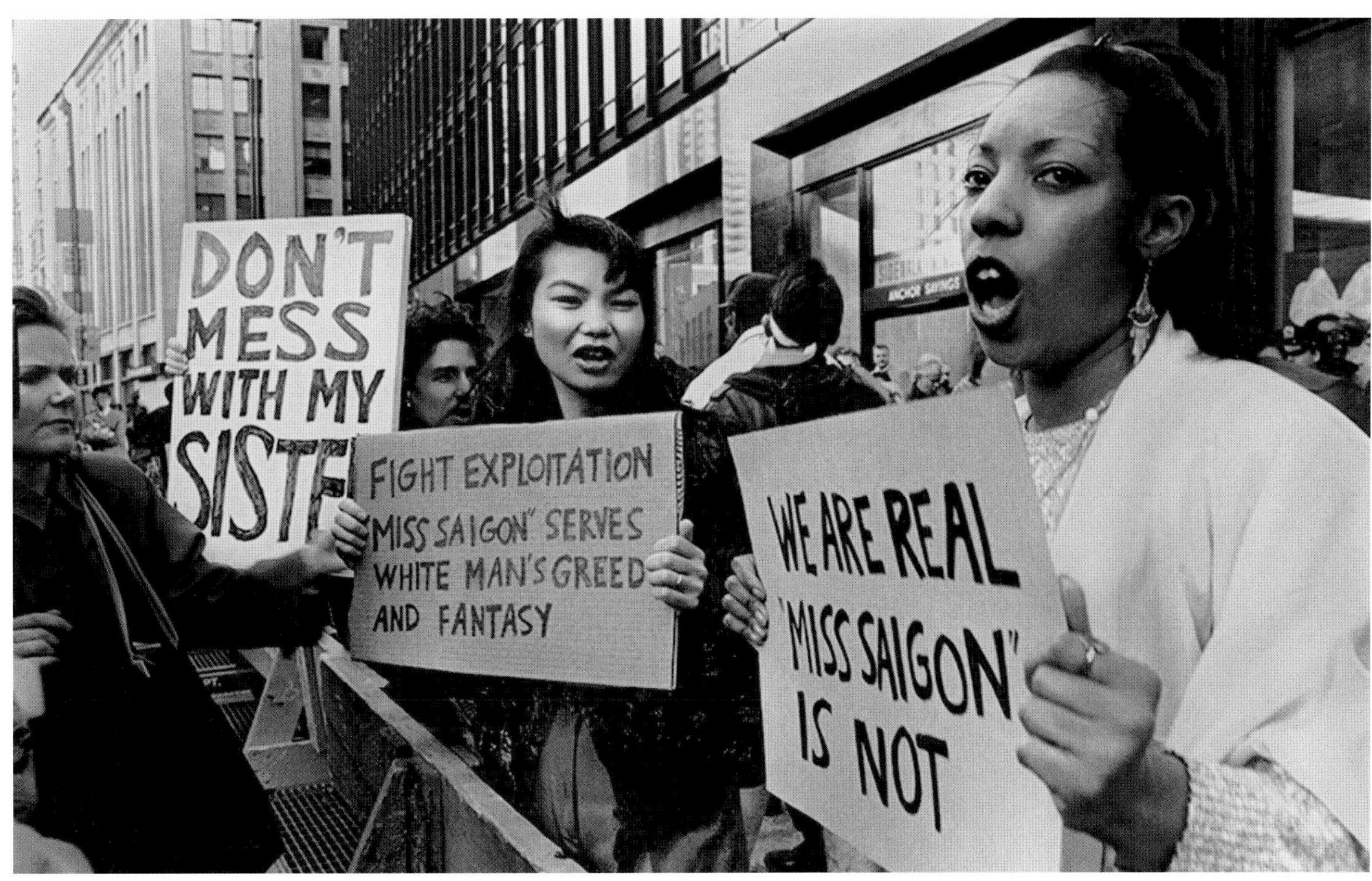

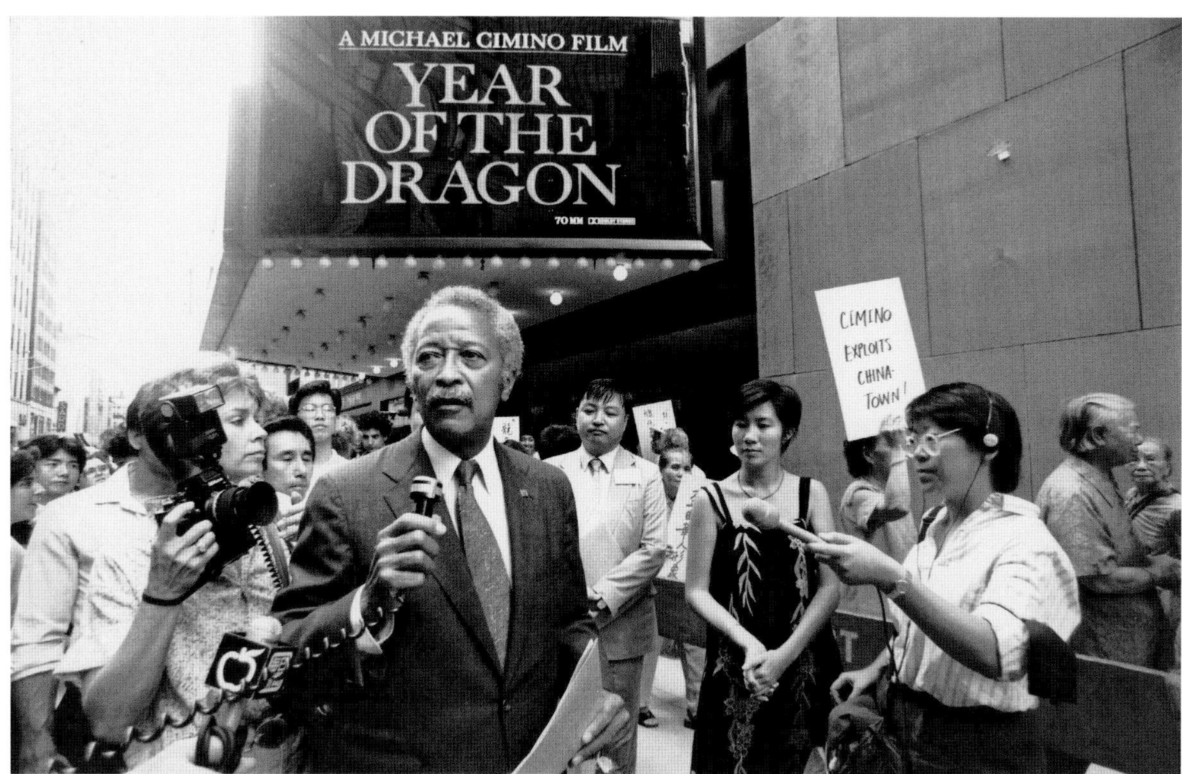

Asian Americans criticized the 1985 film *Year of the Dragon*, directed by Michael Cimino and starring Mickey Rourke, for promoting racist and sexist stereotypes in a violent portrayal of Chinatown gangs. At the film's opening, then-Manhattan borough president David Dinkins spoke at the protest. Times Square, New York, 1985.

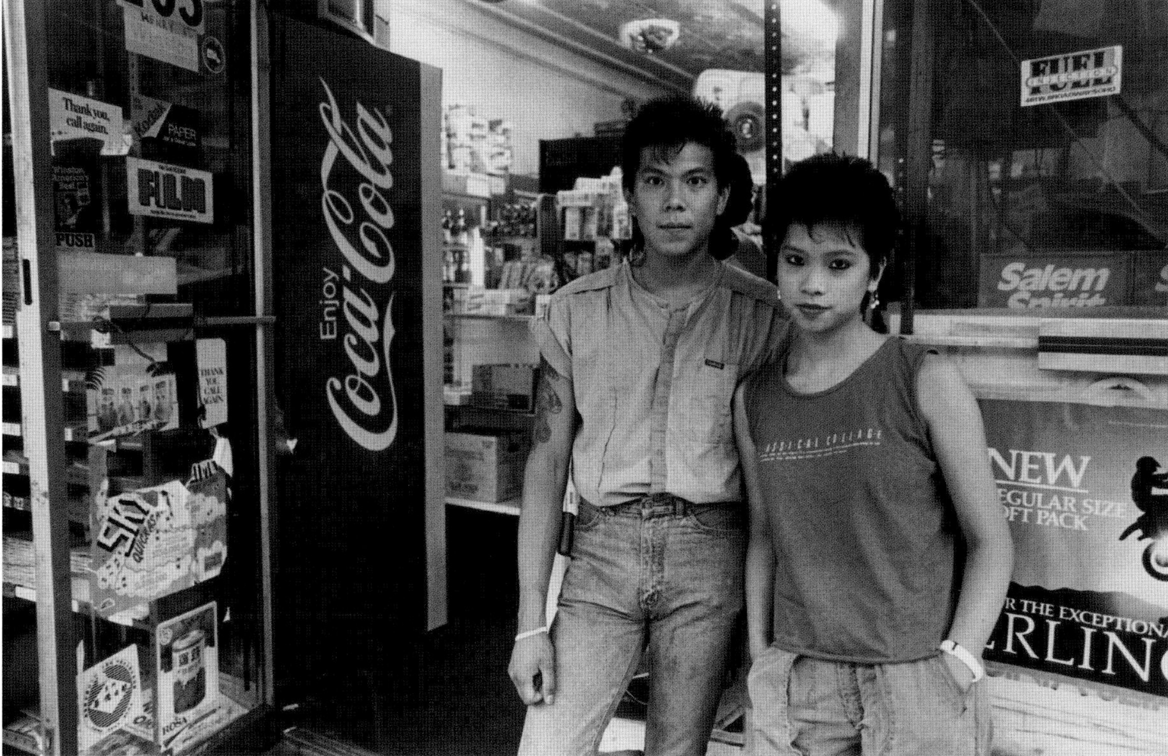

Chinatown locals were hired as extras for *Year of the Dragon*. New York, 1985.

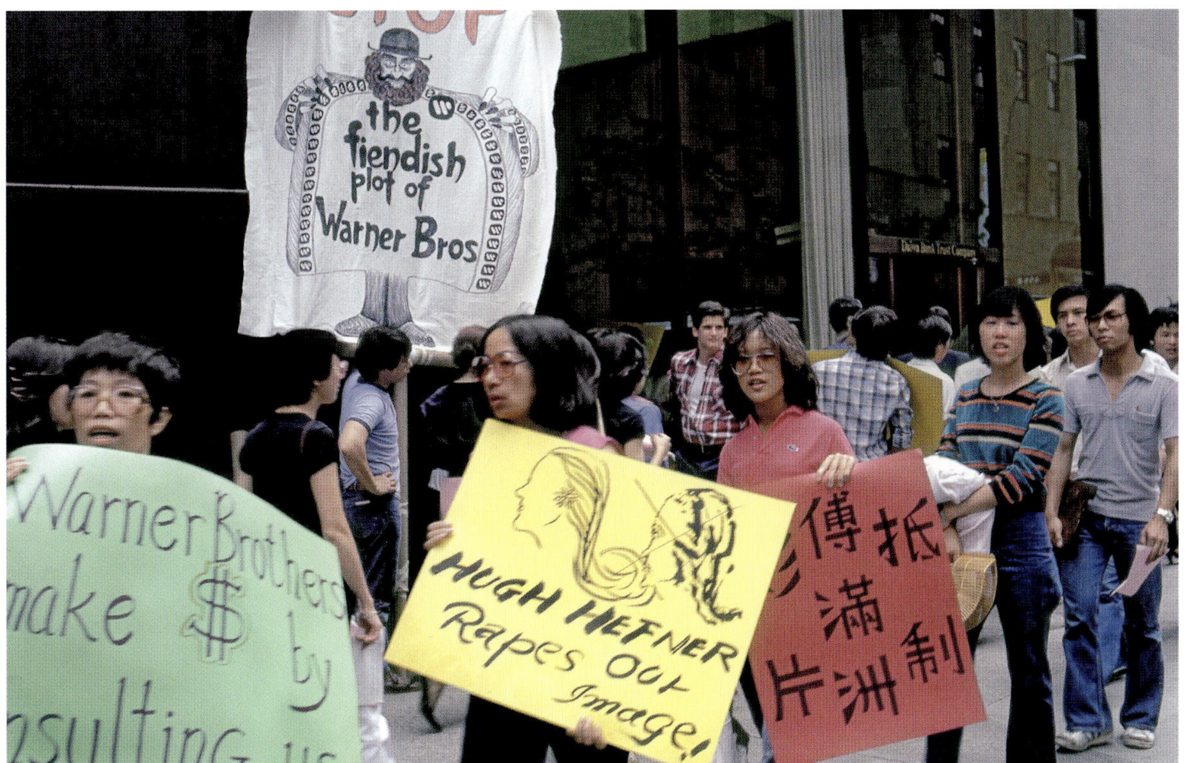

The Fiendish Plot of Dr. Fu Manchu (1980) was written and produced by *Playboy*'s Hugh Hefner and starred Peter Sellers in his last film role. Asian Americans assailed the film for perpetuating the racist "yellow peril" themes embodied in the fictional Fu Manchu, a supervillain character who had a long career in novels (1913–59), television, and film. Critics also panned the film. New York, 1980.

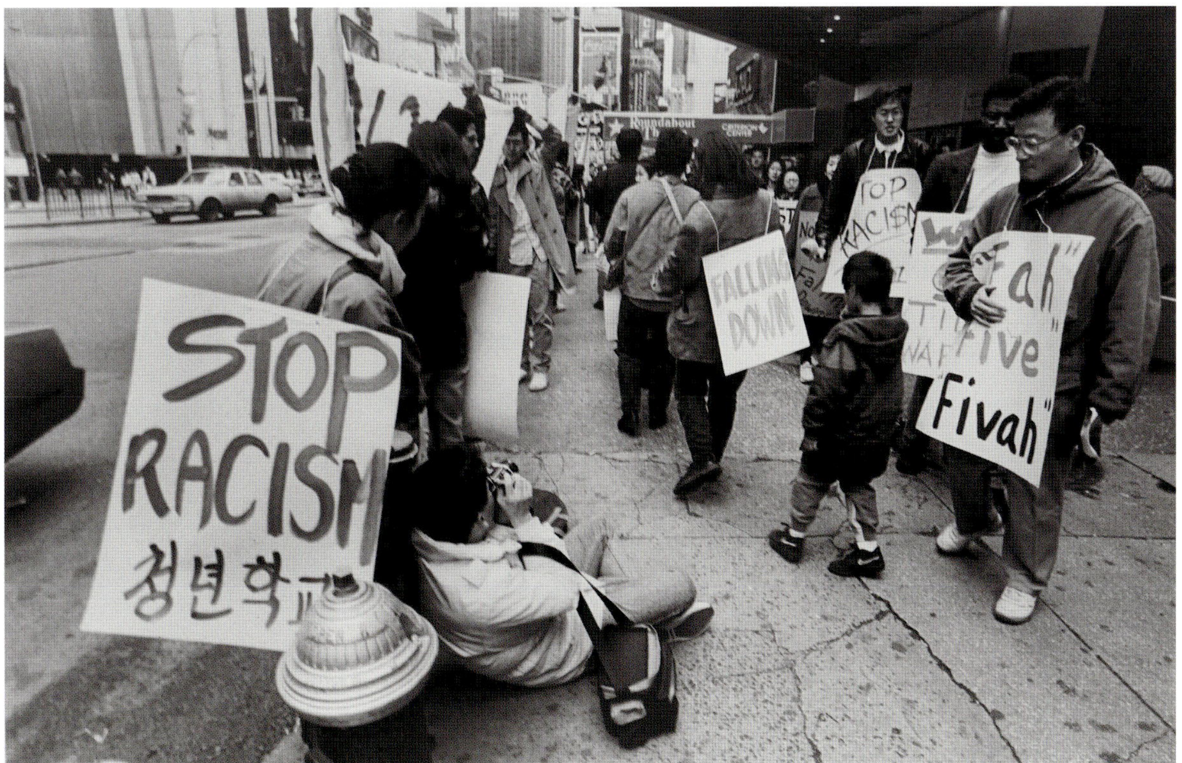

In 1993 Korean Americans protested the film *Falling Down,* in which Michael Douglas portrayed a white man who is frustrated by his own failures and takes it out on the people around him, especially Koreans and other immigrants. New York, 1993.

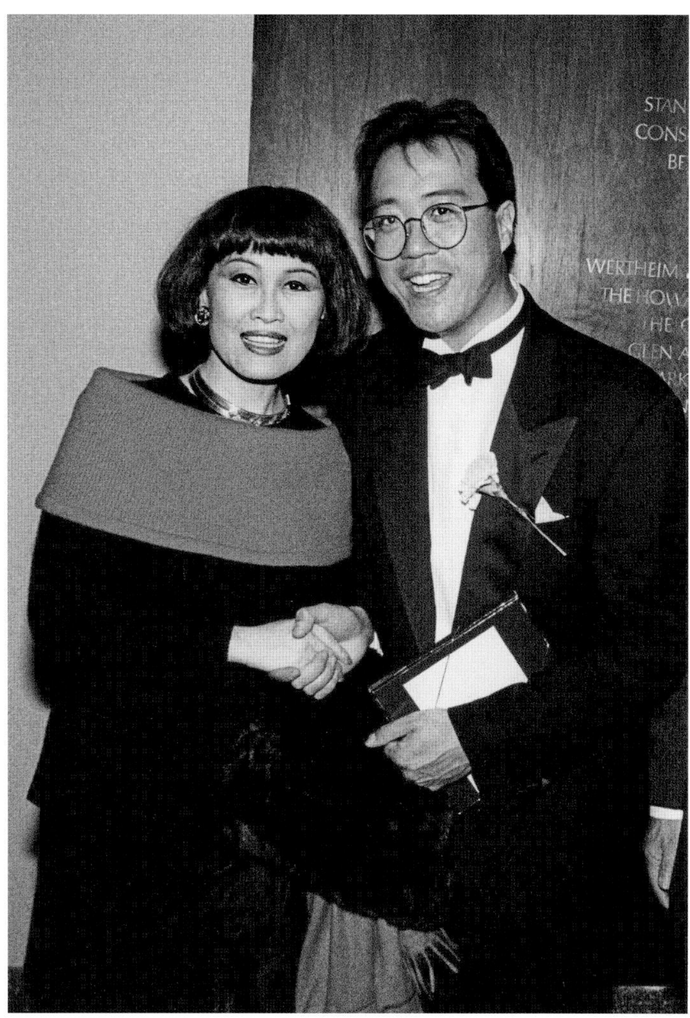

Cellist Yo-Yo Ma and television personality Yue-Sai Kan. New York, early 1990s.

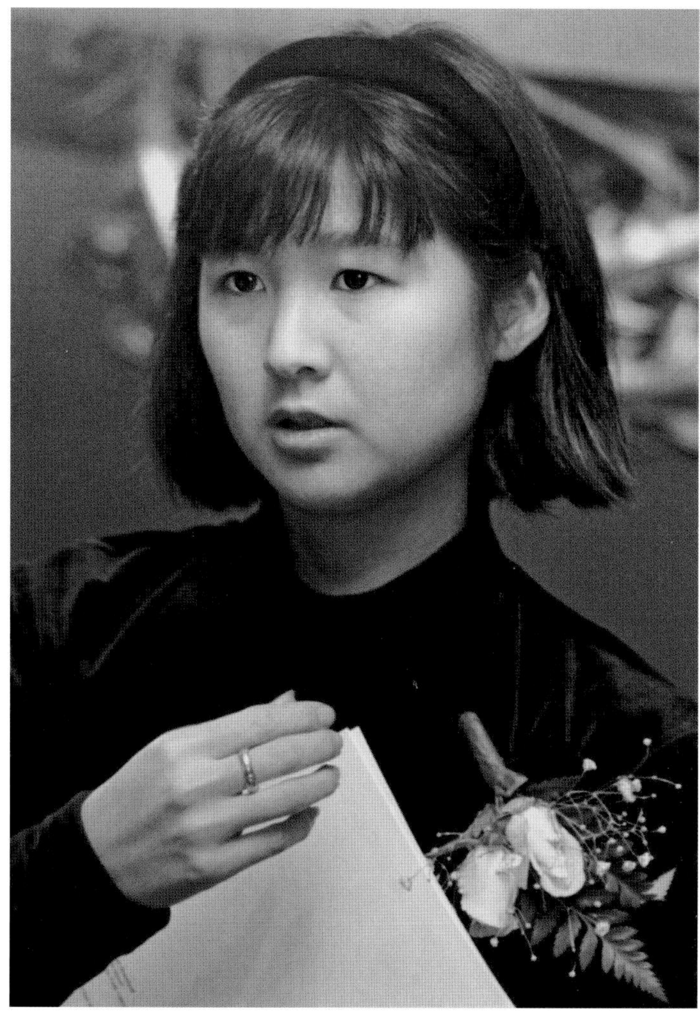

Architect Maya Lin. New York, 1990s.

Filmmaker Ang Lee was interviewed by North American TV, a Chinese cable TV company, during the Asian American International Film Festival and the promotion of his film, *Eat Drink Man Woman*. New York, 1994.

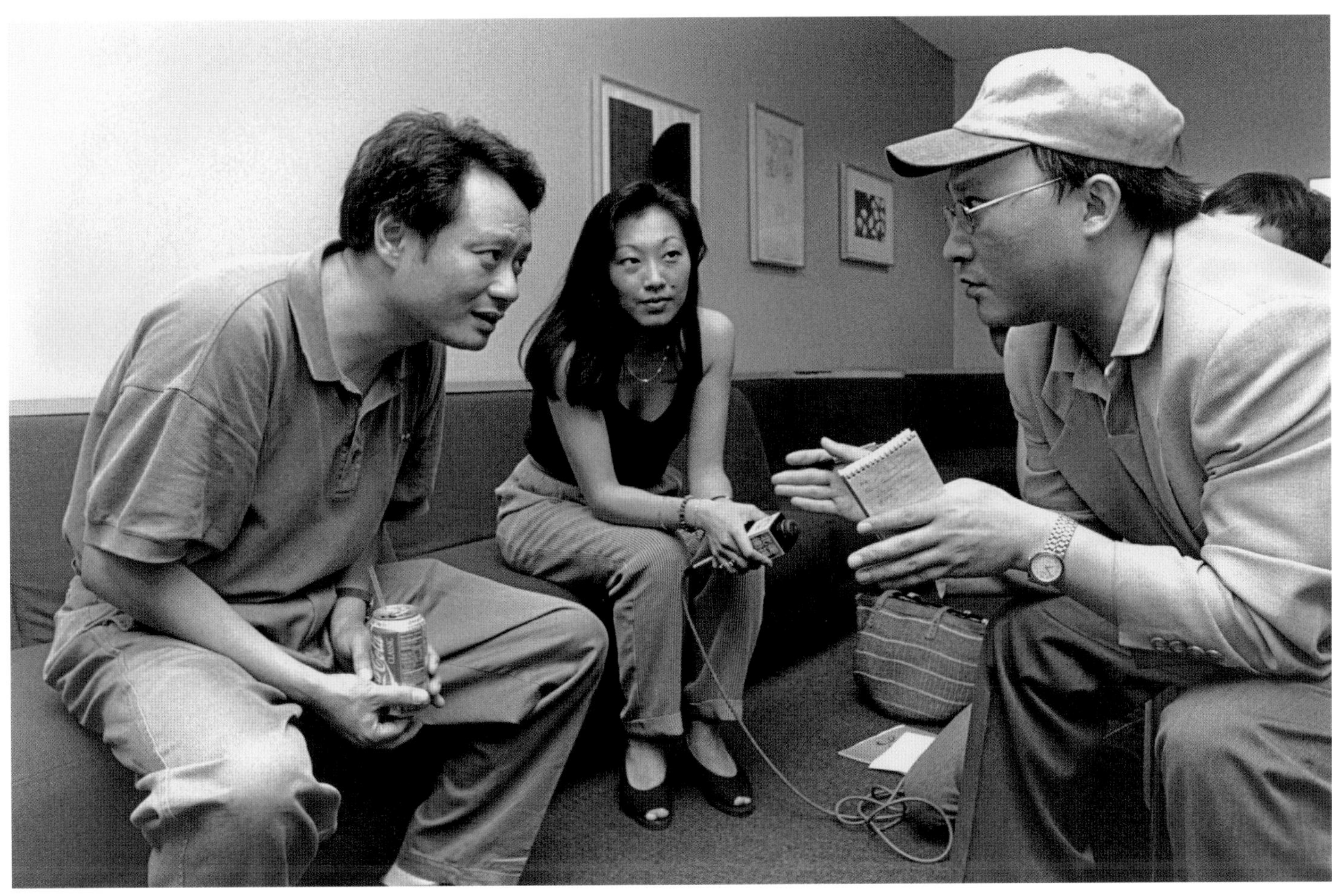

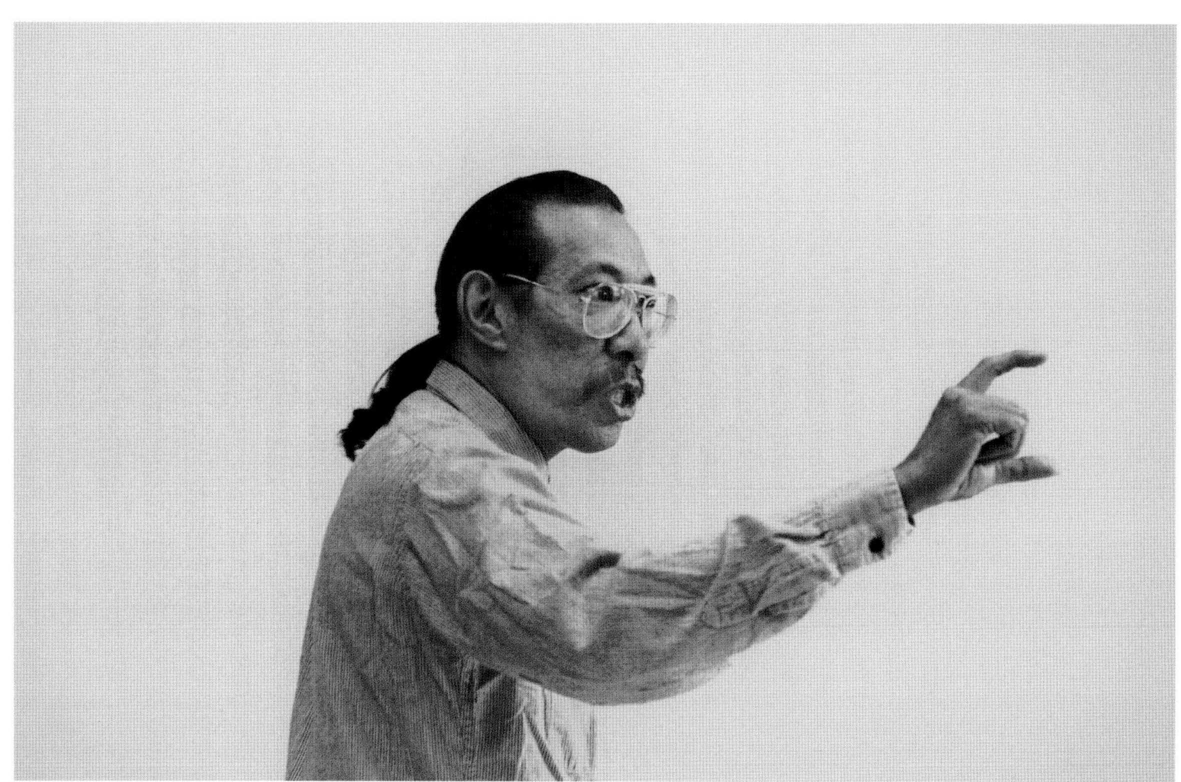

Writer Frank Chin.
Location unknown,
circa 1995.

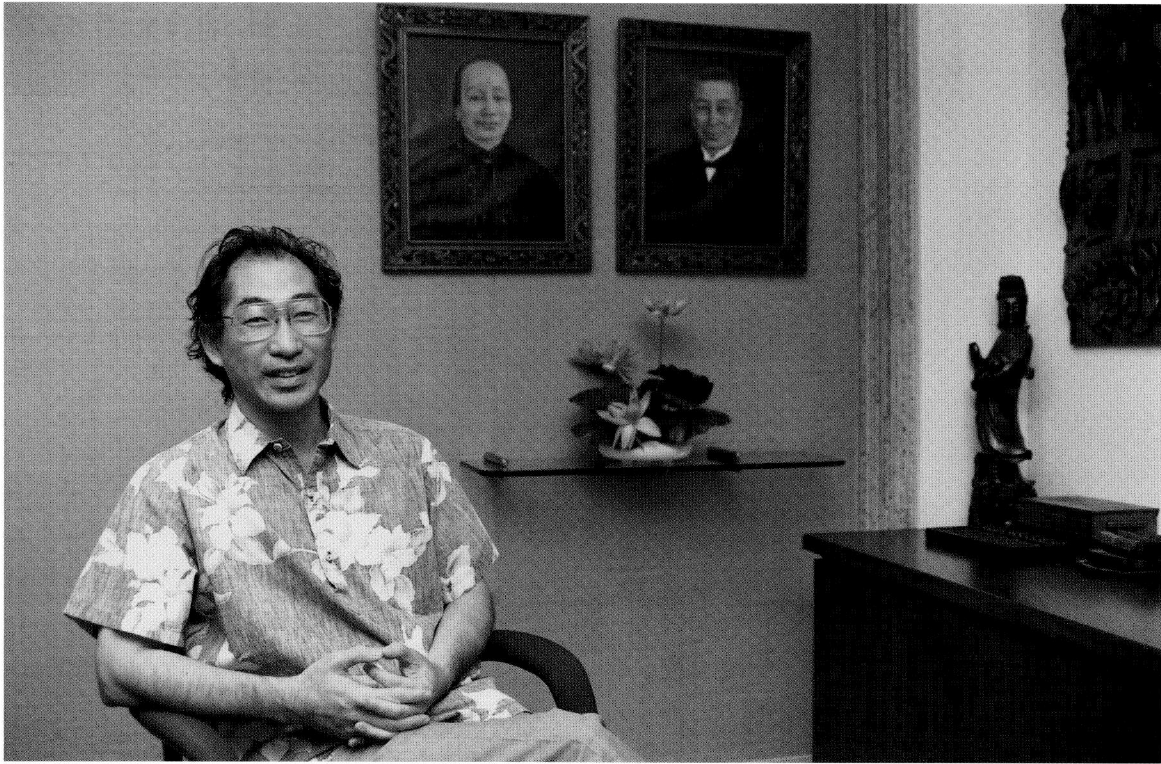

Poet Wing Tek Lum.
Honolulu, 1985.

In 1990 the Pan Asian Repertory Theatre produced an off-Broadway revival of David Henry Hwang's 1980 Obie Award-winning play, *F.O.B.* Directed by the playwright, the production featured Dennis Dun, Stan Egi, and Ann M. Tsuji. New York, 1990.

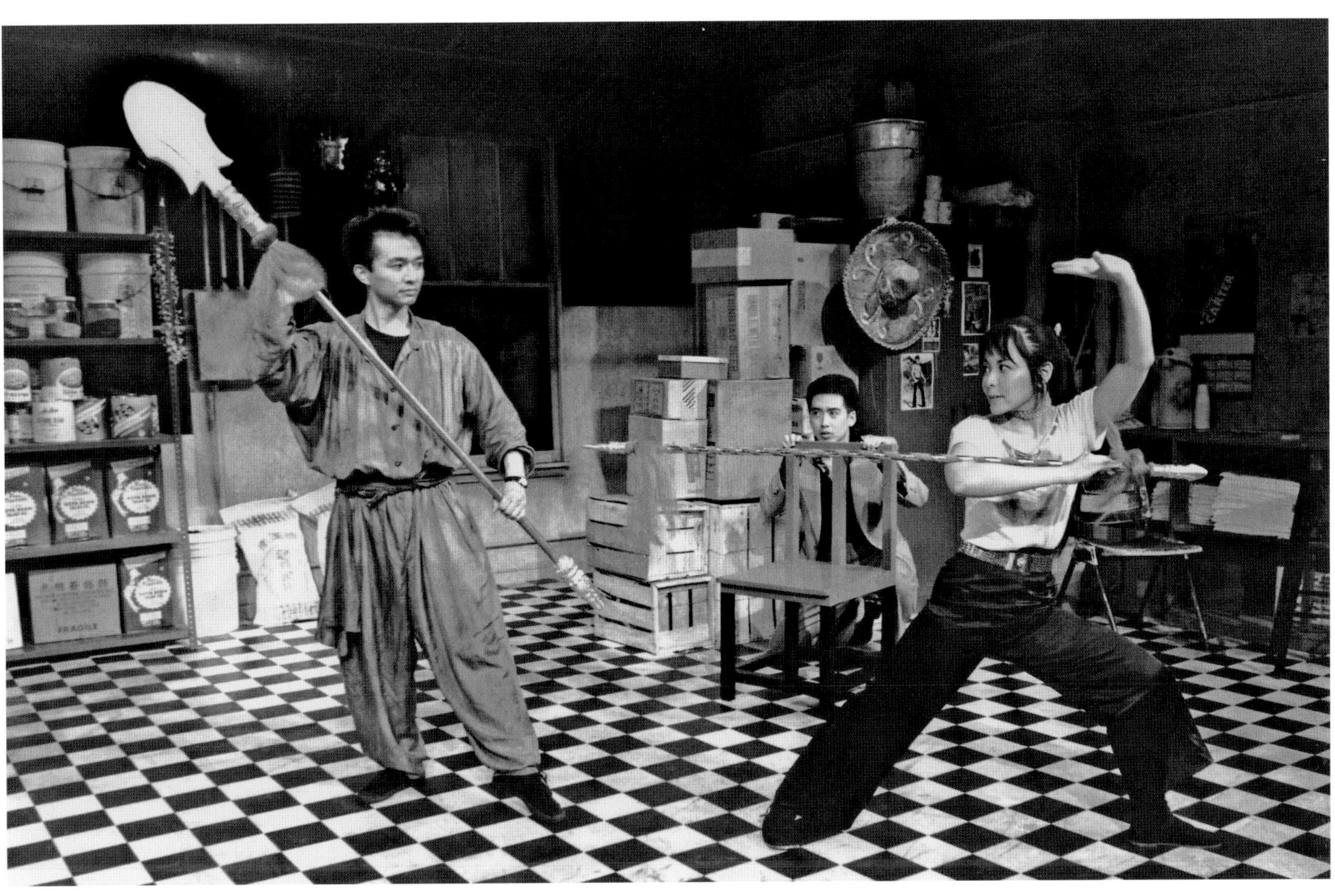

Asian American Journalists Association

TI-HUA CHANG

Award-winning investigative reporter in broadcast and digital journalism

In 1992, Corky Lee approached me with a question that's usually followed by a problem: "Could we talk?"

We were attending a meeting of the Asian American Journalists Association, then just over a decade old. Corky was concerned about the AAJA's membership rules, which he said excluded him from being a full member. I was confused. I had seen Corky at so many AAJA events that I assumed he was a member. Even as we talked, he looked like the quintessential photojournalist, with his ubiquitous SLR camera cradled on one arm and a black camera bag slung over his shoulder. At that moment, I realized that most of Corky's photographs, of what seemed like every event of the Asian American community, were unpaid acts of devotion.

Corky was correct about the rules. The AAJA bylaws required that in order to qualify for full membership, you had to earn the majority of your income as a journalist. Membership entitled you to hold office and to vote in the association's elections. Even though he had attended the 1987 founding meeting of the New York chapter and was one of its most active persons, Corky did not qualify for full membership.

The income requirement reflected the association's desire for acceptance by mainstream media companies. It did not account for the often-excruciating difficulties that most Asian Americans experienced in obtaining and keeping journalism jobs, or for the part-time and unpaid work of activist journalists.

I examined the membership bylaws of the National Association of Black Journalists and learned that this first journalists-of-color organization did indeed account for how hard it was, and still is, for most Black journalists to obtain and retain the ever fewer jobs in the industry. To be a full NABJ member, you only had to work the majority of your time in journalism, not earn the majority of your income from it.

In 1993 I brought the issue to the AAJA board, and to their credit, the board members voted unanimously to change the membership requirement from majority of income to majority of time. That principle remains in effect today.

The AAJA now has more than two thousand members. As a professional association, its goal is to increase Asian American and Pacific Islander perspectives and representation in the news industry. It encourages college students to pursue journalism as a career and AAPI journalists to become news managers and media executives. Its Media Watch site identifies and protests inaccuracies and racial stereotyping in reporting, from demeaning comments about physical appearance

Members of the International Ladies Garment Workers Union protested the firing of Kaity Tong by WABC-TV News. Tong, the first Asian American news anchor in the New York region, had enjoyed the highest ranking in her time slot. New York, 1991.

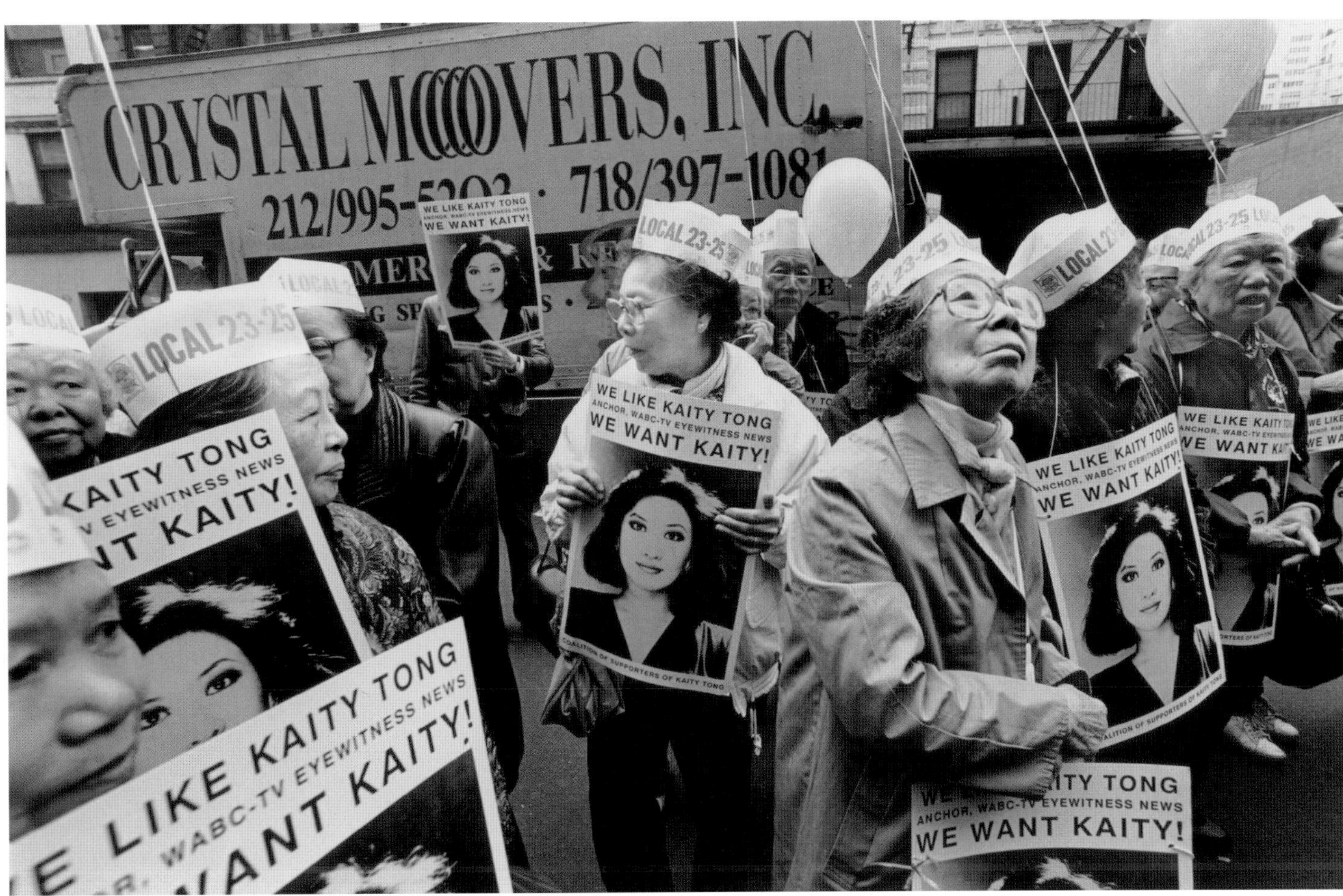

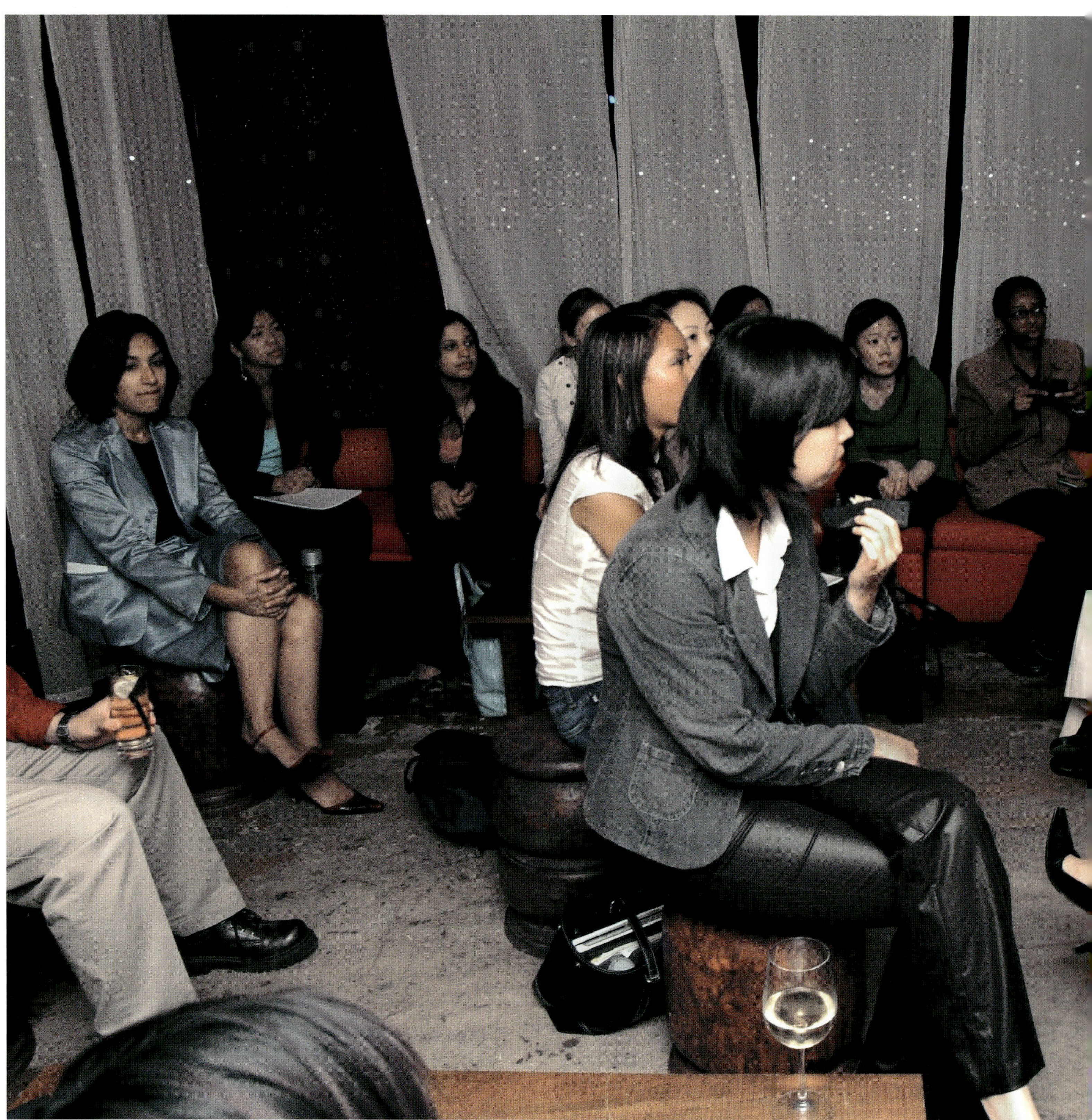

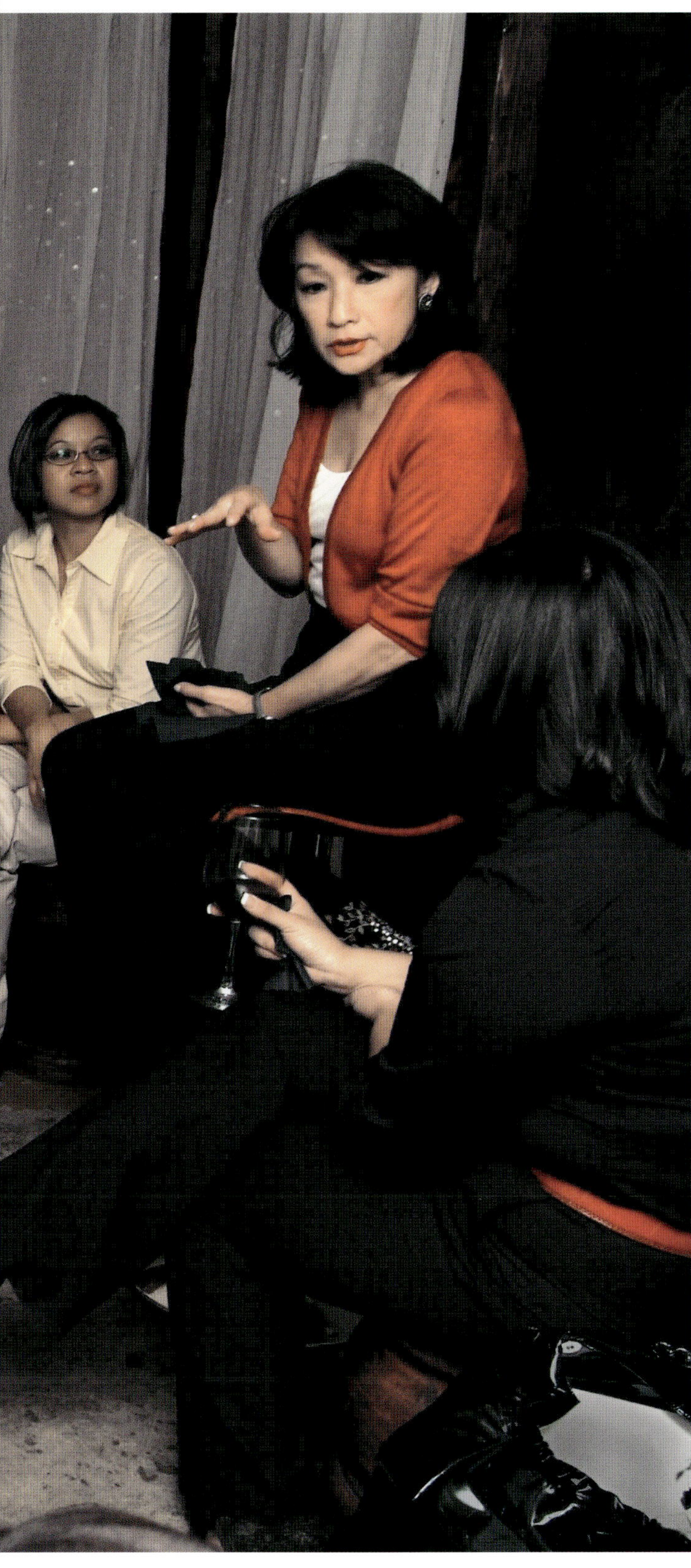

At a private meeting during the Asian American Journalists Association convention, the trailblazing network news anchor Connie Chung talked with other women journalists. New York, 2006.

to mistakes in names. AAPI journalists behind the pen and the lens can work to ensure that news coverage is fair and accurate.

The challenges of representation continue today. A 2022 AAJA study found that Asian Americans and Pacific Islanders are underrepresented in the local television newsrooms of America's twenty largest U.S. metropolitan areas. That finding aligned with a 2022 study by the respected Poynter Institute for Media Studies, which concluded that "newsrooms of all sizes and mediums have mostly stayed white, despite years of declarations and missed goals."

Corky understood the AAJA's impact and captured it with his camera. In 1991, when WABC-TV fired the popular local television news anchor Kaity Tong, he photographed the protests. In 2006, when veteran television news anchor Connie Chung spoke with women members of AAJA, he documented it, providing a stunning inside glimpse of intergenerational solidarity. Corky also coordinated fundraisers for the AAJA, raising thousands of dollars by selling the donated and framed photographs of its photojournalist members (including his own). At the 2022 AAJA convention, the first since the pandemic and Corky's passing, there was no photo auction.

Recently, I asked his brother John if Corky ever told him about his membership struggles. John said that Corky had told him, "Ti-Hua took care of it." That validation reverberates inside me with the weight of a golden spike from history.

Asian American Writers' Workshop

MARIE MYUNG-OK LEE

Writer in residence at the Center for the Study of Ethnicity and Race at Columbia University; author of the novel *The Evening Hero*

In 1991 I left my parent-pleasing job in banking to pursue what I had really wanted to do since age nine: become a writer. My friend Christina Chiu brought me to a meeting of a half-dozen Asian American writers at a Manhattan diner, where they critiqued one another's work. I immediately sank into the comfort and artistic safety of this group, all of them still unpublished but dreamers like me.

I was surprised to learn that New York City, which seemed to have at least one of everything, had no Asian-focused literary organization. If we wanted an artistic community, we would have to create our own. We came up with the name "Asian American Writers' Workshop" for our group. Curtis Chin, who would become the AAWW's first executive director, suggested we hold a reading at the Chinatown History Museum to commemorate the tenth anniversary of Vincent Chin's murder. Pre-internet as it was, we did almost no advertising, but the reading attracted such a large crowd that we had to turn people away so as not to violate the fire code. It was then that we four co-founders—Christina Chiu, Curtis Chin, Bino A. Realuyo, and myself—all in our twenties, realized that our community needed the AAWW.

In 1992 the AAWW incorporated as a nonprofit organization, devoted to "creating, publishing, developing, and disseminating creative writing by Asian Americans." With little capital, at first we shared office space with more established Asian American organizations like the Committee Against Anti-Asian Violence. Eventually, thanks to an NEA grant and corporate sponsors like AT&T, we procured various roving offices: on Elizabeth Street, then in an old Crunch Fitness on St. Mark's. To get the word out, we handed out flyers at Asian American events to anyone who looked receptive. At a lot of these gatherings, I noticed a tall man with a camera seemingly glued to his face. He had attended that original Vincent Chin commemoration reading. He introduced himself as Corky Lee, and we became friends.

Corky's artistic activism was inspirational for our nascent organization. Literary organizations often avoid politics, possibly to make themselves more attractive to donors, but as writers and Asian Americans, we felt that the very existence of our work was inherently political. Many of our early members were entering the Asian American art and/or activism space for the first time. We did not police the seriousness or ambition of their work. We welcomed all styles and themes as long as they didn't harm or demean anyone. We intentionally wanted the workshop to be a place where writers could try out new work, and a refuge from the obstacles and frustrations of the white-dominated publishing world.

Given that the Asian American community was (and is still) made up primarily of immigrants and the children of immigrants, the AAWW's low-cost evening workshops became an alternative to MFA programs. In a single workshop, for example, we nurtured Ed Lin, Lisa Ko, Cathy Park Hong, and Min Jin Lee—and they were taught by the then-unknown Jhumpa Lahiri. In addition, we created our own literary journal, offered fellowships and mentorship, and ran an Asian American bookstore. In so doing, we not only drove Asian American literary work but helped create its community.

The AAWW passed its thirtieth birthday in 2022 and is now run by a new generation of twentysomethings. Min Jin Lee's 2017 novel *Pachinko* has achieved the status of the Great American Novel, Jhumpa Lahiri has a distinguished professorial chair at Barnard, and Ken Chen, a former AAWW executive director, is the associate director of Barnard's creative writing program.

The AAWW no longer runs a bookstore, but twenty-eight-year-old Lucy Yu has stepped into the breach with her own Asian American–focused bookstore in Chinatown, Yu & Me Books. And since Corky Lee is the number one son of Chinatown, the store features two of his prints on its walls.

It's with relief and pride that we see this next generation of artists and activists rising. Corky's iconoclastic example *did* give us a model. He showed us that Asian Americans can raise our voices and make people listen, that we can make noise, get "political," and make art while not needing permission from anyone. We can define ourselves instead of waiting for a white-dominated literary scene to tell us what we are.

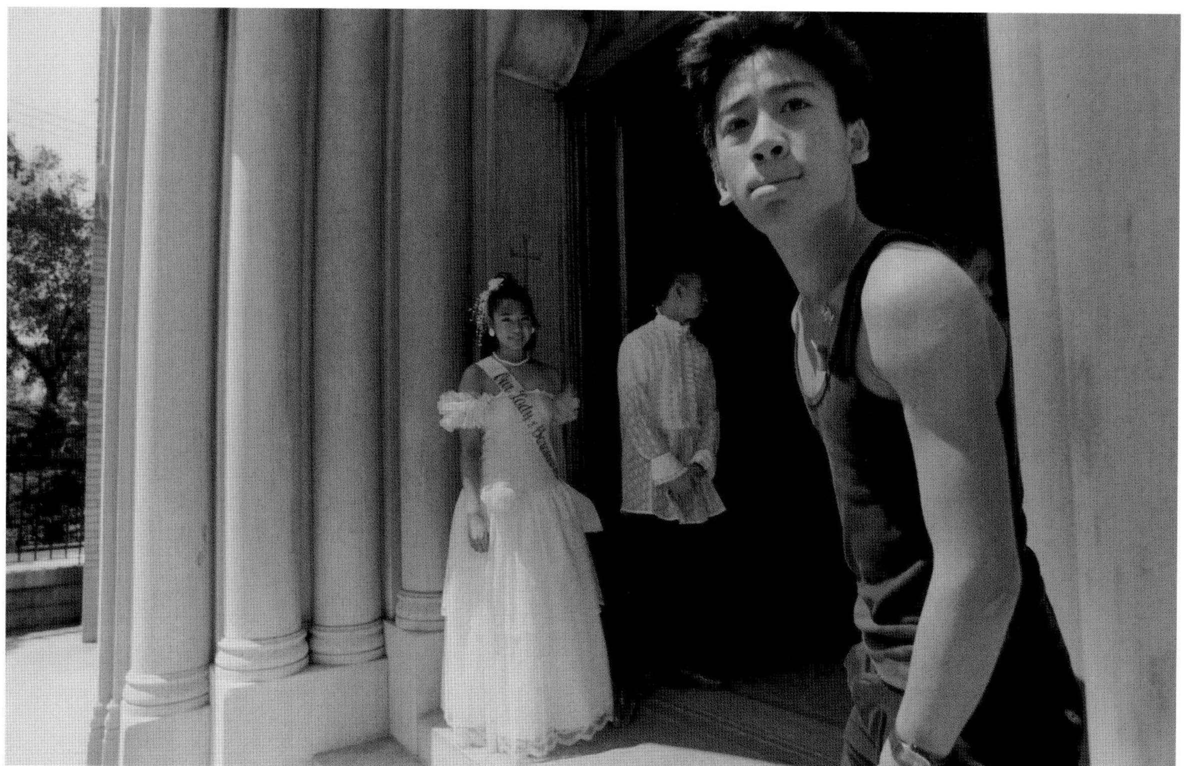

Our Lady of Barangay and friends at St. Mary's Church. Jersey City, New Jersey, 1992.

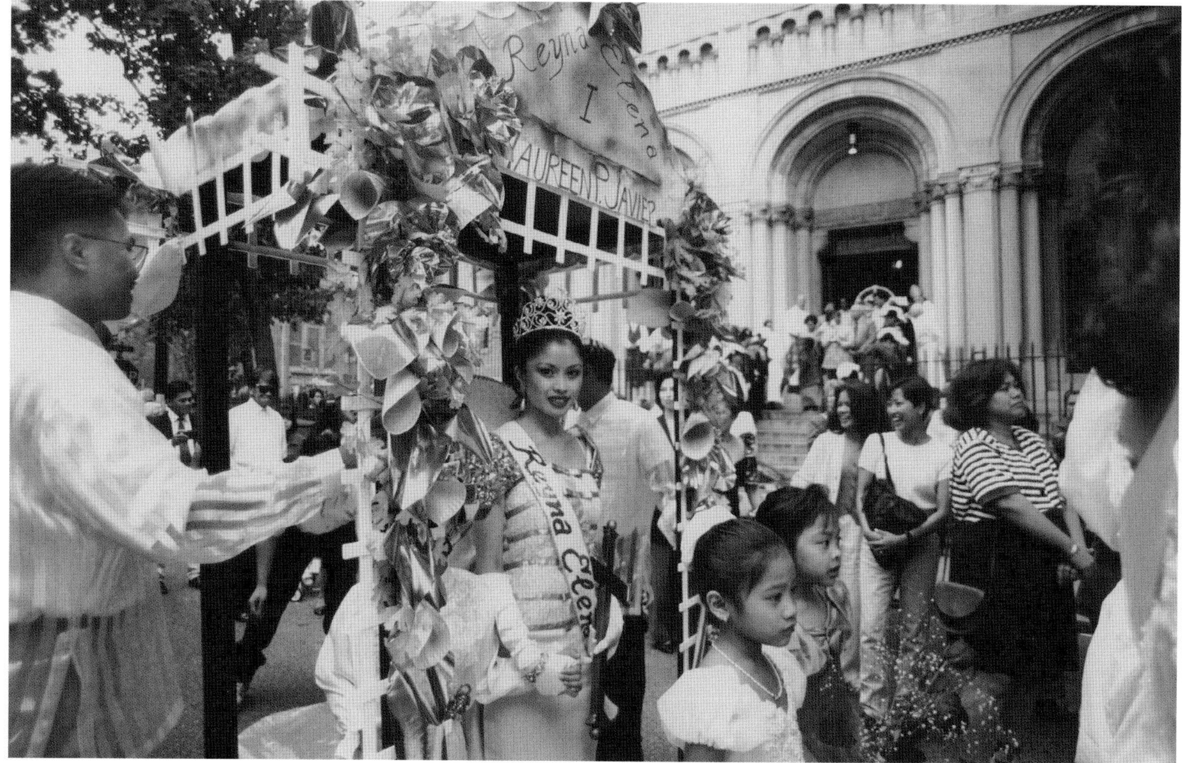

Beauty pageant winner Maureen Javier, crowned as Reyna Elena, leads a procession in the ritual of the holy cross in the northern New Jersey Filipino community's Flores de Mayo festival. Jersey City, New Jersey, May 1995.

The Japanese Folk Dance Institute performed at the *matsuri* (festival of thanks). New York, 1999.

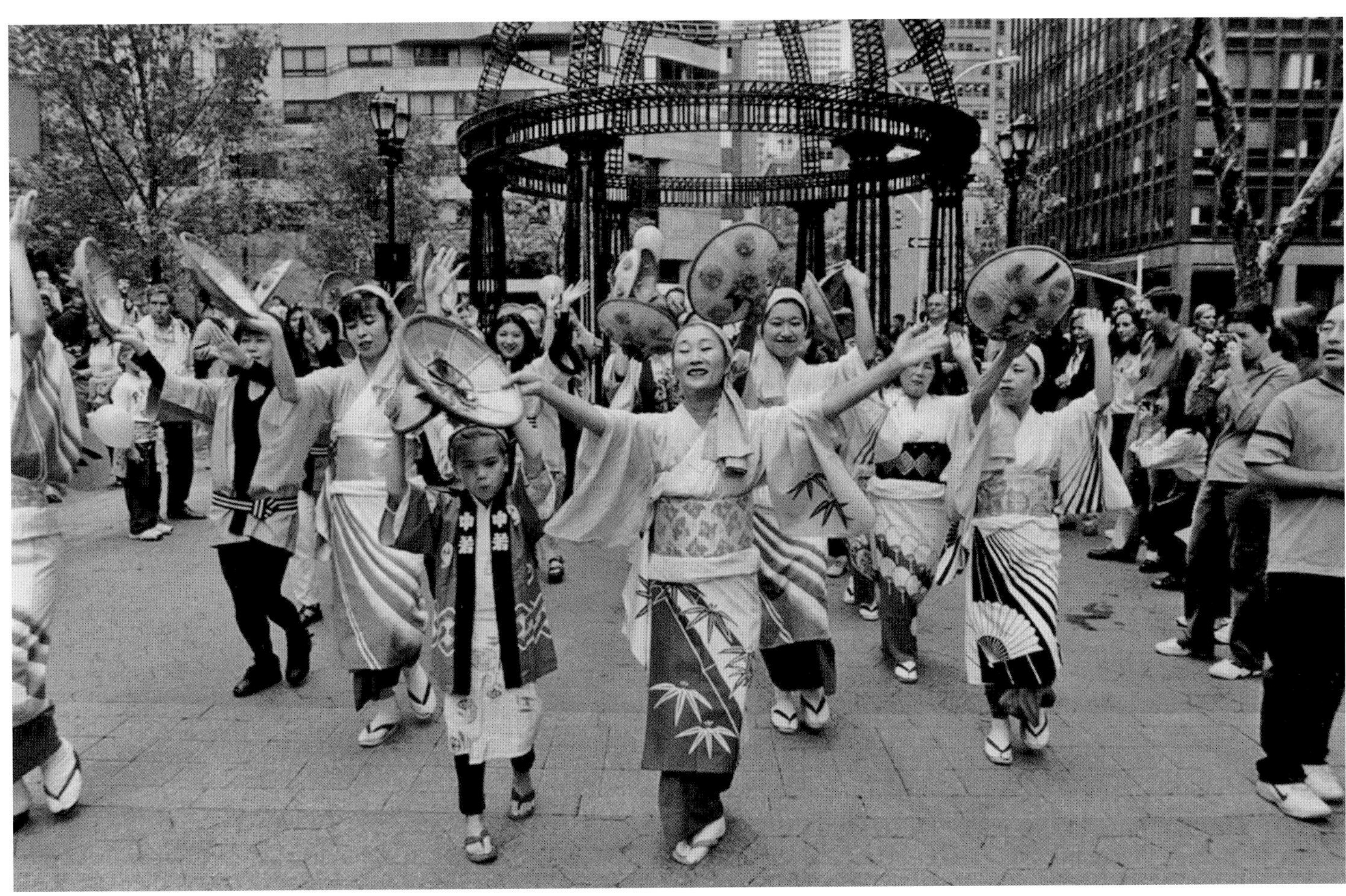

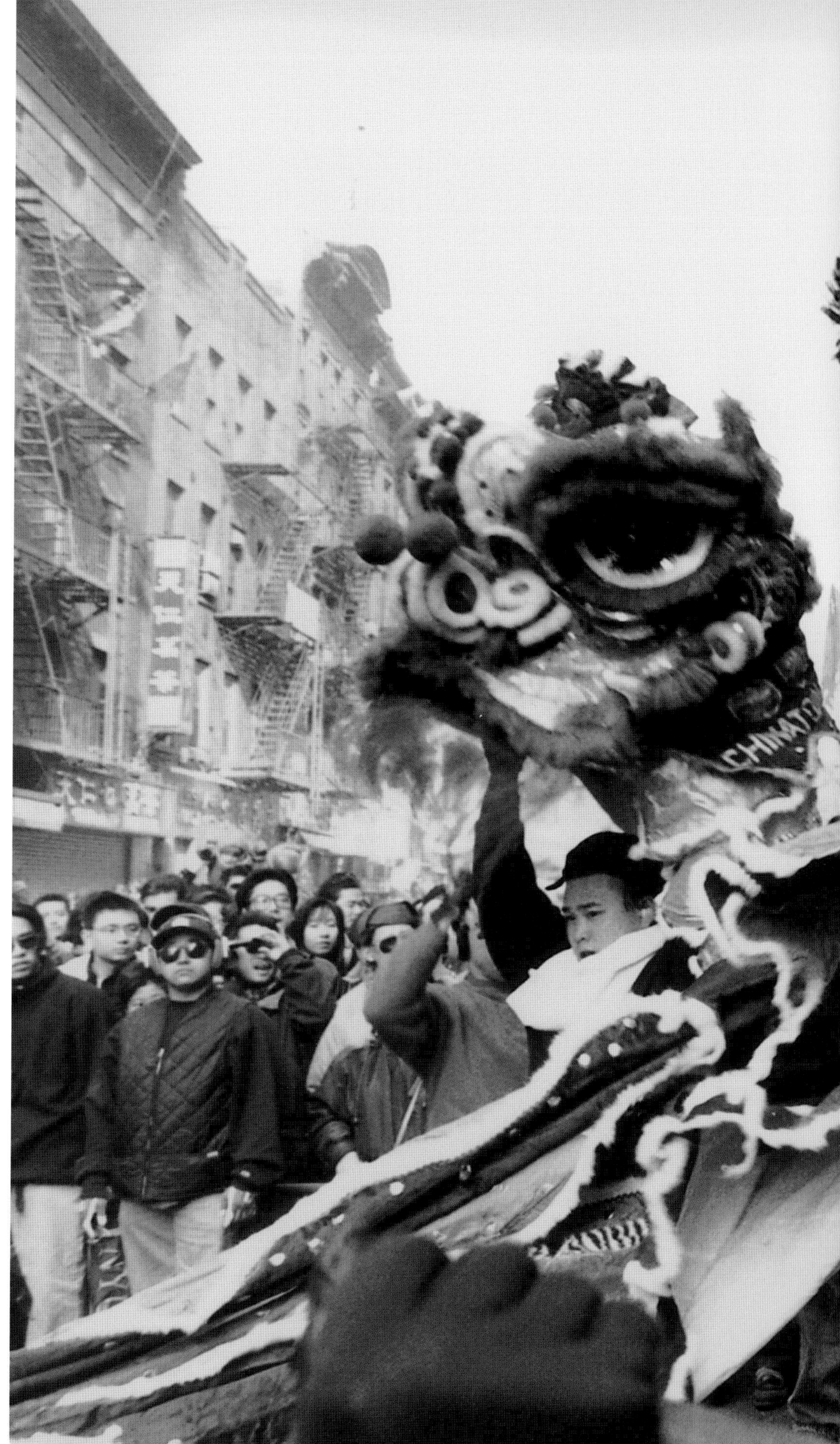

Lunar New Year parade in Chinatown. New York, 1996.

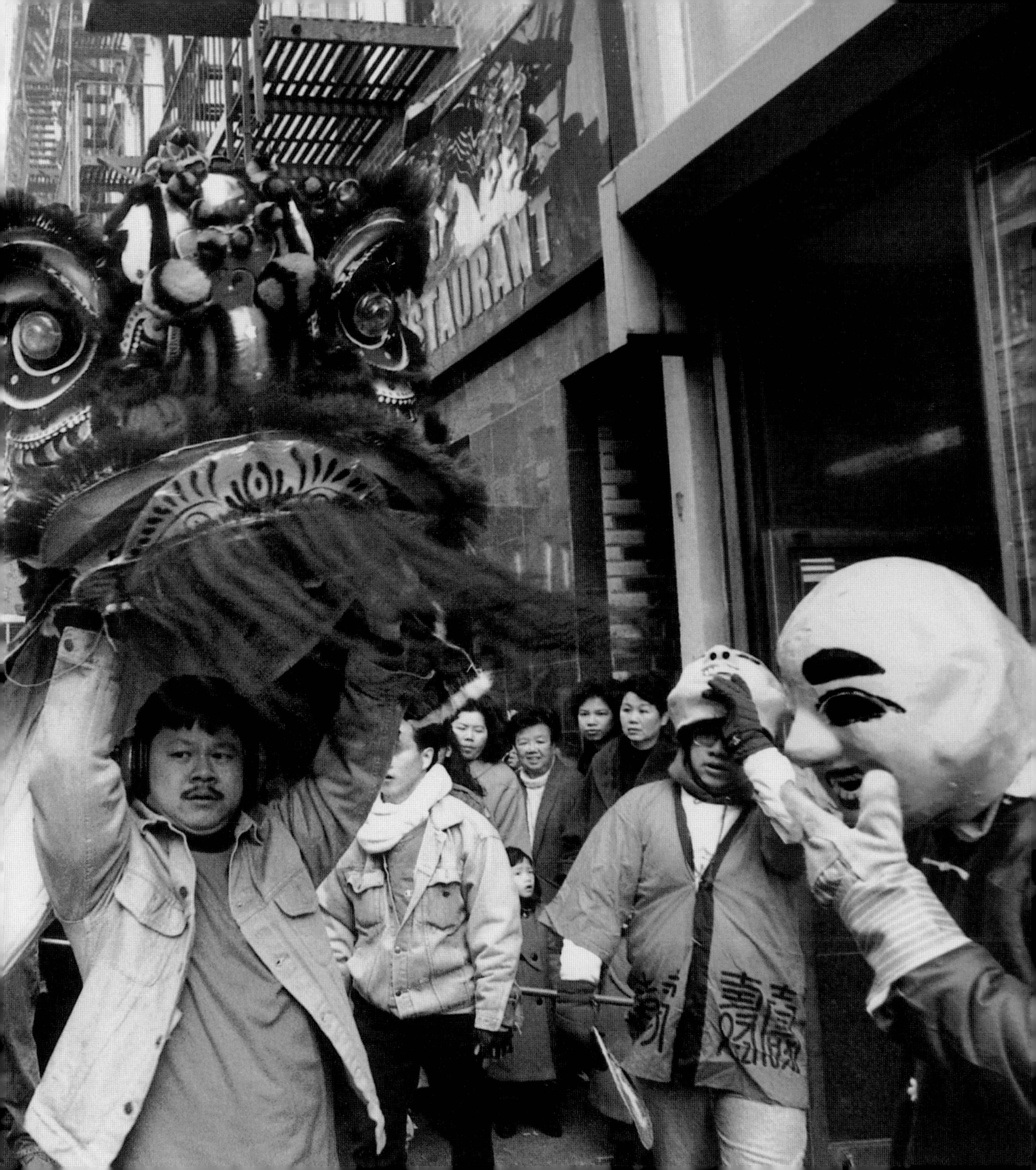
STAURANT

Peeling the Banana

GARY SAN ANGEL
Filmmaker, director, performance artist, and songwriter

In 1995 in New York, sixteen Asian American men, ages eighteen to forty, formed the theater collective Peeling the Banana. Members of our group came from all walks of life: we had a physician and musicians, writers and activists, students and teachers, performers and nonprofit workers. Forming a circle together, telling our individual stories, meant we were no longer silent, no longer invisible, no longer desexualized, the butt of racist jokes. Performing our stories in community was a powerful healing salve to the internalized racism and sexism we faced and an act of defiance to the negative media portrayals, history of exclusion, and antimiscegenation laws that have long shaped the perceptions of Asian men in this country. By sharing our personal truths and delving underneath the surface, we were "peeling" away the layers and rebuilding a picture of what it truly means to be ourselves.

Corky took this photo in March 1996, at our first official show at the Asian American Writers' Workshop. He liked this photo because behind us was an art installation created by Lambert Fernando with different-size penises, a commentary on the stereotype that Asian men have small penises. We both knew that photographing a group of intergenerational Asian men, defying the negative images about us together, was powerful.

At the time, social media did not yet exist, so Corky was our Facebook. His photos put us on the map in the theater scene, and *The New York Times* and *Newsday* covered our show about Asian American men, which was rare in the 1990s. Corky continued to document our group as it expanded to include Asian American women and more LGBTQ participants and sibling groups, Jook Songs at Yale University and Something to Say at the Asian Arts Initiative in Philadelphia. I am indebted to Corky for believing in us and making sure that through his photos, our groups existed and mattered.

The pan-Asian men's performance group Peeling the Banana at the Asian American Writers' Workshop. Behind them is *100 Boys Marching,* an installation by artist Lambert Fernando, part of the AAWW's *Groundbreaking Artists in the Metro Area* exhibition. *Left to right, front row:* John Ko, Gary San Angel, Ken J. Changpertitum, Yongsoo Park, Hugo Mahabir. *Middle row:* Dave Lin, Mike Ishii, Dave Rah, Farhad Asghar, Ed Lin, Ngo Thanh Nhan. *Back row:* Michel Ng, Peter Ong. New York, March 1996.

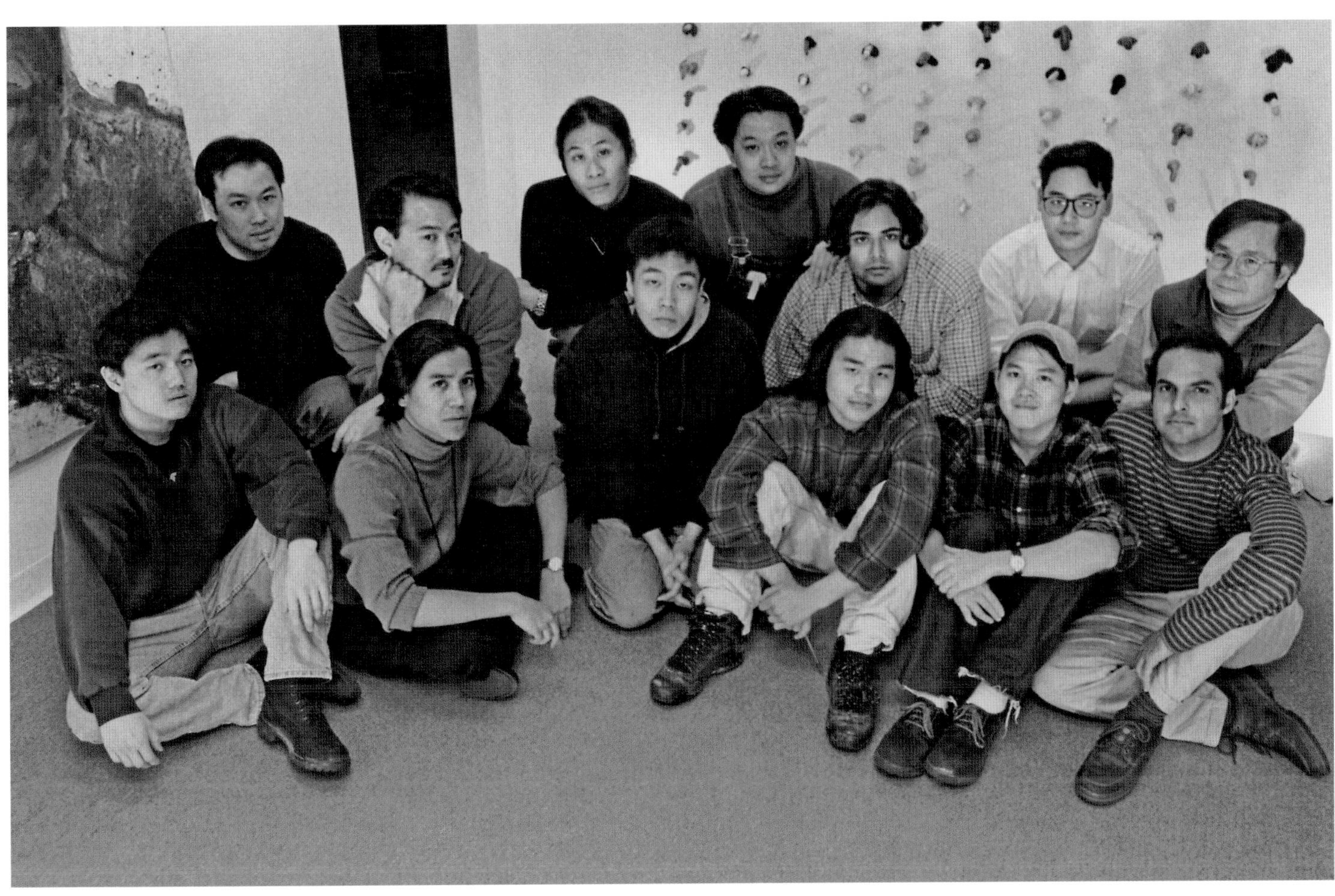

Hip-hop dancers perform for Japanese American Social Services, Inc. New York, 1999.

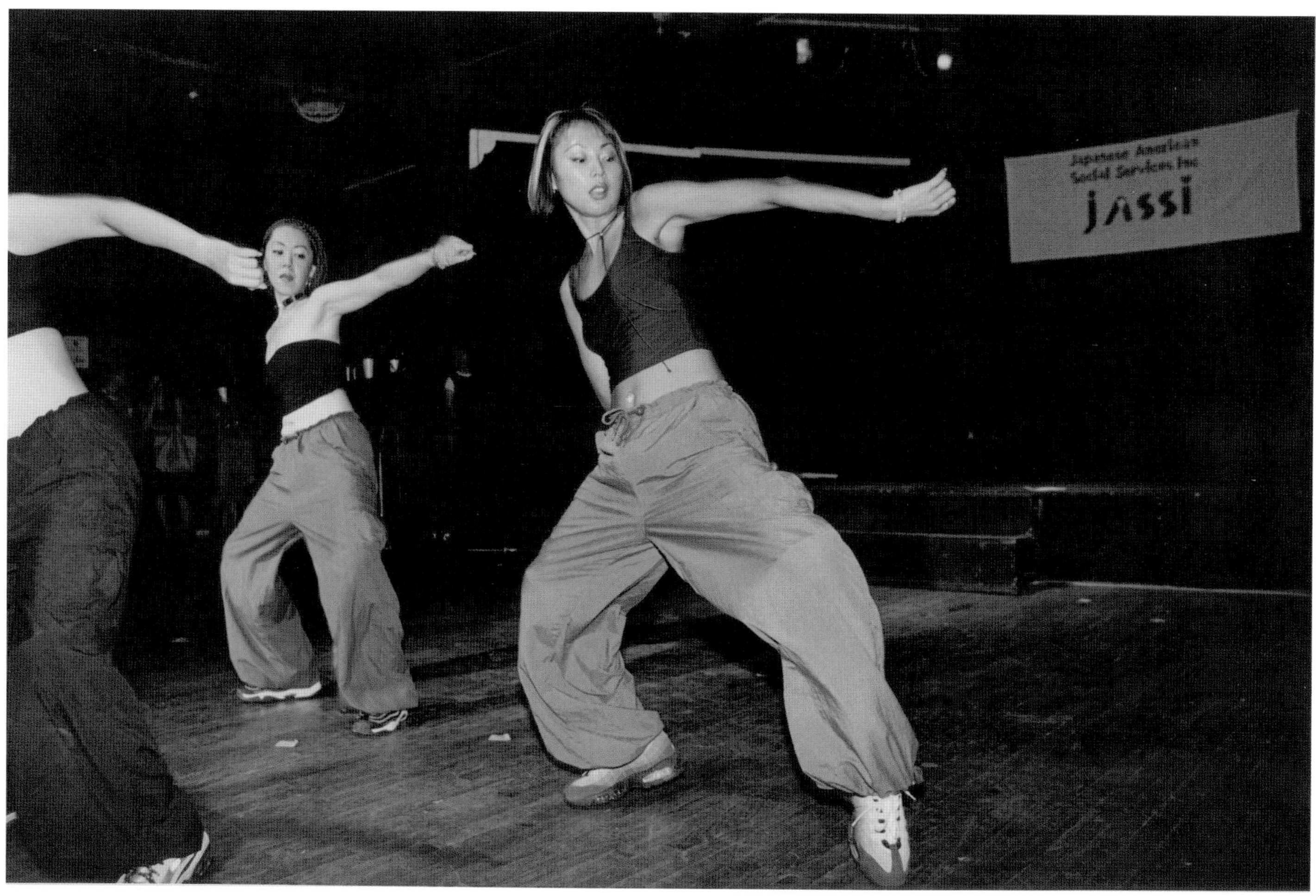

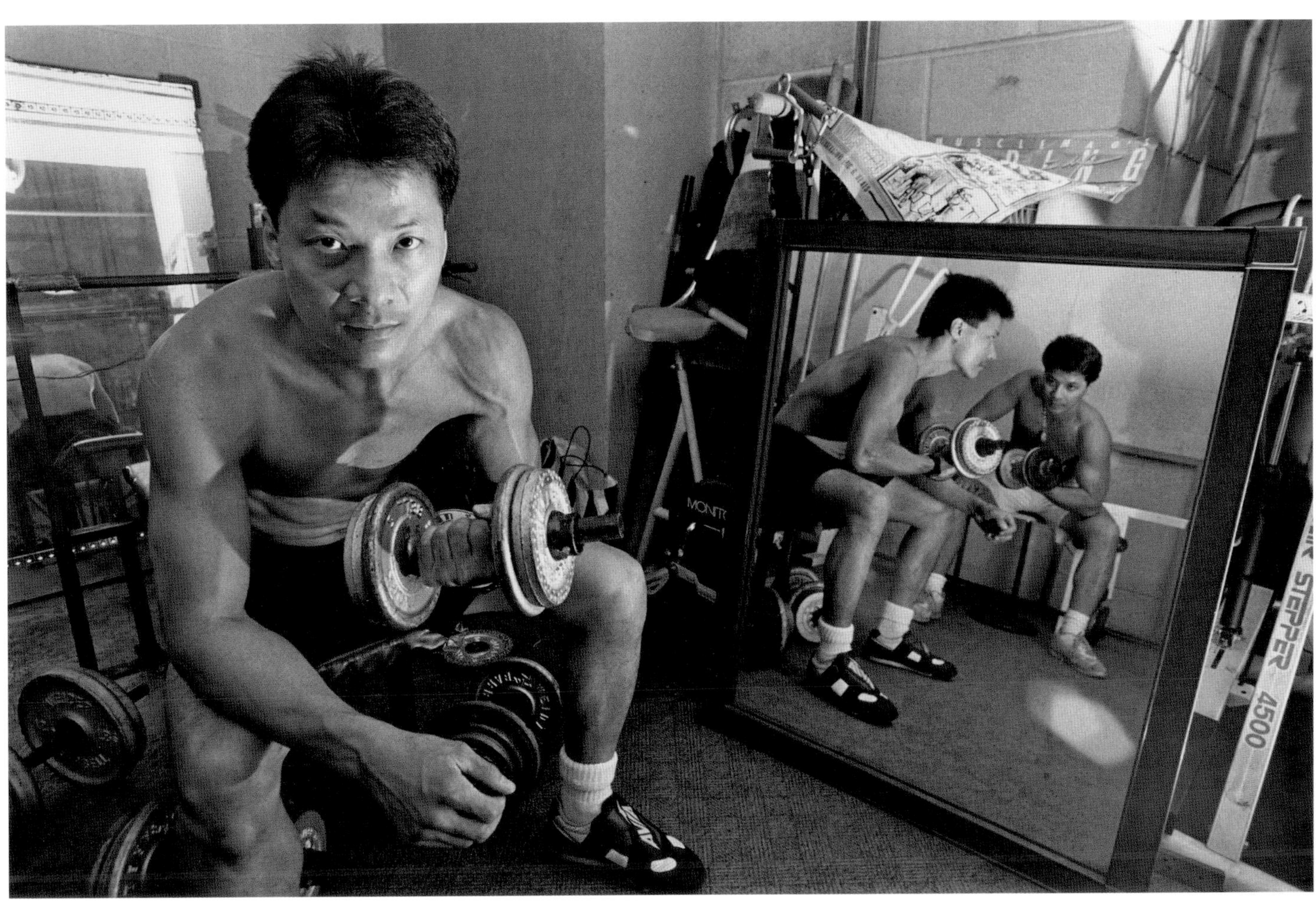

Arthur Ng and his brother Eddie (in mirror), bodybuilders and school custodians and firefighters at P.S. 124 in Chinatown. New York, 1996.

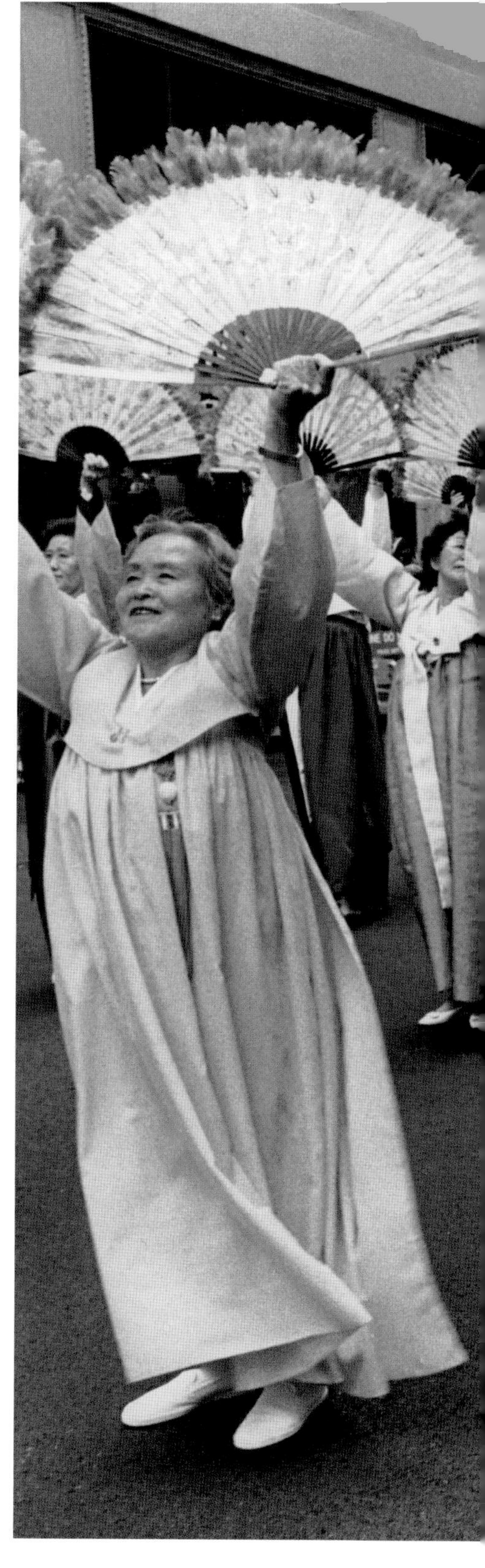

Performers of buchaechum, the traditional Korean fan dance, at the Korea Day parade. New York, 1983.

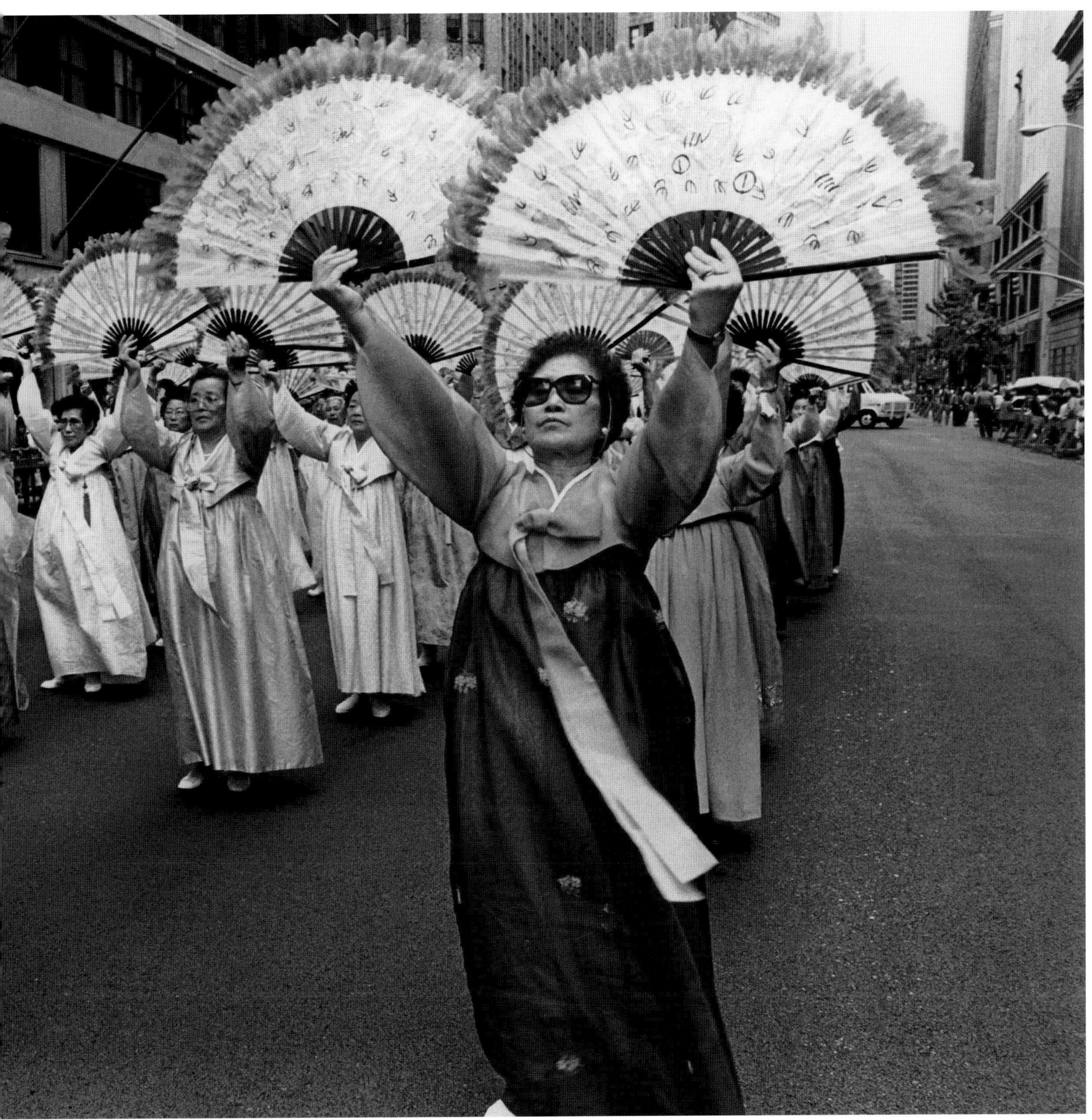

Looking for Corky in the Crowd

POTRI RANKA MANIS
Dancer and performance artist

Corky Lee was a friend, advocate, and documentarian of Kinding Sindaw, the dance and cultural group I founded in 1992. Kinding Sindaw tells the stories of the indigenous people and Moro Muslims of Mindanao, southern Philippines. We preserve and promote the culture, arts, and living tradition of people who resisted Spanish colonization, who were sold by the Spaniards to the United States in 1898, and who are now facing cultural erasure from the encroachment of multinational companies extracting natural resources from their ancestral land.

Corky was a pioneer member of the board of directors of Kinding Sindaw. He nurtured us like a father. I believe he bonded with us because we were a cultural group with artistic sociopolitical content, and our themes encompass how to dismantle and resist the colonial mentality and neocolonialism. He helped us navigate grant funding, photographed everything we did, traveled with us, and stayed with us during rehearsals into the wee hours of the morning to capture our backstage as well as our onstage stories.

Corky took his last photograph of Kinding Sindaw on March 12, 2020, the day of the Covid-19 lockdown in New York. It was the world premiere of a theatrical dance production at La MaMa Experimental Theatre Club, titled *Pananadem*, which means "remembering" in the language of the Meranao. *Pananadem* is a way of looking back across time, to gain inspiration and perspective from one's ancestors. In this tale, old and new align as refugees and displaced tradition bearers recall the legends of *Derangen*, an epic from the indigenous Meranao, the people of Lake Lanao.

Corky, with his camera, was the storyteller of our collective lives. We were not only artist-activists together, we were close friends. He was a part of my life as an immigrant nurse, artist, mother, and activist, and I was a part of his life. In 2001, when Corky's wife, Margie, was dying, I went to their apartment in Queens to bathe her and tend to her wounds and try to lessen her excruciating pain. I persuaded Corky to admit Margie to hospice care. I was there when she passed and saw the enormous devastation in Corky's face. Twenty years later I was with Corky in the ICU when he was hospitalized for Covid. Two precious people in my diasporic life gave me the privilege to be at their bedside in their last moments.

Ever since January 27, 2021, at every rally and demonstration, I and other artists and activists are still looking for Corky Lee in the crowd, looking for him with his camera. His advocacy has gone beyond the islands of New York to the global audience, where the energy of the people immortalized in his photos brings consciousness and a call for solidarity to the world.

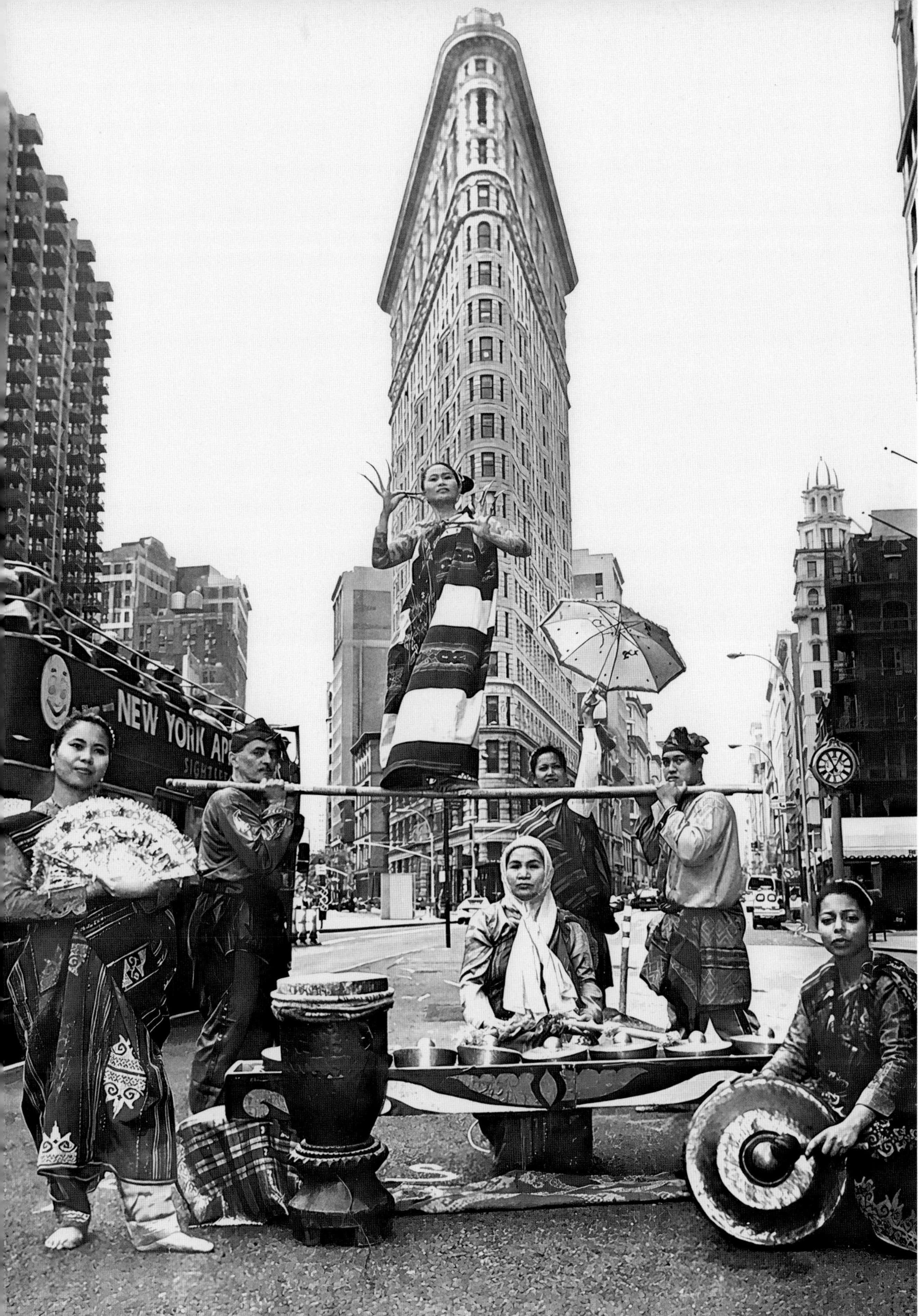

The theater and dance troupe Kinding Sindaw, with Potri Manus (*center*), on Philippine Independence Day. Madison Square Park, New York, 1999.

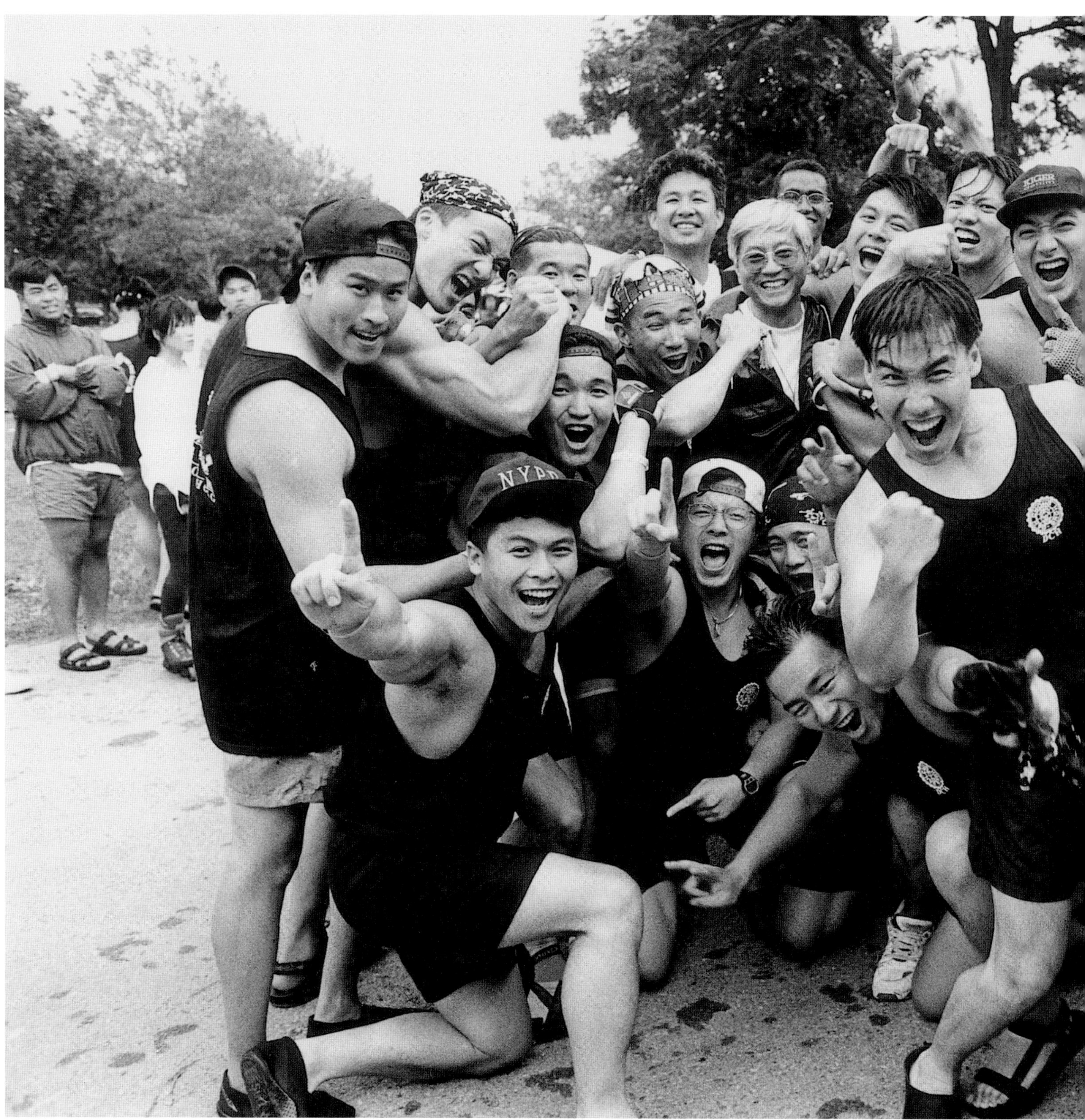
NYPD

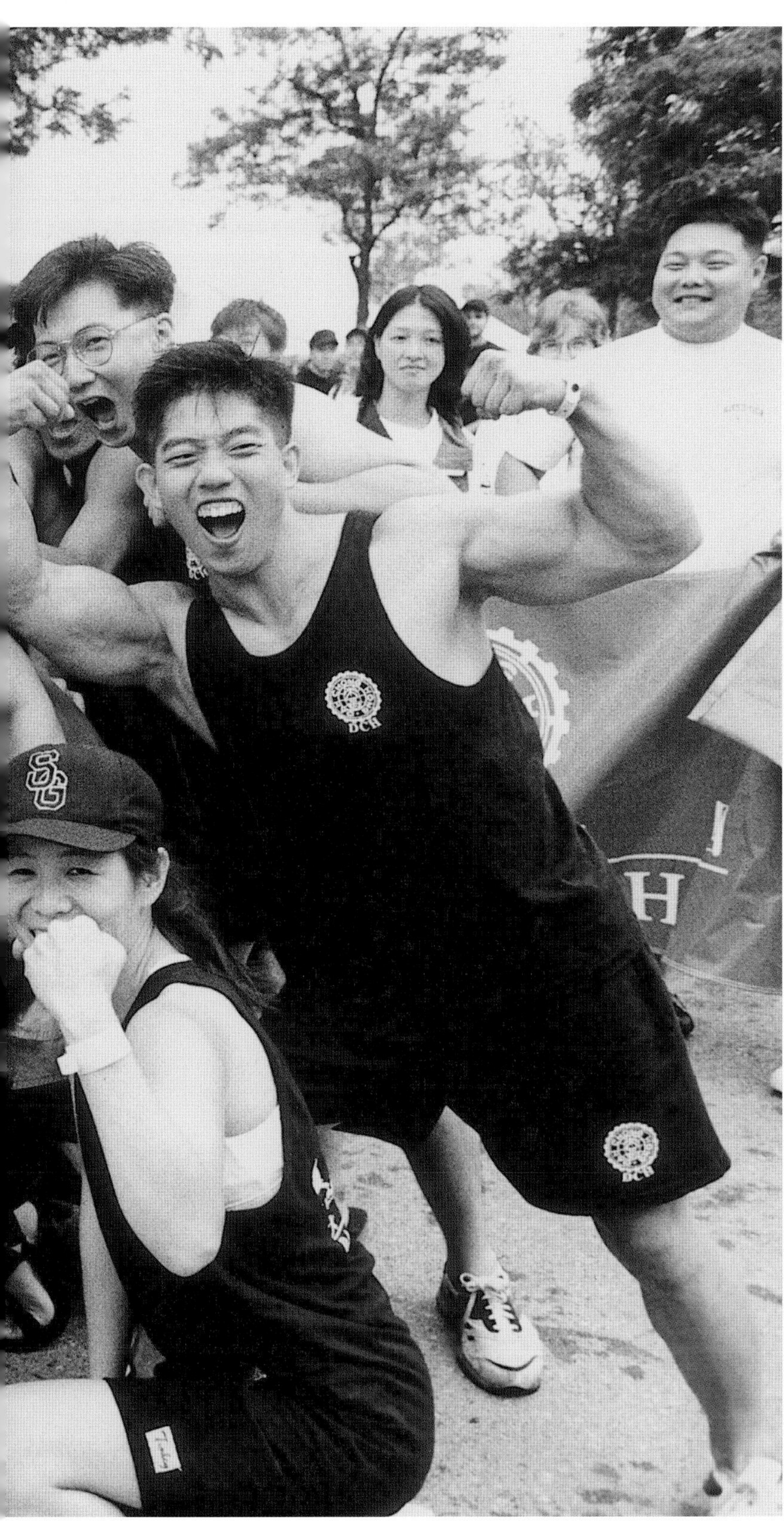

Dah Hong Chong dragon boat club after winning the five-hundred-meter race. Flushing, Queens, New York, 1995.

RESILIENCE

2000s

—2010s

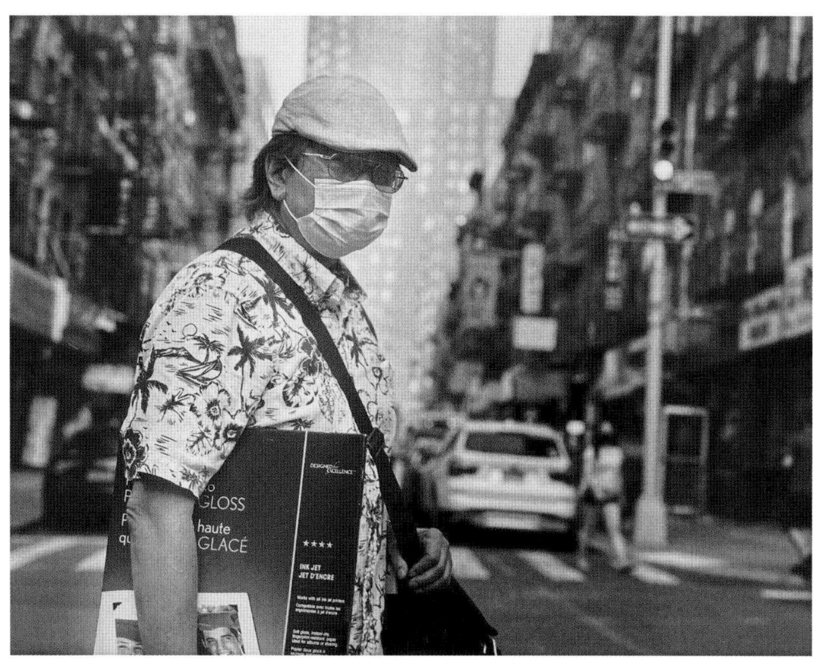

Corky Lee at Mott and Bayard streets in Chinatown during the first year of the Covid-19 pandemic. New York, July 2020.
Edward Cheng

During the 2000s and 2010s, Corky Lee's work continued and reached new heights, despite personal losses and obstacles. His beloved wife of twenty-six years, Margaret, passed away in 2001, from cancer. He continued to cover events, not allowing his troublesome arthritic knees to slow him down. His personal resilience mirrored that of Asian American and Pacific Islander communities as they faced the challenges of the new millennium. Corky's photographs capture the ongoing themes of daily life, political empowerment, and cultural heritage. One can detect in them the same vibrancy as ever and perhaps some maturity, reflecting Corky's evolution as an artist and more broadly the strides made by Asian Americans in politics and the arts.

Owing to his status in Chinatown and in the AAPI movement, Corky was also playing the roles of mentor and organizer. He took photography students and interns under his wing and helped found new community arts organizations, like 21 Pell Street, in the First Chinese Baptist Church in New York's Chinatown. He spearheaded the organizing that brought hundreds of Asian Americans to Promontory Summit, Utah, for an epic photographic reenactment of the completion of the transcontinental railroad.

The defining event at the dawn of the new millennium—for the nation, for Asian Americans, and for Corky—was the terrorist attack on the World Trade Center on September 11, 2001. Spurred by the events surrounding 9/11, themes of loyalty and patriotism became more pronounced in Corky's photography and activism. His poignant portrait of a Sikh man wrapped in the American flag in Central Park, New York, four days after 9/11, was an instant icon. But much more than that famous single photo, Corky took dozens if not scores of photos that featured Asian Americans waving, saluting, and displaying American flags large and small. He was capturing a moment in which waving the flag was the simplest way to convey a message: "We are loyal, we are law-abiding, we are not terrorists, we are immigrants who love America"—a message that was actually more complicated and weightier than the flag alone could bear. Corky's own patriotism was deeply felt but was never jingoistic or pro-war. Rather, it emphasized Asian Americans' belonging to the country.

That sentiment is evident in Corky's documentation of the effects of 9/11 on New York's Chinatown, which was economically devastated because of its proximity to Ground Zero. His photographs appeared in the book *Voices of Healing,* published by the Organization of Chinese Americans. Corky wrote the book's foreword, saying that the "contributions, heroism, and continued determination of Asian Americans and Pacific Islanders to renew and rebuild their lives and communities after September 11" was evidence of "the fabric of a great society. This diverse weave of people who call America home make it kind, generous, giving, and strong."

Corky also expressed his patriotism by joining Chinatown's American Legion Lt. B. R. Kimlau Chinese Memorial Post 1291 (named in honor of an Air Force bomber pilot who was killed in action in the Pacific in 1944). Corky was eligible for membership because his father was a World War II veteran. He wore his American Legion cap around town proudly, as if to publicly honor the nation and his father. He was an active presence at the post and became a beloved "son" of the veterans. In 2016 he joined the campaign to award Congressional Gold Medals to Chinese American World War II veterans in recognition of their military service. Congress finally passed the bill in 2018, and after many delays, Corky's

Corky Lee on a ladder directing the composition of the reenactment photo. Promontory Summit, Utah, 2014. *Scott Summerdorf/Salt Lake Tribune*

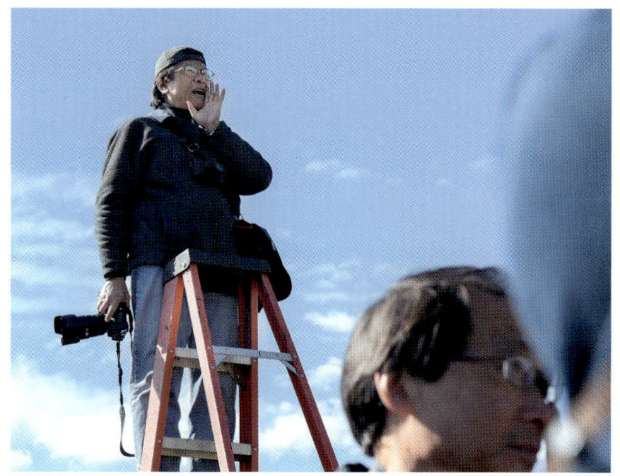

father received his gold medal posthumously in 2021.

Corky continued to photograph Asian American events in the New York metropolitan region as well as the changing scene in Chinatown and beyond. In addition to long-standing issues like labor rights and racism in the media, new themes emerged. In 2005 the National Queer Asian Pacific Islander Alliance formed, reflecting the growing presence and awareness of an Asian American LGBTQ community. Immigration policy, gentrification, and land use, while not new issues, became more prominent. The surveillance and deportation of immigrants, commonly thought to be a concern of the U.S.-Mexico border and Latino communities, affected Asian immigrants as well. The city of New York issued another plan to build a "mega-jail" in Chinatown.

Corky's quest to document Asian America beyond the New York region took him to Chicago, where he visited Devon Avenue, the center of South Asian life there; to the Gulf Coast, to learn about the Vietnamese communities in New Orleans and Biloxi; to Lowell, Massachusetts, and Philadelphia, home to Cambodian Buddhist temples; and to Locke, California, site of an old Chinese gold-rush town. In 2016 he burst with pride when the National Portrait Gallery of the Smithsonian Institution acquired his photograph of Yuri Kochiyama. That year he also visited Beijing and donated eight of his photographs to the Overseas Chinese Museum. Started in 1959, the museum now boasts more than 25,000 items in its collections, donated by Chinese living abroad. The museum keeps two of Corky's works, including his famous police brutality photo, on permanent display.

Corky Lee's pièce de résistance, the photograph he believed was the most important in his entire oeuvre, was the one he took in 2014 at Promontory Summit, Utah, where in 1869 the transcontinental railroad was completed with the driving of the "golden spike." Andrew Russell's famous photograph of the moment, *East and West Shaking Hands at Laying Last Rail,* unceremoniously omitted any representation from the so-called Army of Canton, the twenty thousand Chinese laborers who had made up 90 percent of the workforce on the western line. They had performed the most arduous and dangerous work of tunneling through the Sierra Nevada. Corky

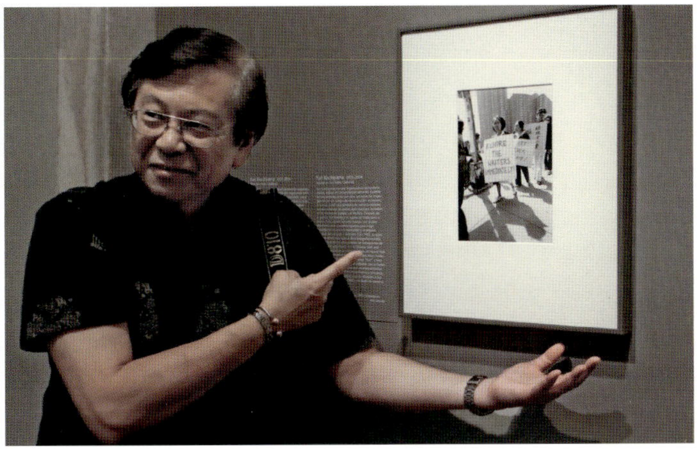

Corky Lee with his portrait of Yuri Kochiyama at the National Gallery of Art. Washington, D.C., 2018. *Shirley L. Ng*

believed it was one of the most egregious erasures of Asian Americans from U.S. history and had long wished to correct it.

In 2014 he organized a reenactment of the "golden spike" ceremony, with 250 Chinese Americans posing in front of the two facing locomotives. The group included direct descendants of Chinese railroad workers—among them Connie Young Yu, a writer and public historian, and Leland Wong, a photographer. Although most of the railroad workers had returned to China after their work was completed, some did settle in the United States or later sent paper sons to America. The Chinese Railroad Descendants Association boasts more than one hundred members.

Corky returned to Promontory Summit every year, establishing a kind of pilgrimage, including the 150th anniversary event in 2019. He did not just compose and photograph the reenactments. He organized the events, drawing on his decades-long relationships and networking in Chinese American communities across the country, in order to bring people to Utah.

Corky's photographs of the 2000s and 2010s represent another chapter in the long struggle of Asian Americans for respect, recognition, and inclusion. But by the 2000s, Asian American politics seemed quite different from those of the 1970s. Though AAPI politics in the 1970s had certainly not been monolithic, they had trended generally toward a liberal and progressive agenda of inclusion. That trend held during the 1980s and 1990s, even against resistance from white mainstream institutions. But by the 2000s and especially the 2010s, there was increased political polarization among Asian Americans. In part, this reflected the growing population of Asian Americans who immigrated or were born after 1965 and lacked connection to the exclusion era and the civil rights activism of the late twentieth century. Contemporary Asian American politics are also influenced by trends in American society generally—growing inequality, scarcer resources, and greater political extremism on both the right and the left.

Various controversies in the 2010s revealed not only differences among Asian Americans but also their increasingly vexed relationship with other communities of color. In 2016, for example, controversy surrounded the case of New York City rookie cop Peter Liang. Liang was convicted of manslaughter (which a court later reduced to criminally negligent homicide) for

Corky Lee (*center*) with Paul Kwan (*left*) and Tommy Ma, marching with the banner of the Sons of the American Legion in the Memorial Day parade. New York, 2018. *Shirley L. Ng*

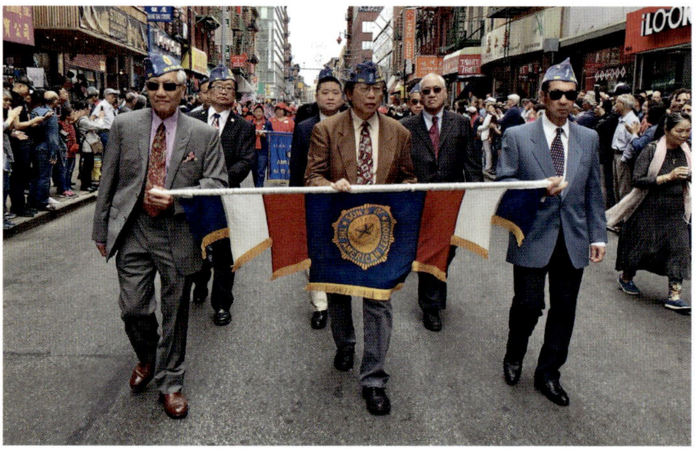

accidentally shooting and killing Akai Gurley, a young Black man, in a Brooklyn housing project stairwell. Many Chinese Americans contended that the police department "scapegoated" Liang in response to criticism that police officers (usually white) were never punished for killing Black people. Other Asian Americans rallied to support the Gurley family and believed that police, regardless of their ethnicity, should be held accountable for their actions.

And although Asian Americans, especially students and young people, marched with Black Lives Matter, some pundits claimed that middle-class Asian Americans were becoming or aspiring to be "white." But the apparent privileges of the professional class experienced a shock in 2020 when the coronavirus pandemic began and Asian Americans, regardless of ethnicity, age, or occupation, came under renewed attack for their presumed "foreignness." All Asian Americans were vulnerable to racist harassment and assault. Some called for more policing and harsher punishments while others advocated for noncarceral approaches (community patrols, social and mental health services, and the like).

Corky continued to work during the first year of the pandemic. Always wearing a mask, he frequently visited Chinatown, which was economically devastated once more. Many restaurants closed early in the day, not only for lack of business but also so workers could return home before nightfall and avoid the risk of becoming a victim of a hate attack. Some restaurants closed altogether. "If you're Asian, you're subject to two viruses: one is Covid-19, and the other is hate," Corky remarked. "The community is in a survival mode, and not enough attention is being paid by mainstream media or elected officials."

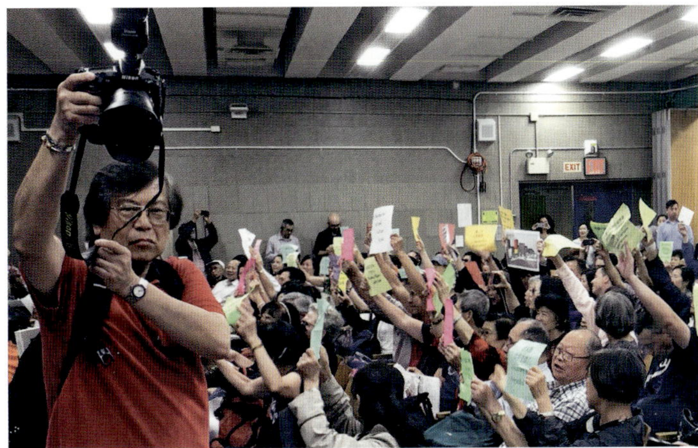

Corky Lee photographs a "no jail" meeting in Chinatown. New York, 2018. *Tomie Arai*

In December 2020, Corky photographed demonstrations protesting the spike in harassment and violent attacks against Chinese and other Asian Americans. On one occasion he fell from a lamppost—a favorite vantage point that he had used for years to photograph protests—which required a trip to the emergency room and several staples to his head. The accident weakened his overall health, but he remained undaunted in his efforts to document the double virus plaguing Asian Americans and to generate solidarity in the community. He documented the work of a community block patrol formed by Chinatown residents and activists and followed a squad of Guardian Angels as they posted signs in the subway stations in and around Chinatown. He participated as well in pop-up photo shows aimed at combating anti-Asian hate while the city's museums and galleries remained closed.

Corky likely caught the Covid-19 virus during one of these outings. He was hospitalized at Long Island Jewish Hospital in Queens, where he passed away on January 27, 2021, at the age of seventy-three. His death struck the community like a thunderbolt. Covid-19 regulations prevented the Lee family from holding a wake or funeral service, and the funeral home allowed only one family member, his brother John, to enter (wearing full protective gear) in order to identify the deceased. A crowd of several hundred people gathered outside, weeping as the hearse pulled away and wended its way through Chinatown. It stopped in front of the Basement Workshop, the American Legion post, and other places that were near and dear to him.

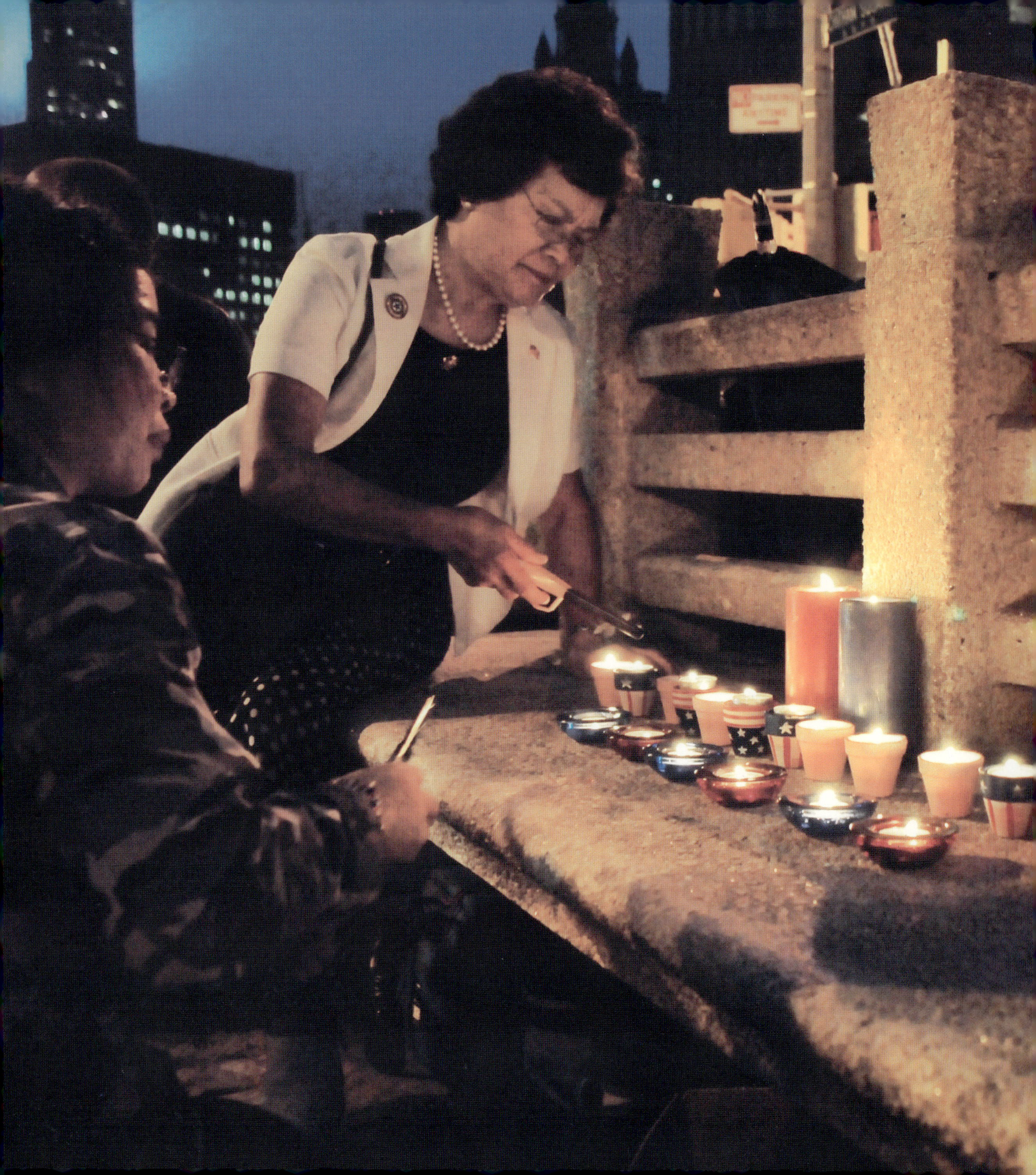

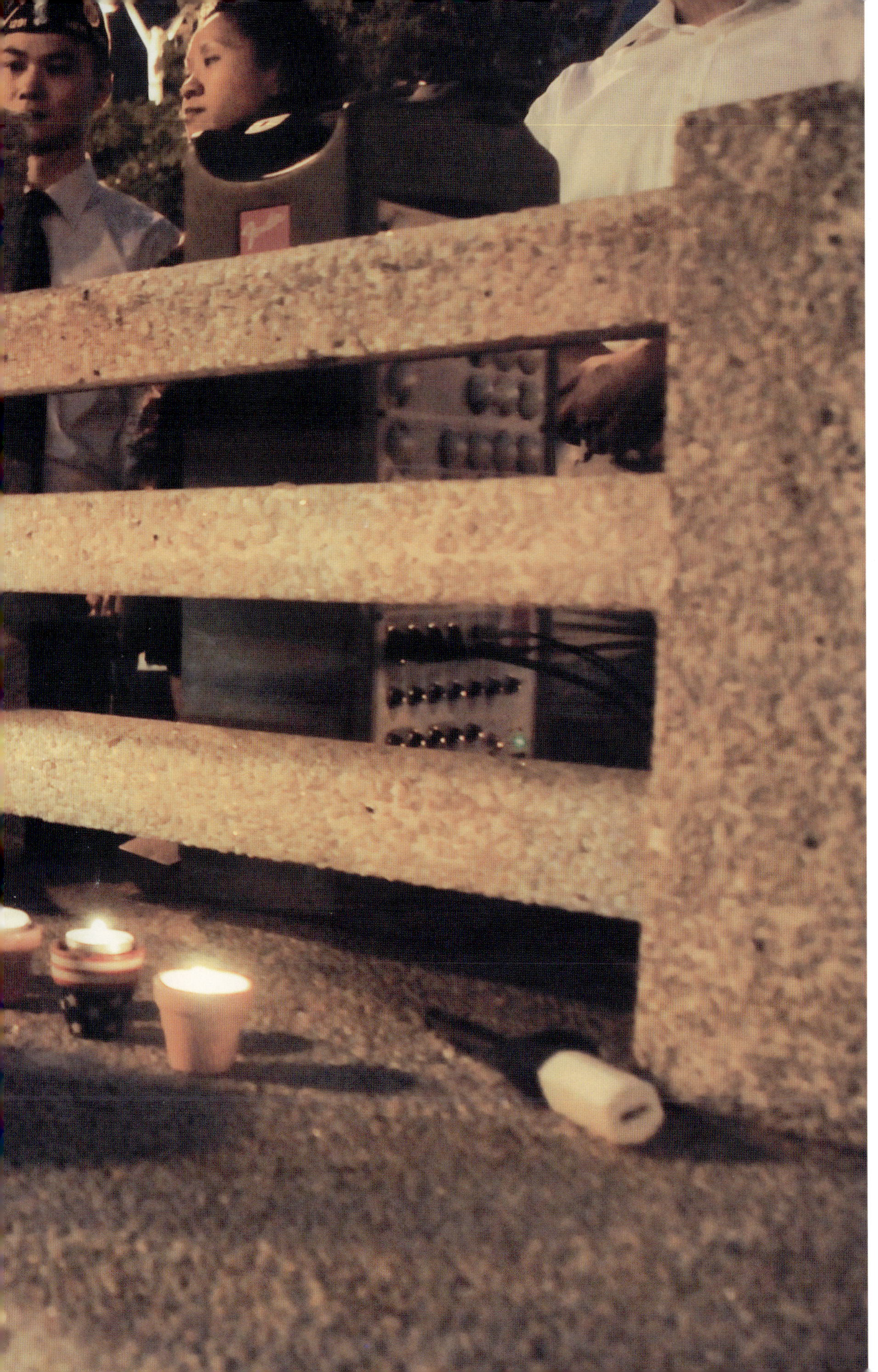

Lighting candles on the tenth anniversary of 9/11 in Chatham Square. New York, 2011.

HENRY CHANG

Author of the Jack Hu detective series

The morning skies are clear over Chinatown as the restaurant chefs fire up their woks. There's a distant explosion high in the air. *Construction crew*, you figure, your tea cooling on the windowsill.

Then another explosion near the first one.

BREAKING NEWS reports a huge fire.

Hurry down to Mott Street and Mosco, and we can see the Twin Towers burning, smoke billowing in the far distance. Helpless, as people emerge from the cloud of ash that engulfs the Financial District and spreads ominously toward Chinatown. Office workers, stunned, in shock, and covered in toxic dust, wander through Chinatown in search of escape. My brother calls frantically; he resides near Ground Zero and has been ordered

All of Chinatown is shut down, cut off, and our world ends at Canal Street. Restaurants closed. Chinese supermarkets unable to restock. Health clinics overwhelmed. Schools, senior centers, day care centers, all closed. Hardworking immigrants suddenly unemployed, adrift on Chinatown food lines.

In this chaos is Corky, with his love of community, determined to document the struggle of the Asian American people who have faced exclusion, internment, hate—people who have nowhere else to go—who survive generations and emerge more resilient than before.

From understated drama to streetwise reportage, Corky seems to be everywhere, dauntless. Boots on the ground. Taking risks to get a better shot, the *best* shot. He captures not only the impact of the crowds at Asian American rallies and demonstrations, but also the sense of pride and defiance in the face of omnipresent anti-Asian hate.

His portraits are reflections of the oppressed, what they endure. But they can also be seen as still lifes, paying attention to the everyday fabric and heartbeat of immigrant lives, capturing hope and resilience in people's faces. The pulse of Corky's depiction of the struggle for justice and equality can be felt in every photograph he took.

In later years, the rallying points have varied, but the course remains steadfast. When a community lacks a voice in the government that ignores and victimizes them, there is a need for change. Corky captured that need in his own inimitable way. He didn't post just the best shots, he posted the *truest* shots. In his photographs he lives on, strong and resilient.

Ground Zero, viewed from the west.
New York, 2001.

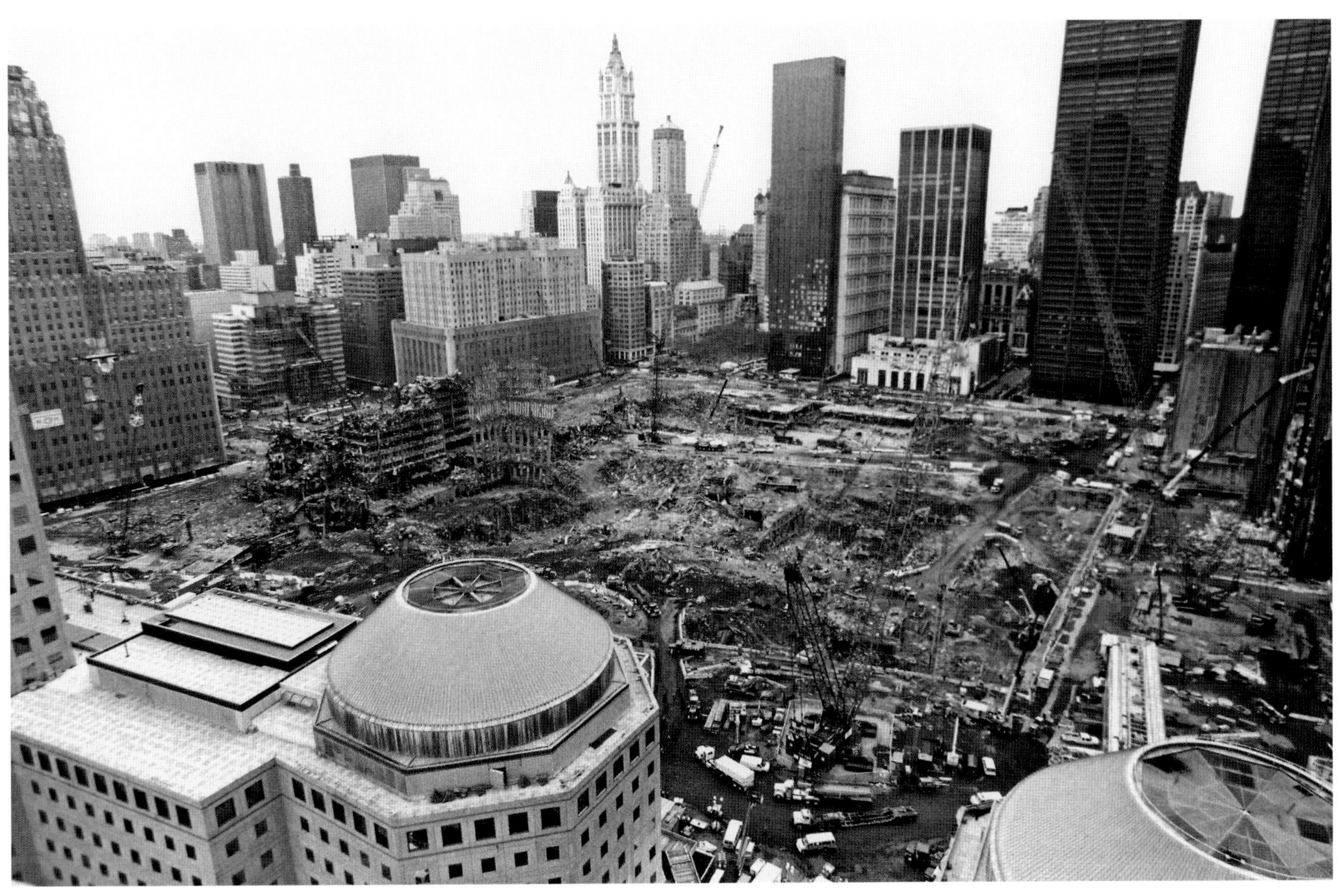

The shrine at Chatham Square, at the Kimlau War Memorial. New York, 2001.

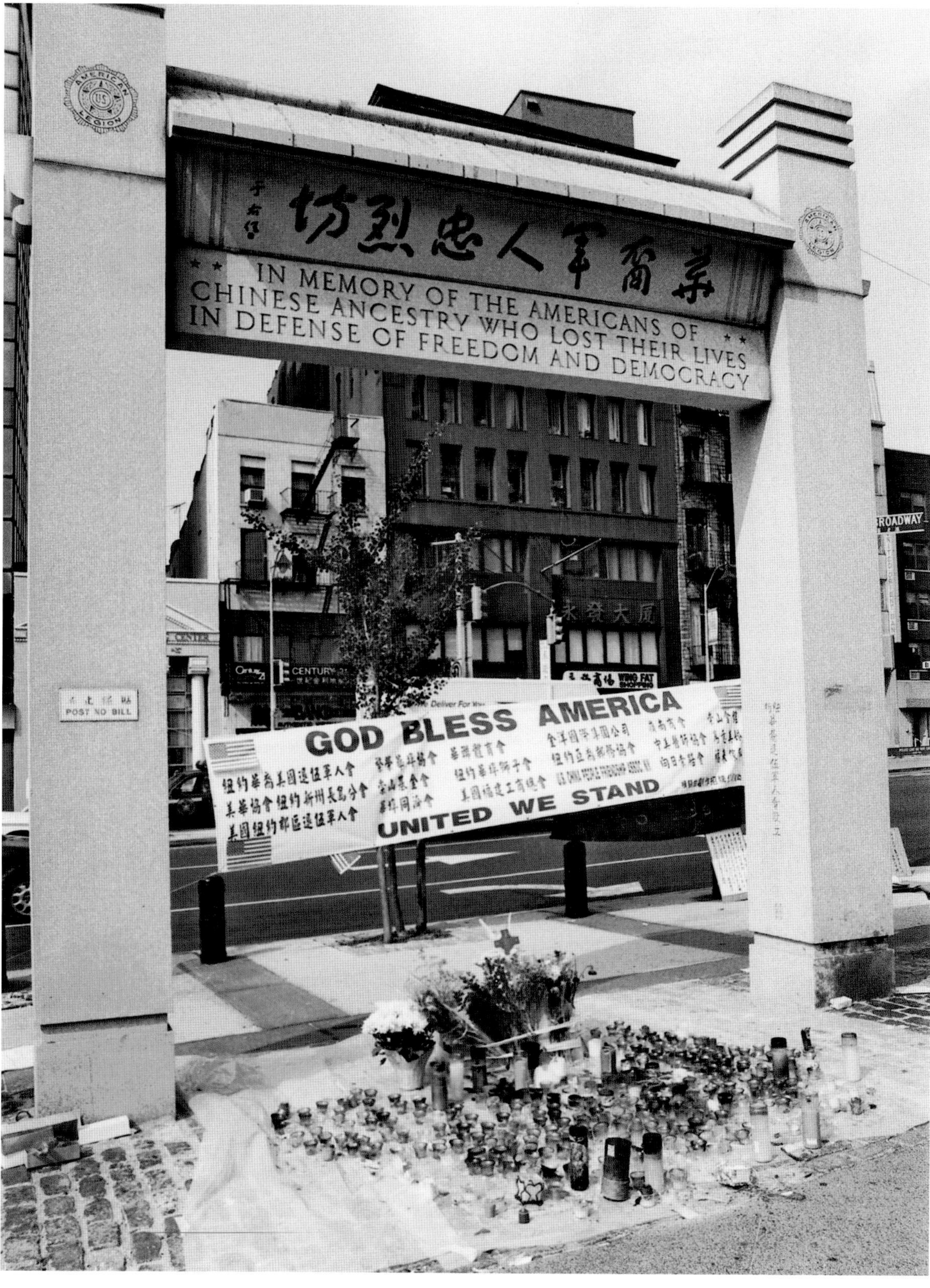

Benny Hom, first responder, Chinatown Dragon Fighters, Engine 9/Ladder 6, New York Fire Department. New York, 2002.

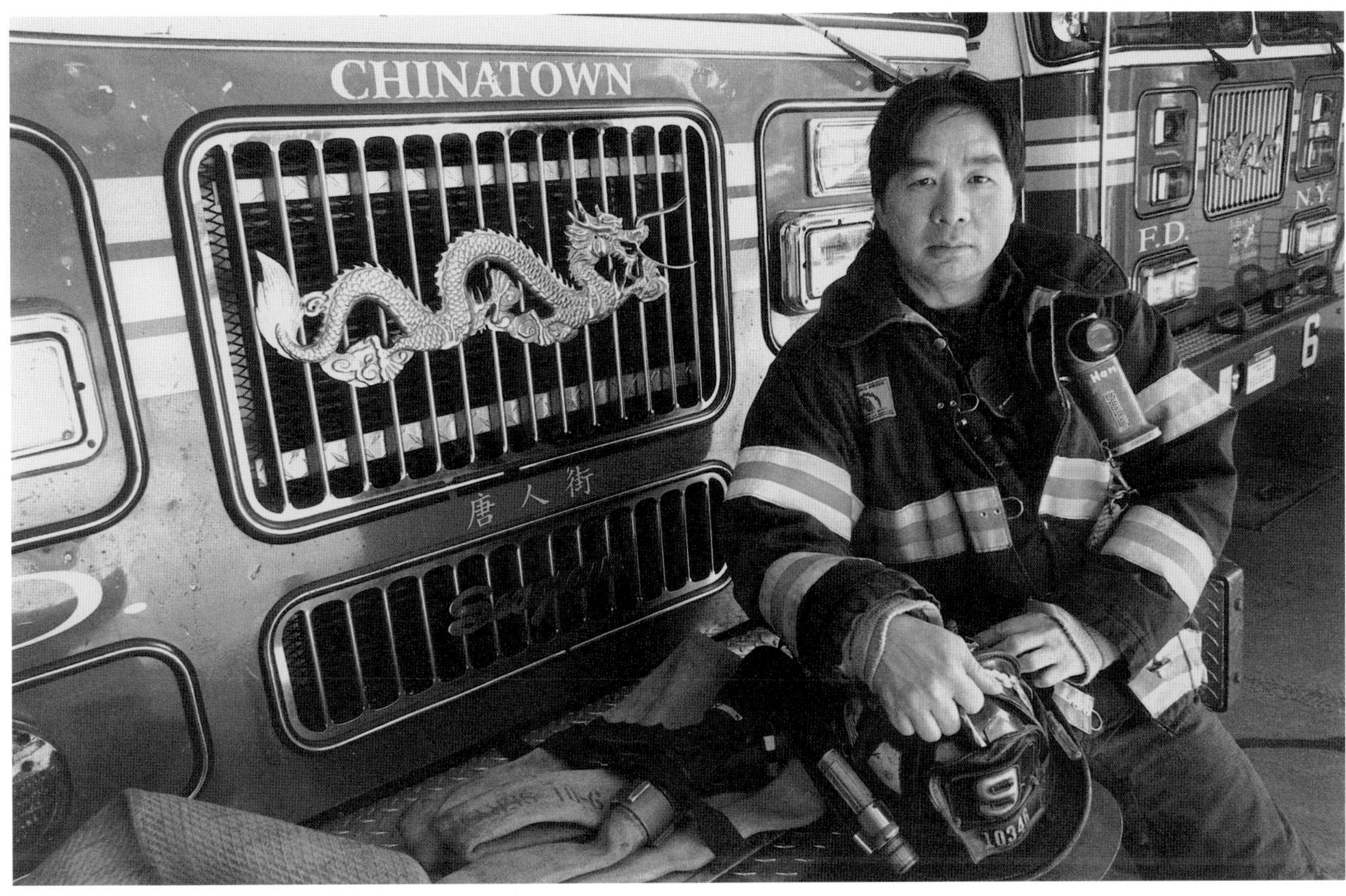

Veronica Jung translated English to Korean for Mr. and Mrs. Seong Soon Kang, parents of Joon Koo Kang, who was killed in the World Trade Center collapse. Location unknown. 2001.

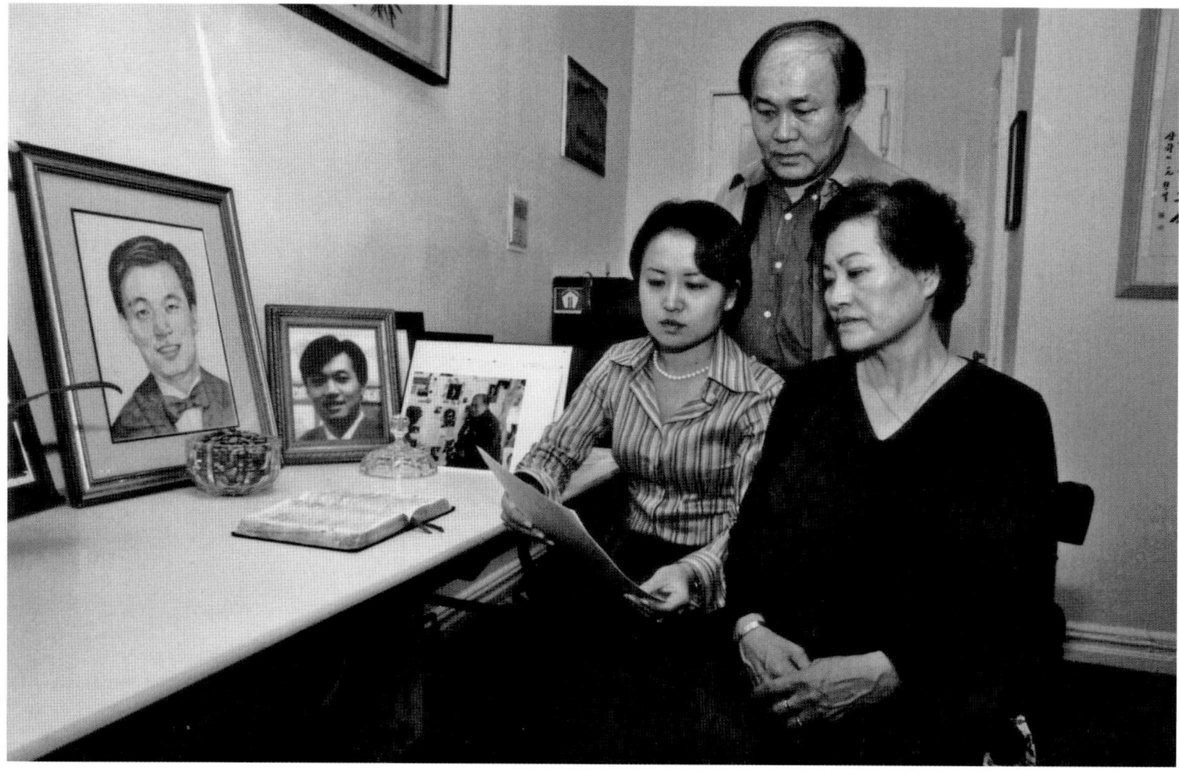

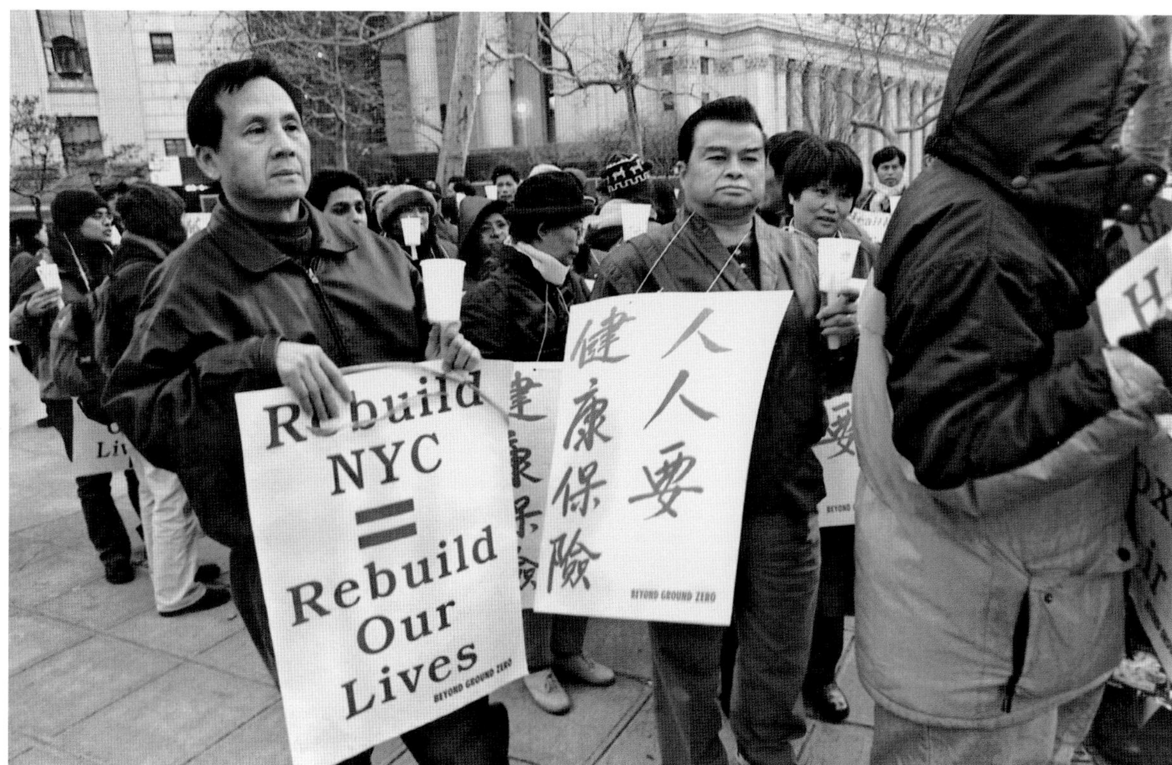

After 9/11, three thousand drivers, restaurant workers, and garment workers who worked in Chinatown north of Canal Street lost their jobs but were denied relief benefits because of stringent federal rules. The sign in Chinese reads, "Everyone Needs Health Insurance." Community pressure won additional relief funds and reformed eligibility standards. A rally at the Ted Weiss Federal Building in Foley Square. New York, 2002.

Jack Chong, a recent CUNY law graduate, assisted Tim Ho, owner of Wo Hop restaurant in Chinatown, with his application for a small business loan in order to stay in business. New York, 2001.

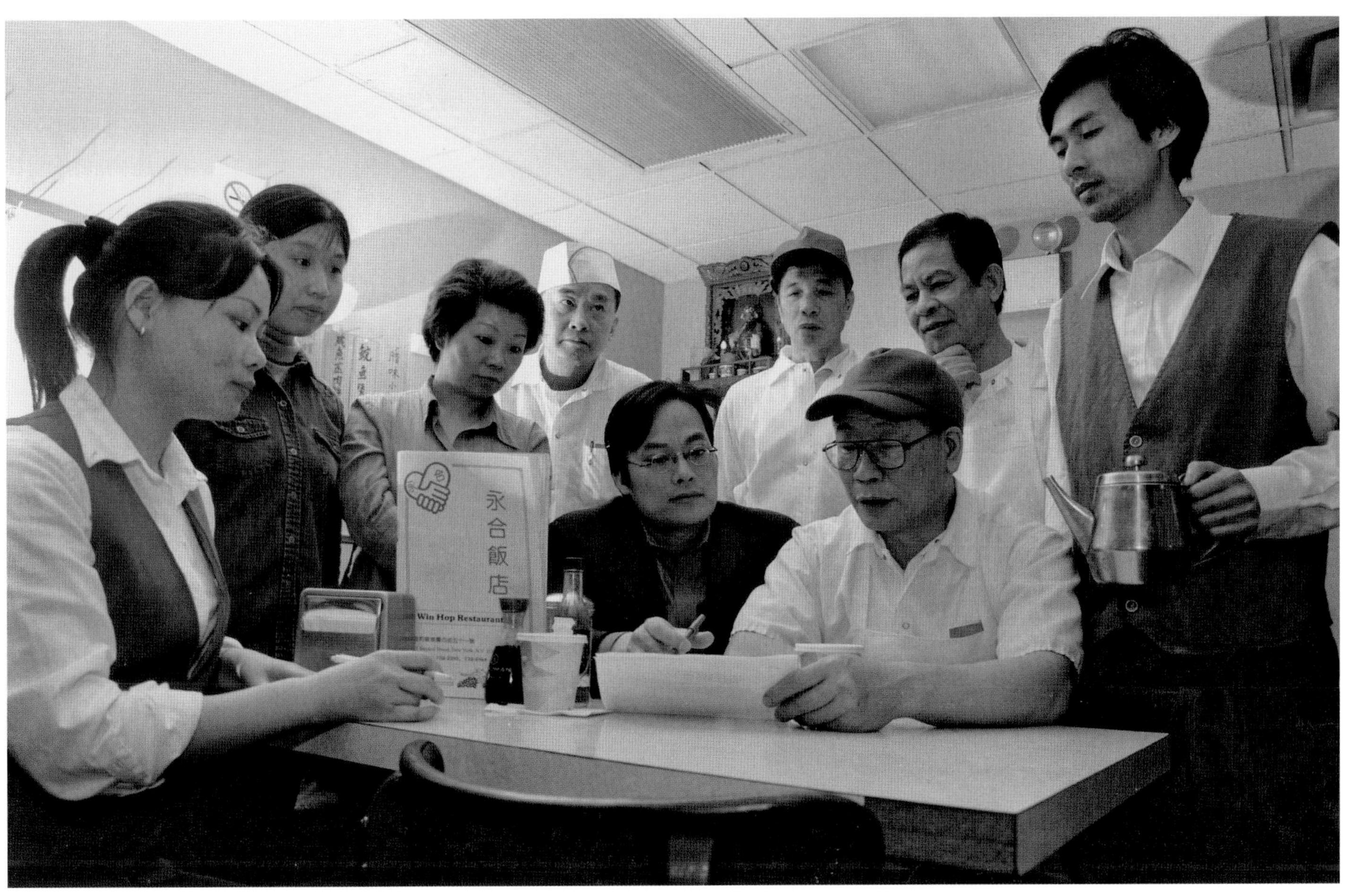

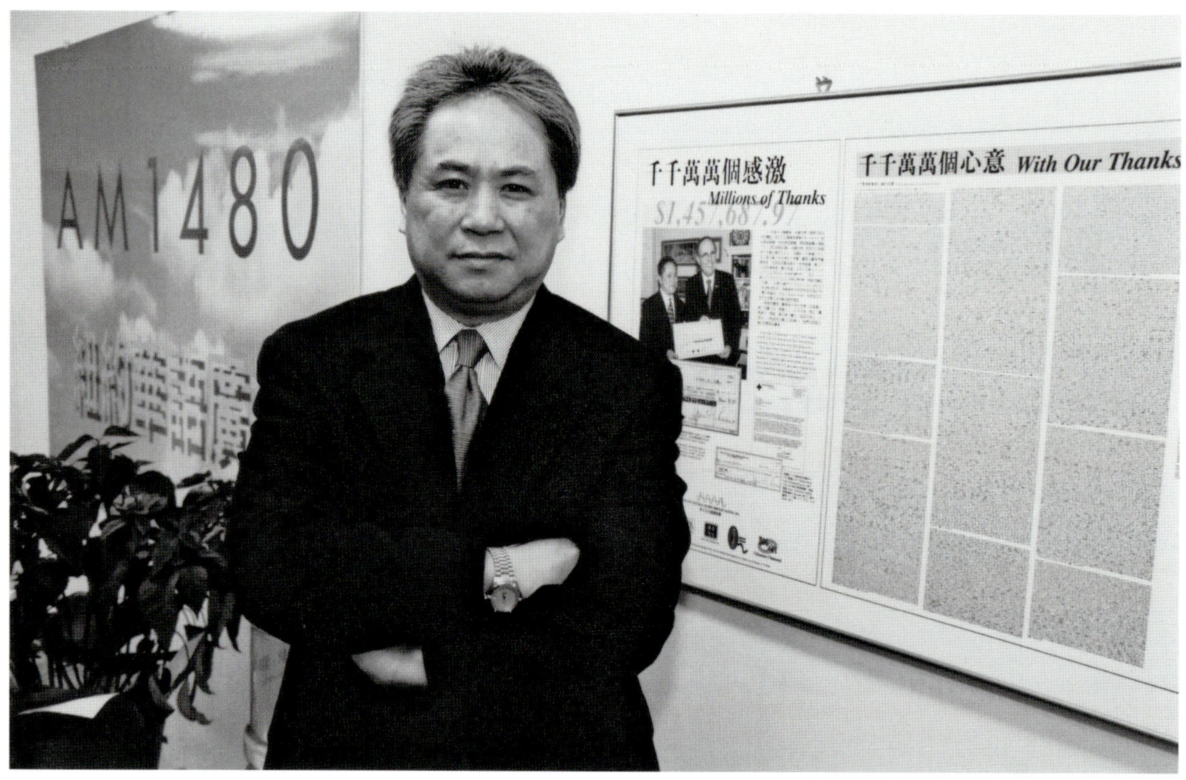

Tony Wong, general manager of WZRC-AM 1480, the Chinese-language radio station, raised $1.4 million from listeners, which he donated to the city of New York for 9/11 victims' families. New York, 2001.

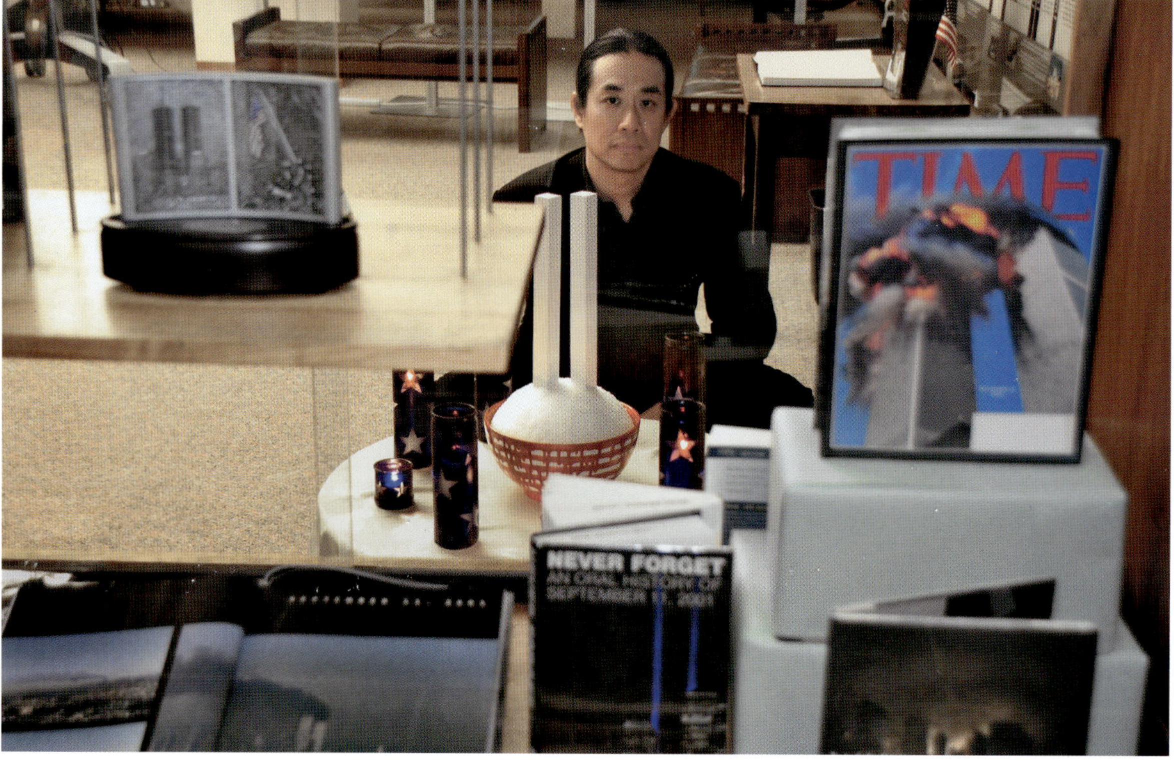

Artist Chee Wang Ng with his site-specific installation at the Pace University Library on the tenth anniversary of 9/11. New York, 2011.

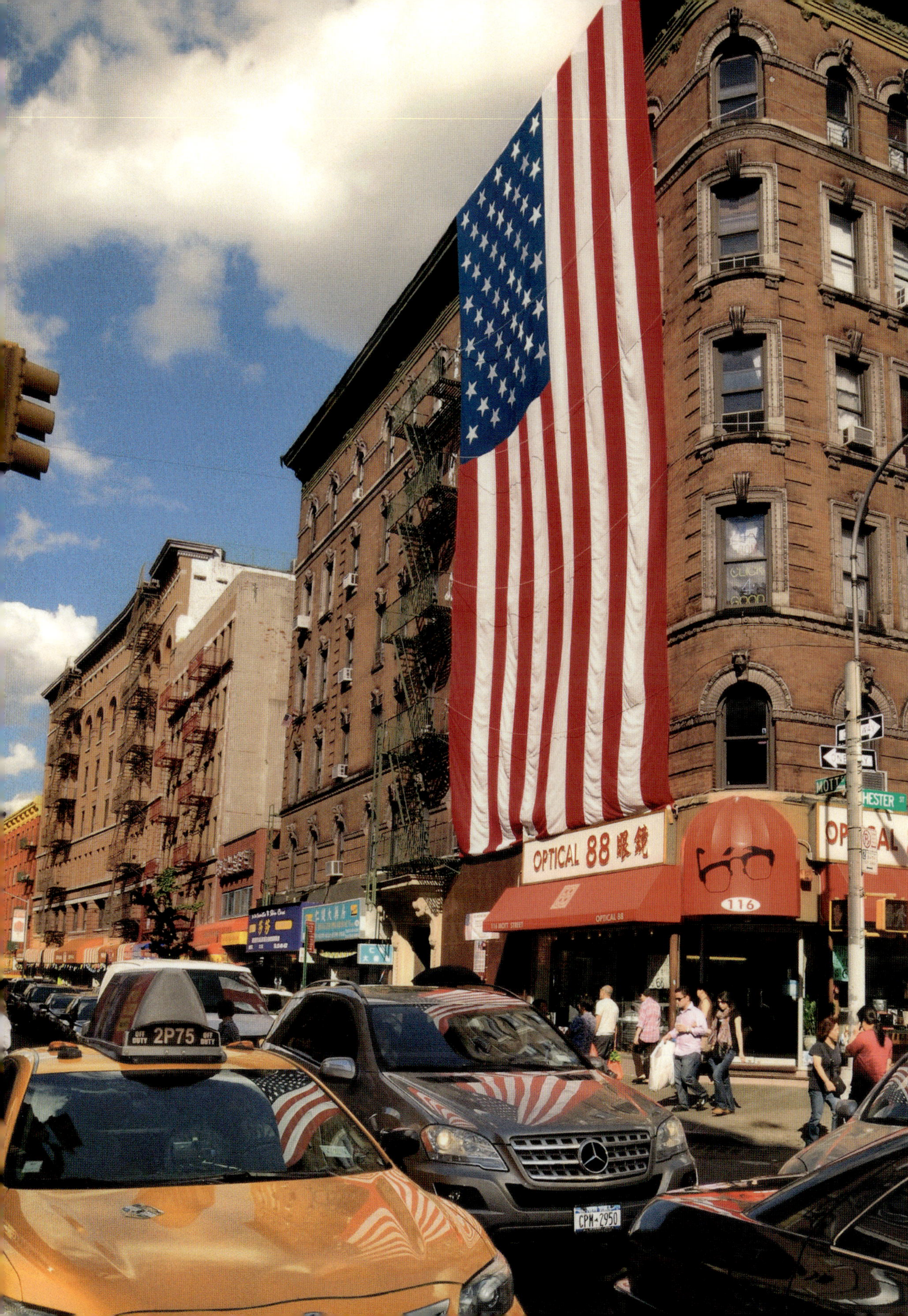

Mott and Hester streets on the tenth anniversary of 9/11. New York, 2011.

Our Never-Ending Vigil

VIVEK BALD

Scholar, writer, and MIT professor; director of the film *In Search of Bengali Harlem*

We're going flag shopping
For American flags
They're staring at our turbans
They're calling them rags

We're going American flag shopping
Red, white, blue on our crib
The neighbors threw rocks at the house
They making it harder to live.

—Heems (Himanshu Suri),
"Flag Shopping," 2015

Corky Lee's photograph of a Sikh American vigil in Central Park after the attacks on the Twin Towers has become one of his most iconic. Years after it was taken, it continues to circulate, as a shadow image of the attacks themselves.

Every time I see it, I feel waves of pain and loss: the pain and loss of that moment—in those days immediately after September 11, 2001—but even more the pain and loss of all that would come for South Asians, Sikhs, Arabs, Muslims, brown folk, immigrants, year after year, in the next two decades and counting.

The roundups, detentions, and deportations; the spying and surveillance in our neighborhoods, our places of worship; the "random" searches at airports; the mosques set on fire; the bullying and abuse of children in their schools and on their playgrounds; the attacks on elders on their evening walks; the pushing in front of trains; the shooting of a teenager on a neighbor's doorstep; the mass shootings at Oak Creek's *gurdwara*, in Indianapolis; the deaths at the border; the pulling of children from their parents' arms; the relentlessness of all those Hollywood villains who looked like us; not to mention the wars; the drone attacks in places where we have families and trace our roots; the immigration ban; and the president who ushered in even more vitriol and violence on top of it all, under the banner of making America "great" again. All this comes to me in a rush, as I look at that single, singular image. Immeasurable pain and loss fill the place inside where there should be anger.

In the foreground, to the left, stands a turbaned Sikh man in his twenties. His presence pulls the viewer in; he is draped in a full-size American flag, draped over his shoulders and held together at his chest by a smaller American flag on a stick. He stares silently forward, past

Lee's camera and the viewer's gaze. His look is grave but, at the same time, weary.

Next to him is a Sikh girl of ten or eleven. She wears an orange scarf over her head, and in one hand, she holds another small American flag on a stick, the kind that crowds typically wave at Fourth of July parades. Her hold on the little flag seems strained. She looks off to the side, toward something outside the frame. One senses weariness here, too, but there's a sharpness—even a hardness—in her young eyes.

Behind the young man and the girl, in a slight blur as we move past the plane of focus, is a row of three older turbaned Sikh men. The elders hold in front of them, at chest height, another full-size American flag, even as all appear to be wearing, pinned to their clothing, one of the smaller flags.

The lower half of the frame is flooded with stars and stripes, with red, white, and blue. The participants in the vigil—and in Lee's photograph—stop the viewer with their demand that they address a deeply significant juxtaposition: of American flags and men with turbans and beards.

When it appears online and in print, the photograph is rarely captioned beyond a few basic contextualizing words: "a Sikh man," "a vigil in New York's Central Park," and "after," or "a few days after," or "in the days after" 9/11. But the specificity of the day is important. It is September 15, the Saturday following the attacks.

September 15, 2001. That day the vigil's Sikh American organizers sent out a press release that called on "all New Yorkers" to join them in a candlelight vigil "to pray for the victims of the World Trade Center and Pentagon attacks that occurred on September 11, 2001."

A "note to the editor" at the end of the press release hints at a grim subtext:

In the days since the horrific incidents at the World Trade Center and Pentagon the Sikh-American community nationwide has seen widespread violence in the form of hate crimes targeted toward many communities, including the Sikhs. . . . As citizens, we cannot support hateful violence in any form and we must have faith that the Government of the United States of America will bring all perpetrators to justice.

The organizers of the Central Park vigil were responding not just to the immense loss of lives in the World Trade Center attacks, but to the spate of violence that had begun to spread across New York City's five boroughs almost immediately afterward, targeting Arabs and South Asians of all backgrounds and faiths. On September 12 in Manhattan and Queens, two elderly Sikh men were beaten by a group of white youths wielding a baseball bat. These "revenge attacks" were serious enough.

But on September 15, as the vigil was being planned, a series of events were unfolding three thousand miles away that would raise the stakes for all us brown folks across the United States.

In Mesa, Arizona, Balbir Singh Sodhi drove to a local Costco to buy potted flowers, then returned to the Chevron gas station that he had opened a year earlier. As he and a group of landscapers were planting the flowers around the perimeter of the station, a forty-two-year-old white man, Frank Roque, left a sports bar down the road. Roque drove his pickup to the station, drew a .380 handgun, and fired five shots at Sodhi out the window of the truck, killing him on the spot. He then drove to a nearby Mobil station and fired on its Lebanese owner, then proceeded to shoot multiple rounds into the home of a local Afghan immigrant family.

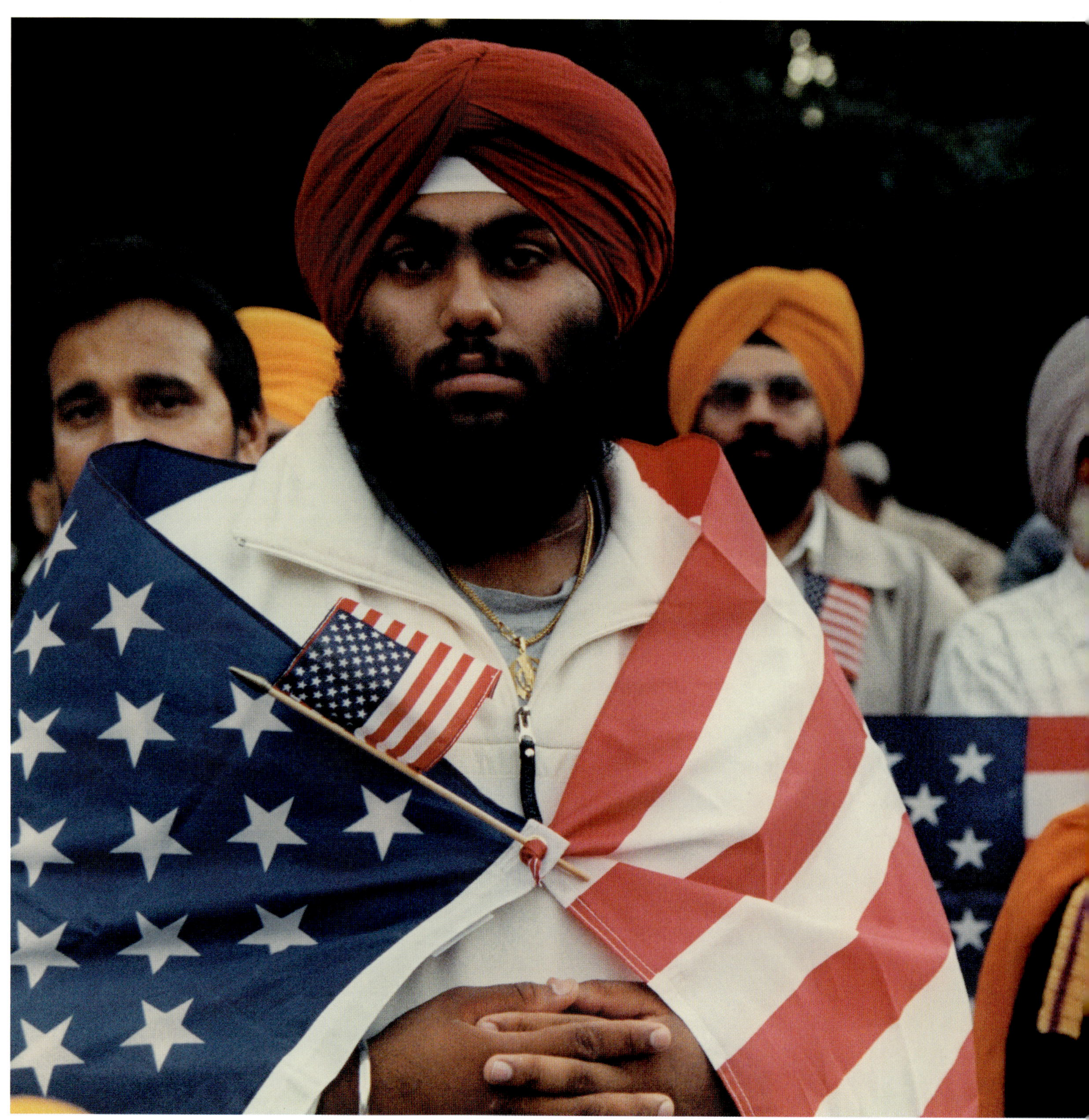

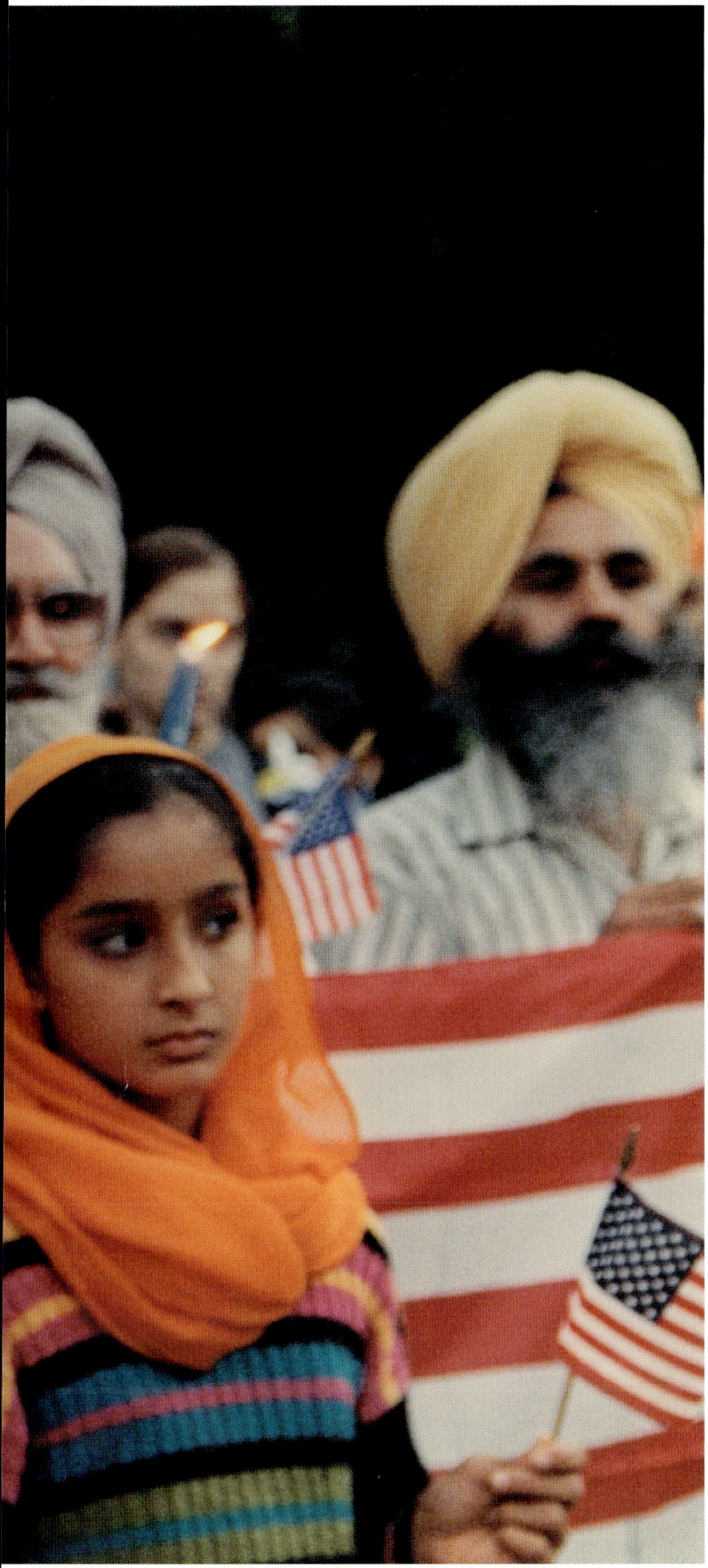

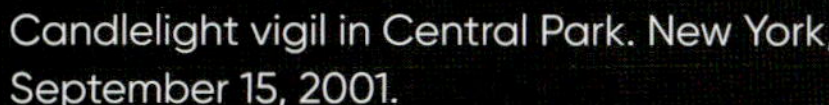

Candlelight vigil in Central Park. New York, September 15, 2001.

The next day the police tracked down and arrested Roque. He is said to have boasted, "I am a patriot" and "I stand for America all the way."

Had news of Balbir Singh Sodhi's murder reached the participants of the vigil at the moment Corky Lee hit the shutter release and took his photograph? It is unclear, but if it had, they would have only just found out. And it would not be until the next day that they, that we, would find out about the murder of Waqar Hasan, a forty-six-year-old Pakistani immigrant and father of three, in Dallas.

Around the time of the vigil, Hasan was shot while making hamburgers in the grocery store he owned. His killer later proclaimed that he wanted "to retaliate on local Arab Americans or whatever you want to call them" and that he "did what every American wanted to do but didn't. They didn't have the nerve."

We're going flag shopping
We're going flag shopping
The kids are throwing stones
We complain but they ain't stopping

And I was there
I saw the towers and the planes
And I'll never be the same
Never ever be the same
I seen things that I never wanna see again
I heard things that I never wanna hear again
And now we're going flag shopping.

After 9/11, in response to racist attacks against Muslims and Sikhs, a teach-in was held at New York University. New York, 2001.

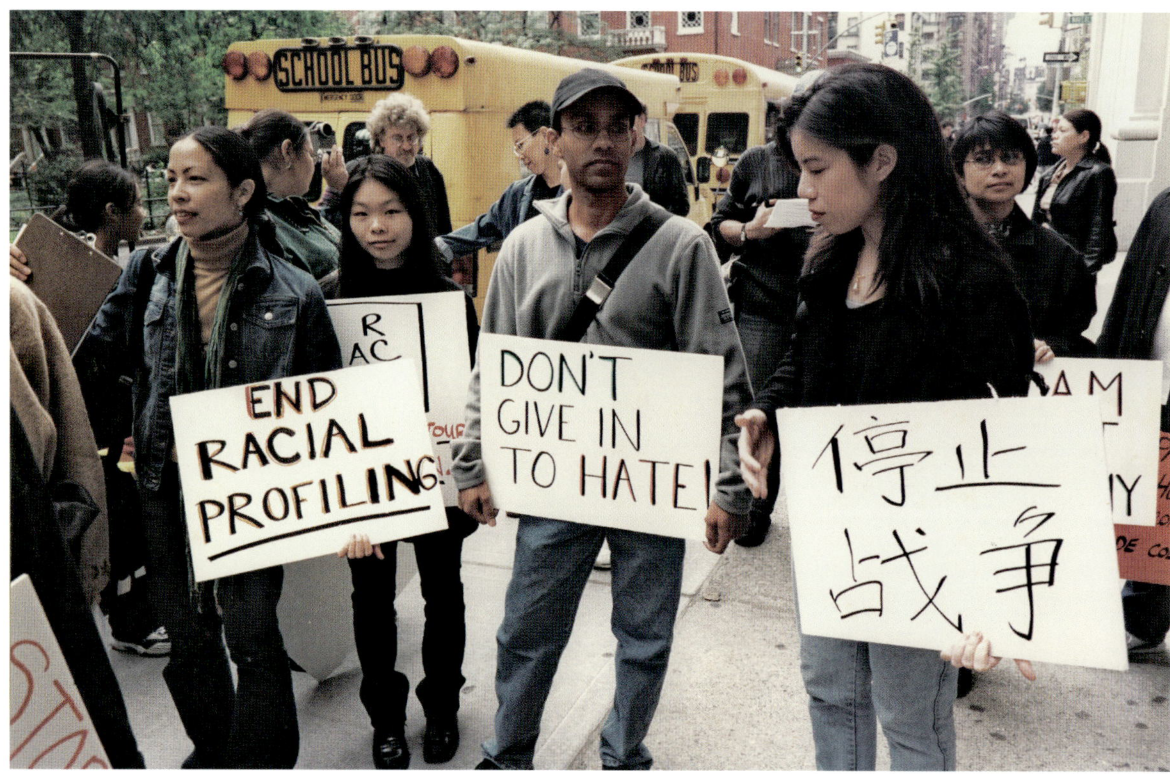

Dr. Sumi Mitsudo Koide, president of the New York chapter of the Japanese American Citizens League, and Indergit Singh, a candidate for city council, attended the teach-in. New York, 2001.

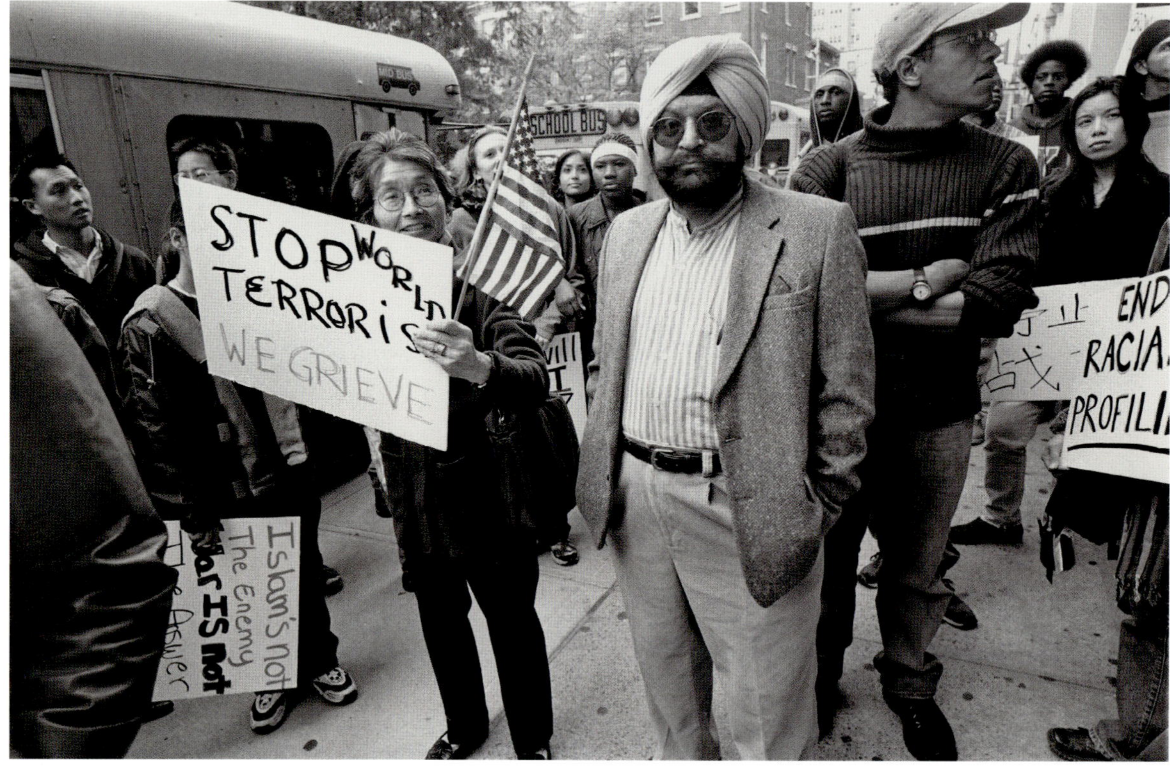

I remember those flags appearing everywhere, overnight. In our communities, it was the most vulnerable who had them first—taxi drivers and street vendors; gas station, convenience store, and corner store workers; those who, in order to support their families, to make their livings, had to come in contact with the public, who had to do so alone and could not afford to take a day off. But the flags went up in front of homes, too, and mosques, temples, *gurdwaras*.

Like the young man in Lee's photograph, our communities had to wrap ourselves in the American flag, as if it were a cloak of protection. As if it would prove our loyalty, our peace-loving nature, our honest, hardworking obedience while images of America's "enemies" who "looked like" us suddenly spread across every television screen and newspaper front page. As if the flag would protect us from the politicians, the commentators, the military experts, the Immigration and Naturalization Service, the FBI, the patriots and citizens.

"We must have faith," said the press release that day, "that the Government of the United States of America will bring all perpetrators to justice." Twenty years and countless lives later, the irony of this statement is painful. American flags are everywhere again, now on pickup trucks even bigger and louder than the one driven by Balbir Singh Sodhi's murderer. Flags are emblazoned on bumper stickers next to images of assault rifles or mounted on poles on the sides of trucks, flapping as they speed by.

I hope that, twenty years on, we've learned that the flag is not, in fact, a protective cloak, that we were never shielded when, out of faith or fear, we wrapped ourselves in its folds to prove our loyalty, doubled down on the American Dream to prove our resilience, or performed as the "model minority" to prove our worth. I hope that we see more clearly the limits of pushing for acceptance in the nation *as it is*, with its ongoing violence and deep inequality. I hope that out of pain and loss, we see our struggles reflected in those of other targeted, marginalized, and racialized communities and that we are ready to build together a more just future, a society *as it should be*.

I look at Corky Lee's photograph, and I'm drawn to the young girl's sharp gaze beyond the frame. I'd like to think she has her eyes fixed on this other, collective future.

South Asians oppose the Bush administration's war against Iraq. Union Square, New York, 2001.

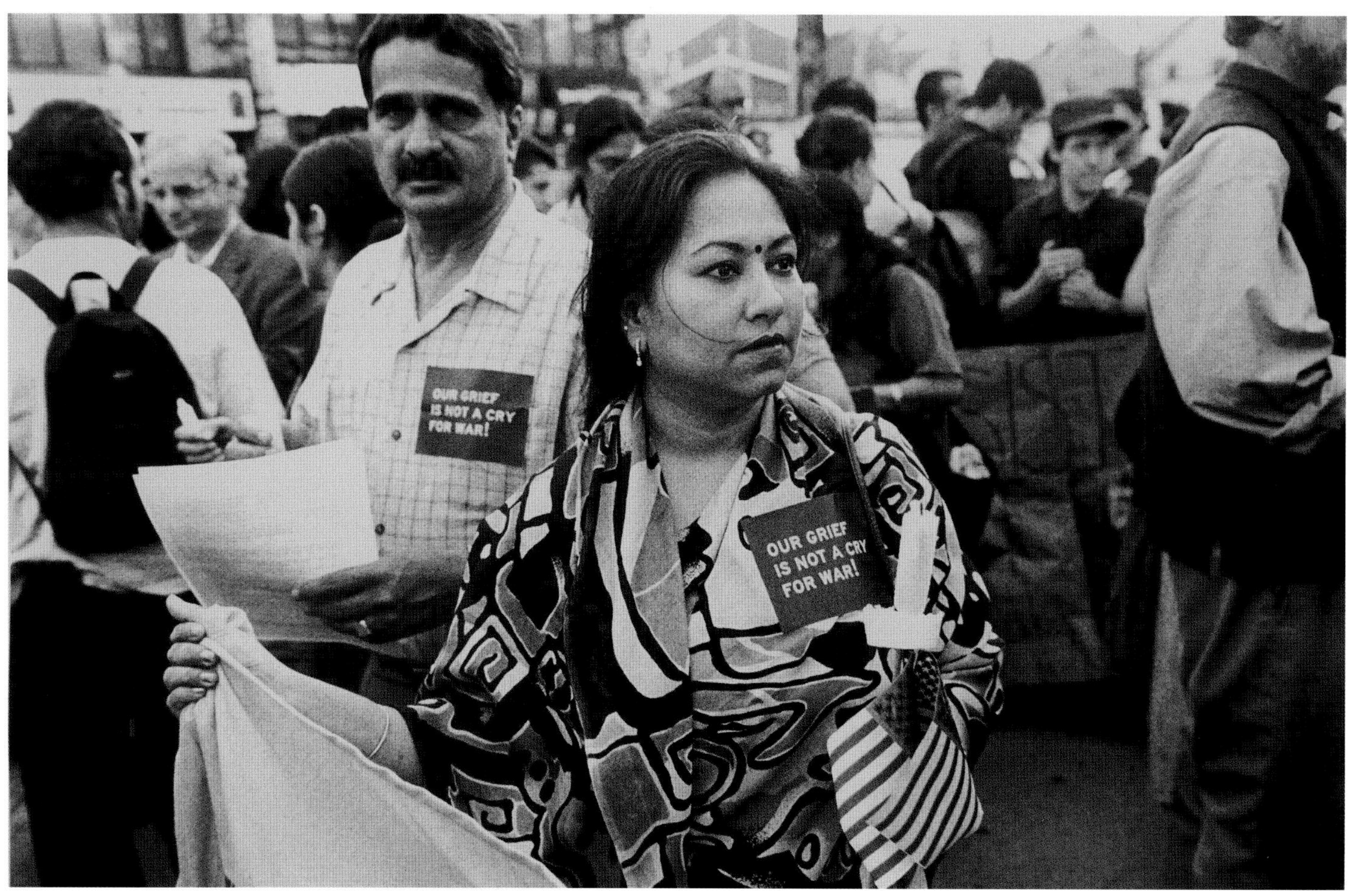

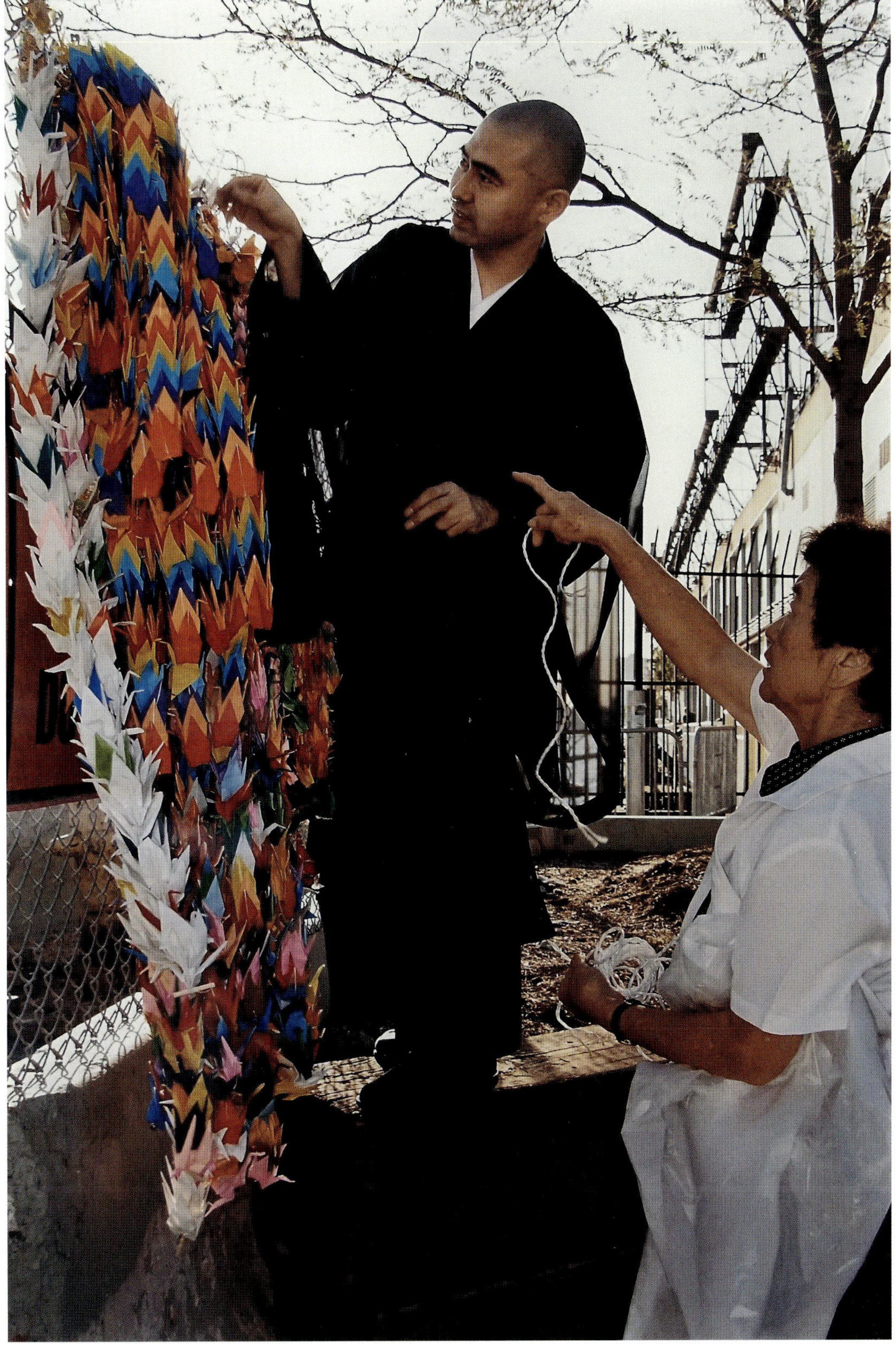

Rev. T. Kenjitsu Nakagaki, the priest of the New York Buddhist Church, hangs one thousand paper cranes, the symbol of peace, at the Japanese Floating Lantern Ceremony, a 9/11 anniversary memorial, at Pier 40 on the Hudson River. New York, 2005.

Corky Lee and the American Legion

BAYER JACK-WAH LEE

Pastor at the First Chinese Baptist Church, New York

I first met Corky at an American Legion parade in New York's Chinatown in 2014. The procession was to begin at Mott and Canal streets and end at the Kimlau War Memorial at Chatham Square. Corky was photographing William Jung, a Vietnam War veteran, sitting on his Harley-Davidson getting ready to ride along the parade. Corky and William looked more like 1960s protesters compared to the veterans in uniforms with their family members neatly dressed for the procession. Later, over lunch, Corky told me his dad was a veteran. Being newly elected as the commander of the Sons of the American Legion (a leadership post that includes the duty to recruit new members), I immediately said to Corky, "Here's the membership application for SAL. Fill it out and cough up the twenty bucks!" He did, and that was the beginning of our friendship.

A few weeks after the veterans' parade, Corky asked me, "Bayer, can you open your church? I have an Anna May Wong DVD that I want to show everyone," as if to say, *I coughed up twenty bucks, now it's your turn.* That was how we came to open our church at 21 Pell Street to showcase works of Asian American filmmakers and for other town hall events.

When I enlisted Corky in the Sons of the American Legion, some old-timers expressed concern. Knowing that Corky had opposed the Vietnam War, they questioned his patriotism. But once Corky started coming to the Kimlau post and showed that he was willing to go beyond the call of duty, he was soon elected commander of SAL. He not only photographed activities of the post but made large prints and hung them throughout the assembly hall for all to see. He tirelessly led a team traveling from the post in New York to Washington, D.C., to lobby for the project that would honor the military service of Chinese American veterans in World War II. Corky was delighted when those veterans finally received a Congressional Gold Medal during a virtual ceremony on December 9, 2020.

Corky was a good shepherd who cared for people and brought them together. After we laid him to rest at Kensico Cemetery in Westchester on February 6, 2021, a young veteran came up with a flag that she had received for her heroism and dedicated it to Corky for the encouraging words that he had given her when they met. We miss Corky so very much. There will never be anyone exactly like Corky to take his place. But we must all come together and continue his legacy. With our cameras and cell phones in hand, we will take pictures and tell our stories, to each other and to those who come after us.

Members of American Legion Post 1291 at the Lunar New Year parade in Chinatown. New York, 2007.

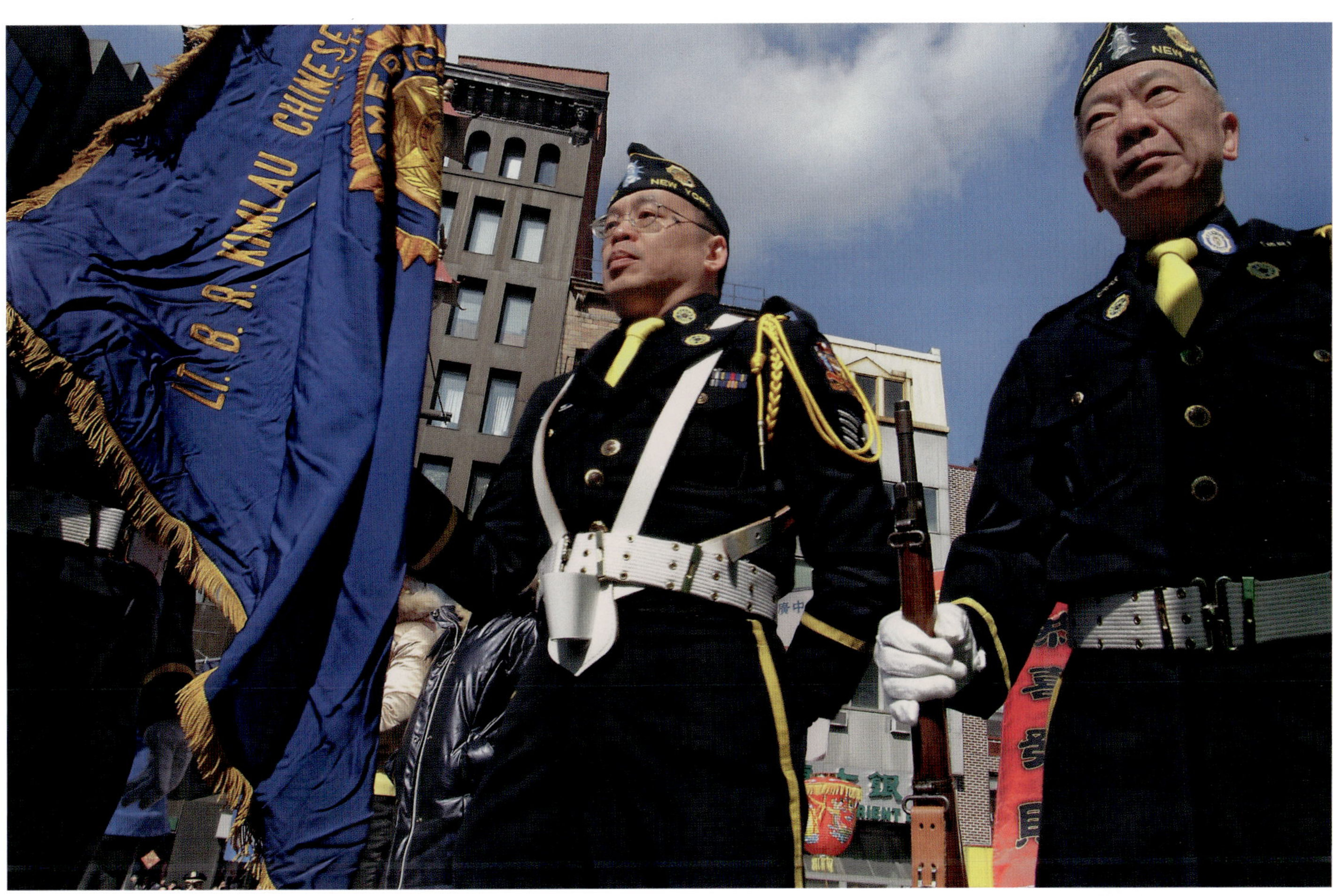

William Jung, a Vietnam War veteran, on his Harley, about to ride with the Chinatown American Legion parade. New York, 2011.

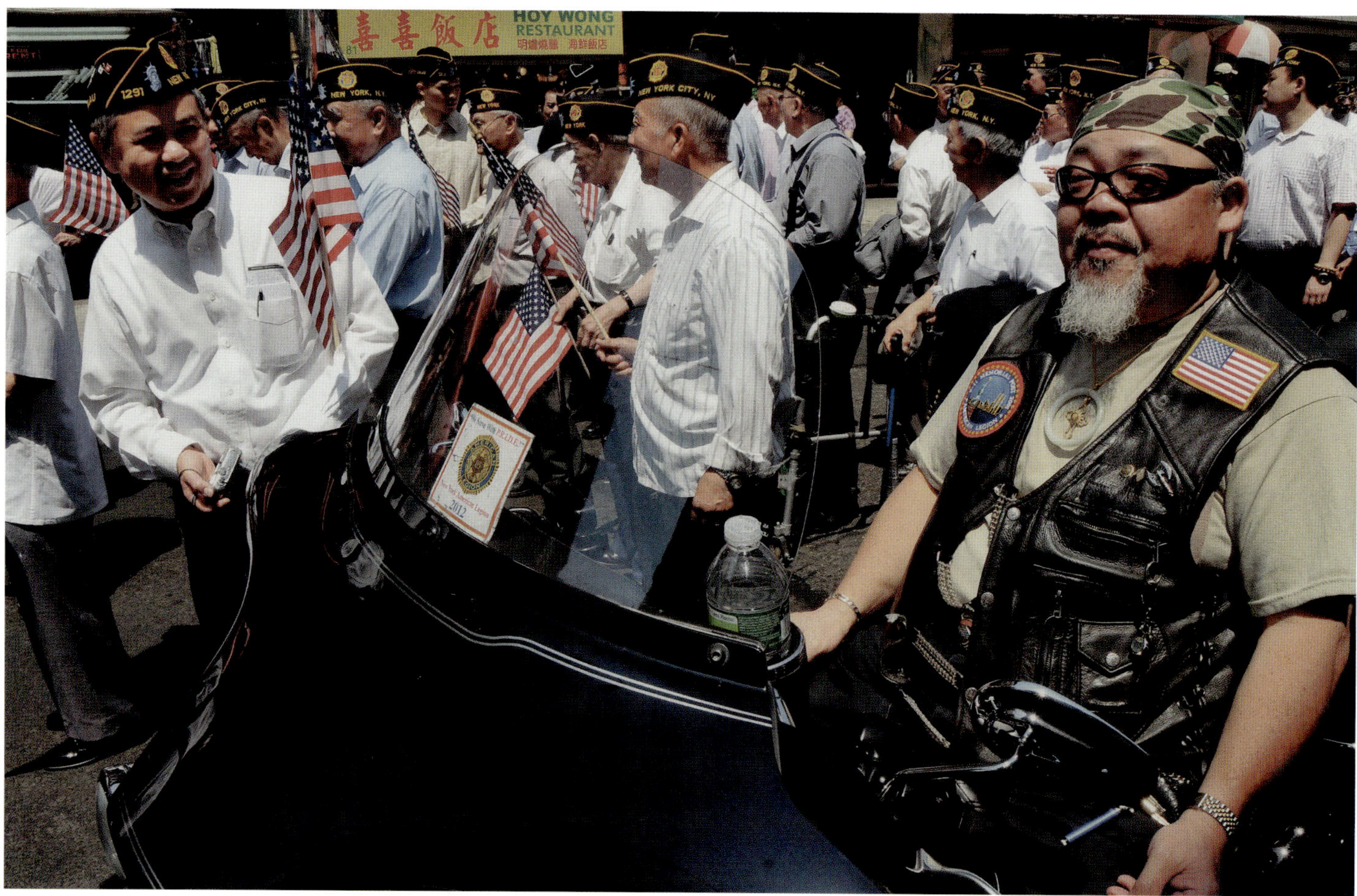

Family members of Chinese American World War II veterans gathered at Lt. B. R. Kimlau Chinese Memorial Post 1291 in support of legislation to award the veterans a Congressional Gold Medal in recognition of their service. New York, 2018.

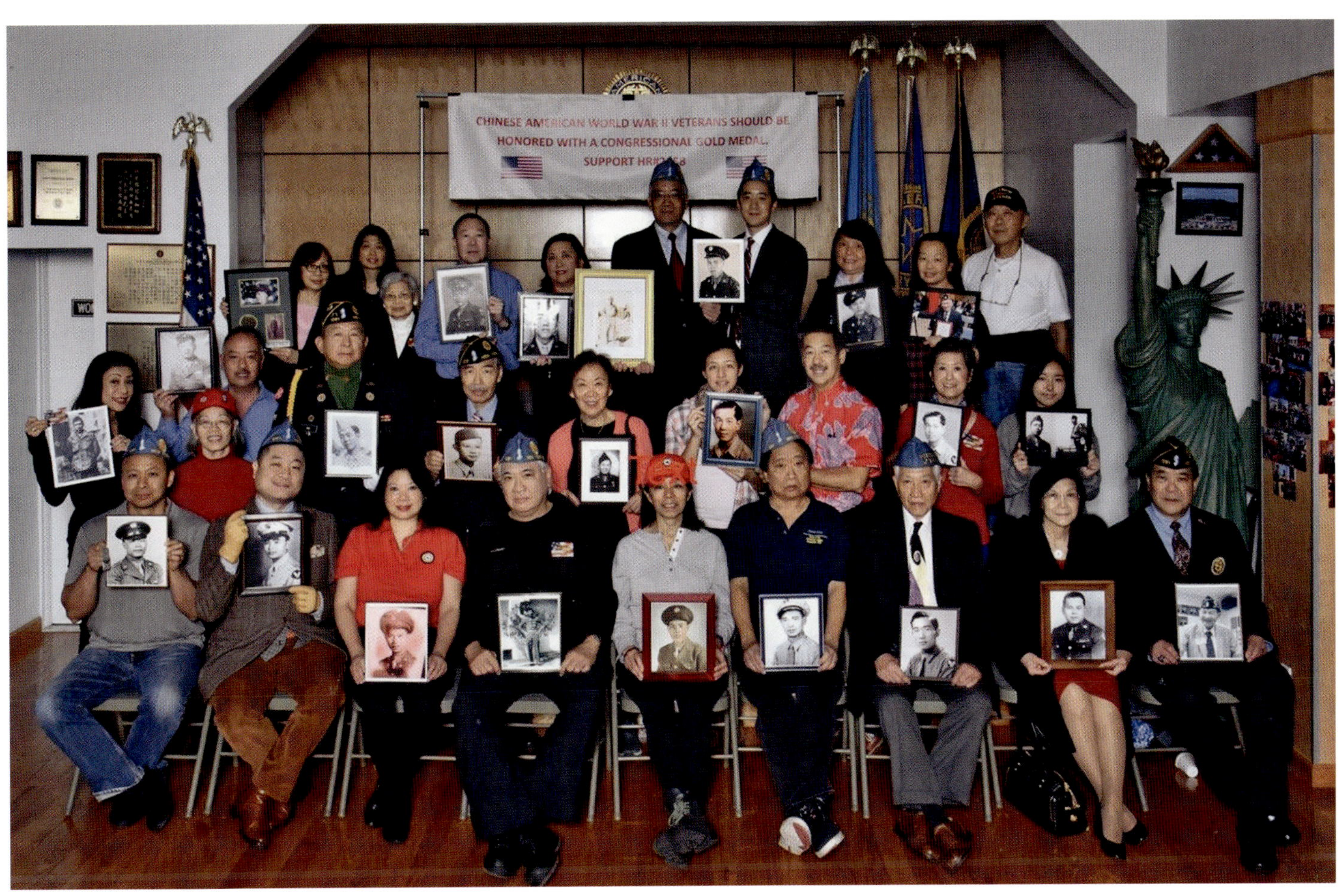

Below: Chinese adoptees in Chinatown's Lunar New Year parade. New York, 2002.

Bottom: Backstage preparations for the New York Chinese Cultural Center's Lunar New Year program. New York, 2001.

Right: Veterans and beauty contestants line up for the Fourth of July parade in Chinatown. The veterans are American Legion Post 1291 members David Louie (*left*, saluting, wearing the "big patriotic parade" sash) and Edward Wong. New York, 2005.

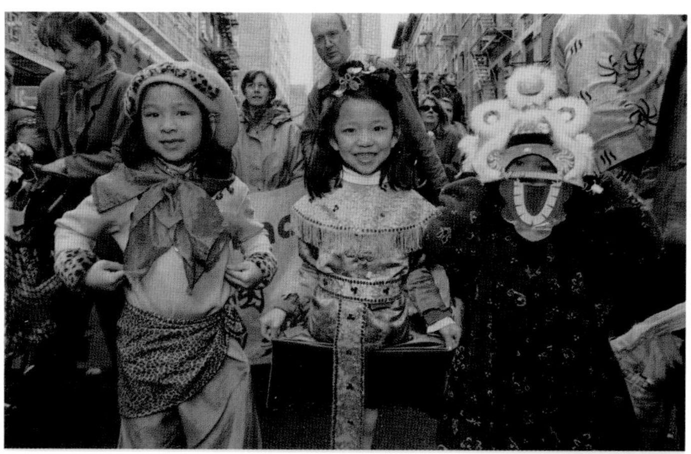

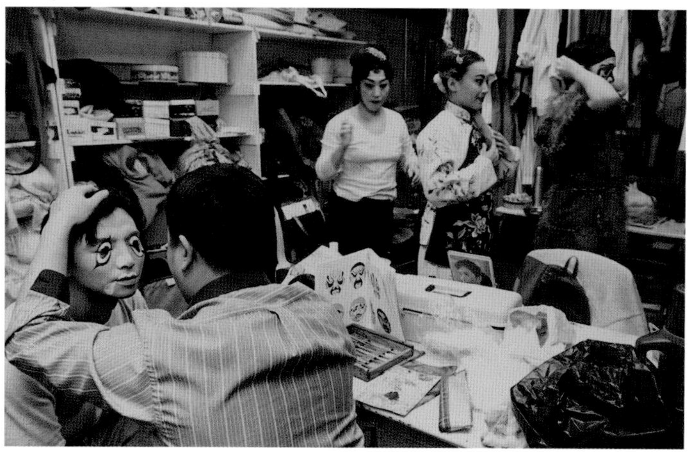

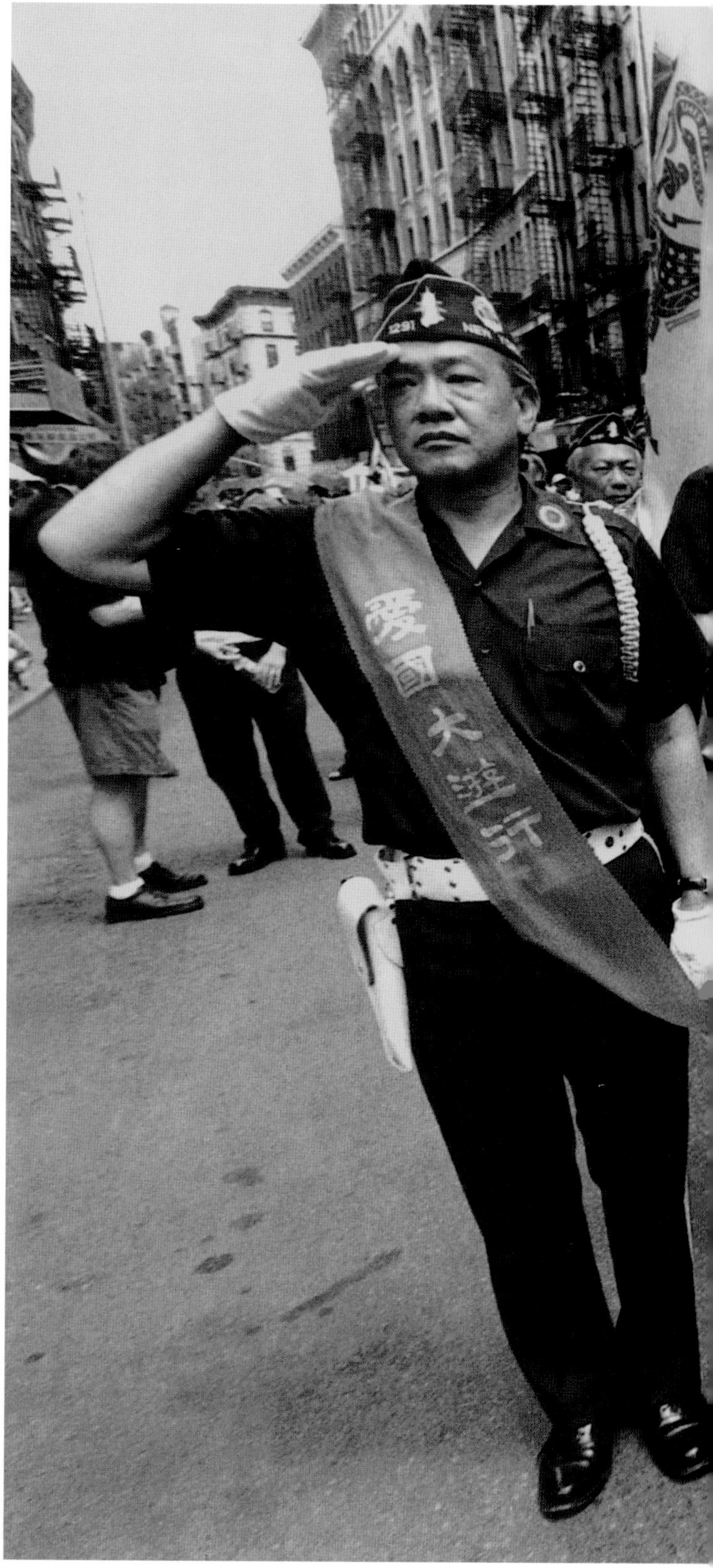

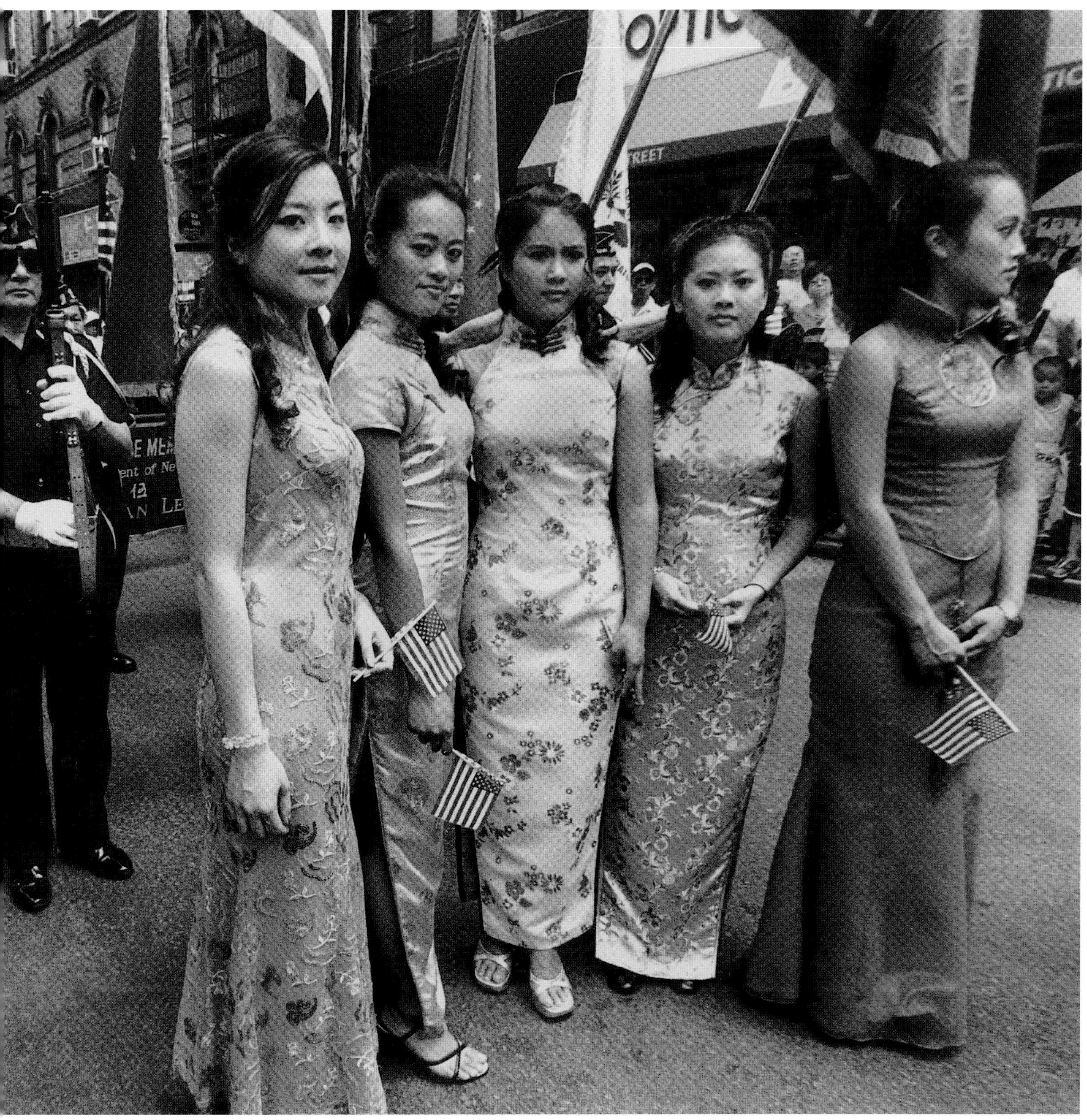

Wen Ho Lee, a Taiwanese American physicist at the nuclear weapons lab at Los Alamos, appeared with activist Helen Zia at a signing of their 2001 book, *My Country Versus Me: The First-Hand Account by the Los Alamos Scientist Who Was Falsely Accused of Being a Spy.* Lee was charged in 1999 with stealing state secrets on behalf of China and detained for 278 days in solitary confinement and without bail. All charges were dropped save for minor ones regarding improper handling of records. Later U.S. district judge Aubrey Parker, who said he had been misled by the FBI, and President Bill Clinton apologized for the government's treatment of Lee. Lee won a $1.6 million settlement in a civil case against the government and media outlets that had leaked information about the charges. New York, 2005.

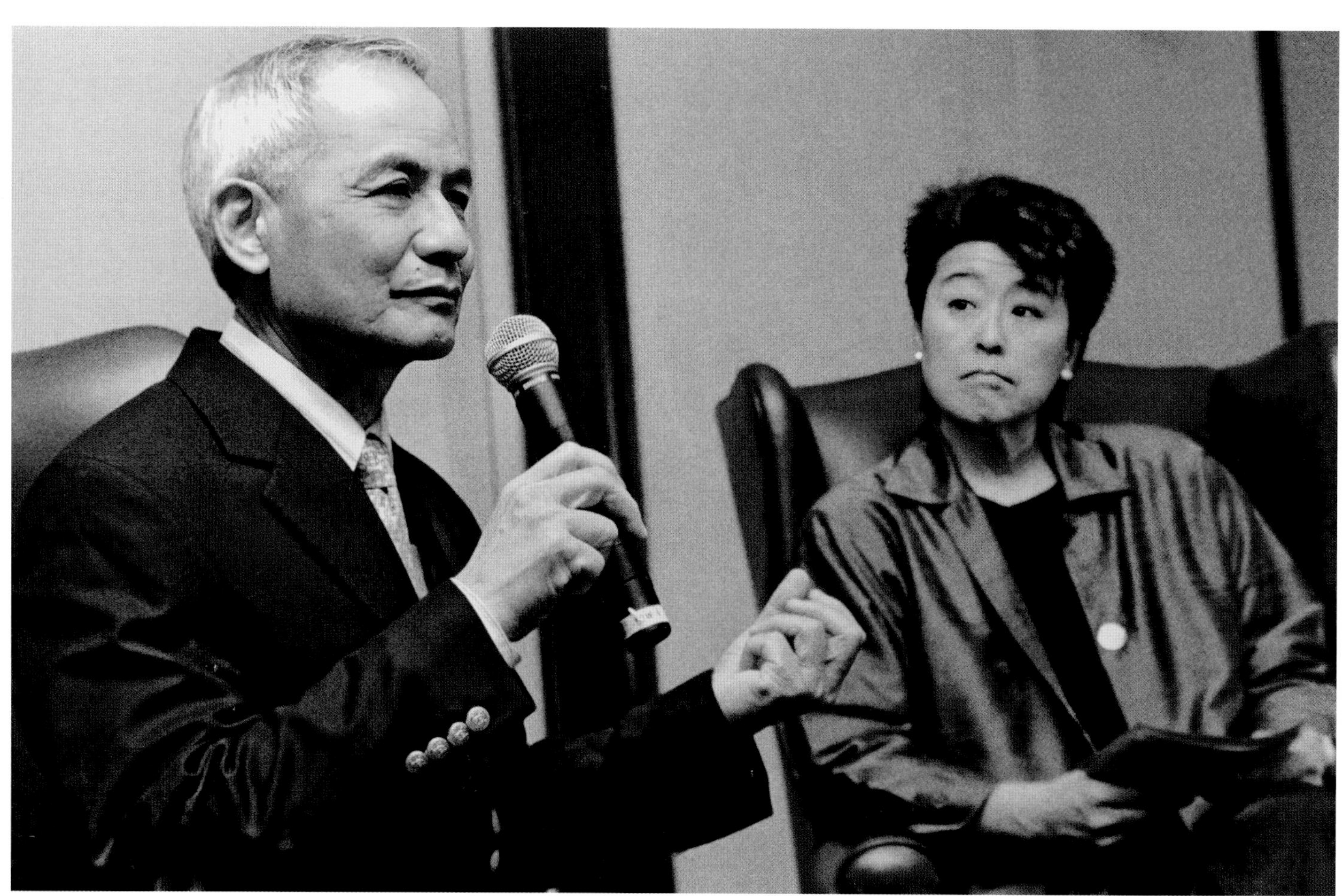

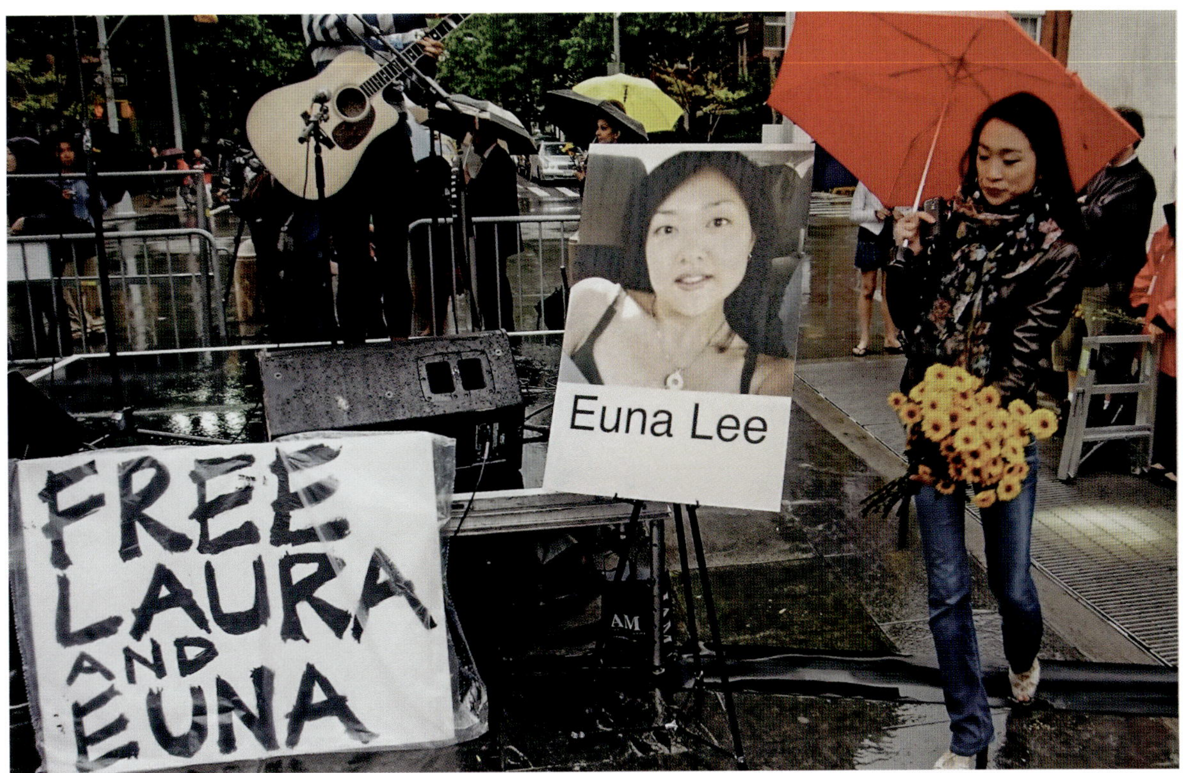

New Yorkers rally to support Euna Lee and Laura Ling, Asian American journalists who were detained after they crossed the border from China into North Korea. They were convicted of illegal entry and sentenced to twelve years of hard labor. Diplomatic efforts, including a humanitarian visit by former president Bill Clinton, led to a special pardon and their release. New York, 2009.

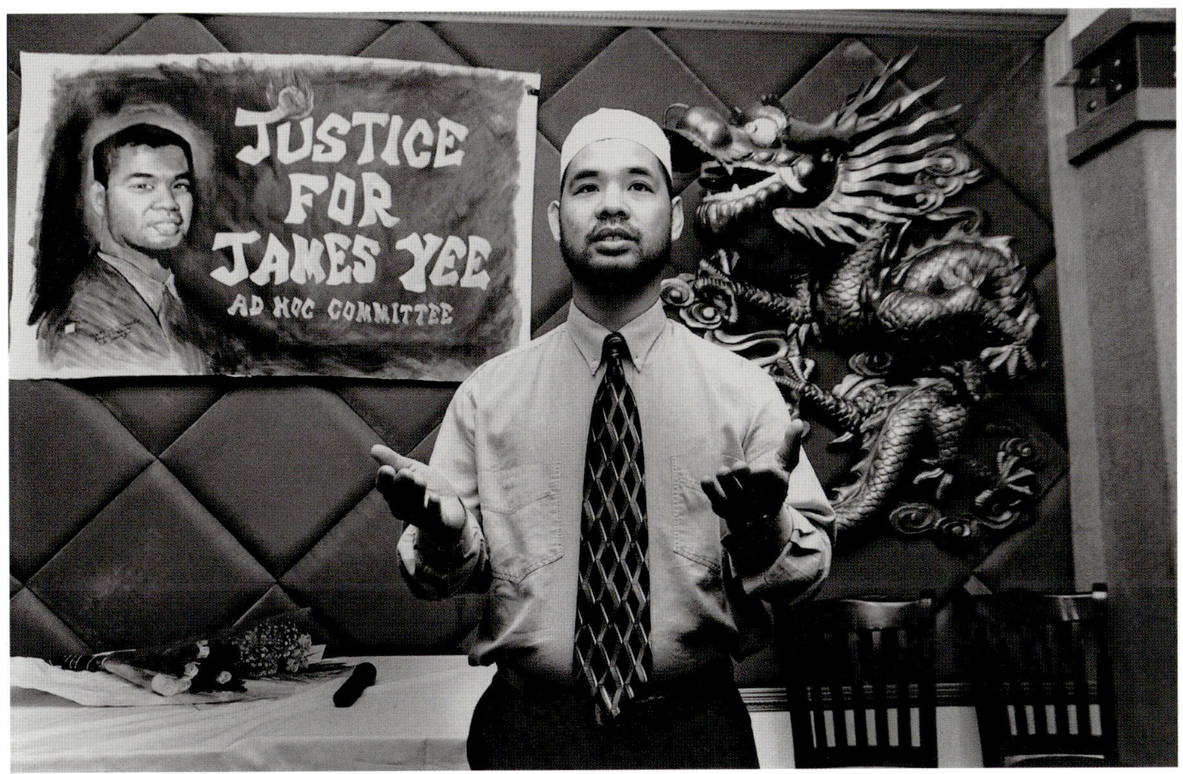

In 2003 Capt. James Yee, a Muslim who was a U.S. Army chaplain at Guantánamo, was charged with sedition, espionage, and other offenses and spent seventy-six days in solitary confinement. All charges were ultimately dropped, and Yee left the military with an honorable discharge. His book, *For God and Country: Faith and Patriotism Under Fire*, was published in 2005. New York, 2005.

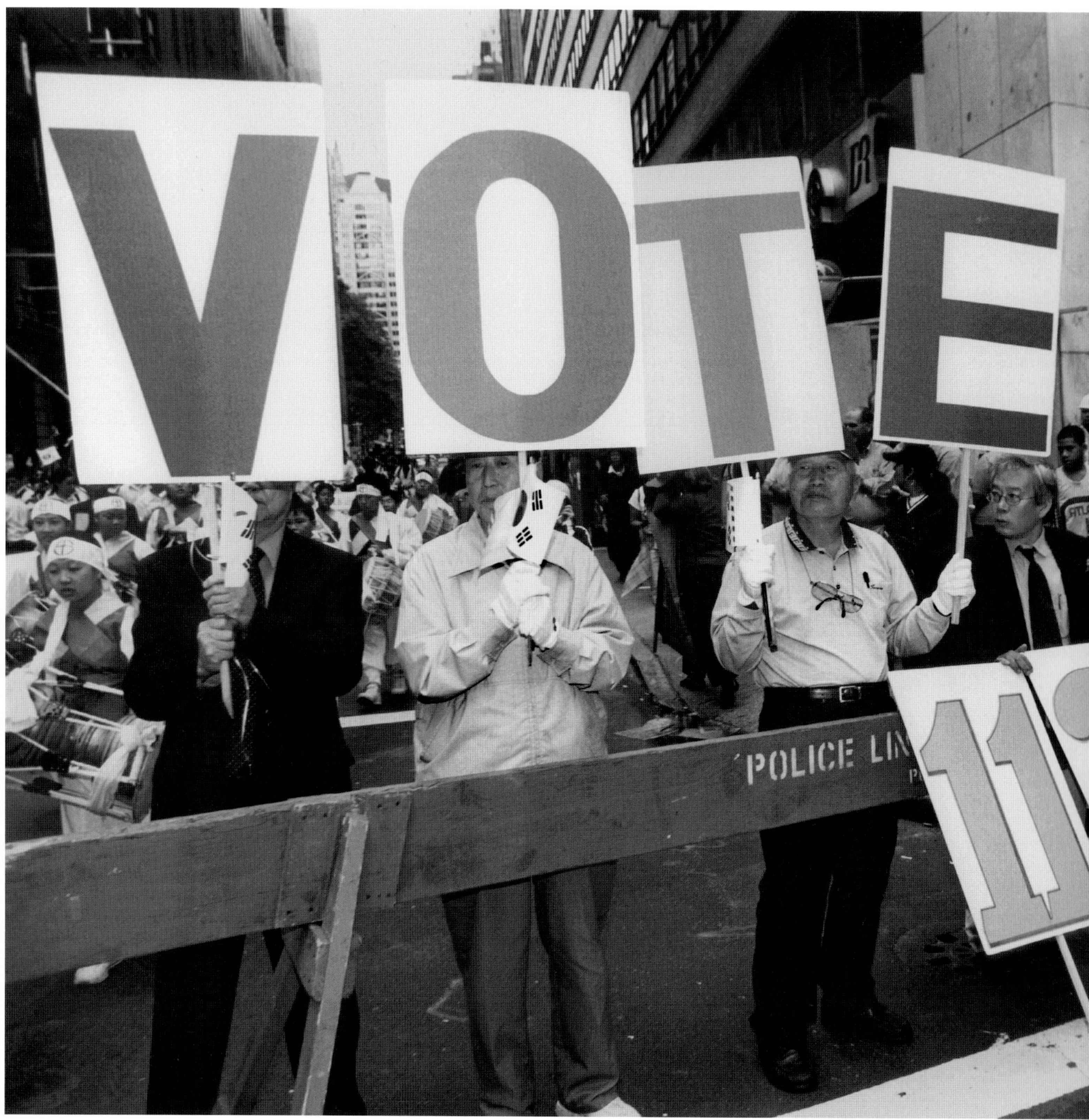
VOTE
POLICE LIN

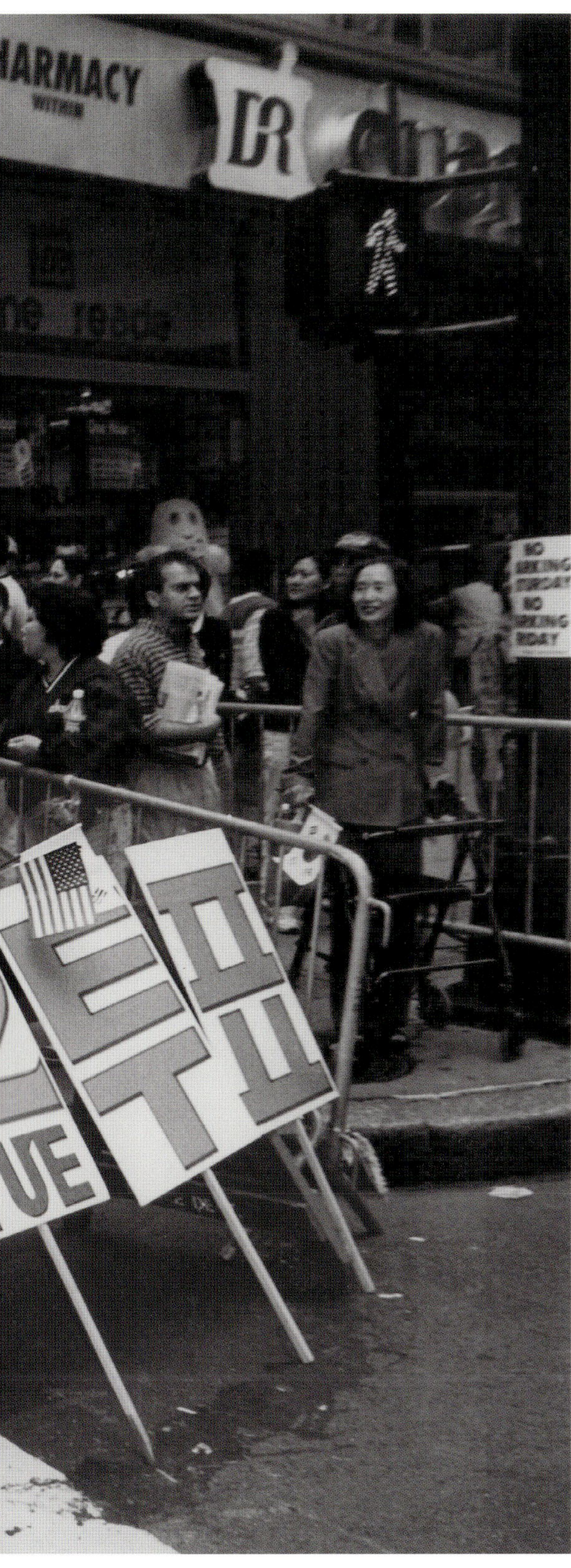

A Korean American voter registration campaign. New York, 2004.

Below: Rithy Uong (*right*), a refugee from Cambodia, was elected to the Lowell, Massachusetts, city council in 1999, the first American of Southeast Asian descent to win any elected office in the United States. During his reelection campaign, he gave Linda Trinh Vo, a professor at the University of California at Irvine, and political scientist Okiyoshi Takeda, from the Association of Asian American Studies, a signed campaign poster. Lowell, Massachusetts, 2003.

Bottom: Jun Choi, son of Korean immigrants and an education specialist, was elected mayor of Edison, New Jersey, the first Asian American mayor of a major city in the state. He served from 2006 to 2010. Edison, New Jersey, 2005.

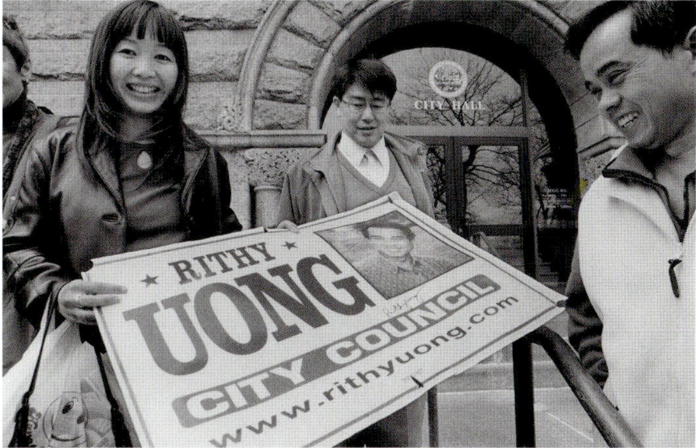

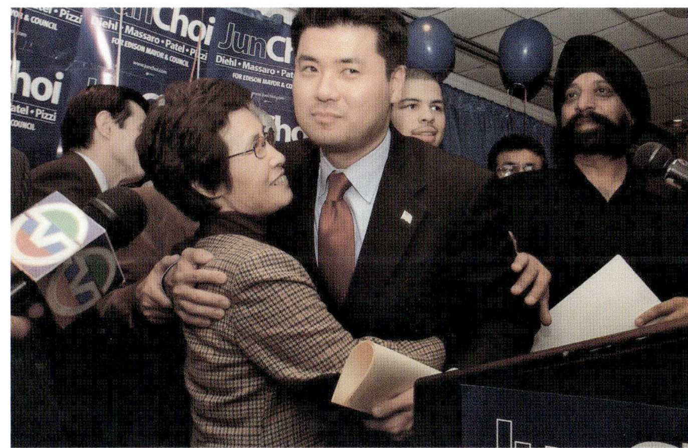

When Hot 97-AM radio played a racist parody of "We Are the World" that mocked victims of the tsunami in Southeast Asia, Ben Chan, a college student and future lawyer, and others protested. The outrage resulted in an on-air apology, the firing of a producer and co-host, and the suspension of others. New York, 2005.

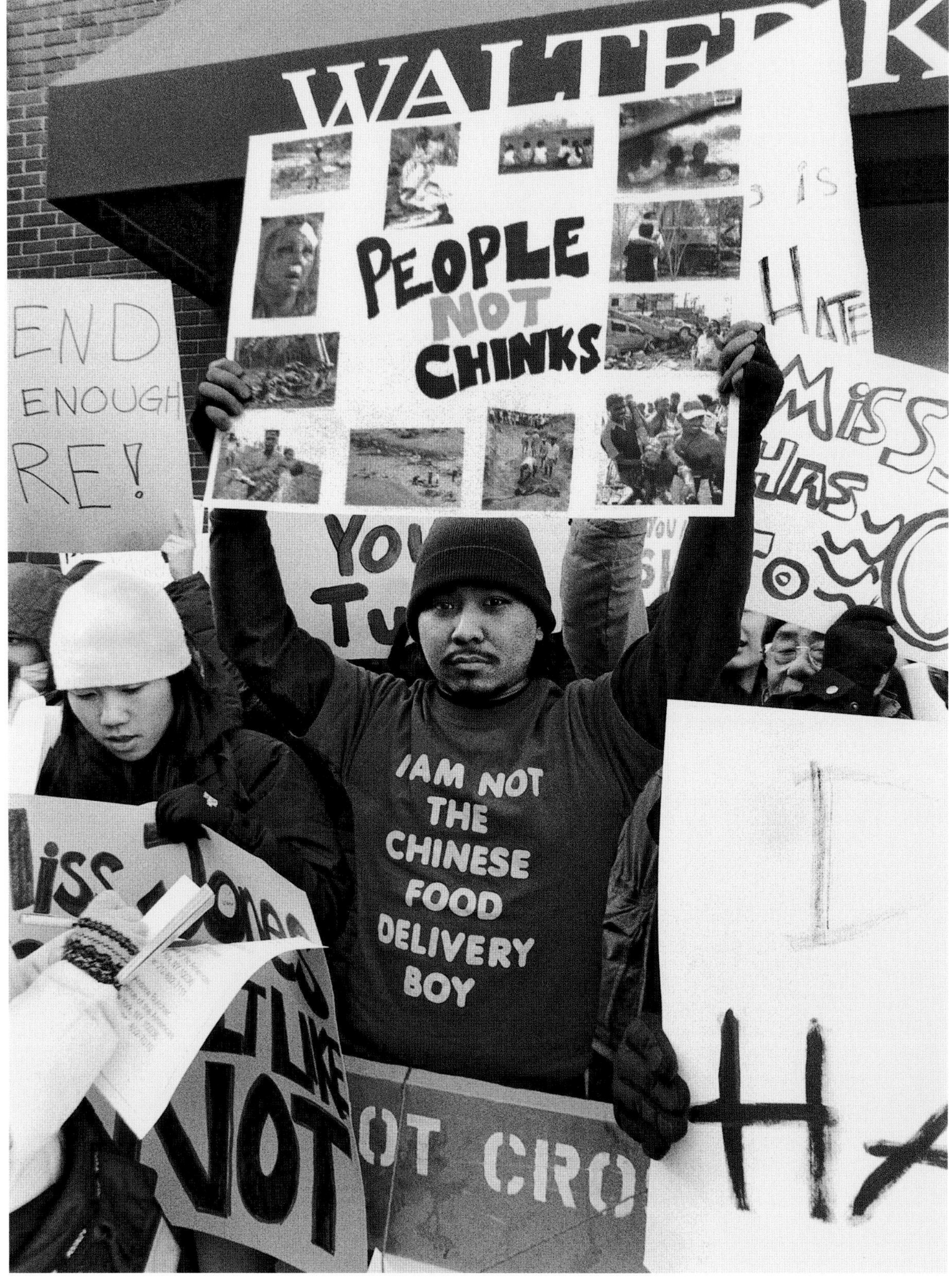

In October 2013 the late-night TV host Jimmy Kimmel aired a pre-taped segment in which he asked schoolchildren for ideas about how to deal with China's rise as a global economic power. A ten-year-old boy said, "Kill everyone in China," to which Kimmel replied, "That's an interesting idea." Public outrage forced Kimmel to apologize, both on-air and in writing. More than 100,000 people signed a petition to President Barack Obama demanding that the show be cut. The White House issued a statement noting the apologies and affirming that the United States welcomed China's "peaceful rise," but saying it could not force ABC to remove the show, on First Amendment grounds. New York, 2013.

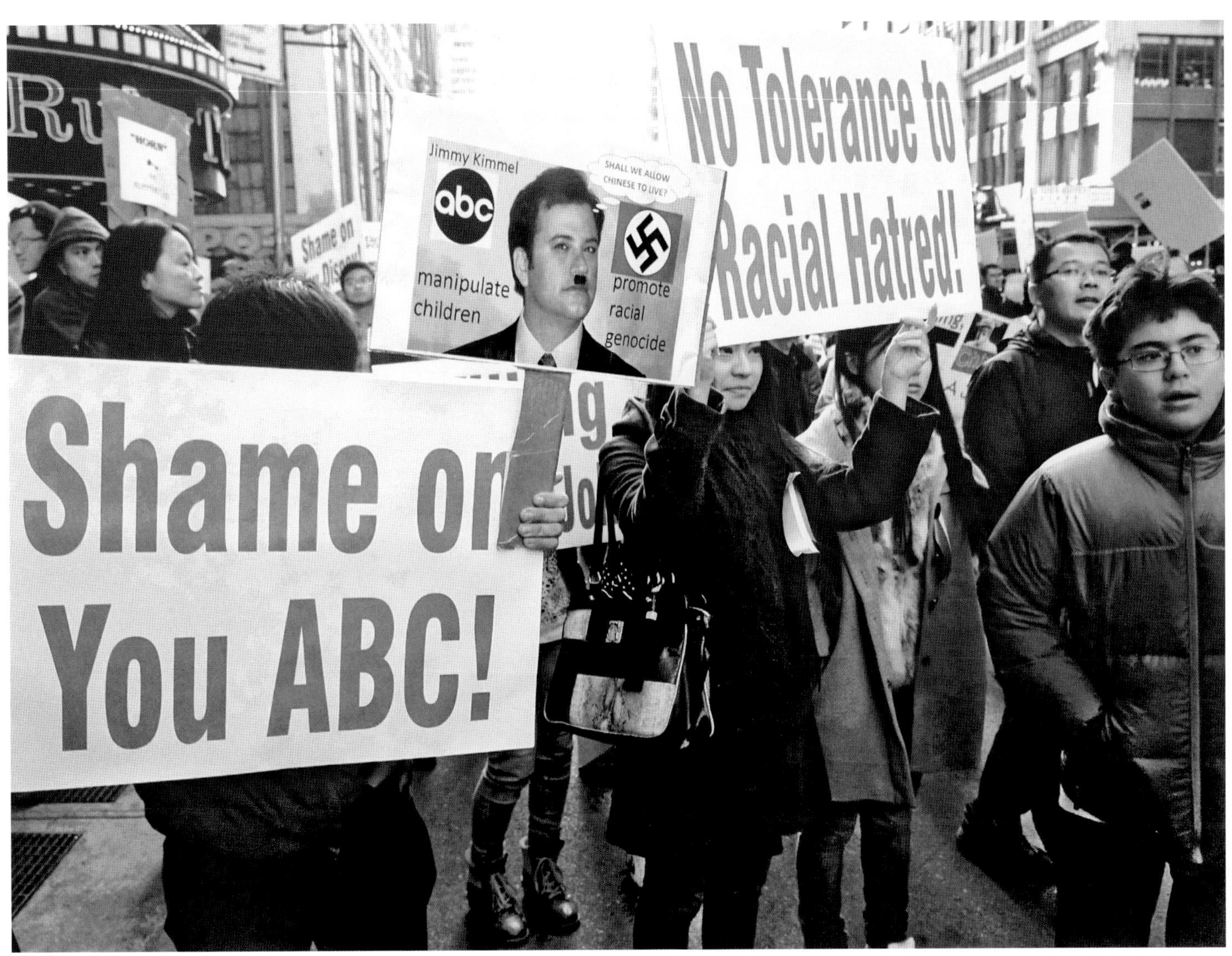

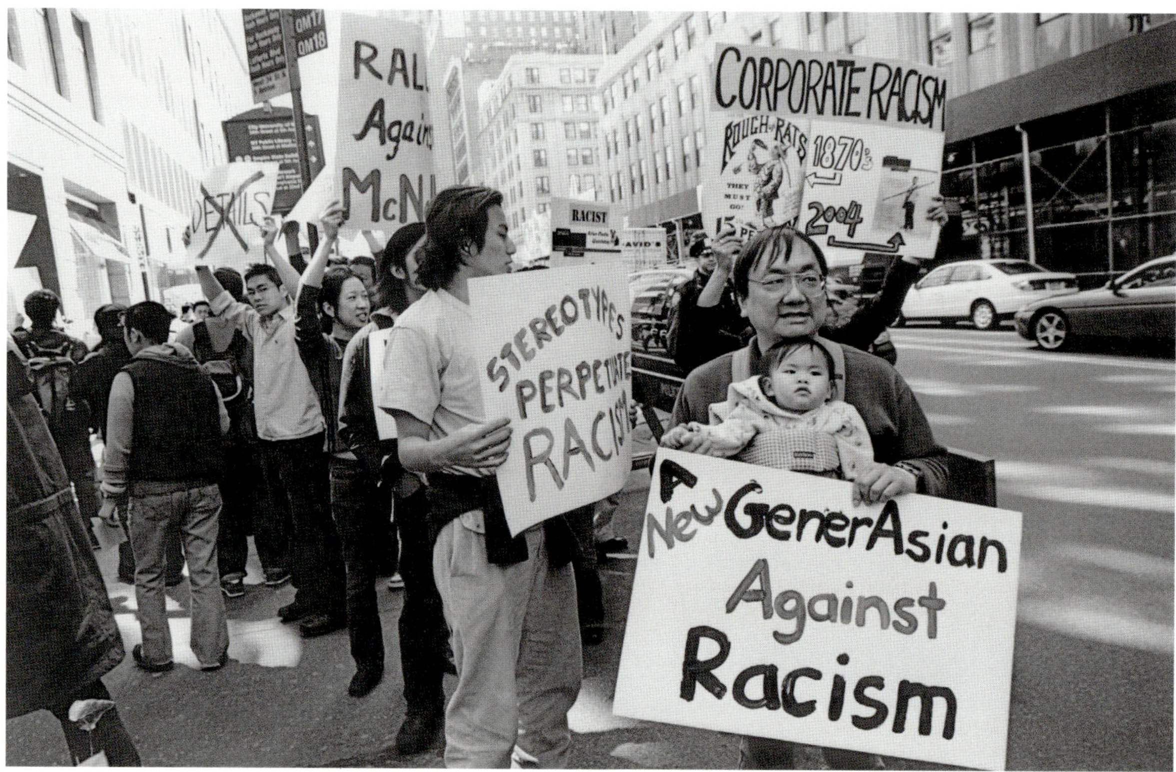

Asian Americans protest a racist and homophobic column in the men's magazine *Details*. New York, 2004.

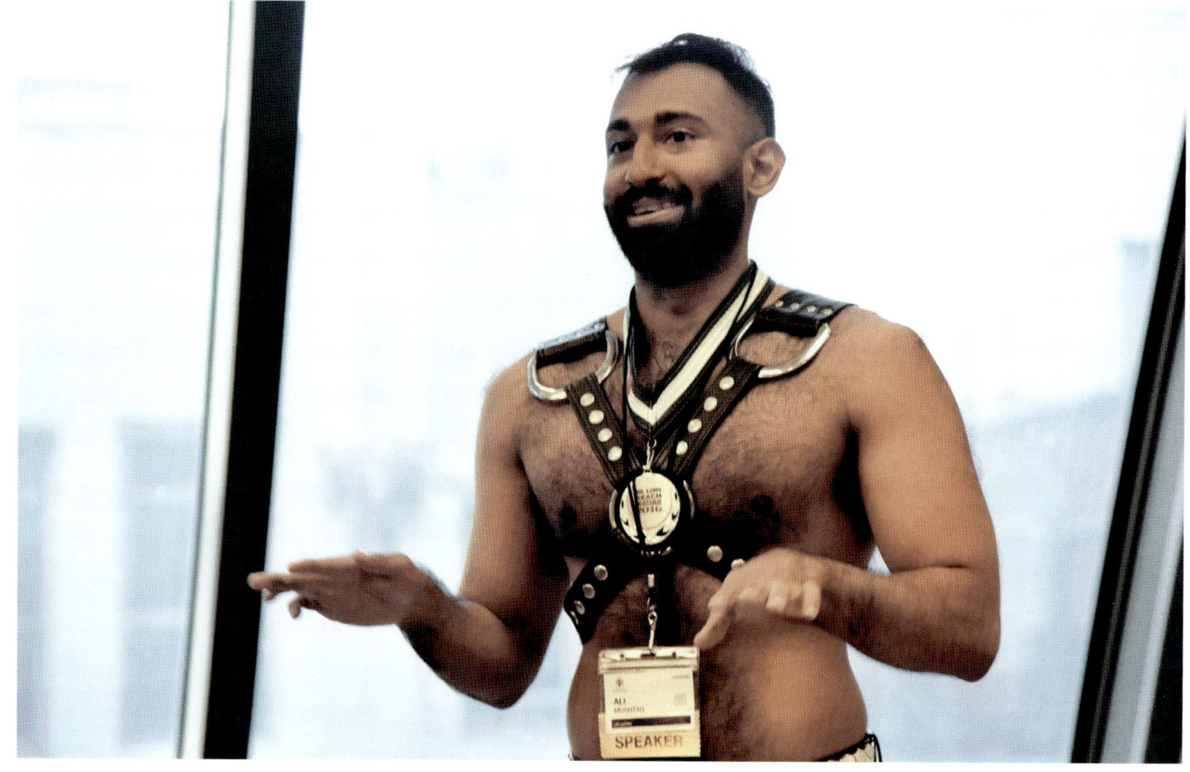

Ali Mushtaq, Mr. Long Beach Leather (2015) and a sociologist, speaking at a workshop of the National Queer Asian Pacific Islander Alliance conference. San Francisco, 2018. *Corky Lee/NQAPIA*

Queer Asian Pacific Islanders support Black Lives Matter at the University of Illinois. Chicago, 2015.

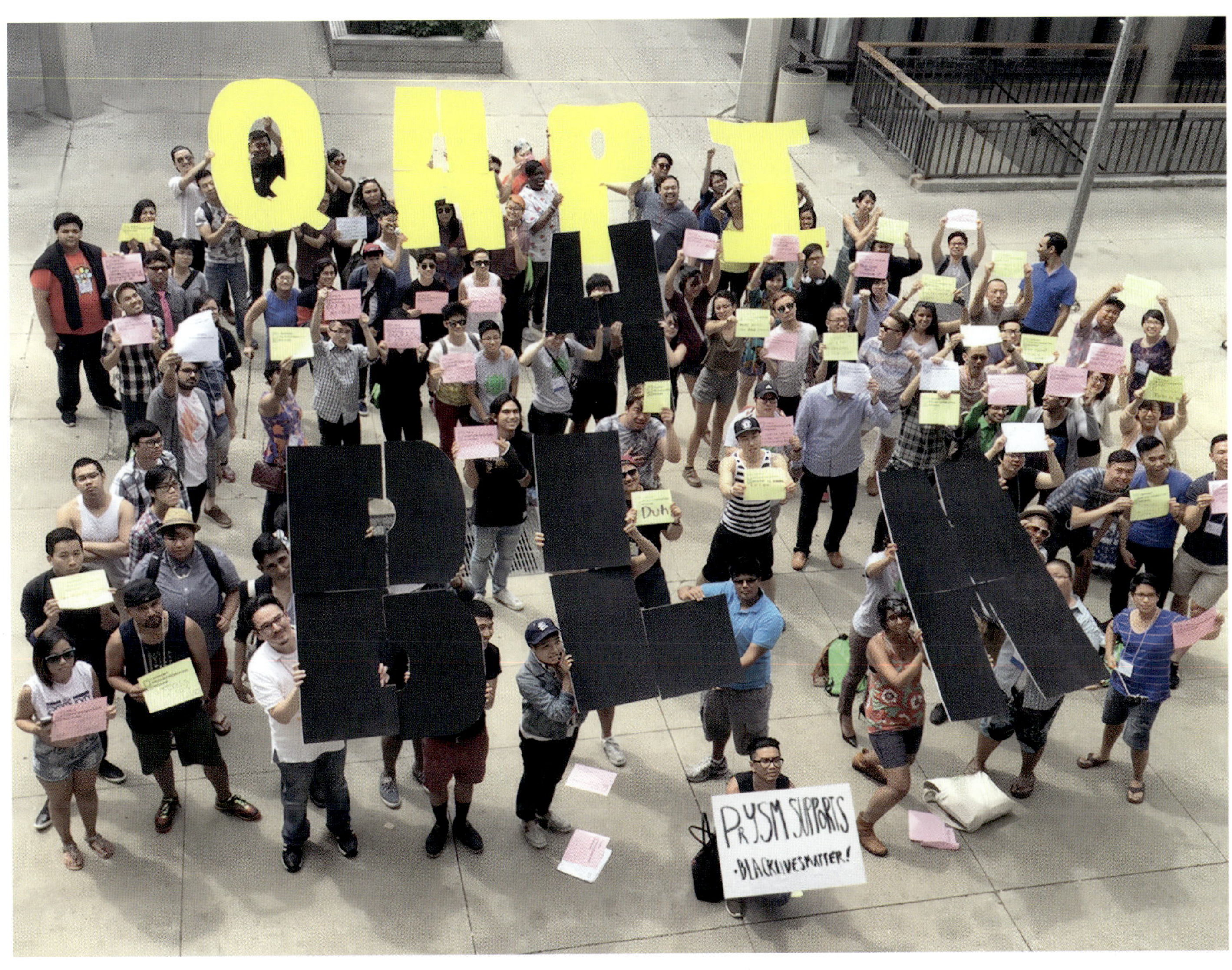

The Emergence of Our Stage

DAVID HENRY HWANG

Playwright, librettist, screenwriter, and Columbia University professor

I didn't remember this photo, even though I'm in it. That Corky Lee preserved images of AAPI events that some of the participants might not fully remember exemplifies the importance of his work. He understood that movements and communities are built from a wide range of people, institutions, and events—visible and publicized, private and intimate. Some might have faded into forgetfulness except that he was there to document them, preserving history for present and future generations.

Thanks to some research, I learned the photo was taken by Corky at the first National Asian American Theater Festival, held at New York's Public Theater in June 2007, produced by the Consortium of Asian American Theaters and Artists. CAATA continues to produce conferences and festivals regularly to this day. This inaugural festival featured more than twenty-five performing artists and companies, including an excerpt from my play *Yellow Face*, which would open later that year at the Public.

From the early days of the Asian American movement, theater has provided an artistic gathering place for our community to explore and imagine emerging notions of identity, politics, and culture. Early institutions included Los Angeles's East West Players (founded in 1965) and San Francisco's Asian American Theater Company (founded in 1973). In New York City, the 1977 birth of the Pan Asian Repertory Theatre led to today's vibrant theater scene, which now includes Ma-Yi Theater Company and the National Asian American Theatre Company.

Corky's documentation of AAPI theater dates to the Basement Workshop in Chinatown, the interdisciplinary political and arts organization founded in 1970. At the Basement he photographed participants in early theater classes led by artists such as the Tony- and Oscar-nominated actor-director Mako. Many of these students, including the actor Tzi Ma, would go on to major careers in stage, film, and television. Back when AAPI actors, dramatists, and stories were largely excluded from Broadway and Hollywood, however, Corky supported and helped make possible the emergence of a stage we could call our own.

My last significant encounter with Corky was in Utah in 2019, at the 150th anniversary of the completion of the transcontinental railroad. Corky's work about the railroad was arguably his most epic. Our encounter was personal, demonstrating the care he showed to friends and colleagues. Before I left, Corky handed me a memento: an old, discarded spike he had found on the ground while trekking along the tracks. To this day, it sits on a shelf in my office reminding me that, thanks to Corky Lee, the past can endure into the present and help to shape the future.

Playwright David Henry Hwang speaks at the first National Asian American Theater Festival at the Public Theater. New York, 2007.

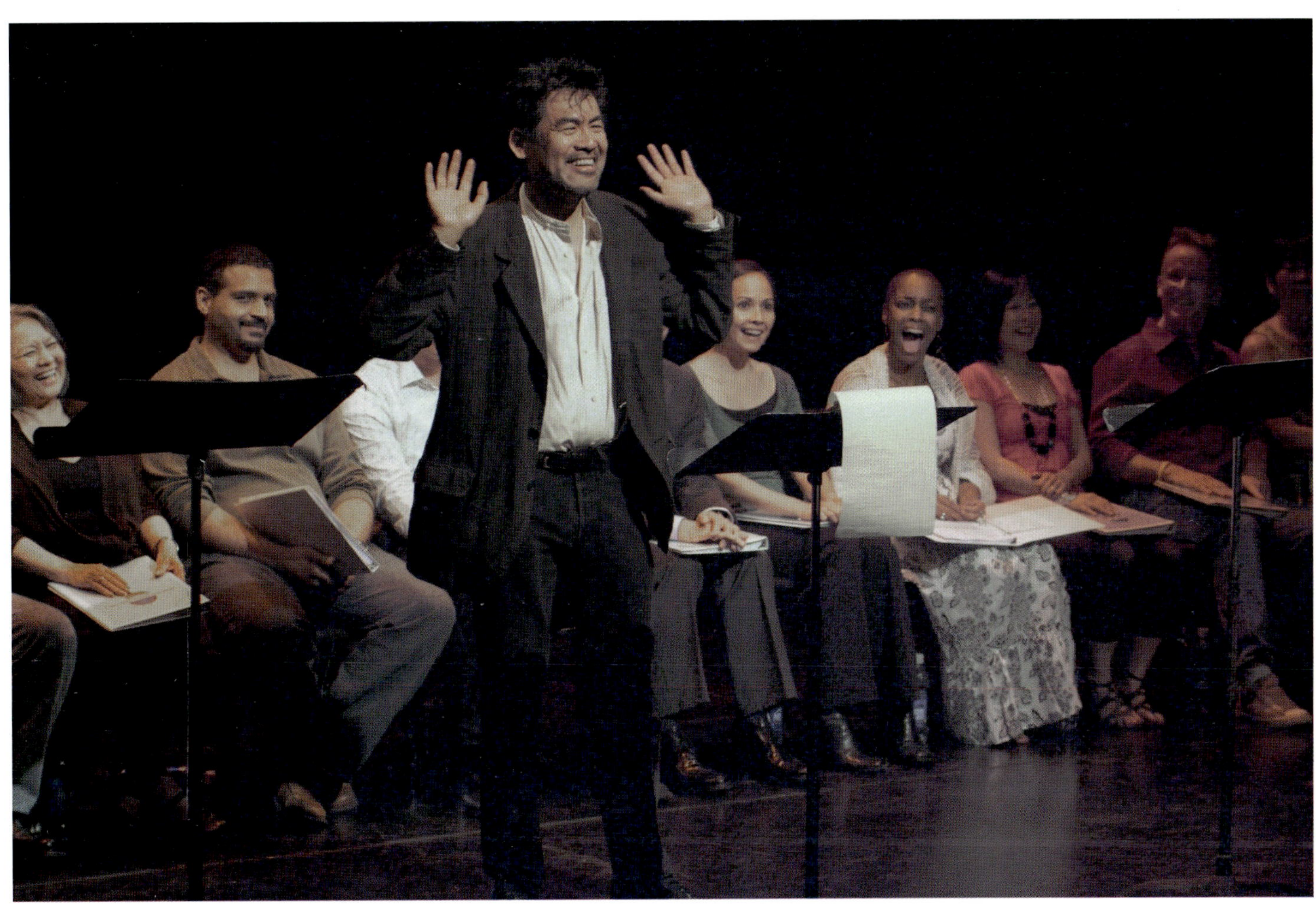

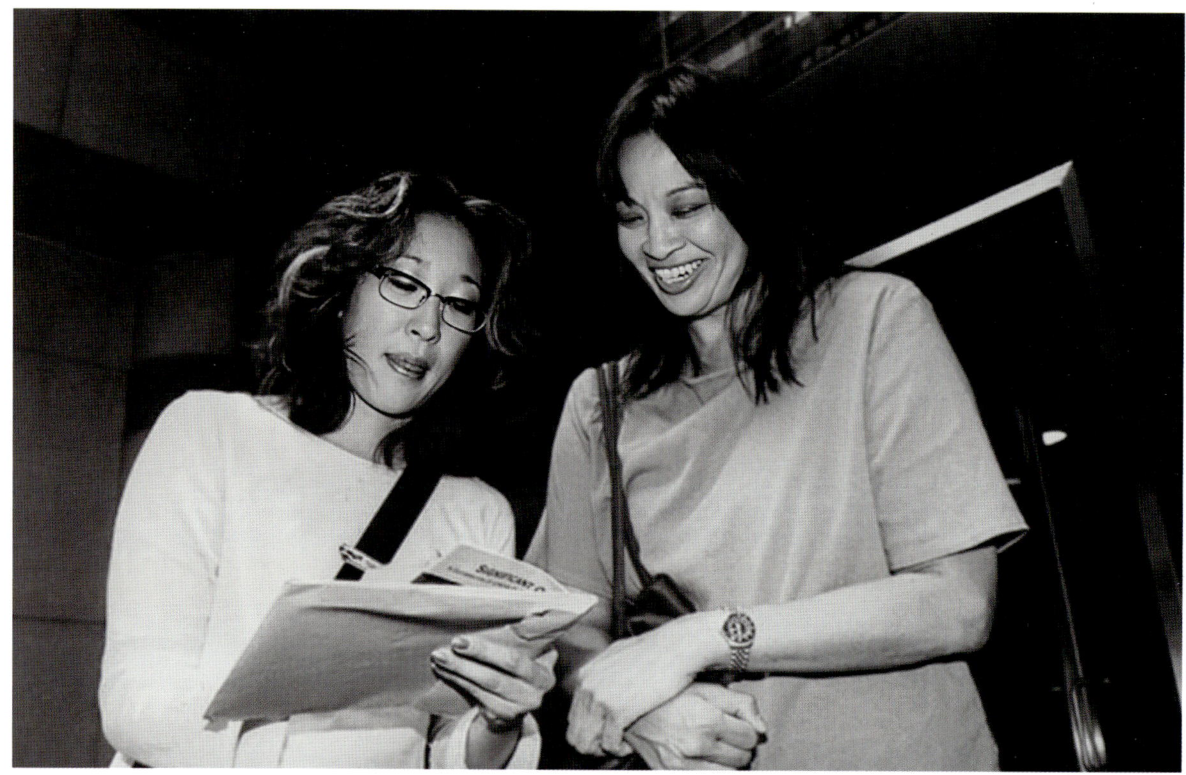

Actor Sandra Oh (*left*) with Margaret Fung, executive director of the Asian American Legal Defense and Education Fund, at a fundraising performance of *Satellites*, a play by Diana Son, at the Public Theater. New York, 2006.

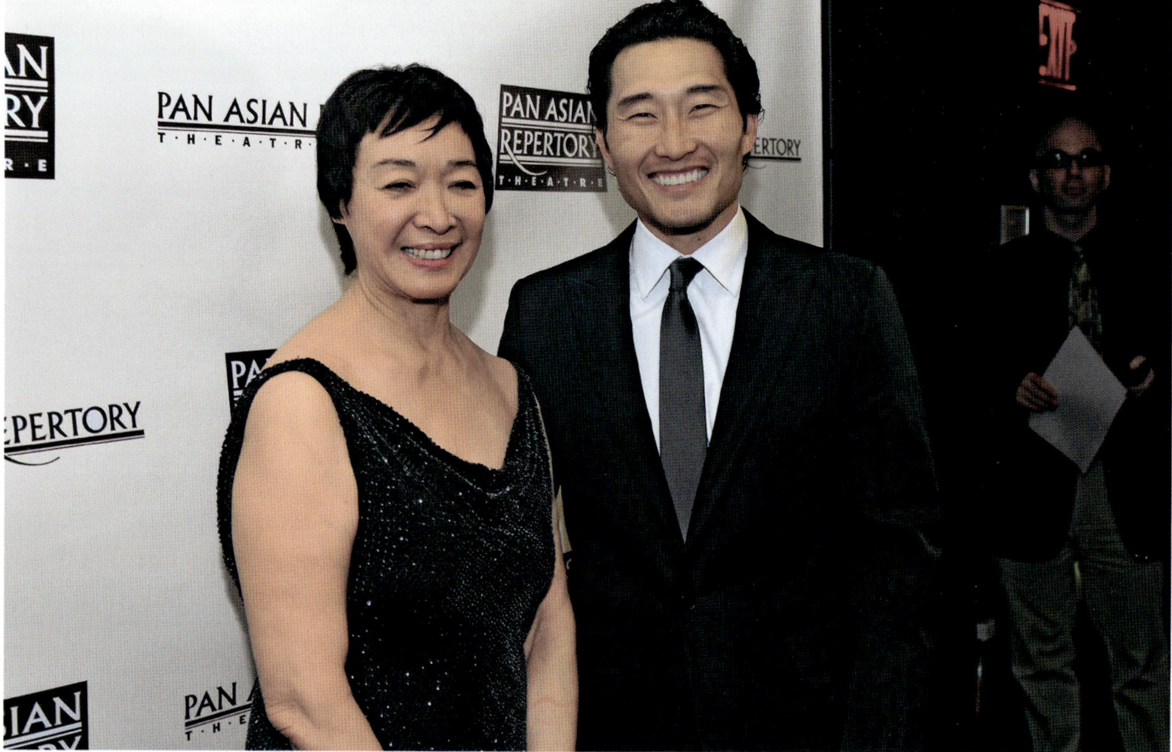

Actor Daniel Dae Kim and Tisa Chang, founding artistic director of the Pan Asian Repertory Theatre, at the Pan Asian's thirty-fifth anniversary celebration. New York, 2012.

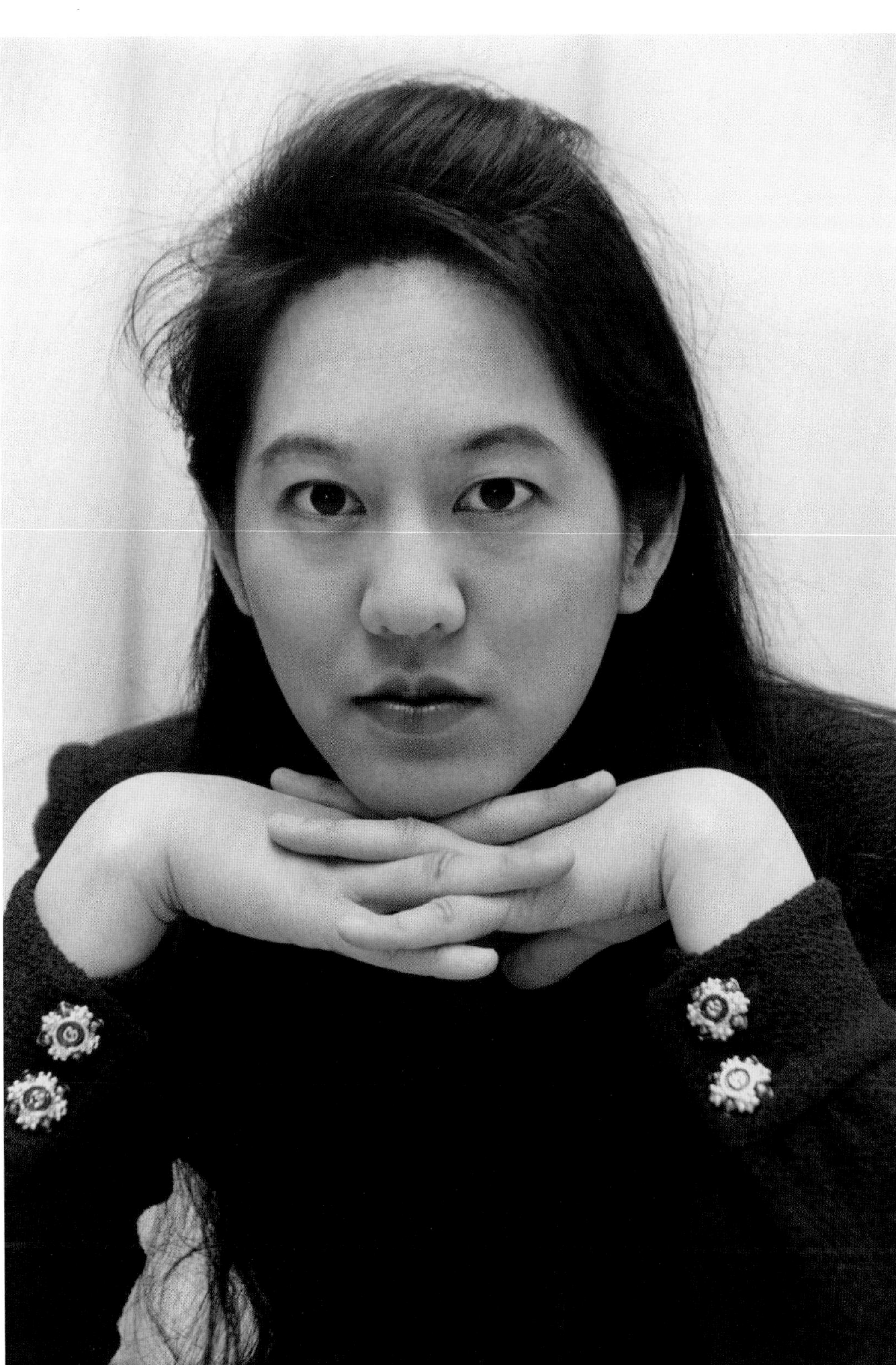

Writer Iris Chang (1968–2004). New York, 2004.

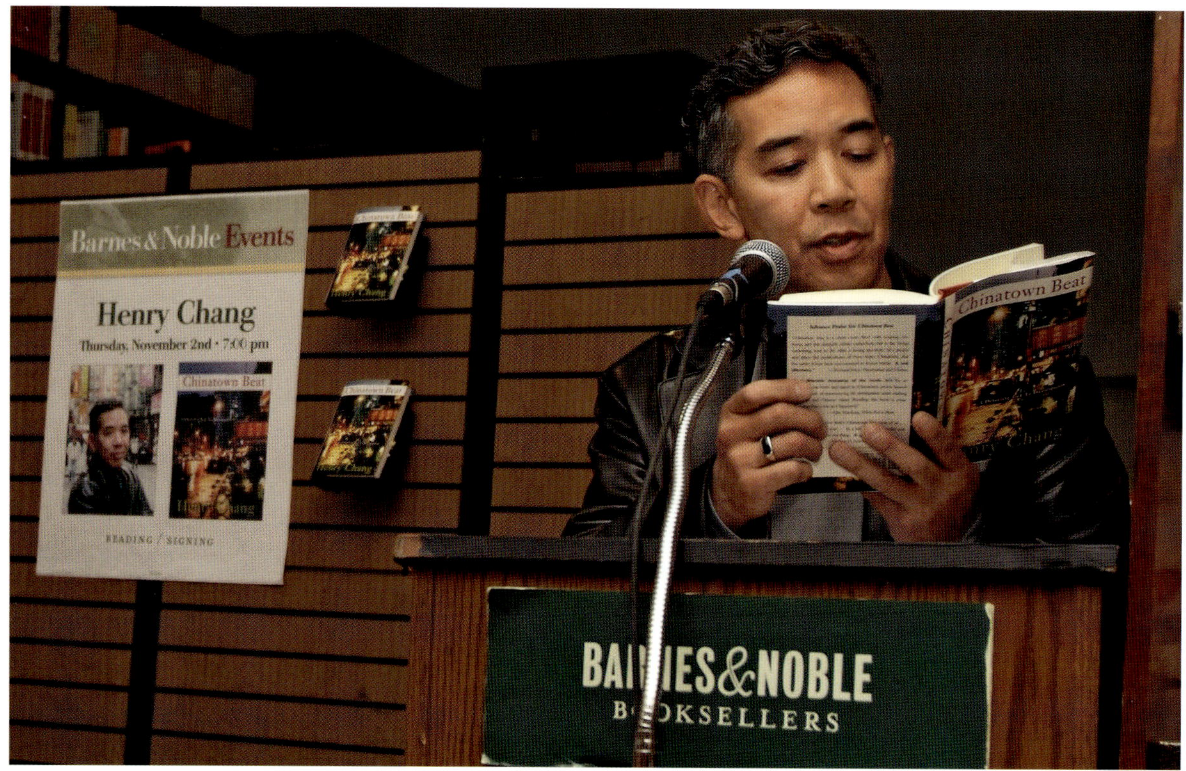

Henry Chang, Chinatown resident and author, reading from *Chinatown Beat,* his first Detective Jack Yu crime novel. New York, 2016.

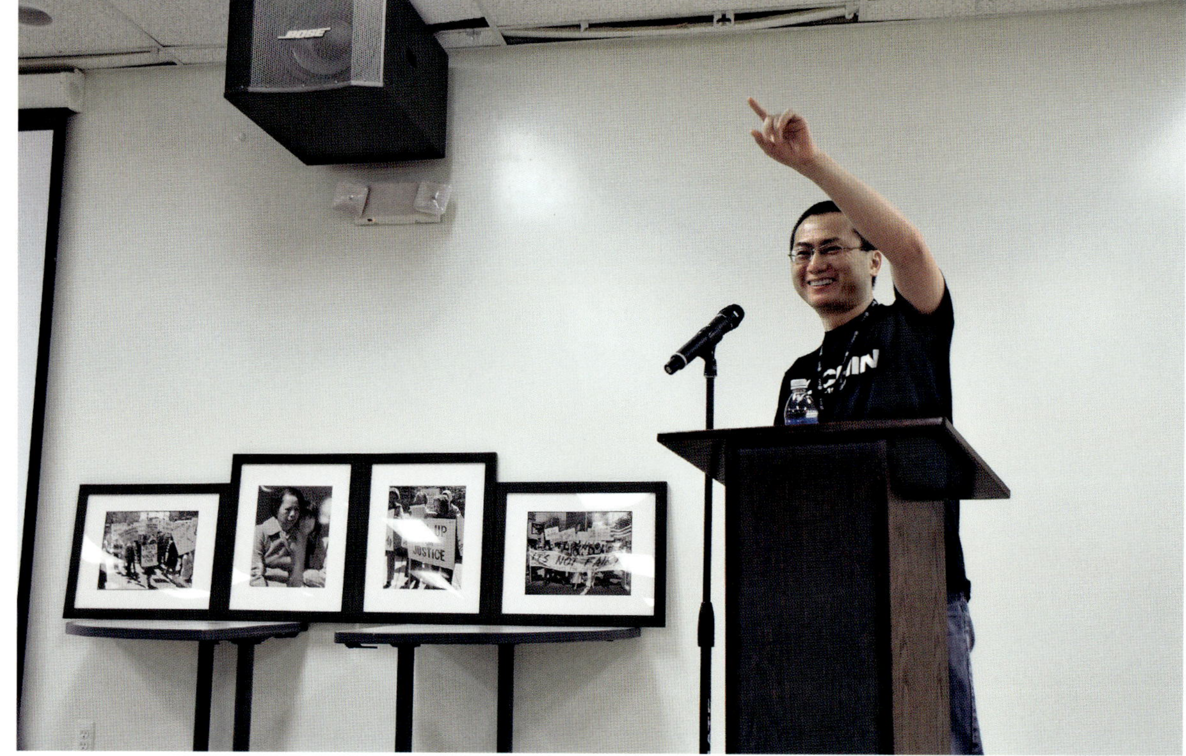

Filmmaker Curtis Chin, who directed the film *Vincent Who?* (2009), speaking at the convention of the Asian American Journalists Association, with a display of photographs by Corky Lee. Detroit, 2011.

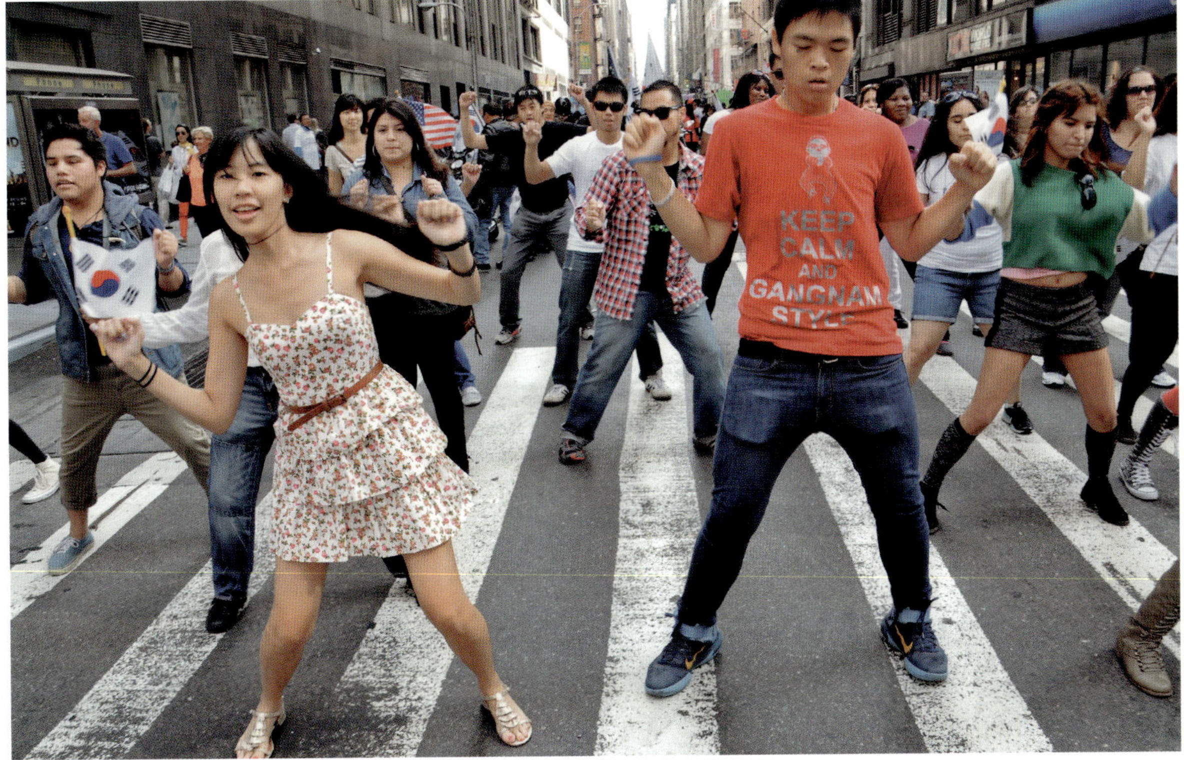

A flash mob performs Gangnam-style song and dance, popularized by the Korean pop singer Psy, before the start of the Korean harvest parade. New York, 2012.

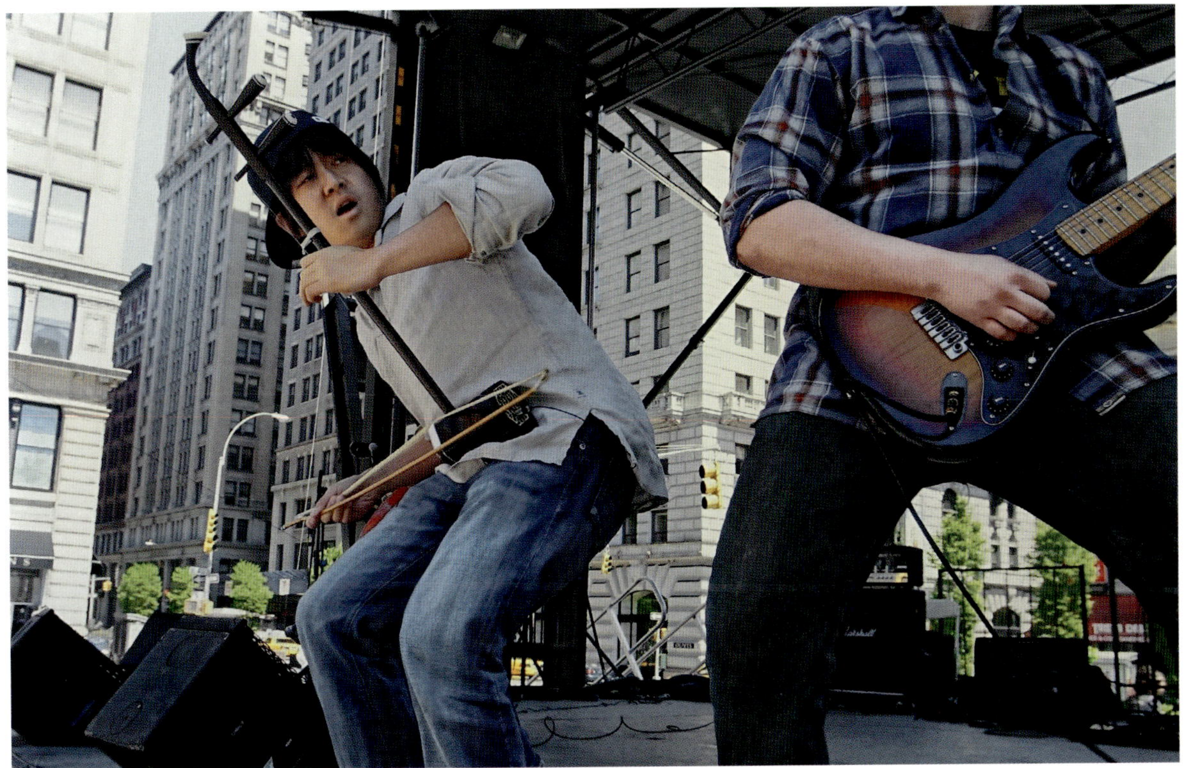

Jack Hsu, front man for the rock group Hsu-nami, is an accomplished violinist. He plays progressive rock, heavy metal, and funk; at times he plays the electric *erhu*. Asian Pacific American Heritage Festival, Union Square. New York, 2008.

Cambodian monks offer the water blessing, the traditional ritual of cleansing and purifying. South Philadelphia, 2013.

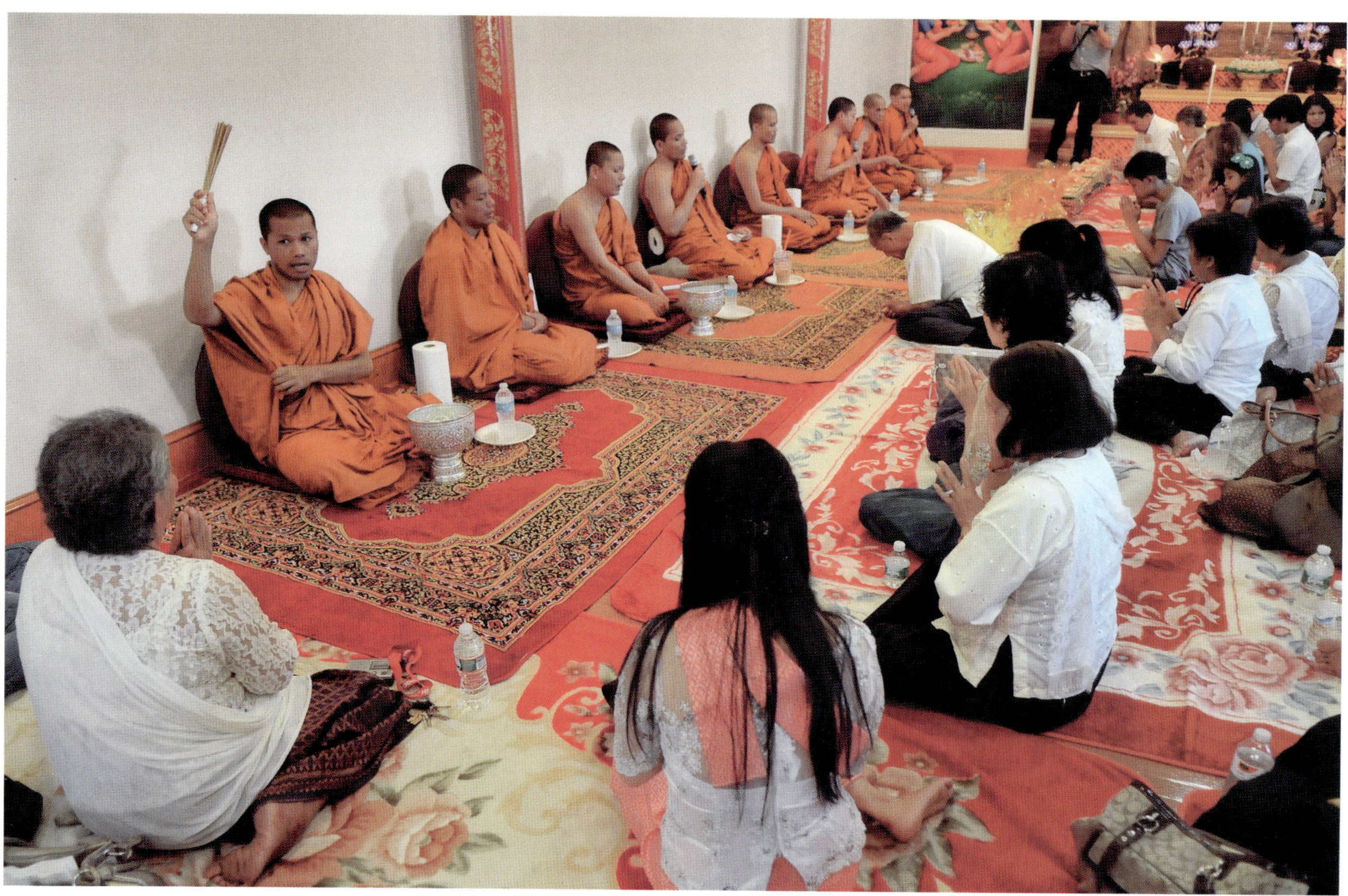

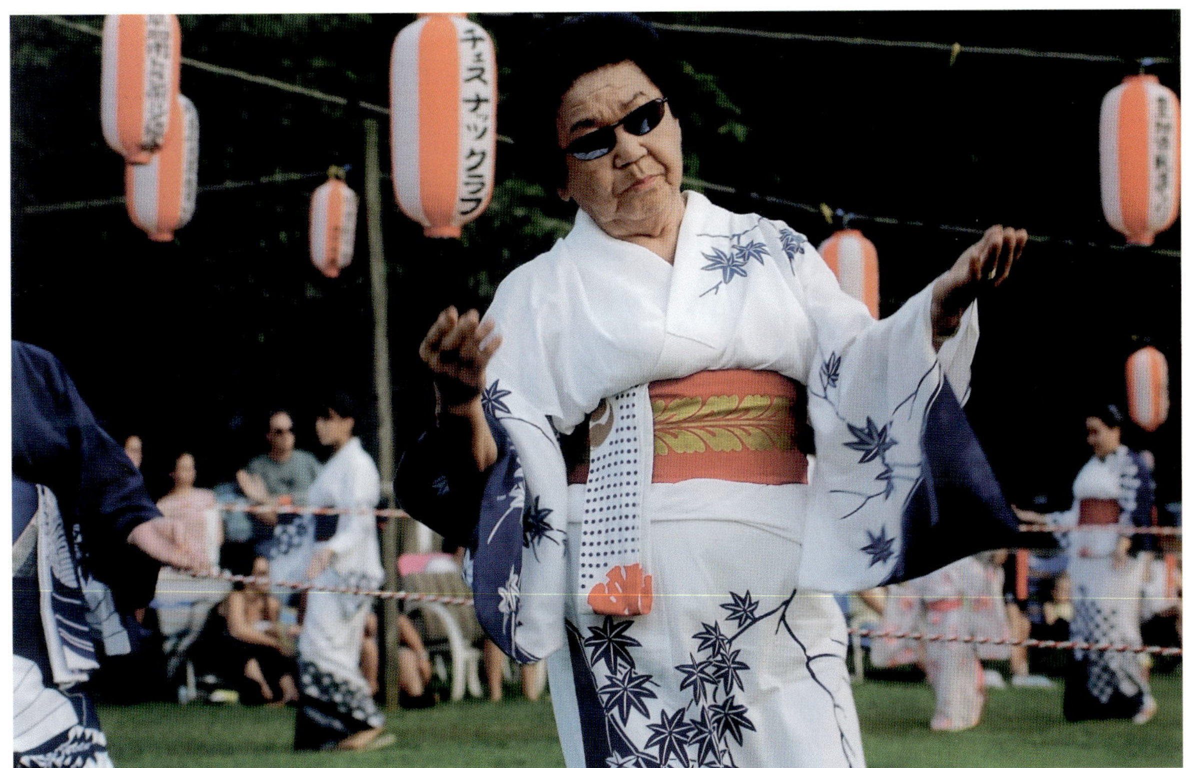

A celebrant at the Seabrook Buddhist Temple's annual Obon Festival. Seabrook Farms, a large commercial farming and canning company in central New Jersey, recruited 2,500 Japanese Americans from the internment camps at the end of World War II. Most later relocated to New York, Chicago, or the West Coast, but a small community remains in New Jersey. Seabrook, New Jersey, 2007.

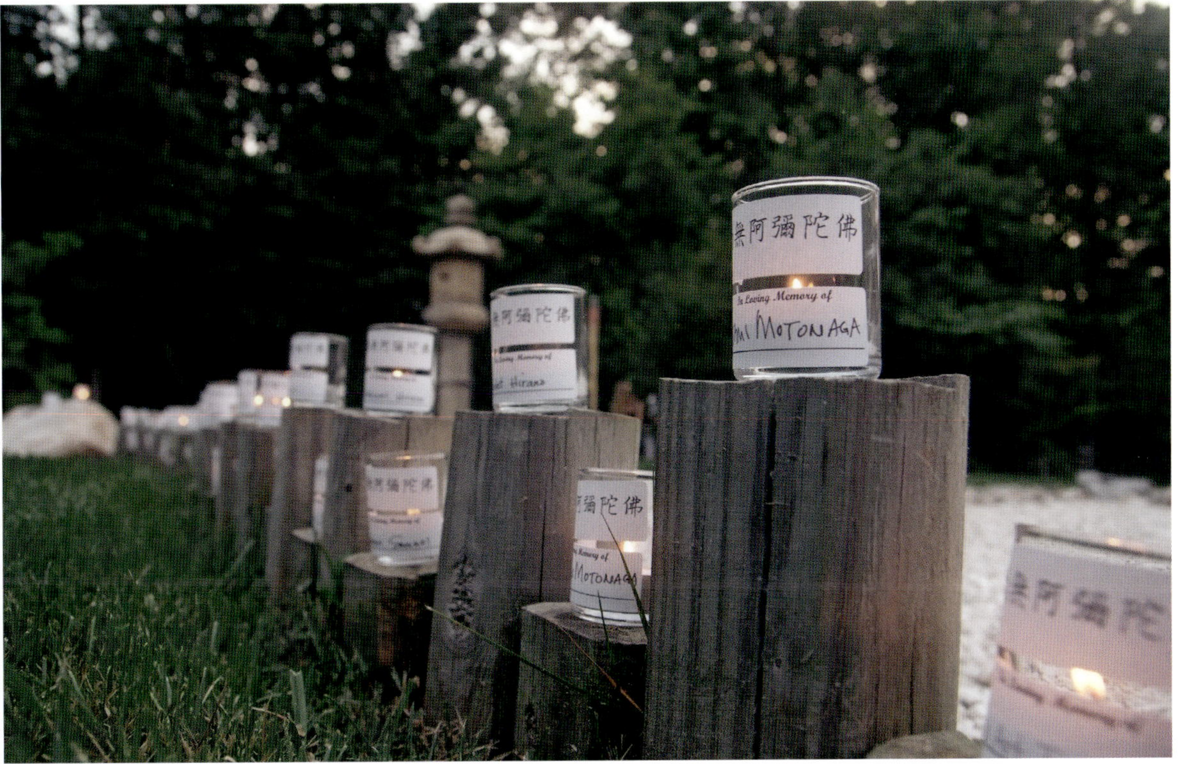

Memorial candles at the Obon Festival at the Ekoji Buddhist Temple. Fairfax, Virginia, 2007.

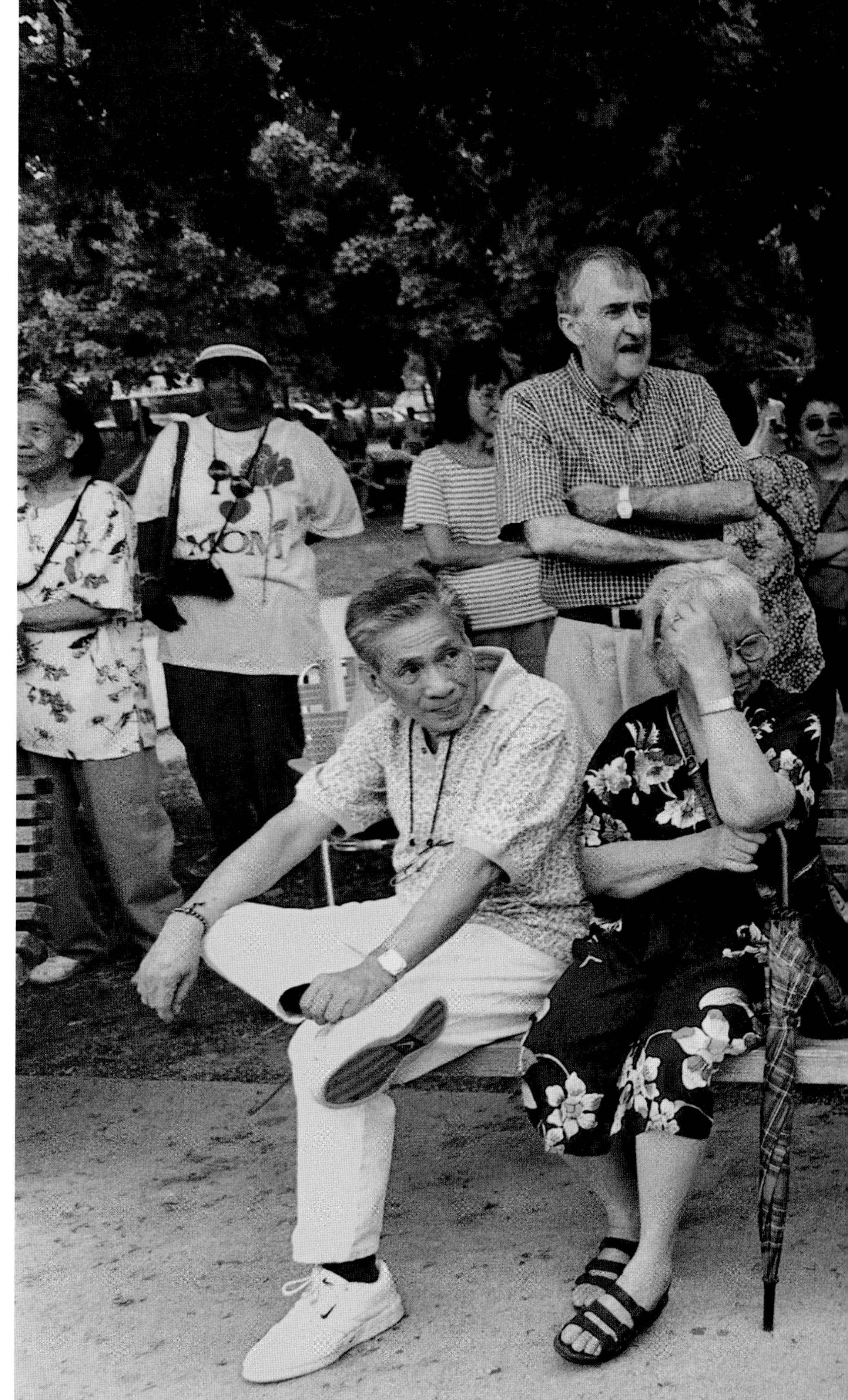

Madame Qi Shu Fang, a Chinese opera singer. Westchester County, New York, 2001.

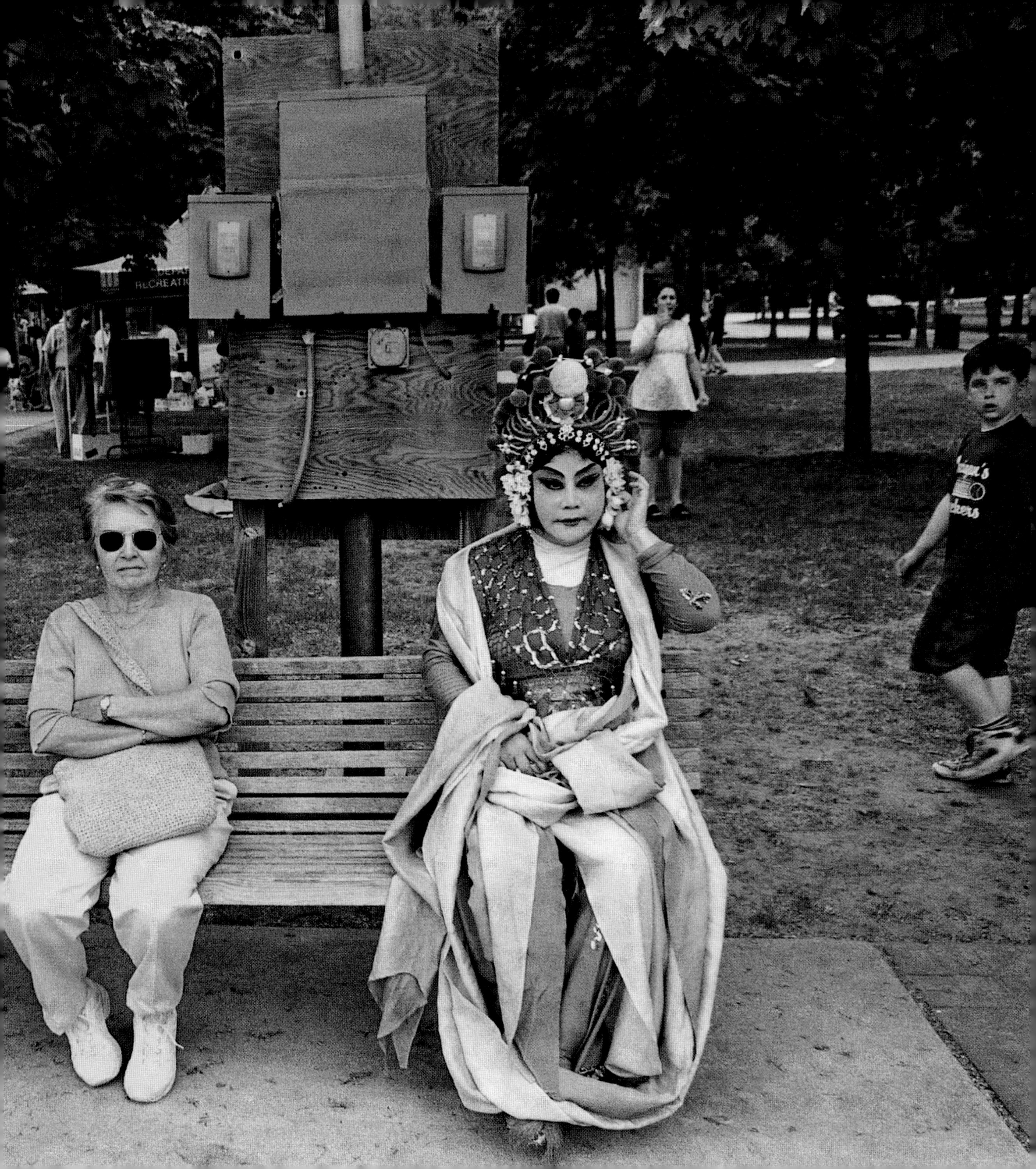

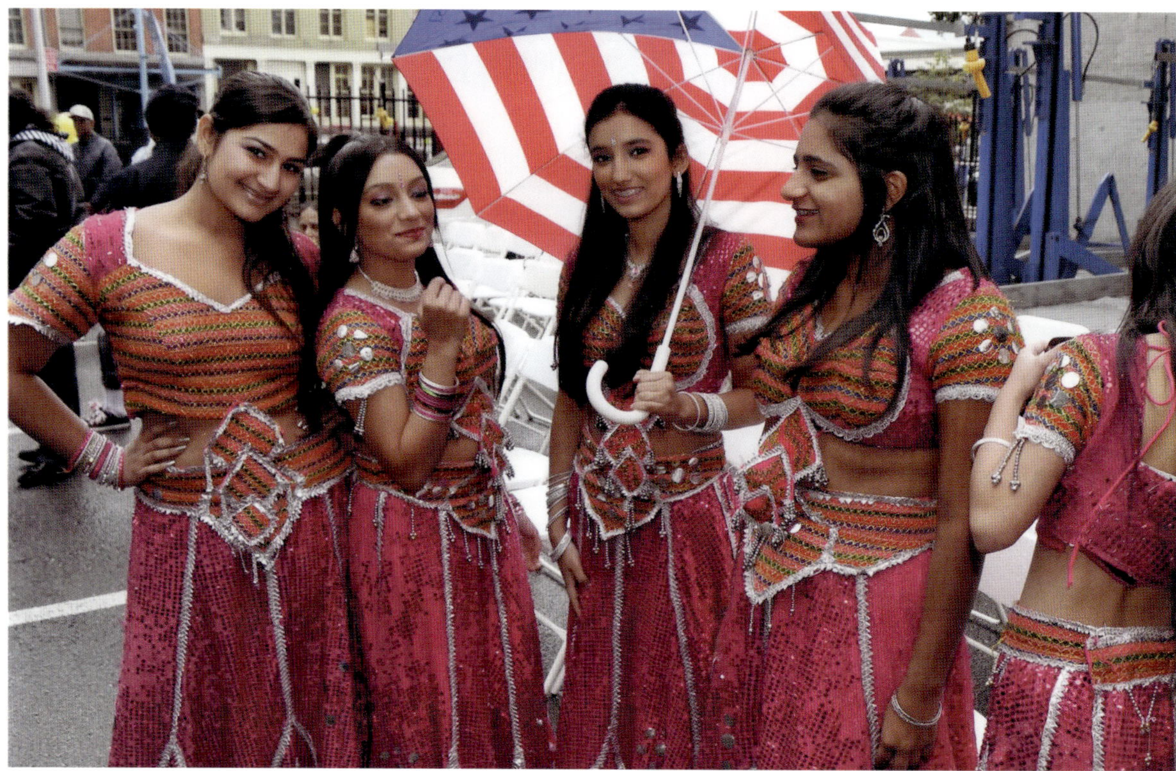

At Diwali, the South Asian festival of lights, at South Street Seaport. New York, 2000s.

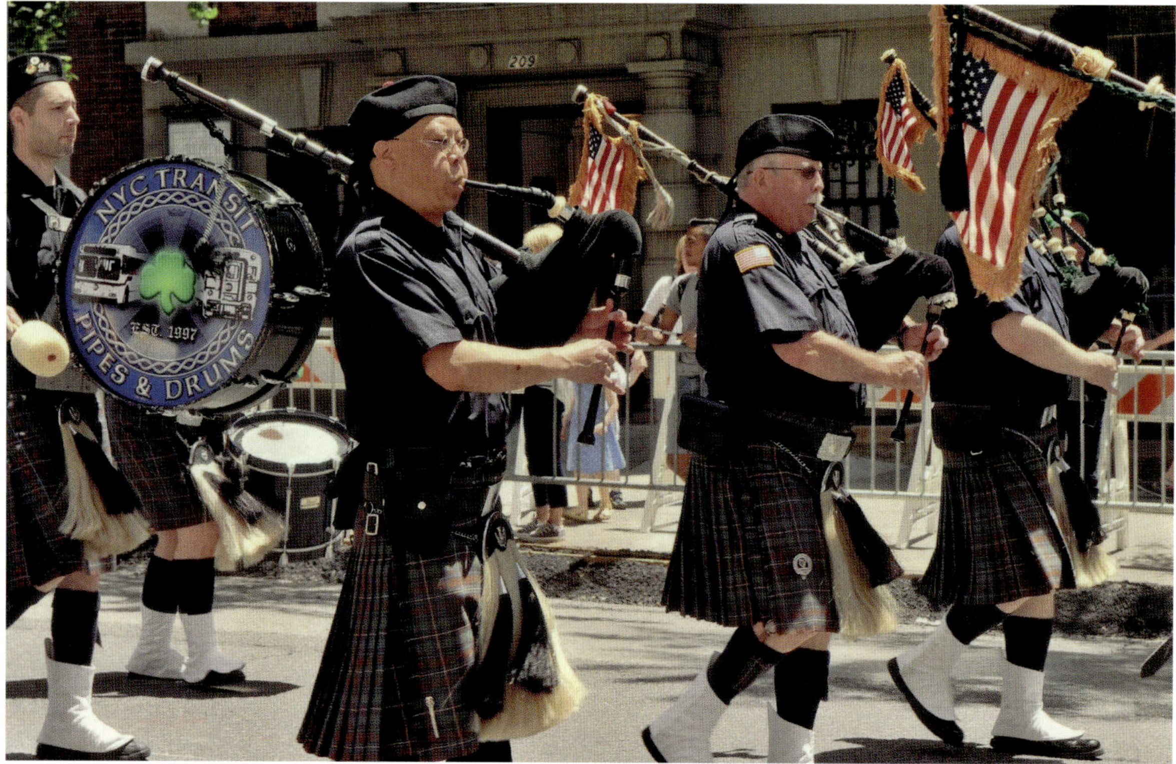

The New York City transit workers union pipes and drums corps marching in the Labor Day parade. New York, 2015.

The Chinese Community Girls' Drill Team of Seattle was founded in 1952 by a Chinatown girls' club called the Chi-ettes, under the guidance of Ruby Chow, a local restaurant owner and community leader. Wearing costumes inspired by the women warriors in traditional Chinese opera, the drill team has been performing military-style routines in summertime parades for seventy years, always culminating in Seattle's Seafair Torchlight parade. Seattle, circa 2000.

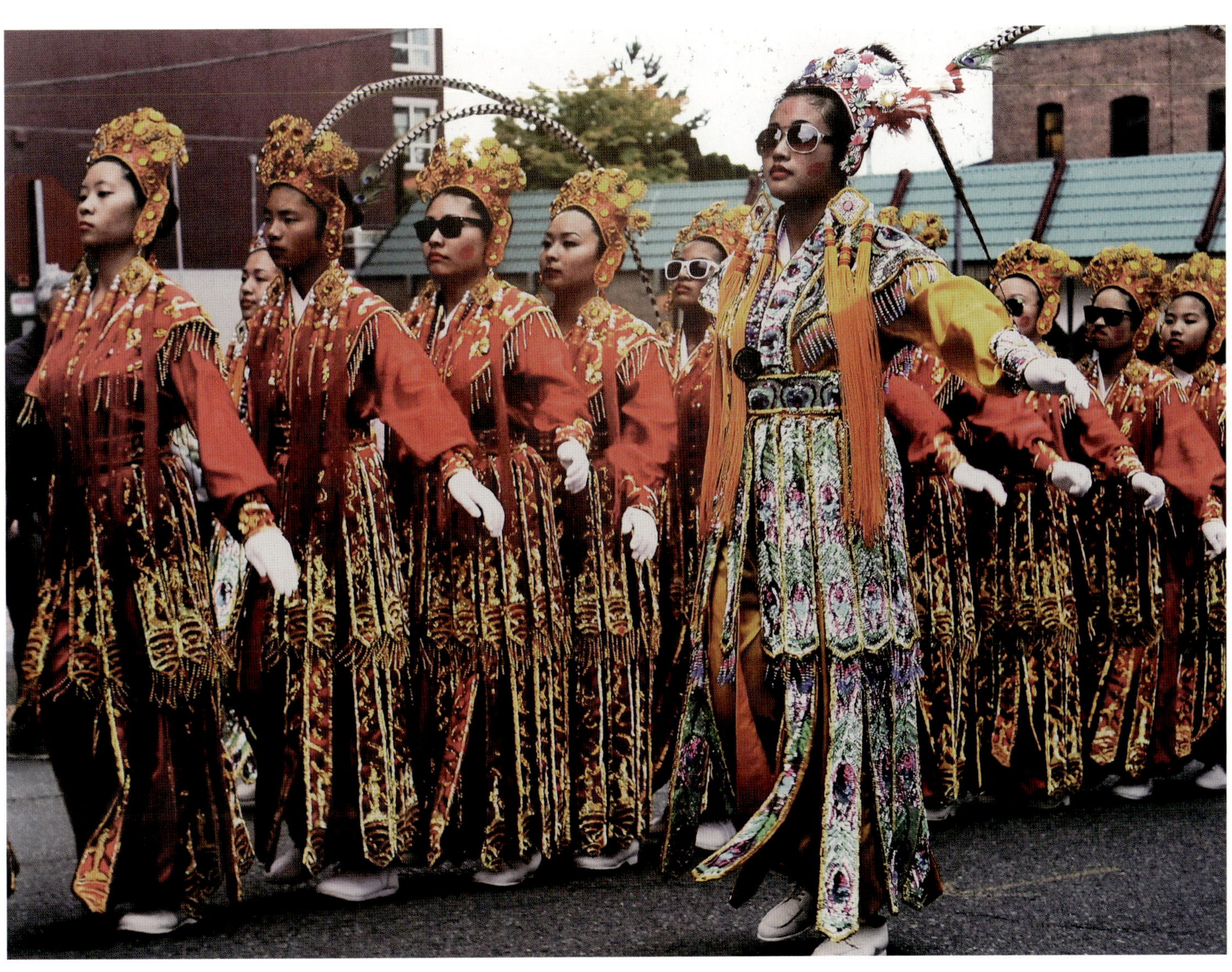

Asian American studies professors Betty Lee Sung (1924–2023) of City College of New York (*left*) and Joyce Moy of the City University of New York (*right*), with May Ying Chen, International Ladies Garment Workers Union officer, at the Association of Asian American Yale Alumni dinner. New York, 2010.

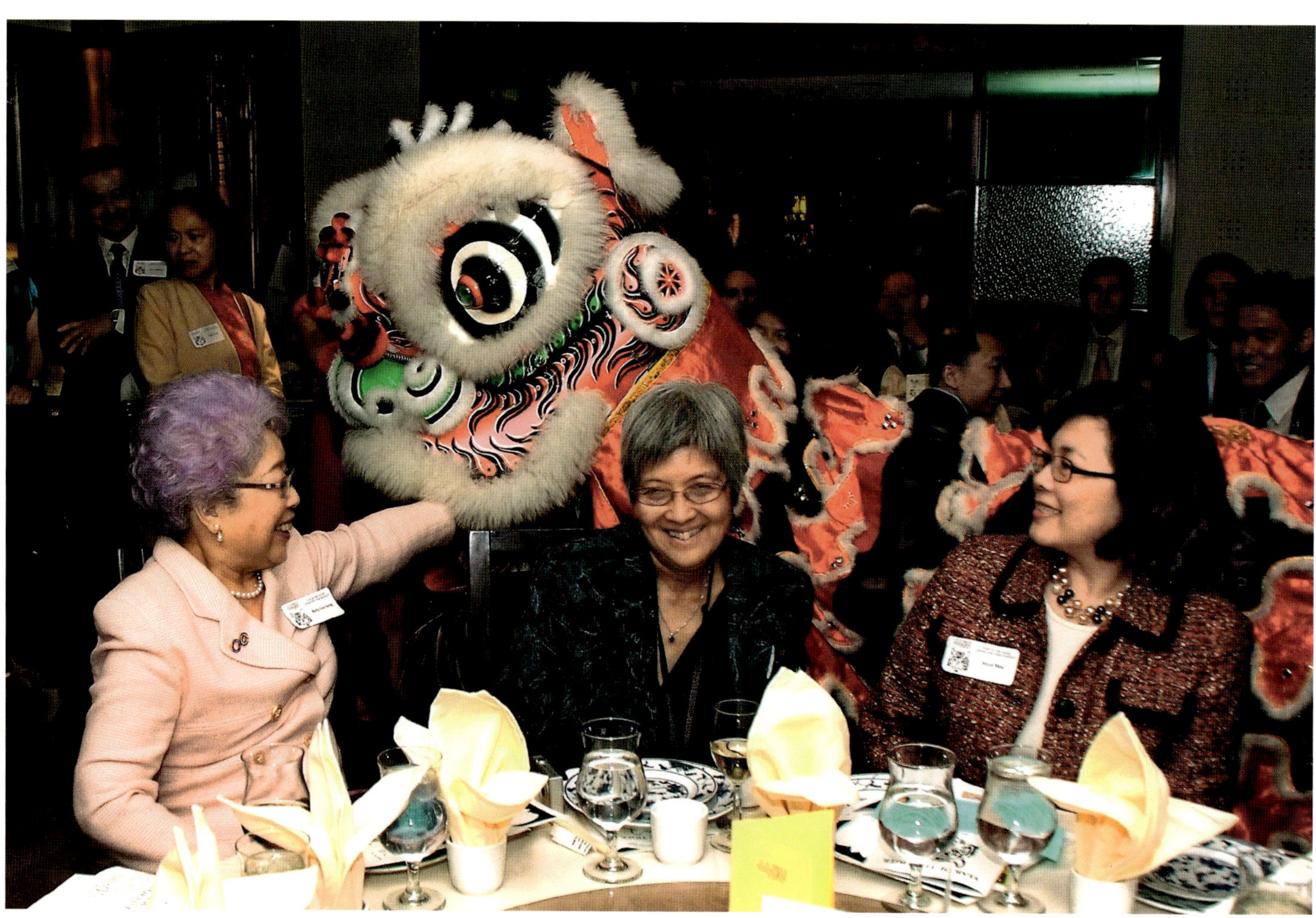

Grace Lee Boggs (1915–2015), a revolutionary activist, author, and feminist, at her book party for *The Next American Revolution: Sustainable Activism for the Twenty-First Century*. Detroit, 2012.

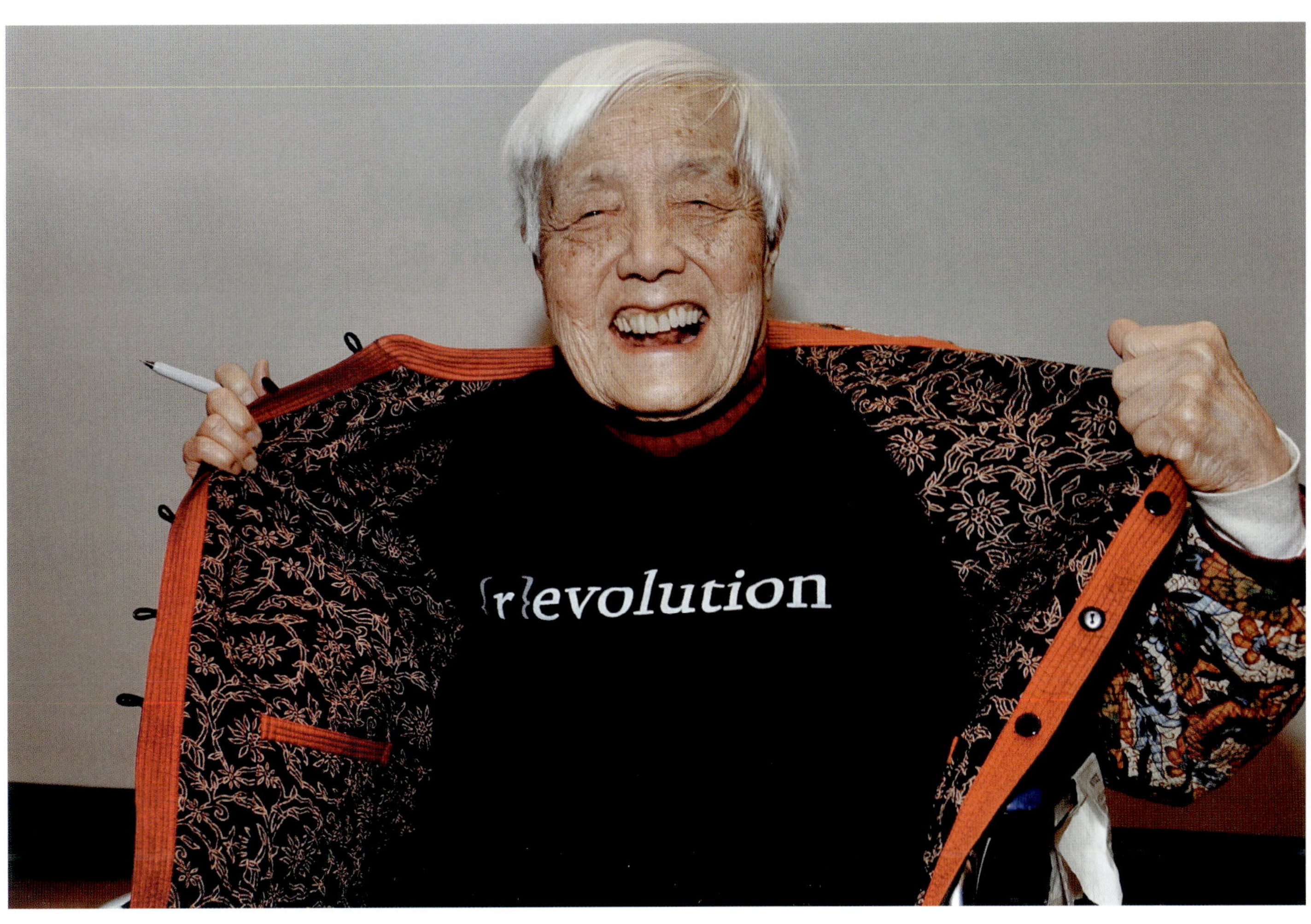

The Railroad in the Chinese American Imagination

GORDON H. CHANG

History professor, Stanford University, and author of *Ghosts of Gold Mountain: The Epic Story of the Chinese Who Built the Transcontinental Railroad*

One date stands out in Chinese American history. On May 10, 1869, the nation celebrated the completion of the first transcontinental railroad with a grand event at Promontory Summit, Utah, where the two competing railroad companies joined their lines. Political leaders hailed the gigantic construction project as marking the end of an era of disunion (the Civil War and the geographic divide of east and west) and the start of a new age in which the country would ascend as a global industrial and trading powerhouse. The railroad would make it possible: travel time from one coast to the other was reduced from six to eight weeks to six to eight days. Coal from the Rocky Mountains was shipped east by rail. European immigrants journeyed west to California.

History books celebrate the Transcontinental, as it was called, as a grand nationalist accomplishment, a marker of American engineering ingenuity and grit. It was seen as the epitome of Manifest Destiny, the justification of the nation's claim to have divine blessing. Those who made it happen supposedly were the officers of the Central Pacific Railroad Company and the Union Pacific.

This narrative is attached to the now iconic photograph, *East and West Shaking Hands at Laying Last Rail*, taken by Andrew J. Russell soon after the end of the Utah ceremony. A throng of white men surround engineers shaking hands, symbolizing the completion of the iron road. Two huge locomotives face head-to-head.

But where are the Chinese? many wondered over the years.

Chinese workers constituted 90 percent of the construction workforce on the Central Pacific, but they do not appear to be in the image. They toiled for five long years, constructing the line from Sacramento eastward to Utah. They conquered the mighty Sierra Nevada mountain range, blasting fifteen tunnels through the solid granite. They laid hundreds of miles of track through the dense forests of California, over the endless high plains of Nevada, and into the blazing sun of Utah. Upward of twenty thousand Chinese worked for the Central Pacific Railroad. Twelve hundred died.

Why were they seemingly excluded from the photo shoot? Wasn't this an insult to their hard labor and to the many other contributions Chinese Americans made to history? (No matter that there is at least one Chinese in the frame: he is front and center but blurred because of his movement. We can't see his face, and so he was invisible to viewers of the photograph through the years.)

Singularly and without peer, Corky Lee came to represent this aggrievement. Corky once said that when he was in junior high school in the 1960s and saw the Russell photograph for the first time, he wondered about the apparent absence of Chinese. Years later, when he was a veteran professional photographer, he decided to act. In a 2014 *New York Times* article, he declared his intention to "commit an act of photographic justice" and called for Chinese and other Asian Americans to join him in a historical reenactment that year. To his surprise, two hundred showed up, including direct descendants of railroad workers. Over the years more and more Asian Americans joined at what became an annual pilgrimage.

In 2014 hundreds of people from around the country and the world came out for that special inaugural event in far-off Utah, north of the Great Salt Lake, to be recorded by Corky's camera. They came to participate in making history and in correcting history. Corky empowered their faces and bodies. When the moment came to reenact the meeting of east and west, he stood high up on a platform to direct the throng. Pushing together, no one wanted to be left out again. Corky, like a grand conductor, asked folks to move this or that way to create a composition resembling the original black and white from 1869. The crowd joyfully cooperated: spirits were high. It is not often that everyday people, and a photographer, can make history.

Corky had touched a nerve in the Chinese American community. He inspired, as well as responded to, the growing sentiment to seek historical inclusion. The month of May became Asian American and Pacific Islander Heritage Month in part to honor the Chinese work on the Transcontinental. Family historians proudly reconstructed their lineages to railroad workers. Community activists from Belleville, New Jersey, to Sacramento, California, formed local committees that called for public recognition of Chinese railroad workers. Scholars and journalists published new accounts of the lives of the Chinese who labored on the Transcontinental. The U.S. Department of Labor inducted Chinese railroad workers into its Hall of Honor, and Congress members called for the issuing of a postage stamp to memorialize the workers.

Chinese Americans have long suffered under the stigma of being perpetual foreigners in the United States. How does one throw off that dark shroud? Attaining recognition in the narrative of the rise of the nation, including in the construction of the Transcontinental, has advanced their effort for inclusion. What could be more American than the railroad, the instrument of modernity in all its physicality, utility, imagery, and even aggression?

Corky's photograph provokes complex, even contradictory, feelings, as art can. One can see a range of sentiments in the diverse crowd, anger against the past insult but also joy in setting the record straight. It's a celebration of shared community and identity, but it also expresses our ambivalence in seeking inclusion in an imperial enterprise. Perhaps most of all, the photograph displays our hopefulness in claiming our place in the country.

Corky was proud of his iconic Promontory Summit photograph; he knew it had been an unexpectedly successful political act. Tragically, the pilgrimages he conducted to Utah ended with his death, but his tangible work, which the world will be able to see forever, lives on and has many lives of its own.

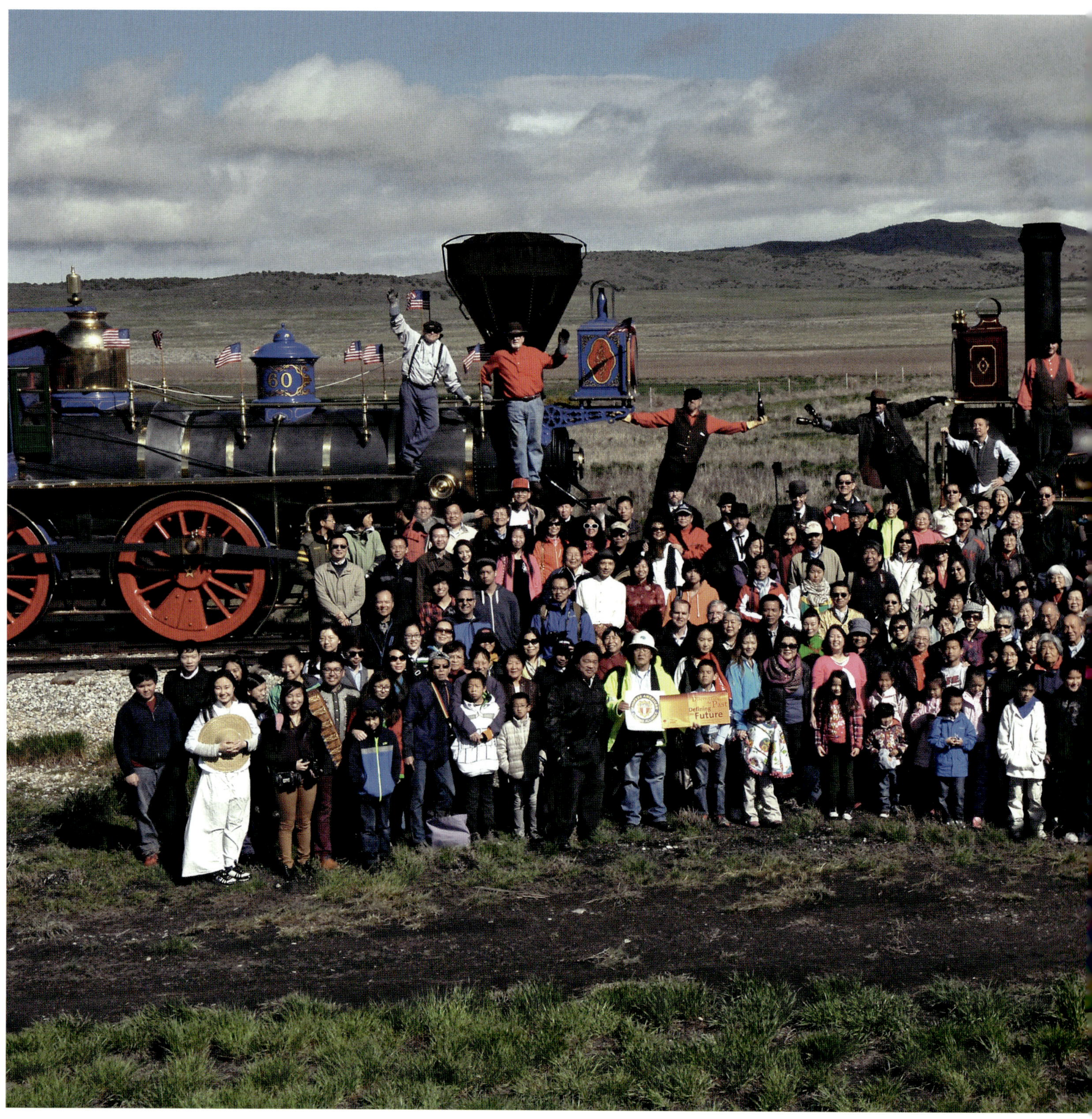
60
Past
Defining
Future

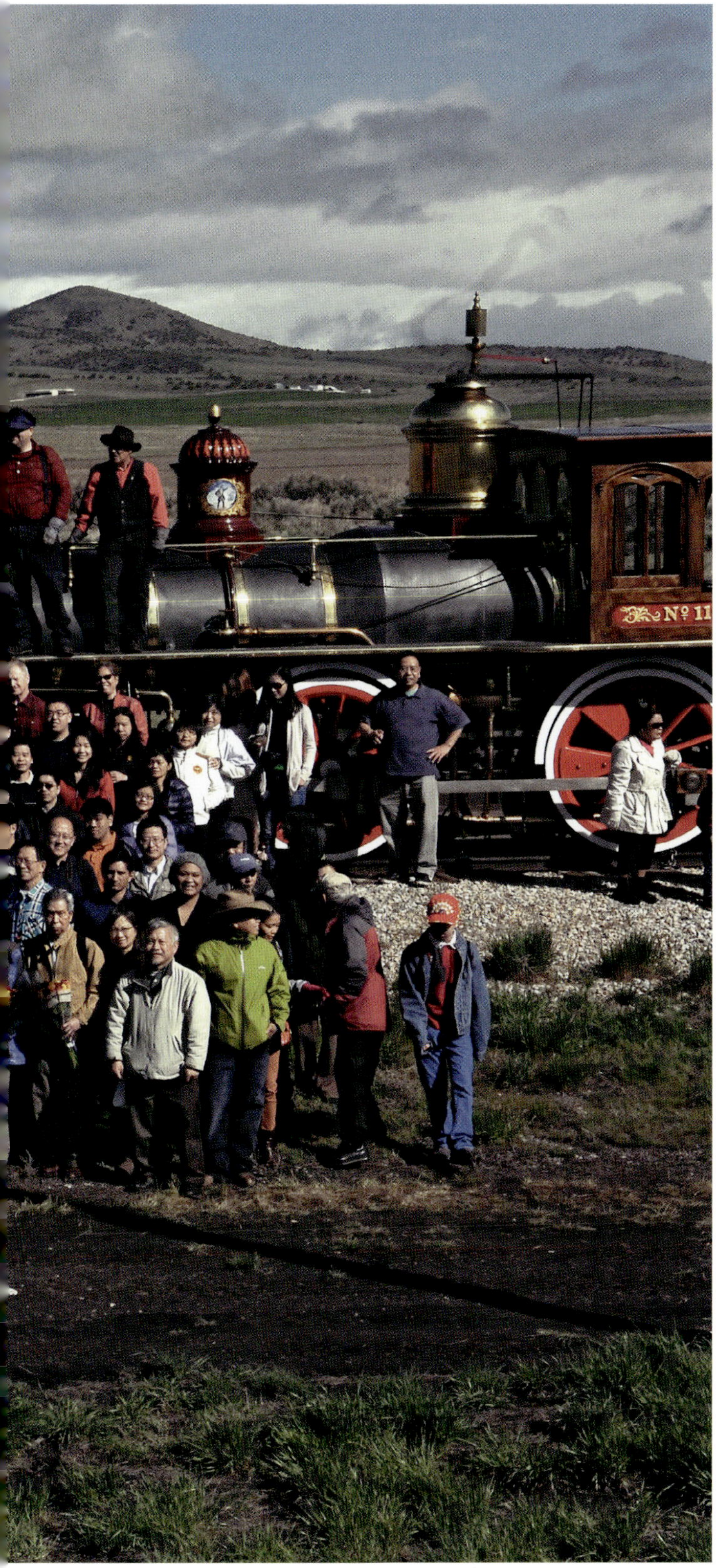

Reenactment of the completion of the transcontinental railroad on the 145th anniversary, with 250 Asian Americans, including direct descendants of railroad workers. Promontory Summit, Golden Spike National Historical Park, Utah, 2014.

East and West Shaking Hands at Laying Last Rail. Promontory Summit, Utah, May 10, 1869. *Andrew Russell*

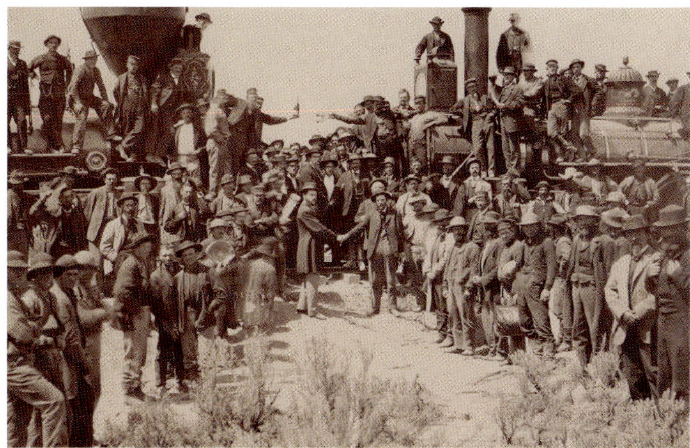

A Buddhist priest gives a blessing at the "Chinese Arch," site of a Chinese workers' encampment near the end of the line. Archaeologists have recovered artifacts (shards of plates, pipes, etc.) there, evidence of the Chinese presence. Golden Spike National Historical Park, Utah, 2018.

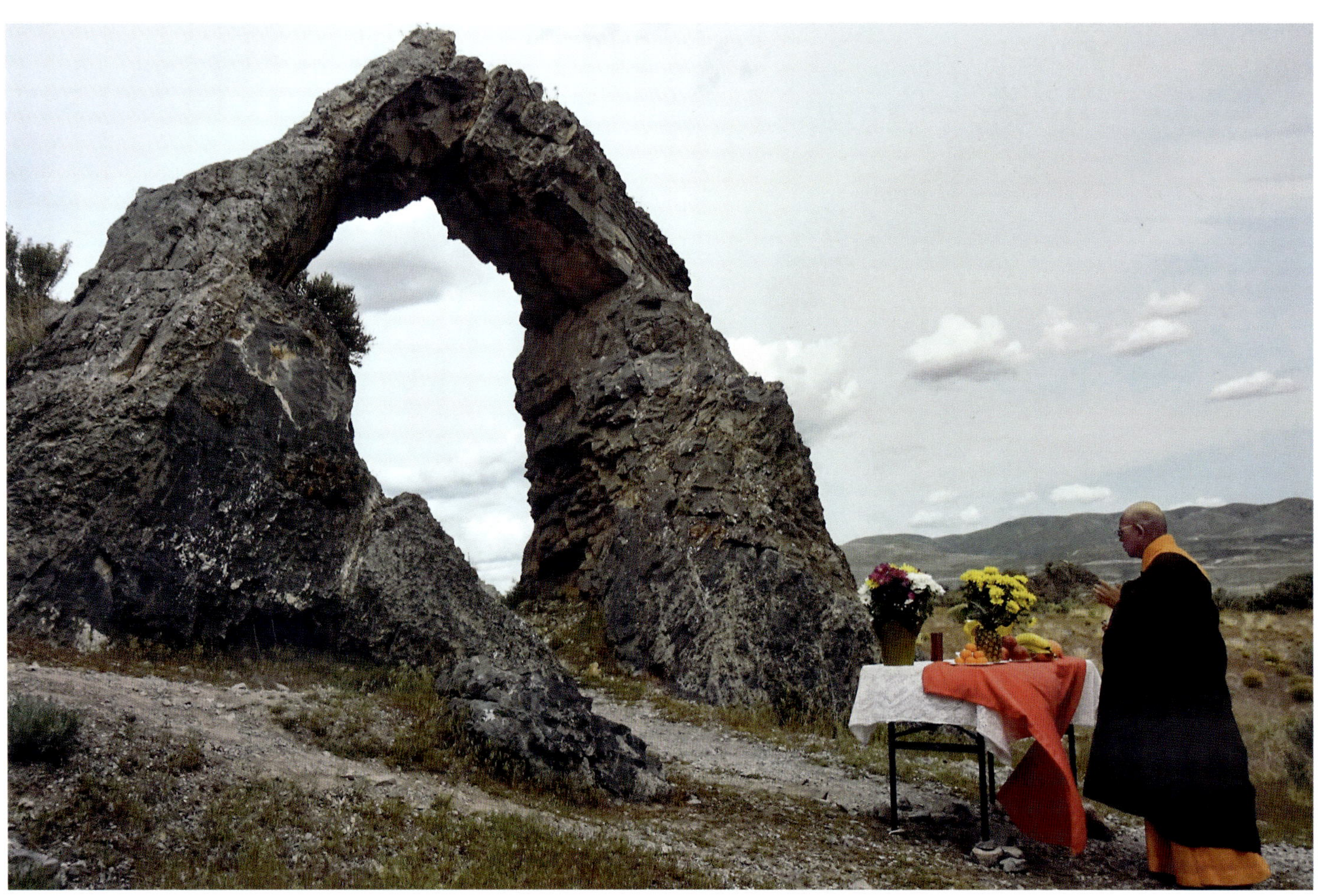

Gathering on the 150th anniversary of the completion of the railroad. Promontory Summit, Golden Spike National Historical Park, Utah, 2019.

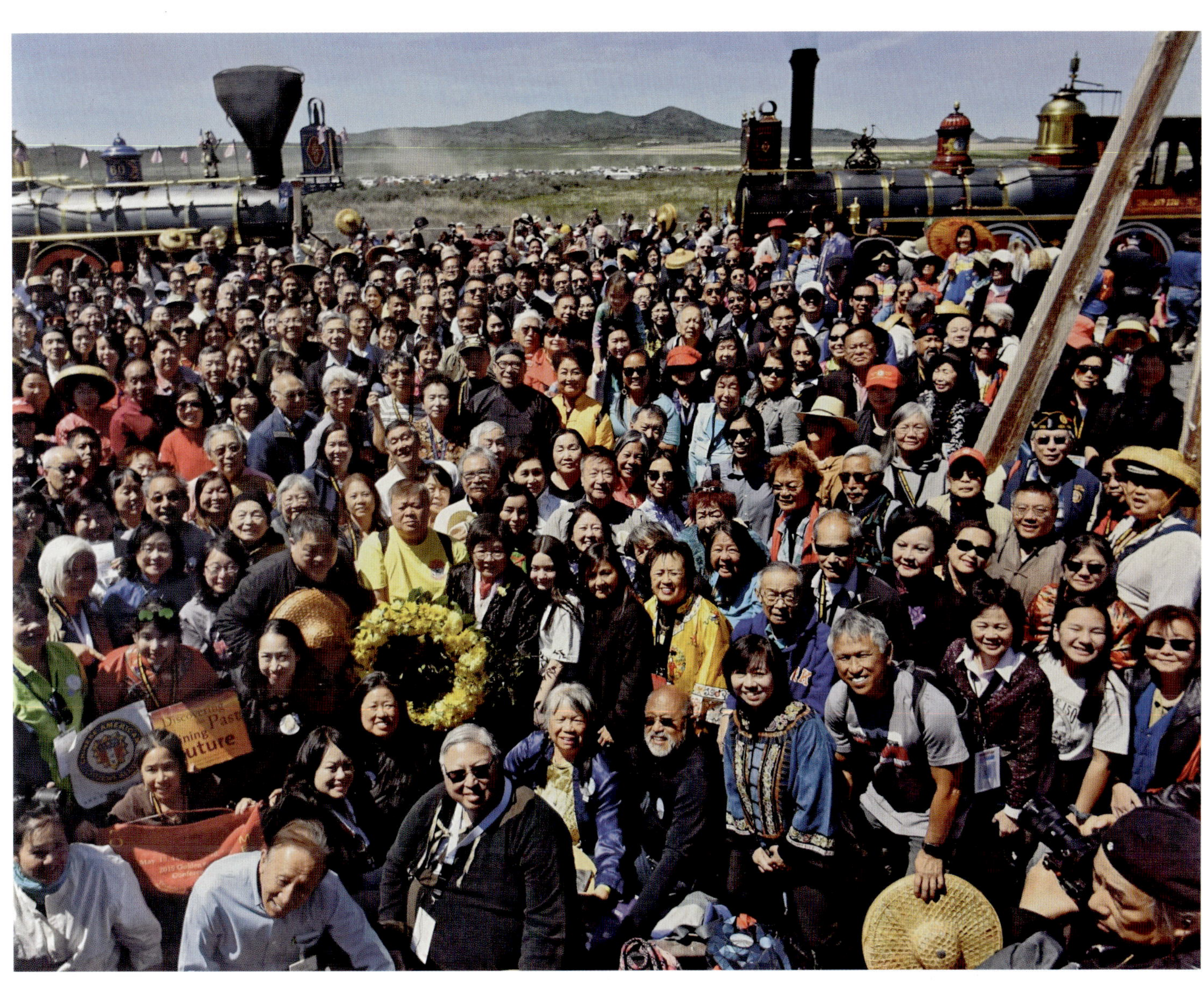

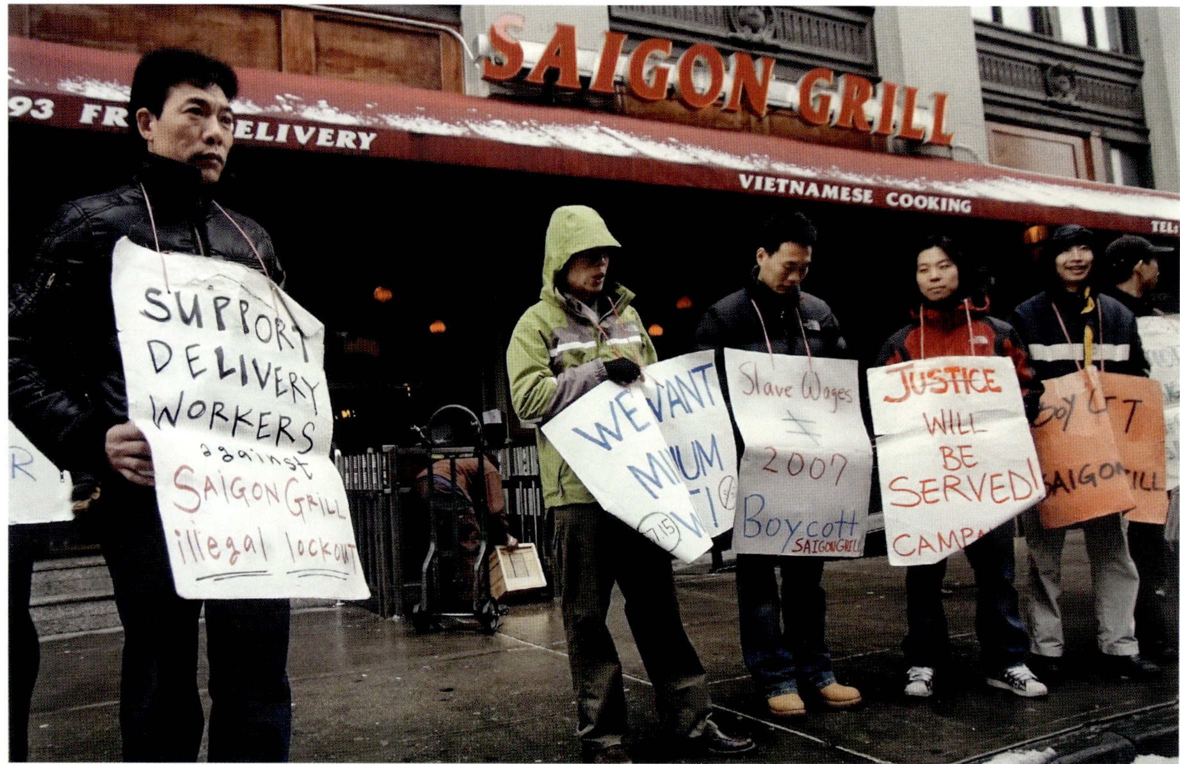

Delivery workers at Saigon Grill, a popular restaurant in Greenwich Village, went on strike to protest their subminimum wages and abusive treatment by their employer. The owner was ordered to pay damages of $4.6 million. New York, 2007.

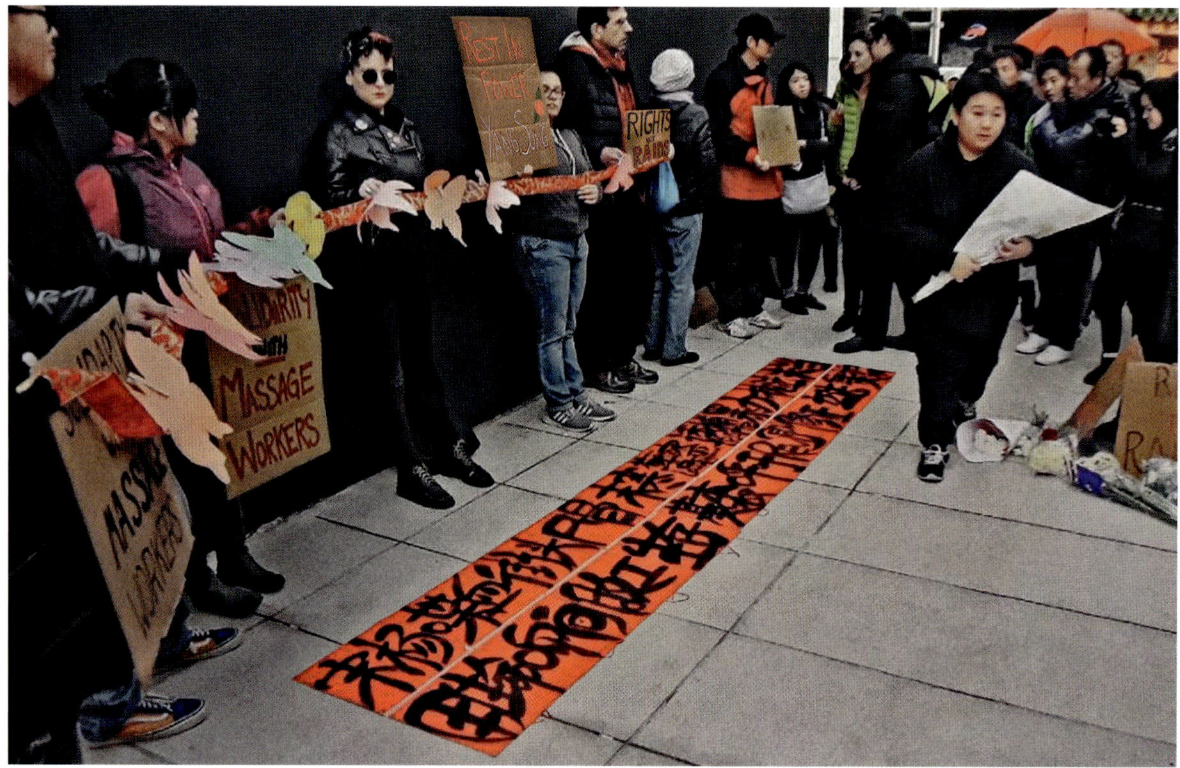

A vigil on the one-year anniversary of the death of Yang Song, who died in 2017 during a police raid on the massage parlor where she worked in Queens. After her death, Asian migrant sex workers and their allies formed the grassroots organization Red Canary Song. It provides mutual aid and advocates for decriminalization of sex work and labor rights. Flushing, Queens, New York, November 2018.

Korean Americans and other Asian American social service groups participate in the annual march against domestic violence. Flushing, Queens, New York, 2011.

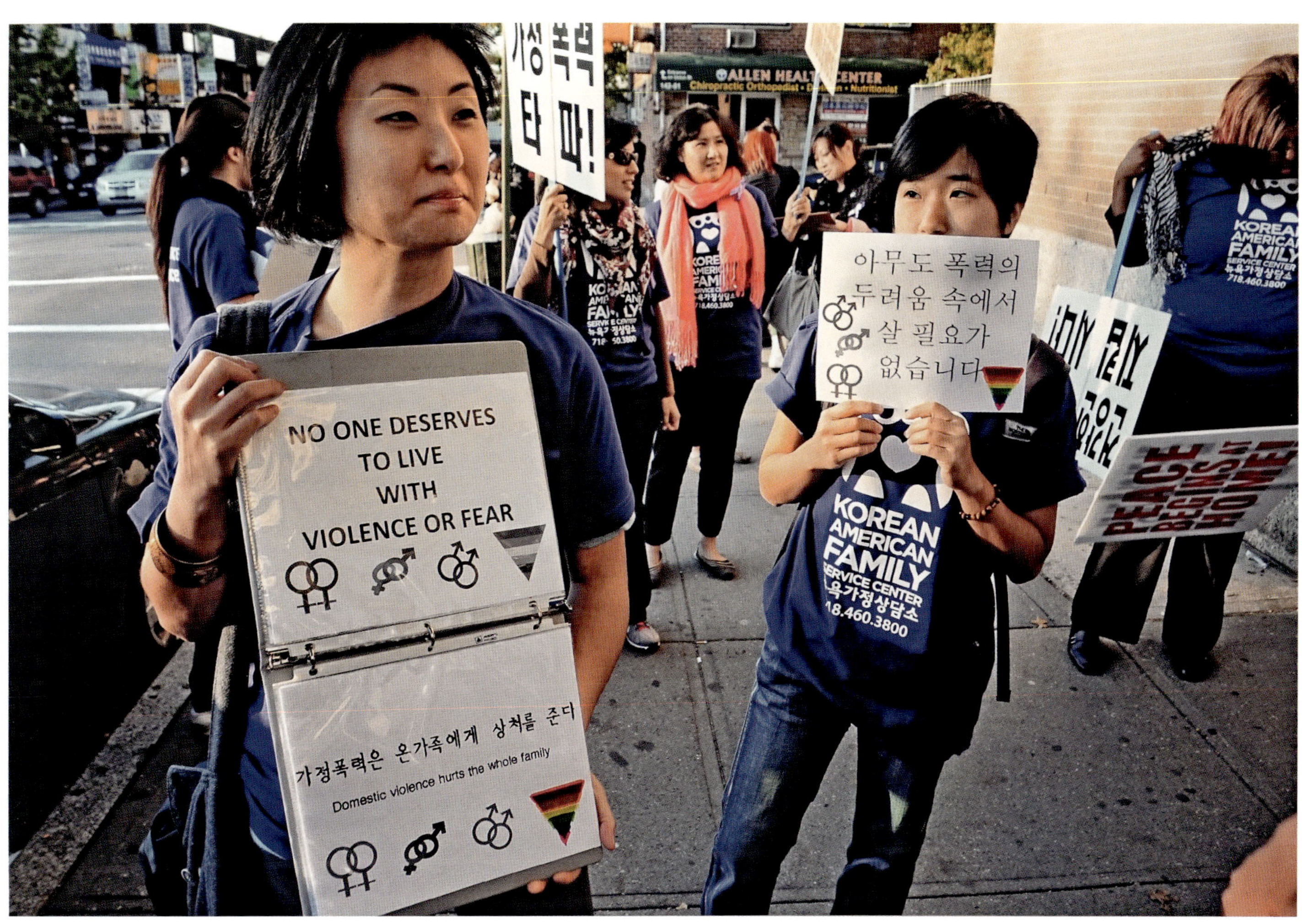

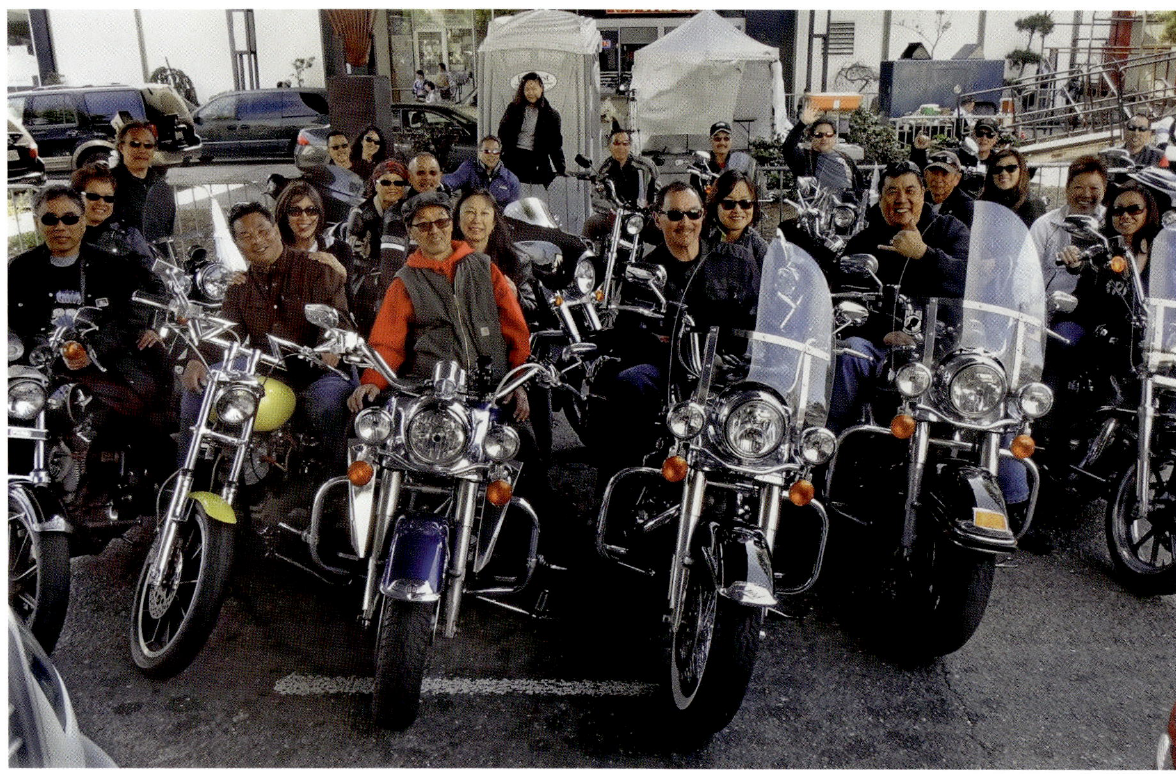

Filipino American Harley-Davidson bikers after the Philippine Day parade. San Francisco Bay Area, 2013.

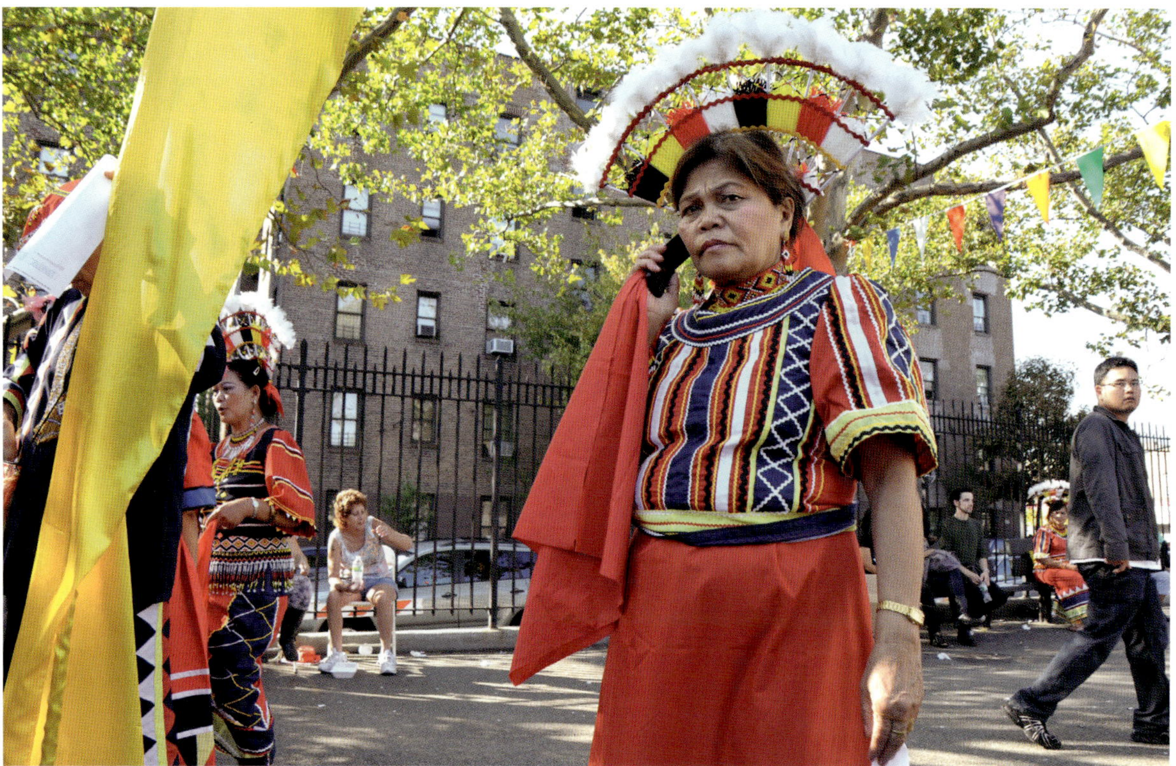

The Bukidnon Kaamulan in America dance group performs at the Filipino Bayanihan Cultural Festival, an event celebrating civic unity and cooperation. Woodside, Queens, New York, 2010.

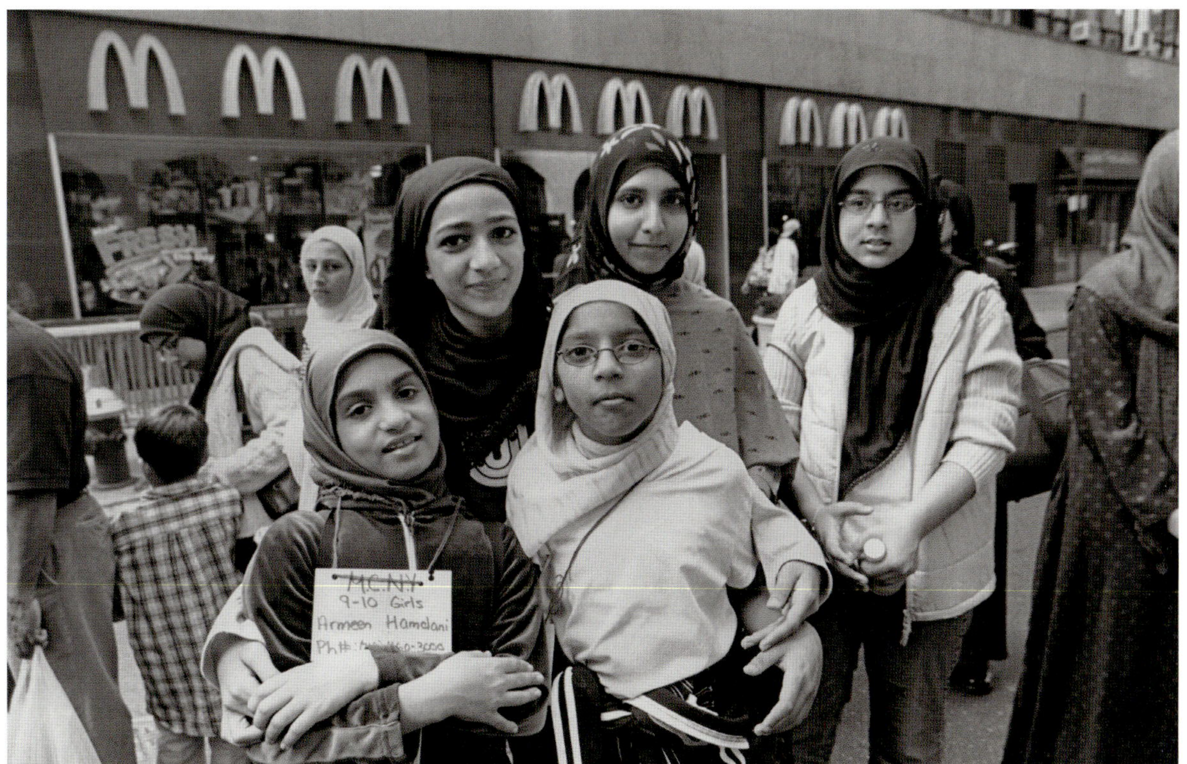

Girls from the Muslim Center of New York at the Muslim Unity Day parade. New York, 2004.

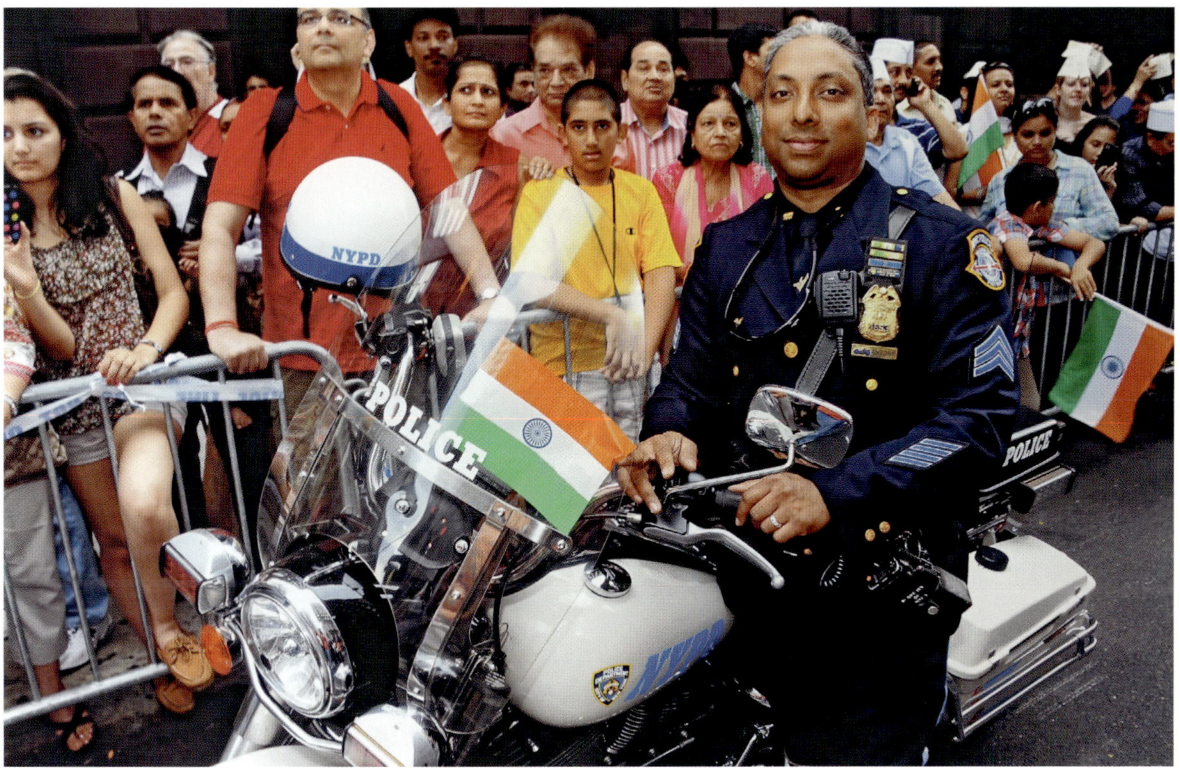

A South Asian police sergeant along the route of the Indian Independence Day parade. New York, 2011.

The New York Chinese Freemasons (*hong qing*) Athletic Club's nine-man volleyball team. The team participates in the annual tournament at venues that rotate among five North American cities. The tournament dates to the 1930s, when it was popular among immigrants from Taishan, China, for socializing and social networking. New York, circa 2015.

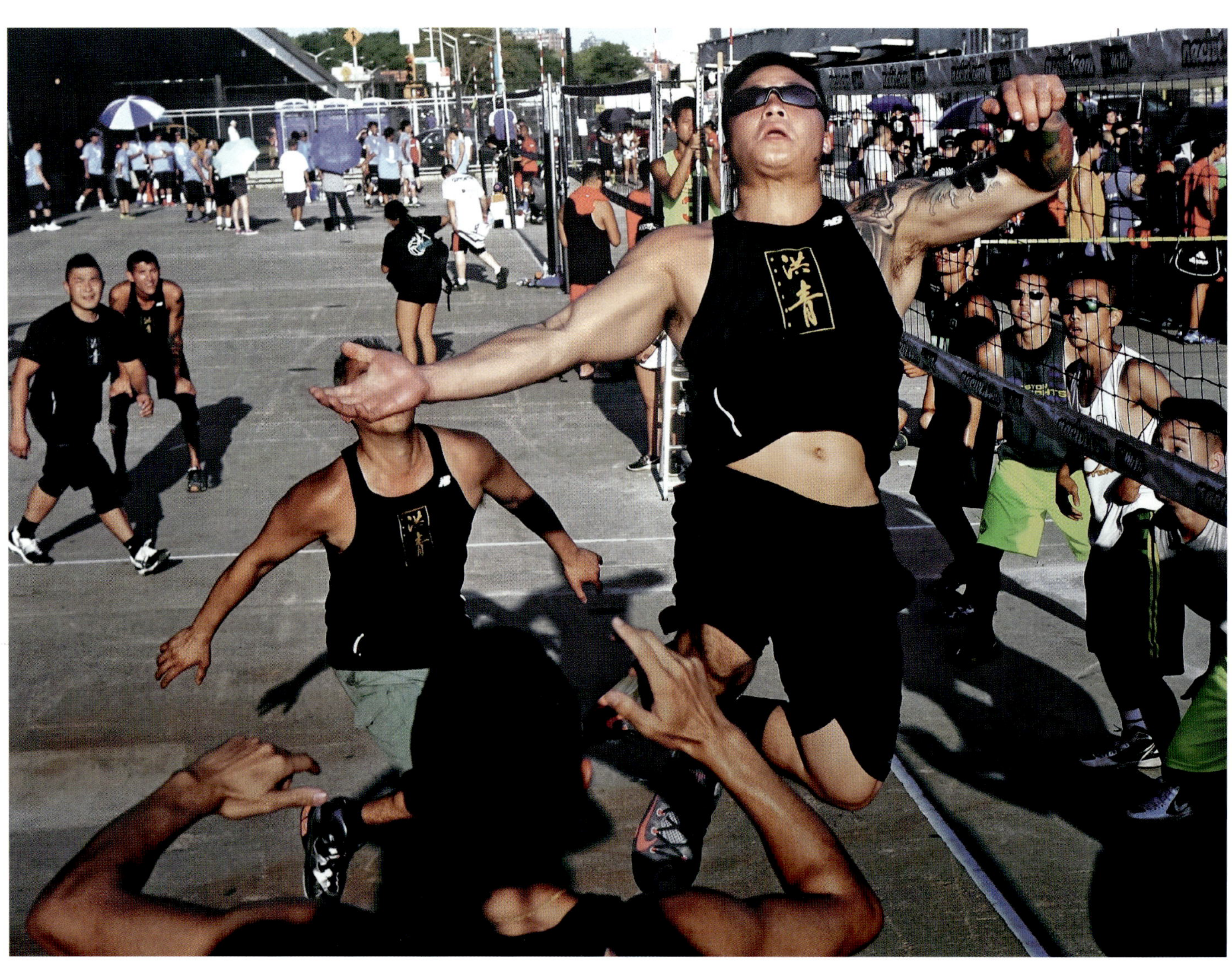

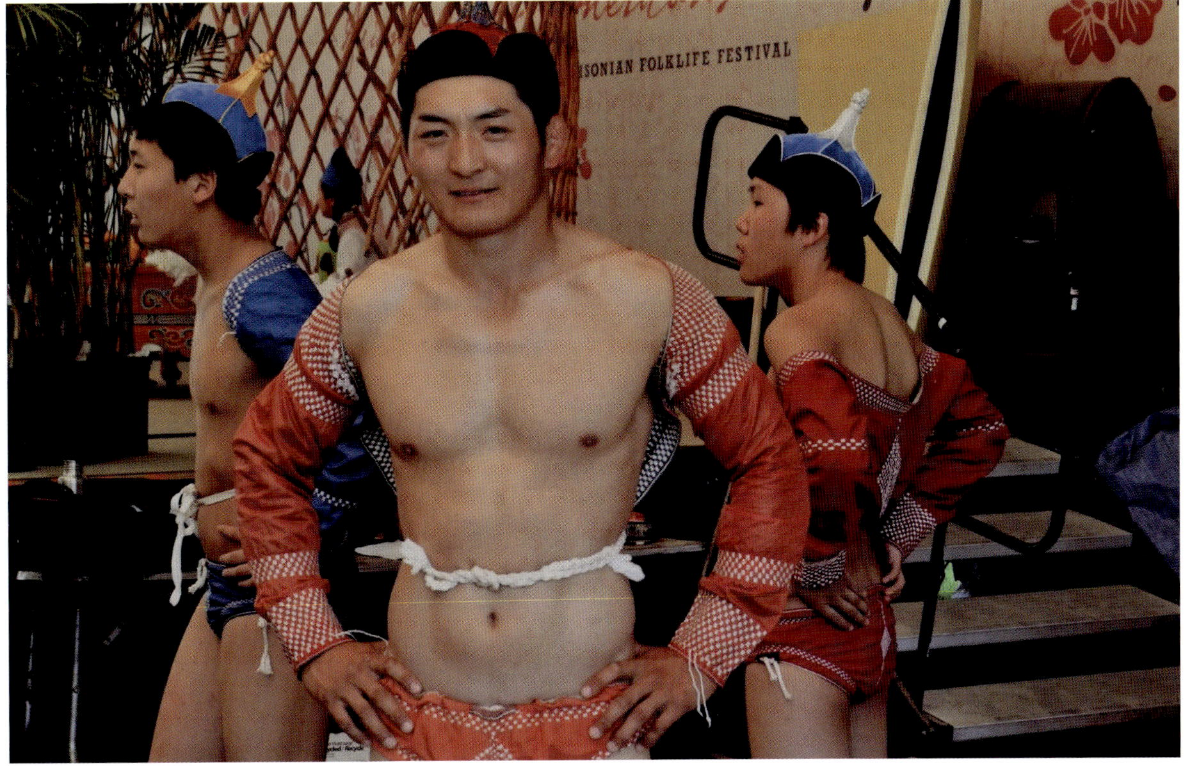

Mongolian wrestlers at the Folklife Festival of the Smithsonian Institution. Washington, D.C., 2010.

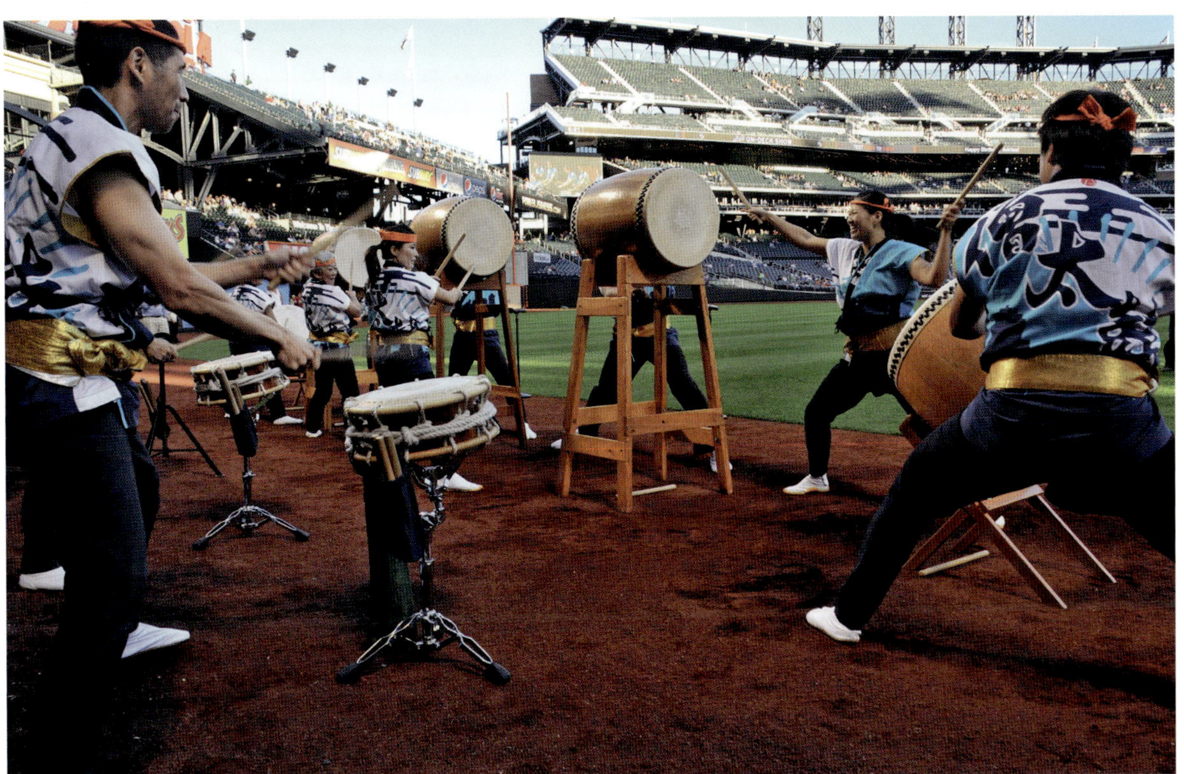

Soh Daiko, New York's oldest taiko drumming group, performs at Japan Heritage Night at Citi Field, one of several pregame ethnic events sponsored by the New York Mets. Flushing, Queens, New York, 2010.

New Orleans

KAREN ZHOU
Photographer

I met Corky at a banquet in Chinatown in the mid-2000s. He had a quick wit, a quirky sense of humor, and an encyclopedic knowledge of all AAPI matters. We soon began to photograph together, both in the New York area and out of town. We visited many places, among them Lowell, Massachusetts; Detroit, Seattle, and Florida; and of course, Utah, which we visited every year for five years to commemorate the Chinese workers who built the transcontinental railroad. To finance a trip to New Orleans in 2010, we photographed a Cambodian-style wedding in Dallas, then hopped onto a Greyhound bus to New Orleans. There I rented a car. It was the worst car possible, with no automatic functions, but we were on a budget.

The purpose of our trip was to document the Vietnamese community in Village de l'Est or, as the locals call it, Versailles. The first Vietnamese had arrived there as refugees in 1975, after the fall of Saigon. Losing everything they had in Vietnam, many started anew and lived for many years on the margins of society. We were curious about how they were faring five years after Hurricane Katrina and in the aftermath of the recent British Petroleum oil spill in the Gulf of Mexico.

When we got to Versailles, we were glad to see that homes had been rebuilt. We saw schoolchildren at a demonstration, protesting the closing of an after-school program. We saw women street vendors selling vegetables. We met and photographed Father Vien Nguyen and his chickens in his backyard. He treated us to homemade chicken soup. We learned that the local Catholic church, Mary Queen of Vietnam, had been instrumental in helping bring Vietnamese families displaced as a result of Hurricane Katrina back to Versailles.

The next day we visited the state unemployment agency. Among the people we met was Hai Minh Tran, a former shrimp fisherman who had turned to welding because the oil spill had ruined the shrimping. Corky posed him with his welding certificate, wearing his welder's helmet, sitting in the open trunk of his car. The helmet and a rice pot in the car trunk represented his ongoing struggle for survival. Later I drove Corky to the docks, where we interviewed and photographed other fishermen.

We had the best of trips together, so it breaks my heart that Corky is gone. I loved every moment of every minute traveling with him and am so blessed that he was in my life.

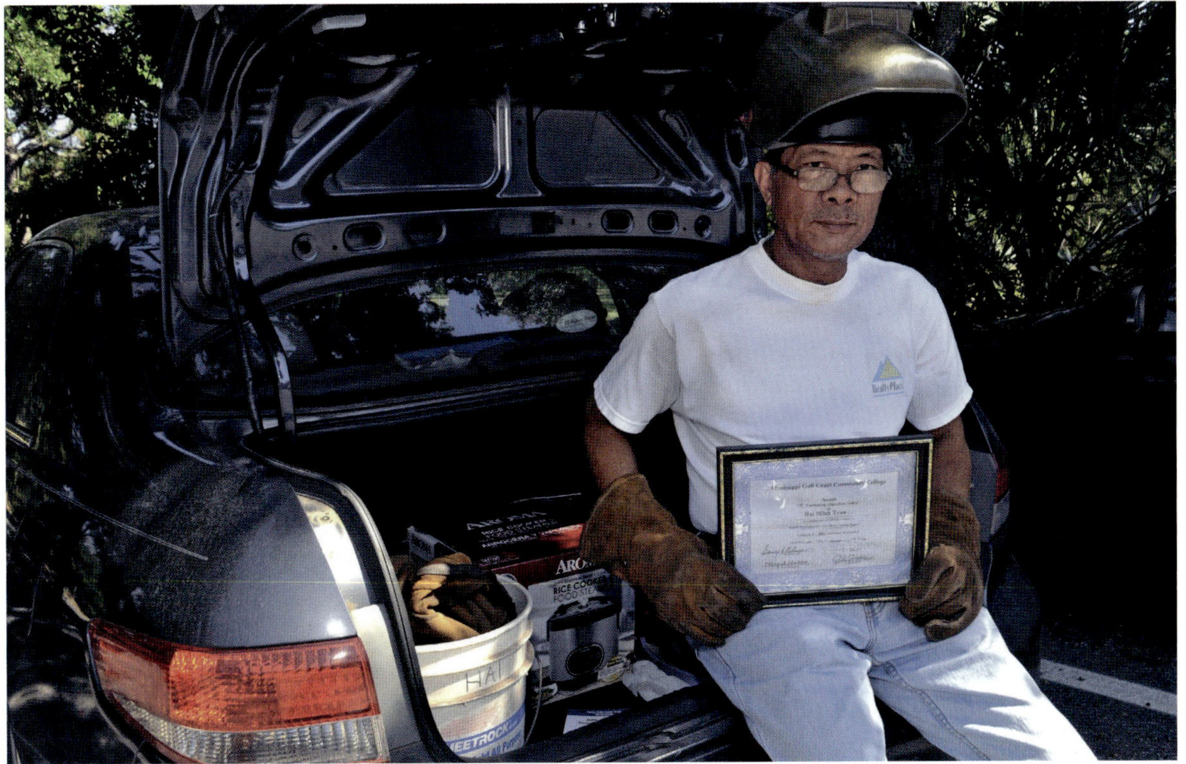

Hai Minh Tran, a naturalized citizen and former shrimp fisherman who turned to welding after the BP oil spill in the Gulf of Mexico ruined the shrimping. New Orleans, 2010.

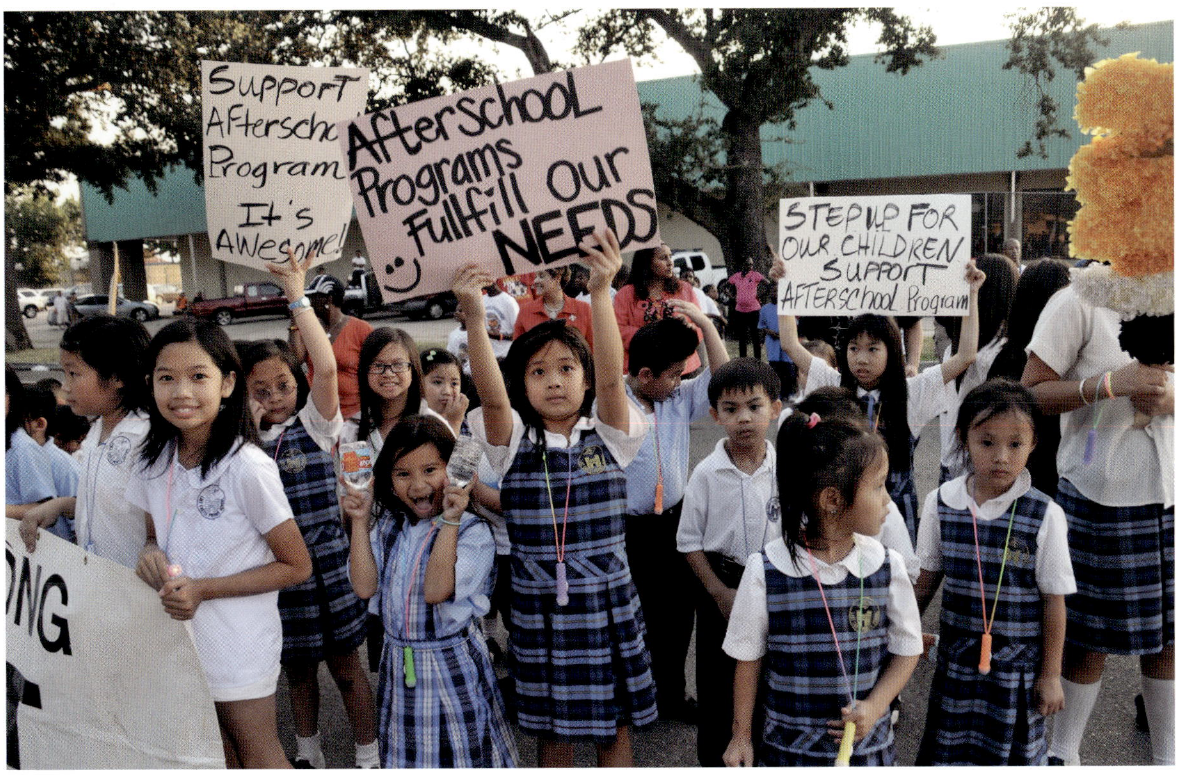

Vietnamese American students demonstrate for continued funding of public and private after-school programs. New Orleans, 2010.

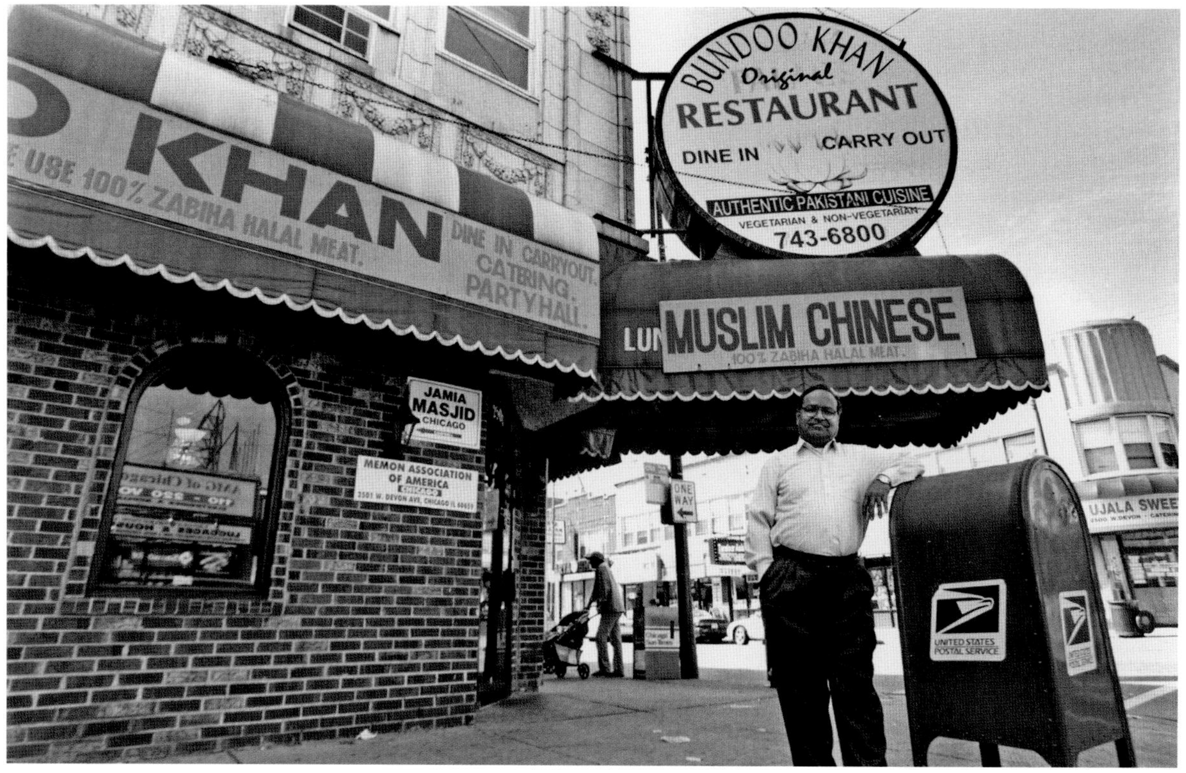

Bundoo Khan, a Muslim Chinese restaurant on Devon Avenue, the South Asian neighborhood. Chicago, 2002.

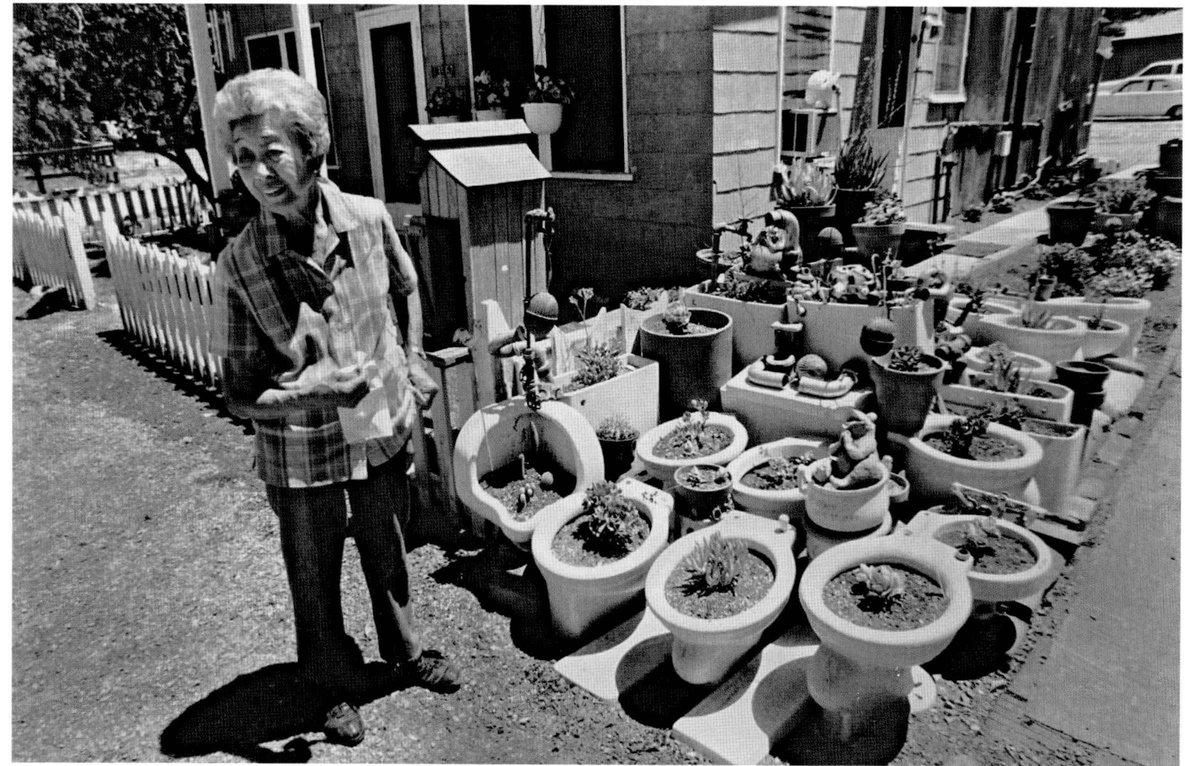

Connie King (1923–2009), the "mayor" of Locke, California, which is considered to be the oldest rural Chinatown in the United States. In 1990 the National Park Service declared Locke a national historic landmark. King, a resident since the 1940s, created a memorial "toilet garden" dedicated to "the Chinese who built the railroads, who built the levees, who planted all the pear trees up and down the Delta." Locke, California, 2007.

Below left: The Golden Gate Fortune Cookie Company. San Francisco, 2013.

Bottom left: Steve Wong, Amtrak conductor. Oakland, 2013.

Below right: A mahjong game at the Hong Lok Senior Center. Oakland, 2001.

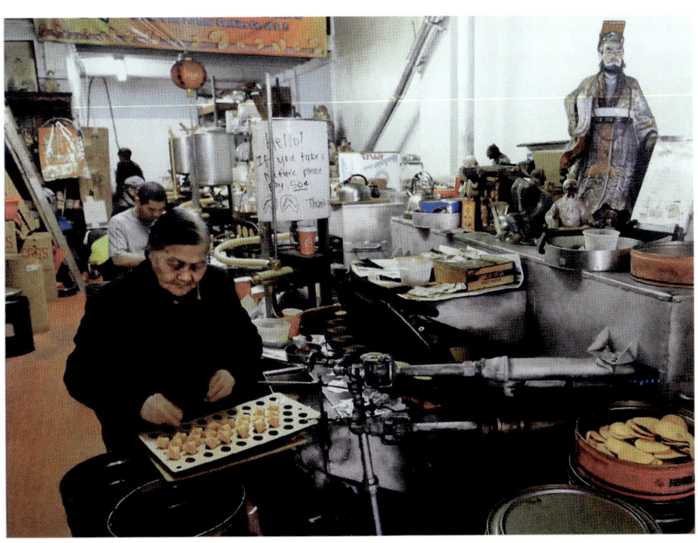

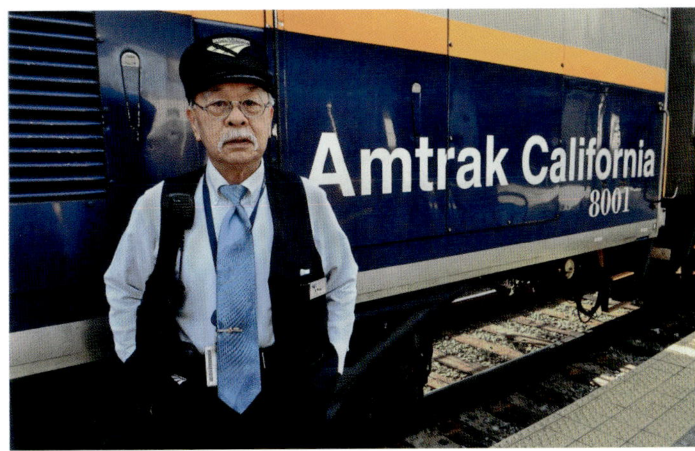

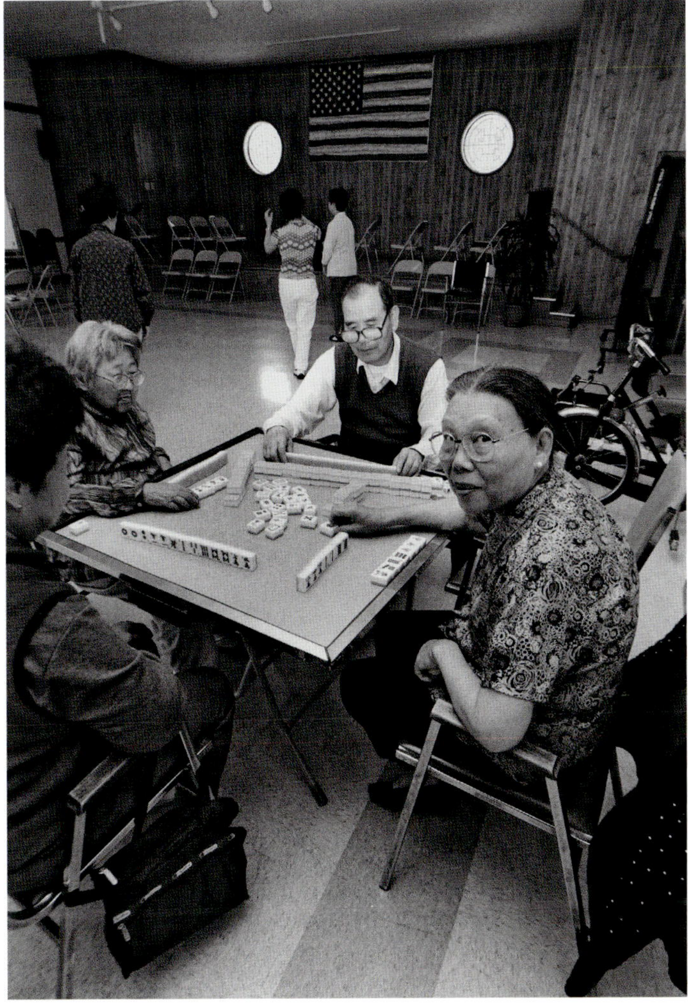

The Hakka are an ethnic minority in southern China. The first U.S. conference of Hakka-Chinese Caribbeans explored their history and culture and strove to change the narrative about who counts as "Chinese." Paula Madison, the author of *Finding Samuel Lowe: China, Jamaica, Harlem,* introduces Sabrina HoSang Jordan *(center)* and Kecia Chin, who wear traditional Hakka *liang mao*, or cooling hats, that women performing agricultural labor wore. The hat's lack of a crown keeps the head cool, and the drape shields the face from the sun. New York, 2015.

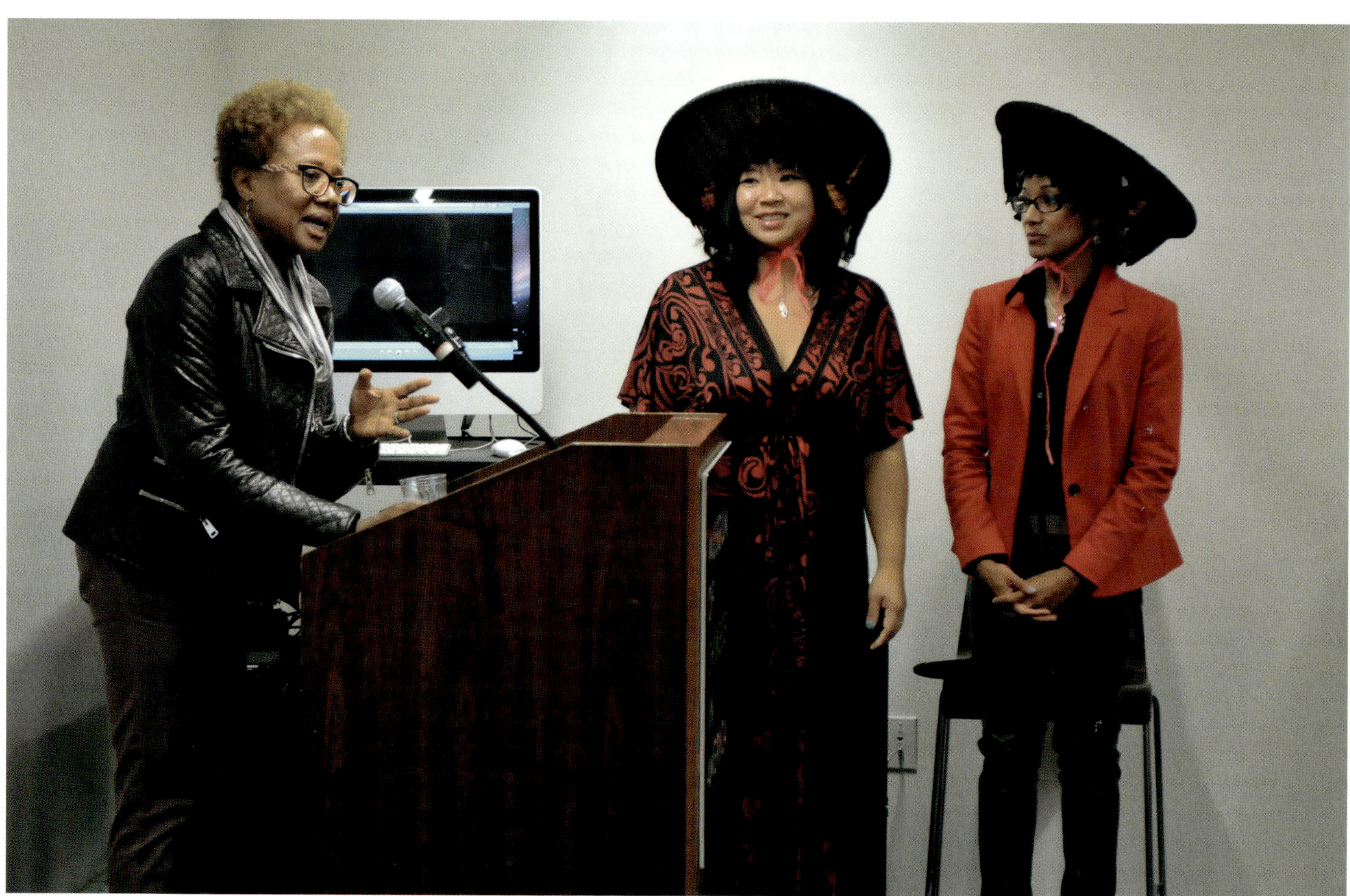

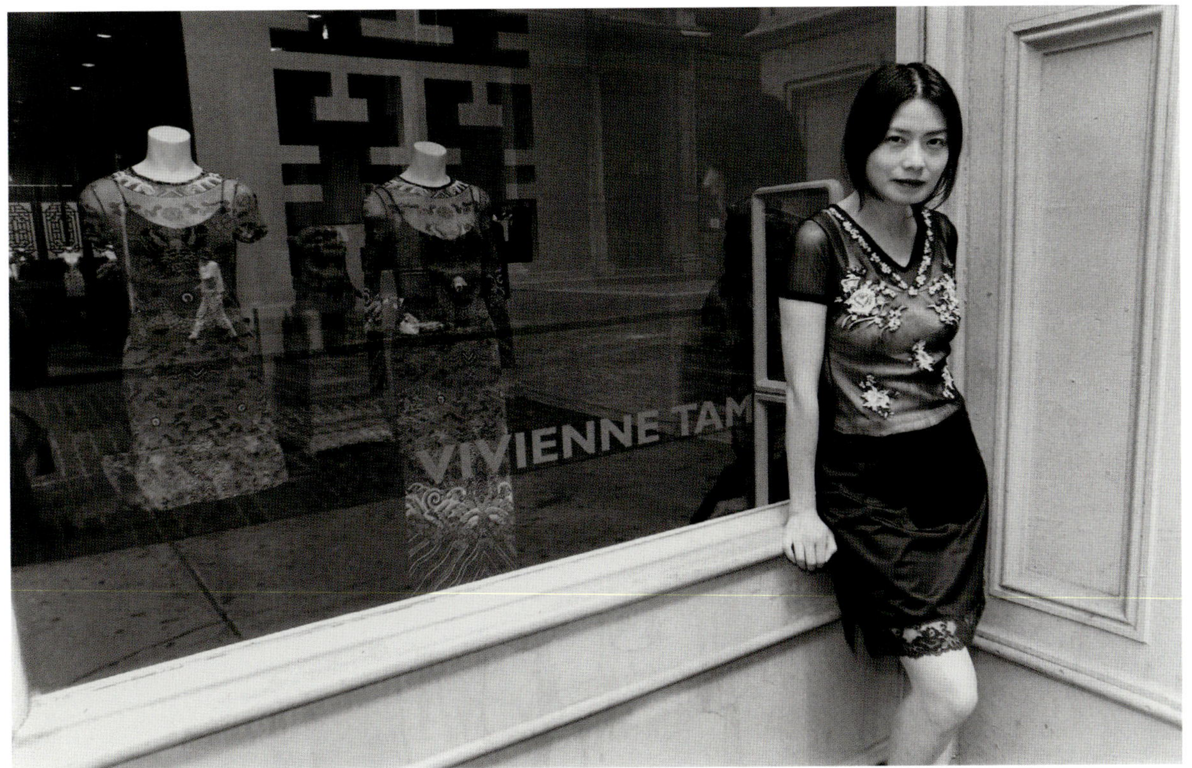

Fashion designer Vivienne Tam in front of her flagship store in SoHo. New York, 2000s.

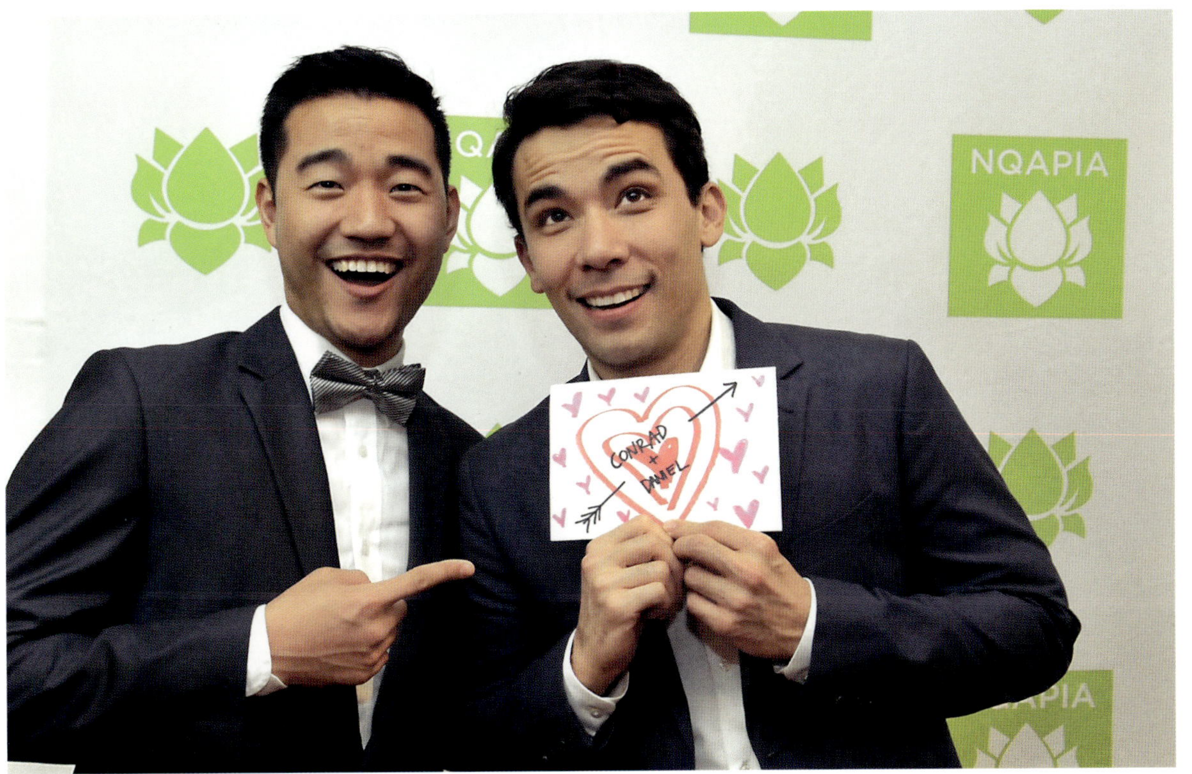

Daniel K. Isaacs (*left*), from Showtime's *Billions*, and Conrad Ricamore, from ABC's *How to Get Away with Murder*, were the first openly gay Asian American television actors. Here they attend the National Queer Asian Pacific Islander Alliance dinner. New York, 2016. *Corky Lee/ NQAPIA*

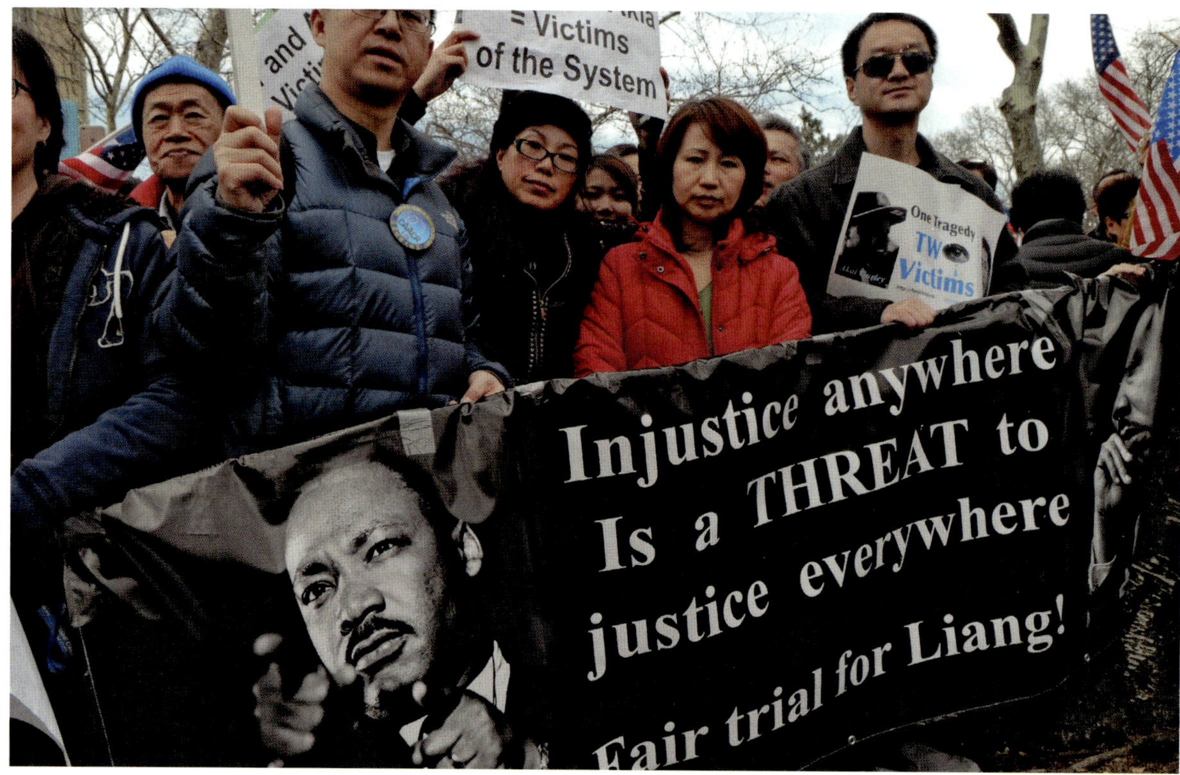

Supporters of former New York police officer Peter Liang, who they claimed was unfairly convicted of the killing of Akai Gurley, a young Black man. Brooklyn, New York, 2016.

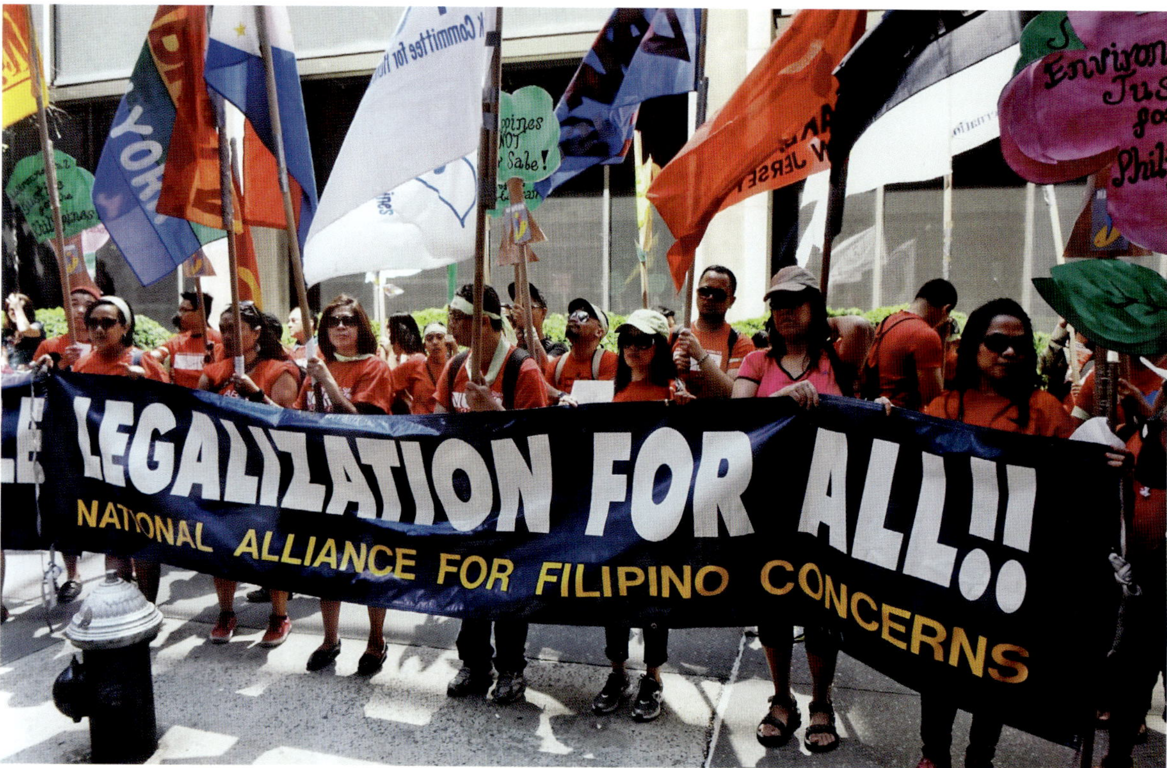

The National Alliance for Filipino Concern demonstrates in favor of legalizing undocumented immigrants. San Francisco, 2016.

Asian Americans participate in the Women's March, which took place the day after the inauguration of Donald Trump. New York, January 2017.

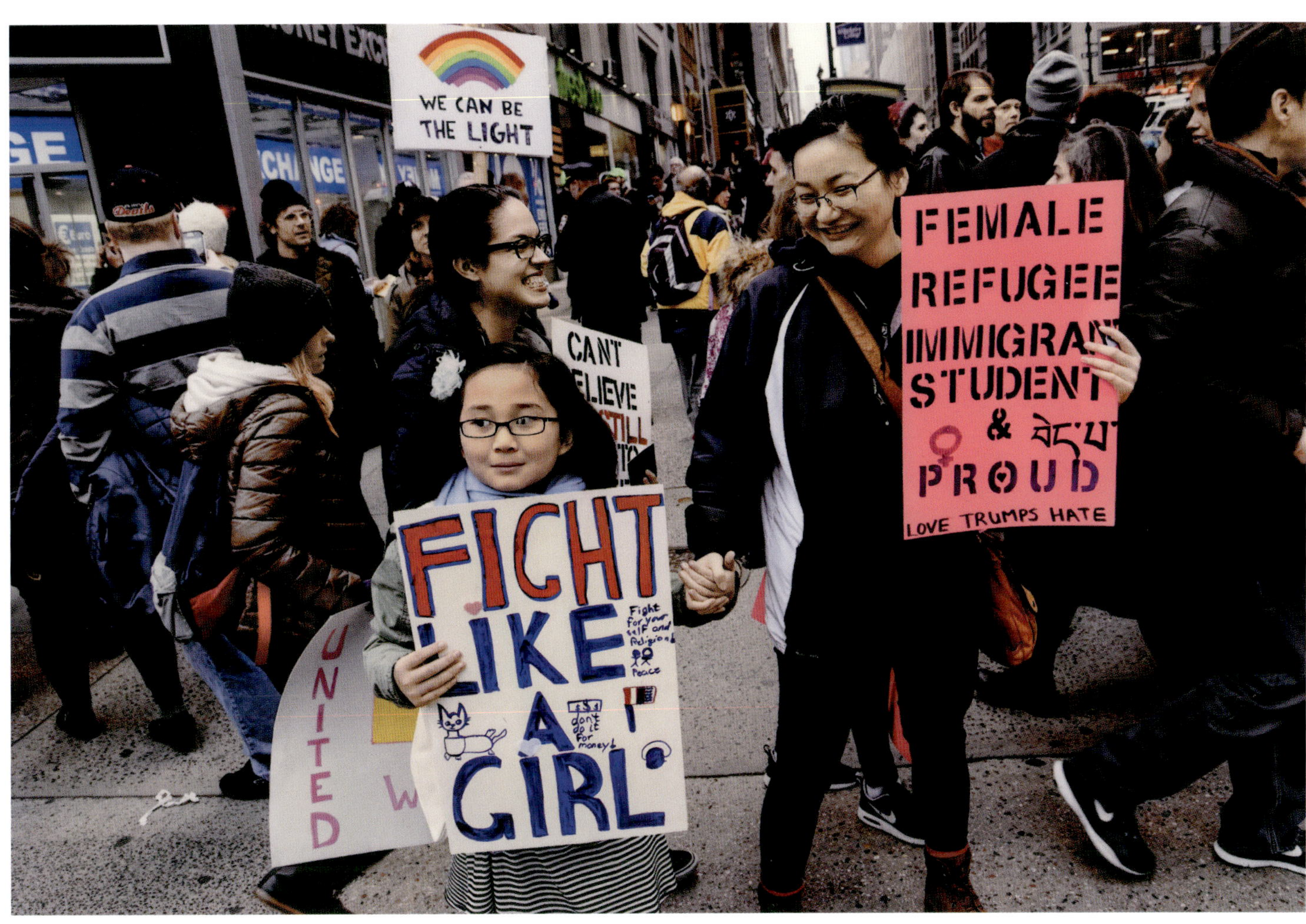

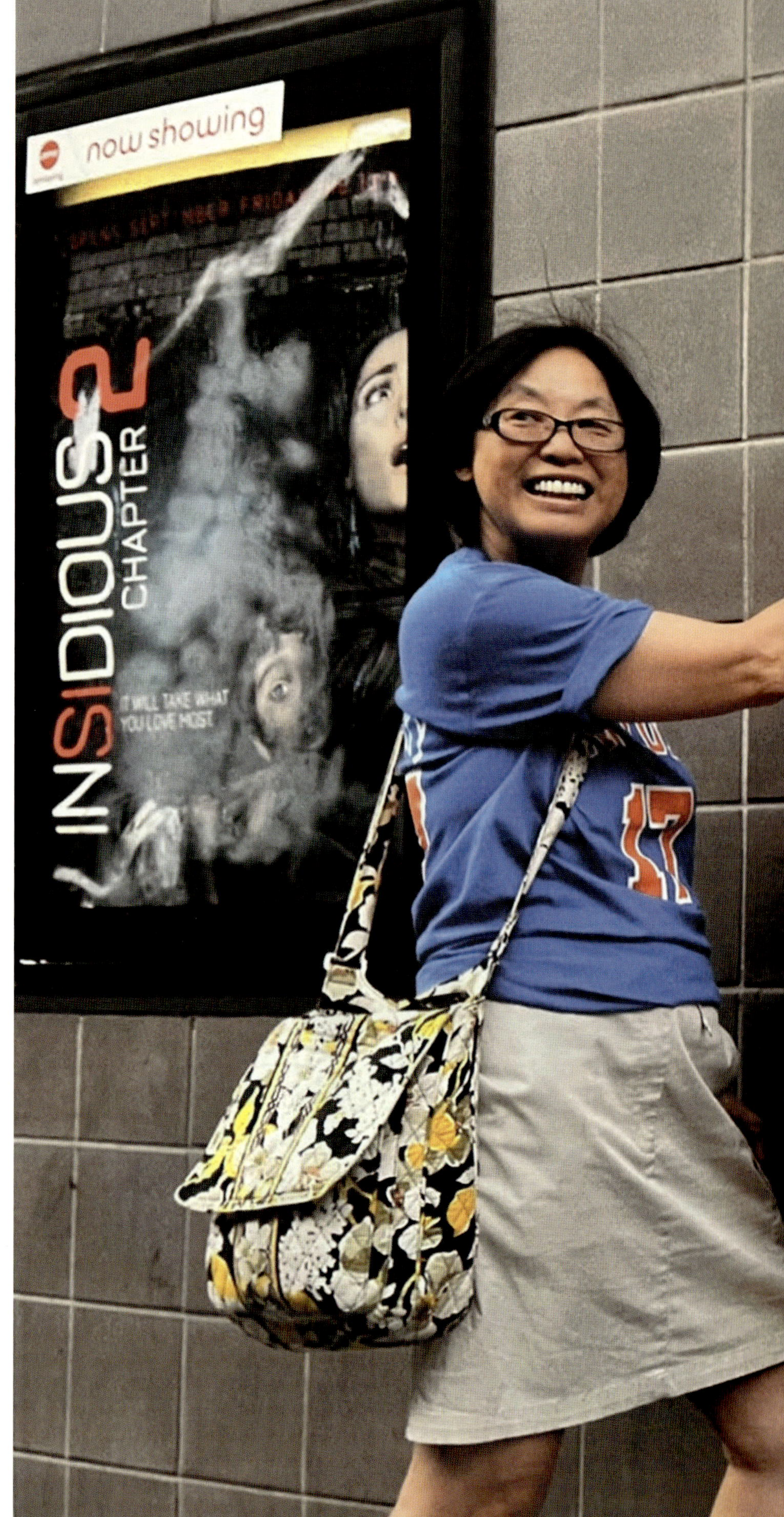

Asian Americans were crazy about NBA basketball star Jeremy Lin. Lois Lee of the Chinatown Planning Council (*left*), with Ruth Lee (*right*) and children Grant Lee and Elyssa Lee. New York, 2013.

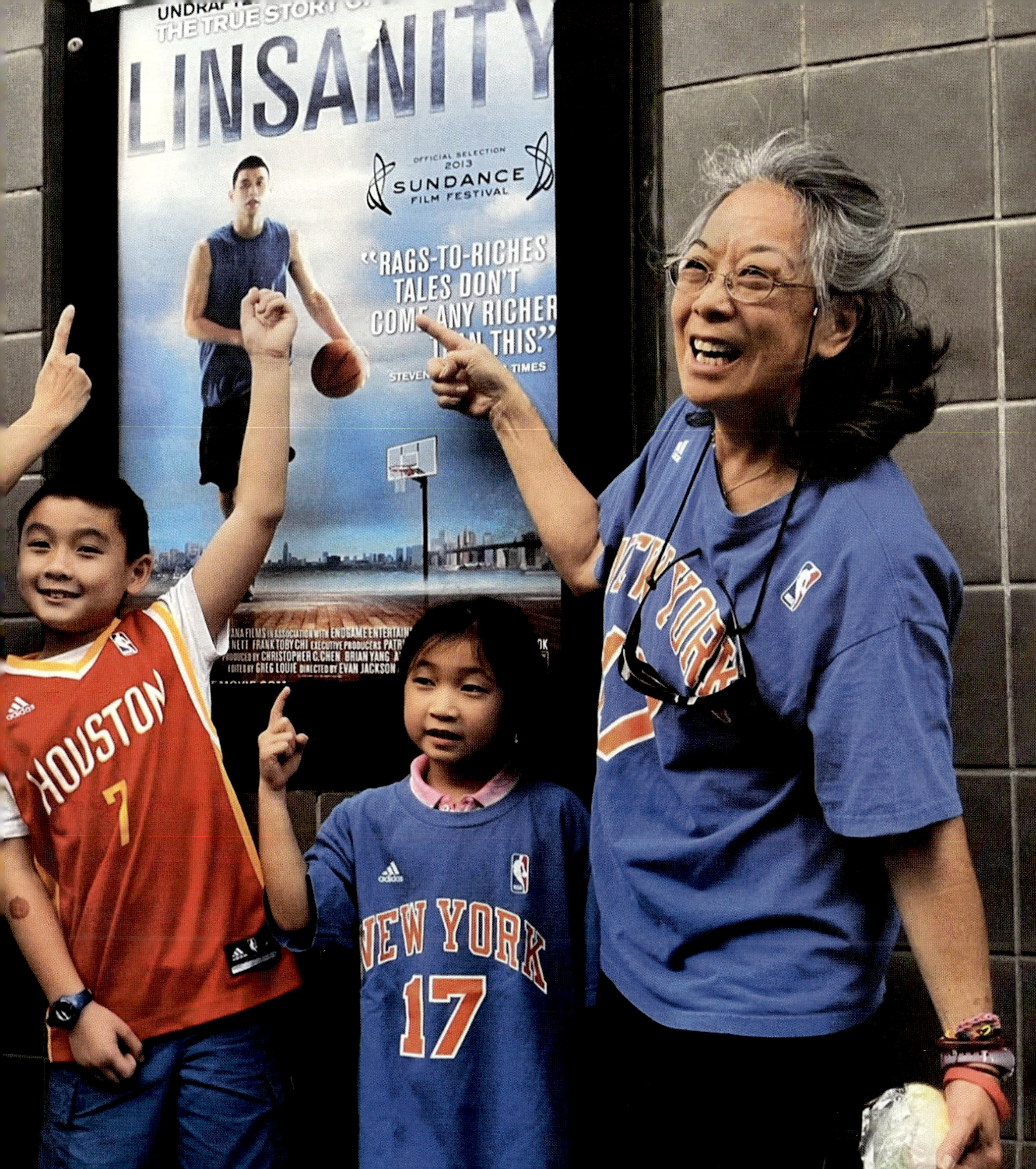
LINSANITY
OFFICIAL SELECTION
2013
SUNDANCE
FILM FESTIVAL
"RAGS-TO-RICHES
TALES DON'T
ANY RICHER
HOUSTON
7
NEW YORK
17

JOANNE KWONG

President of the Pearl River Mart

In 2016 I left my career as an attorney and nonprofit executive to help my in-laws, Mr. and Mrs. Chen, rebuild the iconic Pearl River Mart, the world's first Chinese American department store and a true New York City institution. Their rent had quintupled, and Amazon.com was making brick-and-mortar stores obsolete. And yet Pearl River was no ordinary store. For five decades, it had served as a magical space for Asian Americans and for New Yorkers in general. Perhaps most important, it was a pillar in Chinatown, something to build on and save at all costs.

On reopening night, the weather was crisp and clear. We had spent a frenzied two months finding a space and building it out and reimagining

I spotted Corky with a crowd of people around him. He was hard to miss, with his wide smile, dancing eyes, and animated storytelling style. As a student of Asian American history in college, I recognized his name—there are not too many Chinese guys named Corky—and I knew his work was a big deal.

Given that I was in networking mode, I sidled up to him and jokingly asked if he would mount an exhibition in the small space that would become our art gallery.

I expected a gentle letdown, but to my surprise, he said yes and asked when.

"Two weeks?" I realized how ridiculous this sounded.

He paused a second, considering, and then smiled his signature mischievous smile. "Okay!"

I felt like I had hit the jackpot.

And I had. That spring Corky served as our official artist-in-residence. The show, *Chinese America on My Mind*, included sixty-two images that documented the Chinese American experience over five decades. The photographs were breathtaking and filled with emotion: the horror of a bleeding man hauled off by cops at a police brutality march; the anger of protests after the Vincent Chin murder verdict; the patriotism on display in Chinatown after 9/11; the sheer joy of an entire community during Linsanity; the regal dignity of veterans, po-pos, and restaurant cooks; and the dynamic athleticism of nine-man volleyball competitors and dragon boat racers, to name a few. I couldn't believe it when I came across an image from my own protesting days at Columbia (to establish an ethnic studies program). I didn't make it into the shot, but I was definitely there. And, of course, so was Corky.

Over the next few months, I learned so much about Chinatown's activist history and Pearl River's history, too. The Chens, as busy business owners, had taken few pictures, so it was a blessing that Corky remembered everything in detail, complete with photo references. He began his photography career in 1971, the same year Pearl River was founded. He and the Chens were part of the same activist groups located at 22 Catherine Street, the building that housed both the pioneering collective Basement Workshop and the very first Pearl River Mart. Corky recalled that Mr. Chen had lent him the Pearl River truck to transport lumber for the first Chinatown Health Fair, which eventually became the Charles B. Wang Community Health Center. Corky and Mr. Chen even had identical stories of being investigated by the FBI and using the ruse of dim sum to lure agents to the neighborhood instead of traveling to scary agency offices.

If our gallery was a wok, Corky was the one who seasoned it. He epitomized what it meant to be an artist, a mentor, and a friend. He came every day and always had someone to meet or give a tour to. He made sure to schedule ample time for communal meals before and after all events. He encouraged his friends to get their own work shown, which resulted in some of our best exhibitions by far—those by Arlan Huang, Kam Mak, and Louis Chan. He joked around with our staff and never forgot to encourage visitors to shop downstairs. And he came to every single one of our next shows, always delighted to meet the artist and give his thoughts on the work.

After the completion of the exhibition, I missed our daily talks but still saw him quite a bit. He was everywhere! He'd photograph events on his own dime, and without fail, a few days later he'd drop by with a flash drive of images and a few shots printed out and signed, because he was old school like that. He'd walk right into our "employees only" area, say hi to the Chens, and then poke his head into my office, which proudly displays four of my favorite Corky Lee images on the wall. I can't remember all of what we'd talk about, but we often chatted for a long time, which I never minded. Corky taught me that when friends come to call, you make the time.

I last saw Corky in December 2020, about a week before he contracted Covid. He was part of a group of volunteers who stayed up late two nights in a row to inscribe, hand-dip, and install 250 lights and lanterns as part of the Light Up Chinatown initiative. The lights were meant to make our elders feel safer walking the streets and to help bring back foot traffic for our restaurants and shops. It was a joyous, crisp night, and when the first string of lights flickered on, we all cheered and hugged and took selfies despite the social distancing mandate. I think everyone there on that night will forever be grateful to have had that time with him.

In the years since Corky's passing, so much has happened. Much of it has been pretty bad—a million people have died from the pandemic, divisiveness and inequality increased, random violence and mass shootings continued, inflation rose, Ukraine was invaded, *Roe v. Wade* got overturned. And on a smaller scale, Chinatown itself saw devastating fires, an impending mega-jail, and darkened, quiet streets. Longtime businesses shuttered. The steady drumbeat of attacks on Asian Americans, especially elders, continues.

It's a painful irony that the world in 2023 is probably similar to 1971, the chaotic Vietnam War era when both Corky and Pearl River were starting out. Then as now, the status quo was unacceptable, and then as now, young people organized, took to the streets, and demanded radical change.

I think Corky would have been delighted by the energy coursing through present-day Chinatown. The pandemic and all that ensued has spurred hundreds, maybe thousands, to return to the community and contribute their individual talents. New projects abound, from those addressing food insecurity and neighborhood safety and gentrification, to fun walking tours and arts initiatives and running groups. Not to mention all the kids who stepped up to help their parents modernize longtime businesses. Just as Corky and the Basement Workshop generation were drawn to the spirit and activism of the 1970s, fifty years later Gen Z, millennials, and even grizzled Gen Xers like me feel the same calling.

In June 2021, two dozen friends, contemporaries, and mentees paid tribute to Corky's mission of "photographic justice" by mounting an exhibition entitled *Corky Lee on My Mind* at Pearl River Mart.

On opening night, Corky's friends all gathered, but this time we missed the whirling dervish of energy that was Corky. As I looked around, I marveled that one man had touched so many people and changed so many lives. Corky was an absolute original, but he was also an ordinary guy with a passion for taking photos and bringing people together. If everyone attacked life the way that Corky had, pounding the pavement in pursuit of justice, bringing together friends and neighbors, wouldn't the world be so much better? Wouldn't Chinatown not only survive but thrive?

Corky seemed to be sending us answers through the universe. The centerpiece of the exhibition was a badass image of Corky from his Basement Workshop days, taken by the photographer Bob Hsiang. As people reminisced, cried, laughed, and reconnected around this striking image, Corky seemed to be watching over the hubbub, pleased as always to be a part of the action. In death as in life, Corky was bringing Chinatown together—and urging us to keep moving forward.

Joanne Kwong with lanterns made by volunteers to string across Mott Street for Light Up Chinatown. New York, December 2020.

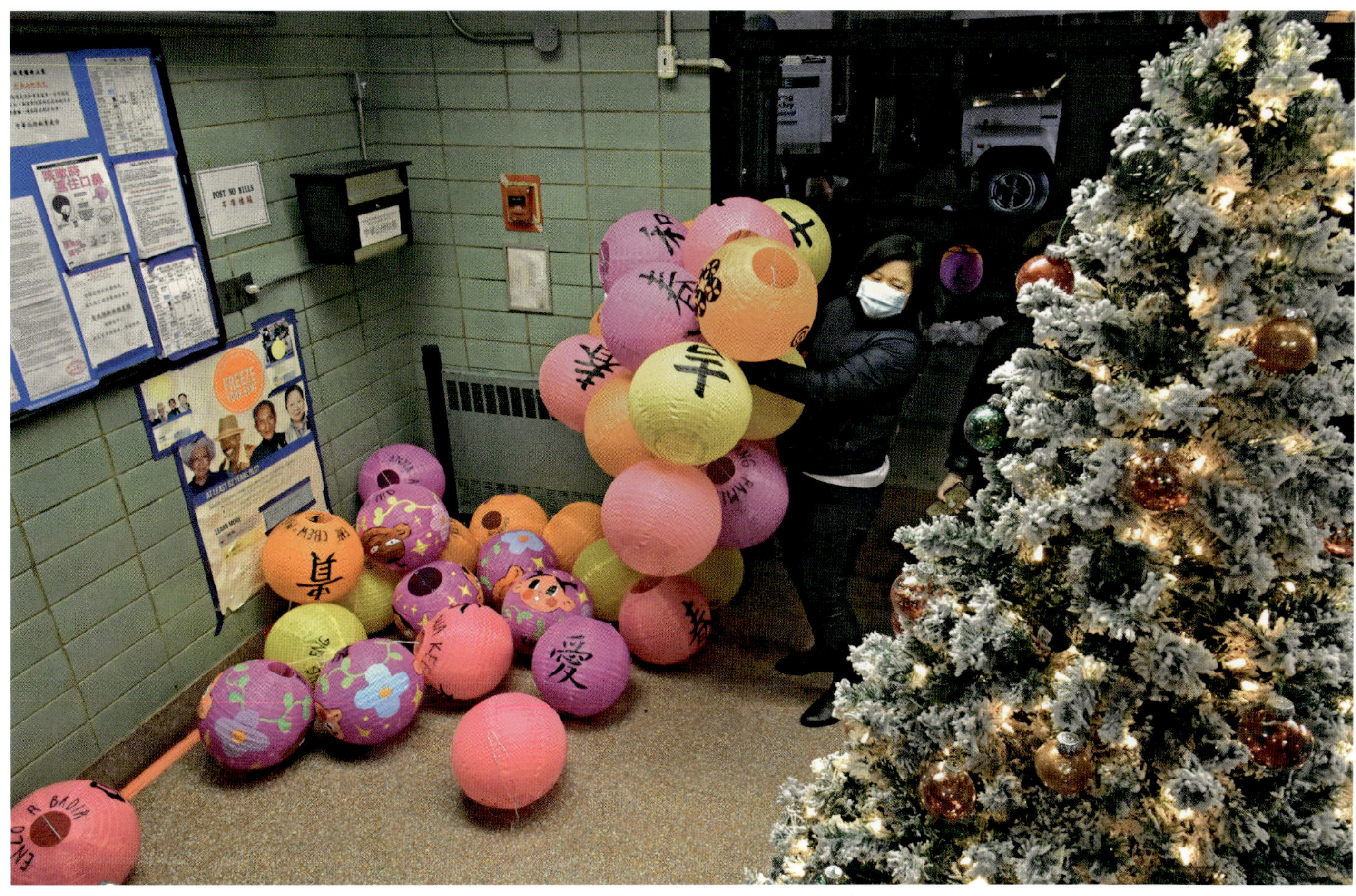

During the first year of the coronavirus pandemic, Corky Lee photographed Chinatown scenes to show the economic devastation it brought to the community and to demonstrate that Chinese people were victims of the virus, not its cause. Small-business people struggled to make a living, some adapting their wares to meet the needs of the moment. Corky asked Chinatown residents to pose in front of their favorite shuttered restaurants, and he photographed responses to anti-Asian attacks, including community patrols and protest demonstrations.

Selling masks and sanitizer on Canal Street. New York, 2020.

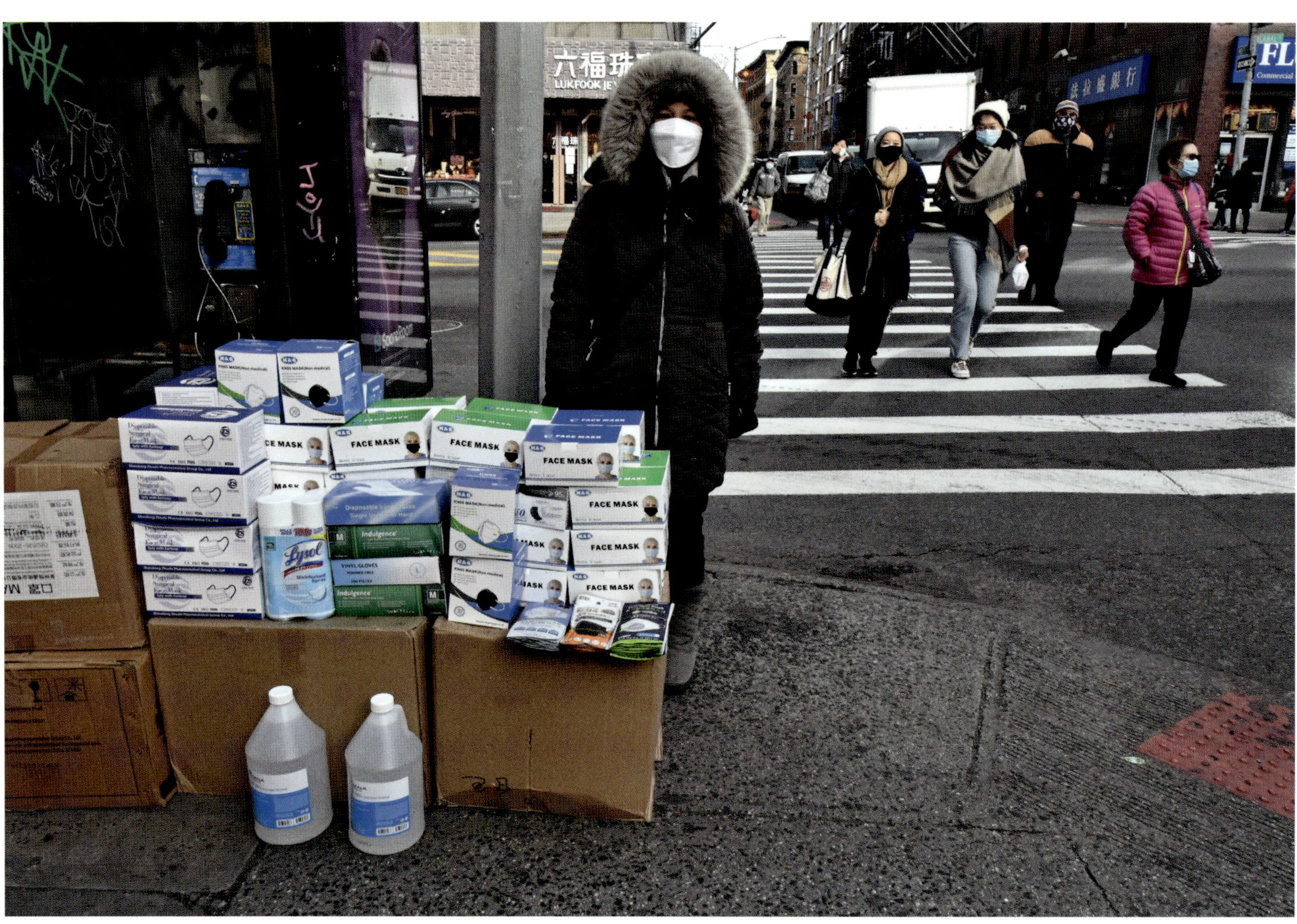

Doyers Street, shut down. New York, 2020.

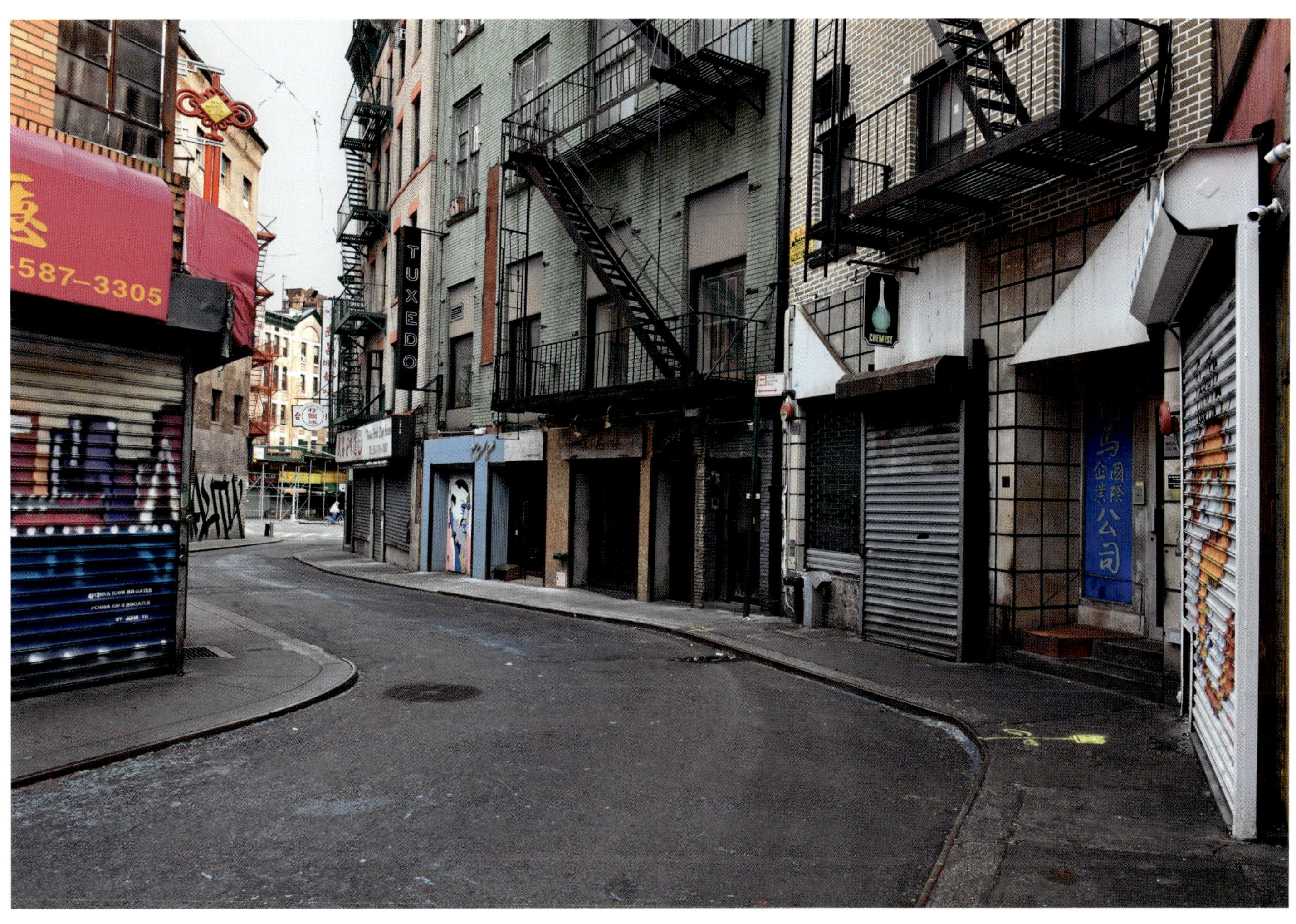

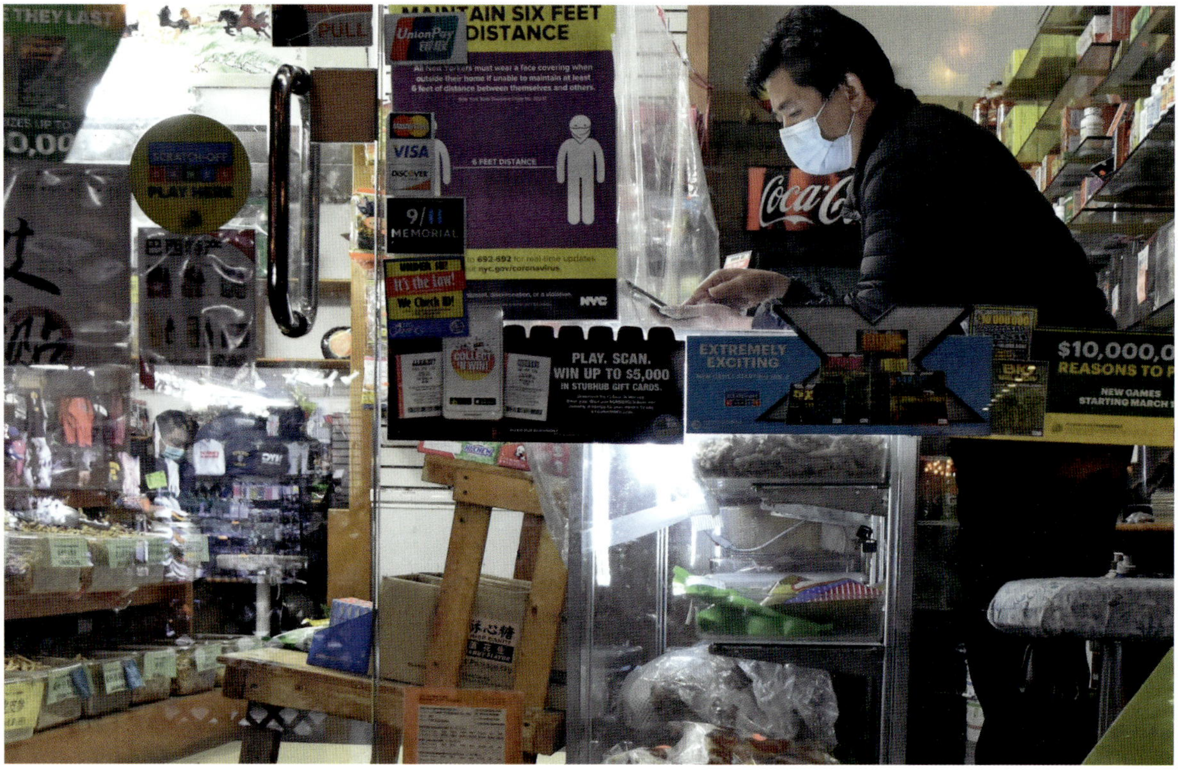

Shop with stalls selling Chinese patent medicines and herbal products. New York, 2020.

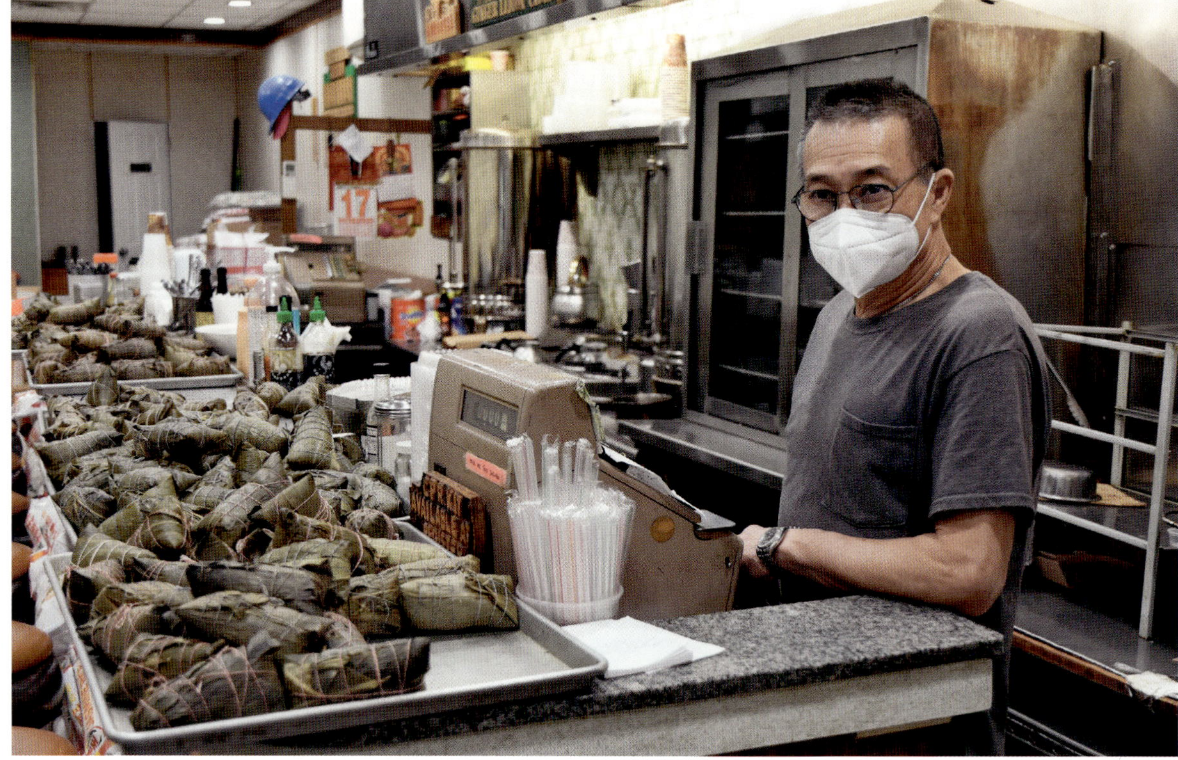

Selling *zongzi* at the Mee Sum Café on Pell Street. The savory sticky rice wrapped in bamboo leaf was a simple grab-and-go food suitable for single handling. New York, 2020.

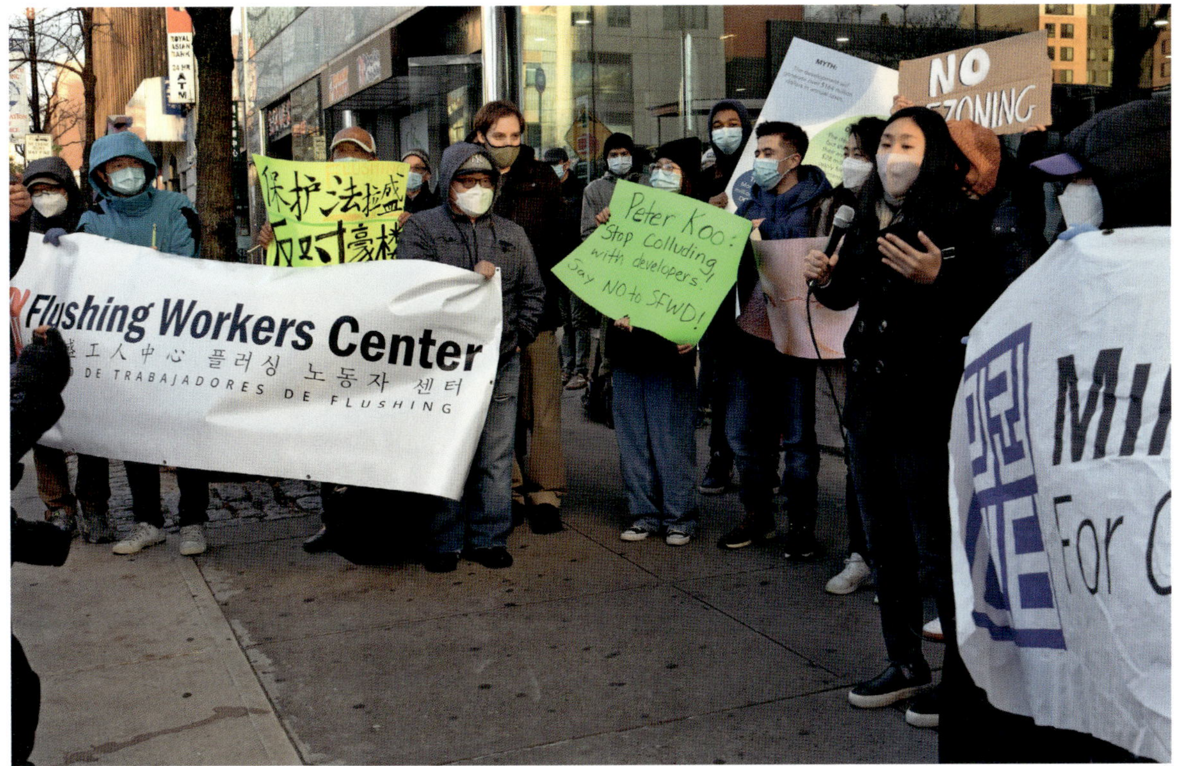

In 2020 a proposed luxury condo development along the riverfront in Flushing, Queens, divided the Queens Asian American community. City councilperson Peter Koo supported the development, while New York State assemblyman Ron Kim, along with labor, tenant, and community groups, opposed it. Queens, New York, December 2020.

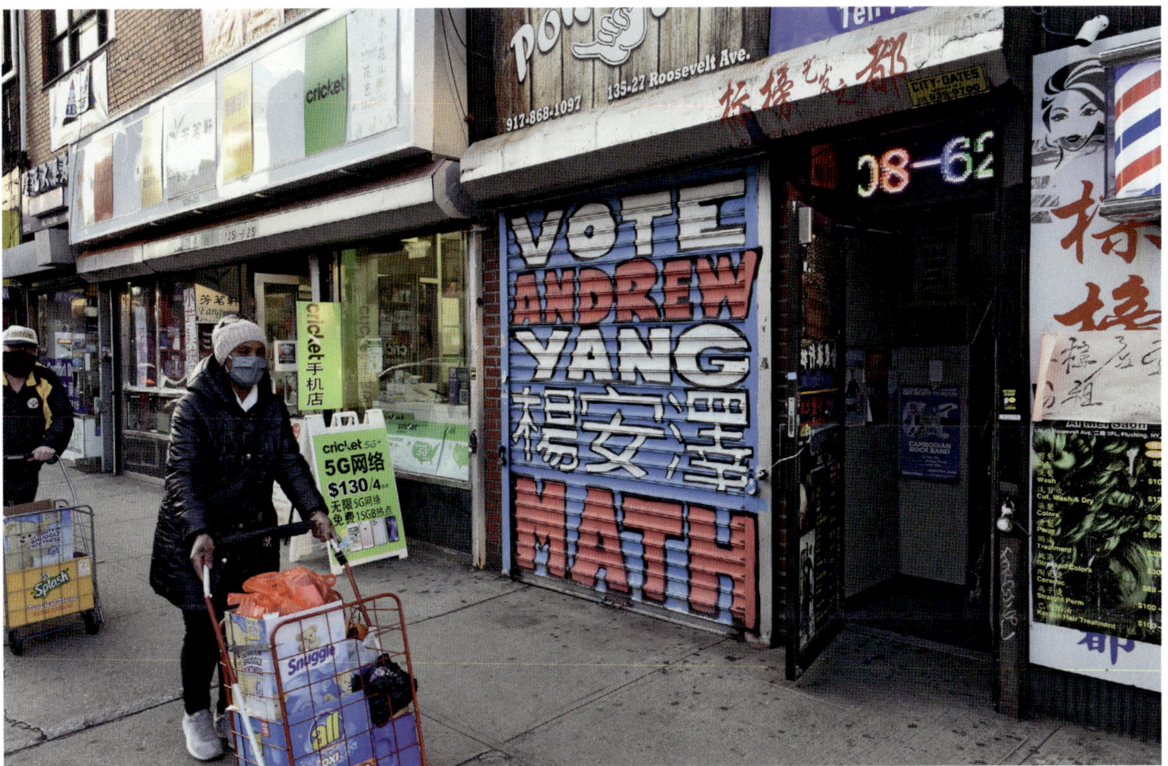

Andrew Yang's bid for mayor of New York received support from many, but not all, Asian Americans. Yang's campaign played on stereotypes of Asians being good at math. Flushing, Queens, New York, 2020.

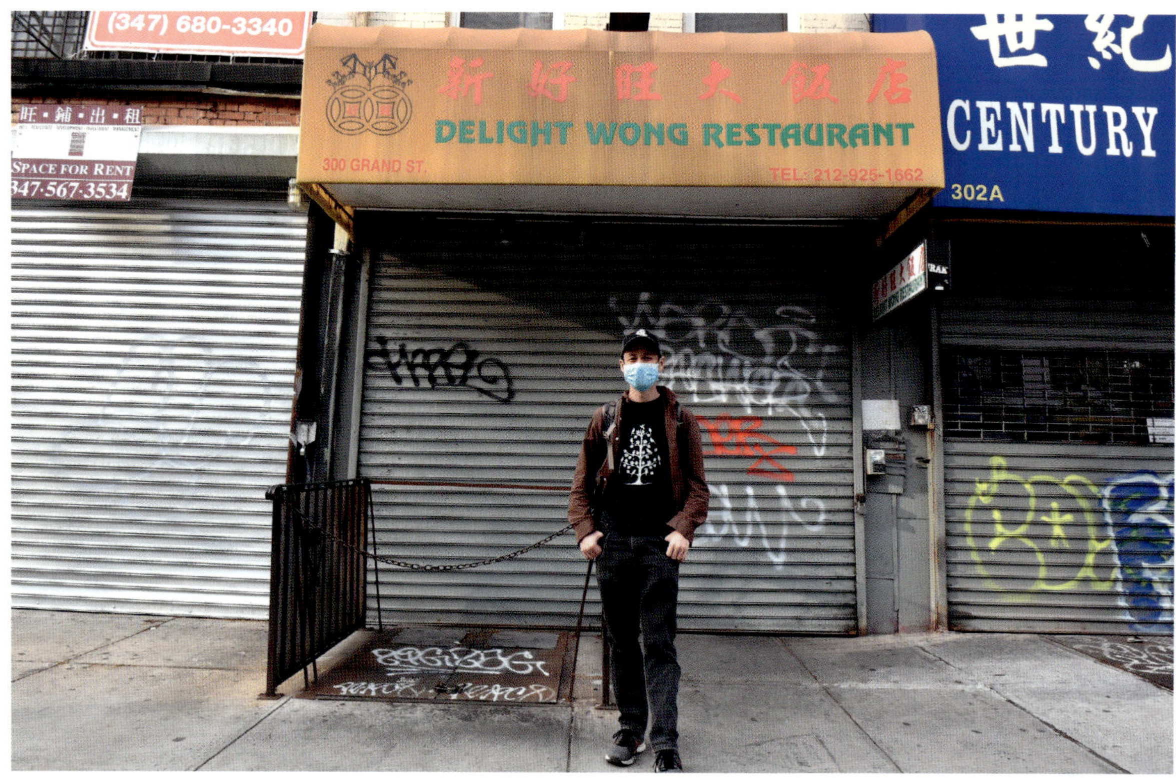

Edward Cheng in front of Delight Wong on Grand Street. New York, 2020.

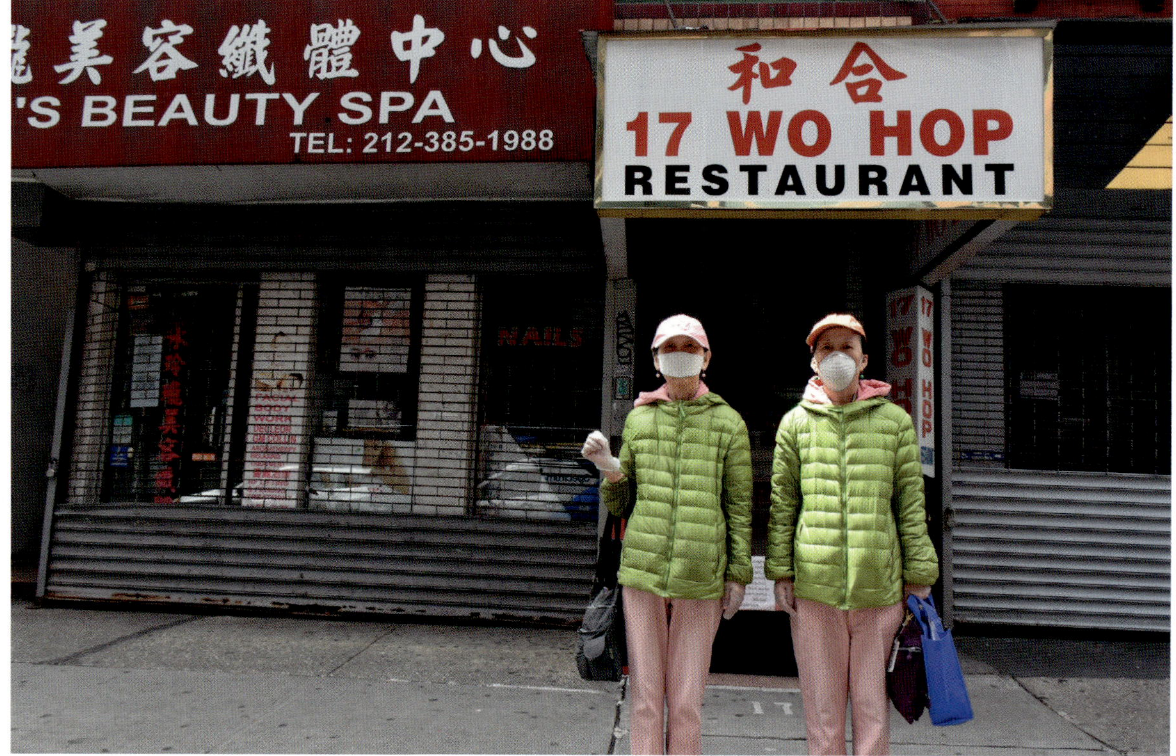

Twin sisters Cassandra Louie Dick and Constance Louie in front of Wo Hop on Mott Street. New York, 2020.

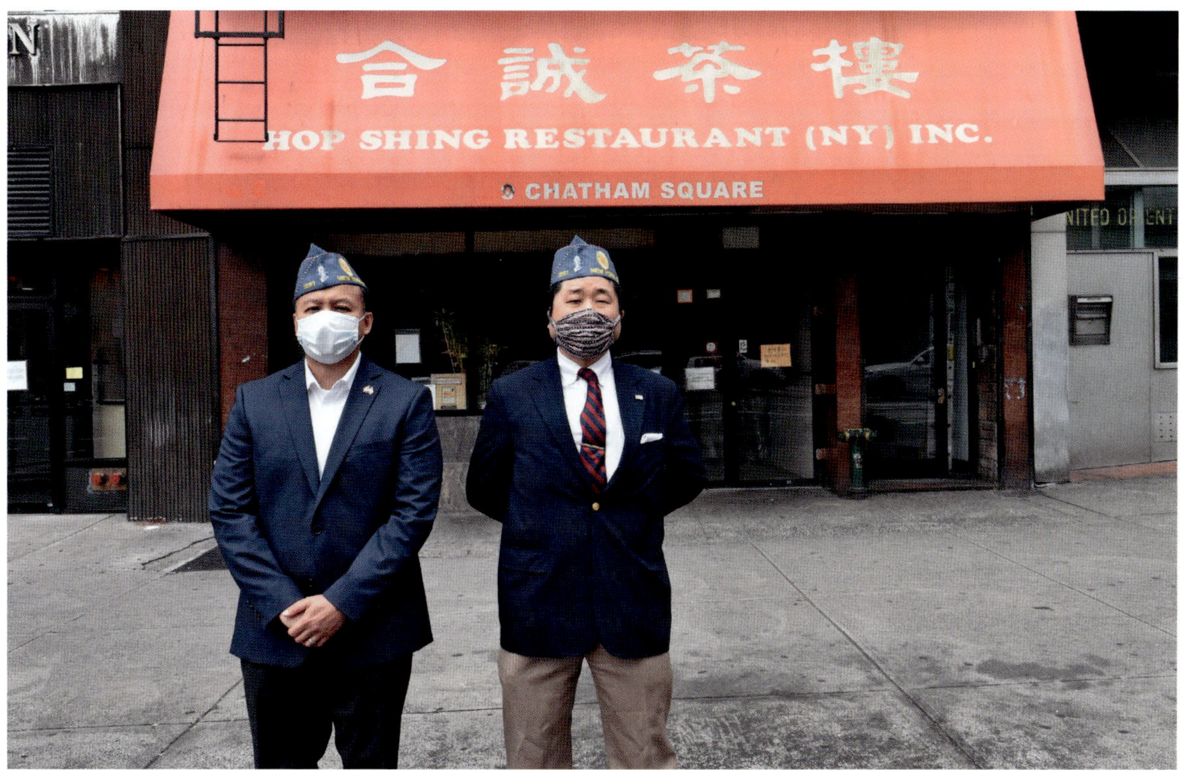

Veterans from the Kimlau Post 1291, David Eng (*left*) and Brian Jung, in front of Hop Shing on Bowery, now permanently closed. New York, 2020.

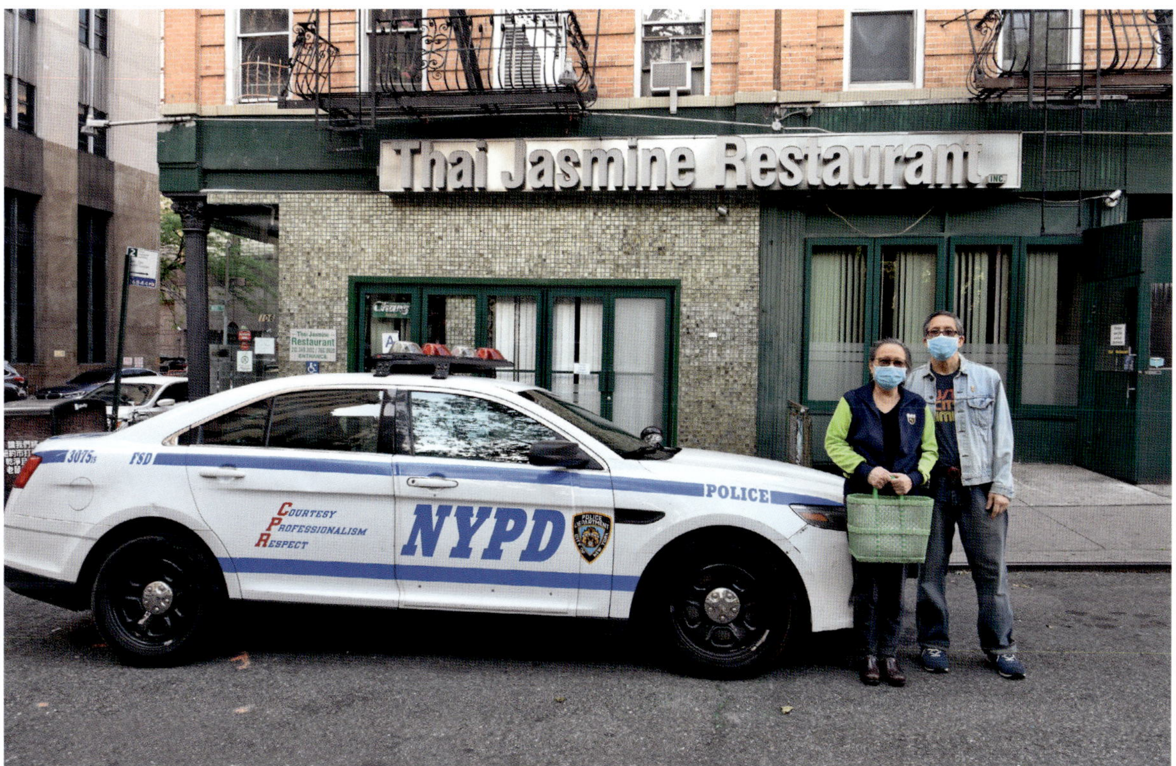

Pamela Lee and Tom Lee in front of Thai Jasmine on Bayard Street, now permanently closed. New York, 2020.

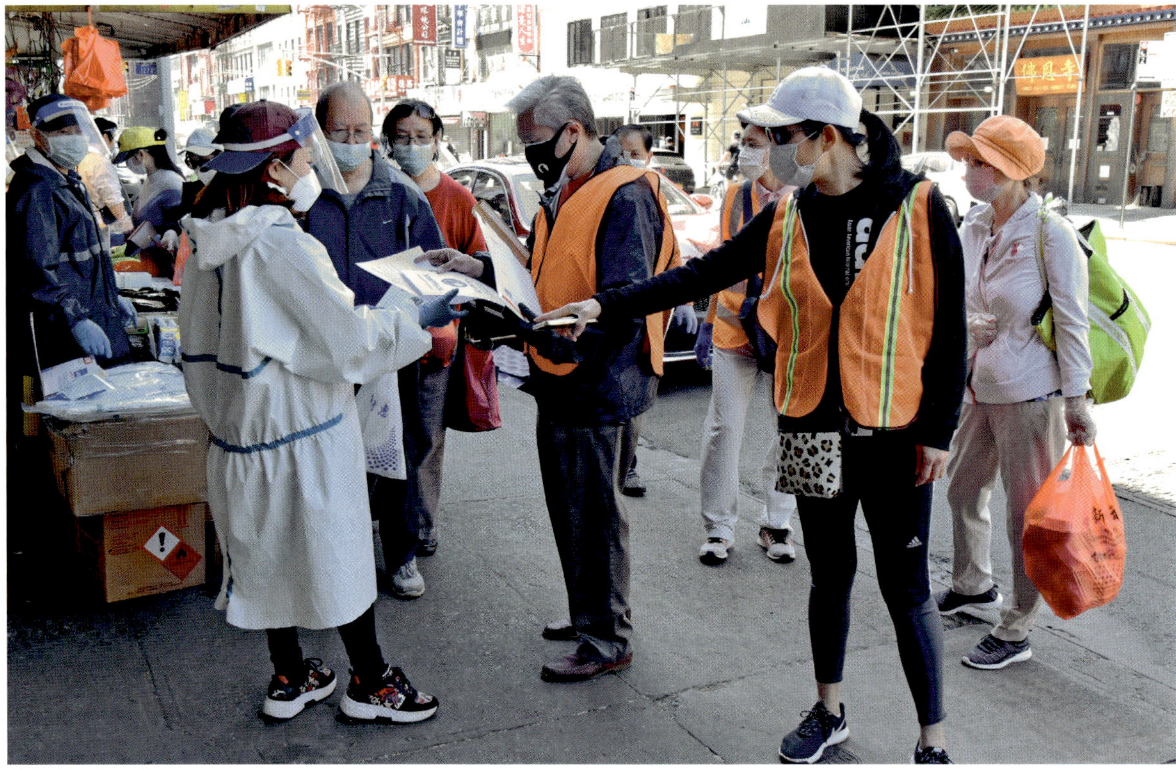

To guard against racist attacks, Chinatown residents formed a volunteer neighborhood block watch that patrolled the community. They also distributed information to educate merchants about safety protocols, urging them to post flyers stating "No Mask, No Service." New York, 2020.

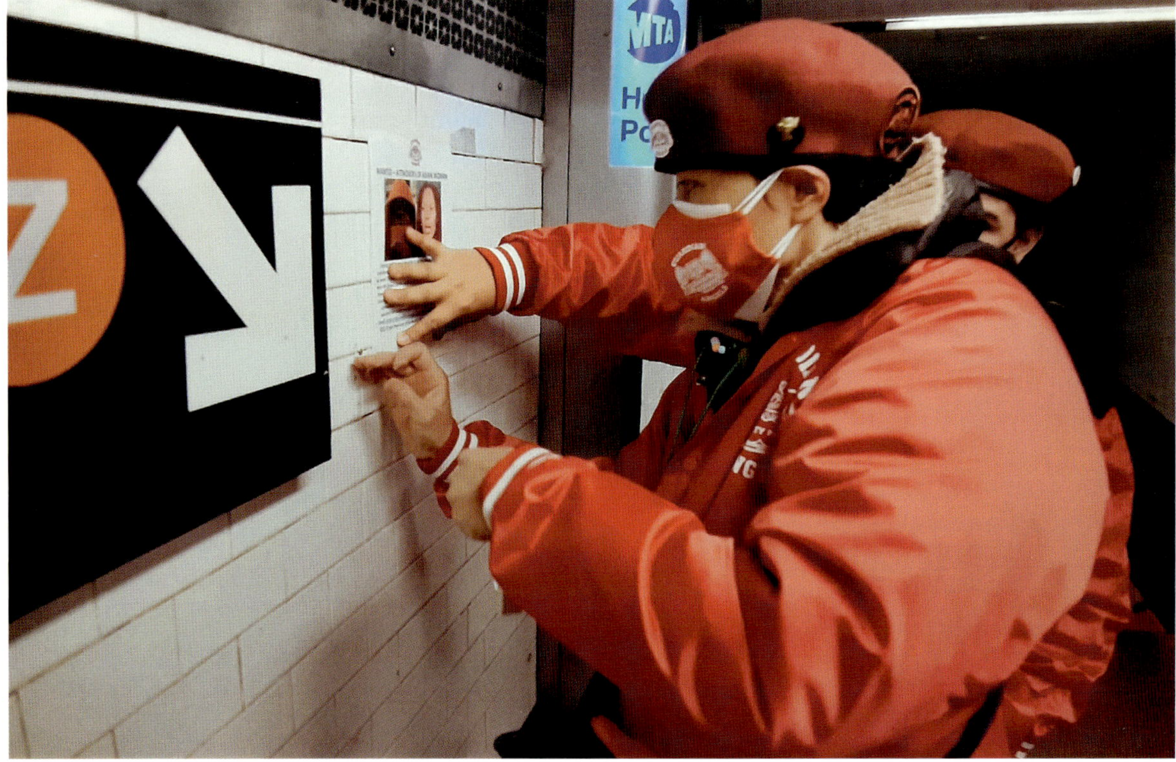

After a Chinese woman was assaulted on the subway, Guardian Angel member Sarah Chin posted a flyer in a Chinatown subway station. New York, December 2020.

Asian Americans protest racist attacks during the coronavirus pandemic. New York, spring 2020.

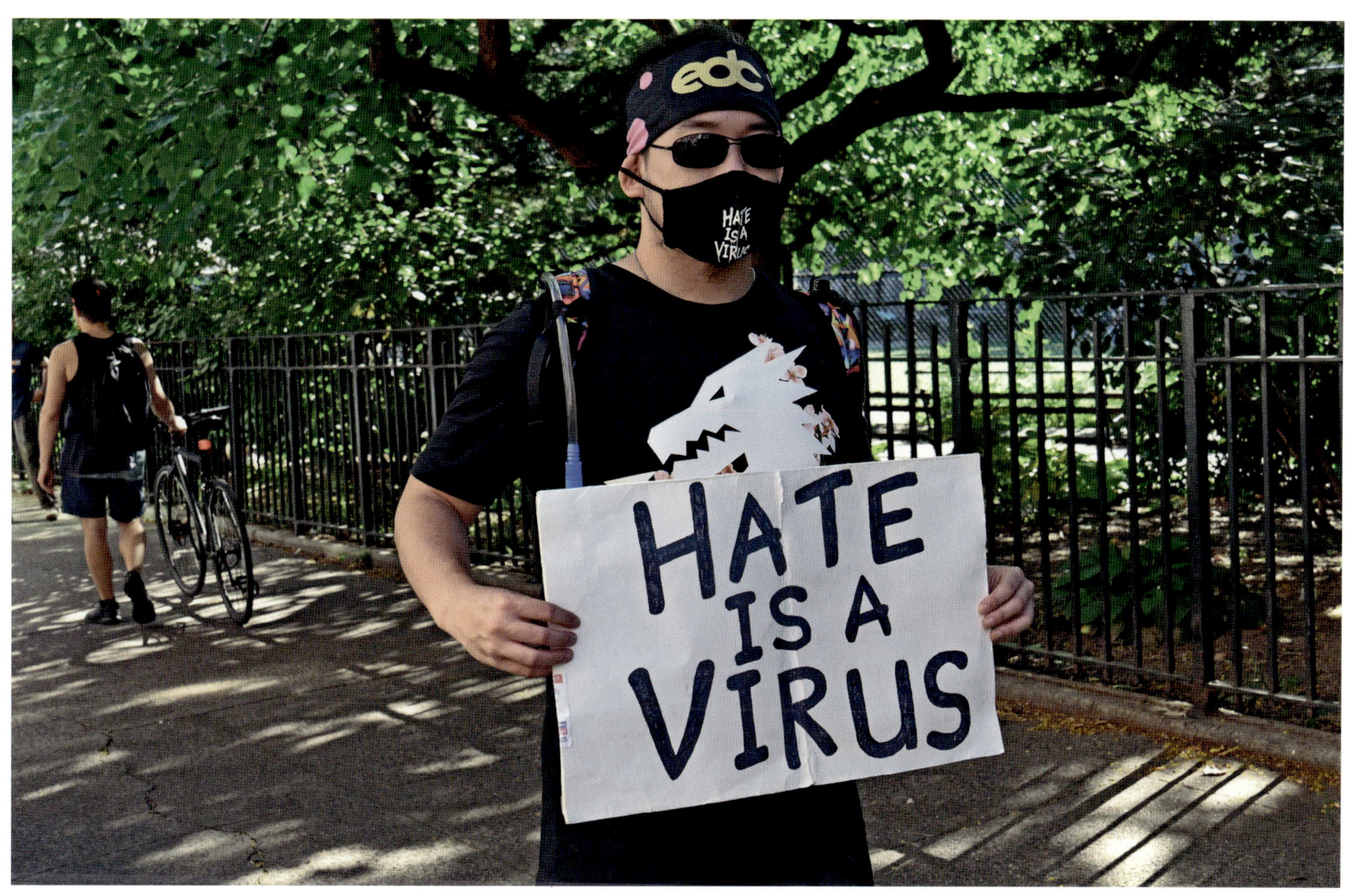

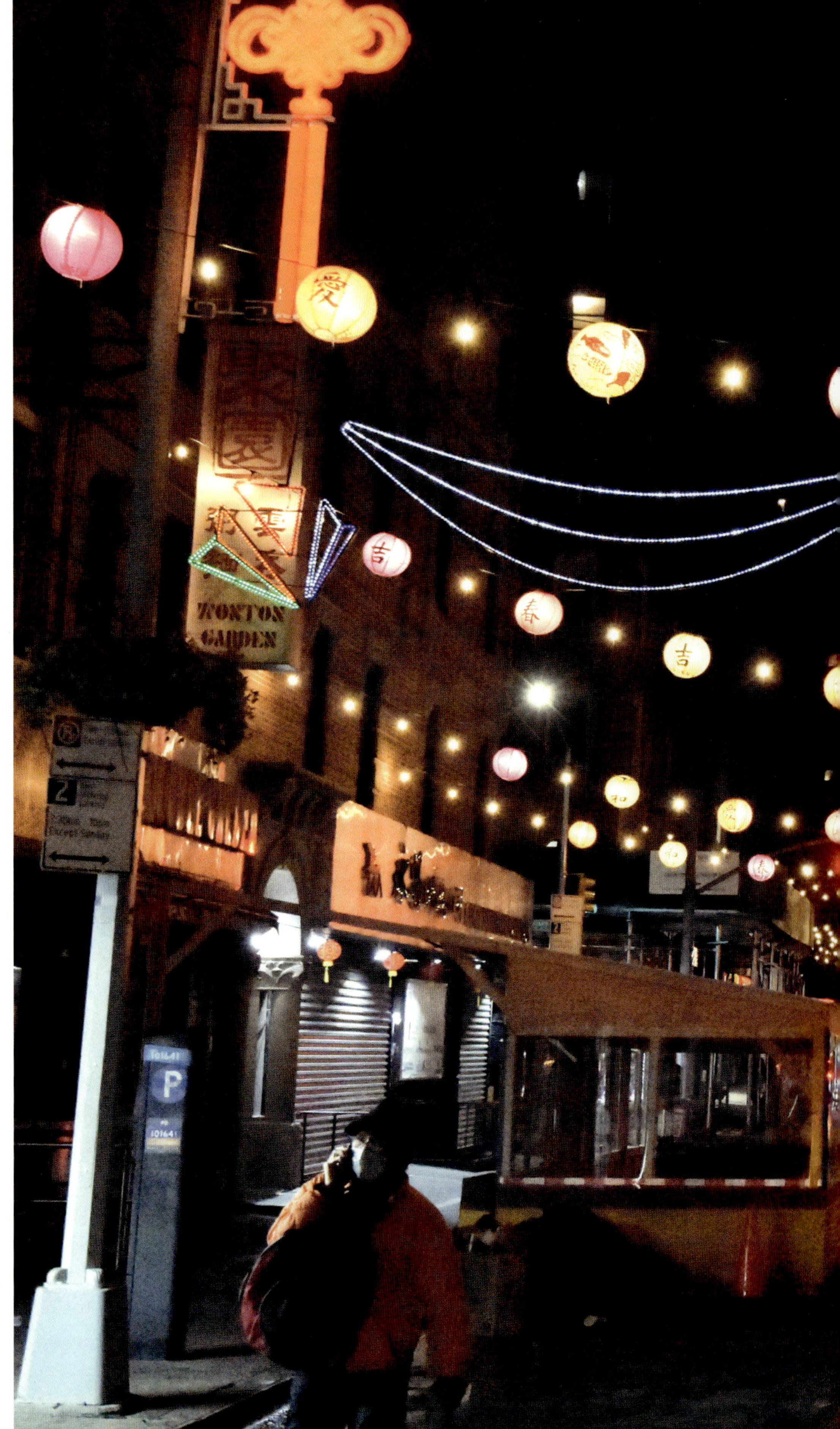

Light Up Chinatown,
on Mott Street.
New York,
December 2020.

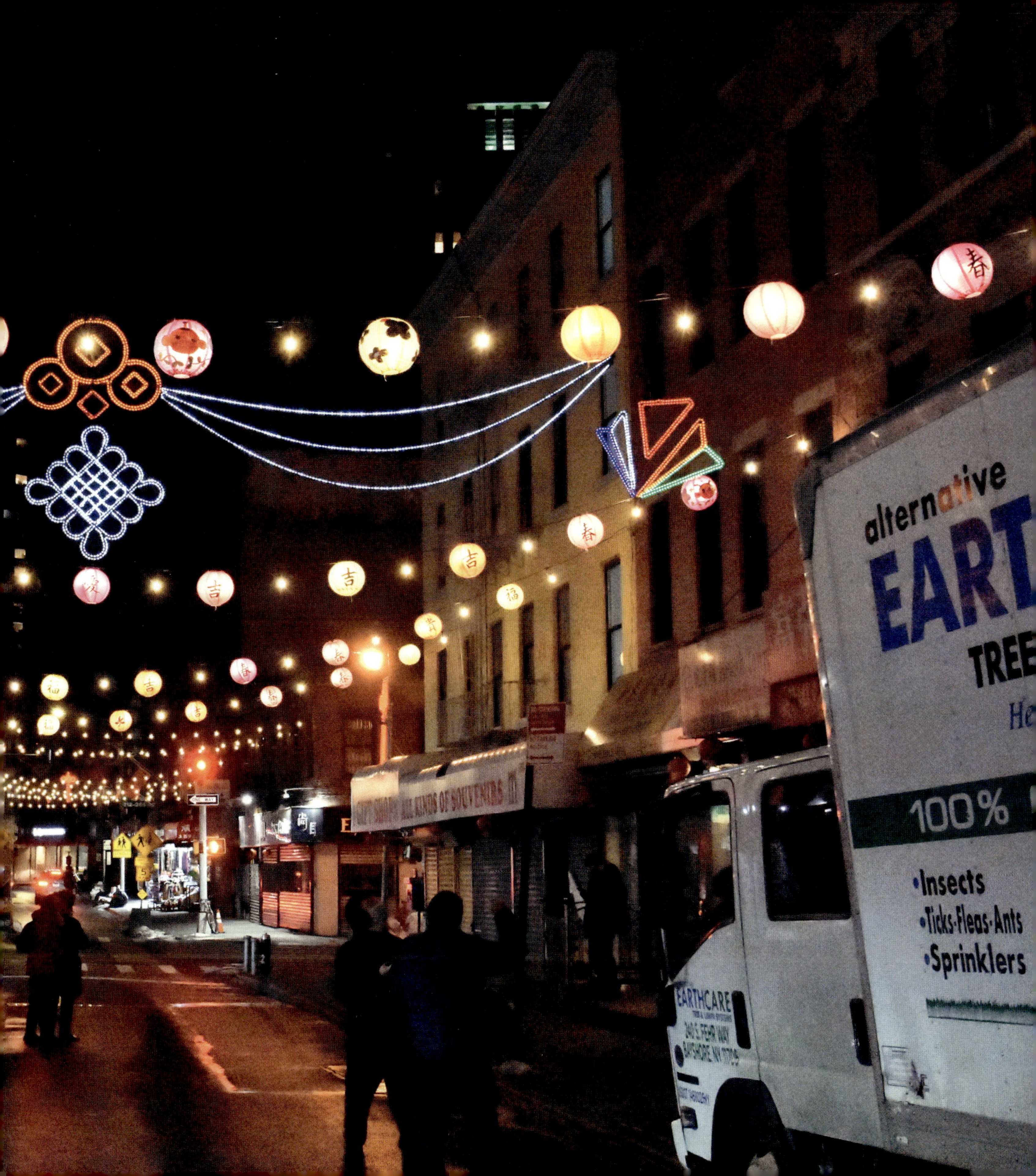

alternative
100%
Insects
Ticks-Fleas-Ants
Sprinklers
EARTHCARE
ALL KINDS OF SOUVENIRS

Epilogue

JOHN J. LEE, CHEE WANG NG & MAE NGAI

Corky Lee's untimely passing in January 2021 left us bereft. He had been a pillar of the Chinatown and Asian American communities, a witness to history, a model of commitment and caring for the people around him and to Asian America, writ large. We felt his loss even more profoundly as racism and violence against Asian Americans continued during what turned out to be a very long pandemic. In 2020 Corky had already documented the ravages of the pandemic on New York's Chinatown and the upsurge in racism against Asian Americans. But he was gone by the time six Asian women were gunned down at Atlanta spas in March 2021.

Anti-Asian hate crimes increased by 339 percent from 2020 to 2021 and continued unabated into 2022. Asian American elders were viciously assaulted in San Francisco, New York, and Oakland, often in broad daylight on busy city sidewalks or in their front yards. In New York, Michelle Go was pushed onto the subway tracks to her death. Christina Yuna Lee was killed in her own apartment in Chinatown. And so many more were harassed verbally and physically. Corky was not there to bear witness, but others picked up his baton. We all try, each in our own way, to continue the struggle against racism, hate, and violence to which Corky dedicated his life's work.

That work necessarily includes preserving and honoring Corky's legacy. This book is the centerpiece of several projects that his estate and others undertook toward that end after he passed away.

In June 2021, Pearl River Mart hosted an exhibition, *Corky Lee on My Mind,* curated by Joanne Kwong, Chee Wang Ng, and Karen Zhou. The title was a riff on *Chinese America on My Mind,* the name of a forty-five-year retrospective of Corky's work that had previously been held at Pearl River in 2017. (That name was itself a riff on Gordon Parks's famous *Harlem on My Mind.*) *Corky Lee on My Mind* did not feature Corky's photos but was a tribute to his accomplishments by twenty-one photographers from across the country, some of them his "OG" comrades, others young artists who were mentored by Corky.

A year later, a second, larger tribute-exhibition took place in the Hon. Charles Sifton Gallery at the federal courthouse in downtown Brooklyn, from May 2022 to January 2023. Organized at the initiative of the Asian American Bar Association of New York, hosted and presented by the U.S. District Court for the Eastern District of New York, and curated by Chee Wang Ng, the show featured the work of more than thirty photographers as well as a small number of photographs by Corky Lee. The exhibition showed Asian American social photography as it had grown and flowered over the decades: Bob Hsiang's photos of the Asian American movement in the 1970s; Marilynn Yee's photos of the Tiananmen Square protests and of 9/11 (published in *The New York Times* in 1989 and 2001); Jeenah Moon's photo of mourners at the Golden Spa in Atlanta in 2021; and Chang Lee's photo of figure skater Nathan Chen skating for the gold at the Beijing Olympics (*New York Times*, 2022). Other works exemplified Corky Lee's style of capturing daily life in the community, like Chien-Chi Chang's photo of a man eating noodles on a fire escape (1998) and Louis Chan's photo of boxers at practice (2008).

Some of the photographs in this book were previewed in a solo retrospective exhibition of Corky Lee's work in 2023 at the Chinese American Museum in Washington, D.C.

The New York chapter of the Asian American Journalists Association, of which Corky was a longtime member, created the Corky Lee Fellowship in Photojournalism. Supported by a grant from Johnson & Johnson, the chapter awarded grants in 2022 to two budding photographers, Fay Chen and Xyza Cruz Bacanti, to tell the stories of underrepresented communities in New York City.

Two films about Corky Lee, long in the making, were released in 2022: *Dear Corky* by Curtis Chin and Kenneth Eng and *Photographic Justice: The Corky Lee Story* by Jennifer Takaki.

In 2023 the New York City Council voted to co-name Mosco Street in Chinatown as "Corky Lee Way," thanks to an effort led by Think!Chinatown and the Organization of Chinese Americans.

Some of Corky's iconic photographs are being

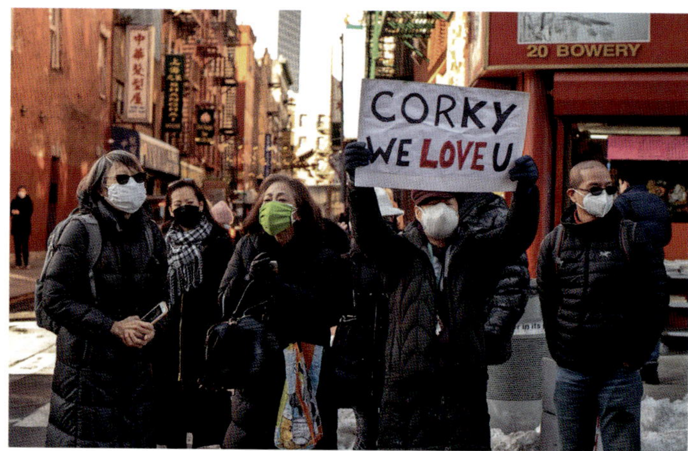

Mourners line the streets of Chinatown to bid farewell to Corky Lee. New York, 2021.
Alan Chin

acquired by institutions for public display. The National Park Service will feature Corky's re-enactment of the "golden spike" photo (2014) as part of a permanent exhibit at the Golden Spike National Historical Park at Promontory Point, Utah.

The Obama Presidential Center Museum, scheduled to open in Chicago in 2025, will feature Corky's photo of students marching against police brutality (1975) in its exhibit "Changing Nation, Changing World."

The estate, which holds the copyright to all works by Corky Lee, continues to grant permission or license for use of his work to students, researchers, nonprofits, and commercial entities. Meanwhile, it is working to create an inventory and catalog of Corky Lee's vast collection, so it may ultimately be entrusted to a major institution, where his photographs will be preserved and made accessible for viewing by all. The estate may be reached at www.corkylee.org.

There will never be another Corky Lee. But in a sense there will be many Corky Lees, inspired by his humanity, his smile, his work ethic, and his commitment to social justice.

About the Photographs

In selecting the photographs for this book, we drew on choices that Corky himself had made for a self-published book in 2011, which he did not complete, and for exhibitions or loans to other projects. These photographs represent what he considered to be his best work.

To that core group we added photographs that Corky took for the historical record but never exhibited or published. Corky was an anti-elitist, and as a general rule he privileged photos of ordinary people and activists over those of celebrities and politicians. We added photos of personalities that help illuminate the history of Asians in American culture and public life.

Corky took many photographs in color—even in the 1970s—but he was inclined to print them in black and white for exhibitions and publication. The reasons are various: the high cost of color printing, the standards of print journalism, and his own aesthetic preference. We present some of his early iconic photos that circulated in black and white in their original color—shot in Kodak Ektachrome and preserved on slides—for the texture of the time that they convey.

By the 1980s and '90s, however, Corky was no longer taking slides; his negatives and prints are almost entirely in black and white. This accounts for the lack of color photographs in the second chapter. Color photos do not regularly reappear until he began using a digital camera in the late 1990s.

Corky composed each photograph as a story, a history lesson. Paradoxically, he did not always record the names of the individuals in his photos. This posed a challenge for us in writing captions. Our research yielded information about some photographs but not all. Corky also dated his photographs inconsistently. When he prepared photos for exhibition, he sometimes wrote dates for the captions that differed from the dates he had penciled on the back of those same photos. In these instances, we did independent research; if we were still unable to identify a definite date, we used the one on the back of the photo.

—Chee Wang Ng and Mae Ngai

Notes

INTRODUCTION

10 **"Do not let anyone":** Corky Lee, foreword to *Voices of Healing: Spirit and Unity After 9/11 in the Asian American and Pacific Islander Community*, ed. Icy Smith (Organization of Chinese Americans/East West Discovery Press, 2004).

12 **"a part of my soul":** Corky Lee, "Chinatown, New York," in *Asian Americans in the Twenty-First Century*, ed. Joann Fuang Jean Lee (New York: New Press, 2008), 157.

AN ABC FROM NYC

22 **They perceived Chinatown:** Anthony Lee, *Picturing Chinatown* (Berkeley: University of California Press, 2001), 7–8.

22 **"I see a different part of Chinatown":** Corky Lee, in *Dear Corky*, dir. Curtis Chin and Kenneth Eng (2022).

23 **When the San Francisco photographer:** Corky Lee, interview by Peter Kwong, circa 2011, unpublished transcript, Corky Lee Archive.

23 **It was a great shot:** Corky Lee, interview by Joanne Kwong, New York, December 17, 2016, https://www.youtube.com/watch?v=Tulk-XfL6SI

24 **In 1979 Corky took a photograph:** Corky Lee, in *Photographic Justice: The Corky Lee Story*, dir. Jennifer Takaki (2022).

ON COMPOSITION

26 **To me, composition:** Interview by Peter Kwong, 2011.

THE BIRTH OF THE MOVEMENT

31 **Although studies in the 1960s:** Karen Tani, "The House That Equality Built: The Asian American Movement and the Legacy of Community Action," in *The War on Poverty*, ed. Annelise Orleck (Athens: University of Georgia Press, 2011), 414–18.

EMPOWERMENT

112 **In a veritable demographic explosion:** U.S. Census Bureau, Census 2000 Brief, "The Asian Population: 2000" (February 2022), https://tinyurl.com/53pxzhrv.

114 **"reluctant to exercise":** Interview by Joanne Kwong, 2016.

114 **By the 2000s, voter turnout:** Jim Dwyer, "Before Victories on Ballot, a Fight to Be Able to Read It," *New York Times*, September 18, 2009.

RESILIENCE

211 **"contributions, heroism":** Smith, ed., *Voices of Healing*, 3.

214 **"If you're Asian":** Corky Lee, in *Photographic Justice*, dir. Takaki.

226 **"We're going flag shopping":** Heems (Himanshu Suri), "Flag Shopping," on *Eat, Pray, Thug*, Megaforce Records, 2015.

227 **"In the days since":** Harpreet Singh and Ajeet Kaur, "Media Advisory: Sikh-Americans Unite for a Candlelight Vigil in Central Park, New York," posted to SikhNet online discussion forum, September 15, 2001, https://www.sikhmatrimonials.com/Sikhnet/discussion.nsf.

227 **In Mesa, Arizona:** Oliver Laughland, "'This Is My Country': How the Family of Balbir Singh Sodhi Resolved to Carry on His American Dream," *Guardian*, September 14, 2021.

229 **"I am a patriot":** Valarie Kaur, "The Ten Year Anniversary of 9/15," September 11, 2011, https://valariekaur.com/2011/09/the-ten-year-anniversary-of-915.

229 **"to retaliate on":** U.S. Senate, *Congressional Record* 153, no. 149 (October 3, 2007) p. S12524.

229 "**We're going flag shopping"**: Heems, "Flag Shopping."

262 **One date stands out:** Sources consulted for this essay include Joanne Kwong, "Corky Lee Interview—Pearl River Mart 17 December 2016," https://otter.ai/u/sFO7xezq7dbD20ETE9Pgk__iM5A; Vanessa Hua, "Golden Spike Redux," National Parks Conservation Association, Summer 2019, https://www.npca.og/articles/2192-golden-spike-redux; Sue Lee and Connie Young Yu, eds., *Voices from the Railroad* (San Francisco: Chinese Historical Society of San Francisco, 2020); Gordon H. Chang, *Ghosts of Gold Mountain* (New York: Houghton Mifflin Harcourt, 2019); and Gordon H. Chang and Shelley Fisher Fishkin, eds., *The Chinese and the Iron Road: Building the Transcontinental Railroad* (Redwood City, Calif.: Stanford University Press, 2019).

EPILOGUE

298 **Anti-Asian hate crimes increased:** Kimmy Yam, "Anti-Asian Hate Crimes Increased 399 Percent Nationwide Last Year, Report Says," NBC News, January 31, 2022.

Selected Exhibitions and Publications

CORKY LEE EXHIBITIONS, 1981–2020

Solo Exhibitions

2020 Untitled pop-up show. Chinatown Organization for Media Awakening, New York.

2018 *Asian Threads, American Weave.* Jorgensen Gallery, University of Connecticut, Storrs.

2017 *Chinese America on My Mind.* Gallery at Pearl River Mart, New York.

2017 Untitled exhibition. AAPI Heritage Month, Asian American Bar Association of New York, New York.

2017 *Chinese Americans: Inclusion/Exclusion.* Organization of Chinese Americans, Seattle.

2014 Untitled exhibition. University of California Regents Lecture, University of California, Los Angeles.

2014 *Corky Lee: Eyewitness to Asian American Activism.* Anschutz Medical Center, University of Colorado, Denver.

2013 *Asian Roots/American Soil.* Charles B. Wang Community Health Center, Stony Brook University, Stony Brook, New York.

2013 *A Place Called Asian America.* Tufts University, Medford, Massachusetts.

2012 *Into the Picture: Images of Asian Pacific America.* Asian Arts Initiative, Philadelphia.

2011 *Asian Pacifically New York: The Photography of Corky Lee.* Queens Museum of Art, Queens, New York.

2009 Untitled pop-up exhibition. University of Florida, Jacksonville.

2008–9 *Asian Roots/American Reality: Photographs by Corky Lee.* Chinese American Museum, Los Angeles.

2005 *Not on the Menu: Atypical Photographic Images of the Chinese Community in New York City.* Colorfax Gallery, Washington, D.C.

2005 *The Movement and the Moment.* University of Michigan, Ann Arbor.

2003 *Not Your Fortune Cookie Wisdom.* Lerner Hall, Columbia University, New York.

2003 *A Photographic Journey with Corky Lee.* New York University, New York.

2002 Untitled exhibition. Pan Asia 2002, University of Chicago.

2001 *Not on the Menu: From Asian Pacific Islander Roots to American Reality.* Museum of Chinese in America, New York.

1998 Untitled exhibition. Ellis Island Immigration Museum, New York.

1997 *Asian Americans: Their Culture, Their Experiences.* American Museum of Natural History, New York.

1996 *Uniquely Filipino.* Cendrillon Gallery, New York.

1996 *Corky Lee: A Photographic Review.* Wall Gallery, John Jay College, New York.

1993 *Roots to Reality.* Harvard University, Cambridge, Massachusetts.

1990 Untitled exhibition. University of Colorado, Denver.

1988 *Uniquely Asian, Coincidentally American.* Gallery, Office of Manhattan Borough President David Dinkins, New York.

1987 *It's Only a Tank: In the Spirit of People Power.* Philippine Center, Philippine Consulate, New York.

1986 *Hawaii: It Ain't Just Sun and Hula Skirts.* Arts for Living Center, Henry Street Settlement House, New York.

Group Exhibitions

2020 Untitled pop-up show. Think!Chinatown, New York.

2017 *Whose Streets? Our Streets! New York City, 1980–2000.* Bronx Documentary Center, New York.

2015 *Beyond Bollywood.* National Museum of Natural History, Smithsonian Institution, Washington, D.C.

2014 *Serve the People: The Asian American Movement in New York.* Interference Archive, New York.

2010 Smithsonian Folklife Festival. Smithsonian Institution, Washington, D.C.

2009 *Asian Pacific Roots in the Big Apple.* Chinese American Arts Council, Gallery 456, New York.

2006 *Queens International 2006.* Queens Museum of Art, New York.

2004 *Queens International 2004.* Queens Museum of Art, New York.

2004 *Kinding Sindaw: Through the Lens.* Philippine Center, Philippine Consulate, New York.

2003 *History of Chinatown.* Museum of Chinese in America, New York.

2002 *Asianlens.* Chambers Fine Art, New York.

1998 *Japanese American Internment Camps.* Ellis Island Museum, New York.

1997 *The Bank (Insider Counting House).* Lower Manhattan Cultural Center, New York.

1996 *Bronx Spaces.* Bronx Museum of Arts, New York.

1991 *Growth of a Dream: The Korean American Experience*. Balch Institute, Philadelphia.

1991 Untitled exhibition. With Ricky Flores. En Foco Gallery, Bronx, New York.

1985 *Hawaiian Chinese Centennial.* City Hall Gallery, Honolulu.

1985 *Gateway Chinatown.* With Wai Fung and Robert Wai Fung. Lane Gallery, Honolulu.

1981 *Not on the Menu.* With Leland Wang. Chinese Cultural Center, San Francisco.

1981 *The Chinese: 3 Views.* With George Potter and Samuel Yette. Martin Luther King, Jr., Memorial Library, Washington, D.C.

1981 *Neighborhoods: Spirit of the City.* New York Urban Coalition, New York.

PUBLICATIONS WITH CORKY LEE'S PHOTOGRAPHS

Aguilar-San Juan, Karin, ed. *The State of Asian America: Activism and Resistance in the 1990s*. Boston: South End Press, 1994.

Asia Society. *Asia in New York City: A Cultural Travel Guide*. New York: Balliett & Fitzgerald and Emeryville, CA: Avalon Travel Publishing, 2000.

Chang, Iris. *The Chinese in America*. New York: Penguin Books, 2014.

Chen, Jack. *The Chinese of America*. New York: Harper & Row, 1980.

Dantzic, Cynthia Maris. *100 New York Photographers*. Atglen, Pa., Schiffer, 2009.

Hongo, Garrett. *Under Western Eyes: Personal Essays from Asian America*. New York: Anchor, 1995.

Hoobler, Dorothy, and Thomas Hoobler. *From Street Fair to Medical Home: Charles B. Wang Community Health Center—Chinatown Health Clinic.* New York: Charles B. Wang Community Health Center, 2011.

Ishizuka, Karen. *Serve the People: Making Asian America in the Long Sixties.* London: Verso, 2016.

Kim, Elaine H., ed. *With Silk Wings: Asian American Women at Work*. Oakland: Asian Women United, 1983.

Kitano, Harry. *The Japanese Americans*. New York: Chelsea House, 1987.

Kwong, Peter. *Forbidden Workers: Illegal Chinese Immigrants and American Labor*. New York: New Press, 1998.

Kwong, Peter, and Dusanka Miscevic. *Chinese America: The Untold Story of America's Oldest New Community.* New York: New Press, 2005.

———. *Chinese Americans: The Immigrant Experience*. Fairfield, Conn.: Hugh Lauter Levin Associates, 2000.

Lee, Joann Faung Jean. *Asian Americans in the Twenty-First Century.* New York: New Press, 2008.

Leher, Brian. *The Korean Americans*. New York: Chelsea House, 1988.

Leong, Russell C., and Don T. Nakanishi. *Asian Americans on War and Peace*. Los Angeles: UCLA Asian American Studies Center Press, 2002.

Light, Melanie, and Ken Light, eds. *Picturing Resistance: Moments and Movements of Social Change from the 1950s to Today*. New York: Ten Speed Press, 2020.

Lin, Ed. *This Is a Bust*. New York: Kaya Press, 2007.

Lin, Jan. *Reconstructing Chinatown: Ethnic Enclave, Global Change*. Minneapolis: University of Minnesota Press, 1998.

Louie, Steve, and Glenn Omatsu, eds. *Asian Americans: The Movement and the Moment*. Los Angeles: UCLA Asian American Studies Center Press, 2001.

Posadas, Barbara Mercedes. *The Filipino Americans*. Westport, Conn.: Greenwood Press, 1999.

Sakamoto, Edward. *Aloha Las Vegas: And Other Plays*. Honolulu: University of Hawaii Press, 2016.

Schlund-Vials, Cathy, K. Scott Wong, and Jason Oliver Chang, eds. *Asian America: A Primary Source Reader*. New Haven, Conn.: Yale University Press, 2017.

Sklar, Morty, and Joseph Barbato, eds. *Patchwork of Dreams: Voices from the Heart of the New America. Jackson Heights, NY:* Spirit That Moves Us Press, 1996.

Smith, Icy, ed. *Voices of Healing: Spirit and Unity after 9/11 in the Asian American and Pacific Islander Community*. Organization of Chinese Americans/East West Discovery Press, 2004.

Song, Min. *Asian America: A Reader*. New Brunswick, N.J.: Rutgers University Press, 2000.

Tung, Stephanie H., guest editor. "Being & Becoming Asian in America." *Aperture* 251, Summer 2023.

Wei, William. *The Asian American Movement*. Philadelphia: Temple University Press, 1993.

Zia, Helen. *Asian American Dreams: The Emergence of an American People*. New York: Farrar, Straus & Giroux, 2001.

Acknowledgments

We are grateful to the many people who helped in the writing and production of this book. We thank everyone who contributed essays, remembrances, and photographs. Your respect and love for Corky shine through in your contributions.

Our biggest thanks go to Virgo Lee, denizen of New York's Chinatown, friend of Corky and John Lee's for fifty years, and adviser to Corky's estate. You worked with us every step of the way on this book. We are grateful beyond measure for your generous advice, logistical support, and patience.

Heartfelt thanks to those who sent us photographs taken by Corky Lee from their collections: Curtis Chin; Marjorie Lee of UCLA Asian American Studies Center; Ed Litvak of Asian Americans for Equality; Yue Ma and Nancy Ng Tam of the Museum of Chinese in America; Paula Madison; Glenn Magpatnay of the National Queer Asian Pacific Islander Alliance; Nobuko Miyamoto; Icy Smith of East West Discovery Press; Eddie Wong of *East Wind* magazine; John Woo of Asian CineVision; Randall Yip of *Asian American News*; and Donald Young and Eurie Chung of the Center for Asian American Media.

Many others helped to identify people, places, and dates in the photographs. Thank you to Benjamin Mo, our intrepid research assistant, who plowed through newspaper archives, sent inquiries, and dug into archival collections. For their help in identifying people and events we thank Tomie Arai, Ti-Hua Chang, May Y. Chen, Michelle Chen, Rocky Chin, Warren Chin, Sayantani DasGupta, Johanna Fernandez, Juan Gonzalez, Jean Hom-Weng, Viola Lasmana, Lorraine Leong, Michael Liu, Wendy Mink, Brian Niiya, Alan Okada, Elizabeth Ou-Yang, Gray Tuttle, Linda Trinh Vo, Benny Wong, Betty Wong, Nancy Wong, Cheryl Yin, Elizabeth Young, Karen Zhou, and Helen Zia.

In the spring of 2021, Jennifer Sit at Clarkson Potter/Penguin Random House reached out to John Lee to express interest in a retrospective book of Corky's photographs. Thank you, Jenn, for *knowing* the importance of Corky's work, and Sandy Dijkstra, for making it happen. We thank Jenn Sit, Aaron Wehner, Francis Lam, Jen Wang, Christine Tanigawa, Kim Tyner, Marysarah Quinn, Monica Stanton, David Hawk, and Natalie Yera at Clarkson Potter for their vision and editorial and design expertise that produced this beautiful book. We are especially proud that Asian Americans are in leadership positions at Clarkson Potter. Your understanding and support are proof positive of the importance of diversity in the publishing industry.

Finally, we wish to express our gratitude to our families, especially Barbara Lee and John New, for their love and support.

Credits

ESSAYS

Ai, Weiwei, "Tiananmen." © 2024 by Ai Weiwei.

Bald, Vivek, "Our Never-Ending Vigil." © 2024 by Vivek Bald.

Chang, Gordon H., "The Railroad in the Chinese American Imagination." © 2024 by Gordon H. Chang.

Chang, Henry, "September 11, 2001." © 2024 by Henry Chang.

Chang, Ti-Hua, "Asian American Journalists Association." © 2024 by Ti-Hua Chang.

Chen, Ken, "Corky Lee's Police Brutality Photographs." © 2024 by Ken Chen.

Chin, Alan, "Chinatown in the 1970s." © 2024 by Alan Chin.

Chin, Rocky. "The Early Days of the Asian American Movement." © 2024 by Rocky Chin.

Chow, Lily, "I Work Very Hard and Love to Be Independent." In *With Silk Wings: Asian Women at Work*, ed. Elaine H. Kim. Oakland: Asian Women United. © 1983 by Elaine H. Kim/Asian Women United of California.

Hsu, Hua, "Foreword." © 2024 by Hua Hsu.

Hwang, David Henry, "The Emergence of Our Stage." © 2024 by David Henry Hwang.

Kochiyama, Akemi, "Internment: 'Never Again Means Now.'" © 2024 Akemi Kochiyama.

Kwong, Joanne, "Corky Lee on My Mind." © 2024 by Joanne Kwong.

Lee, Bayer Jack-Wah, "Corky Lee and the American Legion." © 2024 by Bayer Jack-Wah Lee.

Lee, John J., "Young Kok: 'To Be Praiseworthy of the Nation.'" © 2024 by John J. Lee.

Lee, Marie Myung-Ok, "Asian American Writers' Workshop." © 2024 by Marie Myung-Ok Lee.

Nur, Potrirankamanis Queano, "Looking for Corky in the Crowd." © 2024 by Potrirankmanis Queano Nur.

San Angel, Gary, "Peeling the Banana." © 2024 by Gary San Angel.

Suri, Himanshu (Heems), "We're Going Flag Shopping," in *Eat, Pray, Thug*. Megaforce Records, 2015. Lyrics courtesy Rough Trade Publishing.

Tajima-Peña, Renee, "Asian American Arts in the 1990s." © 2024 by Renee Tajima-Peña.

Zhou, Karen, "A Visit to New Orleans." © 2024 by Karen Zhou.

Zia, Helen, "Vincent Chin and the Long Struggle Against Anti-Asian Violence." © 2024 by Helen Zia.

PHOTOGRAPHS

page 10: Copyright © 1997 Jason Jem

page 12: Copyright © Jook Leung

page 13: Copyright © 2014 Gil Asakawa

page 22: Copyright © David "Dee" Delgado

page 23: Copyright © Stan Honda

page 30: Copyright © Bob Hsiang Photography

page 33: Copyright © Bob Hsiang Photography

page 34: CCTV, Copyright © 1980 Asian CineVision

page 35: Copyright © Thomas Chin

page 115: Copyright © Margaret Fung/AALDEF

page 210: Copyright © 2020 Edward Cheng

page 212: Copyright © 2014 Scott Summerdorf/Salt Lake Tribune

page 213: Copyright © Shirley L. Ng

page 214: Copyright © Shirley L. Ng

page 215: Copyright © 2018 Tomie Arai

page 300: Copyright © Alan Chin

Index

Note: Page references in italics indicate photographs.

Additional credits appear on page 312.

Published in the United States by Clarkson Potter/Publishers, an imprint of the Crown Publishing Group, a division of Penguin Random House LLC, New York.
ClarksonPotter.com

Library of Congress Cataloging-in-Publication Data

Names: Lee, Corky, 1947–2021, photographer. | Ng, Chee Wang, editor. | Ngai, Mae, editor.
Title: Corky Lee's Asian America: fifty years of photographic justice / photographs by Corky Lee; edited by Chee Wang Ng and Mae Ngai
Description: New York : Clarkson Potter/Publishers, 2024 | Includes bibliographical references and index.
Identifiers: LCCN 2023001435 (print) | LCCN 2023001436 (ebook) | ISBN 9780593580127 (hardcover) | ISBN 9780593580134 (ebook)
Subjects: LCSH: Asian Americans—Politics and government. | Asian Americans—Social conditions. | Social movements—United States. | Lee, Corky, 1947–2021. | Portrait photography.
Classification: LCC TR681.A75 L44 2024 (print) | LCC TR681.A75 (ebook) | DDC 770.89/95073—dc23/eng/20230712
LC record: https://lccn.loc.gov/2023001435
LC ebook record: https://lccn.loc.gov/2023001436

ISBN 978-0-593-58012-7
Ebook ISBN 978-0-593-58013-4

Printed in Malaysia

Editor: Jennifer Sit
Editorial assistant: Bianca Cruz
Designer: Jen Wang
Production editor: Christine Tanigawa
Production manager: Kim Tyner
Compositors: Merri Ann Morrell, Nick Patton
Copyeditor: Janet Biehl
Proofreaders: LJ Young, Karen Ninnis
Publicists: David Hawk, Natalie Yera
Marketer: Monica Stanton

10 9 8 7 6 5 4 3 2 1

First Edition